SOCIAL STUDIES

From theory to practice in elementary education

Social Studies

*From theory to practice
in elementary education*

MALCOLM P. DOUGLASS

Claremont Graduate School

J. B. Lippincott Company / *Philadelphia* • *New York*

Preface

How may the school help each boy and girl grow to maturity, thinking and acting responsibly, a contributing member of a free and democratic society? How may every child be helped to achieve a more fully rounded and enriched life, to grow in his awareness of human needs, increasingly sensitive to the aspirations of the infinitely variable yet similar human beings surrounding him on this plane? Traditionally, we have considered these high goals to be central objectives in that aspect of the school's work we have called the "social studies curriculum." We have also been painfully aware that we have fallen far short of our goals, and in response to these concerns we have over the years undertaken to reappraise and redirect our efforts with children in our search for better ways. The orbiting of Sputnik in 1957 brought about the most agonizing reappraisal to date, not only with respect to the social studies but to all curriculum areas of the school. The times cause us to seek, with an increasing sense of urgency, more effective ways of translating theories based upon a rapidly expanding knowledge base into more effective practice.

This book was written in an attempt to draw a closer bond between theory and practice in building a program of social studies for boys and girls. It identifies those ideas considered essential to understanding the foundations for a sound curriculum of social studies in the second half of the twentieth century and suggests ways one might put these ideas into practice in the classroom. The first chapter identifies the goals of social studies and describes important forces at work in contemporary society that should affect our thinking in devising the strongest possible curriculum for today's boys and girls. Chapters Two and Three place social studies in historical perspective and describe the varieties of practice, with their theoretic underpinnings, observable in schools today. Chapter Four contains a discussion of the dimensions of social studies learnings—how concepts, facts, generalizations, values, and skills appear to be most effectively developed. Chapters Five and Six are devoted to a detailed discussion of planning methods for teaching and how creative work with children emerges in the classroom. Chapters Seven, Eight, and Nine consider the major social science disciplines, their contributions singly and in concert to the curriculum of social studies, and how children may learn to think by utilizing concepts and generalizations from these disciplines. Chapter Ten is devoted to a discussion of maps and globes and to ways of helping children grow in their power to read them. Chapters Eleven and Twelve are concerned with using and extending the language abilities of boys and girls in and through social studies. Attention is given both to verbal (reading, writing, speaking, listening) and to non-verbal language abilities. The final chapter considers criteria essential in developing a sound program for assessing the quality of learning that has eventuated from teaching and discusses various techniques of evaluation applicable in the elementary school classroom. Attention is also given to some of the problems inherent in evaluating social studies learnings on a school and district-wide basis.

This book, like every other, represents an indebtedness to many people. In this instance, the finished product is above all else a family affair. The moral and intellectual support flowing from the author's family made it possible to begin and to finish. One also relies heavily upon his teachers in undertaking a project such as this. Above all else, the writer is indebted in this regard to the most effective teacher of all— one's own students, both the very young and the many graduate students it has been his privilege to know. Colleagues at the Claremont Graduate School also have made important contributions to my thinking and, hence, to this book. They do not, of course, bear any responsibility for what is finally written. Not least, there are a number of individuals whose editing, typing, and general assistance prevented a further delay, if not a permanent one, in concluding this task. Deepest gratitude on these accounts is expressed to the following: Mrs. Georgiana Feeney, Mrs. Marny Hubbard, Mrs. Jane Merrill, Mrs. Alberta Files, and William Foskett.

Claremont, California   MALCOLM P. DOUGLASS
February, 1967

Contents

SOCIAL STUDIES

From theory to practice in elementary education

CHAPTER ONE

A Framework for a Social Studies Curriculum

Of all the characteristics which distinguish man from other animals, one of the most remarkable is his abiding interest in others of his species. One may search as far as one likes; still one will not find evidence that other animal life knows or cares about the concerns, interests, and activities of his forebearers, or even, indeed, about other members of his group, his herd, or his flock. But the human being does care and, oddly enough, primitive man often appears to care more than civilized man. Particularly is this true of his desire to know about and to pass on to younger generations the traditions and values of the past.

This desire, this need to know about other people—to examine their past, the human arrangements they have contrived in their search for a better life, their hopes and fears for the future—is a major concern of schools in the late twentieth century, just as it has been since the dawn of history when primitive folk gathered around the fire to hear the tribal patriarch recount for the young the history of the race as he understood it.

The vast changes which have occurred in human society since that time, fantastic as they are, have not altered the importance of teaching the young about the human life which inhabits this earth or about the great events and traditions which have come before. But the explosion of knowledge and burgeoning developments in communicative media characterizing the recent past make the campfire history lesson even more insufficient to the task. It cannot provide the knowledge necessary to live successfully with other human beings, any more than the concept of a flat globe can serve the needs of a space scientist aiming his rocket toward a distant planet.

Introduction

PURPOSES OF THIS BOOK

This book concerns itself with the ways in which this natural curiosity about the human condition, past and present, may be considered in schooling. It considers why children should learn about man's relationships with his fellow man. It is concerned with problems in selecting the things to be studied, with ways in which those studies may be conducted, and with the manner in which successful teaching and learning may be judged. It deals with that area of the curriculum known as "the social studies."

Admittedly, questions of why, what, how, or how well, are not easily answered. Consider, for a moment, that children presently enrolled in elementary schools will live far into the twenty-first century. Life expectancy rates today predict that elementary school children may live well past A.D. 2030. They will enter their most productive years after the turn of the century.

One does not know what kind of world they will live in. However, the years of the current century present some of the most vexing and complex questions ever to face mankind. Schooling *does* make a difference; and since children now in school will assume roles as responsible citizens within the crucial years ahead, it is possible that what is done now may make a significant difference.

Yet, there is uncertainty as to how one should proceed. It is not the intention here to suggest that, in the end, there is only one answer. We live in a pluralistic society. In human affairs, it is not possible to predict behavior precisely. And the study of those affairs, which is a primary concern of the social sciences, provides, at best, ambiguous answers. Consequently, there is always more than one valid answer to any significant question or issue. There is no one best way to plan a curriculum that will lead students to an understanding of human problems. There is more than one way to teach, and more than one way to learn.

In studies of human events and the significance of human actions, one looks both to the past and to the present, to history and geography, and to the other social sciences, for understandings about how and why human beings have arrived at their present estate. Fields outside the social sciences—the arts, the natural sciences, and other areas—provide information relevant to our understanding. But the basis of investigation is the social sciences: history, geography, anthropology, economics, sociology, and political science.

SOCIAL STUDIES: A CONFUSING TERM

In this book, a very specific meaning will be associated with the term "social studies." This becomes necessary because there is little agreement over the meaning of this term. If you were to ask ten people, from as many different walks of life, what the social studies program in the schools is, you would get ten different answers. To the professor of history or one of the other social sciences, the term might well suggest something less than the intellectual rigor that disciplinarians wish to have associated with their studies. Parents often infer that the term means learning to socialize—how to get along with others. Although this is not an undersirable objective, parents often believe that this aspect receives all the attention. Others will say that the social studies is what replaced geography and history—subjects which they feel should be restored to the school curriculum. Even teachers of social studies themselves show a surprising lack of unity in their definition of the term.

For example, how does one respond to the questions: Is social studies singular or plural? Does it refer to content to be taught and learned, or does it refer to a method of teaching? Is it synonymous with *social education, social learning, social understanding,* or *social living?*

SOCIAL STUDIES: WHAT ARE THEY?

To begin, the singular of the term, *social study,* will be defined. *Any inquiry which has as its central focus the study of one or more aspects of man's relationships with his fellow man is a social study.* This definition covers a broad area, but there are other dimensions of the school curriculum which are not included: the natural and physical sciences, mathematics, and languages. Thus, when one inquires into the historic antecedents of our society; into the functions of any of a number of institutions such as the family or government; into geographic relationships in the community, state, or nation; or into the nature of other cultures and their connections with our own, he is engaged in a social study.

Used in this sense, a social study may be distinguished clearly from those inquiries commonly included in elementary schools which do not focus primarily upon human relationships, such as the sciences and mathematics. It must readily be apparent that none of these fields is devoid of social implications or social content, nor is the social study bereft of concepts drawn from other fields. The logic of this definition rests on the *focus of concern,* not on the derivation of the subject matter content. For example, the problem of dealing with the control of nuclear energy is a social one. A person attempting to unravel this problem and to pose solutions for it is therefore involved in a social study. A person attempting to find civilian uses for nuclear energy, however, would be engaged primarily in a physical science study. Similarly, a person engaged in learning a foreign language or one who analyzes a literary work would be engaged in a language study. None of these could be said to be void of social implications or content, but the focus of concern of the learner's activity, regardless of the intellectual level on which he is operating, is clearly different in each case.

Social Studies: Singular or Plural?   Hence, *social studies* merely refers to more than one social study. The *curriculum of social studies,* then, is that portion of the school's activity concerned with the teaching and learning of those socially significant problems, questions, themes, or topics believed to be important to the well-being of our society. Two sets of criteria govern the selection of such themes, problems, questions, or topics which, taken together, comprise the curriculum of social studies. First, standards must be applied to the selection of ideas. It is of first importance to include the worthiest of the concepts, facts, generalizations, values, and skills comprising the widest range of human experience. Second, the learner's ability to make those ideas his own influences the order and range of difficulty of the particular ideas chosen at any particular time.

THE SOCIAL STUDIES VS. THE SOCIAL SCIENCES

In contrast, the social sciences may be identified as those fields of scholarly inquiry which deal with human society or its characteristic elements—the family, the state, the races of man—and with the interrelationships of institutions involved in man's well-being as a member of an organized community. The social sciences, taken singly, deal with special phases of human society. Each is dedicated to the discovery of new knowledge about particular aspects of human social conditions and to the development of specialized means of conducting scientific inquiry into the nature of society. Thus history, as a social science, is concerned with the story of man's existence *and* with developing new ways of discovering knowledge. Methods of discovering and analyzing information of a historic nature are sometimes called the historical method or historiography. The geographer is concerned with the discovery of knowledge which deals with the relationships of things in space *and* with the method of conducting inquiries into that knowledge —called the regional method. Each of the other fields of the social sciences has special means for studying and analyzing data within its particular domain.

The curriculum of social studies draws its content primarily but not exclusively from the social sciences. Of course, other fields of inquiry make important contributions to our understandings of human relationships, both past and present. These ideas, rooted in what are commonly classified as the natural sciences and humanities, cannot be set aside as one thinks about the problem of selecting concepts and understandings to be taught in the schools. However, one turns primarily to the social sciences because these fields of inquiry are most directly related to the discovery of knowledge about human relationships. Even so, because of the differing natures of the social science disciplines themselves, the relevance of the understandings contributed by them to the purposes of the school, and the abilities of children to deal meaningfully with ideas, some of the social sciences make more important contributions to the curriculum of social studies than do others. Those social science disciplines, whose contribution to knowledge is most likely to be utilized in planning a curriculum for boys and girls, include the disciplines of *history, geography, political science (or government), economics, anthropology,* and *sociology.* One should keep in mind that there are a number of other fields frequently defined as social sciences (e.g., social psychology, ethics, education, philosophy, jurisprudence, penology, linguistics); these fields also are of importance in curriculum planning. However, in the pages following, the discussion focuses upon the six major fields of study mentioned here as making the *most direct contribution* as one seeks to evolve a sound curriculum of social studies for elementary school children.

What to Teach: A Major Problem. It is out of this very broad range of scholarly inquiry that the teacher selects the concepts and understandings which he will teach. And it is from these fields that he will be guided in the ways of conducting the various studies in which he engages his children. Studies which are primarily historic in nature, for example, will not only draw much of their subject matter content from the field of history; they will also utilize the methods of research used by the historian. Geographic studies will be guided by the research methods of the geographer and will draw upon what the geographer himself determines to be significant. In a similar manner, the teacher selects from the other social sciences the most important ideas for classroom consideration. He garners, too, notions about modes of inquiry appropriate to the different studies. In this fashion, he erects a framework of valid studies that are readily invested with meaning by his pupils.

Only in the broadest sense is the teacher given guidelines for developing his curriculum of social studies. Most states and local districts, it is true, provide a suggested sequence of studies and offer some ideas regarding possible approaches to them. Although the detail provided the teacher varies widely, in virtually every instance these guidelines for teaching are suggestions, not mandates, to the teacher. Perhaps a factor which "controls" what the teacher is able to do with children more than any other is the range of instructional materials available. With only a textbook, the teacher is severely handicapped. But with a rich variety of materials, the teacher and his pupils can range over a much wider territory; and their studies will have greater depth. The teacher who develops original and creative means of working with children in a social study—the person who is able to teach them in a truly notable way— requires a great many materials and a thorough knowledge of his subject matter. Neither of these is readily available.

On the horizon, however, are exciting new materials. They include both those for use with children in the classroom and those the teacher requires to improve his own competence. Scholars from widely differing disciplines show the beginnings of interest in applying what they themselves know to the problems of teaching children. Providing superior materials calls for cooperative efforts among academic scholars as well as those who possess specialized knowledge of pedagogical principles and those who study the developmental characteristics of children. The results of such joint efforts hold high promise.[1]

The development of new materials will not relieve the classroom

---

[1] Nation-wide efforts in the improvement of social studies are described in *New Current Curriculum Developments* published by the Association for Supervision and Curriculum Development, 1965. See especially Chapter Eight on social studies, written by John U. Michaelis, which reviews thirty-three projects.

teacher of the responsibility of deciding what ideas should be emphasized nor of how the study should proceed. In all probability, such questions will become even more important as the range of possibilities increases and the need to select from that range demands greater care. But the teacher will have better tools and suggestions from which to make these important and continuing decisions.

Why Teach Social Studies at All?

At the outset, it was suggested that a singular characteristic of the human being is his abiding interest in others of his species; that he has always attempted to teach his children about the great events and traditions—about the world as he has understood it. This is as true of highly civilized Western man as it has been of his primitive counterpart. He has not done this simply because there is in every human being an innate curiosity about other people and places. Since earliest times, he has used this natural interest to assure the continuation of his society. Thus, the processes of inducting the young into a community of men have always relied heavily upon teaching children about the principles and values, traditions and beliefs, which give to any group that cohesion essential to the preservation of a society.

Social studies play a special role in this overall objective of inducting young people into the American society. Consider Dewey's assertion that democracy must be born anew with each generation. By this he meant that the underlying values, the knowledge, and the behavior essential to the conduct of our democratic society cannot be inherited. In every case they must be learned, but they are not learned collectively. Each individual must learn for himself the loyalties, the values, and the principles of a free society based on a democratic way of life. Clearly, the subject matter of the social sciences—and hence the concerns of the school, especially in the curriculum of social studies—relates most directly to this objective. Such a lofty goal is not the exclusive domain of the social studies, but the very nature of the subject matter makes this broad objective particularly pertinent. As a committee of the National Council for the Social Studies stated:

The most inclusive aim of Social Studies as a part of general education in the United States is to help young people learn to carry on the free society they have inherited, to make whatever changes modern conditions demand or creative imagination suggests that are consistent with its basic principles and values, and to hand it on to their offspring better than they received it.[2]

Within this broad frame, specific objectives in teaching social studies can be identified. Concerns in this regard have to do with the dimensions of subject matter learning, learning to think, the kinds of skills that are basic to the meaningful use of concepts and understandings, and the development of attitudes and values.

SOCIAL STUDIES: PINPOINTING THE OBJECTIVES

Teaching Content. Every social study is concerned with the teaching of those concepts and understandings which contribute to the overall objectives of the social studies curriculum. This content is drawn primarily from the social sciences. It is the purpose of the elementary school to teach the concepts, facts, and generalizations which are basic to those fields of study. One would expect, therefore, that during the child's elementary school experience, he would gain knowledge of and appreciation for a wide range of understandings in history, geography, economics, sociology, and the other fields of the social sciences.

For a variety of reasons, the important place of subject matter in the elementary school social studies program has not received sufficient emphasis. This situation is now changing. Scholars and educators are beginning to work together to identify major generalizations from the social sciences. Using these generalizations, educators are beginning to provide more detailed guides for teachers. One example of such an attempt has been published by the National Council for the Social Studies. It consists of a statement of fifteen themes which are considered to be a comprehensive description of the scope of the social studies curriculum, kindergarten through grade 14. The themes suggested are as follows:

Themes Representing the Important Societal Goals of American Democracy

1. Recognition of the dignity and worth of the individual
2. The use of intelligence to improve human living

[2] *A Guide to Contents in the Social Studies,* Report of the NCSS Committees on Concepts and Values, National Council for the Social Studies (Washington, D.C., n.d.), p. 1.

3. Recognition and understanding of world interdependence
4. The understanding of the major world cultures and culture areas
5. The intelligent uses of the natural environment
6. The vitalization of our democracy through an intelligent use of our public educational facilities
7. The intelligent acceptance, by individuals and groups, of responsibility for achieving democratic social action
8. Increasing the effectiveness of the family as a basic social institution
9. The effective development of moral and spiritual values
10. The intelligent and responsible sharing of power in order to attain justice ·
11. The intelligent utilization of scarce resources to attain the widest general well-being
12. Achievement of adequate horizons of loyalty
13. Cooperation in the interest of peace and welfare
14. Achieving a balance between social stability and social change
15. Widening and deepening the ability to live more richly[3]

Each theme is supported by a list of generalizations which provide guides to content that pupils should study. Other efforts have been and will continue to be made to specify the range of ideas with which children should come in contact.[4]

Although in the future there will be more such materials, the job will never be completely accomplished *for* the teacher. He will have to adjust his teaching to the maturity level of children, to their prior experience, and to their intellectual capacities for dealing with ideas. Other factors will have to be accounted for as well. The teacher's own knowledge of

[3] Dorothy McClure Fraser and Samuel P. McCutchen, editors, "Social Studies in Transition: Guidelines for Change," Curriculum Series Number Twelve (Washington, D.C.: National Council for the Social Studies, 1965), pp. 11-52.

[4] A notable example is the *California State Framework for the Social Studies,* published in 1962 by the California State Department of Education. This guide to the social studies program contains an extensive list of generalizations from the social sciences which were elicited from social scientists and reviewed by them and educators for accuracy and comprehensiveness. It is being used as a guide by publishers who are preparing teaching materials, by district and county staffs in the preparation of teaching guides, and by teachers who are selecting content for use in their classrooms. See California State Department of Education, "Social Studies Framework for the Public Schools of California" (Sacramento, California: California State Department of Education, 1962). Generalizations appearing in the Framework are reproduced in an Appendix.

the subject matter, the methods he finds most effective for teaching children, and the teaching materials available for his use will influence the content of a particular social study. Nevertheless, such attempts to detail the subject matter emphasis of the social studies curriculum do provide invaluable guides where previously such guides have been scarce.

Also, teachers should exercise care with respect to the part that generalizations, so suggested, may play in developing a social study with children. Young people require an adequate background of concepts and facts, and they need to learn how to put these together in the process of generalizing, if the big ideas are to be invested with meaning. Used in this sense, a concept is considered to be the notions or ideas a person has about particular things for which he has developed an awareness. Words or phrases stand for concepts, but, of course, words are not concepts. Concepts are the ideas which exist within a person. The understanding of facts and generalizations depends upon the child's ability to develop meaningful relationships among the concepts contained in the fact or generalization. Social studies tend to contain a great number of concepts beyond the experience of most children. Awareness of this helps the teacher to focus on the concepts basic to a study; to help children clarify concepts extensively before they delve too deeply into the study of facts and before they develop generalizations about those facts. The specific subject matter content of a study can be understood only when concepts are understood.

In planning a study, therefore, the teacher will seek to clarify in his own mind which concepts, which facts, and which generalizations are most relevant to the objectives of the study, considering the maturity level and age of the children, the materials, and his own understanding of the subject matter as variables. He then works with children to see that the experiences which they have provide ample opportunity to reinforce these learnings so that each child comes away from the study with a number of specific understandings which may easily be labeled "subject matter content."

Teaching Thinking and Problem Solving. A second important objective of any social study is to develop the ability to think and to solve problems. Because it is impossible to teach the entire spectrum of knowledge from the social sciences, and because information once known tends to disappear or, at best, slip below the level of easy recall, a prime target of every study should be to help pupils gain those abilities which help them to become aware—to think about social problems in a continuing way. This is a long-range goal requiring reiteration at each grade level and within each study. If children, growing toward maturity, do not learn to think about problems within the dimensions of the themes suggested above and if they do not have tools for thinking about them, they will either ignore real-life problems or, perhaps even worse, make serious errors because of prejudice and their own inability to deal with problems sensibly.

The processes of thinking have engaged philosophers, psychologists, and many others for centuries. They are so complex that no easy definition of them is possible.[5] However, critical, or reflective, thinking about ideas or problems in a social study is only partly dependent upon the intellectual capacity and maturity of the learner. Although the child appears to pass through developmental stages in which some modes of inquiry are more productive than others, the teacher is also an important influence. His way of approaching a topic may encourage reflective or critical thinking, or it may close all doors to such thought. Jules Henry, for example, suggests that by the time children enter the third grade, many of them have long since ceased to "think" and are only interested in finding out what answer the teacher wishes them to give.[6] The teacher's openness to a variety of ideas, it is agreed, encourages children to think more broadly and creatively. Probably creative thinking is the first step toward critical thinking, and the climate in which this takes place is unquestionably the responsibility of the teacher.

But a second important aspect is problem solving. Over the years, social scientists have developed specific techniques for analyzing problems in their own fields. Historians and geographers, economists and others use specialized procedures to solve problems. These procedures can be learned and they can be adapted for work with even the youngest children. Learning to "think historically" or to "think geographically" is important for the child in social studies since it prepares him to con-

[5] An excellent source in this regard is H. Gordon Hullfish and Philip G. Smith, *Reflective Thinking: The Method of Education* (New York: Dodd, Mead and Company, 1961), 273 pp. See also Isadore Starr, "The Nature of Critical Thinking and Its Application in the Social Studies," Chapter Three in *Skill Development in Social Studies*, Helen McCracken Carpenter, editor, Thirty-third Yearbook of the National Council for the Social Studies, The Council, Washington, D.C., 1963, pp. 35-52.

[6] Jules Henry, "Docility, or Giving Teacher What She Wants," *The Journal of Social Issues*, XI, No. 2 (1955), pp. 33-41. See also his "Spontaneity, Initiative, and Creativity in Suburban Classrooms," reprinted in George Spindler, *Education and Culture* (New York: Holt, Rinehart and Winston, 1963), pp. 215-233.

sider problems which are essentially historical or geographical as he meets them later in school, and later in life.

Teaching Skills. A third major objective of teaching social studies deals with the development of skills. Normally, when one thinks of skills in the school program, it is difficult either to isolate one from another or to assign the responsibility for teaching a particular skill to one curriculum area. Skills in the reading process may be taught in the literature program, in the social study, or even in the arithmetic program. Similarly, study skills and work habits are learned in virtually every phase of school activity. Children learn to work together by virtue of living together in the school and by having a consistent setting which demands excellence in performance throughout the day. The teacher simply cannot turn on training for a skill at one moment and turn it off at the next.

However, although practically every problem of skill development is not peculiar to social studies, there are a few specialized skills which are a primary responsibility of this curriculum area. These are associated with abilities to read maps, to interpret charts and graphs depicting information about human events and conditions, to learn how to collect certain kinds of data, and to gain experience in temporal and spatial thinking. To these concerns, the teacher gives special attention in the social study, recognizing that other curriculum areas may also be utilized to advantage in their development.

Teaching Values and Attitudes. Finally, the social studies curriculum is concerned with the teaching and learning of values and attitudes. This concern has several dimensions. First, it must be recognized that the attitudes and values which have their greatest significance to the child in guiding his behavior are those learned largely outside of school: in the home, in the peer group, perhaps in the church. Children bring these values and attitudes into the classroom where their potency to direct behavior is exceedingly clear to even the casual observer.

A second important observation is that values and attitudes take long to develop and are constantly being modified. Since birth, the child has been deeply immersed in the processes of attitude building; these processes continue in the classroom and as he experiences life outside the classroom. In social studies lessons as in other activities planned by the teacher in school, the child busily engages himself in valuing and attitude building. Consciously or subconsciously, he is asking, "Does this make sense to me?"; "Does it conflict with other ideas I have?"; Is this something I should want to do?"

It is of the greatest importance for the teacher to seek to understand the values and attitudes of the children in his classroom. *Understanding does not connote acceptance of those values and attitudes.* It *does* suggest that the teacher recognize the integrity of the child's value system, illogical or unacceptable as it may appear to him; that he help the child work to bring order within that framework rather than attempting to superimpose another structure from without. Value structures appear to be subject to extreme or rapid modification only under very traumatic conditions—not conditions available to the teacher in the classroom. The teacher must learn, therefore, to live with and use what he has available before him.

Earlier, it was asserted that the most inclusive aim of social studies is to help young people learn to carry on the free society they inherit, changing where change seems desirable in order that the next generation will receive it in better condition than the last. Assuming the validity of this objective, it is readily apparent that the teaching of democratic values is the basic concern of the social studies curriculum. Then, given the conditions under which values and attitudes are learned, certain directions are readily apparent for the teacher. Since values and attitudes are learned gradually and are being modified continuously, the only hope that the child will learn to live by the values of democracy is in living by them consistently and continuously in the classroom. The teacher's behavior must be guided by the basic principles of democratic living. There are many statements which specify these behaviors, so they will not be enumerated here. It is generally agreed, however, that they involve situations in which there is a basic respect for the dignity of the individual, where there is faith in the use of intelligence to solve problems and clarify issues, and where there is belief that reason and persuasion, rather than force, should be used in solving problems and settling controversies.

Can the goals of a democratic society be achieved in classrooms where they are abrogated or ignored? It is very doubtful. Learning in a classroom where democratic principles are emphasized is probably the only way to a lasting effect. That not all teachers have this capacity to direct young people in activities where democratic values are truly observed must be admitted. Some teachers will find it difficult to work with children in ways that are harmonious with the overall objectives of the school in American society; this may hinder the accomplishment of high aims. The resulting problem is understandable; the solutions to it are extremely difficult to achieve.

Another objective related to the teaching of democratic values and attitudes must be considered. In addition to learning *to behave in accordance with* democratic principles, there is a need *to know about* them. The social studies curriculum is therefore concerned with *teaching about* the values and ideals which have given our democratic society its direction over almost two centuries. Learning about such values and ideals is actually a subject matter objective. But its importance is repeated here because the living of democratic principles in the classroom is hollow unless children know what those principles are and how they came to be.

Social Studies in a Period of Transition

When considering the dimensions of a sound curriculum of social studies, it should be remembered that education in America is in a transitional period. The Progressive Era, dominant in the first half of the century, is past. New directions are being charted and new programs of instruction conceptualized. Private foundations and governmental agencies, particularly at state and national levels, increasingly concern themselves in the affairs of the school. Scholars are developing specific curricula; there is support for research that will provide a body of theory by means of which curricula in all fields, including the social studies, may be revised. No classroom teacher will escape this influence nor the influence of those who are increasingly bringing their attention to bear upon the education of the pre-adolescent child.

Three themes, of first importance during this period of transition, have particular pertinence to the development of a sound social studies curriculum: (1) Accelerating change: its meaning for the social studies, (2) Social studies and the curriculum reform movement, and (3) Changing conceptions of learning: their effect on the social studies.

ACCELERATING CHANGE: ITS MEANING FOR THE SOCIAL STUDIES

The most startling, enduring, and troublesome characteristic of the age we live in is *change*. It is startling, not only because the alterations being wrought in our society are affecting every facet of human existence, but also because they are taking place with kaleidoscopic rapidity. Tomorrow will be dramatically different from today; tomorrows a decade hence will be even more different. How they will differ is not known, of course, but one estimate is that "the generation now in school

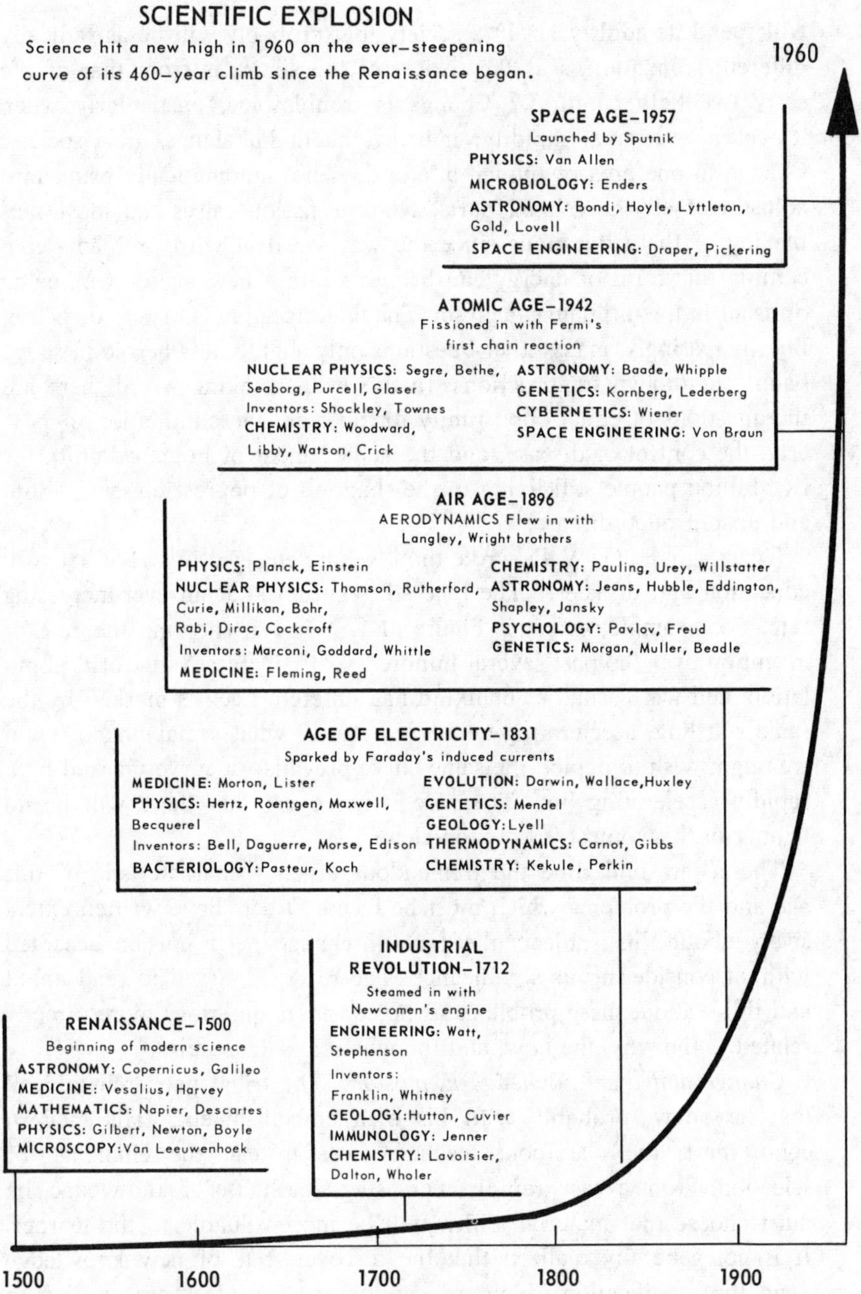

SCIENTIFIC EXPLOSION

Science hit a new high in 1960 on the ever—steepening
curve of its 460—year climb since the Renaissance began.

1960

SPACE AGE—1957
Launched by Sputnik
PHYSICS: Van Allen
MICROBIOLOGY: Enders
ASTRONOMY: Bondi, Hoyle, Lyttleton,
Gold, Lovell
SPACE ENGINEERING: Draper, Pickering

ATOMIC AGE—1942
Fissioned in with Fermi's
first chain reaction
NUCLEAR PHYSICS: Segre, Bethe,   ASTRONOMY: Baade, Whipple
Seaborg, Purcell, Glaser   GENETICS: Kornberg, Lederberg
Inventors: Shockley, Townes   CYBERNETICS: Wiener
CHEMISTRY: Woodward,   SPACE ENGINEERING: Von Braun
Libby, Watson, Crick

AIR AGE—1896
AERODYNAMICS Flew in with
Langley, Wright brothers
PHYSICS: Planck, Einstein   CHEMISTRY: Pauling, Urey, Willstatter
NUCLEAR PHYSICS: Thomson, Rutherford, ASTRONOMY: Jeans, Hubble, Eddington,
Curie, Millikan, Bohr,   Shapley, Jansky
Rabi, Dirac, Cockcroft   PSYCHOLOGY: Pavlov, Freud
Inventors: Marconi, Goddard, Whittle GENETICS: Morgan, Muller, Beadle
MEDICINE: Fleming, Reed

AGE OF ELECTRICITY—1831
Sparked by Faraday's induced currents
MEDICINE: Morton, Lister   EVOLUTION: Darwin, Wallace, Huxley
PHYSICS: Hertz, Roentgen, Maxwell,   GENETICS: Mendel
Becquerel   GEOLOGY: Lyell
Inventors: Bell, Daguerre, Morse, Edison THERMODYNAMICS: Carnot, Gibbs
BACTERIOLOGY: Pasteur, Koch   CHEMISTRY: Kekule, Perkin

**INDUSTRIAL
REVOLUTION—1712**
Steamed in with
Newcomen's engine
ENGINEERING: Watt,
Stephenson
Inventors:
Franklin, Whitney
GEOLOGY: Hutton, Cuvier
IMMUNOLOGY: Jenner
CHEMISTRY: Lavoisier,
Dalton, Wholer

RENAISSANCE—1500
Beginning of modern science
ASTRONOMY: Copernicus, Galileo
MEDICINE: Vesalius, Harvey
MATHEMATICS: Napier, Descartes
PHYSICS: Gilbert, Newton, Boyle
MICROSCOPY: Van Leeuwenhoek

1500   1600   1700   1800   1900

Figure 1—1: Scientific Explosion. (Redrawn from *Time* The Weekly News-
magazine; © Time Inc. 1961)

will spend its adult years in a society that probably will be as radically different from today's as the society of the sixties is from that of the early twentieth century."[7] Change is troublesome, particularly when it occurs with great rapidity; it brings about imbalances in a society. Change in one area of human affairs does not automatically bring into adjustment all the related parts. Nuclear fission raises the most perplexing of these questions since the way we deal with problems concerning this form of energy can bring us into a new age of well-being or usher in the ultimate cataclysm. The final question is of war or peace. But, increasingly, many other questions only slightly less heroic in scope haunt our thoughts and actions. In this ever-shrinking world there are the questions of equal opportunity for all men, the elimination of poverty, the control of disease, and the achievement of human dignity for two billion people still living in the shadows of oppression, starvation, and uncontrolled disease.

Years ago, H. G. Wells wrote that "we are engaged in a race between education and disaster." The race still continues, at an ever-increasing rate. For example, consider Figures 1-1, 1-3, 1-5, showing the rate of invention over the past several hundred years, increases in world population, and war casualties mankind has suffered. Each is marked by the same startling, accelerating curve. No matter what social phenomenon we might wish to depict, the same curve prevails—a curve marked by a rapidly accelerating line. The race is not over: that there will be no winner in this contest is only too clear.

These data underline the tremendous urgency characteristic of this age and the problems which must be faced. Others have written extensively about this subject; the fact of change need not be accepted without considering its significance. The reader is urged to read about and think about these problems as he considers questions more directly related to the why, the how, and the what of social studies.

Change and the Knowledge Explosion. The tribal patriarch told all that he knew, probably with his own embellishments. His modern counterpart, the classroom teacher, faces instead the challenge of selection. From a vast, rapidly increasing storehouse of knowledge, he must choose that material which will be most valuable to the learner. It is not generally realized that the discovery-rate of new knowledge (and the modification of old conceptions as new data are applied to

[7] NEA Project on Instruction, *Education in a Changing Society,* (Washington, D.C.: National Education Association, 1963), p. 7.

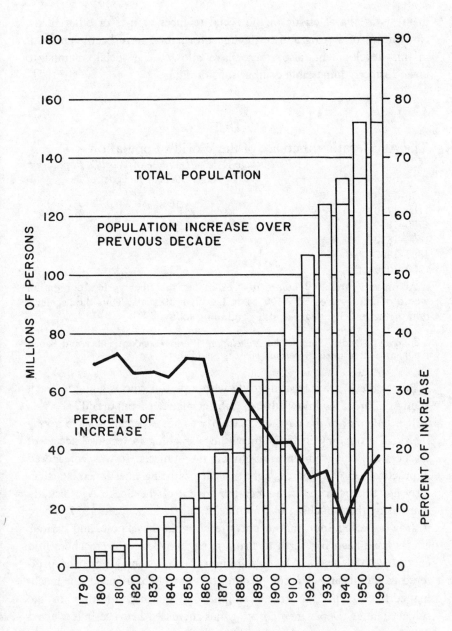

Figure 1–2: Total U.S. Population, Decennial Population Increase, and Percent of Population Increase, 1790–1960. (Reprinted by permission from *Education in a Changing Society*, NEA Project on Instruction, Washington, D.C.: National Education Association, 1963, p. 92)

them) is as characteristic of the social sciences as it is of other fields. New means of storing and retrieving information have been significant in this development, also; these have allowed the social scientist to make formerly impossible comparisons of data.

TABLE 1

The Accelerating Increase of the World's Population

Period	Percentage Rate of Increase of World's Population Over 50-Year Periods
1650–1700 ⎱ 1700–1750 ⎰	16.8%
1750–1800	24.4%
1800–1850	29.2%
1850–1900	37.3%
1900–1950	53.9%

At present rates of increase it is estimated that the world's population would double (increase by 100%) in less than 40 years. Thus the acceleration of the last 300 years is still continuing today.

Source: L. Dudley Stamp, Our Developing World (London: Faber and Faber, 1960), p. 19. Reprinted by permission of the publisher.

But, you ask, what has this to do with a person who is going to teach young children? Is knowledge of subject matter so important?

It is true that in the past, the teacher was not expected to have a very thorough grounding in the subjects he was going to teach. Since most teachers of young children taught all the subjects, it was considered impractical as well. Increasingly this idea is being questioned. Particularly has this been the case since the advent of the Space Age, usually marked by the launching of Sputnik by the U. S. S. R. in 1957. There is growing recognition that teachers teach what they know, and various efforts have been put forth to bring more knowledgeable teachers into contact with elementary school children. Team teaching has been proffered as one means of accomplishing this end. Requirements for teaching certificates include greater emphasis upon more training in the subject matter. Departmentalization has increased because it is viewed as one means of accomplishing this goal.

Another factor which has heightened interest in the subject matter preparation of the teacher has been the suggestion, made by respected educators and psychologists, that young children are capable of dealing

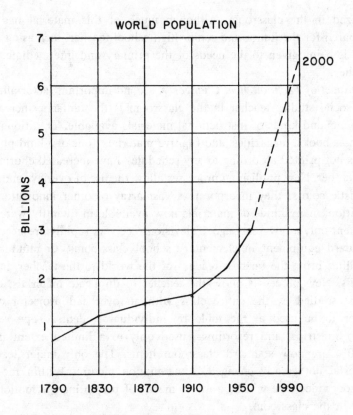

Figure 1–3: World population, at currently projected growth rates, will double before the year 2000.

with social science concepts at much lower levels of maturity than previously believed possible. Bruner's idea that "any subject can be taught effectively in some intellectually honest form to any child at any stage of development"[8] has had the widest kind of distribution; this has led to further demands that teachers obtain a better grasp of intellectual material than formerly. Reinforcing this view are a number of books designed to bring the teacher up to date; to extend his knowledge in various facets of the social sciences; and to suggest ways in which this fresh information (and new interpretations of older data) might be

[8] Jerome S. Bruner, *The Process of Education* (Cambridge: Harvard University Press, 1961), p. 33.

utilized in the classroom. Although much of this material has been prepared for the junior and senior high school teacher, increasing attention is being given to the needs of the primary and intermediate grade teacher.

Impact of Technological Change. A second important factor affecting the social studies teacher in the classroom is the fantastic increase in amounts and kinds of instructional materials available. Traditional aids such as books, magazines, and fugitive materials (one-of-a-kind publications not printed according to any schedule) have increased enormously in number. New publishing processes allow the use of overlays and more realistic colors; they incorporate a vast array of other innovations. In addition, many kinds of materials now available in quantity were nonexistent only a few years ago. Television receivers rapidly are becoming standard equipment in elementary school classrooms. Communication satellites bring the farthest reaches of the world to the teacher and his pupils. New processes allow the teacher to duplicate materials, either to be studied by the entire class with an overhead projector or on paper to be used at the table by individual students. Tape recordings, filmstrips, and recordings, used only to a limited extent in the 1950's, are now standard classroom items. The only major teaching material not greatly changed is the motion picture. Within the next decade, video-tape will be a major means of presenting the motion picture in the classroom.

In the near future lie even more sophisticated teaching materials. Video-tape recorders, automated devices, color television: all these, in combination with already widely available tools, spell revolution for the teaching of social studies. Probably it will never become completely obsolete, but the textbook, already in serious jeopardy as *the* major teaching tool in the intermediate and upper grades, will assume less and less importance. The effect of this change will be widespread since, traditionally, the textbook (and the highly developed Course of Study for the teacher in the primary grades) has defined the nature and extent of the subject matter. As the textbook loses ground as the sole definer of the social study, the teacher's role in this respect will become increasingly important. With a very wide variety of materials to choose from, he will be in a position to develop a series of studies for his pupils unique to his classroom. Variability of media thus encourages a rich variety in the ways children may approach their studies.

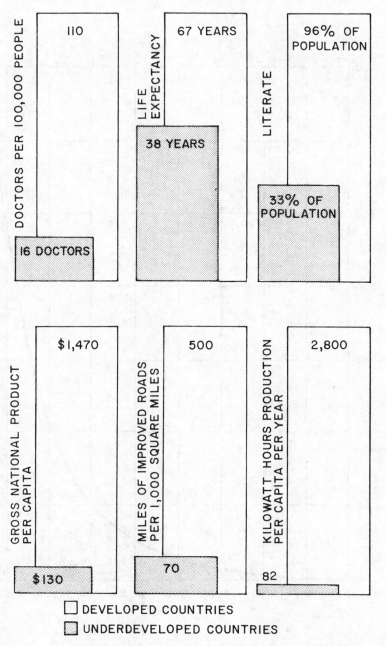

Figure 1–4: The Gap Between the Underdeveloped and the Developed Countries. (Reprinted by permission from *Education in a Changing Society*, NEA Project on Instruction, Washington, D.C.: National Education Association, 1963, p. 103)

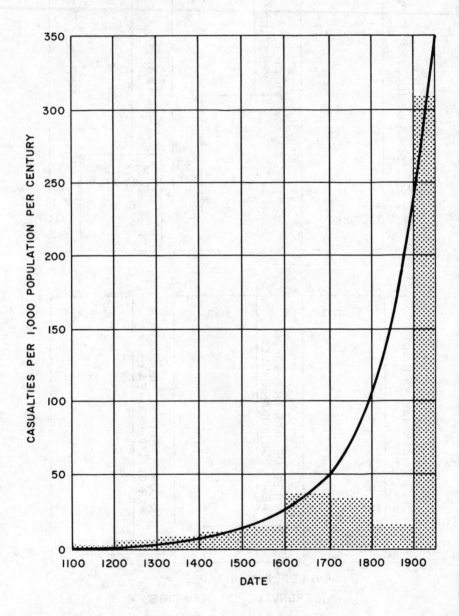

Figure 1–5: The Accelerating Increase of War Casualties. (From: *Technology and Social Change* by Francis R. Allen, et al., Copyright, © 1957, by Appleton-Century-Crofts, Inc. Reprinted by permission of the publishers)

SOCIAL STUDIES AND THE CURRICULUM REFORM MOVEMENT

Any social studies curriculum for children in the sixties and seventies must take into account the fact that a curriculum reform movement is under way. So far, it has had less impact on social studies than on any other curriculum area. How rapidly the movement will affect the content of social studies and the way they are taught will depend in part upon how quickly social scientists attend to the problems of the elementary school. Thus far, scholars have been somewhat loathe to work at this level, preferring to direct attention to the high school. Another unknown element is the amount of federal and state money to be invested in curriculum revision projects. The ultimate effectiveness of the programs which are devised is still another. Will they be appropriate to children's use in a wide variety of school situations? Will teachers use the materials? Only time will answer these crucial questions.

There is no question, however, that, spurred by the close of the Progressive Era and the advent of the Space Age, the curriculum of social studies will undergo marked changes in the years immediately ahead. Enough serious questions have been raised and dissatisfactions expressed to give a clear indication that a sizeable number of educators and social scientists earnestly desire reforms in social studies similar to those already advanced in the teaching of mathematics and science. Goodlad has summarized the situation, saying:

> The general criticism is and has been [of social studies] that both the rigor of separate social science disciplines and the unity of social science have been sacrificed to amorphous studies of man and society or, worse, to a curriculum in "social living" and "life adjustment." Whatever the strength and weaknesses of past and present social studies programs, the future trend is already apparent: the new curricula will emphasize concepts, principles, and methods of the social science disciplines; efforts will be intensified to develop a sequential program from kindergarten through the twelfth grade; and social sciences such as sociology, anthropology, political science, economics, and geography will receive somewhat more attention than in the past.[9]

Of course, a mixture of practice in the way social studies are taught in the schools will continue. However, future trends are apparent. Gradually one will see the advent of materials for teacher and pupil use

---

[9] John I. Goodlad, "School Curriculum Reform in the United States," The Fund for the Advancement of Education (March, 1964), p. 42.

designed to bring about learnings growing more directly out of the social science disciplines. These materials will emphasize modes of inquiry; they will be directed toward helping children grow in their capacities to reason. In some instances, studies will be rooted directly in single disciplines. In others, they will represent an interdisciplinary approach to the study of problems or topics. As such materials become increasingly available, they will have a noticeable effect upon the kind of social studies curriculum a teacher can create for his pupils.

SOCIAL STUDIES AND CHANGING CONCEPTS OF THE LEARNER

A third consideration which affects thinking about developing a curriculum of social studies has to do with conceptions of how the learner learns. Views of the child as a learner have undergone considerable transformation since the end of the nineteenth century, when formal studies of his learning behavior were first initiated. Getzels has pointed out that "at the turn of the century, the dominant . . . conception of the human being as learner was that he was psychologically 'an empty organism' responding only randomly to stimulation, and learning only when specific responses were connected to specific stimuli through the mediation of pleasure or pain."[10] In those times, learning was teacher-centered: the teacher's desk was in the front of the room, the pupils' desks lined in front; all teaching materials were designed to complement the teacher-centered atmosphere of the classroom.

After a time it was recognized that these early theories did not take into account all of the learning behavior observable in a classroom. Conceptions of the learner then began to take motivational factors into account more fully. The learner was viewed as a dynamic organism, not a passive one absorbing knowledge in an environment of stimulus-response regulated by the teacher. Gradually the focus shifted from a teacher-centered classroom to a learner-centered or child-centered one.

The next shift in thinking emphasized the child as a social being. This development became pronounced in the late 1940's or early 1950's and is probably the dominant conception in schools today. In this view, learning is motivated essentially through social interaction. Thus, more

---

[10] J. W. Getzels, "New Conceptions of the Learner: Some Implications for the Classroom," Twenty-eighth Yearbook, *Claremont Reading Conference*, M. P. Douglass, editor (Claremont, California, 1964), p. 11. See also J. W. Getzels, "Theory and Practice in Educational Administration," R. F. Campbell and J. M. Lipham, editors, *Administrative Theory as a Guide to Action* (Chicago: Midwest Administration Center, University of Chicago, 1960), pp. 37-58.

time is devoted to the nature of social interaction and to the study of group dynamics. Classroom activities are planned to involve groups of various sizes, working jointly to solve problems identified by the group with the help (minimally employed) of the teacher.

Getzels emphasizes the point that these conceptions of the learner, although different in certain ways, are also similar in that they emphasize what has been termed a *homeostatic model* of the learner. That is, these views are predicated on the assumption that learning is an activity in which the learner attempts to return to some kind of homeostasis or equilibrium. He wants to solve the problem, to release his energy, because the "normal" state of the organism is one of rest, in which drives to activity are at a minimum. When the teacher presents a problem situation to the learner in such a way that he becomes motivated to find a solution to it, the activity which ensues stems from the desire to eradicate the problem, not because he is activity seeking.

Increasingly, the validity of the homeostatic model is being questioned. Anyone observing a group of children might well wonder why we have been so long in coming to this conclusion. Children clearly appear to be moved to activity purely for the sake of activity. The teacher who does not wish to be inundated with random activity, therefore, seeks to direct the energies of children along "productive" lines. But the question being raised here is whether the child-centered, teacher-centered, or group-centered classroom provides the best framework for thinking about dealing with all that energy. Unfortunately, perhaps the obvious is too often ignored in the search for truth. Since the early 1950's, however, an increasing body of research has been published which suggests that earlier conceptions of the learner were inadequate. In all likelihood the views will be modified again, and attempts to build teaching materials and learning situations will be more in harmony with that fresh view. As Getzels puts it, if

the classroom of the first period to which we referred could be characterized as *teacher-centered,* and the second as *child-centered,* and the one that is just now undergoing change as *group-centered,* the next one may very well be characterized in historical perspective as *inquiry-centered,* as a function of our changing concept of the child as a stimulus-seeking rather than a stimulus-avoiding organism.[11]

Many ideas flow from the concept of the inquiry-centered classroom. For example, if the learner *is* stimulus-seeking, then the nature of the

[11] *Ibid.,* p. 19.

stimulus to be presented to him must be examined more precisely. This means that concepts and principles which educators consider important for the child to learn will be emphasized. There will be decreasing emphasis on socialization and group behavior patterns. Although these concerns will not be cast aside, they will be thought of not as primary, but as concomitant, to the learning situation. Independent modes of learning, group settings for learning, and *ways* of thinking about a given group of concepts and principles will be stressed. It will be necessary to know how social scientists think and how they deal with ideas in their particular fields.

It will then be necessary to study more intensively ways in which elementary school age children think: how they deal with concepts and principles in a given field within the social sciences. For instance, knowledge of how *logical thinking* in children develops must be expanded. The degree to which the child can think about historical ideas, geographical ideas, and concepts from other fields of inquiry must be ascertained.

Educators are not entirely ignorant of these things. Actually a great deal *is* known. Bruner, Piaget, Vygotsky, and others have made major contributions to our understanding of the ways children can think about socially significant ideas. Reference will be made to these and other pertinent sources at the end of this chapter.

When thinking about a curriculum of social studies for boys and girls, one must take into account these harbingers of the future. But usually change does not occur in a drastic way. New conceptions slowly become absorbed into the conventional wisdom; they bring about newer ways of thinking and behaving only as they are tried and tested in the laboratory-classroom. To see how they "fit," one must become aware of what constitutes dominant practice in those classrooms today. We need to know how that practice evolved; to direct our thinking in considerable detail toward methods of working with children which may bring about a blending of what we hope for a curriculum of social studies with the "state of the art" as it exists today. These tasks will be discussed in the remaining chapters.

First, however, a theme important in any discussion of teaching and learning in school should be noted. Perhaps it is gratuitous, in a book devoted to problems of teaching social studies, to emphasize the importance of knowing and understanding boys and girls. Particularly may this be true when one realizes that many of these aspects cannot be taught or learned directly. It is a fact that the growth characteristics of children can be studied. By reading and study, one can gain an understanding of typical behavior, of physical characteristics of various age groupings, of social and emotional development in children. Many good books are available which present this important information, and every teacher should be familar with them.

But beyond this, there is the vital matter of being able to empathize with real boys and girls. Knowing children involves this intuitive capacity to project oneself into the personality of the child—to be able to comprehend in some degree how he feels, to sense the reasons *he* responds the way he does. Ultimately such "knowing" is achieved only through direct experience with children. And it is only possible where there is a true love for them. No one can teach this, but everyone can learn.

The remarks that follow, then, are predicated on this need to "know" children. The objectives in social studies in this respect are the same as they are for every curriculum area of the school. Children need to have a healthy sense of their own worth and a feeling of competence in dealing with life. Teachers strive toward this goal for every child, believing that it can be more readily achieved if each boy and girl is encouraged to develop a zest for learning; if he can gain practice in relating his knowledge to the world in which he lives; if he can be given experience in exercising responsibility. Finally, it is hoped that he also, by following the example set by his teacher, can develop an empathy for others.

For Further Reading

Association for Supervision and Curriculum Development, *New Curriculum Developments* (Washington, D.C.: The Association, 1965). See especially Chapter Eight, "Social Studies" by John U. Michaelis.

Bruner, Jerome S., *On Knowing: Essays for the Left Hand* (Cambridge, Mass.: Harvard University Press, 1962).

Bruner, Jerome S., *The Process of Education* (Cambridge, Mass.: Harvard University Press, 1961).

Bruner, Jerome S., *Toward a Theory of Instruction* (Cambridge, Mass.: Harvard University Press, 1966).

Cremin, Lawrence A., *The Transformation of the School* (New York: Alfred A. Knopf, 1961).

Cremin, Lawrence A., *The Genius of American Education,* (Pittsburgh: University of Pittsburgh Press, 1965).

Fraser, Dorothy McClure, and Samuel P. McCutchen. (eds.) "Social Studies in Transition: Guidelines for Change," Curriculum Series Number Twelve (Washington, D.C.: National Council for the Social Studies, 1965).

Goodlad, John I., *School Curriculum Reform in the United States,* The Fund for the Advancement of Education, March 1964.

Goodlad, John I., *et. al. The Changing School Curriculum,* The Fund for The Advancement of Education, 1966.

Hullfish, H. Gordon and Philip G. Smith, *Reflective Thinking: The Method of Education* (New York: Dodd, Mead and Company, 1961).

National Education Association, Project on Instruction, *Education in a Changing Society* (Washington, D.C., NEA, 1963).

National Society for the Study of Education, *The Changing American School,* Sixty-fifth Yearbook, Part II (Chicago: University of Chicago Press, 1966).

National Society for the Study of Education, *Social Studies in the Elementary School,* Fifty-sixth Yearbook, Part II (Chicago: University of Chicago Press, 1957).

Riesman, David, *Constraint and Variety in American Education,* revised edition (Bison Book, No. 317, 1966).

Whitehead, Alfred North, *The Aims of Education and Other Essays* (New York: Macmillan Company, 1929).

CHAPTER TWO

Social Studies Today

One cannot understand the social studies today without reference to their origins. It is in their past that one can come to understand why this aspect of the school curriculum has become such an important one and why today it assumes the dimensions it does in elementary schools throughout the country. Then, too, it is only by looking to the past that one may speculate intelligently upon its future characteristics.

The term itself has had a relatively brief history, spanning only slightly more than fifty of the three hundred years in which schools have been teaching the subject matter content associated with the curriculum of social studies. Prior to 1914, the year in which the National Education Association convened a group called the Social Studies Committee of the Commission on Reorganization of Secondary Education, the common terms used were the familiar "history," "geography," and "civics." But the origins in this country of the concept that children should be taught in these three areas can be traced to 1642. In that year the Massachusetts Bay Law was enacted, in which it was decreed that all children should be taught "to read and understand the principles of religion and the capital laws of the country." Less than a century later, history and geography joined the early "civics," and it became expected that all students, beginning and advanced, would study these subjects. Jefferson, for example, in writing his famous *Notes on Virginia,* in 1782, urged the establishment of a state system of education, stating that:

instead of putting the Bible and Testament into the hands of the children at an age when their judgments are not sufficiently matured for religious inquiries, their memories may here be stored with the most useful facts from Grecian, Roman, European, and American history.[1]

---

[1] Thomas Jefferson, *Notes on the State of Virginia,* William Peden, *editor* (Chapel Hill: University of North Carolina Press, 1955), p. 147.

And in another instance, he urged that superior students, selected from among all the children who were to begin their schooling under state auspices, be "well taught in Greek, Latin, Geography, and the higher branches of arithmetic."

In 1784, Jedidiah Morse published the first edition of a textbook, *Geography Made Easy,* which was to reappear in almost countless revisions for years afterwards. He prefaced the 1804 edition with these comments about the value and place of geography in the school:

Curiosity is the most prominent feature in the youthful mind, and it is the business of parents and instructors to gratify it; and by skillful management, it may be made to subserve the most useful purposes. No science is *better* adapted to gratify the *rational* curiosity of youth than GEOGRAPHY. Mr. Locke was of the opinion, that "youth ought to begin with this Science as an introduction to their future studies. . . ."[2]

Between 1800 and the Civil War, laws were passed requiring that geography, history, and civics be taught in every public school. But there was a relatively naive conception of the learning process. Grave questions began to arise about the effectiveness of such instruction; these resulted, by the end of the nineteenth century, in a series of attempts at revision. It was recognized that a system wherein teachers were mere taskmasters and where the goal of students was literally to memorize the contents of textbooks presented severe limitations.

Publishers were resistant to change, however; textbooks had become a profitable business. Many geography texts were in print by 1860, and there were some 360 different history text books of the type described.[3] Figure 2–1 shows reproductions of a typical history textbook of the day. Clearly, the teacher using this little book was held responsible for drilling the students so that they could respond correctly to the questions which, with their answers, comprised the chapters of the text. The latter portion of the book, containing a reproduction of the Constitution and other documents, lists 433 questions, arranged serially, which the teacher could use to make certain the pupil memorized the entire text and not merely certain portions of it.

By the time the United States had reached the latter part of the nineteenth century, it had been subjected to the trauma of civil war,

---

[2] Jedidiah Morse, *Elements of Geography* (Boston: Thomas and Andres, 1804), Preface.

[3] Harold Rugg, "The School Curriculum, 1825-1890," National Society for the Study of Education, Twenty-sixth Yearbook, Part I (1927), p. 21.

HISTORY

OF THE

UNITED STATES,

CONTAINING ALL THE

EVENTS NECESSARY TO BE COMMITTED TO MEMORY;

WITH

THE DECLARATION OF INDEPENDENCE,

The Constitution of the United States,

AND

A TABLE OF CHRONOLOGY,

FOR THE USE OF SCHOOLS.

BY BISHOP DAVENPORT.

A NEW EDITION, REVISED, IMPROVED, AND BROUGHT UP TO THE PRESENT TIME,

BY JOHN J. ANDERSON,

PRINCIPAL OF WARD SCHOOL, NO. 16, NEW YORK

Multum in Parvo.

PHILADELPHIA:

URIAH HUNT & SON.

NO. 62 NORTH FOURTH STREET.

CINCINNATI: APPLEGATE & CO

Figure 2–1: Sample pages from a school textbook published in 1850. Teaching methods implied in the organization of the book are evident.

Q. Was the attempt successful?

A. No: the attempt was unsuccessful, and fatal to the brave Montgomery.

Q. Where do the remains of Montgomery now repose?

A. In the city of New York, where, in 1818, they were removed by direction of the state of New York, Congress having ordered a monument to be erected to his memory.

Q. Were the Americans compelled to abandon Canada?

A. Yes: before the middle of 1776, the Americans had entirely evacuated Canada.

CHAPTER IX.

EVENTS OF 1776.

Q. Who held possession of Boston in 1776?

A. The British, under Sir William Howe, who had succeeded General Gage in the command of the English forces in America.

Q. What measures were taken to drive the enemy from Boston?

A. Batteries were erected on several neighbouring hills, from which shot and bombs were thrown into the town.

Q. Which battery was most successful?

A. The one erected on Dorchester Point, which soon obliged General Howe to abandon the town.

Q. When did the British leave Boston?

A. On the 17th of March, 1776, the British troops embarked for Halifax.

Q. Where is Halifax? Which way from Boston? What is the meaning of embark?

Q. What southern city was attacked in June of this year?

A. Charleston, in South Carolina.

Q. What was the result?

A. After an action of more than ten hours, the British were compelled to retire; their ships being much shattered.

Q. Who commanded the British vessels that entered the harbour?

A. Sir Peter Parker.

Q. Who commanded the fort on Sullivan's Island?

A. Colonel Moultrie.

Q. For what is the year 1776 particularly memorable?

A. The Declaration of American Independence.

Q. When was Independence declared?

A. On the 4th of July, 1776.

Q. How many colonies were there?

A. Thirteen.

Q. What were they declared to be?

A. They were declared to be FREE, SOVEREIGN, AND INDEPENDENT STATES. Thus, the political ties between Great Britain and her colonies, were forever dissolved.

Q. By whom was the motion made and seconded?

A. It was made by Richard Henry Lee, of Virginia, and seconded by John Adams, of Massachusetts.

Q. Where was congress then assembled?

A. At Philadelphia.

Q. Who wrote the Declaration of Independence?

A. Thomas Jefferson, of Virginia.

Q. Who was then president of congress?

A. John Hancock, of Massachusetts.

Q. In what were the Americans deficient?

A. In almost everything necessary for carrying on a war.

5

hurled into international affairs, and catapulted into an unprecedented economic growth. General expansion continued at an ever-increasing rate on many fronts: economic, social, and political. This was the beginning of the Progressive Era in American life, and such times and events brought about the re-examination of the manner in which children were taught the social realities. The "old" curriculum no longer seemed to fill the need; therefore, various learned societies between 1892 and 1921 attempted to determine how the traditional history-geography-civics curriculum might be improved at all educational levels. All had concepts of what a person should know to become a first-class citizen in the America of the American Dream. That there were many markedly different recommendations suggests an uneasiness about what one does in fact need to know in order to be a "good citizen"—an uneasiness which continues to the present time. These recommendations or suggestions, summarized in Figure 2–2, were made in the light of three interrelated developments. Without a doubt, these factors provide important base lines for our own thinking as we consider the development of a sound social studies program for children growing to maturity during the second half of the twentieth century. These developments may be encapsulated as follows:

1. The growth of knowledge and research in the social sciences
2. The rise of experimentation in social studies education
3. The Progressive Movement in education and social studies

The Growth of Knowledge and Research in the Social Sciences

Geography and history are the original "social sciences," having their roots as formal disciplines in Greek times. Herodotus (484?-424? B.C.) is generally credited with being the father of history. Strabo (63? B.C.-A.D. 24?) is usually called the father of geography. Of course, even before the dawn of recorded history, early man "recorded" history through his folk tales and tribal customs. Similarly, he became a practicing geographer in wresting from his environment food, clothing, and some form of shelter. It should be noted, too, that Strabo's predecessors had for several hundred years shown a penchant for finding out about the earth and the spatial relationships of things occurring on the earth's surface—the essence of all geographic inquiry—and for recording data in some permanent form. They constructed models of the earth's surface

Name of Committee	Date	Membership of Committee	Third Grade	Fourth Grade	Fifth Grade	Sixth Grade
Committee of Ten N.E.A. A.H.A.	1892 1894	7 Professors 3 Principals			Biography & Mythology	Biography & Mythology
Committee of Seven A.H.A.	1896 1899	6 Professors 1 Principal	Stories from the Iliad, etc.	Biography	Greek and Roman History	Medieval & Modern History
Committee of Eight A.H.A.	1905 1909	4 Professors 2 Superintendents 2 Teachers	Heroes of other times. Pictures of scenes and persons of various ages	American history; exploration to Revolution. Historical scenes and persons in early American History	American History; Revolution to the Civil War. Historical scenes & persons in later American History	European background
Committee of Five	1907 1912	4 Professors 1 Principal	Chiefly Biography: Civics to be taught Grades 1 to 8			
Social Studies Committee N.E.A.	1914 1916	5 Professors 2 Superintendents 10 Teachers 4 unclassified				
Committee of Seven A.P.A.	1911 1916	6 Professors 1 Superintendent	Civic virtues	A study of simple community activities Little textbook work	The Making of the United States	
Committee on History & Education for Citizenship, A.H.A. N.E.A.	1918 1921	6 Professors of History 1 Professor of Education 1 Superintendent 1 Teacher	Discovery and Exploration	How Englishmen became Americans 1607–1783	The United States 1783–1877	The United States. 1877 to date, 1/2 yr Civics 1/2 yr

A.H.A., American Historical Association
N.E.A., National Education Association
A.P.A., American Political Science Association

Figure 2–2: Summary of recommendations for curriculum development. (Reprinted by permission from "Three Decades of Mental Discipline," by Harold Rugg, National Society for the Study of Education, *Twenty-sixth Yearbook*, pp. 48–49)

Committee	Seventh Grade	Eighth Grade	Ninth Grade	Tenth Grade	Eleventh Grade	Twelfth Grade
Committee of Ten N.E.A. A.H.A.	American History and Civil Government	Greek and Roman History with Oriental Connections	French History with background of Medieval and Modern History	English History with background of Medieval and Modern History	American History	One Special period & Civil Government
Committee of Seven A.H.A.	English History	American History	Ancient History to 800	Medieval & Modern History	English History	American History and Civil Government
Committee of Eight A.H.A.	Early American History 1500-1789. Still more Civics	Later American History 1789-1909 (Also some Modern European History)				
Committee of Five			Ancient History to 800 (Econ., Pol. & Soc.)	English History with Continental Connections to 1760	Modern Europe English Connections since 1760	American History and Government (Separately or ratio 3:2)
Social Studies Committee N.E.A.	Geography European History, and Community Civics	American History Community Civics and Geography Incidentally	Political, Economic, & Vocational Civics with History incidentally	Ancient and Medieval History to 1700 (1 yr.); Modern European History (1/2 or 1 yr.); American History since 17th Century (1/2 or 1 yr.); Problems of American Democracy (1/2 or 1 yr.)	An advanced course in Civics (Report does not state in which year to be offered, nor whether 1 or 1/2 yr.)	
Committee of Seven A.P.A.	Community Civics (Emphasis upon functions, but some treatment of machinery of Government,)	American History in its World Setting			The Modern World	
Committee on History & Education for Citizenship, A.H.A. N.E.A.	The World before 1607 (Including Spain in America	The World since 1607 with emphasis on Economic & Social History of the United States	Community & National Activities, incl. Commercial Geography, Civics, Socio., & Economic History	Modern European History since 1650	American History during National Period	Social Economic & Political Problems & Principles

as they knew and conceived of it; these are the forerunners of today's maps and globes. Many of these represent remarkably sophisticated ideas. For example, in Aristotle's time (384-322 B.C.) it was widely agreed that the earth was round, and many models of the earth represented this conception, not to be given credence in the Christian world for hundreds of years. Though many maps developed by the early Greeks appear absurd in relation to what is now known about the earth, even these comprise important historical evidence of man's study about the nature of the earth and his interest in man's occupancy of it. They are significant documents in the study of Greek thought and life.[4]

Except for history and geography, the social sciences as they are known today have their academic origins in the late 1800's and early 1900's. These were times in which study and research in both the physical and social sciences quickened. In the United States, the fields of history, economics, and political science in particular, joined later by the other social sciences, witnessed an extension of research and knowledge which even today continues at an ever-increasing pace. Geography was slower to develop; scholarly endeavors in this field were left primarily to Europeans until the 1920's. In the classrooms of the schools geographic studies stagnated while the stature of history increased. Meanwhile, since little geography was taught in colleges and universities, few teachers were able to develop knowledge in this field. Since teachers teach what they know, this fact explains partially why little that is new in geography has been effectively taught, or learned, in the schools over the past several decades. In turn, it suggests a major problem facing the schools in the second half of the twentieth century: how to include geographic study in fresh and vivid ways in the elementary school curriculum.

Toward the latter part of the nineteenth century, interest in the other fields of the social sciences began to increase. As knowledge was accumulated, specializations grew out of the extant fields. These have become known as the *behavioral sciences,* such as psychology, sociology, and

---

[4] Useful books, for adults as well as children, which deal with map making and the early history of geographical conceptions of the earth (in addition to much other useful and interesting information about the earth) are Lloyd A. Brown, *Map Making: The Art That Became a Science* (Boston: Little, Brown, and Company, 1960); Frank C. Debenham, *Global Atlas: A New View of the World from Space* (Wayne, N.J.: Golden Press, 1958); Leo Bagrow, *History of Cartography,* revised edition by R. A. Skelton (Cambridge: Harvard University Press, 1964); and Leo Bagrow and R. A. Skelton, editors, *Imago Mundi;* a Periodical Review of Early Cartography, The Hague (not published in 1957-58).

anthropology. As scholars sought to study more intensively the nature of differences among men, they were led to establish the fields of psychology (which seeks knowledge of individual behavior) and sociology (the study of the behavior of individuals in groups). Another field of inquiry, social psychology, attempts to unite these two major concerns with human behavior.

By the early 1900's extensive collegiate courses in psychology and sociology were being offered in the liberal arts tradition. At about the same time, the field of education burgeoned. This was a logical answer to the problems presented by an increasingly diverse school population, problems that were in themselves a predictable result of the uniquely American ambition to provide universal education. The study of problems in education is a field closely allied to the social sciences and is emerging as an important discipline during the second half of the present century.

By 1910 psychology and sociology were firmly entrenched as disciplines in the social sciences. Next, anthropology emerged as a field of study. Anthropology bears some similarities to geography; both fields have roots in the physical as well as in the social sciences. As there is a field of study known as physical geography, so is there a field of physical anthropology. Similarly, studies can be primarily focused on cultural geography or on cultural anthropology (also known as ethnology).

As the twentieth century has progressed, each of the social sciences has continued to develop sub-specialties as knowledge about man's social behavior has expanded. No longer can one man become even relatively well conversant in a major part of a given field of study, as was the case not long ago. At the same time, the research tools available to the social scientists have become more refined. Better research procedures and instruments mean that knowledge grows in geometric proportion to the number of research scholars available. Since mid-century, for instance, important tools such as data processing machines, tape recorders, microfilm, television video-tape, jet transportation, and subsidiary inventions which make the whole world immediately accessible as a laboratory for first-hand research have been added to the equipment used in scientific research in the social sciences. Such aids were but impossible dreams at the turn of the century.

What has this tremendous expansion of knowledge and research procedures meant for the social studies curriculum? Above all else, it has made obvious the depth of our ignorance, both past and present, and has tremendously complicated the problem of selecting what to teach boys and girls in our schools. It has become evident in recent years that the process of making choices with respect to *what to study* involves an analysis of each social science discipline to determine *the most critical elements* which ought to be selected for study. It means, also, that not only new subject matter content but also new ways of studying and thinking in the social sciences must be given attention. Learning to *think about* problems in this realm therefore assumes an increasingly important place. Since it is no longer possible to achieve anything resembling mastery of a field, the *processes of thinking* about man's social world become a prime target in teaching. Without this ability, one can expect inefficient if not ineffective behavior from adults as they meet the realities of a social world badly in need of sane thinking and practical problem solving.

The Rise of Experimentation in Social Studies Education

Prior to 1900, the teaching of history, geography, and civics was dominated by memoriter methods. Drill and recapitulation of the textbook in class was the method of instruction in virtually every school. The sudden quickening of national life which occurred toward the close of the nineteenth century, to which reference has been made, included an active search for better ways to educate our children and youth. Participating in this search were William James, notably in his *Talks to Teachers* (1899), and Francis W. Parker, who was an important influence in education—both in Quincy, Massachusetts, where he served as an administrator in public and private schools, and later as head of the Department of Education at the University of Chicago. Perhaps most notable of all was John Dewey, who dealt with social studies in the larger sense in *The Child and the Curriculum* (1902) and *The School and Society* (1900, revised in 1943). Attempts to apply theory in practice resulted in the establishment of experimental programs in both public and private schools. For example, Dewey began his experimental school at the University of Chicago in 1896, and the Parker School, the birthplace of the "project method," was founded in 1901. Other plans were begun in Gary, Indiana, and Winnetka, Illinois. Helen Parkhurst inaugurated the Dalton Plan in 1920. The consequences of this experimental movement are still being felt across the land, and, in fact, around the world. Major ideas about teaching which stemmed from this movement included the following points:

1. Subject matter is most effectively learned when children enter into problem solving activities which make sense to them. When subject matter content is implanted from an outside source, as from a textbook or arbitrary teacher decision, opportunities for the child to become involved in real problem solving are diminished, if not eliminated. Social learnings of all types are therefore best acquired where the classroom becomes a laboratory for learning— where the teacher works with children to provide learning experiences which have as their basis experimentation. The experimental attitude leads to the formulation of hypotheses, at the child's level of understanding, and to the development of generalizations, also at the child's level of understanding. It includes the right to make mistakes as well as to achieve successes.

2. Learning is the reorganization of experience. Education is the process of drawing out, or educing, that which the child knows and helping him to reorganize ideas in the light of new experiences. Experience in the social studies should be within the range of a child's understanding and should be planned with the aim of keeping him constantly on the frontier of his own thinking. Experience is that which helps the child to solve the problem. It may include direct experiencing, such as handling, observing, examining, etc., or it may be vicarious, such as discussing, reading, re-creating through dramatic play, etc. Concrete experiences tend to mean more to children than vicarious ones. However, a variety of experiences are essential to all learning, and as children mature vicarious experiencing becomes the most important avenue for learning in the social studies.

3. Individuals vary widely in physical, social, intellectual, and emotional terms. Individualization of the social studies program so that each child is cast in a problem solving atmosphere holds the best promise for individual growth on all fronts. Teaching which ignores the individual for the norm of the group will likely miss its mark entirely in social studies.

4. Ideals are learned in large part by example. Therefore, the values of a democratic society can best be taught by living those values in the classroom. Autocratic classroom procedures in social studies are inappropriate and prevent achievement of this, a major goal of social studies teaching.

5. Responsibility for learning rests with the learner. If the social studies teacher assumes major responsibility for the pupil's acquisition of knowledge, the pupil is divested of his own responsibility for learning. In the end, only the person who feels responsible for his own learning will develop any real competence as a student of social studies or the behaviors which are associated with the goals of social studies teaching. In this connection, it is fallacious to argue that *some things* must be learned, regardless of the desires of the learner. Learning tasks which do not pose problems to be solved which are of interest and/or concern to the learner will not gain sufficient attention to be solved appropriately.

6. More than one thing is being learned at any one time. In social studies, social behavior accompanies learning of formal content. Skills of writing, reading, etc., accompany reporting, discussion, and other activities. Planning which seeks to take advantage of multiple learning provides all-round learning in the social studies.

The Progressive Movement in Education and the Social Studies

The earlier statements of principle by Dewey, James, and others, which gave rise to the experimental programs to which reference has been made, led in turn to widespread experimentation and study. Thus the new century witnessed the rise of what has been termed the Progressive Movement in education, paralleling the Progressivism which pervaded the entire American culture. The traditional history-geography-civics curriculum was criticized for its wholesale failure to satisfy the principles summarized in the six points above. As a consequence, a search was begun for more functional content and for more effective methods of teaching that content. Researchers turned to the methods of research being developed in the social sciences in an attempt to secure answers to the problems which needed answering.

Research during this period dealt with more precise determinations of social studies objectives, selection of more functional subject matter content, ways in which that content might be better organized for teaching, what methods appeared to be most effective in teaching, and the contributions of different types of instructional materials to learning in the social studies. In addition, attention was focused on improved testing procedures and methods of evaluating learning, particularly with respect to standardized test instruments.[5]

Most of the research and other writing produced during this period supported the six principles for guiding the development of learning situations summarized above. Strong support was thereby given to the "new" education at the expense of "old" or traditional approaches because those conducting the research and writing advocated change in education. They believed that their viewpoint was basically objective, that they were taking their cues from the scientific method, which was then beginning to achieve the support it still largely enjoys.

Supporters of progressivism in education enjoyed the role and advantage of the attacker. Virtually everything they found in conventional settings suffered under their criticism; meanwhile, they themselves had little to defend, for, even at the height of the support for progressivism in education, relatively little actually came into practice in any full-blown sense. But during the most popular years of the movement, "scientific and Progressive thinking" was beyond reproach, and those who believed in solving educational problems through this avenue appealed to a broad segment of the public.

In defense of those who sought to bring about changes in education, it must be said that it was not difficult to become disenchanted with traditional schooling. The cures advocated, although in practice relatively untried at any stage of the movement, appeared reasonable enough. Besides, most of these ideas had been espoused by a notable, although small, group dating from the times of Socrates and progressing through such educational gods as Comenius, Rousseau, Pestalozzi, Herbart and Froebel.

With the collapse of the Progressive Movement in education, which began in earnest sometime after World War II, one might have expected the derrogation of the principles that have been listed here. Not so; the principles were sound. The problem lay rather in the manner in which these principles were, or were not, put into practice. Thus, the Progressives, or those who would desert the traditional approaches to teaching, found themselves in the same awkward position as those they had previously attacked; and they were unable to overcome the attack for similar reasons. Despite the supposed advantages of the methods and

[5] A summary of the impact of this movement on education in general, and the social studies in particular, may be found in *The Scientific Movement in Education*, Thirty-seventh Yearbook, Part II, The National Society for the Study of Education (1938).

ways of science, they were unable to turn good theory into reasonably good practice.

Since World War II, the social studies curriculum has sustained further criticisms and demands for reform. Major curriculum revisions accomplished in the natural sciences and in mathematics at both the elementary and secondary school levels are being cited as the prototypes of changes which will eventually engulf the social studies program. An excellent example at the elementary level is the School Mathematics and Study Group material prepared under the direction of the Greater Cleveland Study Council; another is the series of science units for the primary grades developed by the Science Curriculum Improvement Study at the University of California at Berkeley, under the direction of Robert Karplus, Herbert D. Thier, and others (1964). An examination of the national scene by Martin Mayer in 1963, undertaken to assess the degree of readiness for such change, was sponsored by grants from the American Council of Learned Societies and the Carnegie Corporation.[6] Mayer came to the conclusion that the time was not yet ripe, and he cited three major stumbling blocks to further progress: "(1) reluctance of major scholars to take the time from their own work and to see themselves as educators of children, (2) the lack of intellectual sophistication among people in positions of power in the educational hierarchy, and (3) the *total* inadequacy of teacher preparation."[7] Mayer's comments are strong ones and undoubtedly require tempering. For, inevitably, the future of the social studies must be the product of its past. Right now, we *know* much better than we are able to *do*. The *ideas* which guide us in the development of sound programs in the social studies for boys and girls are not the culprits. If the desired success is not achieved, more of the blame should be placed upon the inability to put theory into practice than upon the theory as such.

Types of Approaches in Social Studies Teaching

Over the years, many different avenues have become recognized as successful ones for teaching social concepts to young children. As one watches teachers at work with youngsters, one is struck by the wide variations which exist from one classroom to another, even within a particular school.

[6] Martin Mayer, *Where, When, and Why: Social Studies in American Schools* (New York: Harper and Row, 1963).
[7] *Ibid.*, pp. 177-178. Italics added.

In viewing the different ways in which one may teach, it may be helpful to attempt to identify some of the major approaches currently used in American schools. Of course, it must immediately be apparent that these various approaches defy any specific designations. Any attempt to categorize methods which teachers find most satisfying in working with children inevitably draws too sharp boundary lines. The reader must take care, therefore, not to attempt to make *every* program fit only one of the approaches to teaching summarized here.

For the purposes of this discussion, four major approaches to the teaching of social studies will be identified:

1. Separate Subjects Approaches
2. Correlated Subjects Approaches
3. Comprehensive Themes or Problems Approaches
4. Social Living or Interactive Approaches

This classification system is useful in identifying the major principles existent in organizing content, selecting instructional materials, and directing pupil activities. It does not imply that a teacher will use one approach exclusively. It is entirely possible, and even highly probable, that the teacher will use at least two of these approaches within a given school year.

SEPARATE SUBJECTS APPROACHES

The traditional approach, the one stemming from the earliest days of free public elementary schools in the United States, organizes the social studies program into separate subjects. History, geography, and government (better known as civics) remain the usual ones considered. In such approaches, content for instruction is selected from each of these three basic social sciences and is, in effect, transplanted into the school curriculum. Selection is based upon what authorities think necessary and proper for pupils to know and upon the pupil's ability to comprehend the material.

If the reader will refer back to the chart showing the recommendations for improving social studies (see pp. 37-38), he will notice that many of the suggestions might be considered as separate subjects in nature. One must also be struck by the implication that separate subject approaches are not deemed suitable for the younger child. No recommendations are made for the primary grades; and most of those suggested for the intermediate years center around the literature of the social sciences, such as biography, rather than around history or geography as such. By the time the child is ten or eleven years of age, subject matter content in its more conventional sense is introduced. When the child reaches his junior high school years, it is presumed that he could profit from teaching which organized content around the fields of historic, geographic, or political studies.

The inappropriateness of the *separate subjects approach* in the earliest elementary school years has therefore been recognized for a long time, even by eminent scholars in the social sciences. It is accepted as an obvious fact that primary school children simply do not have the background of experience *or* the concepts and thought processes necessary to deal with history, geography, or government (political science) as separate subjects. Therefore, few adaptations of this approach are used in the first four years of school (through grade three), but from the intermediate years on through the junior and senior high school, it remains in vogue with the incidence increasing with the number of years the child spends in school. The most common occurrences are at the fourth grade level where state history and geography are often required topics, at the fifth grade level where United States history and geography are universally demanded (usually by legislative edict), and at the eighth grade level where there is also a universally held requirement that children again study United States history, with the addition of some work in civics.

Although topics such as those mentioned are included in the social studies program by legislative action, it is not mandatory that they be studied as distinctly separate subjects. It is the approach to the topic which gives it this designation. Thus this approach is characterized by the manner in which the content is organized. History is presented chronologically and is distinctively set apart from geography or other subject areas. Geography is presented in a regional or topical fashion, is primarily descriptive, and, for the most part, avoids historic considerations. At least, no formal or deliberate attempt is made to draw relationships between the various social sciences as in the correlated subjects approach which will be described.

The content in the separate subjects approach usually is derived from a textbook which in effect organizes that content and determines its sequence. The success of this method is usually determined by assessing how well the pupil has mastered the material covered in the textbook; also, attention is often given to related assignments and other activities growing out of the topics presented in the text.

The term *unit* or *unit of work* is often used in connection with this approach and with the *correlated subjects approach* as well. In fact, it has been applied in many different settings, leading to much confusion. Textbooks which organize their subject matter along essentially historic lines, for example, often use the word *unit* to designate a grouping of several chapters only. In one history textbook, for example, the material appears with these designations.

PROLOGUE • HOW DID IT HAPPEN?
UNIT ONE • BUILDING OUR FOUNDATIONS
   1. Europeans Discover a Large New World
   2. The Spaniards in the New World
   3. Other European Nations Plant Colonies in the New World
   4. How the English Conquered New France
     Let's Think about Unit One
UNIT TWO • THE ENGLISH COLONIES GROW UP
   5. The Colonists at Work
   6. How the Colonists Enriched Their Lives and Leisure Time
   7. The Spirit of Liberty Grew in the Colonies
   8. The Colonies Unite to Resist the Mother Country
     Let's Think about Unit Two
UNIT THREE • FREE AMERICANS BUILD A STRONG NEW NATION
   9. The Colonies Win Their Independence
  10. How the Thirteen Independent States United Under the
     Constitution
  11. The Government Under the Constitution Faces Its
     First Tests
  12. Other New World Colonies Win Their Independence
     Let's Think about Unit Three
UNIT FOUR • A FREE PEOPLE PUSH WESTWARD
  13. Across the Appalachians and on to the Mississippi River
  14. Expanding to the Pacific
  15. Rich Treasures of the Far West Attract Adventurous
     Pioneers
     Let's Think about Unit Four

[8] Oscar O. Winther and William H. Cartwright, *The Story of Our Heritage* (Boston: Ginn and Company, 1962), 800 pages.

This book is typical of the separate subject materials designed for the fifth grader currently in use in schools.

The textbook thus serves as the organizing framework for the "unit of work," but a wide variety of other instructional materials is used in conjunction with it. These additional enrichment-type materials— brought into the classroom to support and extend understandings primarily developed through the text—include motion picture films, maps and globes, filmstrips, flat pictures, realia, and models. From the example given above, it is obvious that the textbook can only give an introductory coverage to important segments of the major topic under discussion. Therefore, no conscientious teacher would rely exclusively upon the textbook to carry the entire burden of content. With the rapid expansion, during the past decade, in quantities of instructional materials, the problems of securing adequate supplements to accompany the text have markedly diminished.

It should be noted here, and reiterated in the discussion concerning the *correlated subjects approach,* that, despite the availability of many fine supplementary materials, there is considerable question as to whether subject matter organized and presented in this manner is the most valuable way to reach intermediate and upper grade children. This is particularly true of historic materials; it may also hold true for geographic and civic ones. The question is not whether any learning at all will take place. It is, rather, whether *adequate* learning occurs and whether the time spent yields commensurate rewards. A number of studies into children's understandings of time concepts, for example, suggests that history, when presented in a chronological sequence of events, is too difficult to understand for the vast majority of pupils in the elementary schools.

CORRELATED SUBJECTS APPROACHES

Widespread recognition of the fact that maintaining separate subject boundary lines is difficult when working meaningfully with young children early led to attempts to unify different fields of the social sciences in various ways. The earliest attempts at such unification of subject matter resulted in various blendings of history, geography, and government (civics). As knowledge increased and other social science disciplines became established, information from those fields came to be included to a limited extent. In selecting content for children to study, various ways of correlating, fusing, or setting out broad fields of concern were proposed. For the most part, however, history and geography provided the major fields in which correlation was attempted. Today, textbooks for elementary school use are frequently representative of this attempt to achieve a blending of history and geography, with some government or civics added. These are designed in the light of what is known about how children grow and learn. The following example illustrates the make-up of textbooks which attempt some kind of fusion or correlation of the subject areas.

UNIT ONE • I PLEDGE ALLEGIANCE
    Chapter   1. What Are the Words in the Pledge?
UNIT TWO • TO THE FLAG
    Chapter   2. The First Americans Had No Flags
              3. First Flags in a New World
              4. English Colonies in America
              5. Thirteen Colonies Grow and Prosper
              6. Unfurling the Flag of Freedom
UNIT THREE • OF THE UNITED STATES OF AMERICA
    Chapter   7. "From Sea to Shining Sea"
              8. Living in the Northeast
              9. The Midland Country
            10. The Southland
            11. The West, a Land of Variety
            12. Two New Stars for the Star-Spangled Banner
UNIT FOUR • AND TO THE REPUBLIC FOR WHICH IT STANDS
    Chapter 13. Americans Decide On a Republic
            14. The Capital and the Constitution
            15. The Morning of America
            16. Our Flag Gathers Stars
UNIT FIVE • ONE NATION UNDER GOD, INDIVISIBLE
    Chapter 17. Americans Live and Worship in Freedom
            18. Our Republic Is Tested and Proved Strong
            19. A Reunited Nation Grows and Looks West
UNIT SIX • WITH LIBERTY AND JUSTICE FOR ALL
    Chapter 20. Liberty and Justice Brings Us the Good Life
            21. From 1900 Until Today
UNIT SEVEN • THE FLAGS OF OUR AMERICAN FRIENDS
    Chapter 22. Knowing Our Latin-American Friends
            23. Canada: A Not-So-Sleepy Giant[9]

---

[9] Franklin Patterson, Jessamy Patterson, C. W. Hunnicutt, Jean D. Grambs, James A. Smith, *This Is Our Land* (Syracuse: The L. W. Singer Company, 1963), 474 pages.

This text is typical of those representing the correlated subjects approach to social studies teaching. The reader is encouraged to consult a nearby curriculum laboratory where various texts may be compared. It will be readily apparent which approach the authors are employing as they prepare their material.

The correlated subjects approach is dominant in the intermediate and upper grade classrooms of the United States today. As in the separate subjects approach, content is set out in advance; the text provides the basic guide and establishes the pattern in which that content is to be covered. Detailed teacher's manuals or teacher's editions of the classroom textbook provide guides for action for the teacher and, at the same time, disclose the intent of the writers of the text in relation to how social studies should be taught.

It should be made clear that, as in the separate subjects approach, correlation of subject matter may occur *without* the domination of the textbook. In such an approach, a wider variety of audio-visual materials and other teaching aids are used to convey the subject matter which children are to learn. Normally in these approaches such a breadth of content is not presented as that contained in the textbook, so it is possible to dwell on a topic for a longer period of time.

Both in the separate subjects approach and also in the correlated subjects approach the text should become one tool among many. It must be admitted, however, that it is difficult to subordinate this teaching tool to equal status with supplementary texts, trade books, reference books, films, and the like. Probably the most effective teaching takes place when the teacher has a firm subject matter background in the topics to be studied. Then he will feel free to deviate from the text, to provide for differentiated work among the pupils in his class, and to make some measure of individualization of teaching and learning possible. Similarly, he will be freed from the sometimes stifling effect of the "suggested activities" section following each major portion of the text. More variety in recitations and discussion, written and oral reports, artistic representations of material studied, and map and globe work may be the result of this approach.

When one recognizes that most elementary school teachers are not directly prepared to teach the subject matter they are expected to teach to children, there is little wonder that the textbook dominates classroom procedures, both in the selection of content to be covered and in guiding the teacher's selection of learning activities. One must also observe that

"*I don't get it.*"

present texts are in many ways superior to their predecessors. In addition, they are being supplemented by a wide variety of printed materials; reference has already been made to the new wealth of other instructional resources.

THE COMPREHENSIVE THEMES OR PROBLEMS APPROACH

The social studies program may be organized and taught in such a way that there is a different focus on the role of subject matter. In this approach, attention is first directed to socially significant themes or problems; these, in turn, determine what that subject matter will be and how the subject matter will be brought in. Hence the pupil studying a problem refers to the content which is appropriate to the solution of the problem as he sees it. This may mean that his data are primarily historic or geographic or drawn from one of the other social sciences, such as economics. Or, it may mean a blending of information from all kinds of sources. It is argued that such approaches are more meaningful to children since the problems identified are more childlike and, therefore, more realistic. Also, the sources to which the child turns for information are varied and can be adjusted to his ability levels. It is also claimed that the teacher may capitalize upon varied sources through highly individualized learning activities.

Two such approaches will be considered here. The *comprehensive themes or problems approach,* discussed in this section, differs from the *social living or interactive approach,* which is discussed in the next, in two important senses. In the former, the basic framework of problems or themes to be studied is determined for the most part outside of the classroom—through the adoption of a state framework, perhaps, or of a county or district social studies guide.[10] Although considerable latitude is provided for the teachers and pupils as they work together, the major areas of emphasis are fairly well decided. Also, it is expected that such study of the theme or problem will occupy a specified portion of the school day. That is, although it is expected that the social studies will permeate the school day to a greater or lesser extent, the teacher is expected to designate from thirty to sixty minutes a day to the study of the area designated.

[10] The rationale for this approach to the problem of organizing the social studies curriculum was developed in the Virginia Study conducted in 1934 and the Santa Barbara Study, completed in 1940. Paul Hanna has led in the further development of this concept, having participated in the original studies. For further details on the principles involved in this pattern of organization, see pp. 70-77.

In the *social living or interactive approach,* on the other hand, the teacher is given only the broadest kind of guide. It is expected that various studies will result naturally, as a consequence of the expressed interests of the children in the class. The teacher is expected to be alert to these interests and to capitalize upon them by encouraging children to study their diverse problems or questions. The teacher's role is less directive than in the other approaches described: it is his responsibility to help children identify problems but not to select the themes or areas to be studied. Also, the studies thus identified are expected to permeate the entire day; they become fused with the problems of living in the classroom and are virtually impossible to separate from the rest of the curriculum.[11]

The *comprehensive themes or problems approach* will now be considered in some detail. The broad framework of this approach usually is predetermined. Although there is no national curriculum center which selects broad areas of emphasis for the country as a whole, Richard Gross found almost universal agreement on these emphases for grades one through eight in a study of common practices in American social studies:

Common Emphases in the Social Studies

Grade I	Home and School Life
Grade II	Community Helpers
Grade III	The Larger Community and Other Communities
Grade IV	State History and Geography
Grade V	United States History and Geography
Grade VI	Other Regions and Countries of the World
Grade VII	History and Geography of the Eastern and Western Hemispheres
Grade VIII	United States History[12]

---

[11] The theory and practice of the social living or interactive approach are best described in two books: Florence B. Stratemeyer, *et al., Developing a Curriculum for Modern Living,* revised edition (New York: Teachers College, Columbia University, 1957); and Alice Miel and Peggy Brogan, *More Than Social Studies* (Englewood Cliffs, N.J.: Prentice-Hall, 1957).

[12] Richard E. Gross, "Social Studies," *Encyclopedia of Educational Research,* Chester W. Harris, editor, (New York: Macmillan, 1960), p. 1301.

Within major areas such as these, local units (the school district or county) develop a framework of topics. The following illustrates one county's decision concerning topics for study (examples are for grades one, three, six, and eight): [13]

Grade One

The statement of the major problems or questions related to the home, school and neighborhood for second grade social studies is not made to indicate a teaching sequence. This is a statement of activities which are themselves interrelated and focus on how the family, school, and neighborhood workers help meet our needs. These or similar activities are used to introduce and strengthen such understandings as how our families meet the needs of health, understanding and affection; how people, including the workers in the neighborhood, work together to make life more satisfying; how all plants and animals need certain conditions for growth and how all people have a responsibility for caring for private and public property.

THE HOME:

How work is shared in the home

The services and duties of each family member

The contribution and needs of pets

How families differ in size, customs, religion and traditions

The tools and equipment used by members of a family

How tools are used and how they are cared for

How families solve problems

How neighborhood families help one another

How families can have fun together

How houses are different and why a home is more than a house

How we make our homes convenient and comfortable

Why all living things have homes

The homes of animals and birds

THE SCHOOL:

Living together at school

Correct preparations for school

How we share work space, equipment and materials in the classroom and on the playground at school

How we care for our health and safety needs at school

How we care for school property and materials

The schoolbuilding and grounds, including the nurse's office, the cafeteria, the custodian's supply room and the principal's office

School personnel and how they help meet our needs

What we do in school, how we share ideas and work with others

Rules and customs of the school

Our responsibilities to other people in the school

[13] Solano County Schools, "Curriculum Guidebook and Elementary Course of Study," Solano County Schools, Fairfield, California (July 1, 1961). Reprinted by permission.

THE NEIGHBORHOOD:

What the land around us is like —the hills, rocks, soil and streams

Ways people change the land by constructing highways, bridges, buildings, streets, parks and recreational facilities

Different uses of the land in the neighborhood

Plants and animals that live around us

How weather affects our neighborhood

COMMUNITY WORKERS:

How workers in the neighborhood help meet our needs—the services of the electrician, the milkman, the plumber, the postman, the garbage collector, the deliveryman and the fireman

The services offered by various stores in the neighborhood

The gas station, the library, the police and fire departments

UNDERSTANDING THE INTERDEPENDENCE OF PEOPLE IN A COMMUNITY:

Our responsibilities in helping workers who help us

How families, schools and civic organizations work together to improve our neighborhood

How we can use and care for private and public property

How we can be good neighbors

Practices that make our neighborhood a healthy and safe place in which to live

Why people work together and the results they achieve

How people learn to appreciate and respect one another's work

Grade Three

The statement of experiences which help children understand how people and communities depend on one another does not suggest a teaching sequence. These or other experiences which show how people work together to provide services, what our community is like, how our community is related to other communities and those features which make for a good community life form the social studies curriculum for grade three. They will introduce and strengthen such understandings as how responsible citizens participate in community activities, how the services of many people are necessary to help us meet our needs, how materials and goods come to us from other places, how we produce and send things to people in other places and how machines make things easier and enable us to have many comforts and conveniences. These experiences should also help children understand the effects of geography on the lives of people and how differences in natural environment affect the work and the recreational activities of people.

A MODERN COMMUNITY:

What our community is like

The complexity of a modern community

How services are provided for the protection and improvement of both natural and human resources

How people communicate

How people and goods are transported

How people produce and process goods

How people control themselves and are controlled by law

How people are educated

How people spend their leisure time

Why pure air and water are important to good health

How good health is related to clothing and shelter

How adequate sanitation facilities protect our health

How doctors, dentists, nurses and others help us

Safety in the home, school and neighborhood is dependent upon the observance of rules and regulations

THE GEOGRAPHY OF THE COMMUNITY:

The geographical features of our community and of Solano County

A concept of the earth as land and water areas

The growing ability to interpret maps of school, neighborhood, community and county

Understanding map directions

LIFE IN A CONTRASTING PRIMITIVE COMMUNITY:

How primitive man carried on simple activities to satisfy his basic needs

An Indian tribe or pueblo

How the Indian protected and improved his natural and human resources

How he transported goods and people

How he communicated

How he produced and processed goods

What arrangements he made for government

Ways of meeting needs in a primitive society compared and contrasted with contemporary industrial life

Provisions the Indians made for recreation and education

The contribution of primitive Indian civilizations to our modern ways of life

Grade Six

The following curricular experiences for the social studies in the sixth grade do not indicate a teaching sequence. Children in the sixth grade have these or similar experiences related to how our country is associated with its immediate neighbors, how certain countries in the Western Hemisphere developed, how all countries in the Western Hemisphere are interrelated and how the Western Hemisphere is related to the world. They will develop and strengthen such understandings as that all human beings have common needs, that the ways of living in all countries are constantly changing as people meet new conditions, that improvements in transportation and communication are increasing interrelationships among countries, that peoples of many countries are learning to understand one another and work together to meet common needs, that human relations are improving as people learn to understand the cultural backgrounds of one another.

CANADA AND ALASKA:

Exploration and early settlement

Historical development

Present relations with Great Britain and the United States

The people and how they live

Similarity of the ways of life in Canada and those in the United States

Relation of the life of the people in Alaska and Canada to their climate

Modern developments in transportation and communication

The natural resources, products, industries and arts of Canada and Alaska

MEXICO:

How the Mexican people satisfy basic needs

The geographical contrasts in Mexico

The effect of climate on life in Mexico

The history of Mexico

The primitive inhabitants of Mexico

The Spanish Conquest

Independence from Spain

The place of Mexico in the history of California

Economic and cultural relations with the United States

The Good Neighbor Policy

Mexican-Americans in California

Mexican influence on the culture of California

OTHER AMERICAN NEIGHBORS:

Major cultures in Central and South America

Ways of life in contrasting cultures

The effects of climate and topography on the lives of people in South America

Products, occupations and modes of transportation

The influences of Spanish, British, French and German settlers in South America

The struggle for freedom by South American countries

The importance of international understanding and good will

The Good Neighbor Policy

THE PACIFIC ISLANDS:

The major cultures on the large island groups in the Pacific

The effect of climate and topography on the life of the people in the Pacific

Products, occupations and modes of transportation on the Pacific islands

COMMUNICATION:

The use of radio

The operation of a radio broadcasting station

The history of communication

The telegraph, telephone and television

The effects of communication on the lives of people in the Western Hemisphere and in the Pacific area

Mass communication and propaganda techniques

THE AIR AGE:

Man's conquest of the air

Types and uses of modern aircraft

The facilities needed
Global geography and air routes
Passenger and freight service
Time and space relationships
Knowledge that all populated
   places in the world are less

than a day from the nearest
airport
The effects of aviation upon the
lives of people in the Western
Hemisphere and throughout
the world

Grade Eight

The experiences in the social studies for grade eight are to help boys and girls understand how our country fosters the democratic way of life, how people meet their needs by participating in groups, how our government reflects our democratic values, how our American heritage continues to grow and how our ways of governing compare with other ways of governing. The experiences listed will help boys and girls strengthen such understandings as that the development of our country depends upon the cooperation of all our people as individuals and in groups; that our way of life has its roots in certain great political experiences; that the basic values of our American heritage include the worth of the individual, the welfare of the group, the equality of opportunity and responsible citizenship; that change is constantly occurring in all areas of human experiences; that our constitution provides for amendments to meet changing conditions; that our country has grown into the role of a leader in world affairs and that we must do more than give lip service to the concept of being a Christian nation in dealing with our enemies as well as with our friends.

Pupils will learn how people meet their needs by participating in groups, in the family, school, community, state, nation and world organizations. They will learn more about the family group and why it is important in a democracy and why each person is individually valued. They will learn about the adolescent group and its purposes; the individual's responsibility to the group and what the group does for him. They will learn about community groups, their characteristic ways of working, and their membership.

OUR DEMOCRATIC HERITAGE:
The functions of government;
   how civic and governmental
   organizations, facilities and
   services affect the adolescent
What the adolescent receives
   each day in protection, privileges and opportunities
Why beliefs in the rights and dignity of the individual is the
   source of our rights and privileges

The basic values in our national
   culture
Why individual responsibilities
   go with rights and privileges
How people's needs are met
   through cooperation and government
How civic and governmental organizations, facilities and services are the outcomes of need
How our American heritage
   grows

How the colonists met the problems of living and government in a new land

How people today are meeting the problems of living in an atomic age

The diversity of our people and the contributions to our growth made by the peoples from many lands

How we continuously use scientific knowledge to improve our way of life

Why the conservation of natural and human resources is necessary for our continued growth

GOVERNMENT IN THE

COMMUNITY, COUNTY, STATE

AND NATION:

The development of the constitution of the United States; the evolution of the idea of democracy through famous documents and the application of the constitution in our life today

The privileges and responsibilities of American citizenship

The institutions which have developed to perpetuate and improve democracy in state and local government

How the basic values of our American heritage have been tested through such events as the American Revolution, the Civil War and the World Wars

How our beliefs and basic values have developed into free education, social welfare practices, customs and institutions for man's benefit

How our values and ideas of freedom have influenced our actions and relations with other countries through the Monroe Doctrine, the Pan-American Union, the Atlantic Charter, the League of Nations, The International Postal Union, the International Red Cross and the United Nations

It is expected, in such programs of study, that the teacher will help children identify the problems or questions which will best stimulate them to look for satisfactory answers. Heavy emphasis is therefore placed on problem solving and the processes of research from the earliest years in school. In addition, direct attention is given to the nature of interpersonal relationships, group processes, and individual responsibility in the total study. Child growth is sought in these dimensions, as well as in the acquisition of subject matter, the development of generalizations, and the learning of such skills as map reading and expository writing. Learning sources of a wide variety are exploited as answers are sought to the questions raised by the class. Books, films, community resources of all kinds, models, recordings, radio, and television constitute important sources for information. The *separate subjects approach* and *correlated subjects approach* are characterized by uniformity of learning tasks; here differentiation is the keynote. And in addition to the more formal means of evaluating a child's progress, informal techniques are used extensively: teacher observation, checklists of activities, pupil self-evaluation, and culminating activities at the end of the study.

The approach the teacher uses is often called the unit method. Although that term is used in many contexts, as pointed out previously, it is in this setting that the term carries the most extended meaning. The major characteristics of the unit include proposing a problem or issue which pupils understand and which raises real questions in their own minds, conducting a search to gather information, generalizing with respect to evidence gathered, and drawing conclusions and formulating additional questions which call for further study and analysis. The unit method includes, as well, consideration of the nature of human relationships which further the development of the study, how the study may be related to the other tasks of the school, and concern for the development of democratic values and skills. In other words, it describes a *process of study* rather than the *subject matter for study*. It should be repeated that in this approach, the teacher normally has great flexibility in delimiting the topic, in selecting the approach which will be used, and, in fact, in studying those questions and problems within the broader topic which are most relevant to the children in the particular classroom. In the Solano County guide, reproduced in part above, it should be noted that at every grade level the teacher is reminded that the material "does not indicate a teaching sequence." Every comment in the guide suggests that the teacher should adapt the material to the particular situation in which he finds himself. This is characteristic of the comprehensive themes or problems approach.

When this method is used, frequently the themes or problems selected will become the "core" of the total daily program. The teacher will then use the contents and activities which surround the social studies program as the primary source for practice of the various language skills—reading, writing, speaking, and listening. In addition, he may rather systematically relate other areas. For example, physical education may be taught, in part, through folk dancing, when that activity expresses part of a culture under study; music can be taught through songs which are related to the unit topic; and art may be learned as a consequence of drawing murals or through the use of other media which relate directly to the social study. Literature may be taught through reading fiction and non-fiction dealing with the topic under scrutiny; arithmetic skills are practiced in connection with construction and other related activities. Not *all* of the school day is concerned with the social studies, but the unit method does provide many opportunities for relating knowledge and understanding from many different curriculum areas to the social study.

A majority of the schools in the United States have, within the past twenty-five years, adopted a *comprehensive themes or problems approach*. This circumstance readily becomes apparent as one examines courses of study from school districts and governmental units throughout the country. How then, can one explain the apparent incongruity between this statement and a previous one: that most teachers of intermediate and upper grade children use a correlated subjects approach in their teaching? The answer lies in the fact that the textbook continues to dominate the work of the teacher; this is primarily because neither private nor public education can yet provide a sufficient variety of teaching materials to make the teacher feel secure about departing from this anchorage. The teacher finds it necessary to rely more heavily on the textbook than he would like. And, where the teacher feels that his own subject matter background is weak, he prefers to rely upon the "authority" which the text provides, rather than on his own judgment in determining what is most important to teach and most important for children to learn. Therefore, textbooks have been written to serve a double purpose: to organize content and to present it authoritatively either in a separate subjects or correlated subjects approach and to select that content for presentation in the text which also fits the majority of courses of study. Hence, one sees courses of study which provide for a comprehensive themes or problems approach being supported by textual materials which are within the broad framework of content but which organize subject matter differently than would be the case if the "unit method" were to carry the responsibility for the approach in which children would become engaged in the study.

Recently, it should be noted, publishers have been providing a much wider range of supplementary and other materials, and these are finding greater use in the school. The primary grades have always had a greater variety of materials from which to draw since it is generally accepted that a subject-centered curriculum is inappropriate at this level, and the materials provided have always been written with this in mind. But the trend toward publishing varieties of supplementary materials in social studies is now expanding at the intermediate and upper grade levels.

Paperback books and hardbound materials which treat particular topics in depth are both inexpensive and of high quality. In the future, they will enable the teacher to exercise more freedom in his teaching. He will no longer be bound by the limited amount of teaching tools available to him.

SOCIAL LIVING OR INTERACTIVE APPROACH

Some educators have felt that learning the ways of a democratic society—the mores and traditions, the knowledge and understandings, and the skills and behaviors—is too often thought of as being the responsibility of the social studies alone. They believe that the approaches described above have over-emphasized the separateness and uniqueness of subject matter content and have raised artificial barriers within the school curriculum. It is their contention that problems and issues are often selected with relatively little regard for either children's understanding or for child interest. They point out that learning occurs where vivid, first-hand experience calls for immediate translation of thought into action. This process of interacting between the child and his environment is viewed as the key to learning the ways of democracy. Therefore, the quality of childhood experience in and out of school receives heavy emphasis. Content is not ignored, but much importance is placed upon the judgment of the teacher and the class in selecting that which will be most useful to study.

The *social living or interactive approach* to social studies considers character education as a responsibility of the total daily, weekly, and yearly program of the school. It holds that:

The older debates as to whether science or social studies should be the core of the elementary school curriculum no longer seem pertinent. Social learning should be at the center, and most individual and group studies that contribute to such learning draw upon all the sciences for information. Since the natural and physical sciences in this case are being put to social uses, the term social studies is still appropriate. In the same way, arithmetic and other communication skills are put to social uses within a study even though the learning of them is approached in additional ways in the school program.[14]

This program, then, places heavy emphasis upon interpersonal and

---

[14] Alice Miel and Peggy Brogan, *op. cit.*, p. 140. See also Florence B. Stratemeyer, *et al.*, *Developing a Curriculum for Modern Living*, second edition revised (New York: Teachers College, Columbia University, 1957).

intergroup problems of daily living and upon the quality of those experiences which children have with other human beings. Wide choice is provided with respect to what shall be studied. Immediate problems or issues which are topical and grow out of day to day living provide the main vehicle for initiating a study. An airline strike or questions about minority rights raised during discussion of current issues in desegregation may begin a class on a new social study. Or, the natural curiosity of children expressed through questions raised in a casual discussion may be the impetus. How roads are built, what happens in the town's civic center buildings, why their town was founded, or how they might improve the appearance of their school or neighborhood are the types of questions which might give rise to further study and analysis. It is the responsibility of the teacher to help children develop socially useful concepts and generalizations through these studies. He helps them apply facts learned in particular studies to a wide variety of situations in and out of school. His long-range objectives are therefore similar if not identical to those of all other social studies teachers. He merely seeks more immediate, first-hand means to achieve these goals.

The flexibility and possibilities for choice in this approach are too overpowering for many people. They feel that it leads to chaos and lack of continuity. Proponents insist, however, that teacher and pupil initiative in deciding what to study and when to study it provides opportunities for fostering continuity in social learning for every individual and that other programs are lock-step devices which prevent each child from moving ahead as rapidly or as well as he might in his understanding of social affairs.

Unquestionably there is considerable misunderstanding about this approach to social learning. All those who question its validity as a means for teaching children about social realities are encouraged to observe and talk to teachers who undertake this approach with their children in the classroom before drawing conclusions about its effectiveness. Any approach can be badly abused. Poor teaching in social studies, like good teaching, can be found where each of the approaches described here is used.

In this chapter, the social studies as they exist in their infinite variations throughout the United States have been discussed, looking first at some of the historical data necessary to understanding the sources of this curriculum area in the schools. It was pointed out that the term "social studies" is a relatively new one, having its origin in the period immediately following World War I, but that the teaching of socially significant ideas, as well as man's concern for studying social phenomena, is as old as man himself. The next consideration was the impact of the period of experimentation and scientific study in education, which preceded and paralleled the Progressive Movement in American life, beginning in the late 1800's. It was noted that studies of child development and consideration of the objectives of the school in the light of a new and powerful nation caused educators to attempt to build a new framework to guide us in the social education of the young. The influence of the Progressive Movement in education itself upon the development of the social studies curriculum in the schools was discussed.

Next, the four main approaches now being widely used by teachers in the United States were described: the *separate subjects approach,* the *correlated subjects approach,* the *comprehensive themes or problems approach,* and the *social living or interactive approach.* Differences between each of these approaches in teaching were noted, with the admonition that, in practice, it would be difficult to find any of these in its "pure" form. Attention will now be given to factors which must be considered in developing a balanced social studies program, regardless of the approach which may be used in the classroom.

FOR FURTHER READING

Cremin, Lawrence A., *The Transformation of the School* (Alfred A. Knopf, 1961).

Estvan, Frank J. and Elizabeth W. Estvan, *The Child's World: His Social Perception* (New York: Putnam, 1959).

Gross, Richard E., "Social Studies," *Encyclopedia of Educational Research,* C. W. Morris, ed. (New York: Macmillan and Company, 1960), pp. 1296-1319.

Mayer, Martin, *Where, When, and Why: Social Studies in American Schools* (New York: Harper and Row, 1963).

Miel, Alice and Peggy Brogan, *More Than Social Studies* (Englewood Cliffs, New Jersey: Prentice-Hall, Inc., 1957).

Metcalf, Lawrence E., "Research on Teaching the Social Studies," Chapter Seventeen, *Handbook on Research in Teaching,* N. L. Gage, ed. (Chicago: Rand-McNally and Company, 1963).

National Education Association, *Focus on Social Studies,* Report from the 1965 Department of Elementary School Principals Annual Meeting (Washington, D.C.: NEA, 1965).

National Society for the Study of Education, *Curriculum-Making: Past and Present,* Twenty-sixth Yearbook, Part I, 1926.

National Society for the Study of Education, *The Scientific Movement in Education,* Thirty-seventh Yearbook, Part II, 1938.

Stratemeyer, Florence, *et. al., Developing a Curriculum for Modern Living,* second edition revised (New York: Teachers College, Columbia University, 1957).

CHAPTER THREE

Criteria for Developing a Balanced Curriculum of Social Studies

A problem which every teacher faces, irrespective of the approach to the social studies he may undertake in his classroom, is that of providing a well-balanced program for his pupils. He needs criteria against which he may judge the worth of the program he plans with any particular group of children. Such assessments are made both in terms of the yearly program, for which the teacher is most directly responsible, and of the total plan of studies developed for children as they progress through the various levels of the school.

Patterns to be considered and provided for by the classroom teacher become more complicated as the world becomes increasingly complex. Factors of choice in curriculum building, such as those dealing with scope and sequence, are of first importance to the social studies teacher. In these times, he is called upon more and more often to cope with involved legal provisions, unavailability of adequate materials, and markedly atypical classes of several varieties.

Determining Scope and Sequence in Social Studies

Social studies may be evaluated in terms of their "scope" or breadth (sometimes called the *what* of the curriculum) and by their "sequence" or order in which topics are taught (sometimes termed the *when* of the curriculum). Quite naturally, the criteria one selects will reflect what he believes to be most important in teaching and learning. The criteria for evaluating scope and sequence are important for all levels of educational planning: in the classroom, in the elementary school, at district and county levels, and at the state level (the governmental unit responsible in our society for establishing and maintaining the public school).

Different loci of responsibility exist for private education; still it is true that each level has a responsibility for developing a sound social studies curriculum. Programs which develop without an overall plan or pattern are likely to become disjoined and unrelated, if not chaotic. The consequences for learning are apparent.

The need to coordinate some systematic approaches to content selection in the social studies has been discussed for many years. Early examples of attempts to reach accord on this problem were illustrated in Figure 2-1, in which it was shown how, at the turn of the century, the various committees of Ten, Seven, and Eight sought agreements as to the nature of the "best" social studies program. This search has continued. Thus, county and state departments of education in many instances play very direct roles in outlining, in broad strokes, the total social studies program within their jurisdiction. Curriculum guides, social studies "frameworks," and other statements are published by these agencies to help school districts and teachers to organize their programs according to accepted principles. Often instructional materials, such as textbooks, are recommended by these governmental agencies to implement the county or state course of study. There is even a sizeable professional body which feels that state participation in curriculum development is not sufficient. Since 1958, particularly, proposals have been considered for establishing some sort of national curriculum in the social studies.[1]

Unfortunately, many classroom teachers do not consider that they are responsible for the development of sound social studies scope and sequence, particularly outside their own grade levels. Such decisions are usually rendered by curriculum supervisors and administrators. Teachers might well become more concerned with this problem, for what can go on in the classroom is influenced markedly by district, county, and state pronouncements on what constitutes adequate scope and sequence. Since freedom to teach depends upon being informed about the options open to the teacher, blindness to the reasoning behind the selection of emphases in the social studies inevitably

[1] See Paul R. Hanna, "Design for a National Curriculum," *Nation's Schools,* LXII (September, 1958), pp. 43-45. Some reactions to this proposal appear in "What Leaders Think About a Design for a National Curriculum," *Nation's Schools,* LXVI (November, 1958), pp. 54-56. Further discussion of the issues appears in Allan A. Siemers, "A National Social Studies Curriculum," *Social Education,* XXIV (November, 1960), pp. 305-306; and Paul R. Hanna, "Proposed: A National Commission for Curriculum Research and Development," *Phi Delta Kappan,* XLII (May, 1961), pp. 331-338.

restricts the ways in which the teacher may implement his classroom program. Lack of this important information allows the teacher to assume that he *must* teach in a certain manner. This is read primarily as a mandate to cover a certain amount of content, in a prescribed order, using prescribed materials. Since most curriculum guides are prepared to provide only suggestions for teaching rather than required mandates, the uninformed teacher believes his hands are being tied when in fact they are not.

THE SOCIAL FUNCTIONS AND EXPANDING COMMUNITIES CONCEPTS AS CRITERIA FOR SELECTING A SOCIAL STUDIES PROGRAM

The most common criteria used in the United States today for determining scope and sequence in the social studies curriculum are the social functions or basic human activities (for scope) and the expanding community concept (for sequence). There are many ways in which the social functions may be stated. One widely-used list is that developed by Paul R. Hanna:

1. Protecting and conserving life, health, resources and property
2. Producing, distributing, and consuming food, clothing, shelter, and other consumer goods and services
3. Creating and producing tools and technics
4. Transporting people and goods
5. Communicating ideas and feelings
6. Providing education
7. Providing recreation
8. Organizing and governing
9. Expressing aesthetic and spiritual impulses.[2]

Hanna casts these basic human activities against the expanding community concept. Maintaining that each person holds citizenship responsibilities in a number of different communities, he states that every pupil should study these communities. Beginning with the family community, the child moves outward to the school and neighborhood communities. Following this, he studies the local community and then the state, region of states, national, and international communities. When charted, the emphases fall into place as follows:

[2] Paul R. Hanna, "Generalizations and Universal Values: Their Implications for the Social Studies Program," Chapter Two in *Social Studies in the Elementary School,* Fifty-sixth Yearbook, Part II, National Society for the Study of Education (Chicago: University of Chicago Press, 1957), p. 46.

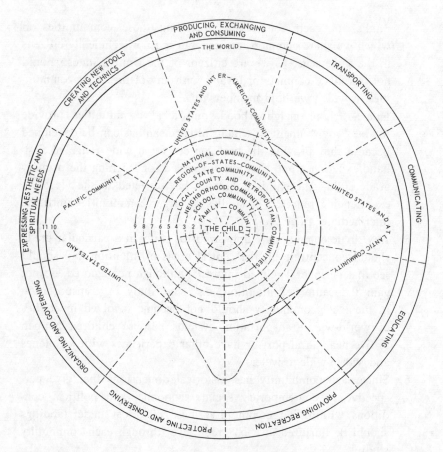

Figure 3–1: Basic Human Activities Superimposed on Expanding Communities of Men. (Reprinted by permission from Paul R. Hanna, et. al., *Geography in the Teaching of Social Studies*, Boston: Houghton Mifflin Company, 1966, p. 86)

In outlining the manner in which this type of scope and sequence should be utilized, Hanna presents six guiding principles:

1. The particular sequence of expanding communities should be followed in logical order.
2. Each expanding community should deal with the same list of basic human activities; but each study will treat those activities according to the interests and problems pertinent to that particular community.

3. Studies of each community, including those communities in which we share common interests but are not technically citizens in the same sense as we are citizens of the United States, should not introduce conflicts of loyalty with any of the other communities in which we hold membership.

4. Home, school, neighborhood, and local communities provide the best environment in which initial meanings can be developed because they provide the best sources for a wide range of first-hand experience and should be reserved for teaching the primary grade child—the child should not be subjected to the vicarious experiencing required of studies of larger communities until the intermediate grades.

5. Any single community emphasized for study in a particular grade should concentrate on the central areas of attention and should see that peripheral related interests, although not ignored, do not gain the center of attention, e.g., the study of transportation in the local community should not become involved in studies of world-wide transportation systems because children happen to live near an airport or have other experiences with jet planes and world-wide travelers.

6. Since each community has historical dimensions that give perspective to contemporary social, economic, and political conditions within that community, these historical understandings should be nurtured at each grade level through each community study.[3]

Criticism of These Criteria. This approach to designing the social studies curriculum has been criticized on several points:

1. The expanding community design is highly logical but only partly psychological when viewed from the standpoint of the learner. To insist that the child's view of the world and his ability to study and comprehend it must progress from one community to another, from a smaller "community" to an ever larger and more en-

[3] Adapted from Paul R. Hanna, "Society-Child-Curriculum," in *Education 2000 A.D.* Clarence W. Hunicutt, editor (Syracuse: Syracuse University Press, 1956), pp. 183-189. This chapter develops the rationale for the expanding community-social functions approach to the development of a design for the social studies curriculum. See also Paul R. Hanna, *Focus on the Social Studies,* A Report from the 1965 DESP Annual Meeting (Washington, D.C.: National Education Association, 1965), pp. 28-45.

compassing one, is too rigid and uncompromising. A child's interests and abilities are much more flexible and capable than this; his understanding of spatial relationships extends outward earlier than the present plans provide. Maximum learning will not occur where children are "locked in" to a study of home, school, neighborhood, and community for the first three or four years of their school life.

2. To study only one "community" in a year, such as the neighborhood or state "community" as is commonly suggested for the second and fourth grades, prevents the child at either level from becoming oriented to the broadest aspects of society. Children in the primary department should have opportunities to study communities reserved for middle and upper grades in this scheme. Similarly, upper grade pupils should have an opportunity to study topics normally reserved for younger children, when they have the added maturity which age and experience bring.

3. The communities and topics which are developed within those areas too often lead to superficial, overly broad studies. Children need to study intensively rather than extensively. Theoretically, intensive studies might accrue from the expanding community emphasis, but, in practice, too often unit topics are vacuous and burdened with too many complex concepts. Excessive verbalism is therefore too common in such studies. Units lack the problem focus essential to study and good thinking.

4. The framework suggested leads to crystallization of the curriculum. Topics become out-dated rapidly, and the suggested sequence and scope perpetuates the out-dated material rather than encouraging its elimination. This approach discourages the utilization of current issues and tends to eliminate consideration of controversial material and that which is likely to be fraught with the greatest interest and meaning for children.

5. Topics suggested because of their universal importance are broad generalizations of social problems, relatively meaningless in application to particular children in a specific classroom. Content which is determined by experts at a distance from the teacher, who do not know the teacher and his pupils, suggests a scope and sequence which will fail to come to life in the classroom.

6. Defining scope according to the basic human activities leaves areas of human concern untouched. The following critical topics

would not develop, for example, if the scope were described only through application of these criteria: the world-wide population explosion; race problems at home and abroad; the nature of ideological conflicts between the free world and the slave world.

The advocates of the expanding community-social functions approach counter these criticisms with several of their own. Major advantages of this type of design, in addition to those presented above, include:

1. The design ensures comprehensiveness. The major citizenship responsibilities and the types of activities in which all men engage are presented to all children in those schools in which this design is observed. Thus, common elements are presented to a large number of pupils, providing a commonality of experience necessary for the development of a citizenry with common goals.

2. The scope of any social study can be evaluated at any time merely by applying the criteria of social functions or basic activities to the curriculum in the classroom. The teacher is therefore provided with an immediate tool to help him determine the adequacy of content emphases in his social studies program.

3. The design helps bridge the gap between subject matter and and the daily life of the pupils. Pupils may center their studies on problems which are real to them, and the design helps them and their teacher reach into fields of the social sciences for content which is related to the problem they seek to resolve.

4. The expanding community concept is, in actuality, psychologically *the* sound approach. At the same time, it presents a logical organization within which those concepts and generalizations which should be held in common in American democracy may be taught. To argue that children are capable of understanding more complex cultures at greater distances is not supported by research.

5. Most criticisms of the expanding community concept might be leveled at any design. The design does not in and of itself prevent creativity and originality in teaching. It merely provides a framework on which the teacher may build; it does not guarantee the quality of that teaching any more than does any other design.

Obviously, most discussion about the validity of this approach centers around the notion of the expanding community concept. This is not surprising since various approaches to selecting the scope of the program may be adapted to the sequence which one selects. The entire logic of the expanding community concept rests upon the acceptance of the sequence; this lack of flexibility is unacceptable to many people.

However, an analysis of current practice in social studies throughout the United States reflects the impact of this point of view upon American education. The emphases found by Gross were noted in an earlier chapter. Preston discovered similar emphases, the most common subject matter being as follows:

Grade I   Home, school, pets
Grade II   Community helpers
Grade III   Food, clothing, and shelter
Grade IV   Type regions of world; U.S. history; community
Grade V   U.S. geography; U.S. history
Grade VI   Latin America; Canada; Asia; Europe[4]

A recent comprehensive study to determine a modern "framework" for social studies illustrates how the expanding community concept has been adhered to in California. In preparing this frame, social scientists, educators, and lay leaders were called upon during a period of more than five years. Social scientists were asked to delineate content in terms of basic generalizations about their fields. Educators, upon the general advice of lay leaders, then detailed a sequence of topics within which these generalizations might be studied by children.

Grade Level Allocations
Kindergarten Through Grade School

Grade Level	Theme
Kindergarten	The Immediate Environment: Relationship of the Neighborhood to Home and School
	A. The Home and Family: Their Relationship to Community Activities
	B. School Life and the School Plant
	C. The Neighborhood: Relationship of the Neighborhood to Home and School
Grade One	The Home, School, and Community: Responsibilities and Services
	A. Relationship of the Home to the Community
	B. School Activities and Pupil Responsibilities

---

[4] Ralph C. Preston, *Teaching Social Studies in the Elementary School,* revised edition (New York: Holt, Rinehart, and Winston, 1960), p. 33.

C. Needed Services in the Community

D. Effect of the Natural Environment on Ways of Living

Grade Two   Our Community and City: The Interrelatedness of Community Life

A. Ways in Which People Meet Needs in Producing, Processing, and Marketing Food

B. Ways in Which People Meet Needs in Producing, Processing, and Marketing Clothing

C. Production and Exchange of Goods and Services Between Communities

D. Effect of Natural Environment and People on Each Other

Grade Three   Effect of Growth and Change on Communities: Differences Among Communities in the State, in the Nation, and in the World

A. The Changing Community: Forces in the Present and the Past

B. Communication and Cooperation Between Communities

C. Utilization of the Natural Environment in Rural and Urban Areas

D. Differences Among Contemporary Communities in California and Those in Other Parts of the Nation and the World

Grade Four   California: Its Relationship to the Western States, the Nation, and the World

A. California Today

B. Early California: Periods in its Development

C. California as Part of the Far West, the United States, the Pacific Area, and the World

D. A Contemporary California Community Compared with a Community in an Oriental or African Culture

Grade Five   The United States: Its Growth and Development; Its Future as a World Power; and Its Relationships with Canada

A. The West and Other Parts of the Nation

B. The Origin of the United States

	C. Development of the United States
	D. The United States and its Future
	E. Interrelationships of the United States and Canada
Grade Six	Overviews of Global Geography of the World and Study of Life in Latin America
	A. Global Geography, with Emphasis on the Effect of Scientific Discovery on Life in the World Today
	B. Interrelationships Among Countries of the Americas
	C. Selected Latin-American Countries
Grade Seven	The Mediterranean Area Life in the World Today: and the Middle East; Europe; and the European Backgrounds of the United States
	A. Interrelationships Among Countries of the Mediterranean Area, the Middle East, and Europe
	B. The Mediterranean Area and the Middle East
	C. European Nations
	D. Studies of Selected Cultures
	E. The European Backgrounds of the United States
Grade Eight	The United States and Our Heritage
	A. The People of the United States
	B. Contributions of Individuals and Groups to Developments in the United States and to Our American Culture
	C. The Emergence and Continued Usefulness of Basic Principles and Ideals
	D. Contributions of Natural Resources, an Expanding Economy, and Scientific Advances to Developments in the United States
	E. Services to the People by the Federal, State, and Local Governments; Responsibilities of Citizens
	F. The United Nations[5]

[5] California State Department of Education, "Social Studies Framework for the Public Schools of California," prepared by the State Curriculum Commission (Sacramento, California: 1962).

This social studies framework, developed through the work of the California State Curriculum Committee, has had wide impact on schools throughout the United States. It is to be expected that revisions will be made from time to time; nevertheless, there can be little doubt that these concepts of grade level allocation represent a pioneering effort of continuing nation-wide importance.

OTHER APPROACHES TO A BALANCED SOCIAL STUDIES PROGRAM

Preston has suggested another approach to checking balance in the social studies curriculum. Maintaining that children should intensively study a few things, he further claims that these should be ordered in such a fashion that children will approach major social studies themes from a variety of aspects or positions. Preston suggests four categories of studies appropriate for elementary school children. The first of these is community studies; the second, social processes (as discussed above); the third is regions and cultures; and the fourth includes studies of the past. Rather than using social functions alone to describe the scope of the social studies program, Preston utilizes these categories as one of several criteria by which teacher and administrator may decide whether a sensible scope is being defined. No specific rules are set forth to control sequence as in the expanding community concept. Although one moves from the known to the unknown—generally from the first-hand environment of the learner to more distant locales in time and space—the proper sequence is determined by the educator who is engaged in planning a program for a particular group of children.

Framework for Determining Degree of Balance in the Social Studies Curriculum[6]

	Kinder- garten	Grade 1	Grade 2	Grade 3	Grade 4	Grade 5	Grade 6
The Community							
Social Processes							
Regions and Cultures							
The Past							

[6] Preston, *op. cit.*, p. 45.

Examples of categories of studies that could be inserted in the blanks of the chart:

Community	Social Processes	Regions and Cultures	The Past
Community survey	Protection Conservation	Homeland Minority culture	Origin of special days
Comparison of communities	Production Distribution	Neighboring society	Early American Indians
Community history	Consumption Invention	Unknown, remote society	Early explorers Colonial period
Community service	Transportation Communication	Stable, democratic society	Westward movement Ancient civilization
Community planning		Isolated society	Medieval period

Preston points out that, although it is not necessary to include each type of study at each grade level, it is desirable to provide a reasonable balance of all studies throughout the elementary school years. In examining what is going on in the schools, he concludes that it would be desirable to provide studies of *regions and cultures* and of the *past* for children in the primary grades to a greater extent than usually found. Similarly, more *community studies* and *social process studies* should be included in the intermediate grades. It will be noted in examining the *California Framework for the Social Studies* that community and social process studies dominate in the primary grades and that studies of the past and of regions and cultures are emphasized in the intermediate and upper grades.

Another plan for the social studies curriculum is presented by Clements, Fielder, and Tabachnick,[7] who suggest that the method of inquiry varies according to the sources available. Different peoples, events, and places need to be studied in different ways. Topics are suggested that will encourage and permit the study of all four categories of social study: the Now and Here, the Now and There, the Then and Here, and the Then and There. All of these should be studied in some manner by all children, during every year, and at every grade level.

It is not difficult to find material for the Now and Here; this facet of social study suffers from an embarrassment of riches. "Living men can talk and respond," the authors remind us. "If we listen to only a few, what are the risks in generalizing about the diversity of responses we

[7] H. Millard Clements, William R. Fielder, and B. Robert Tabachnick, *Social Study: Inquiry in Elementary Classrooms* (Indianapolis, Indiana: Bobbs-Merrill, 1966), pp. 153-237.

obtain? What distortion is inherent in any capsule statement we devise?
... What to attend to? What to ignore?" It is this selection problem that
faces teachers when they lead their children in study of the men and
events of their own time and place.

Now and There presents other difficulties and decisions. One of these
is knowing when he has moved beyond the everyday experience of his
class. Children living in the inner city may never have seen the rural
countryside, and "farms and villages thirty miles away are far away from
their experience." The authors point out that to such children, even
another part of their own city will provide Now and There experiences.

In studying the Then and Here, school children can practice the craft
of the historian when delving into yesterday's people and events in their
own locality. The study of the Then and There is of particular importance to Americans, for their past is truly *then* and *there*.

Clements, Fielder, and Tabachnick believe that inquiry, search, and
discovery provide some of the most authentic human adventures available to men. They quote Paul Tillich, who observed that "the fatal
pedagogical error is in throwing answers like stones at the heads of
people who have not asked the questions." Imaginative use of the themes
presented here provides one way to avoid this basic problem.

These approaches to social studies curriculum design provide more
flexibility in selecting appropriate content for study at the school and
district level. It may be true that they do not contain the detail of the
expanding community—social functions criteria (and thus the written-in
assurance of breadth or comprehensiveness); but many persons believe
that individuality and creativity are sacrificed unless such flexibiliy is
provided in the design. Such educators maintain that removal of the
responsibility for making choices operates negatively upon the teacher,
causing his program to be less effective in every respect.

Schools adopting this type of scope and sequence design rely more
exclusively upon subjective judgments of teachers and administrators
in deciding whether the program represents a good balance for those
teachers and those children for whom it has been developed. They do
not think it necessary to ensure uniformity to the extent the California
Framework suggests. They would be inclined, as a consequence, to resist
attempts to define a national curriculum in the social studies; they would
find little reason to question the validity of professional judgment
about the quality of a particular design. This implies, also, that school
districts would vary with respect to the details of the scope and sequence

appropriate for different locations. There is enough unanimity concerning the nature of child growth and development, and the types of studies which are socially significant, that diversity would not be as great as many people might think.

THE PROBLEMS APPROACH TO BALANCE

Another approach to designating scope and sequence deserves attention. Many educators resist any formal designation of sequence, contending that such patterns, when put into practice in the classroom, ignore child interest and need to a great extent; that such programs of study become only verbal interchanges and are of little consequence in affecting the lives of children. This manner of teaching was described earlier as the *social living or interactive approach* to social studies. The selection of sequence, in this instance, is made by the teacher and his colleagues in a given school, working with a particular population of children. It should not be interpreted that this automatically creates an entirely chaotic, incidental, or accidental result in teaching and learning. Much attention has been paid to designating the scope of programs of this nature. But scope is defined more in the nature of personal–social problems of childhood than in terms of subject matter or broad societal need. Different avenues to the identification of personal–social problems or issues at different stages of life, from infancy to old age, are reflected in the phrases *areas of living, persistent life situations, imperative needs,* and *problems of living.* Stratemeyer and her associates, for example, developed a list representing an analysis of "persistent life situations, those situations that recur in the life of the individual in many different ways as he grows from infancy to maturity."[8] They point out that:

the persistent life situations . . . listed are in no sense a basis for fixed curriculum units; nor are they the only ones at which a school faculty might arrive. Normally every area, and practically every persistent situation within that area, will be faced in some form at each grade level. . . . The intensity of study of a specific life situation, as well as the way in which it will be approached, depends on the needs of the particular pupil group. The . . . list should never be used to prescribe the order in which learners should face these persistent life situations or the grade levels at which they should be focal.[9]

[8] Florence B. Stratemeyer, *et al., Developing a Curriculum for Modern Living,* second edition revised (New York: Bureau of Publications, Teachers College, Columbia University, 1957), p. 115.
[9] *Ibid.,* pp. 165-166.

The persistent life situations are listed under three major categories: (1) situations calling for growth in individual capacities; (2) situations calling for growth in social participation; and (3) situations calling for growth in ability to deal with environmental factors and forces. Part of the last major category is reproduced here to indicate the comprehensiveness with which such situations have been analyzed:

Situations Calling for Growth in Ability to Deal with Environmental Factors and Forces [10]

NATURAL PHENOMENA

A. Dealing with Physical Phenomena

Adjusting to Atmospheric Conditions	Adjusting to weather conditions Adjusting to conditions of air, moisture, sunlight
Using the Earth's Surface and Contents	Dealing with topographic features Conserving and using natural resources
Adjusting to Factors Conditioned by the Structure of the Universe	Understanding factors conditioned by relative motion in solar system Exploring the nature of the universe

B. Dealing with Plant, Animal, and Insect Life

Producing and Using Animal Life	Producing, caring for, and controlling animal life Using animal products for human welfare
Controlling and Using Insect and Related Forms of Life	Controlling and using insect life for human welfare
Producing and Using Plant Life	Producing, protecting, and controlling plant life Using plant products for human welfare
Controlling and Using Bacteria and other Microscopic Organisms	Providing immunity to and the positive use of microscopic organisms

[10] Reprinted with the permission of the publisher from Florence B. Stratemeyer, Hamden L. Forkner, Margaret G. McKim, and A. Harry Passow, *Developing a Curriculum for Modern Living* (New York: Teachers College Press, 1957). © 1947, 1957 by Teachers College, Columbia University.

C. *Using Physical and Chemical Forces*

Producing New Forms through Physical and Chemical Change	Using physical and chemical change Adjusting use of materials to their properties
Conserving Materials	Preserving materials
Using Physical Forces	Adjusting to physical forces Using sources of energy Using and adjusting to light and sound

TECHNOLOGICAL RESOURCES

A. *Using Technological Resources*

Using Tools, Machines, and Equipment	Using common tools Selecting and using the tools and machines of a trade
Using Household and Office Appliances	Using equipment to conserve human energy
Using Instruments of Communication	Using effective means of communicating with individuals or groups
Using Means of Transportation	Using effective means of transporting people and materials

B. *Contributing to Technological Advance*

Encouraging Technological Advance	Supporting experimentation
Using Technological Resources for Maximum Social Good	Using resources in keeping with social values

ECONOMIC—SOCIAL—POLITICAL STRUCTURES AND FORCES

A. *Earning a Living*

Providing for Work Needs of Society	Assuring that needed work will be done Deciding what work to do
Achieving Effective Workmanship	Assuring adequate work standards Providing good working conditions
Assuring the Rights and Responsibilities of Workers	Securing adequate remuneration Assuring other benefits, rights, and responsibilities
Managing Money	Budgeting income Saving and investing Borrowing money

B. Securing Goods and Services

Making Goods and Services Available	Securing effective distribution
Buying and Selling Goods and Services	Deciding where to buy or sell Determining quality Determining a fair price Deciding on means of payment

C. Providing for Social Welfare

Working in the Family Group	Providing secure relations Sharing family responsibilities
Participating in Community Welfare Provisions	Sharing in protective measures Sharing in community welfare efforts
Using Government to Guarantee Welfare	Providing and using public services Providing and using legal protections Controlling use of natural resources

D. Molding Public Opinion

Providing Adequate Educational Opportunities	Participating in organized education Providing and supporting other educational agencies
Using Instruments for Disseminating Information	Interpreting information Using appropriate means of presenting a point of view Acting on issues involving freedom of press

E. Participating in Local and National Government

Electing Government Representatives	Nominating and electing candidates
Securing Effective Government Organization	Considering effectiveness of existing organization Appraising work of representatives
Making and Enforcing Laws	Taking responsibility in making and changing laws Cooperating in enforcing laws
Providing Financial Support for Government	Determining amount and sources of income Determining use of government income

Stratemeyer and her associates have developed activities appropriate to early childhood, later childhood, youth, and adulthood for virtually every sub-category. For example, they suggest the following learning situations in the last category listed above, "Participating in Local and National Government": [11]

	Early Childhood	**Late Childhood**

E. PARTICIPATING IN LOCAL AND NATIONAL GOVERNMENT

| *Electing Government Representatives*

 Nominating and electing candidates | *Sharing in the selection of classmates for special responsibilities*—Voting for class committees; sending delegates to student council; choosing delegate to meet with assembly committee; helping decide which persons should be trusted with special responsibilities in class; discussing what one should take into account in suggesting people for special jobs ... | *Using appropriate procedures in nominating and electing candidates*—nominating and electing candidates for student council; considering special qualifications needed for particular jobs— electing captain of baseball team, editor of school paper; discussing whether secret ballot should be used to elect class officers; planning campaign speech as candidate for student council office; discussing qualifications of prominent candidates for local or national elections; finding how parents get information about candidates; finding why adults must register to vote; finding what voting machines are like, how parents cast their votes ... |
| *Securing Effective Government Organization*

 Considering effectiveness of existing organization | *Identifying the prominent members of local and national government*—Finding how class representatives take part in student council; asking what is done by President, governor, mayor; asking about prominent officials discussed by family or friends; asking about pictures of Capitol, White House ... | *Finding how government groups are organized* — Deciding how long class officers should remain in office; appraising effectiveness of present structure of student council, staff of school paper; finding what kind of work is done by mayor, governor, President, other prominent local and national officials; finding how Consti- |

[11] *Ibid.*, pp. 316-321. Reprinted by permission.

tution of this country came to be; visiting state legislature, meeting of city council; studying differences between Senate and House of Representatives; finding how school board, park commission, other local groups change or improve opportunities to go to school to work or play; discussing work of ambassadors and other members of Department of State mentioned in the news; finding what it means for a country to have a king or queen; discussing relation of Canada, Australia to British Commonwealth of Nations...

Youth	Adulthood

E. PARTICIPATING IN LOCAL AND NATIONAL GOVERNMENT

Understanding and applying the principles involved in nominating and electing candidates—Helping nominate and elect representatives to student council; acting as member of nominating committee for club officers; discussing process through which political candidates are selected; following procedure of national political rally to nominate presidential candidate; discussing qualifications of candidates for local or national offices; considering local procedures which regulate registration for voting; taking part in local drives to get all voters to register, to cast their votes; discussing how ballots are cast, how votes are counted; comparing election procedures with those of other countries prominent in the news...

Taking an active part in the selection, nomination, and election of government candidates — Deciding what qualifications a candidate for office should have; considering respective qualifications of several nominees for office; deciding whether to work actively in political party; holding office in local branch of political party; taking part in nomination of candidates; considering efficacy of local procedures to register voters; deciding what action to take on measures which restrict the right to vote; evaluating proportional representation or other election procedures unique to the given community; deciding whether to electioneer for a candidate; helping plan methods of securing large turnout to vote at elections; considering what points of view are represented by various parties...

Understanding major issues involved in securing an effective organization of government personnel—Helping set up constitution of student council or class organization; considering needed changes in existing council organization; discussing organization of local and national governments; finding how present structure of the national government came to be; discussing news releases on appointments of cabinet members; discovering what municipal positions exist in local community; finding how to proceed to get driving license; deciding which government departments to write to for special information; working with members of Department of Agriculture on demonstration farms; finding how the government is organized to work with those of other countries; securing information about the organization of governments of other nations prominent in the press; tracing the history of democratic forms of government . . .

Acting to secure and maintain an effective government organization—Discussing how long local officials should remain in office; discussing effectiveness of local organization of mayor and council; taking action on proposals to hire a city manager; evaluating presidential appointments to government posts; discussing effectiveness of the work of Department of State in international problems; appraising proposals to put emergency powers in hands of President; considering specific proposals to increase government efficiency; taking action on measures to secure continuity of personnel in government departments; deciding which department to go to for assistance on special problems; deciding what measures should be taken to assist other countries desiring democratic forms of government . . .

	Early Childhood	**Late Childhood**
Appraising work of representatives	*Making informal appraisal of the work of classmates to whom responsibilities have been assigned* — Deciding whether special committee has done its work well; discussing how to tell if special jobs are well done; deciding whether a special delegate has spoken well in assembly; discussing appropriateness of proposals of lunchroom committee, other special committee; considering how well persons responsible for an all-school service did their jobs the previous week . . .	*Finding how local and national groups may follow the work of their representatives* — Discussing reports of student council representatives; making suggestions for new committees on basis of work of those retiring; discussing press and parent comments on work of prominent political representatives; following congressional vote on a major issue of local or national significance; following actions of town council or school board in providing new playground or other special provisions for young people . . .

Making and Enforcing Laws	*Sharing in agreements necessary to effective home and school living* — Helping decide desirable conduct in halls; setting up policies for use of room library table; helping set up lunchroom regulations; coming to agreements as to how many people can share in one kind of work; discussing fire regulations; helping formulate and post important classroom rules; reaching family agreements about playtime, care of toys, time for going to bed ...	*Finding what general procedures are followed in making laws* — Helping set up regulations necessary for effective class living, family living; visiting state legislature; discussing how Congress votes on bills; finding what it means when President vetoes a bill; following vote of city or town council on proposal in which one is interested; discussing parent, press, or radio comments on prominent national bills; learning how regulations of school are developed ...
Taking responsibility in making and changing laws		

Youth

Understanding what is involved in evaluating the work of representatives — Discussing effectiveness of work of student council or other selected group in school or college; following activities of political representatives as reported in the press, magazines; finding how to follow voting records of representatives; discussing state or national legislative action on prominent bills; discussing value of the *Congressional Record* in providing full reports of debates ...

Understanding the procedures through which laws are made—Following progress of an important bill through Congress; discussing importance of public action in securing support for a bill; discussing effect of amendments or riders on bills of public concern; considering purpose and importance of presidential vetoes; discussing press or radio reports of methods through which

Adulthood

Taking active part in appraising the activities of local and national representatives — Following records of representatives; interpreting press reports of speeches, of activity by representatives on committees; deciding when to write to congressional representative urging special action; deciding when to expect representative to support interests of a local group; deciding what congressional action should be expected from minority and majority representatives in Congress; considering effectiveness of local government; following publications of local and national groups in which appraisals are made of work of representatives ...

Taking a responsible part in the making and changing of laws — Following progress of a bill through Congress; deciding when to write to representatives urging that a bill be passed; considering effect of proposed amendments or riders; considering wisdom of presidential vetoes; discussing action of House and Senate committees in revising bills; discussing proposals to amend controversial bills are held up; studying proposed reforms of Congress; discussing methods through which the Constitution can be revised; discussing methods through which treaties are ratified; participating in establishing school rules and regulations; comparing methods by which democratic and totalitarian governments achieve their ends; comparing actions of dictators with those of democratic leaders . . .

the Constitution; discussing proposed changes to harmonize divorce laws, traffic laws, other laws under control of states; taking an interest in legislation which has no immediate relation to one's personal or economic interests; discussing effectiveness of present methods of ratifying treaties . . .

Cooperating in enforcing laws	*Obeying the laws which affect one's immediate conduct*—Cooperating in carrying out class, school, or home agreements and regulations; respecting property rights; learning to obey traffic laws; finding what to do on streets with stop and go signs; asking about work of local policeman; finding what is done by traffic policeman; understanding school fire regulations . . .	*Cooperating in and finding what general organization exists for law enforcement*—Finding what adults mean by "Bill of Rights"; investigating game, traffic, other laws which affect one's immediate conduct; serving as member of safety patrol; taking responsibility for self and others in carrying out school policies; finding what work is done by FBI, state and local police; discussing current methods of punishing criminals; finding what function is served by judge and jury in court . . .
Providing Financial Support for Government Determining amount and sources of income Determining use of government income		*Identifying the main kinds of taxes with which one has personal contact* — Finding what is meant by income tax; finding purpose of local or national sales or luxury taxes which one pays; owning a savings bond, postal savings certificate . . . *Finding the general use of taxes with which one has contact* — Finding what is being done with special sales tax which one pays; finding who pays for public buildings, parks, teachers' salaries, free school supplies; finding how policeman, mailman, fireman are paid . . .

Youth	Adulthood
Understanding the general principles and organization through which laws are enforced and cooperating with agencies of law enforcement — Investigating traffic, curfew, marriage, and other laws directly affecting one's conduct; finding what laws exist for protection of life and property of all; investigating history and present implications of Bill of Rights; discussing progress of a case of national importance or local interest through Supreme Court; discussing proposed appointments to Supreme Court; considering proposals for reform in penal institutions; discovering way in which local juvenile or domestic relations court functions; investigating respective responsibilities of state and federal police, district attorney, local and state courts; discussing proposals for an international court, international police force . . .	*Cooperating with agencies of law enforcement for the protection of self and others* — Finding what laws protect property rights; learning local and state traffic laws; obeying current income tax laws; deciding what steps to take to appeal to courts in case of dispute; discussing effectiveness of work of grand jury, district attorney; taking action to secure constructive treatment of juvenile delinquents; performing jury duty; deciding what action to take on proposals for an international court, an international police force . . .
Identifying major issues regarding the sources of government income — Discussing effects of sales, luxury taxes on various income groups; discussing issues involved in determining rate of income taxes; considering purposes of corporation, excess-profits taxes; considering relation of tax load to widening functions of government . . .	*Taking action in determining policies regarding the sources of government income* — Deciding whether to support proposed sales tax; considering value of proposed luxury taxes; discussing national proposals to vary rate of income tax; deciding whether to support proposed state or local income tax; considering means of enforcing excess-profits and corporation taxes; discussing rate of proposed property taxes . . .
Understanding major issues involved in decisions as to government expenditures — Discussing reported salaries of various government officials; investigating proportion of government income devoted to police and fire protection, to education; sharing in community efforts to finance better roads, parks, improved sanitation; helping publicize school bond issue or tax levy; discussing issues involved in national proposals for expenditure of funds on public works, unemployment insurance . . .	*Sharing in setting policy regarding the use of government income* — Taking action regarding salaries of government officials, of government employees, of teachers; discussing proposals to limit the national debt; deciding whether to purchase a house in a community where there is a high tax for community improvements; deciding whether to support an increased tax levy, bond issue, for schools; deciding whether to support proposals for unemployment insurance, for national medical care . . .

To assume that persons advocating such a broad approach are accepting an academically weak program—one that is neither intellectually rigorous nor thought provoking—is unwarranted. Any approach, whether it be this one or another described earlier, is likely to fail whenever the teacher is inadequately prepared, or when he is unaware of the objectives sought. There is no "safe" way to educate children. Thus it is impossible to protect them from failure to learn by means of adopting any single system or approach. Real teaching occurs only when children learn well.

Unquestionably, magnificent work with children has been accomplished by faculties approaching social studies based upon these "persistent life situations." Such approaches fail when teachers are lacking in self-assurance, knowledge of subject matter, and understanding of children.

Perhaps it is true that approaches such as this one have earned their negative reputations. In part, this has been due to abuses of the system and poor teaching. But cannot it be also true because such an approach represents rather a radical departure from the conventional? Education is a conservative institution and usually radicalism therein is viewed with suspicion.

GENERALIZATIONS AS ADDITIONAL CRITERIA IN DEFINING THE SCOPE
OF SOCIAL STUDIES

The identification of generalizations from the social sciences has received much attention in the recent past as a further means of defining the scope or breadth of the social studies curriculum. The idea that scholars in the various social science disciplines should be solicited for expressions which reflect their views of the important problems and ideas in their fields is not new. The various committees of the American Historical Association, the American Political Science Association, and others, to which reference was made in the previous chapter, represented the beginning steps in seeking from scholars advice about appropriate subject matter for children in school. In 1927, however, Hockett took the next step in the process by seeking more detailed guides to the selection of subject matter content through the development of a bibliography of works by "frontier thinkers"—those people judged to be eminently qualified to evaluate the significance of facts and events in the social sciences—and, from these works, extracting the problems and issues about which the scholars had written.[12] There resulted a list of 396

[12] John A. Hockett, *A Determination of the Major Social Problems in American Life,* Contributions to Education No. 281 (New York: Teachers College, Columbia University, 1927).

problems and issues of American life, many of which are still largely pertinent, suggesting the validity of this approach to content selection. Following Hockett, Billings undertook an even more extensive analysis of the social sciences for generalizations and concepts basic to the social studies curriculum.[13] Incorporating the idea of the "frontier thinker" into his study as Hockett had done, he analyzed books in each of the disciplines of the social sciences which had been recommended by experts. Billings derived a list of 888 mutually exclusive generalizations which he analyzed for central themes. Through further analysis, these themes and their supporting generalizations were ranked in order of importance. The primary use found for these first analyses of content from the social sciences was by Harold Rugg and his associates in the 1930's. Through systematic reference to these sources, they succeeded in developing a series of highly successful textbooks and related study materials which were used in many classrooms throughout the country. They subsequently lost favor, not because the materials were poorly written but because much of the material was viewed as highly controversial in nature. Explication of many of the generalizations and problems identified by social scientists resulted in the presentation of social problems and issues which many adults in America apparently did not want their children to know about.

It was not until the 1950's that this initial impetus to draw systematically from the frontier thinking of the social sciences took on further life. A series of studies at Stanford University was in the van of this new movement.[14] These studies represent the most comprehensive attack to date on the selection of generalizations from the social sciences for use in curriculum building in the school. However, other efforts are following.[15] The most extensive statewide effort is the previously men-

---

[13] Neal Billings, *A Determination of Generalizations Basic to the Social Studies Curriculum* (Baltimore: Warwick and York, Inc., 1929).

[14] The first of these was Douglass' *Interrelationships Between Man and the Natural Environment for Use in the Geographic Strand of the Social Studies Curriculum* (Stanford University, unpublished doctoral dissertation, 1954). This was followed by a series of several dissertations which sought generalizations from the social sciences which were applicable within the basic human activities. Other dissertations have subsequently been developed relating to these basic investigations. Information concerning them may be secured from Professor Paul R. Hanna, School of Education, Stanford University, Stanford, California.

[15] See, for example, "Social Studies in Transition," National Council for the Social Studies, Washington, D.C., 1965) to which reference has already been made in the preceding chapter. See Appendix I for partial listing of the generalizations suggested by the National Council for the Social Studies.

tioned California Framework.[16] In preparation more than five years, a major element in the work involved meetings with social scientists drawn primarily from the colleges and universities in the state. These scholars were asked to contribute the most important ideas from their disciplines. Ultimately these ideas were refined and sifted until each of the major social science disciplines was represented by several generalizations—157 in all. The generalizations are offered in this guide as supplementary to a scope and sequence which is essentially oriented toward the expanding community—basic human activities concepts. They have particular relevance to curriculum building because each one may be utilized at a variety of grade levels. For those who are writing a curriculum or preparing textbooks and other materials, these generalizations provide guides which allow planned repetition and reiteration of understandings at more mature levels. In this sense, particularly, such efforts to identify generalizations represent an important step forward in deciding what to teach in social studies.

Some Dangers in the Uses of Generalizations. It has been suggested that the identification of important generalizations in the social sciences has particular significance for the curriculum builder, for the textbook writer, and for the person preparing other instructional materials for ultimate classroom use. It is valuable because it provides a content focus which is generally agreed upon; it helps clarify goals in preparing materials for the teacher. However, there are fewer direct uses for the classroom teacher, and even some dangers. Although there is a detailed discussion of the nature of generalizations and the processes of generalizing in a subsequent chapter, it should be pointed out here that generalizations are of little value to the person who is unfamiliar with the concepts and facts which undergird them. If the teacher is not competent enough to cope with those important elements of subject matter, he is in great danger of treating such generalizations as fact and of teaching them as facts. Generalizing results from finding relationships among specific bits of information. Without those recallable understandings and pieces of information, generalizations are virtually meaningless and will be remembered only when memorized. In addition, they are soon forgotten. Of course, for the teacher who knows his material well, generalizations serve the same function as they do for the person who prepares

---

[16] *Social Studies Framework for the Public Schools of California,* prepared by the State Curriculum Commission, California State Department of Education (June 1962), 109 pp. The sequence of studies suggested in this report is noted in Chapter Two. Generalizations included in it can be found in an Appendix.

Reprinted by permission from *The Instructor*.

materials for child and teacher use: they focus attention on the important, they guide him in his consideration of the ways he can lead children
to think about the major ideas and issues in a given area. They clarify
teaching goals, help prevent forays into interesting but irrelevant concerns, and provide important guides for determining pupil progress in
developing skills and understandings.

The dangers for the teacher become even more serious ones for children. In their studies they must deal with meaningful units of ideas, and,
for the pre-adolescent, this means extended experience with realistic,
concrete, highly specific materials. And, since children do not generalize
readily of their own accord, the teacher must devote considerable skill
and attention to the processes of seeing relationships among these
experiences. Since generalizations themselves tend to be abstract, un-
specific, and relevant only when they illustrate particular conditions—
in a sense the *antithesis* of childhood experiencing and learning—it may
readily be seen that generalizations cannot be presented full-blown,
ready to be unquestionably accepted by eager minds. The teacher must

view generalizations covertly, finding ways in which children may "discover" them as a consequence of their own thinking. The processes by which this discovery takes place are many, but the problem is one of understanding. If the teacher's understanding is inadequate or insufficient, then the use of generalizations in guiding the selection of content in the classroom will be at best confusing.

Other Factors Influencing the Choice of Scope and Sequence. Important factors other than those previously discussed are influential in determining the content and sequence of social studies experiences which a teacher may plan in a particular classroom. Three vital factors have to do with the legal provisions in force in the school district, county, or state; the availability of instructional materials; and the atypical class.

LEGAL PROVISIONS

Every state has written into its laws, either by legislative act or by decree of a duly constituted authority such as a state or local school board, measures which deal with the social studies curriculum. It is generally agreed that such provisions are usually proscriptive, i.e., they serve as restrictions and prohibitions rather than as permissive regulations governing the teacher's work. Thus they are not helpful to the able teacher. There is, in addition, a question as to whether it is possible in the first place to legislate any guarantees about educational quality or content with a reasonable degree of success. Probably the best that can be said about such provisions is that in many cases they do little harm. Normally, legislative requirements initially enacted to form a base, or *minimum* performance, in practice establish maximum *requirements*. Thus, they tend to be self-defeating. This is often the case with respect to legislation dealing with social studies.

Legal provisions deal with diverse topics. They include questions concerning the number of minutes of instruction provided each week, the grades in which certain topics are considered, and the topics to be covered. One of the most widely adopted requirements deals with the teaching of United States history in the fifth and eighth grades. Others designate holidays to be observed through directed school activities, loyalty oaths to be sworn to by teachers, the selection of textbooks and supplementary books, instruction in "manners and morals" and the like.

A well planned program invariably meets the spirit as well as the letter of the law. Unfortunately, many teachers feel that their program is hamstrung by various legal requirements and do not believe that they are free to plan the best program of which they are capable. Therefore, legal provisions tend to stifle creativity and to hinder the development of sound study programs. Every teacher should become cognizant of the legal provisions attached to the teaching of social studies in his district by studying local, county, and state regulations, available in printed form through the school principal or superintendent. It is to be hoped that such regulations will be interpreted broadly rather than narrowly, since they were enacted in the first instance to provide general rather than specific guides to teaching.

AVAILABILITY OF MATERIALS

Where textbook-centered teaching is the rule, the question of the availability of appropriate materials is rarely raised. The choice of textbook settles that question, not to be reopened seriously until a new text is sought. Where multiple materials are employed in teaching, as is usually the case, the question immediately arises as to whether instructional aids sufficient both in quantity and quality are available for the pupils in a given class and suited to their particular maturity level. Teachers may wish to depart from a former emphasis; for example, by introducing culture studies of a Far Eastern or African area in the primary grades. They may wish to include a study of modern European nations in the seventh grade. It is not unusual to find a marked shortage of study materials in these topics, and in such an instance it would behoove a faculty to move slowly. Desirable as the general topic might be, interested as the pupils might become, sufficient instructional aids must be reasonably available if the study is to be successful. It is well to delay moving into new fields of study until an adequate supply of materials is guaranteed, unless it is possible for class and teacher to collect enough material in the process of study. In the meantime, some limitation will be felt by both teachers and pupils with respect to the range of studies which might be undertaken in a particular classroom.

THE ATYPICAL CLASS

Especially in larger towns and cities, classes are often found which do not conform to the patterns curriculum designers had in mind when formulating scope and sequence for the teaching of social studies. In areas of extremely rapid growth, combination or "split" classes may be formed in which two grades are housed in a classroom under the direction of one teacher. This condition poses the problem of deciding how to handle content, particularly the sequence of that content. Repetition of content should be avoided, and yet sequence must be planned so that children will experience the general content areas and types of studies which the school district believes important. For example, what does the teacher of a fourth and fifth grade combination class do where it is required that state geography and history be taught to fourth grade students and United States history be taught to fifth grade pupils? It is unwise to teach each group as though there were, in fact, two classes in the room, each covering its own content. Teaching this way virtually requires a textbook memoriter approach. Time allotments are such that neither group will spend a sufficient portion of the school day in studying social studies content. Moreover, it requires that the teacher group for teaching and develop teaching plans, quite beyond reasonable demands upon his time. One way of coping with this problem is to plan curricular experiences for such groups over two or more years so that desired content will be included at some time during the period the pupils will be together. A minimum amount of shifting from one group to another is advisable during this time, also, since continuous regrouping of students is likely to create a disjointed social studies program. In addition, emphases can be arranged that probe new aspects of some studies which have been previously undertaken. New views of familiar broad topics can be extremely rewarding and certainly not repetitious. Often these are more valuable than the original learning experience.

Combination or "split" classes should not be undertaken lightly where a fairly strict scope and sequence is envisaged. They can, however, forcibly produce a flexibility in manner of teaching and in selection of content which the typical, rigid, graded hierarchy might never achieve. There are a few schools in the United States which are deliberately planning for multi-graded or—an even more extreme departure— ungraded classrooms. The problems in planning for social studies teaching and learning in these situations are much the same as those facing the teacher who finds himself assigned a combination class. Programs must be planned for particular groups of students rather than for "grades" within a system, and these plans must be developed for a longer period of time than the usual one year. The development of more original programs, more creative teaching, and content designed for particular groups of students is therefore encouraged.[17]

The Culturally Different Class. Another phenomenon which demands adjustment of the social studies program, regardless of the framework within which the teacher works, is the class composed of groups of socially and culturally different children. These also are normally found in large communities. But they are also found in smaller towns, especially where such grouping has occurred by administrative decision; i.e., where some attempt has been made to group children according to ability—or "homogeneously." Emphasis here is upon socially or culturally deprived youngsters, for although they may be selected for a "slow" class on the basis of group intelligence test scores or by the teacher's judgment of ability, these children do not in fact represent the true lower range of ability. Their test scores in no small measure are a consequence of lack of opportunity for those crucial experiences learned outside of school that lead to success *in* school. In other words, they are not necessarily less intelligent but are certainly lacking in those experiences and understandings valued in most United States schools today.

Where "homogeneous" grouping is attempted on bases other than intelligence, it is indeed rare to find groupings based upon ability in social studies. Usually reading is the criterion. Sometimes arithmetic ability is used. Needless to say, grouping according to these standards of homogeneity does not produce a class homogeneous in its interests or abilities in social studies. The most homogeneous factor, regardless of the criterion employed, is often interest in learning in general and behavior in conformity with, or at odds with, what is conceived in our culture to be appropriate for school work. Thus "low" groups are usually distinguished by a lack of interest in learning and by the presence of a larger than usual number of behavior problems. Accompanying these qualities is a low standard or group norm with respect to the goals sought by the school. More often than not, teachers who work with groups of this type rapidly become discouraged. It is difficult to instill a love of learning, a desire to find out, and an enthusiasm about new

---

[17] Trends and issues in the social studies for teachers and schools engaged in programs which depart from the conventional graded hierarchy found in most elementary schools in the United States are discussed by John I. Goodlad and Robert H. Anderson in their book *The Nongraded Elementary School,* revised edition (New York: Harcourt, Brace, and World, 1963). See especially Chapter Five, "Modern Theories of Curriculum and the Nongraded School of Today and Tomorrow," pp. 79-101.

ideas discovered where such ideas are meaningless to children in the first place. The teacher who works with such groups starts at a much different level of understanding and interest and has a much more tortuous route to travel. The conventional social studies curriculum often prescribes content to be learned and suggests teaching procedures to be employed that are almost totally out of step with these pupils and the realities of their lives. The children who fit this description require an extremely flexible social studies program, one which places major focus upon developing an experiential background which illuminates and explains the ideas and ideals valued in our culture. Standards of behavior, moral precepts, and conceptual development in these groups are at variance with societal expectations.

Only teachers who understand and empathize with these differences should be assigned to teach this type of atypical class. They should be provided with the widest range of choice in planning the social studies program for them. Success in the early years should mean that the youngsters can become integrated into the more usual social studies program at a later time. Teachers who prefer the *social living or inter-active approach* to social studies can make a major contribution to this segment of our school population, which probably includes as much as 25 per cent of students in some communities and rarely lower than 15 per cent of the usual school enrollment.

The Advanced Class. Some elementary schools serve high socio-economic areas in which there is a disproportionate number (in relation to the expected occurrence in the general population) of exceedingly capable children. Classes comprised of the youngsters whose achievement, experience background, and general capacity for work is exceptionally high will present the teacher with other special problems in planning a challenging and worthwhile program.

There are, as well, a few other atypical types of classes. Most large elementary schools indulge in some form of homogeneous grouping. Where the problem class, previously described, is formed there may be a group of exceptionally high achievers—children highly motivated to learn who have done well in school. "Cluster grouping" is another arrangement under which such a group may come into existence. In this situation, the school deliberately "clusters" together those children whose capacity for learning has been well demonstrated.

In planning a social studies program for the gifted, the teacher should keep in mind that these children far exceed their peers in verbal abilities and in the rapidity with which they absorb information and ideas. Their interests freely range over a wider landscape; they require much less time to gain the major concepts and generalizations involved in the study. Often they display a remarkably well-developed sense of humor. These realities may be met with delight or pain on the part of the teacher. Anyone finding himself in the position of teaching a class, a sizable proportion of whose pupils fall within the "gifted" category, should become acquainted with the basic research in this area and make a point of keeping up with it.[18]

FOR FURTHER READING

California State Department of Education, *Social Studies Framework for the Public Schools of California.* Prepared by the State Curriculum Commission (Sacramento, California: California State Department of Education, 1962).

Clements, H. Millard, William R. Fielder, and B. Robert Tabachnik, *Social Study: Inquiry in Elementary Classrooms* (New York: The Bobbs-Merrill Co., Inc., 1966).

Getzels, Jacob W. and Philip W. Jackson, *Creativity and Intelligence* (New York: John Wiley, 1962).

Goodlad, John I. and Robert H. Anderson, *The Nongraded Elementary School,* revised edition (New York: Harcourt, Brace, and Company, 1963).

Hunnicutt, Clarence W. (ed.), *Education 2000 A.D.* (Syracuse, New York: Syracuse University Press, 1956).

Jarolimek, John and Huber M. Walsh (eds.), *Readings for Social Studies in Elementary Education* (New York: Macmillan Company, 1965).

Joyce, Bruce R., *Strategies for Elementary Social Science Education* (Chicago: Science Research Associates, 1965).

[18] The best known studies are by Lewis M. Terman and others. They are reported in *Genetic Studies of Genius,* 5 vols. (Stanford: Stanford University Press, 1925-   ). Recent important studies, particularly useful for our purposes, are Jacob W. Getzels and Philip W. Jackson, *Creativity and Intelligence* (New York: John Wiley, 1962); and David C. McClelland, *et. al., Talent and Society* (Princeton, N.J.: Van Nostrand, 1958); and Ellis Paul Torrance, *Education and the Creative Potential* (Minneapolis: University of Minnesota Press, 1963).

Lee, John R. and Jonathan C. McLendon (eds.), *Readings on Elementary Social Studies: Prologue to Change* (Boston: Allyn and Bacon, Inc., 1965).

Massialas, Byron G. and Andreas M. Kazamias (eds.), *Crucial Issues in the Teaching of Social Studies: A Book of Readings* (Englewood Cliffs, New Jersey: Prentice-Hall, Inc., 1964).

McClelland, David C., *et al.*, *Talent and Society* (Princeton, N.J.: Van Nostrand, 1958).

National Education Association, *Focus on Social Studies,* Report from the 1965 Department of Elementary School Principals Annual Meeting (Washington, D.C.: NEA, 1965).

Preston, Ralph C., *Teaching Social Studies in the Elementary School,* revised edition (New York: Holt, Rinehart and Winston, 1960).

Sowards, G. Wesley (ed.), *The Social Studies: Curriculum Proposals for the Future* (Chicago: Scott, Foresman and Company, 1963).

Stratemeyer, Florence, *et al., Developing a Curriculum for Modern Living,* second edition revised (New York: Teachers College, Columbia University, 1957).

CHAPTER FOUR

Dimensions of Learning in Social Studies

P rior to the turn of the century, before the beginning of what has become known as the Progressive Era, virtually all teaching was based on a simple idea—an idea which has yet to fade entirely from the scene. It was believed that a direct, causal relationship existed between knowledge on the one hand and appropriate behavior as a citizen on the other. Knowledge of American history, geography, and civics produced the "good citizen." It made little difference *how* one learned; the important thing was the amount of information one had at his command.

A simple definition of knowledge was also widely adhered to. Facts were considered the fundamental learning unit. Acquisition of facts was therefore equated with acquiring knowledge. In seeing to it that the pupil learned those facts necessary to good citizenship, the teacher's task was viewed as being relatively simple. Virtually every lesson in the textbook was gauged to assist the pupil in memorizing information. Using this material, the teacher conducted recitations in which the pupils vied with each other to see who could best remember the information in the textbook. Paper and pencil assignments required the ability to recall the material in the text. Great value was placed upon exact repetition, and teaching ability was judged by the results of the tests which required pupils to repeat the encantations which the class had gone through so many times under the teacher's directions. It was the heyday of the spelling bee, the declamation of Washington's Farewell Address or some other famous statement, and the recitation of memorized facts from books such as Warren's *Common School Geography,* first published in the 1860's but used widely for more than five decades thereafter. A glance at the reproduction of the old history book appearing on pp. 33-35 brings the old classroom to life.

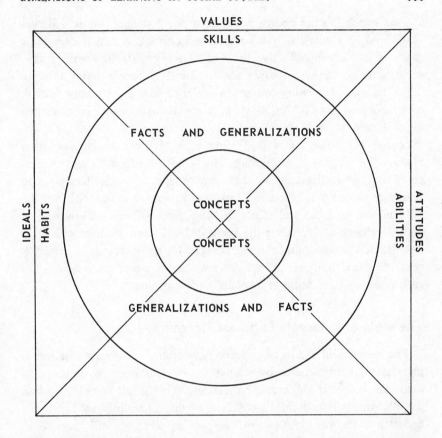

Figure 4–1: Knowledge and understandings in social studies are linked together. They may be thought of as discrete parts, but in learning they are interrelated and interdependent as this figure suggests.

By the end of the 1800's it had become obvious that this kind of instruction, so widely used in the schools, was not achieving the high goals held for it. For one thing, pupils seemed to be forgetting almost immediately afterward the information so laboriously learned. And as for securing a citizenry which behaved in accordance with traditional democratic principles, the robber barons only exemplified a problem which obviously had deep roots in American life. Thus, the search was joined—a search having many facets but chiefly directed to the basic question of how to improve teaching so that the goal of an increasingly effective citizenry might better be realized.

This search has not ended, nor is there much danger that it will ever really end. But there is much valuable information which can guide teachers in planning effective ways of working with boys and girls in social studies. More is known about educating people today than in 1900. Instead of viewing content in social studies as primarily factual, educators now see that, in addition, it contains certain social concepts, generalizations, and skills and is concerned with values and the processes of valuing as well. Within each of these dimensions other matters that require consideration can be identified: the kinds of concepts and generalizations children are capable of understanding and learning; the ways to teach and learn the processes of generalizing; the influence of attitudes and ideals in developing values; and the role of skill development, including the kinds of habits and abilities which are essential to the development of meanings with regard for socially significant ideas and understandings. All are entwined and interrelated, but each deserves consideration in planning for teaching.

The Role of Concepts in Social Learning

The nature and extent of concept development in young children is increasingly being studied by scholars; it is assuming more importance than ever before in the minds of teachers. This is not surprising when one recognizes that a child's concepts or understandings set the limits and define the possibilities with respect to what he will be able to study meaningfully. Concepts truly may be said to provide the basic building blocks of the social studies program. If teaching is to be successful, children must understand the key concepts in the study. If important gaps occur in the child's comprehension of concepts which are central to the development of major ideas in the study, then one can expect that his understandings will either be seriously diminished or, perhaps, disappear almost entirely. Where many concepts which are unknown to the child are used, he will in all likelihood be engaged in what appears to be meaningless activity. The consequences of this to the child should be obvious; it is, however, very easy to be *unaware* that the child does not understand. It is, in truth, very difficult to know whether another person comprehends an idea or not.

As used here, the term "concept" refers to the notions or ideas a person has about some thing for which he has developed an awareness. Social studies concepts are those classes of ideas which refer to man in relationship to others of his species. Words, expressed singly or in short phrases, convey the meaning encompassed by a concept, but, of course, the word is not the concept itself. Words are merely convenient symbols that each of us uses to represent a cluster of ideas about something. It is this understanding within the mind to which one refers when speaking of a concept.

In considering the types of social studies concepts children need to know, it might easily happen that all ideas which have the slightest social content might be included. Taken to its logical conclusion, this might mean that *all* concepts would be included. However, it is more relevant to limit this discussion to those types of concepts which are likely to carry the meaning content of the social studies curriculum in elementary schools. Even so, the quantity and variety of concepts about which children should develop an awareness is amazingly great. In the following list, for example, Wesley has suggested twenty-one different categories under which social studies concepts might be classified. Examples of concepts within each of these categories are shown following each major type of concept. One could extend each of these almost indefinitely.

1. Action (mail, load, fight, transport, discover, harpoon)
2. Agency (store, terminal, bank, fireman, council, jury)
3. Behavior (cooperate, conserve, embezzle, lie, cheat, vote)
4. Change (expand, renew, revise, propose)
5. Communication (telephone, exchange, semantics, language, television)
6. Custom (holiday, more, tradition, game, rite, ceremony)
7. Entity (animal, city hall, man, house, mountain)
8. Group (herd, gang, political party, school, pressure group)
9. Ideal (faith, democracy, charity, love, equality)
10. Institution (family, school, government, state, university)
11. Instrument (ballot, mace, courts, constitution)
12. Invention (satellite, constitution, vaccine, rifle)
13. Obligation (contract, taxes, treaty, debt)
14. Place (location, ocean, distance, island, continent, India)
15. Process (election, jurisprudence, refining, manufacture)
16. Profession (teacher, engineer, secretary, scientist, employee, judge)
17. Quality (faithful, honest, friendly, kind)

18. Relationship (brother, father, husband, proprietor, partner)
19. Situation (prisoner, witness, observer, downtrodden)
20. Status (wealthy, public, private, culturally deprived)
21. Time (score, generation, future, hours, century)[1]

Obviously, these classifications are not exclusive. Some concepts might be listed under several categories. In addition, other concepts appear as nouns under one heading, as verbs under another, all with slightly different meanings. But such a list *is* useful in indicating the breadth of the ideas included in the social studies program and the possibilities for semantic pitfalls for both teacher and pupil.

Without direct and continuous attention to the development of concepts in the social study, learning activities planned by the teacher are likely to become meaningless to the pupils. That this represents a real danger is indicated by research findings of the past fifty years which have sought information about the quality and extent of children's conceptions of the social world in which they live. One of the earliest of these studies was conducted by Scott and Myers.[2] It was found that, although children might respond accurately to questions which required them to name or identify concepts, they encountered great difficulty in explaining the meaning or significance of those concepts. For example, when children were asked to name two explorers, many were able to do so. But when they were asked to explain the meaning of the word "explorer," only a few could tell the investigators what it actually meant to them. Other studies since reported have corroborated these findings. Seemingly many children are placed in a learning situation in which they verbalize adequately enough to *appear* to understand. However, upon examining the amount of meaning the child has—the real extent of his understanding—it becomes evident that he is not likely to have the degree of comprehension which he first appears to possess.

An interesting guide to thinking about this problem of understanding is contained in Bloom's *Taxonomy of Educational Objectives*.[3] A simpler classification system which suggests the various levels of understanding

[1] Adapted from Edgar B. Wesley and Mary A. Adams, *Teaching Social Studies in Elementary Schools,* revised edition (Boston: D. C. Heath and Company, 1952), p. 293.
[2] Flora Scott and G. C. Myers, "Children's Empty and Erroneous Concepts of the Commonplace," *Journal of Educational Research,* VIII (November, 1923), pp. 327-334.
[3] Benjamin Bloom (ed.), *Taxonomy of Educational Objectives,* Handbook I: *Cognitive Domain* (New York. Longmans, Green & Company, 1956).

a person might attain is presented by Bradfield and Moredock, who point out that using a performance scale of this type presupposes that the teacher knows what kinds of prior experiences the children have had. If the teacher is not that familiar with the past learning experiences of his pupils, he is likely to be misled into thinking that a child is performing on Level IV when he is actually operating at Level II.

Performances Indicating Different Levels of Understanding of a Given Subject

Level   *Performance*

I   *Imitating, duplicating, repeating.*
      This is the level of initial contact. Student can repeat or duplicate what has just been said, done, or read. Indicates that student is at least conscious or aware of contact with a particular concept or process.

II   *Level I, plus recognizing, identifying, remembering, recalling, classifying.*
      To perform on this level, the student must be able to recognize or identify the concept or process when encountered later, or to remember or recall the essential features of the concept or process.

III   *Levels I and II, plus comparing, relating, discriminating, reformulating, illustrating.*
      Here the student can compare and relate this concept or process with other concepts or processes and make discriminations. He can formulate in his own words a definition, and he can illustrate or give examples.

IV   *Levels, I, II, and III, plus explaining, justifying, predicting, estimating, interpreting, making critical judgments, drawing inferences.*
      On the basis of his understanding of a concept or process, he can make explanations, give reasons, make predictions, interpret, estimate, or make critical judgments. This performance represents a high level of understanding.

V   *Levels I, II, III, and IV, plus creating, discovering, reorganizing, formulating new hypotheses, new questions and problems.*
      This is the level of original and productive thinking. The student's understanding has developed to such a point that he can make discoveries that are new to him and can restructure

and reorganize his knowledge on the basis of his new discoveries and new insights.[4]

Another way of looking at the problem of identifying the kinds of concepts with which children must deal in a meaningful social studies program is suggested by the work of Brownell and Hendrickson.[5] Here the reader is asked to view particularly the problem of learning concepts at three apparent levels of difficulty. As suggested by Bradford and Moredock those concepts which deal with the immediate, real world of the child tend to be more readily learned than those which are remote and impersonal. The following chart suggests the differences in degrees of difficulty, or abstraction, at the same time emphasizing the fact that this is a continuum, rather than a situation in which clear lines of demarcation distinguish one concept from another.

Personal referents directly related to the life-space and experiences of the learner	Impersonal referents indirectly related to the life-space and experiences of the learner	Ideas and ideals with no concrete referent points either in time or space for the learner
More easily taught .... More difficult to teach		
More readily learned .... More difficult to learn		
Examples: animal, bus, store, river, to-day, family, trip, toy, cloud, seashore, mountain, street, etc.	Examples: business, manufacturing, trade, boundary line, state, company, tomorrow, etc.	Examples: democracy, cooperation, conservation, prejudice, peace, attitude, citizenship, faith, etc.

Major difficulties are encountered in developing concepts which are concerned with impersonal referents and with ideas and ideals. Since concepts can exist only in one's mind, it is inevitable that there will be some confusion between the meanings and the labels given them: either the printed symbol or spoken words. Whereas children may learn to

[4] James M. Bradfield and H. Stewart Moredock, *Measurement and Evaluation in Education* (New York: Macmillan, 1957), p. 204.

[5] William A. Brownell and Gordon Hendrickson, "How Children Learn Information, Concepts, and Generalizations," Chapter Four, in *Learning and Instruction*, Forty-ninth Yearbook, Part I, National Society for the Study of Education (Chicago: University of Chicago Press, 1950), pp. 92-128.

give appropriate responses to direct questions with respect to that class of concepts indicated above as pertaining to impersonal referents, such as the example from Scott and Myers, a different problem exists in connection with those concepts which relate primarily to ideas and ideals. Thus, children are admonished to "cooperate," to be "democratic," and the like. Yet they may have little notion of what these terms really mean. Often, they interpret them to mean "doing what the teacher wants me to do." This tendency to "second guess" the teacher has been studied by Henry.[6] He found that teachers, often unwittingly, provide verbal and *non-verbal* "signals" or "cues" to correct answers in their discussions with children. An effective "short circuit" is set up in such situations. Children are "taught to find the answer the teacher wants and to give it to her" rather than to clearly think it through to an appropriate intellectual conclusion.[7] This encourages meaningless verbalization; it poses a problem all teachers must constantly guard against. The solution to this problem is to listen carefully to what children talk and write about. The child must clarify his own thinking; obvious verbalization can neither be ignored nor put aside until a "better time" without fatal consequences. Thus the rule: the teacher listens, the pupil expresses his thoughts; then the level of understanding is evaluated, and the teaching-learning situation is adjusted to improve the development of understanding.

The amount of meaning involved with respect to any given concept is strictly an individual matter. Since only individuals comprehend concepts, there is no such thing as "group understanding," except as a summation of all that is understood by the individuals in a given class. For any concept, the level of understanding for a particular pupil might be plotted along a continuum, such as that illustrated.

(ZERO) O _____ N (MAXIMUM)

The pupil's understanding of the concept might be plotted at one point on one day and at another the next day. The quality of experiences which he has, both direct and vicarious, will affect the degree to which his level of understanding increases. Two other factors condition the range upon which this scale operates: the intellectual capacity of the learner and his maturity. For example, a third grade class studying the local community becomes involved in a consideration of how the town

---

[6] Jules Henry, "Docility, or Giving Teacher What She Wants," *The Journal of Social Issues,* XI, No. 2 (1955), pp. 33-41.

[7] *Ibid.,* p. 40.

is governed. Pupils' concepts of local government change as a result of a trip to the city hall, class discussion, and the contributions of a city councilman, the city manager, and the police chief, who come to the class as resource persons. The degree of change in meaningfulness of such concepts as "fire protection," "city council," "laws," "elections," etc., will be affected by the *individual experiences children have* in connection with these activities *in relation to* any prior experiences they may have had with respect to these concepts. The degree to which concepts change is further affected by such matters as the intellectual capacity of each child, his motivations and interests with respect to the topic studied, his general maturity, his values, attitudes, and other unpredictable variables.

Social studies concepts are learned out of school as well as in the classroom. Some of them, such as those associated with the functions of the city council or mayor, the state or United States history, are learned primarily through school experiences. Others, those related to the work of such persons as the mailman or fireman, are learned both in and out of school. Still others, such as the role of the church in the child's life (and perhaps the work of the minister), are learned almost exclusively outside of school. In some instances, this is as it should be. With other kinds of concepts, the learning takes place outside of school, in informal groups, when it probably should be taught by one of the major social institutions: the family, the church, or the school. These concepts have to do with the controversial elements in our society. Examples are sex education, information about crime and corruption in all segments of private life, controversy in politics at all levels, and the problems of war and peace. Preston points out these constitute the reality of social life in addition to that which is normally included in the school curriculum. He suggests that the school is remiss by choosing to ignore what he terms these and other "harsh social realities." And he maintains that there has been a real "divorcement of school content in the social studies from [these] social realities."[8] The net effect of this, in Preston's view, one which is shared by many others, is that, just as there are many important social concepts which are *not* considered by the school, there are many other significant ones which are glossed over, so that teaching of them becomes "euphemistically and evasively presented [and] the content . . .becomes insipid and uninviting."

[8] Ralph C. Preston, "Children's Reactions to Harsh Social Realities," *Social Education,* Vol. XXIII, No. 3, (March, 1959), pp. 116-117+.

This warning has validity. Undoubtedly, present social studies programs often omit certain concepts which should be considered; conversely, they frequently spend far too much time on other concepts for which out-of-school experiences provide a firm base. Thus classroom teaching covers material already well known to pupils. Studies will have more significance and meaning for children when they reflect more closely the reality of the situations in which children live and learn. The reader is urged to think about those kinds of concepts which presently are best learned in school, those that should be learned outside of school, and those which he believes are not being taught at all (and which should be taught) to all children in our society. If one were to make a representative list of concepts in each of the three categories, what kinds of changes might these deliberations bring about in the social studies curriculum?

In summary, it may be observed that there is much research yet to be done before an adequate understanding of the nature of learning with respect to concept development in young children is gained. But at this time, the following generalizations appear to have validity:

1. Social studies learnings *not* based upon an understanding of the concepts involved lead to meaningless activity and temporary learning.
2. Wide variations exist in the degree of understanding of given concepts within specific classes. Usually, the differences within a class will greatly exceed the differences of the averages between classes.
3. Concepts that are directly related to the experience of the learner are more easily comprehended than those that are indirectly related. The most difficult concepts to learn are those which have to do with ideas or ideals for which there are no direct referents either in time or space.
4. The amount of meaning involved with respect to a given concept is an *individual* matter. Understanding of specific concepts changes with appropriate direct and vicarious experiences.
5. There is a constant danger of verbalism where social studies concepts are concerned. It is possible for a child to use a concept in an *apparently* meaningful context with little understanding, or with a totally incorrect conception, of its meaning.
6. Children tend to express their understandings of concepts in concrete, personal terms.

7. Social concepts are learned both in and out of school. Teaching should be planned to capitalize upon adequate out-of-school learning and to overcome inadequate or inaccurate out-of-classroom concept development. Attention should be given to those concepts of importance that are either ignored or avoided by the school because of their controversial nature.

8. Attention needs to be given to the orderly development of basic concepts, from the kindergarten upward, in the school curriculum. An example is the sequential arrangement of concepts known to be necessary in map reading.

Learning Social Studies Facts and Generalizations

In addition to concepts, the subject matter content of social studies is expressed in terms of facts and generalizations. Traditionally, great value has been placed on learning this type of material; particularly is this true of those classes of information termed "facts." This is because social studies facts are more easily identified in the public mind than are generalizations; they tend to be less controversial because it is easier to assess whether a person has knowledge of a given "fact" than whether he has grasped a generalization.

Although it is not possible to make a precise differentiation between a social studies "fact" and a "generalization," which would apply in all instances, a practical distinction can be made between the two. A social studies "fact" may be viewed as a statement of a condition, a situation, or an occurrence which deals with (1) man as a physical being or with his environment, (2) with what he has said or written, (3) with what he has done or is doing, (4) with ways he has felt and thought or presently thinks and feels. A "fact" relates to a specific instance whereas a "generalization" may be viewed as a statement of a relationship between two or more concepts which has broad applicability.

Unlike concepts, then, facts and generalizations are stated in so many words. One struggles with words, with statements of facts and generalizations, with gestures and other non-verbal modes as well, to communicate his concept of a particular thing, but it will never be possible for him to do anything more than use his verbal and non-verbal language to express the ideas or concepts he possesses about the things around him for which he has been able to develop an awareness. The nature and scope of prior experience determines which concepts one will have and how well developed they will be. In college, an example of inadequate knowledge converted into a communication effort is sometimes called "a snow job." But beyond the obvious problem of "not knowing what one is really writing or talking about" lies another. An appropriate experiential background is necessary if one is to make new associations and create new meanings out of subsequent experience. This principle is true for all persons. For example, two statements following are drawn from a professional book in educational psychology.[9] The first statement is from the first chapter, the second from the last chapter.

First Statement, First Chapter	We begin with what seems a paradox. The world of experience of any normal man is composed of a tremendous array of discriminably different objects, events, people, impressions. There are estimated to be more than 7 million discriminable colors alone, and in the course of a week or two we come in contact with a fair portion of them. No two people we see have an identical appearance, and even objects that we judge to be the same object over a period of time change appearance from moment to moment with alterations in light or in the position of the viewer. All of these differences we are capable of seeing, for human beings have an exquisite capacity for making distinctions.[10]
First Statement, Last Chapter	Much of our commerce with the environment involves dealing with classes of things rather than with unique events and objects. Indeed, the case can be made that all cognitive activity depends upon a prior placing of events in terms of their category membership. A category is, simply, a range of discriminably different events that are treated "as if" equivalent. In the preceding chapters, we have been concerned with the nature of psychological categories and with the strategies by which people come to discover what cues they can appropriately use for inferring the category membership of objects and events they may encounter.[11]

The experience of the reader in traversing 231 pages is absolutely essential to the comprehension of the second statement. The speed with which the teacher moves and the ability of the learner (in part his prior experience and in part his intellectual capacity to comprehend) determine the extent to which the learner can understand the facts presented in

[9] Jerome S. Bruner, et al., A Study of Thinking (New York: John Wiley and Sons, Inc., 1956).

[10] Ibid., p. 1.

[11] Ibid, p. 231.

the second statement and, ultimately, the material contained in the last chapter of the book.

Like concepts, therefore, facts and generalizations range from relative simplicity to immense complexity. In planning a social study, it becomes the teacher's problem to provide learning situations in which children of varying intellectual capacities and experience may move ahead in their understanding at different rates and levels of complexity as illustrated by the following continuum:

```
. . . . . . . Relative simplicity              Relative difficulty
        (Zero) 0 . . . . . . . _____ . . . . . . . N (Maximum)
. . . . . . . . . . . . . . . . . . . . . facts. . . . . . . . . . .
            . . . . . . generalizations. . . . . . . . . . . . . . .
```

Care must be taken to consider facts not so much as ends in themselves but as means to an end. The process of remembering tends to cause all of us to cast off specific information as time goes on—to forget the details. Generalized notions of our experiences are the major residue of all learning. Still, the quality of those general ideas depends upon the richness of the original learning experience. To ensure quality in social studies, children are provided with learning experiences which make sense to them but which keep their thinking on the frontier of their ability. Direct experiencing is important; this includes such activities as study trips to places and things they are learning about. Of equal importance to younger children (and of greater import to older pupils as they begin to consider problems which are not available for such direct observation) are reading and discussion. Reading is valuable not only as an independent activity, but also as an aural one in groups—that is, listening to the teacher and other pupils as they read aloud pertinent materials. Such activity should be followed by appropriate discussion; too much stress upon questions by the teacher and answers by the pupils must be guarded against. It is out of such "stuff" as this that facts are learned and generalizations developed, for it remains true that "there is no expression without expression."[12]

Facts provide the basis for developing sound generalizations. The

---

[12] This aphorism dates, at least, from the turn of the century when William James wrote: "No reception without reaction. No impression without correlative expression, — this is the great maxim which the teacher ought never to forget." *William James Talks to Teachers on Psychology: and to Students on Some of Life's Ideals* (New York: Henry Holt and Co., 1901), p. 33.

process of generalizing follows this general pattern: (1) the learner is led to discover in one context or another a series of facts; (2) at first, these facts appear to have little or no relationship to one another; (3) with the addition of another piece of evidence—another fact, perhaps— and with or without the assistance of the teacher, a guiding rule or common attribute is observed; (4) the learner formulates the rule or attribute in his own mind—he generalizes from the data he has discovered or observed—and sets out to test the extent of its applicability; and (5) finally, he determines to what degree the generalization appears to him to be valid.

Generalizations dealing with social phenomena are characterized by the relatively limited area in which they may be said to be true and by the fact that they change. When generalizations are stated as principles or laws, they are more widely applicable. However, facts constantly are in the process of change, and, hence, the generalizations which may be evolved from them are always subject to some degree of modification. Apparently, the development of universally applicable principles will have to be left to the more precise sciences. Of the following statements, for example, some are presently true, some were true at one time, and some are true only for certain locations. Which statements need correction? How recently has this information, or fact, become inaccurate? How soon again will it likely change? Which statements represent factual conditions and which are generalizations? How widely applicable are the generalizations? Are they likely to change soon? Can they be ranked according to their difficulty on a scale similar to that shown above? Can the incorrect statements be modified so that they are again accurate expressions of fact or relationships (generalizations) for the time and place in which you are reading this material?

1. The world population is aproximately 2.75 billion people.
2. The legal speed limit is 65 miles per hour.
3. The United States is a republic.
4. We are engaged in a race between education and disaster.
5. The death rate increases in the winter time.
6. Thomas Jefferson was our third president.
7. My father is a community helper.
8. Mountains provide barriers to trade and communication between people everywhere.
9. The fireman helps protect our home from fire.
10. Man destroys the balance of nature everywhere he goes.

11. The Civil War began in 1861 and extended to 1865.
12. We adjust our activities according to the seasons as well as to the climate and weather in a particular location.
13. The concept of the frontier in American life, which has played such an important part in our thinking, is all but gone.
14. Socrates died in 399 B.C. but his words live on.
15. The extent of man's utilization of natural resources is related to his desires and to his level of technology.
16. The sequence of human activities and culture patterns is related to geographic location and accessibility and to the particular time in which human beings live.

The problems encountered in evaluating accuracy and difficulty of material in such a list as that appearing here are typical of the day to day questions which every social studies teacher must raise. In addition is the major question of which facts and generalizations are most appropriate to the development of understanding about a particular problem or topic. Also, judgments must be made with respect to the ability of the pupils to understand those facts and generalizations. This already formidable task is further complicated by the problem of selecting learning materials appropriate to the age and maturity of the pupils. This includes not only the selection of reading materials, but the entire range of possible learning sources, including audio-visual materials (tape recordings, filmstrips, motion pictures, etc.), study trips, and resource persons to be utilized in the study. Detailed suggestions for the different levels of elementary school work in the social studies will be found in later chapters. However, social studies teaching is conditioned by local and regional differences, problems, and opportunities. Teaching guides, courses of study, and other area references should be consulted for assistance in making wise choices.

WHAT SHOULD BE THE ROLE OF FACTS IN THE SOCIAL STUDIES PROGRAM?

Social studies programs in recent years have been under increasing pressure to emphasize so-called basic facts. It is a popular conception that pupils should gain from social studies instruction a knowledge of key facts, if nothing else; there is widespread belief that this is not happening. This is particularly true of historical information, but increasingly in the past fifteen or more years there has been a concern that children learn certain types of geographical information. Public concern has been expressed over the "lack of knowledge" evidenced by products of our educational system. As a consequence, much criticism continues to be directed toward the school. This is not a new development. There are records of the same sort of criticism dating at least as far back as the 1850's.[13] Nor is this to say that such criticism is totally unfounded. The inability of the American public to show any great degree of historical or geographic literacy is well established.[14] In answer to this problem, a number of scholars have directed their attention to identifying the most important factual information which should be taught by the school.

Recognizing the transitory nature of most factual information, as indicated above, they have compiled lists, which might serve as minimum standards lists for schooling, of specific names, dates, places, and events considered "essential" for understanding the American heritage and the place of the United States in the world today. As one might expect, the contents of these lists vary widely, reflecting as they must the particular interests and concerns of the person compiling it. No definitive report of this kind can be achieved; this is not to say that such efforts are useless.

Meanwhile, classroom teachers of social studies are confronted by a dilemma. Different theories of learning have implied varying emphases on kinds of information which should be learned. Out of this diversity have emerged two major points of view. One, representing cognitive theories of learning, emphasizes insight, problem solving, and the creative nature of the thinking process. The other consists of stimulus-response theories, in which trial and error, habit formation, and the more mechanical aspects of learning receive primary attention.[15] The minds and forces which have shaped educational policy during the past fifty years have been influenced markedly by cognitive theories of learning. Thus, increasing attention has been given to the role and development of generalizations in the social studies. This emphasis has been badly misunderstood both within and without the profession. Because scholars suggest that more attention be given to the development of

[13] The report of the first school survey, conducted in Boston in 1845 under the direction of Horace Mann, decries the lack of geographic knowledge of the pupils. See O. W. Caldwell and S. A. Courtis, *Then and Now in Education* (New York: World Book Company, 1925), pp. 186-190.

[14] See, for example, Benjamin Fine, "U.S. College Students Flunk in Knowledge of Geography," *Journal of Geography*, L (November, 1951), pp. 334-341.

[15] For the best exposition of influential theories of learning today see Ernest R. Hilgard, *Theories of Learning*, second edition (New York: Appleton-Century-Crofts, Inc., 1956).

generalizations, they are widely interpreted as believing that facts are unimportant. Thus, it is currently believed that teachers are being asked to forsake the teaching of facts. Actually, this is a false argument; the development of generalizations in a child's mind depends upon his ability to muster his knowledge of specific information or facts and to establish a generalized relationship among them. Generalizations developed in any other way become meaningless and are soon forgotten.

Hence, factual information must be given a central place in the social studies *provided it is considered at the level of understanding of the child.* The key words in this sentence are italicized for it must be recognized that what appears to be *fact* to the adult may well be meaningless verbiage to the child. Generalizations can never emerge in a child's thinking if the basic elements, the concepts and facts, are not understood.

Even today, it is desirable for a majority of our citizens to know specific types of information, quite apart from the role of such information in the development of generalizations. Basic democratic principles and cultural values find support in factual information of this type by providing permanent referent points upon which thinking about present and future problems depends. It is not wrong for the school to participate in teaching procedures which secure this type of knowledge. The principle of overlearning may be applied, for example, in situations where basic information is keyed to more important ideas and generalizations. This principle, stated simply, calls for teaching well in excess of that point at which mere recall is possible. When repetitive practice is employed in the overlearning of such information to the point of automatic response, opportunities for repetition or practice will fix what has been learned with a relatively high degree of permanence. In learning the names and locations of the fifty states, for instance, the teacher might well use a procedure in which an outline of each of the states is first studied intensively for its geographic features. Pictures of the states can then be flashed on a screen, much as the outlines of airplanes were during World War II in enemy airplane identification training. Pupils seek to recall the name of the state flashed before them and to locate it on a desk map. Continuous practice over a period of two or three weeks, for fifteen or twenty minutes per day, results in an ability to locate and identify the fifty states with a high degree of accuracy. Retention of this information is high when a re-test occurs a year or more later. Knowledge of this type is essential to any historical or geographic study of the

United States; therefore, it is most appropriately taught at about the fifth grade.

There are other types of social studies information which might be taught with a view toward considerable permanence. Knowledge of certain dates, personalities, events, situations, and places provides keystones in a particular study. Teachers in a school or school district should give attention to identifying those facts and skills which are considered in this category and make provisions for long-range articulation for those they consider most important. Care should be taken that such a list not grow to a great length, for this will defeat the purpose. But when a reasonable selection has been made, based on the importance of the information and on the abilities of children to learn it, decisions can be made at which points it will be introduced and when review and additional practice can be provided throughout the school experience of the child. The reader is urged to consider those specific items of information which in his belief should fall into this fact-category. What criteria justify their selection and what teaching techniques are most appropriate to successful teaching and learning of the material so chosen? By using original teaching ideas, particularly those which utilize unusual materials and devices (such as the tachistoscope in map reading as described above), the drudgery—and lack of success—in teaching various types of arbitrary associations and facts can be overcome.

WHAT IS THE ROLE OF GENERALIZATIONS IN THE SOCIAL STUDIES?

It has been pointed out that a generalization is a statement of a relationship between concepts which has broad applicability. Generalizations are derived from studies of specific instances. Bright children tend to require fewer such examples to arrive at valid generalizations than do less intellectually gifted children. The richness or depth of understanding of generalizations depends upon the variety of experiences, both direct and vicarious, which a child has and upon his ability to grasp the significance of those experiences. It is entirely possible to gain factual information with little or no generalizing emanating from such experiences. Or, it may easily happen that a child's understanding of the relationships which are expressed as a generalization may be badly distorted. The quality of understanding is dependent upon the types of activities designed by the teacher to foster the development of generalizations from specific information. To clarify meaning and to encourage thinking which leads to the development of a generalization, the teacher plans total-class and small-group discussions, provides opportunities for written and oral presentations, and seeks in every possible way to involve children in the organization and expression of their own ideas. Constant probing of the depth of understanding of concepts contained in the generalizations used and alertness to opportunities to broaden the base of understanding through reading, writing, speaking, and listening lead to more accurate thinking and the development of the power to generalize.

One must never forget that it is the *child* who develops the generalization. It is he who must go through the steps of acquiring knowledge of the concepts and facts which are the foundation of the generalization before he can invest it with meaning. Because there is a great range of subject matter in the social sciences from which to select content, there is a natural tendency to try to cover too much in the time available. The consequence is an inclination to select too broad a range of content, to place emphasis upon generalizations which are representative of a far greater range of subject matter than pupils can deal with sensibly. Too often, this forces the social studies teacher to teach generalizations as though they were arbitrary associations—meaningless facts committed to memory, to concentrate on too high a level of abstraction for adequate understanding. This trend should be resisted and in its place one should seek to understand more clearly the place of generalizations within the total framework of content in the social studies program.

To secure such understanding, generalizations identified as important in the content of a social study should be analyzed for the concepts and factual data basic to them or their understanding. Recognition that understanding grows and develops, that it does not come into full flower at once, leads to planning for recurring emphases throughout the grades. Social studies generalizations learned in the lower grades are refined and broadened later. From rather limited generalizations, the pupil is encouraged to draw inferences and to expand his understanding so that it finds expression in more broadly applicable statements and ideas of relationships. For example, generalizations about the family might find expression in a child's thinking as he matures and studies in the following developmental sequence of ideas:

Generalizations About the Family

Overarching generalization: The family is the basic social unit in society, taking different forms in different cultures, but the basis upon which the total culture is built.

"Almost everyone has a family."

"One important thing a family does is to help each other."

Primary Grades: "Some families in our community are unable to take good enough care of their own needs for food, clothing, and shelter."

"Members of families in other countries and in other times helped each other as they do today."

"The family, with the church, is the important institution in teaching religion."

Intermediate Grades: "Other cultures have different forms of family life than we do in our country."

"Although family life has taken different forms throughout the history of man, it is the oldest social grouping."

Upper Grades: "Because we consider the family so important in our country, state and federal laws have been passed to help protect it."

Because generalizations are such an important outcome of the teaching-learning process in social studies, the quality and quantity of learning in this dimension is extremely important to the teacher. Successful teaching occurs when the teacher has a clear conception of the generalizations important to a particular study and then plans learning experiences in a way that allows each child to progress in his own development of these generalizations. Individual differences within a class make uniform understanding or growth in comprehension of generalizations impossible. The teacher seeks to help each pupil advance at his own rate and assists him to progress as far as he possibly can in formulating pertinent generalizations.

Learning Values Through Social Studies

Values are the standards held by individuals and groups. They help each individual to define what he believes is best for him by providing guides by which judgments of worth are made. The *process of valuing* is what everyone goes through when he makes judgments about people, things, events, or ideas encountered in day to day living. Although much valuing may be at a high level of awareness, a great deal of it occurs at subconscious levels. For example, the conscientious voter in local or national affairs gives careful thought to the arguments, proposals, and statements of purpose which are propounded by different sides in political contests. Such thinking requires a careful evaluation of the arguments for and against a particular issue in the light of the values held by the voter. Race prejudice, in contrast, derives from emotional sets and biases, few of which are recognized by the person who is deeply prejudiced. Such thought and the action which stems from it are the consequences of subconscious, emotional responses rather than intellectual ones.

Social studies teachers constantly must take into account the fact that children, like adults, are deeply involved at all times in developing their own value structures. The problem facing the social studies teacher, therefore, is not whether values will be learned but what their quality will be. Traditionally, a heavy responsibility has been placed upon the social studies curriculum for teaching particularly those values associated with the ideals, attitudes, and behaviors esteemed in a democratic society. Such terms as the following carry the meaning which stimulate thinking about values or standards of right or wrong, good or evil, better or best:

45 Value-Laden Terms

Conservation	Freedom from fear	Import duties
Respect for others	Represenative	Buy American
Socialism	government	Republican
Yellow journalism	Eggheads	Pledge of Allegiance
Democracy	Confederacy	AFL-CIO
Sex education	Iron Curtain	NRA
Spiritualism	Jews	Loyalty oath
Cleanliness	War	Nationalism
Immigration quotas	Muckrakers	Civil War
Free speech	Genocide	Freedom of assembly
Good manners	ICBM	Bill of Rights
Religious freedom	Big Stick	Democrat
State's Rights	Christian nation	Comintern
Republic	NAACP	White backlash
Culturally deprived	Communism	Athlete
	Scholarship	

This list includes terms that are heavily weighted with values throughout the American culture. What are some ideas you might wish to include as being of particular importance? Obviously, not everyone would agree that those included here, or those which might be added, are in fact either the most important ideas or that they should be given the same degree of value. But all would agree that every person should have a well developed sense of values with respect to most of the ideas indicated above. In addition, some common agreements about additional values, behaviors, and attitudes to which every citizen should ascribe value should be achieved. The selection and teaching of such values therefore becomes a major problem for the social studies curriculum.

How well has the school succeeded in teaching these and other values most directly associated with the objectives of the social studies curriculum? All the evidence indicates that learning in this dimension of the social studies has been poorest of all. Since World War II, particularly, there has been an overwhelming accumulation of research reports which suggest that the school continues to exercise no measurable positive influence upon students in learning those values (the attitudes, ideals, and behaviors) upon which it is generally agreed that a democratic social order depends. Sheldon, for example, reports a study in which it was discovered that:

The completion of high school courses in Civics or U.S. Government *is not* related to any of the attitudes measured in this study. There is *no* evidence of any *positive* effect of such courses of study upon the beliefs of the pupils so far as freedom guaranteed by the U.S. Constitution is concerned. . . . The implications of these findings are:

A significant segment of U.S. high school seniors do not agree with the freedoms guaranteed by the Bills of Rights. About *one* student in *five* disagrees (on some items of the questionnaire, the proportion of respondents in disagreement runs far higher).

The students who reject freedom tend to accept authoritarianism.

The same students tend to classify themselves as the best Americans, and supporters of American democracy.[16]

This not to say that, universally, conscientious teachers are not successful in teaching values as well as concepts, facts, generalizations, and skills associated with social studies content. However, the number of studies indicating findings of this nature are growing, and their pessi-

[16] Kenneth Sheldon, "Summaries of Significant Research," *Social Education,* Vol. XXIII, No. 1 (January, 1959), pp. 30-31, in a review of an unpublished doctoral dissertation by Roy E. Horton, Jr., titled *American Freedom and the Values of Youth,* Purdue University, 1955. See also John C. Weiser and James E. Hayes, "Democratic Attitudes of Teachers and Prospective Teachers," *Phi Delta Kappan,* XLVIII, No. 9 (May 1966), pp. 476-481.

mistic conclusions are in line with those appearing here. Apparently, pupils learn most of their significant values out of school, often in an incidental fashion. There is serious cause to question the quality of learning taking place under these conditions and to bring sharply into focus the problem the school faces in making effective the teaching and learning of those values upon which a democratic society is based.

How does the social studies teacher assure himself that values *are* learned by his pupils? To learn *about* our own values and those of other cultures does not differ basically from the way any social studies concept is learned. But it is the *process of valuing* which must be considered in teaching if basic ideas of good or bad, right or wrong, better or best are to be developed. At this time, enough is not known about this process to warrant drawing unchanging conclusions. Yet so important is the process that it constitutes one of the major research frontiers of the behavioral sciences. Educators turn primarily to those fields, seeking suggestions for practice in the classroom.

Research in the behavioral sciences stresses the point that the school shares in the development of values with other agencies and institutions. Today, as has been pointed out, the role of the school is a minor one. To become more effective, the school must adopt practices which are known to produce better results than those currently used. The conclusions appearing in the following paragraphs appear to be warranted from the data at hand.

Although it is readily agreed that a child's conceptual framework is developed through experience, a different approach is used when values are involved. That is, children are guided in developing concepts for many things through direct experiencing (such as might be accomplished on a study trip) or through vicarious experiences (seeing flat pictures, filmstrips, or motion pictures; reading books; and examining and perhaps building models). However, concepts heavily weighted with value are usually taught dictatorially. Through the "injunction method," the child is told that he should cooperate, for example; and the child is considered successful in acquiring this value when he conforms to the teacher's wishes, standards of conduct, and the like. The child is quick to learn that there are certain values which it is best to assume (or at least appear to assume) in order to please the teacher or other adult authority figure. The child quickly becomes a fine parrot, in the meantime going about his own business in perfecting a value structure which makes sense to *him* and which, in his immature view, operates sucessfully. This process is well established by the time the child is eight or nine years old. It does not take long for the schism to be established between knowledge about values and the development of behavior in accord with those values. For example, in the following responses to the question, "Tell as many ways as you can in which people cooperate," the tendency to give it back to the adult in terms and behaviors valued by adults is clearly established. Few of the responses indicate the children have an operationally sound understanding of the values implied in the term "cooperation":

Kindergarten[17]
Not to push them down.
Not to step on toes on purpose.
*Help everyone get well.
Not to let them go when people do something bad.
Setting table when Mother asks.
*If somebody hurt, carry them to teacher.
Put all tools away before you sit in circle.
Not fight with brother.
Leave people alone when they're working.
Remember rules in line.
Stay on playground.
*Get Jane's crutches.

First Grade
Be quiet.
Be careful of people in line.
Be nice.
Wash dishes right away.
Do work before play.
*Do work that needs to be done so we can have good time together.
Be quiet when somebody talks.
Sit still, not bother people.

Pick up my toys.
Bring garbage cans to house.
*Help hold pieces of wood.
Listen.
Ask permission before going to washroom.
Do what they are told.
Listen in the circle.

Second Grade
Sit nice.
Sit like ladies and gentlemen.
Might help other people.
*If you are invited out to dinner, you might wash or dry the dishes.
Being quiet.
Listening.
Doing your work.
Staying in your seat.
Listen.
Don't move around in the circle.
Don't talk out of turn.
Take turns in games.
*Play together in games.
Obey.
*When people do things that they know will help other people.
When you do things when you are first told.

[17] From a preliminary study by Southern Section Social Studies Committee, California Association for Supervision and Curriculum Development. An asterisk has been placed before those responses indicating instances where the child has a good understanding of the value involved. Reprinted by permission.

Third Grade
*Doing everything for each other.
*Helping each other.
*They don't fight.
They do their own work.
*Be friends.
*Get along together.
*Liking everybody.
*Helping people.
Teacher helps us if we get stuck.
*Children help each other.
Once in awhile they are real good to their children.
They (children) don't have gangs.
They mind all the rules.

Fourth Grade
When people don't act noisy.
When children mind their parent.
When someone does not get mad too easily and lose his temper.
When you ask them to do something and they do it.
Go finish your arithmetic.
Go get clothes off the line.
Go feed the dog.
When Mother tells you to do something and you do it.
Eating food you don't like.
Taking out music book when teacher says to.
When I am at my father's store and don't bother him he says I am cooperating.
When they do things when they are asked to do them.
*If there is a lot of things to do, to help without being asked.
When on a boat fishing and the guy tells you to be quiet, do it.
*Pay attention to others.
Mind teacher.
Quiet when teacher is out of room.
Not get up until teacher says to.
Do what they are told.
Do what they are supposed to.
You do what teacher says and not argue.

Listen to what teacher says.
Obey orders.

Fifth Grade
Do as they are told and stuff.
Go where they tell them to.
They are not supposed to copy off others.
Do as your mother and father tell you.
Never steal.
*Play together and talk together.
Sing together.
Read together.
Paint and draw together.
*Live together by being friendly.
They listen.
Do what they are told.
If someone asks you to do something, you do it.
When you cooperate with someone you do what they ask.
If someone wants you to empty the wastebasket, you do it.
Cooperate in games and sports.
*They work together.

Sixth Grade
*In games, play by rules.
In class, don't talk.
Mind parents.
Mind teacher.
People go along with you.
*Working together.
*Play together.
*Helping others.
Being quiet in school.
Minding teacher.
Mind Mother.
Follow orders from your elders.
*Like in clubs, do your part.
When teacher asks you something, do it.
By doing things people ask them to do.
*By saying nice things about people instead of awful things.

*Hawaii cooperates by giving us part of their sugar.

*Japan trades with us.

*People cooperate in their communities.

When there's a war or anything people come around and warn people when there's an air raid.

*They help people out a lot, like the nurses working for the Red Cross.

*Going someplace to help people out.

Doing what teacher wants you to do.

*Not hurting other people.

People in the U.S. not revolting against the government.

Seventh Grade

We cooperate by not talking in class.

Not being rude to the teacher.

Do what you are told to do and not gripe about it.

If any elder asks you to do something, do it if it is the right thing to do.

*On a basketball team take your turn.

By sitting still.

By not talking out.

By doing what the teacher says.

By raising your hand when you want to talk.

*By offering to help.

*By playing fair.

Eighth Grade

*Government is run by cooperation of the governed.

Armies and navies discipline by cooperation.

*UN countries cooperate with each other.

*Friendships are cooperative.

*If two people can't get along with each other, how can two countries, or two worlds?

*Some people don't understand what democracy means we have to show them by having good government and living better ourselves.

Values will be best learned when children are given opportunities to explore concepts of value *at their level of maturity* with the same degree of objectivity that characterizes the consideration of concepts in other dimensions of the social studies. Valuing of the kind desired occurs in social studies teaching where problems are analyzed, solutions proposed, and action taken which appear to pupils to be appropriate, and where the consequences of these ideas and behaviors are evaluated by them. Key words italicized above reiterate that successful teaching depends upon teacher knowledge of the types of problems which pupils at the various levels of maturity in the elementary school are capable of handling. Sixth or seventh grade pupils obviously will be able to deal with some problems which kindergartens or first graders cannot. And, inevitably, pupils differ widely from one school to another, even within a particular school district. At any level, this means that children should be allowed the privilege of making mistakes. The old adage to the effect that we learn through our mistakes as well as through our successes has urgent application here. Nevertheless, the "injunction method" of teaching is incompatible with this point of view, since it does not provide the learner with an opportunity to make a judgment concerning the importance or applicability of a given value. If the teacher does not feel that he can place his trust in the deliberations and decisions which pupils thoughtfully reach, and upon which action is taken, then values will constitute a minor portion of the content of instruction in his classroom.

For these reasons, the modern social studies classroom is characterized by ways of teaching and opportunities for decision making which encourage the pupils to make judgments. For example, the following types of experiences are considered to be critical in helping children develop their value structures in the social studies program.

1. Much discussion and analysis of value-laden terms
2. Careful attention to helping each pupil understand *what* is to be studied and *why* it is important to undertake the study
3. Cooperative development of plans for studying a topic, problem, or issue
4. Much personalized teaching through the use of a wide variety of groupings of pupils within the class and through individualized responsibilities for study
5. Group involvement on a systematic and continuous basis for evaluating progress and for modifying plans wherever appropriate as the study continues
6. Opportunities for "role playing" in a wide variety of situations
7. "Democratic atmosphere" prevails throughout the program, not merely when the teacher finds it convenient
8. Many opportunities for expressive activities: writing, speaking, drawing or painting, dramatizing, etc.
9. Utilizing a wide variety of learning resources, emphasizing the importance of self learning and the uniqueness of each pupil's knowledge of a topic or problem in the social study
10. Attention to topics which are emotionally charged

The Importance of Skill Development in Social Studies

Skills make possible the most efficient development of *meanings*—of the concepts, facts, generalizations, and values which comprise the objectives of social studies teaching. But skill development itself unfolds best where it is closely associated with meaning. Hence, skill development in the social studies is inextricably entwined with the other dimensions of content which the teacher includes in his social studies program.

The term "skill" refers to one's ability to perform a complex act. In the social studies, the learner must call upon a wide variety of skills. Although some of these skills are used rather broadly throughout the school curriculum, there are others in large measure restricted to the social studies program itself. The pupil lacking in skill development in either aspect is without question seriously handicapped. Of those skills which find application in all areas of the curriculum, the most important to the social studies are those associated with the reading process and other language skills (listening, speaking, and writing), learning to work in groups, and study skills. Those skills confined more strictly to the social studies program itself must be taught by the teacher primarily in this curriculum area, without relying upon other institutions to teach them. Such skills include:

1. Map reading and interpretation of other graphic materials
2. Abilities in formulating generalizations about socially significant ideas
3. Employing research methods in the identification of problems and in proposing means by which those problems might be attacked
4. Developing abilities associated with locating and gathering information and in organizing and evaluating it, including the utilization of various types of special reference materials such as almanacs, encyclopedias, audio-visual materials (motion pictures, filmstrips, flat pictures, etc.), museums, resource persons, and libraries
5. Interpersonal relationships, including the ability to work in small groups, participate in discussions, prepare and present oral reports

CONTRIBUTIONS OF KNOWLEDGE ABOUT HOW PEOPLE LEARN
TO TEACH SOCIAL STUDIES SKILLS

Research findings in the learning of skills have been summarized by Burton into four principles which can serve as guides to the teacher in thinking about the skill program in the social studies.

1. Skills are not isolated mechanisms which can be learned apart from real situations and then automatically applied in real situations. Skills are extensions of meaning; procedures for making understandings

operative. Skills are learned better, therefore, when closely associated with meanings.

2. Skills are not acquired readily in advance of need or of meaning and familiarity. The repetitive practice or drill through which facility develops must be preceded by a period of integrative practice. Facility is not the aim of this preliminary activity; rather, familiarity and insight are sought. The integrative period should include several contacts, some tentative trials, conversation about or more formal diagnosis of mistakes, questioning, handling, "fooling around." Repetitive practice is then accompanied by increasing insight into meaning and pattern. The time for and number of repetitive drills are reduced under these conditions. The term "trial-and-error" is, in some quarters, being dropped in favor of "retrial-with-insight." The evidence seems to warrant special emphasis on insight and understanding in all practice.

3. Skills are not, as commonly thought, fixed unchanging routines which may be acquired through unthinking repetition. Skill performance is inherently variable, from person to person and from situation to situation, and differs in terms of position in which it is performed.

4. Research shows that children who have had considerable contact with drill which grew out of their own needs, i.e., was meaningful, will acquire a principle very important on upper levels, namely, that drill or practice is a necessary and sensible activity. The end in view, or the use of the skill, removes drill from the dull routine of repetition and gives it meaning and sense.[18]

TYPES OF SKILLS TAUGHT IN THE SOCIAL STUDIES

In planning for skill development, the teacher may think about the types of skills and abilities he wishes to teach in a variety of ways. The largest number of concerns listed would be intellectual skills and abilities—those associated with locating and gathering information, evaluating information and ideas, formulating generalizations, proposing solutions to problems, determining next steps in a study. Certain motor and social skills associated with the intellectual aspect are also important. Motor skills include those activities in which a person engages when he records, receives, or communicates ideas. Reading and writing, expressing ideas through pictures, maps, charts, and graphs, oral discussion and reports, and aural (listening) skills each involve certain types of motor activity and require that those skills be developed fully enough to be useful to the learner if they are to support his intel-

[18] William H. Burton, "Implications for Organization of Instruction and Instructional Adjuncts," Chapter Nine in *Learning and Instruction*, National Society for the Study of Education, Forty-ninth Yearbook, Part I (1950), p. 246. Reprinted by permission.

lectual inquiry. Among these motor skills are abilities to remain quiet, to be capable of receiving oral directions or information from the teacher or other children in the class, to write legibly, to handle various art media, to speak clearly—the whole range of physical development and skills required to accomplish the tasks the teacher sets before the class or the child requires of himself. Social skills include those activities which indicate that the child has a facility in personal and human relationships. In the social studies program these consist particularly of abilities for working in groups of various sizes, for fulfillment of leadership roles in groups of varying numbers, for participation in group discussion on both an informal and a formal basis, as a member of a panel or symposium, under the terms of parliamentary procedures, and the like, as well as on less structured bases. Teaching these skills begins in the kindergarten and extends upward through the grades. Each teacher at each level can make a contribution to such skill development in the three facets described here: the intellectual, motor, and social development of the child.

Although a logical progression of increasing difficulty might be used to describe some skills (for example, map reading), many social studies skills cannot be described satisfactorily in this manner. Group process skills, particularly, are difficult to describe in quantitative terms alone, since the quality of such participation is highly situational and does not lend itself to objective evaluation. Motor skills are most likely to yield to a logical analysis, therefore, with intellectual and social skills, in that order, resisting analysis into logical parts and application to a sequence of learning activities based upon the maturity of the learners.

The breadth and complexity of skills directly related to the social studies program are suggested in a list developed by Tyler. Such a list is useful in enumerating the skills to be taught in a social study or in evaluating progress of pupils upon the completion of a particular study. According to Tyler, skills, abilities, and habits in social studies are employed:

1. In analyzing problems
2. In collecting facts and other data
   2.1 Skill in selecting dependable sources of data
   2.2 Ability to observe carefully and listen attentively
   2.3 Ability to read critically
   2.4 Ability to discriminate important from unimportant facts
   2.5 Ability to take notes
   2.6 Ability to read charts, graphs, tables, and maps

3. In organizing and interpreting data
   3.1   Skill in outlining
   3.2   Skill in summarizing
   3.3   Ability to make reasonable interpretations
4. In presenting the results of study
   4.1   Skill in writing a clear, well-organized, and interesting paper
   4.2   Skill in presenting an oral report
   4.3   Ability to prepare a bibliography
   4.4   Ability to prepare charts, graphs, tables, and maps
   4.5   Ability to write a critical book review
5. Ability to do independent thinking
6. Ability to analyze argument and propaganda
7. Ability to participate effectively in group work
8. Good work habits—planning time, efficient use of time
9. Ability to interpret a social situation, to recognize motives and needs of others
10. Ability to foresee consequences of proposed actions.[19]

SKILL DEVELOPMENT IN THE CLASSROOM

Like other things learned in a good social studies program, skills are not learned in one or two class sessions. They take time to develop and require many situations in which the pupil practices and reviews his progress. This is true whether the particular objective is primarily an intellectual, motor, or social skill or ability.

To plan an effective skill program in social studies, the teacher needs to develop and keep at hand a list of specific ideas about the major skills in which he wishes his pupils to become more adept through a particular study. He then is equipped to plan for the practice and review which is associated with the various types of skills he is attempting to further in his pupils. When his purposes call for increased skill in collecting facts and other data, for example, as he plans his social studies work with children he finds opportunities for a wide variety of activities to support this objective. Such activities are adjusted to the level of maturity of children; appropriate ones are available at any level.

Pupils in the early grades, studying neighborhood and community life, can become expert in searching out information from varied sources such as books in the classroom, at home, and at the public library; from

---

[19] Ralph W. Tyler, "Curriculum Organization," Chapter Six in *The Integration of Educational Experiences,* National Society for the Study of Education, Fifty-seventh Yearbook, Part III (1958), p. 119.

resource persons or pictures in a variety of sources. But they must become habituated to both searching for information and using it in the classroom. The teacher's role is to help children see the value of seeking out information from a wide variety of sources. This he can do only if he assiduously avoids the role of final arbiter of the validity of information which is being sought and displays an *attitude of respect* for the activities of his researchers. He must place genuine value on the worthwhileness of gathering such information in the first place. To do this, information sought out must be used. That is, it must be talked about, evaluated, and related to the purposes of the overall study. Therefore, it is important to provide opportunities for researchers to present their findings from time to time in oral, written, and pictorial form.

Older children are generally able to work for greater lengths of time with more abstract material. This is not universally true, and adjustments must be made for particular classes or for groups of children within a class. It should always be kept in mind that the types of reference materials used should depend upon the major questions which are being asked. Textbooks serve useful functions, primarily at the beginning of a study, in orienting learners to a problem. No textbook contains sufficient detail to satisfy the needs of a class in developing research skills for collecting facts and other data. The same is true of the other intellectual skills and abilities which are developed in a social studies program. To use the textbook as the major source for information means that the program will be weak in developing those intellectual skills, habits, and abilities in which elementary school children should become well grounded.

The preceding discussion of but one aspect of skill development in the intellectual realm is intended to illustrate the opening statement above, that *skill development in the social studies is inextricably entwined with the other dimensions of content which the teacher intends to include in his social studies program.* Further illustrations of how these elements are interrelated will be discussed in subsequent chapters. In addition to the other intellectual skills indicated above, there are important motor and social skills to be learned. Like the skills most closely related to intellectual activities, motor and social skills are learned best when the teacher plans for their development and provides continuous practice and review. A child does not learn to represent what he has learned with maps or charts unless he has many opportunities to record information in this manner. He does not learn to read social studies material more effectively through the textbook alone, but only by having many opportunities to read widely and deeply those sources containing information which he needs to have. Such sources may be printed, hard-cover books, but should not be exclusively so. They include as well pamphlets, filmstrips, magazines, materials written by himself and other children, and even, perhaps, things written by the teacher for his pupils.

Social skills develop where there are continuous opportunities to practice and review them. Children learn to work in groups by having opportunities to work as members of variously sized groups and by evaluating the quality of the work accomplished. A child learns to take part in panel discussions as a consequence of participating actively as a member of a panel. Most of the experience a child has in school is as a member of a large group of thirty to forty children. Such experience can be valuable in developing social skills, but he also needs to gain experience as a member of various other groups—small work groups of from two to six members, larger discussion and planning groups, information giving groups such as panels and symposiums, and debate and other "teams" designed to test the validity of opposing points of view with respect to significant issues. Such skills are not only immediately useful in helping children to learn socially significant material; they also provide opportunities to learn valuable skills. Utility in this respect may be tested from two standpoints: (1) as means of furthering each person's social education, i.e., continuing his intellectual growth toward better understanding of man's social problems; (2) as a means of improving social intercourse and encouraging the development of wholesome personalities, in contact with social realities. These objectives will only be achieved as the teacher provides specific experiences with a wide variety of group activities in the social studies classroom.

FOR FURTHER READING

Association for Supervision and Curriculum Development, *Human Variability and Learning*, Walter B. Waetjen, ed. (Washington, D.C.: ASCD, 1961).

Association for Supervision and Curriculum Development, *New Dimensions in Learning: A Multidisciplinary Approach*, Walter B. Waetjen, ed. (Washington, D.C.: ASCD, 1962).

Association for Supervision and Curriculum Development, *Perceiving, Behaving, Becoming: A New Focus for Education*, Yearbook 1962 (Washington, D.C.: ASCD, 1962).

Bruner, Jerome S., *et al.*, *A Study of Thinking* (New York: John Wiley and Sons, Inc., 1956).

Combs, Arthur W. and Donald Snygg, *Individual Behavior*, revised (New York: Harper and Brothers, 1959).

Erikson, Erik, *Childhood and Society*, revised edition (New York: W. W. Norton Company, 1965).

Flavell, John H., *The Developmental Psychology of Jean Piaget* (Princeton, N.J.: D. Van Nostrand Company Inc., 1963).

Holbrook, David, *The Secret Places* (London: Methuen & Co., 1964).

Holt, John, *How Children Fail* (New York: Pitman Publishing Company, 1965).

Henry, Jules, *Culture Against Man* (New York: Random House, 1963).

Hunt, J. McV., *Intelligence and Experience* (New York: Ronald Press, 1961).

National Society for the Study of Education, *Child Psychology*, Sixty-second Yearbook, Part I (Chicago: University of Chicago Press, 1963).

National Society for the Study of Education, *Theories of Learning and Instruction*, Sixty-third Yearbook, Part I (Chicago: University of Chicago Press, 1964).

Phenix, Phillip H., *Realms of Meaning* (New York: McGraw Hill, 1964).

Phi Delta Kappan, "Special Issue: The School's Responsibility for Moral Education," XLVI No. 2 (October, 1964).

Russell, David H., *Children's Thinking* (Boston: Ginn and Company, 1956).

Rosenblith, Judy F. and Wesley Allinsmith (eds.), *The Causes of Behavior: Readings in Child Development and Educational Psychology* (Boston: Allyn and Bacon, Inc., 1962).

Spindler, George (ed.), *Education and Culture* (New York: Holt Rinehart and Winston, 1963).

Thelen, Herbert A., *Education and the Human Quest* (New York: Harper and Brothers, 1960).

Vygotsky, L. S., *Thought and Language* (Cambridge, Mass.: Massachusetts Institute of Technology, 1962).

White, Ralph K. and Ronald O. Lippitt, *Autocracy and Democracy: an Experimental Inquiry* (New York: Harper and Brothers, 1960).

CHAPTER FIVE

Planning the Social Study

Ideally, teaching inspires children to probe deeply and significantly into their studies. Where such inspiration occurs, pupils experience an inward drive to learn; they derive great personal satisfaction from the effort expended in study. When a visitor enters a classroom where the teacher has released children's energies in this manner, the phenomenon is clearly manifest. Children are well organized. They are thinking for themselves. They have identified problems they understand and which they will attempt to solve. The activities they engage in are directed to the solution of those problems. A sense of accomplishment pervades the room. What has happened before in the class is logically related in the pupils' minds to what is presently being done and to the anticipated next steps of the study.

The teacher's role in such a classroom is immediately noticeable. His is the role of coordinator, helper, questioner, listener; he is teaching, not instructing. This is not a passive role. Nor is it predicated upon a laissez-faire philosophy of following the lines of least resistance in which children are allowed to do whatever seems best at the moment. It is positive and dynamic; it gives every evidence of careful, systematic planning. The teacher has made his preparations well in advance of actual teaching. As teaching progresses, teachers and pupils plan together. In this classroom, the teacher sees his role as that of an *arranger* of conditions within which children think and learn for themselves. In other words, the teacher knows what he must do to establish the conditions for learning, and he knows what things pupils must do for themselves. In this chapter, the nature of the plans that the teacher makes in advance of actual teaching; the planning and decision making that occur as teaching progresses will be discussed in this and the following chapter.

Social Studies and Units of Work

A word should be interjected here about the terms *unit, unit of work,* and *unit method.* These terms were applied to social studies programs which were developed as a reaction to the strictly subject centered curriculum that reached its zenith around 1900. Today, these terms are so widely used, and in so many different contexts, that there is little agreement as to their precise meaning. Generally speaking, at the elementary school level *unit* and *unit of work* are synonymous, referring to those learning experiences which children have as they study a significant topic, problem, or issue. *Unit method,* in contrast, has come to mean the manner in which those learning experiences are organized. Each term is so lacking in exact meaning that, in this book, a simple term has been chosen to describe what it is children do when they explore socially significant subject matter: study. How one organizes a study, and how he prepares himself to teach it, varies according to the subject matter and the purposes of the teacher. In dealing with content derived from the social sciences, there are several aspects which usually must be considered in planning for teaching and in teaching itself. These are discussed in the remaining pages of this chapter.

Teaching Plans and Teaching

The first step in planning a study does not involve children directly. This is the stage at which the teacher builds his own resources for teaching, where he gathers the ideas and materials he will need in working with his pupils. In this process he first identifies the general area of concern for study, then expands his knowledge of the important subject matter content; he identifies the subject matter likely to be important for his pupils to learn, develops his objectives for teaching it, plans a wide variety of learning activities to support the development of the subject matter of the study, and gathers teaching materials. He plans ways in which the study may be evaluated. All of these guides can be more or less formally prepared, written down, and kept in one place.

Teaching the study is another matter. The plans which the teacher draws up with children are developmental: they are determined from day to day, according to the actual progress of the pupils in the classroom. The teacher, prior to embarking on the study with the pupils, has prepared himself so that he feels comfortable in planning *with* children.

He has anticipated enough contingencies so that a variety of learning experiences can be employed in realizing the objectives for teaching it. Each study, as it comes to life in the classroom, is a unique experience, never to be exactly repeated again. The resource materials constantly are added to and refined as time passes, making it possible for the teacher, as he works with one group of children and then another, to improve his skill at tailoring the study to meet the needs and abilities of children as they vary from one year to the next.

Building Resource Materials for the Study

Decisions must be made, information gathered, and ideas examined prior to teaching. The steps involved are described below.

THE TEACHER SELECTS THE GENERAL AREA OF CONCERN

School districts generally adopt a course of study or "framework" for social studies which indicates in broad outline what the scope and sequence of studies will be. Sometimes this course of study is planned within the individual school district.[1] More often, counties, large cities, and states work out a course of study based upon the expanding community-basic functions concept, areas of living, or some other scheme— which the local district either adapts to its own purposes or adopts outright. However, within these very general statements,[2] it is necessary for the teacher to select the specific area of emphasis. "Community" studies call for identifying a particular community and for determining emphases within that broad topic; state studies obviously will vary similarly. Always, the local situation influences how a study might be approached and what material will be pertinent: regional and hemispheric studies, studies of other cultures, or studies of particular political, economic, and social institutions. If sufficient depth is to be achieved, even further emphasis may be necessary. For example, the following topics were drawn from a group of resource studies for various grades prepared by teachers:

Geography of the Eastern States (fourth)
Our Creative Community: As It Is, and As It Was (third)
Early Exploration and Settlement of the United States (fifth)

---

[1] Consult a nearby school district curriculum office for examples of courses of study.
[2] One such statement is reproduced on pp. 75-77 of Chapter Three.

Transportation in Our Community (second)
Ships, Harbors, and Cargoes (second)
Mexico, Its People and Heritage (sixth)
The Story of the Development of Our Country (fifth)
The Problems of Southern California (fourth)
Free World Alliances (sixth)
World Trade (seventh)
Civilizations of the Old World (sixth)

Where teachers have considerable initiative in selecting areas of emphasis, at every level of the school a balance should be maintained between studies involving relationships in time and in space and those focusing upon man's institutions and processes. Moreover, the scope of studies undertaken by children ought to be checked against the several criteria for breadth: the social functions, areas of living, persistent life problems, and imperative needs curricula.

It is best for the teacher to have a considerable range of choice in selecting specific topics or problems for study for at least three major reasons. First, the maturity and experience levels of children vary widely, even between classes of the same grade within a school and, certainly, between one school and another. Second, in selecting a topic for study, the availability of teaching resources must be considered. Such resources consist of talented citizens, library facilities, texts, reference books, audio-visual materials, and other sources for learning. When there is a dearth of such teaching resources, it is better not to attempt a study which meets all the other criteria for an appropriate choice. Third, the teacher must have some knowledge and interest in the subject matter of the study and be willing to learn more about it. Appropriate choices in all likelihood will be made where these criteria are observed, regardless of whether the school demands close adherence to an adopted course of study or whether it leaves up to the teacher considerable responsibility for deciding topics.

THE TEACHER EXTENDS HIS UNDERSTANDING
OF THE TOPIC OR PROBLEM AREA

When the broad topic has been selected, the teacher reviews what he knows about it. How shall he find out what he still needs to know in order to feel adequately prepared to teach? Now it may seem strange to insist that teachers not only know the subject matter of the study they plan to teach, but like it as well. Too often it is said that elementary school content is *so* elementary that teachers of young children really do not need to know very much, let alone to develop any genuine scholarship in those social sciences which contribute to understanding of the studies taught. There is a widespread notion that the satisfaction of teaching young children must come from sources other than those associated with the love of learning. Rather, the satisfactions of teaching young children are sometimes said to come almost exclusively from the warmth of human interaction which prevails in the elementary school classroom. This attitude is particularly prevalent in the primary grades, decreasing as the aging process among pupils goes on. Henry, in commenting on this problem, states that the attitude in the American culture seems to say:

> If the teacher cannot love the subject matter, let her at least love the *subjects,* i.e., the children! At this point we are confronted by [a] . . . paradox in elementary school teaching, for while in the University we demand of teachers of philosophy that they love philosophy, of teachers of physics that they love physics, and of teachers of anthropology that they love anthropology, we do not require that elementary school teachers have the same love of language skills, arithmetic, etc., that the scientist has for his sciences or the humanist for his art, but demand rather that the elementary school teacher *love* children. I would urge that this emphasis originates in the fact that we do *not* expect our school teachers to love their subject matter, and so, instead, we make it compulsory that they love the children. Only when this antinomy has been removed so that the teacher . . . is in love with his subject matter, because the content . . . is a joy to both teacher *and* children, will such teaching be completely worthy of a human being, for it will draw on *all* his capacities.[3]

A special quality pervades the classroom in which the teacher loves and knows his subject matter. The scholar's attitude of inquiry, study, and thought is transmitted to children, largely without words, where the teacher-scholar is found. Such a person is at all times keenly aware that he does *not* know it all, and this attitude, the posture of honest inquiry, is reflected in his work with children and in their efforts throughout the study. Under these ideal conditions, children do not develop the notion that the teacher knows everything. The teacher, in turn, does not fear saying, "I don't know." Out of this climate come learnings based upon discovery and a mutual search for solutions to children's questions. It must be recognized that most elementary school teachers teach many

³ Jules Henry, "Reading for What?" *Claremont Reading Conference, Twenty-fifth Yearbook* (Claremont, California: The Claremont Graduate School, 1961), p. 21.

"America's leadership must be guided by the lights of learning and reason—or else those who confuse rhetoric with reality and the plausible with the possible will gain the popular ascendancy."

—John F. Kennedy

subjects. However, this does not preclude the development of a modest degree of scholarship in any elementary curriculum field, nor does it render unattainable the attitude of inquiry associated with true scholarship. The dichotomy between love for knowledge of subject matter and concern for the welfare of children must be broken in *all* areas; particularly is this true in social studies.

THE TEACHER IDENTIFIES THE UNDERSTANDINGS BASIC TO THE STUDY

When the teacher has sufficient adult insight into a topic, then he is ready to identify those understandings and skills fundamental for its comprehension. The understandings that are central to the development of any study consist of those concepts, basic facts, core generalizations, and central ideals and values best suited to the study in question. The skills consist of those behaviors or habits needed for the pursuit of the study and of those which may best be developed through it.

One of the major difficulties in teaching any social study is that of verbalism. Often children use words with little or no understanding of their meaning.[4] To overcome the problems of verbalism, the teacher must clearly have in mind the nature and extent of the understandings necessary in beginning a study as well as the types of understandings which best can be developed through it. The teacher begins by identifying basic concepts. It is extremely important that the nature and extent of the conceptual development of children be assessed with respect to a particular topic before moving ahead with it. As the study progresses, the teacher finds opportunities to extend and deepen these concepts and to introduce others which are important. It is from this conceptual base that an understanding of facts is derived, and from which the child is led to generalize. The importance of ascertaining the initial level of understanding before proceeding with other material is illustrated in this experience of a mother and her five-year-old.

The child had been given a booklet at school by the teacher, who had in turn received it from the local police department. In it, drawings and a simple text explained that children should not accept rides, candy, and so forth, from strangers. On each page a person, referred to as a stranger, was depicted offering bribes and behaving in a manner certain to arouse suspicion in an adult, if not a child. The comic book format, with simple text and pictures, had been gone over by the class with the teacher, page by page, before it was taken home. When the mother saw her child come into the house with the booklet, she thought the idea of distributing information like this a good one and so she in turn went over it with the child, reading the text and pointing out the pictures. When she had finished, her youngster looked her full in the face and posed the one question she had not anticipated. "Mother," the youngster asked, "what is a stranger?"

Failure to understand this, the fundamental concept contained in the story, meant that, at best, the rest of the material was meaningless. But there is a significant sequel to the story.

After the mother had explained as best she could, and the child seemed satisfied, the matter was dropped. But a few days later, the mother was walking home from the nearby store when she met a friend whom she had not seen in some time. In approaching home, the mother stopped and chatted with her friend, all the time under the surveillance of the five-year-old, who had been playing in front of the house. When

---

[4] It was pointed out in Chapter Four, "Dimensions of Learning in Social Studies," how little one may take for granted when considering the problem of verbalism in social studies.

the chat ended, and the mother started into the house, her child came up to her and said, "Mother, was *that* a stranger?"

Errors just as gross as this one, in the understanding of seemingly simple ideas or concepts, have been noted by researchers at every grade level of the school. It is a serious error for a teacher to assume how much a child really knows until he can grasp the extent of the child's understanding.

Too, this illustration points up that understanding of concepts is developmental. Children constantly are expanding their understanding of them, even though the concepts are not being taught directly. The basic nature of the questions raised by the child in this illustration should serve to point out, too, that failure to understand ideas which adults take for granted are understood can lead to meaningless verbiage. *The need to help children clarify their concepts at every stage in the development of a study cannot be stressed too strongly; as a consequence, they will have a clear understanding of what the key concepts in a particular study may be.*

Identifying Key Concepts. Identifying key concepts need not be a difficult task. For example, one fifth grade teacher worked out this list of concepts which he felt to be central to understanding the Civil War period. He used this list as a handy reference for himself as he developed the study with his pupils, constantly checking with it to ascertain how well the children in his class seemed to be extending their understanding of these ideas. The words representing the concepts were listed in two columns, one for those standing at the beginning stages of the study and one for those which he expected would be introduced and extended as the study progressed.

Key Concepts in a Study of the Civil War Period

Concepts for the initial stages of the study	Concepts to be introduced and extended as the study progresses
slavery	Whigs
The North	Republicans
The South	House of Representatives
slaveholders	Senate
political party	Admission to the Union
congress	ratify
debate	dissolution

Union
statehood
District of Columbia
Constitution
territory
Supreme Court
fugitive
President
oath of office
civil war
victory
nation
republic
government
campaigns (Presidential,
   military)
courts
votes
justice
federal government
politics
nomination (nominee)
law (s)
majority
minority
Negroes
loyal
economy

secession (secessionist)
Amendment to the Constitution
compromise
parallels
act (legislative)
Democrat
treaty
Slave Trade
Unionist
filibuster
proclamation
emancipation
homesteads
sovereignty
abolitionist
due process of law
treason
doctrine
ordinance
tidewater
Piedmont
neutral
railroad system
industrial economy
agricultural economy
invasion routes
enlist
rebellion
independence
Confederate
retreat
assassination
impeachment
reconstruction
carpetbaggers
scalawags

Each teacher can readily develop his own list of key concepts. The ones he selects will depend upon what kinds of experiences the pupils in his class have enjoyed prior to this study. The interests and knowledge of the teacher will also be reflected in the concepts emphasized. Such a list will never be used as a vocabulary check for children but, rather, will serve as a check point for the teacher as he works with children, trying to find out what is in their minds, determining what may be appropriate ways to expand the horizons of their thought.

How does one find out what *is* in a child's mind? He finds out through asking qustions and through giving the child a multiplicity of ways in which he may respond or show what he knows. He may talk it out with the teacher, or in a group of other children. He may express his ideas creatively through writing, through art, music, or drama. He may use concrete objects to explain his ideas.[5] One should keep in mind, as noted previously, that there will be no impression without expression, and it is unquestionably the role of the teacher to present a variety of opportunities in which expression may be possible. Children often cannot verbalize clearly enough for their own, or for adult, satisfaction. Particularly in these circumstances should concrete objects be available in the classroom. A child should have an opportunity to demonstrate with objects as well as to express himself verbally.[6] The use of concrete objects, although more time-consuming, often will provide the most accurate impression of what a child knows and what he has learned.

Identifying Core Facts and Generalizations. Just as the teacher identifies key concepts, so also must he attempt to record some of the core facts of the study. These constitute the major body of understandings which every teacher hopes all children will learn to some degree as a result of the study. These understandings are not taught didactically, after being previously identified by the teacher. They are learned in the course of the study to fill an authentic need. In planning the resource materials, the teacher must ask himself, "What are a few of the most important facts that children might learn through this study?" He then

[5] One recent study demonstrated that, when children are asked to explain their conceptions of common terms appearing in a sixth grade textbook, they will tend to score higher on an objective test of understanding (a multiple-choice test) than when they are asked to define the same concepts with concrete objects. Children of higher intelligence in this study tended to obtain scores more nearly alike (between objective tests and tests requiring the use of concrete objects) than children in the lower ranges of intelligence. It may be concluded from these and similar data that children in the lower intelligence range should have more opportunities to explain themselves using concrete objects whereas children in the upper range may be relied upon to express their ideas or concepts almost as well through verbal activities as through concrete ones. See Paul Schiele, Jr., *An Analysis of Children's Concepts of Common Sixth Grade Social Studies Terms* (Claremont, California: Unpublished master's thesis, Claremont Graduate School, 1961), 102 pp.

[6] These encompass the entire range of tactile materials which may be used in a classroom: paints, construction paper, globes, maps, rulers and yardsticks, crayons, clay, etc.

guides the teaching-learning situation so that these few facts are given sufficient attention to assure reasonable permanence.[7] These are not the only facts which will be discovered by a class. Rather, they represent those which warrant special attention in the teacher's opinion. He then uses these and other facts to help children generalize. Clear distinctions have been drawn between concepts, facts, and generalizations in Chapter Four. Keeping these distinctions in mind, then, the teacher attempts to identify those core facts and generalizations which, in his opinion, ought to be learned by most of the children in his class in the course of any given study. A sixth grade teacher, conducting an inquiry about Mexico, might list such statements as the following to represent the kind of factual information he desires his pupils to have at the study's completion:

1. Mexico has a population of approximately 35 million.
2. Almost half of Mexico lies in the equatorial belt; Mexico lies nearer to the equator on the globe than the United States.
3. Mexico is a country considerably smaller in size than the United States; it is approximately one-quarter as large.
4. The Rocky Mountains continue into Mexico, where they are called the Eastern and Western Sierra Madre Ranges.
5. In Mexico, corn is the staff of life. Indians developed it from *teo cintl,* a wild plant, many years before the explorers came to this country.
6. Mexico is divided into three distinct climatic zones: the hot lands along the coast and in the lowlands, called *tierra caliente;* the temperate area on the central plateau, called the *tierra templada;* and cold mountain lands known as *tierra fría.*
7. Less than an eighth of the United States' population are farmers; in Mexico, half the people are engaged in farming for a livelihood.
8. Spanish, though it is the official language of Mexico, is not spoken by more than 100,000 Mexican Indians. Fifty-six Indian languages are current in Mexico at the present time.
9. *Mestizos,* a mixture of Spanish and Indian peoples, form three-quarters of the population of Mexico.
10. Mexico's divisions are similar to those in the United States: there are twenty-nine states, a Federal District, and two territories.

[7] See Chapter Four, pp. 118-119, for a discussion of overlearning and the problem of securing some permanence of information.

11. Mexico's system of representation is not unlike that of the United States: it consists of an executive (president), a legislative body (Chamber of Deputies), and a judicial one (Supreme Court).
12. Mexicans are served by a nation-wide telephone and telegraph service.
13. Mexico has a national railway system that connects major cities and seaports.
14. Electric power and irrigation are being developed by both private and public enterprises.
15. Eighty-five per cent of the air passenger traffic in Mexico is handled by three Mexican-flag commercial airlines.
16. The Mexican government is making a concerted effort to improve transportation and communications systems.

Children are not expected to learn these facts verbatim, but one would assume that this type of specific information would be known to a large majority of the pupils in the class, along with many more specific items of information, by the conclusion of the study. These, then, are materials the teacher can use to check on himself and on his pupils. Teachers of lower grades will also find such a listing helpful, provided it is gauged to the maturity level of the children.

The teacher then selects some key generalizations which may be developed throughout the study. A second grade teacher, for example, identified these generalizations as important as she planned a project concerning the production, processing, and marketing of food:

1. Most foods come from green plants.
2. To maintain health, all of us require a variety of foods.
3. It takes the effort of many different workers to supply us with food.
4. Laws concerning food affect our health and must be strictly enforced.
5. We must know about which foods require refrigeration.
6. It is important to wash fruits and vegetables.
7. It is possible to cook, can, or freeze many fruits and vegetables.
8. Food we eat grows in several ways: above ground, below ground, and in water.
9. To grow, plants need soil that contains the proper ingredients, water, and sunlight.

10. In any given place, the kinds of food grown are affected by the climate.
11. Farmers in this country have a dramatically different life now because of modern machinery.
12. New types of machinery and modern ways of processing food mean that fewer workers can produce more food.

Identifying Central Ideals and Values. In similar fashion, the teacher examines the topic or problem to be explored for its central ideals and values. A study of the Revolutionary War period will lend itself to the teaching of certain of these. A study of state geography will provide an opportunity for others to be emphasized. Obviously, the overall balance in the curriculum design becomes very important here. In previous pages, the difference between the need to *learn about* ideals and values and the need to *behave in accord with* those values was pointed out. Both elements must be considered here. One teacher listed the following ideals and values as growing out of a study of one community:

1. There is strong desire to carry on the tradition of responsible citizenship set by early settlers.
2. There is appreciation of the fact that this community is beautiful and unique.
3. There is recognition of the value of citizens' working together for common needs.
4. There is tolerance of those who diverge in any way from the average.
5. Cooperation *and* individuality are considered important.
6. Creativity in all fields is encouraged and enjoyed.

Identifying the Skills Most Closely Associated with the Study. The final step in outlining significant content involves some specification of the types of skills which must be employed by children as they undertake their work. These skills cover a wide range of abilities. Some may be introduced for the first time; others may be strengthened through practice. The use of certain types of reference materials, interview techniques needed in obtaining information from talented citizens or resources in the community, utilization of maps, globes, and charts, human relations skills, and methods of reporting and evaluating information learned suggest the breadth of skills which might be appropriate in a particular study.[8]

Again, one study will lend itself to the development of certain skills better than will another. A third grade study of children living in different cultures around the world will call for extensive consideration of skills involved in reading the globe. A first grade study of the immediate neighborhood will necessitate direct attention to field work skills. A sixth grade study about Canada's relationships to the United States might embroil a class in debates or symposia as well as in report writing. Thinking through those skills which the teacher feels evolve naturally from a particular study provides the "advanced warning" needed to teach them well. In studies of various regions of the United States, for example, one teacher noted these skills as central in the development of understanding:

Skills for Regional Studies

I. We need map skills.
  A. It is important to grasp pictorial and semi-pictorial symbols.
  B. Perceiving is important too. We need to perceive:
      1. Distance
      2. Direction
      3. Position
  C. We need ability to *locate,* using equator, poles, North-South and East-West lines.
  D. We must understand the relation between man and his environment based on simple map skills.
  E. Reading is important. We need to be able to judge:
      1. Altitude
      2. Depth of water
      3. State and national boundaries
      4. Relation between land and water
      5. Scale
      6. Relation between slope of land and direction toward which rivers flow
      7. Location of poles and equator

[8] An excellent presentation of the nature of social studies skills and the manner in which they may be taught is contained in *Skill Development in Social Studies,* Thirty-third Yearbook, National Council for the Social Studies, 1963.

       8. North and South directional lines; East and West directional lines
       9. Earth as a sphere

II. We need research skills.
  A. We must learn how to use reference books; be familiar with:
    1. Title page
    2. Copyright
    3. Table of contents
    4. Index
    5. Appendix
    6. Glossary
  B. Skimming is a useful skill.
  C. We need to be skillful at critical reading: maps, pictures, globes, books.

III. Planning and working together are important too. We must become adept at:
  A. Planning individual and group activities
  B. Expressing, interpreting, using information and ideas
  C. Problem solving
  D. Participating effectively as a member of a group
  E. Evaluating individual and group progress

IV. Thinking critically is important. We must become skilled at:
  A. Grasping main ideas
  B. Forming and creating sensory images
  C. Making associations concerning
    1. Natural and man-made features
    2. People, places, things, processes
    3. Real places and things and symbols for them
  D. Comparing and contrasting
  E. Perceiving relationships to do with time and sequence, class, cause-effect, analogous, part-whole
  F. Making judgments and drawing conclusions
  G. Organizing and summarizing
  H. Generalizing
  I. Remembering and evaluating

Why the Planning of Content Is Important. Careful and systematic planning of content has a purpose; it is to bring to social studies a deserved rigor and intellectual honesty. Too often in the past the nature of the organized knowledge taught through the social studies curriculum has been ignored. It has proved easier to let subject matter specialists present content ready-made (resulting in the subject-centered curriculum). In other cases, educators have ignored the disciplines and developed a project-centered curriculum (in which activity seems often to have been an end in itself). These are the two easy solutions. A more difficult task by far is to secure the benefits of both—to identify the elements of the content fields in a particular study and to plan teaching so that children are allowed to move in their own thinking in such a way that they discover content through their own intellectual efforts. This implies a method of discovery, to which reference has been made and about which more will be said shortly.

The problem in overall planning of a social studies program is to make provisions for an appropriate variety of studies, the result of which is a defensible scope and sequence. The teacher's unique problem is to think through the substance of each study he will teach so thoroughly that children will be led to an understanding of the content and to an appreciation of the discipline behind the content.

Foshay has expressed this well.[9] He feels that a discipline is a way of creating knowledge and that it may be characterized by its "domain," or particular concern. It is also characterized by its history and by the generalizations it states as truths. Thus, chemistry may be said to deal with chemical phenomena, according to the rules of science; both rules and "domain" are products of the history of the field. The same thing may be said for geography or mathematics; indeed, for any discipline. But, Foshay reminds us, some scholars, for example physicists, have been telling us that it is possible for the young to approach a discipline *directly*.

The idea that disciplines may be approached in a direct manner is very powerful, and it is very different from the subject-centered approach teachers are familiar with. It should not be called subject-centered; this name does not accurately describe it. Instead, it attempts to involve children in learning in an active, rather than in a passive, way. It helps them "to grasp the intellectual means through which knowledge is discovered."[10] Hence, the task should not be to ask a mathematician, for example, "What should be taught in the first grade, what in the fifth." Rather, it is necessary to learn how to ". . . ask them

---

[9] Arthur W. Foshay, "A Modest Proposal," *Educational Leadership*, Vol. 18, No. 8 (May, 1961), pp. 511-515.
[10] *Ibid.,* p. 513.

to tell us what kinds of generalizations are appropriate to the disciplines they know well, and what is required if these generalizations are to be discovered by students."[11]

In an Appendix, the reader will find a listing of books for further reading, selected from several fields of the social sciences. These comprise a basic list of resources for the teacher wishing to expand his knowledge of the content commonly taught in the schools. They will also assist in identifying key concepts, facts, generalizations, values, and skills. For further assistance, the reader is urged to contact social scientists at neighboring colleges and universities. They can be of invaluable assistance in directing attention to other worthwhile materials.

THE TEACHER DESIGNATES THE OBJECTIVES OF THE STUDY

The teacher, confident that he understands the topic well enough to teach it, certain that he has outlined the major dimensions of the subject matter which children will discover and use as the study progresses, is now ready to identify the major objectives or purposes of the study. Sketching out the reasons why a study should be undertaken gives an overall direction or course of action for the teacher. It prevents him (and his class) from becoming overly concerned with detail. The teacher thereby provides himself with a gauge for evaluating how well the major purposes of the study are being accomplished.

In examining resource materials prepared by those active in social studies, often one finds that the statements of purpose are vague and ambiguous. There is confusion between the overall purposes of social studies (such as were described in Chapter One) and the purposes of any specific study. Ideas that would have meaning in another, broader context become meaningless platitudes under such circumstances. Therefore, such statements as:

Fostering a concern for the needs and problems of others in order that we may bring about changes consistent with our democratic ideals,

or

Instilling a sense of responsibility in the individual toward governmental functions and their impact on daily living,

or

[11] *Ibid.*, p. 515.

Stimulating the ability to think critically and creatively in all situations involving human relationships,

are better left to those who are concerning themselves with a total program of social studies. The teacher who seeks to prepare himself for teaching his own classes would be better advised to spend his time on more specific matters. Statements of general goals have been worked out by many teachers and social scientists; they are available in a wide variety of places.[12] At the classroom level, the teacher is most concerned about these questions: "Why should I teach *this* study? What do I expect children specifically to gain from it? What purposes do *I* hope will be served when we have concluded our study? What can I say *now* that will help me judge whether we have reached the goals initially set reasonably well? Are the overall purposes of this study compatible with the broad goals of social studies in my school?" Below are listed the goals or purposes for two studies developed by different teachers at different grade levels. They illustrate the very practical level at which objectives may be stated:

Objectives for a Study:
How People Lived in Early Arizona

1. We shall try to find out how man adapts to his environment; how he has obtained freedom from its restrictions in many ways; how he has learned to control it, in other ways.
2. We shall attempt to discover how the natural environment (topography, climate, natural resources) influences man as he goes about meeting his needs and conducting his activities.
3. We shall work at developing empathy with people of other times and places; we hope to see similarities as well as differences.
4. We shall increase our knowledge of our own environments; in the course of our study it will expand from home, to community, to state.
5. Arizona's wealth of natural and human resources is remarkable; we shall try to be aware of these factors, as well as the problems involved in fully realizing the potentialities of our state.

[12] One of the most comprehensive statements of this type is that prepared by Nolan C. Kearney and associates in *Elementary School Objectives, a Report Prepared for the Mid-Century Committee on Outcomes in Elementary Education* (New York: Russell Sage Foundation, 1953). See especially pp. 59-95. Also, refer to large city, county, and state courses of study in social studies.

6. We shall scrutinize the differences between a simple handicraft culture and a modern machine culture.

7. We hope to enjoy the realization that our state has a dramatic and colorful history; we shall learn fully to appreciate our cultural heritage as Arizonans.

8. We shall increase our awareness of how Arizona's early Spanish citizens contributed to our culture, and enhance our appreciation of today's Americans of Mexican heritage.

9. We shall hope by the end of the study to be more effective and better informed citizens of Arizona.

Another study, developed initially for second grade children, sought the following goals:

Goals of a Study of the Local Community of Oakdale

1. To learn more about the unique qualities of our community; its physical and cultural makeup; its beginnings and early years and how it is changing.

2. To learn how the ideas of the early founders of Oakdale affect the Oakdale of today.

3. To study the Oakdalians of the '90's and compare them with Oakdalians of today.

4. To increase the feeling that active responsibility for a better community is the duty of every individual.

5. To learn more about cooperation and that communities are interdependent in many ways.

6. To realize that creativity was an important element in the founding of Oakdale.

7. To realize that change is a constant in our lives.

8. To understand that, as citizens, we must utilize concepts of conservation, safety, creativity, and responsibility.

9. To develop our skills in other subject areas through the many activities of our study.

10. To stretch our minds; widen our horizons.

THE TEACHER IDENTIFIES A BROAD RANGE
OF POSSIBLE LEARNING ACTIVITIES

There are many avenues children may take as they are led to discover the major ideas of a particular study. Reading a book, listening to a recording, watching a television program, interviewing a person outside of the classroom, seeing at first hand how a thing works or looks, seeing and discussing a filmstrip, planning, writing, and acting in a play, participating in a panel discussion, planning and drawing a mural, or making a map are but a few of the many activities favorable to learning. For most teachers good ideas for teaching do not flow easily and at the moment of need. Careful thinking must be done in advance about the different types of experiences and media that will contain good potential for achieving the goals of the study. Successful field generals map the moves which may be necessary during a battle if confusion in the ranks is to be avoided. It seems, then, that the teacher's problem is not unlike the general's. Moreover, there is no reason for learning experiences in a social study to be dull, drab, overly repetitious, or pointless in the child's eyes *if* the teacher has thought out in advance a good variety of appropriate learning activities. To have more ideas than he can possibly use with a class gives the teacher the opportunity to entertain a wide variety of possibilities suggested by his class. Such choice provides children with the freedom necessary for deciding how to attack the problem or question raised in their group—the first step toward discovery and real learning.

Special Plans are Laid for Initiating the Study. One of the primary concerns of any teacher is contained in the question, "How do we get started?" Young children have many interests, and it is not difficult to get any group of youngsters enthusiastic about a study. But getting the desired focus and developing plans so that a fairly long-range study can get under way calls for special planning. Considerable attention is given to initiating the study so that the problem or area of concern is clearly defined in children's minds, so that they are motivated to discover all they can about it in order that some overall direction and purpose are secured.

Ideas for initiating a study fall into three major categories. First, the teacher collects materials and ideas for creating an attractive room environment. Pictures, displays of artifacts, and other items that will add to the attractiveness and relevance of the study are collected. These materials do not need to be extensive or overly colorful, but they should provide the teacher and children with foundation materials for later stages of the study. Second, a variety of ideas about teaching materials are collected which may be used to arouse interest in the study and help define clearly and directly the topic of the study. These materials should be of a type that will help children gain the broad view they will later use as a reference point during that portion of the study when detail and depth are emphasized. Motion pictures, trade books, and filmstrips are some of the media most widely used to this end. Third, the teacher collects ideas about how he will employ these materials in the initiation of the study. With ideas about a wide variety of ways to involve the class in a study, the teacher will feel more comfortable as he sets out to read the signs of interest and events he may capitalize upon in beginning the study.

Beginnings should be simple. A class may start its study of the community by taking a short walk, returning to discuss what they have seen, what they are sure about, and what they do not know. Another study might be initiated through discussion stimulated by a large picture which has particular relevance to the study. A motion picture, artifact or model, a particularly good story which the teacher reads to the class may provide the right vehicle for opening up an area for future inquiry. One fifth grade teacher, for instance, begins a study of the founding decades in American History by reading and discussing with her children the Declaration of Independence. She tape records the session, using it later to help everyone appreciate the degree to which understandings and insights have grown, as the class reads biographies of the great men who helped mold the Constitution and thence to study and discuss the Constitution itself. The point is that one does not need a great range of materials to begin; nor should they be displayed all at once, preparatory to a beginning, in a pyrotechnic of color which fills the room with every conceivable resource the teacher has been able to discover. A key statement, such as the Declaration of Independence, a motion picture, or some other material representing adequately the scope of the problem or questions to be explored in the study, forms the basis for a good beginning.

Ideas for Learning Activities during the Course of the Study are Gathered. The teacher then proceeds to gather as many relevant ideas as he can for learning experiences that he thinks will most directly contribute to the purposes of the study. These ideas might be recorded in a variety of ways. Formal lists will help the beginning teacher. Probably less formality is required as the teacher gains experience in the classroom. The important point is that the teacher should have many ideas about relevant activities and that he should think specifically about these matters before he enters a classroom to work with children in a particular study.

Ideas for teaching come from many sources, and creative teachers are constantly on the lookout for new or different ways of working with children. One of the most fruitful sources of teaching ideas is one's fellow teachers. Through sharing with others notions about the worthwhileness of particular learning resources, comparing notes on successes and failures, and discovering new possibilities for classroom teaching as one talks with his colleagues during the day, more good ideas than could possibly be used will suggest themselves. Since one must select from a range of choices, there are difficult decisions to make about the potential of one learning activity over several other good ones.

From the many ideas which present themselves, then, one makes judgments about their appropriateness or power in carrying children toward the goals of the study. Another factor is also considered, and that has to do with selecting a variety of learning experiences. Even the most inherently interesting activities become dull and ineffective means for learning if repeated too often. Too many motion pictures, too many discussions, even too many study trips will rapidly reduce a potentially effective means for teaching to a very low level. In conjuring up ideas for learning activities which may be utilized as a study progresses, therefore, it is important to remember that children, not unlike adults, are easily bored if the lesson today is too much like the ones that have come before.

In the following illustration, a series of powerful learning experiences were combined in a manner which maintained high interest. It is an account of a study developed to introduce children at the intermediate grade levels to the importance of one particular geological formation in their lives. It utilized as basic activities (1) two "experiments" for the most part conducted by the children, (2) viewing slides made especially for the study, (3) going on a study trip, (4) collecting soil samples, and (5) making maps. The objectives of this "Study of the Alluvial Fan" were to introduce boys and girls to the physical characteristics of an alluvial fan and the manner in which human beings living on such a fan might utilize its resources and how they, in turn, were influenced by the physical formation of this particular landform.[13]

For persons living in the southwestern part of the United States, or in other relatively dry areas around the earth, alluvial fans are a

[13] See "The Alluvial Fan, a unit for upper elementary students," by Billie Vincent, Dale O. Merrill, and John S. Shelton (Claremont, California: 1963).

commonplace. They are not found in areas where there is ample rain-fall except in a very minor way. A dictionary description of an alluvial fan states that it is "a fan-shaped alluvial deposit formed by a stream where its velocity is abruptly decreased as at the mouth of a ravine or at the foot of a mountain." In other words, one sees alluvial fans where rains have washed the soil and rocks down from the mountains, leaving them in a fan-shaped deposit in which the point of the fan issues from the mouth of the ravine. They occur in a variety of sizes. The one we intended to study in detail measures about ten miles in each of its longest dimensions.

During the study, we engaged ourselves in a series of activities designed to lead us to an awareness of the fact that our homes and schools, the places where we were spending most of our sleeping and waking hours, were situated upon a large alluvial fan. We were seeking, as well, to learn how our lives were affected by this phenom-enon, and how we in turn were having an effect upon it. First, then, we sought an understanding of the size, shape, and physical composition of the fan; and second we hoped to move on to the human element, to an appreciation of the many subtle and not so subtle relationships which the people living on this particular fan were having with each other and the environment around them. The basic activities planned included: directly experiencing the slope of the land created by the fan through such activities as a bicycle riding experiment and through encouraging hikes in the area; mapping experiences emphasizing the development of an awareness for slope through the study of a small area on the fan; viewing slides of the region under study to extend familiarity with the fan; conducting experiments demonstrating ways alluvial fans come into being; going on study trips to view at first hand the physical and human aspects of man's occupancy of the fan; and collecting soil and other samples of natural and man-made evidences from the alluvial fan itself. There were, in addition, some specially prepared reading materials and worksheets.

The study began with the bicycle experiment. Every member of the class was urged to get on his bicycle, or borrow one, after school to find out which ways it was possible to coast. Much to their amaze-ment, they returned the next day to report they could coast toward the west (everyone had previously thought the east-west axis was quite level) as well as along the familiar north-south axis since the apex of the fan was in a northerly direction from the school, and was, of course, the higher elevation. This discovery led to speculation about the causes of this strange condition. They then became involved in a discussion of how aware they were of things they were experiencing directly every day. This led to a challenge by the teacher to see if they could draw a reasonably accurate map of the school playground. Despite the fact that many of the children had been in the school for several years, general failure was experienced—their maps were really surprisingly inaccurate. This, in turn, led to careful exploration of the school yard and the discovery not only of its size and shape in more realistic terms but to the fact that it sloped in a similar fashion to the streets where they had tried their coasting experiment with the bicycles.

From this point onward, we studied colored slides taken of the area and discussed all of the possibilities we could think of which would account for the land being in slope in such a seemingly peculiar way. Gradually, the concept of an alluvial fan emerged. We conducted experiments with a small box, some water, and soil containing a liberal distribution of a variety of sized rocks and pebbles. We saw how alluvial fans could be created and we developed some generalizations about flow of water, the size of soil particles which might be moved, and the general composition of alluvial fans.

At this point, we began looking around us to see how our lives might be affected by the fact we lived on a fan. We also began to study the resources available to us as a consequence. We took a study trip over the fan, including a deep pit which had been dug by a company engaged in extracting and crushing rock in supplying builders in the area. By examining the layers of different kinds and sizes of deposits, we could get an idea of how much water had come out of the mountain to deposit the rocks and sand, and soil in the centuries past. We collected soil samples, noting that the base or lower end of the fan had the finest soil and that it grew progressively more sandy and rocky as we climbed to the apex of the fan. Then we went up into the canyon from which all that material had come over so many years. We studied the kinds of plant growth and looked for evidences of animal life, thinking about the importance of these to the things that had gone on down below. This experience vividly called to the children's minds the importance of ground cover in controlling erosion.

As the study progressed, we became increasingly aware of the ways human beings had been using the area. We noticed that different kinds of crops grew at different elevations. Some of this was due to changes in temperature and some of it because of differences in soil. Generalizations about man's ability to utilize his environment began to develop. We became cognizant, too, of the network of roads in the area and their relationship to the size and shape of the fan. We studied the big dam which had been erected by the Corps of Engineers at the apex of the fan, we learned why it had been built there, and we became aware of the location of homes and industries, seeing that a great "wash" area had not been chosen for building sites until the dam was built. These discussions and forays into furthering our understanding of the region in turn gave rise to other questions, some of which we had time to pursue. For example, we became increasingly interested in the source of our water supply, in the factors which influence the growth of certain agricultural crops, and in the ways other alluvial fans in our region—those in unoccupied desert areas and in urban regions—affected and in turn were affected by human activities of different kinds.

The study took about a month. We spent some time on it almost every day. Besides discussing and experimenting with the things around us, we did some writing about our discoveries. And although the class time was fairly limited, we did discover that a great deal of learning was taking place outside of the classroom. We made some maps of the area, showing places of interest and hikes which might be taken, and sent them home. As a consequence of this assistance and because of the high interest which was generated among the children, many family outings were conducted over the week ends. The children enlisted their families in explorations of the region, returning to places we had been or had pictured in our slides and going to others we didn't have time to see or talk about in class. So these "extra-curricular" activities were reported on in class, enriching the work we were doing immeasurably.

In studies to extend over a longer period than that described above, it is frequently desirable to utilize one or two major activities which provide a focal point, where information gathered can be collected and summarized. A classroom textbook, one written primarily by the children with perhaps some additions by the teacher or pertinent material reproduced from another source, is one such activity. The ease with which materials of all kinds can be duplicated makes it possible for every child to have his own copy of the book in his possession as the study progresses. Built over a period of time, the textbook serves as a record of the developing study and stands as evidence of learnings experienced by the class. Creating a large map, with information constantly being added to it, serves the same purpose as the classrom textbook for studies which emphasize geographic inquiry. For older children, the development of a time line helps organize information, aids in recall, and assists in the development of a sense of chronology. Younger children will find value in building scrapbooks containing pictures and stories cut from magazines and other sources as well as their own drawings and written materials.

Parent communication is important to the progress of every study and can be encouraged through periodic distribution of "letters" or bulletins (perhaps in the manner described in the illustration above). Short explanations written by the teacher may tell of the work the children are doing. By collecting comments about some aspect of the study, perhaps with the aid of a tape recorder, and duplicating them for distribution, parents can sense what is being studied and become aware of the general level of understanding of children the age of their own. They will also be enabled in making comparisons of their child's performance; but since only first names appear on the sheets which the teacher prepares, the usual invidious personality issues are avoided. These "letters" to parents may also contain brief explanations of the overall nature of the study in which their children are engaged. Included also from time to time may be suggestions for family excursions or discussions which would enhance their child's understandings. Information about the nature of assignments which are being made, when pupils are expected to complete them, and other guides for developing standards for work done in and out of school may be included in these letters to parents.

Since parents frequently have only very vague ideas about the nature of the social studies curriculum, establishing some kind of communication system helps extend their understandings and, as a consequence, their interest and support of this important aspect of their child's school work. Of greater long-run significance for the child, however, is the matter of giving him assistance in establishing good work habits. Frequently, the social study is the major curriculum area through which children are expected to learn to establish long-term study plans. That is, it is here the child first meets the challenge of planning his work

over a period of time. It is expected, as well, that he will learn to
organize himself for obtaining information and frequently for producing some tangible product, such as a story, report, or other written
material. At the intermediate and upper grade levels, fairly extensive
papers are sometimes prepared. All children need help in developing
the independent study skills which activities of this kind demand.
Obviously, parent awareness of class expectations becomes increasingly
important in assisting the child. Like everything else, however, the
communication system can become cluttered when too many bulletins
are sent home. Some prudence is called for, consequently, or little
attention will be paid them when, or if, they arrive at their intended
destination.

Because teaching ideas do not flow as readily in the classroom as
they do in the relative quiet of those hours which can be devoted
to thinking about and anticipating teaching, the importance of thinking
ahead has been emphasized repeatedly. It is necessary to develop as
many ideas as possible, recognizing that only a fraction of them will
be used. Without many alternatives from which to choose, one's opportunities for being a flexible, creative worker with children are severely
limited. Once a topic or problem area has been identified for study,
many specific ideas will present themselves. There is no need to fear
that not enough good ideas will be at hand provided enough time has
been given to planning.

The general nature of the preparatory work which is necessary in
thinking about getting ready for teaching has been considered in this
discussion. Beyond the point of developing many ideas, it is important
to select those learning experiences which are most relevant to a particular study. And, in the process of deciding how to work with boys
and girls, thought needs to be given to choosing those activities which
appear to have power in the sense that they are inherently of interest to
boys and girls. In the several chapters which follow, sources of
materials, teaching ideas, and means of assessing progress toward the
desired goals in teaching in the various dimensions of the curriculum
of social studies are discussed in greater detail.

THE TEACHER BUILDS A BIBLIOGRAPHY OF RESOURCES FOR TEACHING

Building a reservoir of teaching materials and resources is also the
concern of the teacher. A majority of these will be ones which he may
find useful in the classroom as the pupils move through the study. But

he will also find helpful a list of professional resources to which he may turn for additional information needed as the study continues. Listed below are types of resources the teacher will need and use. Information about these resources can be obtained from a variety of places, including the district curriculum library, the school office, catalog listings (different types of reader's guides exist for motion pictures, filmstrips, free and inexpensive materials), the local chamber of commerce, a nearby college or university library or curriculum laboratory, fellow teachers, and others that will occur to him.

Learning Resources for Children

1. Textbooks	8. Radio and Television
2. Supplementary Texts	9. Study Trips
3. Reference Books	10. Talented Citizens
4. Trade Books	11. Maps and Globes
5. Motion Pictures	12. Realia and Models
6. Recordings (disc and tape)	13. Flat Pictures
7. Filmstrips	

Professional Resources for the Teacher

1. Books contributing to an understanding of the subject matter content of the study
2. Materials for teacher use with children: prose, poetry, music, dance
3. Sources of information about teaching methods

In subsequent chapters, extended discussions of each of these major resources for teaching and learning may be found. This list may be of use in the sense that it provides the major categories within which one would wish to obtain information and ideas. It is appropriate to attempt to secure lists of resources for each of the categories listed.

THE TEACHER MAKES PLANS FOR EVALUATING THE
PROGRESS OF PUPILS

The final step in preparing to teach a social study is the identification of the means for judging individual and group progress toward the goals of the study. The teacher asks himself, in this regard, what types of instruments and what means seem to lend themselves most effectively to this end. Some of them will be more or less formally contrived.

That is, they will consist of written responses to questions posed in a variety of ways. Others will be less formal. Teachers' observations and anecdotal recording of those observations may constitute one such method of evaluating progress. Evaluation should include both formal and informal types of assessment, although there will be a heavier emphasis upon informal evaluation in the first four grades of the school. During the past decade or two, particularly, formal testing has not been widely used in social studies evaluations, although there has been great growth in the use of these tests in many other areas of the curriculum. Emphasis in social studies has been upon the more subjective or informal means, and it would appear that in many classrooms little critical assessment of progress has been used. This has occurred because there was not a clear perception of what children were expected to learn. Emphasis upon social behavior and growth in the processes of acquiring values has overshadowed other types of learnings. These are admittedly extremely difficult to assess because it is hard to establish norms by which judgments can be made. However, where the teacher clearly holds in mind the goals of the study and the full dimensions of content, he provides himself with much more specific guides for assessing learning in any particular social study. Thus, if he has identified some of the crucial concepts, significant facts, important generalizations, key ideas and values, and skills that should be developed in the process of the study, he will have much less difficulty in determining appropriate means for evaluating the achievement of the pupils individually and as a group.

There is an educational platitude which states that "evaluation is a continuous process." This means simply that one does not judge achievement at the end of a study alone but that one constantly assesses progress in order to modify teaching procedures so that learning will become more effective. Furthermore, evaluation should not cease at the end of a study. One of the major problems in all learning is forgetting. Although forgetting appears to be a natural human phenomenon, the teacher who finds after several weeks have elapsed since the conclusion of a study that little, if any, residue is left in his pupils' minds should re-examine his teaching procedures. Forgetting is enhanced under certain circumstances. It is not wise to continue procedures which result in more than a reasonable amount of forgetting.

Research reveals that meaningful learning situations, i.e., those in which *pupils see a purpose in what they are doing,* cause children to increase their understanding of a subject *after direct teaching ceases.* Forgetting increases unduly where learning activities are not meaningful, i.e., when the goals for learning are not clear to pupils. The most formal as well as the most "progressive" approaches to teaching may be subject to such criticism. Therefore, it is well for the teacher to check up on himself and his pupils some time after a study is completed. During the course of the study, one would be well advised to make a point of asking his pupils as they work on individual or small-group assignments what they are doing and why they think they are doing it. Any confusion or ambiguity reflected in the replies of children should lead him to a reassessment of the study and to getting a rational purpose established in the minds of the pupils.

Before beginning a social study, therefore, some thought should be given to these questions and some tentative plans made for evaluating the progress of the study. This can best be done by listening to pupils. Listening in some cases will be accomplished by requiring fairly formal written materials; in others, questions will be asked and direct answers sought. In other instances, less formal techniques will be utilized. The means will vary according to the study and the maturity of the children. More extensive consideration is given these questions in Chapter Six.

The Significance of Careful Planning

Considerable stress has been placed here upon careful preparation because it is seen as the most important single key to successful teaching of social studies. "Staying one jump ahead of the class," or "Learning right along with the children," seldom, if ever, provide the kinds of learning situations elementary school children deserve. Although occasionally a teacher will be forced, for one reason or another, to embark upon a study without adequate preparation, such situations as a general rule do not augur well for children. Administrators should make every effort to see that teachers do not have to face children under such circumstances.

Planning of the type described here does not connote the formal preparation of resource materials. Although it is probably good experience for a beginning teacher to prepare at least one, and preferably two or three, resource guides for his personal use, the purpose in such formalized preparations is to encourage one to begin to think automatically of the major tasks to be accomplished before the teaching of any study can actually begin. Master teachers have learned through experience that the steps outlined in the early portions of this chapter are necessary to the successful development of a study. They are not likely to omit consideration of any of these aspects. How they gather materials and information varies according to the person and according to the topic for which they are preparing. The ultimate test of any such procedure is its practicality to the teacher as he works with children in the classroom. Thus, teachers with considerable experience build picture files, collect card catalogs of films and their sources, acquire knowledge about sources of local information, spend much time in the district curriculum library reading and analyzing books and instructional materials of all kinds, read and take courses in content fields related to the studies which they teach, and so forth. The beginning teacher does not have the advantage of time and experience which the master teacher has. His efforts in preparing for teaching a social study, therefore, usually require more systematic and seemingly formal approaches to building a resource for teaching than those of his more experienced colleagues.

Finally, it may clearly be seen that planning in all its many facets is an essential skill for the teacher whose aim is excellence. The amount and kind may vary according to the school in question, the children being taught, the breadth and length of teacher experience, and the particular study under scrutiny; but, in all cases, for the development of a strong curriculum of social studies in elementary schooling, planning is a prime factor.

FOR FURTHER READING

Clements, H. Millard, *et. al., Social Study: Inquiry in Elementary Classrooms* (New York: The Bobbs-Merrill Company, Inc., 1966).

Fraser, Dorothy McClure and Samuel P. McCutchen (eds.), *Social Studies In Transition: Guidelines for Change,* Curriculum Series Number Twelve, National Council for The Social Studies (Washington, D.C.: NCSS, 1965).

Hill, Wilhelmina (ed.), *Selected Resource Units in Elementary Social Studies: Kindergarten-Grade 6,* Curriculum Series Number Eleven,

National Council for the Social Studies (Washington, D.C.: NCSS, 1961).

Hunicutt, Clarence W. (ed.), *Social Studies for the Middle Grades: Answering Teachers' Questions,* National Council for the Social Studies (Washington, D.C.: NCSS, 1960).

Litfinger, Delores E., *Social Studies Instruction at the University Elementary School, U.C.L.A.* (Berkeley: University of California Press, 1965).

Miel, Alice and Peggy Brogan, *More Than Social Studies* (Englewood Cliffs, N.J.: Prentice-Hall, 1957).

Sears, Pauline and Vivian S. Sherman, *In Pursuit of Self-Esteem* (Belmont, California: Wadsworth Publishing Company, 1964).

Stratemeyer, Florence, *et. al., Developing a Curriculum for Modern Living,* second edition revised (New York: Teachers College, Columbia University, 1957).

Wilcockson, Mary (ed.), *Social Education of Young Children: Kindergarten and Primary Grades,* Curriculum Series Number Four, National Council for the Social Studies (Washington, D.C.: NCSS, 1956).

CHAPTER SIX

Teaching the Social Study

The world is the elementary school child's oyster. His interests are catholic, often intense, and easily aroused. The problem in teaching children of this age is not so much how to interest a child in a topic but how to encourage him to think and study about it. As a first order of business, we need to think with considerable precision about how children move into a social study and how they learn socially significant content.

Shall We Educate or Instruct in the Social Study?

Roger Burlingame points out the difference between "education" and "instruction," a distinction which has pertinence for thinking about the best ways for working with children in social studies.[1] As Burlingame states:

Instruction is putting in (or, as we now say, "building in"); education is drawing out. The instructor puts in facts or skills in the hope that they will stay in the pupil's mind at least until the examination. One may be instructed in drawing or cooking, in economic law or mathematics, in jurisprudence or engineering. A student may gain a high degree of proficiency in these things without ever becoming in the least educated.

Education is a two-way street. Unless the teacher can provoke original and dynamic thought in the student, no education will have taken place. The student must not merely answer questions, he must ask them. The word *why* must be forever on his lips, and he must not accept the teacher's answer until he recognizes its truth.

---

[1] Roger Burlingame, "If You Weren't Educated — Here's Why," *Think,* 25, No. 10 (October, 1959), pp. 32-34.

The question that must be asked when thinking about teaching social studies is: what kind of balance is there going to be between education and instruction? Criticisms of the schools indicate that there is a serious imbalance between the two, that instruction dominates in classrooms, from kindergarten to the college. This does not mean that instruction has no place in the classroom, for it certainly does. However, it is essential to look with care at teaching approaches in an effort to learn different and better ways to work with children so that both these goals may be reached.

The goal of education is not to train children to be parrots. How can they be taught to *think,* not repeat what they think teachers want to hear? This formidable task may be tackled in a variety of ways.

First, children may be encouraged to use both inductive and deductive reasoning. They may learn from teachers that analytical thinking is highly valued, but that intuitive thinking is equally valued and desirable.

Concepts of reasoning and thinking developed by scholars in other fields may further illuminate these questions. For example, in Chapter One reference was made to Getzels' definition of *presented problems* and *discovered problems* and the difference between them; Getzels suggests that discovered problems might well receive greater emphasis in the classroom. Guilford opposes *convergent thinking* to *divergent thinking* in his attempt to aid teachers in framing questions for children to consider as they study. The former process encourages all the children in the class to respond more or less similarly; the latter brings forth many different answers to the questions raised.

Finally, one may give earnest consideration to the capacity of children to think logically. A good deal of work and thought has gone into the nature of children's thinking. Bruner, Vygotsky, and Piaget (an American, a Russian, and a Swiss, respectively) provide knowledge about the differential nature of children's thinking and about different maturity levels. What these ideas may mean for the social study should be considered.

INDUCTIVE AND DEDUCTIVE REASONING IN THE SOCIAL STUDY

In logic, inductive thinking is the process of reasoning from parts to wholes, from particulars to generalizations. Deductive thinking is that process of reasoning which moves from the general to the particular, from generalizations to specific facts which support or refute or, more likely, modify the initial premise. Children should experience both modes of thinking or reasoning from the earliest years in school, since both procedures have value in problem solving.

There is general agreement that more ways to encourage inferential or inductive processes are needed. Schools have tended to overdo deductive modes; that is, there has been much more of the "this is what is" (generality) followed by "why it is so" (specifics which support the premise) than there has been of the "what is this?" (several questions of a highly specific nature) which leads to "what sense do all these things make when they are put together?" (generality). For example, in studies of community helpers—essentially an economic study of the local community—the mailman, the milkman, and a number of other persons are identified as "community helpers." Then children are directed in studies which tell about these helpers: who they are, what they do, why we should be grateful for their assistance. This is all right as an introduction, but what of the community helpers who are never identified by the teacher? Chances are they will go unnoticed. As a consequence, pupils will be very likely to have a limited view of the economics of their community because, of course, all members of a community are "community helpers."[2]

An inductive approach to a study of "community helpers" would start at the other end of the continuum. Children might begin with the question, "What people in our town are important to us?" Then, perhaps, "Why are they important?" "What do they do that makes a difference to us?" Or, they might ask, "How do our mothers and fathers make a living?" Any number of different questions might arise. The objective is to explore the basic idea that people work; that they work at different jobs and in different places; and that communities of people, occupied in different pursuits, depend upon one another economically, socially, and politically in developing and extending a satisfying life for all. To what extent can the child generalize about the role of "community helpers" in such an approach? The only answer is, "It all depends upon the maturity of the children, the kind of community they live in, the resource materials available for study, and the skill and knowledge of the teacher."

[2] For an extended discussion of this problem of teaching incorrect or incomplete ideas in the area of economic education, see Committee for Economic Development, *Economic Literacy for Americans: a Program for School and for Citizens* (New York: February, 1962).

It is not suggested that this study, or all other studies, should employ a purely inductive approach. The major question concerns balance— the balance between inductive and deductive modes, between studies, and within the daily planning and working with children which the teacher controls.

A warning must be issued about the inductive mode. Obviously, it is a more open-ended approach. Where it is the major approach of the teacher, a study could travel in any one of a number of directions; the daily lesson might lead to any number of topics and activities not readily suggested by the deductive mode. The teacher must be prepared to go with his pupils in any one of these deductions, provided only that they appear fruitful for the study. Often, the teacher is not well enough prepared, or sufficiently at ease with children or their parents, to accept the responsibility an inductive approach entails. It is safer to define the area to be explored so that the class does not wander too far from the teacher's plan. Perhaps the flexibility, even looseness, in this approach is one reason the deductive mode is the more common one. Perhaps this situation will challenge the more venturesome as they think about ways of working with children.

INTUITIVE VERSUS ANALYTIC THINKING IN THE SOCIAL STUDY

Ideally, children will be encouraged to think both intuitively and analytically. Intuitive thinking is that process by which the pupil apprehends the probable solution to a problem without recourse to reasoning or knowledge. An intuitive leap is made from the known, through a mass of data, to a hypothesis or solution. Intuitive thinking is learned by experiencing situations in which the teacher encourages children to make informed guesses. It calls upon the child to think creatively, to exact from his mind ideas which have not consciously been there before. The teacher encourages intuitive thinking by asking open-ended questions for which no one right answer seems immediately evident. For instance, the query from the teacher might be: "What do you think that is?" "How did it get there?" "What is it for?" "Why was it put there?" Questions like this might be applied to anything from the light switch on the wall to a statue or to a plaque on a nearby building. Or, a series of "What if?" kinds of questions could be appropriate: "How would the settlement of the midwest have been changed if the Mississipi River flowed east-west rather than north-south?" Or, "What kind of climate would the western United States have if there were no Rocky

Mountains or Sierra Nevada Mountains?" Or, "What would happen if only babies could have milk?" The possibilities are endless; the kinds of responses doubtless will prove surprising and fascinating. These are the kinds of questions from which children pose hypotheses. From these hypotheses, or proposed solutions, the pupil obviously must support or refute evidence by means of some detailed analysis of revelant data. Intuitive thinking is always followed by analytical processes.

In contrast, analytic thinking refers to the process of studying a topic in terms of its components or its constituent parts. It is the process of obtaining facts and organizing them into a body of related material. Thus it is an essential element in any thinking process characterized by any kind of precision. Children can engage in analytic thinking, provided that the referent, or evidence to which they turn, is understandable to them. Understanding for younger children is heavily dependent upon their ability to utilize first-hand experience. They need to see electrical wiring being put into a house in order to understand that there is a connection between the switch and the light. They cannot *imagine* the connection. However, older children can use materials which call for vicarious experiencing. Map study evokes answers to the problem of a river running in another direction or of mountains presumed no longer to be in existence; it also helps one to build an imaginary land or to draw one's own map, showing a new direction for the river. It is easy to push even the nine- to thirteen-year-old beyond his capacity to handle the processes of analytic thinking, however.

Again, there should be emphasis on *balance* in considering these ways of encouraging children to think about the things around them. Intuitive processes alone leave too many questions unanswered. Analytic processes alone prevent the child from seeing the whole for the parts. Many specific questions rarely form of themselves in the child's mind. Problem setting and problem solving can take place only where both kinds of questions are woven into the daily web of study.

CONVERGENT AND DIVERGENT THINKING

Another way of looking at the methods which have been devised for working with children is expressed in the terms *convergent thinking* and *divergent thinking*. Guilford has developed these concepts to suggest that teachers can pose questions or plan activities with children in two ways: (1) everyone can be directed toward the same or similar answers (encouraging convergent thinking) or (2) the study can be planned to develop a rich variety of acceptable responses (divergent thinking).[3] He suggests that learning experiences for children should include both kinds. A useful technique for discriminating between convergent and divergent activities is to list the kinds of questions or activities belonging to each category.

Questions Which Encourage

Convergent Thinking	Divergent Thinking
Who was Nathan Hale?	Who was the most brave of all the
What kind of things can you buy at the grocery store?	Revolutionary heroes?
Where is the XYZ Dairy?	Suppose you wanted to go to the XYZ Dairy. What is the best
Who said, "Don't fire until you see the whites of their eyes?"	way to get there?
Locate New York on the map.	Can you write a story telling what it would be like to live in a house built under the sea?
What characteristics of location do the largest cities of the world have?	
Why are colors used on maps?	What similarities are there between the ways streets are laid out in our town and latitude and longitude on our world map?

Activities Which Encourage

Convergent Thinking	Divergent Thinking
Taking a multiple-choice test.	
	Writing an essay examination.
Answering the questions at the end of the chapter in the text.	Debate on the issue: The "one man-one vote" rule in apportioning state legislatures is a good one.
	Talking on an assigned topic.
	Writing an essay on a topic of your own choice within the general framework of the study.
	Listening to a group of pupils discuss a topic before the class.
Improving a toy or other object by making one addition to, or change in, it.	Thinking of unusual uses for familiar objects.
Finding one best word to describe something you are studying.	Planning the classroom arrangement for better use of space and equipment.

[3] J. P. Guilford, "The Three Faces of Intellect," *The American Psychologist*, Vol. 14 (1959), pp. 469-498.

At times the world seems compulsively concerned with conformity. There are powerful forces at work, particularly in our own society, which encourage people to think alike, act alike, even talk alike. In many respects, this trend runs counter to the American tradition of placing a high value on originality, creativity, and nonconformity. Hence the school's role in perpetuating a democratic society cannot exclude the responsibility for developing individual talents in original and creative ways. Many experiences in divergent thinking must be included in the social study if the school is to remain true to these values.

PRESENTED PROBLEMS AND DISCOVERED PROBLEMS

Another way of looking at the conditions which the teacher creates to develop children's thinking and reasoning abilities is contained in the concept that problems may be studied in basically different ways. Getzels, for example, suggests that one can make a useful distinction by thinking of those problems that are basically *presented* as being opposed to those which involve some form of discovery.[4] He indicates that in the following problem situation three levels may be distinguished between the "presented problem" at one extreme and the "discovered problem" at the other:

1. The teacher teaches the material from a chapter in the textbook about how the state became a part of the Union by assigning children to read certain pages. At the conclusion of the chapter is a series of questions to be completed by filling in the blank spaces. The child is directed to complete the questions.
2. The teacher does not begin with the textual material but begins instead by posing the problem: What do you suppose things were like when our state became a part of the Union?
3. The teacher asks such questions as: What might have happened if (stating a condition crucial to the process of becoming a part of the Union or the state in question) had not taken place? Or, going beyond the particular subject of statehood, What problems would our state have if its most important crop (or product) could be grown (or manufactured) more cheaply elsewhere? Or, What would conditions be like here if the average elevation,

---

[4] J. W. Getzels, "New Conceptions of the Learner: Some Implications for the Classroom," *Twenty-eighth Claremont Reading Conference Yearbook* (Claremont, California: Claremont Graduate School and University Center, 1964), pp. 20-21.

temperature, rainfall, soil composition, etc. were much different than is now the case?

Getzels suggests that:

In the first type, the problem is given—it is presented—and there is a standard method for solving it, known to the problem-solver and to others, guaranteeing a solution in a finite number of steps. All the student has to do is plug the given data into the given statements or phrases to find the answer. It is essentially a problem of *retrieval.*

Consider the second type. The problem is still given, i.e., still presented, but no standard method for solving it is known to the problem-solver, although known to others. Here it is by no means a problem of retrieval. It is rather a problem in *reasoning* on the part of the student until the solution he propounds matches the solution the teacher knows.

What now of the third type? Here the problem itself remains to be identified or *discovered* by the student as well as by others, including the teacher. An attempt at inventiveness, at "going beyond the information given or known" must be made by all concerned, and this requires a very different kind of intellectual skill yet.[5]

Much, perhaps most, teaching today deals with the first type of problem, perhaps some with the second, and virtually none with the third. Getzels asserts that the latter two types of problems are often avoided or turned into "type one" problems; therefore young people are not led to acquire experience with the more innovative and creative aspects of learning. Particularly is this true of intermediate and upper grade classrooms; the high school fares even more poorly. And, he argues, "teaching must deal not only with *presented problems* requiring for solution conformity to known standards, but also with *discovered problems* requiring for solution the risk of inventiveness and creativity on both the student's part and the teacher's part."[6]

The Method of Discovery

Several concepts have been presented here about children's thinking and the modes of various reasoning processes, indicating that they have value in considering ways of working with children in social studies.

[5] Adapted from Getzels, *op. cit.*
[6] Getzels, *op. cit.* See also J. W. Getzels, "Creative Thinking, Problem Solving, and Instruction," Chapter Ten in *Theories of Learning and Instruction,* Sixty-third Yearbook, Part I, National Society for the Study of Education (Chicago: University of Chicago Press, 1964), pp. 240-267.

These ideas have been presented in an either-or framework, as if they were true dichotomies. The questions have been posed like this:

Shall we educate or shall we instruct?
Shall reasoning be by the inductive or the deductive mode?
Shall thinking be intuitive or analytic?
Shall we employ procedures which encourage divergent or convergent thinking?
Shall we work with problems which are either presented or discovered?

For purposes of clarifying meaning, it is useful to distinguish sharply between concepts such as those presented above. But when one thinks of putting such ideas into practice in the classroom such distinctions necessarily must be blurred. The *balance* which seems most appropriate for the best learning might best be called the *Method of Discovery*. In this approach, the teacher attempts to blend all these ways of reasoning and thinking; his goal is that of working and problem setting in a way that will turn the classroom into a learning laboratory for children.

What are the characteristic features of the Method of Discovery? It is extremely difficult to describe *exactly* what sets off one classroom situation from another—what distinguishes a classroom in which the Method of Discovery is present from the one where it is absent. The atmosphere of the learning laboratory where the Method of Discovery is in use can be experienced in its reality only when one is present in person. One can, perhaps, recall a teacher who was skillful at creating this climate in the classroom. One may have been fortunate enough to have studied under such a teacher.

It may be argued that some teachers are born, not made. These are the ones who need no textbook or fancy materials. They build their program out of the life about them—from their own experiences, from those of the children in their classes. It all seems so natural and unattainable for the teacher who feels he is not so gifted. Perhaps one is too self-deprecating if he believes that these gifts are given to but a few and that he cannot attain them.

Some examples drawn from real life experiences will help the reader to grasp the feeling of the Method of Discovery. Then, let him look about for examples in his own experience, for teachers in his own community whom he may observe and from whom he may learn. The examples will be divided into three types: (1) experiences which might characterize the Method of Discovery in the initial stages of a study, when pupils are first sensing its dimensions, getting the feel of its depth and breadth, searching tentatively for an understanding of the approaches they will employ in successfully exploring it; (2) experiences children may have as they move into the data gathering stage; (3) examples of ways teachers have worked with children in the concluding stages of the study. It is in this stage that the major generalizations are most likely to be developed, hypotheses proved or disproved, and new areas for inquiry opened up.

INITIATING THE STUDY

The initial stages of the study are designed to encourage interest in the topic or problem and to explore its dimensions. It is the time to hypothesize about the subject, to engage in some intuitive thinking, to find out what the children in the class already know, and to begin collecting some notions about questions that seem important enough to be subjected to more detailed scrutiny. It is a period of much *question asking* and of little *question answering*. The first concern is to find out what is already in the children's minds; next, it is to interject just enough new information from a wide variety of sources to guide them in profitable directions. It is the teacher's purpose to help the children get a broad view of the problem; then they will be able to decide themselves which questions are most deserving of their further exploration.

Children will not always make what seem to the teacher to be the "best" choices. Teachers must exercise judgment in deciding whether children should be guided away from a potential blind alley, but too much interference of this sort dulls curiosity and enthusiasm for learning. Not enough can lead to much wasted energy. However, children should not be entirely prevented from making poor decisions. Learning comes from analyzing mistakes as well as successes. Limiting children to only "right" decisions can be just as unfortunate as encouraging them to move in directions most likely to produce failure. The art of the teacher is apparent in the way he guides children at this stage of the study, and no one route can be recommended that will assure him and his class of a safe journey.

One major objective of this period of exploring, goal setting, and organizing for action is to clear away the misunderstanding which may characterize children's concepts about the subject of the study. As part of the initial stage in this Method of Discovery, the teacher plans to learn how much children know about the concepts upon which understanding of the study will be built. Thus, he asks many questions, builds upon responses in an attempt to probe more deeply into understandings through increasingly complex questions, encourages children to think and read about some of the more significant ideas which they have discovered, notes instances where understanding seems lacking or incorrect, and, in general, attempts to build the framework of understanding that will be necessary for the erection of a broader, more complicated structure of ideas.

This period may last from a few days to several days. Usually noted down somewhere—often on the chalkboard—are the questions, the proposed solutions, and the problems which are anticipated as the study progresses. In subsequent discussions, they will be altered or removed; new items will be added as clarification proceeds in the pupils' minds. Children with experience in this approach to learning will be able to move more rapidly into the study than those who have not had practice in making decisions and in thinking through problems.

When questions are raised, either at this or later stages of the study, the wish to answer them immediately seems to be a natural human propensity in adults, especially, perhaps, among teachers. Teachers should all resist this inclination—but encourage it in the children. What are some of the possible answers to this question? What do we really know about the topic? What evidence can we muster to bring light to the topic? Where can we find it? How might we go about getting it? Do we need to know anything in advance of searching out the answer to this question? What different kinds of research need to be done? Who shall do it? The Method of Discovery takes form from these kinds of questions; the result is inquiry which has significance in the minds of children.

As indicated earlier, when initiating a study based on the Method of Discovery the beginnings do not need to be overly complicated. In the preceding chapter, it was noted that one class of fifth grade children commenced their study of the founding decades in American history with a careful reading-discussion of the Declaration of Independence. The teacher tape recorded this experience, replaying portions immediately and saving the entire tape for later listening. In this way, the boys and girls were given an opportunity to judge their own progress during the course of their study. The teacher may find this an effective way to introduce the major ideas to be considered in the overall study. Interest mounts as the reading gets under way; then open discussion of the many important ideas that emerge is all that is needed to produce enthusiasm. Even one class meeting of this type could provide a dramatically eye-opening beginning.

Bruner describes another possible start for a study utilizing the Method of Discovery in his book, *The Process of Education*.[7] A sixth grade class, having covered a conventional unit concerning the social and economic geography of the southeastern states, was introduced to a study about the north central region in a different manner. They were asked to locate the major cities of the area on a map containing physical features and natural resources, but not place names. "The resulting class discussion very rapidly produced a variety of plausible theories concerning the requirements of a city—a water transportation theory that placed Chicago at the junction of the three lakes, a mineral resources theory that placed it near the Mesabi range, a food-supply theory that put a great city on the rich soil of Iowa, and so on."

Still another example is offered by Foshay. He describes the encounter of a class ready to engage itself in a study of the post-Civil War period. How does the teacher direct this encounter?

He asks of children . . . that they be producers of knowledge, not mere passive consumers of it. He raises with them the question, therefore, "What kinds of events after Lincoln would be most worth knowing?" (Does this seem too advanced? You should see how children handle it!) "Now," he goes on, "how can we discover what these events were?" (We can read, ask, search, tell one another.) "What do historians say they were?" (Not one historian—several, for not all historians choose to deal with the same events, and the sooner we understand this, the more liberated we are from a naive view of our past and of the historian's place in understanding it.) "What are the principal ways the period has been interpreted by the historians?" "What information do you think the historians might include that they appear to have omitted?" "Why do you suppose they omitted this information?" "Because they couldn't find it?" "Because it didn't fit with their interpretation?"[8]

Now consider a study designed for younger children. Clements, Fielder, and Tabachnick, presenting the informal accounts of a teacher,

[7] Jerome Bruner, *The Process of Education* (Cambridge, Mass.: Harvard University Press, 1961), pp. 21-22.
[8] Arthur W. Foshay, "A Modest Proposal for the Improvement of Education," *Educational Leadership*, Vol. 18, No. 8 (May, 1961), p. 512.

suggest the following beginning for a study of "The City."[9] The teacher
in question had noticed how proud and self-conscious young elementary
school children tend to be about their new school clothes. She therefore
commented on the newly-purchased apparel as well as on less noticeable
purchases such as new library books, paper supplies, and a new kick
ball. The many things purchased by the children's families were discussed; almost immediately a lively controversy ensued. "What do you
buy if you pay rent?" "Is buying when you trade stuff with a pal, like
at a party?" "You get good things saving blue stamps!" After a day or
two the members of this class were more willing and able to grapple
with the problems of buying and selling in the city; they were intrigued
to realize how little they really knew about these subjects, even though
they had been in stores, and even made their own purchases, many
times.

There are many ways that younger children may be engaged in essentially the same type of inquiry. For example, in the outstanding
film, "Learning Is Searching: A Third Grade Studies Man's Early
Tools," prepared by Vassar College, an encounter by a group of primary
children with the evolution of tools and machines is described. A portion of the script paints a vivid picture of the ways in which one third
grade became involved in that study.

It is early in the school year; the setting is a New York City school. We
are going to follow a class of 24 third graders; we've worked out a plan for
their year of social studies. The starting point has already been set by the
teacher; the class is to consider the use of tools. We first spend a few days
linking up topics to the child's experiences. A wooden playhouse built by
last year's class has been left at the children's request. What tools were
used to build the house? Saw, hammer, screw driver. What tools did you
see on the way to school? What tools are you using right now? What about
a pencil? What tools do you have at home? A knife, and a fork and a
spoon.

On other days the group goes out of school to look for tools used in the
neighborhood. The children's interest is already keen, but they must become
clearer about just what a tool is. They must define their terms. The teacher
asks pointed questions: How long would it take to dig this hole with your
hands? How would your hands feel? How long would it take with shovels?
Some other important questions come up: "Is the bulldozer a tool?" "Is
the machine the same thing as a tool?" The teacher is providing the

---

[9] Millard H. Clements, William R. Fielder, and B. Robert Tabachnick, *Social
Study: Inquiry in Elementary Classrooms* (Indianapolis: Bobbs-Merrill Co., 1966),
pp. 158-160.

children with the opportunity to make real discoveries of their own. He is helping them go back and forth from their own experience to direct observation, to discussion.

In this particular study, the pace is more leisurely. More time is used to set the scene. It is intended that it will continue over a fairly long period of time. Were one to attempt to categorize it as to type of study, it would more nearly fall within the frame of reference which was described as a *social living* or *interactive approach* to social studies in Chapter Two.

As the study proceeds, questions become more general. What are some things you do with your hands? What have people done when hands were not enough? The children, sitting in a circle, discuss this until they narrow and define their area of inquiry. They put aside consideration of complex machinery like bulldozers and cement mixers in order to look at simple hand-powered devices like screwdrivers and brooms. In doing this, the children are completing what adults would call the problem setting phase of their search—they have decided what a tool *is;* they are moving from mere mechanics to a consideration of the vital place of tools in men's lives.

MOVING INTO THE STUDY ITSELF

As relevant questions are identified and means of securing answers to them are suggested, a commitment to action is implied. In talking with children and in probing their ideas about ways in which solutions might be reached the teacher will find it valuable to refer from time to time to his own list of ideas which he has developed to help point the way toward activities most likely to lead to their goals for the study. Occasionally, the teacher may suggest directly an approach to gathering information which the children have not considered or a manner of synthesizing and reporting ideas gained from research. Some other specific suggestions may be made. Usually, however, the teacher seeks to draw from children their own ideas; his role is to help them relate those ideas to the task at hand.

Thus, the class moves into a period of study in which information is gathered and evaluated with respect to its relevance to the questions being raised. Modification of questions and of areas of concern occurs as children become better informed about the topic. Groups are formed to gather and report on the several aspects of the study in a manner appropriate to the topic and to the maturity levels of the children. The whole class holds frequent—often daily—discussions to review the work of various groups, to set goals for the day and the days ahead, to get suggestions for further refinement of the questions or topics under consideration, and to coordinate the advancement of the study in general.

During this period, the teacher constantly refers to the resource materials he has prepared in advance. He asks himself how well each child appears to be progressing in his understanding of the concepts significant to the study. He notes the ability of each child to recall and make use of factual information. He gives specific practice in generalizing or drawing conclusions about the matters under study through discussion, reporting, and other activities. He helps the children shape concepts into facts, and facts into broad generalizations and understandings. He notes development in the areas of valuing and skills. He adjusts his work with the class as he goes along according to his judgments about the best work of which they seem capable under his direction. At the same time, he recognizes that learning comes slowly. Startling changes will not be noted instantly; he demonstrates his understanding of this phenomenon by his patient ways with children. In this respect, he values development in ways of thinking and dealing with problems as much as the apparent acquisition of subject matter. Some examples drawn from classrooms at this stage of development may help to clarify understandings of the ways children and teachers may work together.

For example, at this stage of the study of man's tools, the children are eagerly wrestling with the special problems that have arisen in the course of their study; they begin to realize that they are swiftly re-enacting thousands of years of human history. They reach out eagerly for fresh ideas. Thinking is hard work, especially when you are only eight years old. It is not easy to sit still for long periods; diverse activities must be included.

Because of all this hard thinking, and because they have been offered all sorts of social and sensory experiences, these children are strongly motivated to consult relevant books. They have their own questions to answer. At this time no motivation will be necessary; the children will be eager to learn to use the library. Nor will the offer of help with study skills be rejected; now children will need these skills for work that is meaningful to them.

One problem the children have been struggling with is the matter of how to fasten handles to tools; they do this in a direct, specific way by actually trying out various materials such as grass and leather. Finally this problem is resolved to their satisfaction; now others await them. What sort of tools do farmers use? The children once again try tentative solutions, make observations, consult authorities (two of the school's custodians were formerly farmers), compare what they *think* with what they *find* in books and organize their information. In discussions, they get down to the basic purpose of the plow and conclude that primitive man must have begun with simple, pointed scratching tools.

A few weeks later, the children are enjoying the tools they have made with their own hands. They need times like this to assimilate their learnings.

At this point, the teacher gives them a chance to prove their new skills, to test their fresh knowledge. He takes them to a wild and unpruned corner of a nearby park: the class is asked to pretend that this setting is a wild jungle, and that here they must cope with the unknown with their bare hands. Children happily fling themselves into this project; in an instant they are primitive cave-dwellers. Every bit of the knowledge they have absorbed in the past weeks comes into use as they make decisions, create weapons and housekeeping tools, build houses, and determine what their relations will be with neighboring tribes.

Books may play an even greater part in similar studies made by older children. In the study of the founding decades of this country, to which reference has already been made, an experience of central importance was the reading of a number of books (including historical novels and biographies) about such people as Washington, Jefferson, Madison, and Franklin. As the discussion progressed and as the major ideas identified at the outset increasingly were invested with meaning, other experiences were utilized. Motion pictures, such as the three outstanding Omnibus films, "One Nation," "One Nation, Indivisible," and "Liberty and Justice for All," were viewed and discussed. A professor from a nearby college agreed to talk with the class about some of the people of this period about whom he had specialized. A number of trips and excursions were made, both by individuals and by the group, to discover new information in nearby libraries. The clarification of ideas resulting from these experiences led to other projects, such as writing, drawing, and painting, and to more meaningful discussions. In this manner, the children brought to life one historic period, primarily through activities which encouraged them to identify themselves with the men and women who were influential in molding our nation and its history.

The main work of any study progresses for an indeterminate period of time, from a very few weeks to perhaps three or four months. Naturally, the length of time involved will have considerable effect upon the number and variety of learning experiences in which pupils are able to become engaged. There appears to be a trend, however, toward shortening the length of time devoted to any particular study. This is related to the trend toward identifying more specific topics or problems about which classroom inquiry is conducted. The feeling appears to be emerging among educators that the extensive study, which is usually associated with very broad problems or questions, such as a study of conservation, of farm life, or of a large geographic area such as South America (all commonly appearing in the curriculum of social studies in the United States), covers so much territory that children have difficulty in relating the many generalizations important in such inquiries. As a result, the generalizations tend to lose meaning. It *is* difficult to concentrate upon a very broad objective for very long, be it a visual or an intellectual one. Thus, studies which present a more manageable set of questions and problems may be investigated more directly by planning relatively fewer classroom activities. However, probably all would agree that these not only may, but must, be chosen for their greatest impact if social studies learnings are to be vivid and long-lasting.

CULMINATING THE STUDY

The purpose of any social study might be described as bringing about a "satisfaction of demand." In the process of a study, the skillful teacher helps children, through a series of learning experiences, to satisfy their initial demand for knowledge and understanding. Thus it is the teacher who must also decide when this initial demand has been met adequately.

Indications that a study is maturing or ripening to the point of conclusion, and that it is time for a new area of study, come in subtle ways. A prime indicator is the quality and nature of the children's thinking about the topic that has been the focal point of the study. There comes a point in the study process when the act of generalizing becomes easier for children. Relating facts and concepts becomes a more natural undertaking; children begin to put together ideas about the subject in question with less direct assistance by the teacher than before.

Culminating activities of a more or less formal nature are indicated when the teacher senses that it is time to conclude the study. The more or less formal observance of the end of a study is important to children. They need to know when a thing is done, and the "official" observation of a conclusion makes this possible. Drawing together all that has been discovered, reviewing it, and perhaps sharing it with others yields keen personal satisfactions—educational benefits which should not be over-looked. Probably children measure their own achievements through such activities more than at any other time. The teacher, too, can learn much about the progress his pupils have made.

Part of the culmination may consist of a written or oral examination. This should not comprise the total recognition of the end of the study, however. The opportunity to recapitulate and review may take a variety of other appropriate forms, e.g., writing and presenting a play or a formal report, conducting an open house where friends and parents may view the results of work undertaken in the class, presenting a "program" depicting the major learnings of the study, or planning short special presentations for the class itself or for others in the school on topics within the major study of special interest. The possibilities are legion; they will flower quite naturally out of the study itself.

In the examples from actual classrooms which follow, an impression of satisfying conclusions may be gained.

As the concluding activity for several seventh grade classes which had studied different countries around the world, a model United Nations Day was held. At the beginning of the year, each class had undertaken studies of different countries so that, between all the classes, a wide cov-erage of the major countries of the world had been accomplished. In conducting a model U.N., the children divided themselves into the major delegations represented in the General Assembly. They studied the rules applicable in the conduct of the General Assembly and developed an agenda based on questions then before the Assembly in New York. A retired resident in a nearby community who had served in an official capacity with the United Nations agreed to moderate the meeting. In late spring all of the seventh grade students met to conduct their mock assembly meeting in the multi-purpose room. Since there were ten seventh grade classes in the school, over 300 young people were present. They spent the entire day in the meeting, following the agenda agreed upon, listening to debate on the various items, and voting on matters before them. They attempted to represent the views of the countries they represented that day and voted according to their under-standing of the official views of those countries. The boys and girls literally became citizens of other countries around the world. They argued international questions with intelligence and with fervor. Their involvement was total and intense, their conduct beyond reproach, and their experience one which will live with them for years.

We look again to the study of tools. How shall it be concluded? The children decide that there is to be a special kind of exhibit. Not only will the children display all the articles which they have made, but they will also give reports about what they have been doing and why they have been doing it. The furniture is pushed to one side, and the culminating work begins. The class will have two showings—one for the entire school and one for the parents.

In preparation for the exhibit, each child must crystallize his individual findings. In preparing his report he tests his understanding by communicating his learnings to his peers. He gains practice in listening, too, as he thoughtfully checks the accuracy of the other reports in rehearsal. The day of the exhibit is exciting: the tools are demonstrated, the exhibits are displayed, and the reports are given.

Many original and meaningful activities took place in the third grade study of "The City" previously discussed. As a culmination, the teacher in question took the class on field trips to visit three different types of small industries nearby—a furniture factory, a toy producer, and a small supplier to the automotive industry—to consolidate their burgeoning knowledge about making, producing, buying, and selling. With their new sophistication, the children were able to bring much more to these trips than would have been possible a few weeks before.

Learning like this can never be a simple process. Both the teachers and the children are aware that they are doing something important. What is significant here is not the "end product" but the process of intellectual growth and the excitement of the search. This way of teaching, this way of learning, is really a method of research. The first three steps—knowing the original area of interest and defining the specific problem, seeking practical tested solutions to the problem chosen, and formulating and recording the evidence—are followed by the drawing of valid generalizations.

MOVING TO THE NEXT STUDY

Each well-planned and well-taught study raises more questions to answer, more areas for inquiry than a class possibly can handle. Each pertinent question asked, for which some answers are secured, leads to several more. Consequently, at the conclusion of a study there are usually a number of questions outstanding which may lead boys and girls naturally into the next study planned for them. There are times when the work that is to follow is quite unrelated to that which has come before. In such cases, or for work being planned at the beginning of the year when all are relatively unacquainted, additional thought will need to be given to ways of beginning. However, children generally are inherently interested in any valid topic if it is presented in a vivid and straightforward way. It is primarily this zest for learning which carries children from one area of inquiry to another and manifests itself in enthusiasm for attacking whatever problems appear.

HOW LONG SHOULD A STUDY BE?

No strict rules need be observed with respect to the length of time a class is involved in a particular study. Generally speaking, the older the pupils, the more able they are to focus on a large topic to be studied over a long period of time. There are exceptions to this. Boys and girls who have had experience with inquiry centered studies will much more likely be able to maintain interest and drive toward a successful conclusion over a longer period of time than those whose background has been primarily textbook centered. Nevertheless, it is probably true that too much time is allocated for individual studies. This comes about for several reasons:

1. Text materials, usually presented in book form, cover a great deal of territory. It takes a fairly long time to read and study with any degree of thoroughness the material contained in the average textbook. Where reliance is placed upon the text as the main source of subject matter content, the class will be required to spend several months before completing its work. Such long-term commitments frequently exhaust the teacher's enthusiasm for the topic, to say nothing of the pupil's. Publishers, in response to this situation, are now making available in increasing numbers "supplementary" texts and other publications which center on aspects of the traditional, larger topics. These allow a class to limit the extent of their study; they help relieve the problem of too voluminous materials bound within the covers of one book.

2. One tends to perseverate satisfying activities. Although it is always best to terminate any lesson and any study while interest runs high, there is a natural reluctance to do this. But it is well to cultivate one's terminal facilities. Enthusiasm generated for one study carries over to subsequent ones, as has already been demonstrated.

3. Traditionally, courses of study have blocked out very large topics or problems. Most curriculum guides suggest three or four major studies in a given year; usually two or three are stipulated for the intermediate years. Such a designation of study emphases may result in dividing the amount of school time available by the number of studies to be undertaken, a logical but dubious practice commented upon by C. Northcote Parkinson. In his First Law he asserts that "Work expands so as to fill the time available for its completion."[10]

School curriculum problems should not be solved by the application of Parkinson's Law. On the other hand, selection of very broad topics for study is not the solution either. The teacher must find other ways to limit the scope of the problems confronting his pupils.

In contrast, it may be noted that social studies materials now being developed (such as Project Social Studies, and other similar attempts to evolve more useful and relevant materials for classroom use as a result of the curriculum reform movement) are focusing on shorter time intervals. Although these have not been widely adopted, evidence is mounting that shorter term studies provide children with the opportunity to study narrower subjects in greater depth. At the same time they maintain a reasonable view of the overall problem. These materials will not be adopted by large numbers of schools immediately; it is to be expected that for some time more traditional patterns will continue to be followed.

4. Each subject tends to be taught every day; even in the so called self-contained classroom, the curriculum tends to be departmentalized. As a consequence, time allotments, once decided upon, normally are followed every day. It is desirable to devote time to the social study according to need, rather than to again apply Parkinson's Law. However, the *fact* of a daily schedule and the *need* to utilize the time allocated undoubtedly attenuate many studies beyond their usefulness to children.

Given the generalization that most social studies last too long, an exception must be mentioned. Some topics lend themselves to a continuing, irregular patterning of inquiry. Older children particularly are

[10] C. Northcote Parkinson, *Parkinson's Law and Other Studies in Administration* (Boston: Houghton-Mifflin, 1957), p. 33.

likely to find this approach valuable. A study of local government might continue throughout the year. Elections, actions of city commissions, and community issues to be resolved mainly in the local political situation might be studied from time to time along with some other particular studies designed to be carried out on a relatively short-term basis. Other examples of long-range studies in which a class might be engaged include following a particular piece of legislation or, perhaps, a movement to establish a forest reserve or national park, a political campaign, the weather and climate of a region, or observing the construction of a building, highway, or public facility.

It seems apparent that if present trends hold, the curriculum of social studies in the future will consist of *more studies,* with a *sharper focus.* The goals for teaching and learning will be more clear. Time allotments will be more flexible. On some days the study may encompass half or perhaps all of a given day; at other times there will be no work directly undertaken in this area.

THE SOCIAL STUDIES LESSON

The course taken by intellectual inquiry cannot be plotted precisely in advance if it is to be productive of thought and dedicated to the notion of discovery. Although the general outlines of a study certainly may be delineated with considerable precision, the daily lesson is worked out *with* children as inquiry progresses. It is helpful to plan completely in the broader sense; if this is done, "target dates" will allow comparisons of estimated progress with what is actually happening in the classroom. Such comparisons yield valid data on the adequacy of one's own planning, as well as giving information about the appropriateness for the pupils of the pacing of the work.

After a study is under way, most daily lessons will consist of a period of planning with children to determine the tasks for the day. This is followed by a period of research, construction, report writing, dramatic play—whatever is appropriate to the tasks to be accomplished. This then will be followed by an assessment of progress and decisions about the next tasks. Thus, the next day's planning is in part accomplished by the class at the conclusion of the present day's work.

Since it is to be expected that the length of the social studies period will vary, as will the portion of the school day to be devoted to this curriculum area, a great variation from one classroom to another may also be expected. Yet, since the concerns in social science education are at least equivalent to those of the other major curriculum areas, it is to be expected that decisions respecting the average amount of time to be devoted to the social studies will reflect a reasonable balance. Not infrequently, concerns with reading development, the skills of writing and other aspects of language, and plans for an emphasis on mathematics consume so much time that the social studies curriculum gets summary treatment. Still, the language curriculum may find a strong ally in the social studies. All other curriculum areas can also find a place within their broad framework.

When the daily lesson plans specify work in the social study, many teachers decide to utilize the first part of the day for that purpose. This procedure has two advantages. First, during the remainder of the school day opportunities to relate the subject matter of the study and the skills associated with it to other areas of the curriculum are provided. Also, it provides children with a ready source of "things to do" after they have completed their work. Third, it places *one* subject area which relies heavily for its development upon interpersonal classroom contacts at a time of day when children are alert. At this time, they will be most likely to be able to cope with those problems that inevitably arise when human beings work actively together. Later in the day, when children tire, it is often best to reduce the opportunities for such contact and, hence, the possibilities for conflict, by planning work which essentially children must do alone, e.g., spelling, arithmetic practice, handwriting, and reading.

From time to time, specific needs will be identified that will cause the teacher to plan lessons designed to help develop the skills and understandings required. For example, as the study develops, certain map skills may be central to understanding, or a class may appear to require further experience in outlining. The techniques of report writing may require attention as a class moves into the study. The teacher decides what needs are present in a given class and plans a lesson or lessons designed to achieve this desired end. At times, such lessons may be planned for the entire class. At other times, they will call for the participation of a portion of the class; the others may continue their work in the study or, perhaps, in another curriculum area. It is not mandatory for all children in the class to work on the social study at the same moment, just as it is not required that arithmetic be studied by everyone at the same time. In these circumstances, the teacher may identify ten or twelve pupils who need special instruction. The teacher may call these pupils together, invite any others who need review to attend, and leave more advanced students free to pursue their own concerns. Such an approach has been called "grouping by invitation." Teachers who are particularly eager to individualize children's learning experiences have found it highly successful.

Grouping Procedures

That learning activities do not need to be identical is such an important fact that it bears repetition. Diversity of talent and interest exists in every classroom. The topics selected for study are broad; they may fruitfully be attacked from different angles. When different children explore different aspects of a problem at any one time, they have the opportunity to become aware of a broader range of ideas than they would were everyone simultaneously engaged in the same assignment. It is not often necessary or desirable for each child to learn equally well each thing that is brought up, discussed, or studied in detail in the classroom. Although the teacher will identify some common learnings which he hopes all will assimilate as best they can, these learnings or understandings should not constitute the total content of the social studies curriculum. If pupils are to achieve insights into the nature of the social science disciplines—methods of thinking and working with information —situations are required in which ideas from several sources are secured, analyzed, and compared; from this, conclusions are drawn. A variety of activities is basic to the achievement of this goal.

This is not to imply that the class should always work in small subgroupings. Such groupings, often termed "committees," have become the mark of the "modern" social studies classroom. This is unfortunate, for it has encouraged the formation of groups or "committees" within a class as a matter of course rather than where authentic need exists. It encourages teachers to slight the fact that much valuable work can be done when the entire group works together. Although learning takes place with reference to groups, this does not mean that all learning experiences have to be planned with particular groups in mind. As children grow older, they need time to reflect, to think, and to work on their own. Individual study carrels, increasingly found in junior and senior high schools experimenting with flexible scheduling, provide for this need of children to be alone at times.

Therefore, in thinking about grouping, the primary group is the total class. Smaller groups may be formed when a genuine need is perceived by the teacher. Independent study should also be provided for. Any social study should be characterized by a combination of these: there should be activities in which at times the total class works together, other times when individuals and small groups will pursue special projects. The balance between total-class and small-group activities will vary according to the study itself, acording to the extent of the class's progress in that study, and according to the experience of both teacher and pupils in working together.

Teachers must have considerable organizational ability if they are to guide children's work when they become involved in small-group activities. This is essentially an administrative problem, requiring the teacher to keep in mind clearly what the purpose of each group is and what success its members are achieving in their work together. If either pupils or teacher are inexperienced in this sort of working together, caution must be exercised lest groups or "committees" be formed too early in the study. It is best to begin with short-term groupings, perhaps those who can accomplish their purpose during one class period. Confidence comes with experience. Groups will evolve naturally and easily that will work well together for longer periods if careful attention has been paid to initiating short-term groupings.

Whether the temporary groups formed within the social studies classroom are of short or long duration, children require careful guidance at every stage of group activity. This is true at every age or grade level. Each time the group gathers to do a task, they should set their goals. The teacher in this situation helps the members of the group to review past progress, to outline the day's projected work, and to relate the long-range goals of the study to what they are doing. Particularly at first, this may take considerable time. It is a mistake, however, to slight this aspect of group work; doing so is bound to lead to wasted time as pupils attempt to accomplish the tasks they *believe* have been assigned to them. One day of careful goal-setting, even though it appears to consume too great a time, will assist children in clarifying goals and purposes in the days ahead. If this is done, less time will be required during future classroom meetings to accomplish this aspect of group work.

There should also be time for some evaluation of work accomplished at the close of every small-group session. This is true, as well, of social studies lessons which are essentially total-group activities. Reviewing the work accomplished in each session helps children compare their progress with the goals set at the beginning of the period. Consequently, they will have a better view of what they wish to complete during the next period. Evaluation in this context merely means providing an opportunity for the members of the group or their chairman to indicate to the teacher and the rest of the class what they have accomplished and what they have yet to do. In situations like this the teacher also obtains valuable guides with respect to learning problems which have arisen as group work proceeds. These may include the need for certain types of materials, the resolution of inter-personal problems, the identification of areas in which special help may be required. An additional value derives from the fact that bringing ideas to a verbal level carries with it a commitment to more efficient future work. It provides an opportunity for self-evaluation of that which has been accomplished, and it gives the remaining members of the class and the teacher an opportunity to make constructive criticisms which the group may find helpful.

Both planning and evaluation usually will be a total-class activity. Children learn from each other as well as from the teacher, from textbooks, and from other materials in the classroom. However, to learn from one another, pupils must have opportunities for interaction and communication. Group activities are also dignified by recognition in the total-class environment, and healthful competition is encouraged between groups and individuals as they work to fit their individual parts of the study into the whole.

HOMEWORK

Working on the social study outside of the regular classroom is an appropriate activity at every level. Naturally, tasks given to the very young child must be of a very specific nature. Reporting one definite item of information, such as where the father works, or bringing something, such as a summer trip souvenir, to school will be as much as the young child can remember for an overnight task. Children from the third grade on, however, may engage in more demanding activities.

Work done by the child at home in connection with his social study should have strong creative elements; nevertheless, it is much easier for the teacher to give out rather arbitrary assignments. Because of this, there is always danger that homework will become busy work, i.e., the child is required to complete a mimeographed page asking him to list classes of factual information, or he is asked to engage in some other activity which can be assigned with minimum discussion and, it is hoped, confusion to all the children in the class. Since it is impossible for the teacher to evaluate all the homework which children do, this work is usually collected by the teacher and never returned to the children. At best, it becomes a part of a notebook or a collection of things the child is required to keep. When viewed at the end of a study, such efforts have the monotonous conformity of mass production a modern industrialist might envy.

It is under such circumstances that home tensions mount, often reaching the breaking point both for the child and for his parents. Arguments ensue and constructive attitudes are undermined. Not only does this comprise an overall threat to mental health, but it also gives children the notion that completed blanks, paragraphs copied from textbooks, encyclopedias, and other sources are to be valued over their own ideas and their efforts at communicating them. Such assignments are reminiscent of the days when the mind was viewed as a muscle requiring constant exercise. Teachers who dote on such assignments and parents who equate them with education always retreat behind the old cliche: "It is good for you." Nothing could be further from the truth.

Homework can be creative and interesting. But to be so it must be highly individualized. Although *on occasion* it may be valuable to make similar total-class assignments for all, at most times there will be other kinds of work that can directly contribute to the study in which the class is engaged and which will encourage the development of the individual's intellectual powers. Examples of these activities include study trips to various sections of the community; preparation of oral reports that encourage children to use a variety of visual and auditory procedures and forms of presentation (i.e., a play, a symposium, a debate, poetry), interviews conducted after school, the reading of biographies and other books which contribute to the social study on a "self-selection" basis, the construction of shadow-boxes, the painting of pictures, or clay modeling. There are many more. Some faculties who are particularly interested in building more creativeness and interest into their social studies assignments have discusssed the types of things which children can do outside of school. Listing these activities under such headings as "Most Creative" and "Least Creative," they have unearthed many original ideas for the pupils in their classes. Often the by-product of such activity at home is increased pupil interest in the classroom during school hours.

The ideal homework situation, then, is one that encourages individuals or small groups to undertake things outside of school hours that contribute directly to the work being done in the classroom. Total assignments should be used, but sparingly. The most desirable type of activity is one growing logically out of the class work.

The commentary comprising this and the preceding chapter has been of a general nature. Specific activities, goals for teaching, and procedures to be worked out with children take on meaning as one considers the particular types of inquiry in which boys and girls become involved. In the three chapters following, teaching objectives and samples of learning activities drawn from the major content areas are presented.

FOR FURTHER READING

Darrow, Helen F., *Social Studies for Understanding* (New York: Teachers College, Columbia University, 1964).

Frazier, Alexander (ed.), *Freeing Capacity to Learn: Papers and Reports from the Fourth ASCD Research Institute* (Washington, D.C.: Association for Supervision and Curriculum Development, 1960).

Goodlad, John I. and Robert H. Anderson, *The Nongraded Elementary School*, revised edition (New York: Harcourt, Brace and Company, 1963).

Guilford, J. P., "The Three Faces of Intellect," *The American Psychologist*, Vol. 14, (1959), pp. 469-498.

Hullfish, H. Gordon and Philip G. Smith, *Reflective Thinking: The Method of Education* (New York: Dodd, Mead and Company, 1961).

Jarolimek, John and Huber M. Walsh (eds.), *Readings for Social Studies in Elementary Education* (New York: Macmillan Company, 1965).

Lee, John R. and Jonathan C. McLendon (eds.), *Readings on Elementary Social Studies: Prologue to Change* (Boston: Allyn and Bacon, Inc., 1965).

Miel, Alice, (ed.), *Creativity in Teaching* (Belmont, California: Wadsworth, 1961).

National Council for the Social Studies, *Social Studies in Elementary Schools,* Thirty-second Yearbook (Washington, D.C.: NCSS, 1962).

National Society for the Study of Education, *Individualizing Instruction,* Sixty-first Yearbook, Part I (Chicago: University of Chicago Press, 1962).

National Society for the Study of Education, *Theories of Learning and Instruction,* Sixty-third Yearbook, Part I (Chicago: University of Chicago Press, 1964).

Zirbes, Laura, *Spurs to Creative Teaching* (New York: G. P. Putnam's Sons, 1959).

CHAPTER SEVEN

The Method of Discovery: Historical Studies

Lhe past is neither unknown nor incomprehensible to the young child. From his earliest days, it exists as a natural part of everyday life. Even before entering school, he becomes aware of the past, of the existence of history, through a wide variety of avenues. For example, artifacts of the past surround him in his daily life. Some of these material remains of the past are part of the home environment. They may be highly prized, such as a grandparent's picture, various kinds of home furnishings, a diary, and other physical remains which the child can see and touch and talk about with his parents. Other material remains are seen in the neighborhood where the child lives. Old homes, perhaps only a foundation that once supported a house, old trees, automobiles of various vintages, and other objects like them are seen every day. Other artifacts of the past are to be found in the public library, in the museum, or in other public and private buildings. They exist as forceful reminders that people have lived differently in different times and places.

Children have two other extremely important sources in their everyday lives from which to acquire concepts about the past. These are the motion picture and television. Although these media are thought of primarily as sources of entertainment for children in an out-of-school setting, it cannot be denied that much learning takes place when children view them. Unfortunately, much of what is presented is either inaccurate or distorted. But these media *do* exist; children *do* watch them, sometimes with a frightening tenacity; and, good or bad as they may be, children will be influenced by them. A casual examination of the available fare reveals that an unusually large number depict the past in one way or another. Westerns, "period" motion pictures, even Laurel and Hardy films fall into this category.

"No matter what you saw on television, General Custer, Daniel Boone and Abe Lincoln were not all in love with the same Indian girl!"

Reprinted by permission from Saturday Review and John A. Ruge.

Books can provide another incidental, yet important, source for learning about the past. In recent years, particularly, the field of children's literature has contributed a large number of books of high quality which deal with the past in one way or another. For example, two recent winners of the Newbery Medal for distinguished children's literature were presented to authors whose books were essentially historical.[1] A recent bibliography of books for use in the elementary school

[1] Scott O'Dell, *Island of the Blue Dolphin* (Boston: Houghton Mifflin, 1960), 184 pp.; Elizabeth George Speare, *The Bronze Bow* (Boston: Houghton Mifflin, 1961), 255 pp.

social studies program lists 191 titles of books for children telling of the past.[2] Thus, ideas about the past, about people and the ways they have lived, their problems, their differences from and similarities to people living today are becoming increasingly available to children whose recreational reading habits are well developed. In addition, of course, they added an important dimension to the sources to which the classroom teacher may turn when he is helping children increase their understanding of the past and its meaning for them now and in the future.

The Place of History in the Elementary School

Living, as children do, in a world where the past is part of everyday living, one might have expected studies that deal with the past to have been a natural part of the school curriculum from the earliest grades. It has been pointed out in previous sections of this book that this was not the case. Prior to the advent of the Progressive Movement in the United States, history in school mainly consisted of memorization of past events. Indeed, it often consisted of memorizing the entire textbook. General dissatisfaction with the result of such instruction led to numerous suggestions for reform. But, as Rugg points out, reform was based upon theories of how people learn, theories that were coming under increasing attack.[3] In a chapter titled "Three Decades of Mental Discipline," Rugg presented the chart reproduced in Chapter Two. His purpose was to show the nature of suggestions for curriculum revision, most of which dealt with the historical aspects of the social studies curriculum, believed to be basically faulty by him and by other Progressives.

Rugg, his contemporaries, and many educators who were to follow him raised pertinent questions about the efficacy of instruction as it was then being conducted. The extent to which elementary school children could really "understand" history was challenged in virtually every quarter. The claim was made that elementary school youngsters have neither the interest nor the "time sense" necessary to understand history,

---

[2] Helen Huus, *Children's Books to Enrich the Social Studies*, rev. ed., National Council for the Social Studies, Bulletin No. 32 (Washington, D.C.: The Council, 1966), pp. 23-56.

[3] Harold Rugg, "Three Decades of Mental Discipline," *Curriculum Making Past and Present*, Twenty-sixth Yearbook, National Society for the Study of Education, Part I (1927).

that historical studies should be postponed until at least the junior high school years. Many studies have appeared to support these contentions over the years.[4]

Such arguments reflect a basic misunderstanding of the nature of history and the methods of inquiry that are involved in studying the past. Certainly, there are many aspects of history too advanced to have meaning for children. That is true, also, of many adults. But history is found in many forms and can be approached in many ways. Local history, state and regional history, United States and world history, and many other aspects of man's past can be studied in ways which have great significance for children. The problem is not whether history shall be taught but, rather, how to present it. When the manner of presentation is solved, history in its best sense can be taught from the beginning of the school experience of every child. But under such conditions it must always be in terms which are understandable to children.

When does history become understandable? Many of the ideas of history come as part of the ordinary process of growing up in the American culture. These include acquaintance with past events, the development of understandings of relationships of those events to the present and future, and the understanding of human problems as they have existed in other times and places. Unquestionably, it must be remembered that some of these understandings are quite erroneous; many are incomplete or otherwise inadequate. Furthermore, varieties of cultural backgrounds, opportunities, and childhood experiences cause the quality and extent of these experiences to vary widely. But they *do* exist as strong, though primarily incidental, factors within the general culture. Teacher planned experiences rest upon the same type of foundation but with the correcting factor of content selection and planned presentation: bringing children into contact with things which carry valid meanings *for them*. One noted historian commented that history will be understandable to the youngest children in the elementary schools when:

. . . it is presented in the form of concrete examples—material remains, physical representations of material remains and of actions, verbal description and narration rich in material for imagery, mental states directly and obviously related to things which can be clearly imagined. Elementary his-

[4] Some of the pertinent research is reviewed by Ralph H. Ojemann, in "Social Studies in Light of Knowledge about Children," *Social Studies in the Elementary School*, Part II (Chicago: University of Chicago Press, 1957), pp. 76-119.

tory, whatever its content, is history brought within the sensory experience of children. Any other history is advanced. History presented in the form of abstract appraisals of men or things is advanced history. It may, therefore, be argued that the problem of grading history is essentially a problem in presentation. A fact presented in one way is elementary; the same fact presented in another way is advanced.[5]

History presented as chronology is advanced history and does not belong in the elementary school. Rather, historical studies should be placed in a period, and children should be able to live in that period for a considerable length of time. Preston agrees with this point of view in commenting:

History that consists in surveying vast spans of time in a single school term with emphasis on the sequence of events has little justification in the elementary school. Where sufficient time is allowed, however, for the learner to linger and become immersed in the detail of the period—the character of the people, customs, dress, language, literature, art, science, games, and education—history becomes one of the most fruitful sources of social studies content.[6]

In other words, historic studies come alive for children only when the teacher avoids that which is too abstract to have meaning for the child and draws, instead, upon first-hand experience and the wonderful world of imagery to provide the base upon which relationships, understandings, and empathy are developed. The determination of whether the historic study is too complex or advanced must be made through analysis of what children appear to understand well. But it is generally appropriate to consider those things for which immediate referents are available or that represent in the child's mind sufficient reality to have meaning to be satisfactory. When one goes beyond these matters in the classroom, verbalism and meaninglessness appear.

Examples of ways in which historical concepts and facts may be approached at several different grade levels are presented in later sections of this chapter. Meanwhile, it should be kept in mind that all studies possess historical attributes. Inquiry emphasizing geographic concepts or ideas drawn from the other social sciences, the natural sciences, art, or any other area that make a contribution to the curriculum cannot

[5] Henry Johnson, *Teaching of History*, revised edition (New York: Macmillan, 1940), p. 103. This is essentially a forerunner of Bruner's thesis that any subject can be taught at any level if it is properly presented. See Jerome S. Bruner, *The Process of Education* (Cambridge, Mass.: Harvard University Press, 1961).

[6] Ralph Preston, *Teaching Social Studies in the Elementary School*, revised edition (New York: Holt, Rinehart and Winston, 1964), p. 41.

be fully understood without reference to their historical aspects. First, however, one should probe into the nature of the discipline called history so that one may catch a glimpse of the dimensions of this field of inquiry in its mature state. In this connection the nature of the content of history and the methods the historian employs in plying his trade will be considered. For the teacher who would teach a social study whose content is rooted in the past must understand and appreciate the goals and ways of the historian if he is to be successful in working with young children.

THE NATURE OF HISTORY

The word "history" has many meanings. Commonly, it is used in at least two senses. First, it is used to refer to all that has taken place in the past. Beard calls this *history-as-actuality:*[7] all that has ever been thought, felt, imagined, said, or done by human beings. Second, history refers to the *story* of what has happened. In this sense, it is the written material which purports to place the facts of history (or history-as-actuality) in relation to one another. In a way, the story is like witnessed history. But it is more than merely placing historical facts in relation to one another within the general framework of a chronology. *Written-history* always incorporates the notion of interpretation. The writer of written-history, in other words, is concerned not only with the *what* and *when* of events and conditions; he is also interested in their *significance*.

The problem of establishing the what, the when, and the significance of historical events and conditions focuses upon a third use of the word "history" which is less commonly noted but which is of great practical importance to the teacher as well as to the historian. In reading written-history, the question must always arise as to whether the historian has his "facts" correct. In addition, the reader must always ask whether the relationships established are valid and whether the interpretations the writer gives his data are sound.

Because the historian deals with events and conditions in the past, he must employ special methods to help him secure his facts and to analyze them in as objective a manner as possible. The past obviously cannot be brought back and analyzed in its original sense. Unlike the natural scientist, the historian cannot create events, study them, and then check

[7] Charles A. Beard, "Grounds for a Reconsideration of Historiography," *Theory and Practice in Historical Study: A Report of the Committee on Historiography,* Bulletin 54, Social Science Research Council (New York: The Council, n.d.), p. 5.

THROUGH HISTORY WITH J. WESLEY SMITH
"I doubt if a runt like you, Bonaparte, has any qualification for leadership—but I'm giving you a try as acting corporal."

Reprinted by permission from Saturday Review and Mrs. Burr Shafer.

upon his original observations by re-creating the exact conditions again. Instead, he must rely upon other means for searching out data and interpreting them. "History," then, in this sense refers to the manner in which the person who would understand history-as-actuality goes about his studies. This process is more precisely termed the *historical method* or *historiography*. It provides the guides for dealing with the facts of history-as-actuality—the bridge between written-history and history-as-actuality.

A fourth use for the word "history" has special significance for the school. In this sense, history refers to the *collective memory* of a people for the past. It consists of all sorts of memory traces, collective and individual: myths and legends, folk tales, facts, generalizations, values, hearsay remembered either from actual experience or stemming from formal educational experiences—all of the things comprising a people's understanding of the past. The pattern and accuracy of these memories vary from one culture to another and within various sub-cultures. In a culture which provides for the extensive education of its children and youth, this aspect of history should reflect the impact of the school.

The significance of this kind of history should be obvious, for man tends to rely heavily upon it for guidance in day to day living and in making decisions about the future. For example, it is to these recollections that individuals turn when they say, "The lesson of history is . . ." or "If history is to be our guide . . ." etc. Statements prefaced by allusions to the past, real or imaginary, have great influence upon other people as they search their own storehouse of memories to seek affirmation or denial of the course of action being urged upon them.

It is easy to become too complacent about the effectiveness of formal educational institutions within the American culture to teach the knowledge and understandings of history which scholars deem important. There is apparently a feeling among the public that the more history taught, the more learned. The validity of this assumption must be challenged, for the existence of this relationship has not been established. It is the quality of teaching, not the amount, which is the critical factor. And all must realize that, although a great deal of history is taught in our elementary and secondary schools, the amount learned in relation to the time spent represents an extremely inefficient educational operation.

In order to support strongly the amount and quality of history-as-the-collective-memory of the American people, more effective and efficient ways of teaching must be found. One approach that is increasingly being suggested lies in the learning of history-as-actuality in essentially the same manner as the professional historian learns it. Of course, the principles of child growth, development, and learning must be observed. However, the methods and sources for studying history which are useful to anyone, child or adult, who would gain an understanding of the past cannot be neglected.

KINDS OF SOURCES WITH WHICH THE HISTORIAN DEALS

The historian learns about the past through various kinds of traces which cast light on man's past existence. These traces include written records, oral traditions (as in balladry and folk tales), relics of all kinds—any bit of evidence which provides clues to man's past actions, thoughts, or feelings. Some of the records that have been left behind exist because of a deliberate effort to provide men living in a subsequent period with information about a particular time. Other sources are representative of the time but have not been deliberately devised as a record of the event or condition. Newspapers, works of art, material objects, such as furniture are examples of this type. The range of such sources is virtually endless; however, the following list may help suggest the breadth of possibilities that the historian considers in his studies and which children, with their teacher, may use in their investigations of the past.[8]

1. Narrative types of sources
   (a) Inscriptions (e.g., the Rosetta Stone)
   (b) Genealogical material (pedigrees, family trees, dynastic tables, lists of officials, etc.)
   (c) Calendars
   (d) Annals and chronicles (newspapers, magazines, other periodicals, etc.)
   (e) Histories of any kind conceived as records of the past
   (f) Biographies
   (g) Autobiographies, memoirs, diaries, journals, letters
2. Official records
   (a) Government records (local, county, state, national, international)
   (b) Private organization records (church, lodge, business, etc.)
3. Oral sources
   (a) Rumor, anecdote, historical proverb
   (b) Popular tradition (i.e., oral transmission of incidents or events from the past)
   (c) Historical ballad
   (d) Saga
   (d) Myth
   (f) Legend
4. Pictorial and figured sources
   (a) Monuments (pyramids, temples, churches, commemorative tombs and historical memorials, such as paintings, frescoes of historical scenes or persons, garments, gems and goldwork, etc.)

[8] Adapted from Gilbert J. Garraghan, S.J. *A Guide to Historical Method* (New York: Fordham University Press, 1946), pp. 111-113.

(b) Ornaments (painted or sculptured work of historical content on buildings, historical pictures on parchment or in books, historical details on coats-of-arms, etc.)

(c) Graphic materials (maps, topographical sketches, plans of towns and cities, anthropometric measurements such as fingerprints, etc.)

(d) Photographs (photostats, microfilm, motion pictures, flat pictures, etc.)

(e) Phonographs (discs, tape recordings, etc.)

This list is merely representative of the broad range of sources which are of value to the historian as he studies and thinks about the past. The teacher of young children will want to test his inventive capacity. He can find ways to make it possible for children to study the past realistically by thinking of the widest range of sources available in the classroom. In a study of colonial America, for example, what kinds of sources could children examine and analyze which would lead them to a better understanding of that period? What kinds of sources would be appropriate to a study of your state history? Keeping in mind that children of elementary school ages require "first-hand" experience with the materials of the past, what kinds of sources are more appropriate than others?[9]

THE LOCATION OF SOURCES

It is a popular misconception that the historian secures all the information he uses in his studies from deep inside some musty library. Although the library is an important resource, it is certainly far from being the only one of significance to which the historian turns as he seeks information about a particular topic. Primary sources, particularly, are to be found everywhere if the eye is discerning enough. Old diaries and letters, artifacts of all kinds, still reside in large quantities in the hands of private citizens. Often the people who possess these historical treasures are unaware of their value for telling us about the past. The historian constantly is alert to leads which will guide him to these unknown treasures. In the recent past, he has become increasingly interested in oral history: the recounting of important events and

---

[9] The reader is encouraged to become familiar with the idea of thinking about the broadest range of sources which could be made available to children with respect to historical studies, remembering Henry Johnson's admonition reproduced on pp. 200-201.

situations actually experienced by people through use of taped interviews. In addition there are still in existence, in the everyday world, many traces of the past. Old buildings, furniture, paintings, coins, stamps, monuments, clothing, ruins, and other articles that have weathered the passage of time are available for study. Then, too, museums have been established as collecting points for such items; restorations of old buildings and equipment have been undertaken. These provide, with varying degrees of authenticity, materials for building an understanding of the past.

Still, it is true that for the historian the library serves as a major source. Even within this institution will be found an increasingly varied number of resources. Modern means for collecting, storing, and reproducing authentic copies of rare materials are changing the nature and quality of even the smallest library's holdings. No longer must rare volumes be found only in a few great libraries. Modern copying devices make authentic copies available to all. Microfilm, tape and disc recordings, authentic models and reproductions, photographs and paintings are more commonly available for studying the past. Thus it is becoming increasingly possible for the classroom teacher to bring into his room a wide variety of first-hand materials which he can use to make the past come alive for children.

DISTINGUISHING BETWEEN PRIMARY AND DERIVED SOURCES

This wide-ranging variety of sources to which the historian turns have been described as being of two general types: original, or *primary sources,* and *derived sources.* The distinction between the two is important as a guide for establishing historical fact, as will be seen later. Primary sources may be the direct material remains of a particular period, or they may be the impressions or expressions recorded about that period by first-hand observers. They include the actual artifacts of the time, such as official documents, coins, roads, bridges, buildings, paintings. They may include the personal memories of events actually observed and the reports of eyewitnesses, as well. All other sources of information are called derived sources. These may be termed secondary; that is, they are accounts based upon primary sources. Or, they may be tertiary; that is, they are based upon secondary sources. The degree of removal from the primary sources may, it is obvious, extend to the nth power.

It is not uncommon for a source to be, by turns, a primary one and a derived one. Few persons write exclusively of that which they directly observe. Their material is more often a combination of direct representation and of observations based upon the reports of others. In the same fashion, derived sources may be partly secondary, partly tertiary, etc. In addition, a source may be *primary* for one purpose and *derived* for another. An editorial in a newspaper, for example, serves as a primary source for reflection of that paper's attitude toward, or conception of, an event or condition. Rarely, however, is an editorial based upon the first-hand experience of the writer. In the examples following, which are primary sources and which are derived? Under what circumstances might a particular source serve as primary, and under which circumstances would it most likely be derived? In which instances might the source be a mixture of primary and derived sources?

Benjamin Franklin's *Autobiography*
A photograph of Abraham Lincoln
Upton Sinclair's book, *The Jungle*
The Holy Bible
Rodin's sculpture, "The Thinker"
The town of Williamsburg, Virginia
A Tale of Two Cities, novel by Charles Dickens
The Declaration of Independence
The World Almanac
The Dead Sea Scrolls
de Tocqueville's book, *Democracy in America: 1835-1839*
The Republic of Plato
The Biennial Survey, U.S. Office of Education
Parrington's book, *Main Currents in American Thought*
The medieval English song, "Greensleeves"
George Bancroft's book, *History of the United States*

ESTABLISHING THE CREDIBILITY OF SOURCES

Whether the source is a primary one, or whether it is to some degree a derived one, the historian asks himself this basic question with respect to every shred of evidence he uncovers: how authentic and credible is this source? If he fails to seek an answer to this question, his *history* is most likely to become *his-story* instead, one that is more likely to approach the level of backfence gossip than to result in a penetrating commentary upon man's past.

When the historian's judgments about a source are made fairly and in sufficient detail, the process of establishing the credibility of the souce is called the *critical method*. The researcher, in applying this method to any particular piece of evidence, asks these fundamental questions:

Is this object or piece of writing genuine?
Is its message trustworthy?
How do I know?

This leads to an unfolding series of subordinate questions:

1. Who is its author or maker?
2. What does it state?
3. What is the relation in time and space between the author and the statement, overt or implied, which is conveyed by the object?
4. How does the statement compare with other statements on the same point?
5. What do we know independently about the author and his credibility?

The point of these questions is easily grasped:

1. If the document or the coin is forged, it has no value as the thing it purports to be. Gauging the truth of the statement is obviously assisted by a knowledge of who made it.
2. Similarly, it is essential to ascertain with more than ordinary care what the document states and what may be inferred from it. As in law, false conclusions are ruled out by the good judge.
3. The value of a piece of testimony usually increases in proportion to the nearness in time and space between the witness and the events about which he testifies. An eyewitness has a good chance of knowing what happened; a report distant from the event by only a few years will probably be more accurate than one separated by a century.
4. A single witness may be quite accurate, but two witnesses, if independent, increases the possibility of eliminating human fallibility. If a dozen reports already exist, a thirteenth just discovered is compared point for point with the others in an effort to resolve puzzling allusions or contradictions, to strengthen or destroy an interpretation.
5. What can be learned about the author's life and character helps make up our judgment on several of the previous points. If we know his life we can answer the queries: Was he there? Had he the expertness to appreciate the facts? Was he biased by partisan interests? Did he habitually tell the truth?[10]

[10] Jacques Barzun and Henry F. Graff, *The Modern Researcher* (New York: Harcourt Brace, 1957), pp. 134-135.

To repeat: it is best that all historical sources constantly be subjected to the *critical* method. The authenticity of any source is always open to further discussion. The credibility of the source, as well as the reliability of the meaning it carries, is always subject to individual interpretation. Each historian must satisfy his own standards and develop his own conceptions of the meaning of material. In the mature historian, such standards are high; wherever possible, such scholars work from primary sources. Obviously, the elementary school pupil cannot aspire to such scholarship. Nevertheless, it is important that a beginning be made. In helping children to think historically, the teacher tries wherever possible to direct them toward the question of credibility. The objective is to establish early the rudimentary elements of the critical method so that it will become habitual. Hence it becomes a natural part of class activity to ask such questions as these: How do we know that *that* particular building was one of the first to be built in our town? How may we tell whether this author can be relied upon to tell the true story? What sources tell us that this event actually *happened* the way it is reported to us? How responsible are these sources? What parts of this story are we certain about, and which parts are not conclusively known?

Historical thinking employs the critical method to verify sources and to come to some conclusions about the probabilities of truth. Children are able to learn early that absolute assurance about the facts of history is a rare phenomenon. When two independent primary sources are in agreement about an event, a higher probability for truth can be established than when only a single primary source is consulted. Derived sources are generally not as valid for establishing historical truths as are primary ones. The farther removed the derived source, the less likely is it to be useful to the historian. Thus, emphasis usually falls upon the assumption of *probability* that a given event actually happened rather than upon absolute *assurance*. In the study of history, if this question is not raised both with adults and also with children, a critical approach will, in all likelihood, be missing almost entirely. Thus, although highly specific facts of a certain kind, such as the date of Washington's second inauguration, usually are easily established beyond reasonable doubt, the more significant events or conditions, such as the climate of opinion in the new nation at the time of inauguration, are not as easily established. For these reasons, the historian realizes that most of the fundamental questions he raises must be couched in terms of probabilities rather than certainties.

THE MAJOR OBJECTIVE: HISTORICAL INTERPRETATION

But historical criticism is merely a means to an end. The major purpose of historical research is to attach significance to the notable event itself. The facts of history call for interpretation, for generalization. In this process, the historian of any age or maturity asks: what do these facts have to do with each other and what do they mean today? What may they mean for the future? Do they carry the same meaning today as they did twenty years ago? Fifty years ago? So the fundamental questions which the mature historian asks himself are essentially the same as those the young historian must ask. It is not so much a question of differences *in kind* between their research activities as it is differences *in degree* of sophistication of the topics they study.

Generalizing about historical events is bound up not only with knowing facts but also with knowing causes. No event occurs without antecedents. Therefore, to generalize about the relationships which exist among specific events, one must have knowledge of the elements preceding and influencing their occurrence. Assigning appropriate weights to the causal factors in history is a subtle and complicated process. No precise measuring instruments are available, as they are in the natural sciences, for evaluating known causal factors. For example, one cannot rank precisely the significance of the events which led to World War II. Even less shattering experiences fail to respond to exact measurement. The elements leading to the defeat of a local school bond issue, the factors that provide a narrow margin of victory or defeat in an election, the forces leading to a murder or suicide all require subjective judgment. And in reaching conclusions, in generalizing from the facts, it must immediately become clear that, not only is it difficult to establish the relative importance of the various known antecedents to a given event, it is often impossible to discern all of them. All the causal factors in a given situation are not known. Thus the problem of the historian in dealing with a past which cannot be recalled completely becomes complicated.

Changing Interpretations of the Past. It is disturbing to many people to note that history is being re-written constantly. Apparently the significance which the historian attaches to past events is never static. In the layman's view, something is wrong when this occurs. Why isn't history, once written, good enough to last? Aren't historical "truths," once discovered, universals which should stand the test of time?

There are two important aspects of this problem that are pertinent here. First, when thinking of the past, whether one is a historian or not, one's thinking takes place in the light of all temporal experiences. The values, interests, and concerns of the interpreter—his whole experience—are likely to be reflected in selecting important data from less important data and in establishing relationships among them. Thus, when looking back upon the past, the present condition may be expected to act as an ever-changing leavener on one's thinking. For example, views of the Louisiana Purchase are now, during the second half of the twentieth century, considerably different from those held during the first half of the nineteenth century. Similarly, views change about the significance of events such as the proclamation of the Monroe Doctrine, World War I, the Bolshevik Revolution, the Emancipation Proclamation.

Closely interrelated with the influence of the present condition on the interpretations of the past is the fact that new evidence may be discovered. This new evidence casts another light upon the original event and the conditions surrounding it. Or, subsequent events alter the meaning of the original happening. The passage of time is one of the kindest friends the historian has. It is not true, as many popularly believe, that history written in close conjunction with the actual events themselves is more likely to be authentic than that produced after many years have passed. New data, new insights gathered as a consequence of other experiences, the objectivity that comes with time alone give the historian ample grounds for re-examining and re-interpreting the past.

THE HEURISTIC ABILITIES OF THE HISTORIAN

Central to the success of any historian's venture into the past is his heuristic ability—the sixth sense which leads him to the right source at the right time. No historian can function well without a highly developed heuristic capacity, this ability to ferret out the information he requires to solve his problem.

Actually, historical research is not unlike everyday detective work. Ellery Queen and his real-life colleagues are, basically, historians. All primarily work on an inductive method. Known facts are put together in new combinations and patterns in an effort to reach novel generalizations about man's past experience. Searching out the facts, establishing their authenticity, finding new relevant information, and possessing enough insight to propose new generalizations or refinements on others require an imaginative researcher. For many people, historical research can be just as exciting as any piece of detective work. Although it must be granted that some appear to come into this world already endowed with more imagination than others, there is little question that imagination can be developed through appropriate practice. Similarly, the heuristic in the study of history can be extended through practice. Therefore, in the training of a historian much stress is put upon researching problems that require the student to employ his imagination in getting answers to a historical problem. The first graduate course in historiography may include finding the answers to these problems: When was gold discovered in California (the exact date is unknown); What kind of man was John C. Fremont (actually a very complex personality not well understood); and, how do we know whether all of the facts listed in an undocumented chapter of a book on the muckrakers (a derived source) were true? Subsequent work in the field requires searching out quotations from unknown sources, attempting to authenticate statements of fact for which no source was known, and so forth. Such training provides a solid base of experiences upon which the historian draws in his day to day work. Like all other professionals, historians are made, not born. The capacity for sensing where to go, where to look, and what to look for is one no historian can do without. One needs intuition to proceed when, in solving a historical problem, he really does not know which turn is the correct one.

It is neither possible nor practical to probe all of the aspects of the art and science of historiography or to provide in this volume more than an introduction to the nature and values of history. Certainly, a knowledge of this field is essential if one hopes to teach young children effectively. The reader is, therefore, referred to the books on the nature of history and the historical method listed at the conclusion of this chapter. Such material should help the reader develop a fuller sense of this important discipline and provide additional guides to the teaching of historical concepts and understandings.

BUILDING UNDERSTANDINGS OF THE PAST

Children develop historical concepts and understandings through a wide variety of classroom experiences. Some of these are formally designed: a major area of exploration is determined in advance, and the teacher guides the total development of the study on a more or less systematic basis. This is particularly true beginning with the third grade and extending throughout the remaining school years. Common studies of this type are those centering on local and state history, various aspects of American history, the study of an ancient civilization, or the strivings of early man. Such studies extend over varying periods of time. In some instances, the entire year may be devoted to one or more of these topics. Usually, however, shorter periods of time are involved, perhaps from one to three months.

However, many opportunities to develop and extend concepts and understandings of the past exist *outside* of the formal framework of a study. Current events call for an understanding of their antecedents. Holidays and other special observances provide vehicles for building a picture of the past. And, of course, the incidental matters arising out of pupil interests, as they are noted through the day to day living of the classroom, are always pregnant with possibilities of this type.

Regardless of the framework within which the teacher is working, the only meaningful approach is a direct parallel to the way the mature historian works; that is, by searching out sources of information, establishing their authenticity and credibility, and drawing generalizations concerning the data at hand. This means that problem finding and problem solving form the central core of learning activities. The teacher, working from the experiences and existing understanding of the children in the classroom, relates all new ideas to that core.

Historical Understandings In the Primary Years

In earlier portions of this chapter, it was proposed that many significant historical concepts could be considered meaningfully by boys and girls in the earliest years of school *if* these concepts were related directly to the real world of childhood. Some of the difficulties in telling what actually is in a child's mind were considered: to comprehend the extent of a child's knowing is always difficult. When trying to assess his understandings about the past, it poses even more problems. A constant exchange of ideas about the past, between the teacher and his pupils, should be maintained. This is the best way to facilitate the growth of understanding of how teachers may adjust teaching methods to achieve a better "fit" between the learning situation and the child. By saying and demonstrating in a variety of ways what he knows, the child tells the teacher about the quality of his understanding. At the same time, he firms and extends the concepts in his own mind.

As the nature and extent of historical understandings that can profitably be understood by children is considered, it may be useful to observe that boys and girls in the primary grades have already absorbed a wide variety of understandings about the past. For one thing, it is readily apparent that the child's extensive capability in using past and future tenses demonstrates an awareness of temporal relationships. It is also evidence that he can speak meaningfully of events and situations which have occurred previously. Not only does he speak of the past, but the stories he tells and writes are predominantly organized in a historic or temporal sequence. In addition, he is rapidly learning to utilize words which stand for the days of the week and the months of the year. Most primary children commonly employ in their everyday speaking vocabularies such important carriers of temporal meanings as the following:

winter	new	after
old (older)	while	year
"olden" times	remember	week
long ago	last (week, month, year)	awhile
tomorrow	used to be	been
were	once (upon a time)	begin (beginning)
was	ancient	history
before	old-fashioned	since
spring	worn out	past
happened	then	other (day)
time	month	during
sometime	season	early
calendar	today	late
springtime	until	expect
change	fall	now (then)
clock	another (day, week)	often
daily	so	went
date	recently	when
had	started	

Apparently, then, the experience of growing up, of acquiring the ability to speak and communicate, leads all children to use many words indicating the passage of time. It is through this vocabulary, and the experiences upon which it has been built, that the teacher will plan his ways of helping children grow in their understanding of the past.

This is not to suggest that the primary child can gain an unlimited grasp of historical ideas; there are clearly important limits set by maturational factors in reasoning-thinking capacities. Generally, the early school years provide fewer *formal* studies of the past than is the case during the intermediate and upper grade years. Periods of inquiry into historical ideas usually will be brief; there will be little attempt to probe the depths. There are two major types of classroom experiences to be exploited in accomplishing the goal of extending understandings of historical ideas at this level of the development. First, every inquiry in social studies provides opportunities for thinking about the past. Second, the holidays and other celebrations which are observed at the local, state, and national level provide a setting for considering historical ideas.

Since historical ideas form an important basis for any study, one can hardly ignore this aspect in considering any topic with primary children. In studies of the home and neighborhood community, for example, children can recognize some of the effects of the flow of time and build their awareness that some things are older than others. They see a variety of buildings about them; certain kinds of evidence attest to the fact that some have been in existence longer than others. Paint wears thin; boards need to be replaced. One can see new houses being built, discuss the causes for repairs, observe differences in construction and consider the causes. Thoughts concerning the roles of family members provide first-hand examples and vivid experiences leading to growth in understanding about the past. Older and younger brothers and sisters, parents, grandparents, and other relatives occupy different positions in the time cycle; knowledge of this helps children extend their understandings of people, events, and relationships which exist between them in time. Studies of the community and the people who live and work in it yield further opportunities. A visitor to the classroom may describe how his work has changed as new inventions have been made available in his field. Toward the end of the primary years, some special studies may be introduced which are more specifically focused on a past period. Here, children should have the opportunity to live in a past period long enough to absorb the feeling of actually being a part of it. Primarily, this is accomplished through dramatic play, role playing, imaginative stories—all the devices which draw primarily upon the child's imaginative, rather than his logical, powers.

Holidays, special events, community, and school-wide observances provide the second important avenue for thinking about the past. Discussions and other activities in connection with such observances as Lincoln's or Washington's birthdays, Flag Day, Columbus Day, Veterans Day, and Memorial Day are particularly fruitful *provided*, again, that one does not assume that the child's understanding of these particular occasions for honoring the past is greater than it actually is. Again, the importance of engaging the child's imaginative capacities should be emphasized. Impromptu plays, dialogues, murals, and role playing are a few of the major types of imaginative engagements in which children can profitably participate. It should be noted, however, that there are dangers here. The tendency to emphasize the more romantic observances (Valentine's Day, Mother's Day) and to spend excessive amounts of time on events which are observed intensively in the home (Christmas is perhaps the prime and most difficult example) frequently serve only to detract from the curriculum of social studies. There are others which deserve fuller attention, e.g., election days; admission day —observed only in certain states; birthdays of noted Americans; days which are local or state in origin frequently by-passed but worthy of attention; observances of "weeks" devoted to particular problems; and finally, holidays such as Independence Day that normally occur when school is not in session, thus providing a challenge to find ways in which attention may be drawn to them at other times of the year. Among the many general holidays and other occasions which Americans observe, the following events are especially fruitful sources for expanding children's historical understanding at every level of schooling.

Feb. 12	Lincoln's Birthday		Arbor Day (various
Feb. 22	Washington's Birthday		dates in different
May 30	Memorial or		states)
	Decoration Day		Admission Day (various
July 4	Independence Day		dates in different
Sept. 6	Labor Day		states)
Nov. 2	General Election Day	Dec. 15	Bill of Rights Day
Nov. 11	Veterans or	Sept. 17	Citizenship Day
	Armistice Day	Feb. 1	National Freedom Day
Nov. 25	Thanksgiving Day	Feb. 15	Susan B. Anthony Day
		Oct. 24	United Nations Day

In addition to the activities planned in the classroom, the value of study trips in extending historical understandings must be reiterated. The study trip provides one of the richest sources of materials and memories available. In the weeks that follow, children will contribute many ideas which were learned on their study trip. Nothing read about, or even seen in a film, carries the impact of a genuine experience. If the sites of great national events are not located nearby, other ways of experiencing history are available. Every state and every town has its own history, which is related to the history of the country. Visiting the sites of historical interest, seeing the things used in another time, examining the monuments and buildings is a vivifying experience, one which deepens the child's interest in history.

Developing Historical Understandings in the Intermediate and Upper Grade Years

Incidental and opportunistic teaching continue to be appropriate in the intermediate and upper grade years in helping children develop historical understandings, just as in the case with younger boys and girls. However, these experiences obviously do not constitute the whole curriculum of social studies during any portion of the elementary school years. As children reach the age of eight or nine, however, the past becomes a more fertile time for engaging the child's thought on a systematic basis. Keeping Preston's warning in mind, nonetheless, that children must be allowed to "linger and become immersed in the detail of the period,"[11] studies of the past can be made of a wide variety of topics and problems. The most commonly observed studies at this level are state and local history, a primitive culture of the past, American history, aspects of European history, near-eastern history or ancient history. World developments, especially since Sputnik, have caused many school districts to introduce studies of other portions of the world, particularly those of Southeast Asia and Africa. Although many of these are contemporary in focus, and are more accurately described as geographic studies, the historical elements within them should not be slighted.

When one plans a study to emphasize a past period, he faces the problem of making that period, the people, and the facts and conditions of their existence real to his pupils. It is particularly at this juncture

[11] Preston, op. cit., p. 41.

that the teacher will find it valuable to go to the materials and the approaches of the historian. Recall the four definitions given for history earlier in this chapter. First, *history-as-actuality* was discussed; all of the things that man has ever done, thought, or felt. In determining the study which children will undertake, the teacher is deciding what aspects of history-as-actuality children can and should know about. One should make judicious selections in this respect, for it is obviously impossible to know more than a small portion of history-as-actuality.

Second, *written-history* was identified as the story of man's occupancy of the earth at some time or period in the past. It is someone's story of history-as-actuality. From it, one learns what happened at some other time and place and how to relate the significance of those events to events of today. It is also, of course, something which individuals construct or write. Children will consult written-history, but they may also prepare their own written-history. Third, the *historical method,* or *historiography,* which provides the rules or guides for dealing with the facts of history-as-actuality as written-history is prepared was considered. It is the bridge between what has happened and the story told of that event. It will help children as they deal with the facts, purported and substantiated, of the past.

Finally, history as the *individual and collective memory of a people* was discussed. For the teacher, this aspect of history refers to the *residue* of learning: what is left when teaching is done. When one compares the residue with what one thinks ought to be there, this definition helps to establish goals or objectives for teaching and, subsequently, to evaluate the effectiveness of work with children. As one approaches any historical study, or course of studies within which historic ideas are identified as important in overall learning, he should keep these four meanings for "history" in mind.

GENERALIZING IN HISTORICAL STUDIES

In Chapter Four, distinctions were drawn between concepts, facts, and generalizations. A *concept* was defined as the constellation of ideas a person has about anything. Words are commonly agreed upon symbols which *stand for* concepts but *are not actually* concepts. A *fact* was defined as a statement of a relationship between two or more concepts which has specific applicability; i.e., it deals with one instance, situation, or condition, as: "George Washington was Chairman of the Constitutional Convention held in Philadelphia in 1787," generally accepted to be true. *Generalizations* were identified as statements of relationships which have broad applicability. Generalizations which are thought to be universally true, or nearly so, are often referred to as rules, principles, or laws. Most generalizations in the social sciences have much more limited applicability and do not belong in this category. The following are examples of historical generalizations that intermediate and upper grade children are capable of developing through the study of specific facts:

Compared with the whole span of man's existence, the time during which he has been struggling to achieve freedom and dignity has been very short.

We cannot understand the present unless we know about the past; also, the past has a great influence on the present.

History is important in helping us prepare for social and political life.

We better understand what our present thoughts and actions might be when we are aware of the historical background of our society.

Change has always been a condition of human society; the tempo of that change has enormously increased in the recent past.

Brotherhood and peaceful cooperation were two of the earliest historical ideas; so were conflict and hostility.

Most races and cultures, from the beginning of recorded time, have made some contributions to our present civilization.

Man has been motivated over the years not only by material needs and wants, but by ideals as well. The value systems of all ages show a persistent demand for a moral standard.

What more specific generalizations might be developed as one studies a particular aspect of man's development?

It has been pointed out that one develops historical generalizations as a consequence of discovering related facts. This discovery can occur primarily in an inductive setting, in a deductive one, or in a combination of the two. In the method of discovery, children develop generalizations primarily through inductive techniques. After the facts are determined and their relationships are related meaningfully, it is the pupils who draw the inferences. The tendency of the teacher to "clinch" the discussion (that is, to state the generalization) is relinquished in favor of the pupil's inferential reasoning.

Self-discovery is opposed to the desire of the teacher who would "cover ground," or "move on." The time required to provide for pupils to express their ideas fully is incompatible with this notion of teaching. Where patience is lacking, or where pressures are exerted by school authorities to cover subject matter, the method of discovery must necessarily languish.

KINDS OF SOURCES WITH WHICH CHILDREN CAN DEAL SUCCESSFULLY IN HISTORICAL STUDIES

The wide variety of sources with which historians deal in their studies of the past were suggested in earlier portions of this chapter. Generally speaking, these are the same materials to which the young historian turns. But this provison must be added: the more "concrete" or real to the child the better. Therefore, historical studies that utilize artifacts, the "real things" of a period, are better than things which purport to represent the period. Those materials or sources which appear real to the child help him to exercise his imagination. For example, here is a list of possible sources out of which ideas of a period could be developed. Some will appear more "real" to children than others. On a piece of paper or a chalk board, list the most meaningful to the left, the least meaningful to the right. Put the ones about which you have some doubts in the center.

An actual reproduction of a letter
A printed copy of the same letter.
A piece of authentic furniture of the period
A picture of a chair in which an important figure of the period was
   known to have owned and used.
Pictures of houses: paintings and photographs
Pictures of exterior and interior reconstructions of houses
Stories told by persons who lived during the period being studied
Phonograph records of someone reading a speech or letter from the
   period
Motion pictures of the actual event
Fiction based on the period
A detailed account (non-fiction) told by a derived source
Textbook presentation of the period
A ballad from the period
Motion picture based on the period

What additions could be made to this list? What generalizations about teaching could be drawn from the experience of attempting this type of classification of sources for young children?

LOCATING HISTORICAL SOURCES FOR CLASSROOM USE

The sources to which the historian turns will also prove useful in the classroom. Ones appropriate for classroom use are not difficult to locate. The teacher and his pupils will look for them in three major places. First, there is the wealth of material normally available through school channels: motion pictures, recordings, flat pictures, texts and supplementary books, models, children's literature—the whole range of items which a well equipped school district provides. Standards for well equipped social studies teaching are still far too low, even in districts that pride themselves on adequately assisting teachers. Furthermore, many impoverished school districts and many very small districts, in which there are only one or two schools, exist which do not provide the variety and quality of teaching materials desired by most faculties.

However, two other important sources, if imaginatively tapped, can in most instances make up for what is lacking. These consist of parent resources and those to be found in the community at large. Increasingly, parents of the children in the classroom are providing a reservoir rich in things and ideas: parents who have traveled to the places being discussed, a father whose hobby is studying aspects of the topics being considered, homes where treasured items have been passed from one generation to another, families in which grandparents, and even great-grandparents, provide sources to be utilized in one way or another. In one community a father whose avocation was astronomy visited the fourth grade in his neighborhood school each year; he became expert at judging what fourth graders understand and relish. Another parent, a geologist, visited the class of his daughter each year, upgrading the difficulty of the material presented as the children themselves progressed. In like manner, historical data and samples may be presented to children. A mother may bring a collection of toys handed down from great-grandparents or grandparents. Cradles, flatirons, and washtubs used by children long ago in imitation of parental pursuits convey far more than the patterns of play of a given era. Carefully preserved old newspapers and costumes worn for special events may similarly be shared. A local newspaper editor or reporter will be happy to tell children how modern history is made and recorded. It will be helpful if such visitors are told ahead of time about the length of time allotted for them, the attention span of the children, the advisability of a free time for open questioning, and the differences between children and adults in ways of showing interest and graciousness. The children may be helped ahead of time to know what behavior will be expected of them in a given situation. A drummer with four children of his own who will let each child in the class have a turn at his drums will tolerate behavior different from that expected by a violinist with a Stradivarius. In addition to building a bond between home and school of inestimable value to the child who is most directly involved in this sharing of things and ideas, the family resources can provide authentic and worthwhile sources of historical information rich in meaning to children.

Beyond the family and the school lies the richest resource of all for the creative teacher: the community itself. Museums, libraries, people engaged in special work relating to the study going on in the classroom, historical restorations, original artifacts of all kinds, public records, and many other possible sources of information are within reasonable distance of a majority of classrooms. From less accessible sources one may secure vast quantities of valuable materials free of charge. Only a letter is required, a telephone call, or a visit by the teacher to an office. Embassies, corporations, small businesses and government agencies are but a beginning. Publications provide information on sources of free and inexpensive materials on a wide range of topics.[12] It is truly astonishing how rich are the resources within a short distance of most elementary schools for those who are willing to look.

In summary, the method of discovery is particularly applicable to the study of history. To engage children in meaningful historical inquiry, the following generalizations should be observed in arranging learning situations:

1. Children enter school with understandings about the past. If the teacher builds on these understandings, much can be done in developing and extending historical concepts earlier in the school experience of the child than one might suspect.
2. Many sources of information about the past outside of the school are affecting the growth and development of concept formation about the past. Not a few of these are responsible for developing incorrect concepts.
3. As in every other aspect of social studies teaching, a constant awareness must be maintained concerning the adequacy of the child to understand the ideas being discussed. The best way for

[12] See, for example, the *Educators Guide to Free and Inexpensive Materials,* published yearly by Educators Progress Service, Randolph, Wisconsin. Another source, not widely enough used, is the yellow pages of the local telephone book.

the teacher to assess the adequacy of understanding is through observing what the child says or does. Many opportunities for self-expression through many channels should therefore be provided.

4. If children are to develop an understanding of *history-as-actuality*, they must be provided an opportunity to study a period for a considerable length of time. "Covering ground," particularly when subject matter is organized along strictly chronological lines, is detrimental to the development of adequate historic concepts.

5. Children develop an understanding of history by applying the principles of the historical method. Such an approach to the study of historical ideas suggests emphasis upon inductive-intuitive approaches, but not to the exclusion of deductive-analytic thinking.

6. Although historical understandings are taught at every level of the school, studies which involve an extended period of time are not appropriate until the third or fourth grade.

7. The most meaningful sources in historical studies are those for which direct referents may be found in the everyday environment of the child. Such sources for historical studies are to be found in abundance not only in the well equipped classroom but among parents and within the community as well, if teacher and children look for them.

For Further Reading

American Council of Learned Societies and the National Council for the Social Studies, *The Social Studies and the Social Sciences* (New York: Harcourt, Brace & World, 1962).

Billington, Ray Allen, *The Historian's Contribution to Anglo-American Misunderstanding* (New York: Hobbs, Dorman & Company, 1966).

Barzun, Jacques and Henry F. Graff, *The Modern Researcher* (New York: Harcourt, Brace & World, 1957).

Bloch, Marc, *The Historian's Craft* (New York: Random House, 1964).

Collingwood, R. G., *The Idea of History* (New York: Oxford University Press, 1956).

Commager, Henry Steele, *The Nature and the Study of History* (Columbus, Ohio: Charles E. Merrill Books, Inc., 1965).

Hunt, Erling M., *et al.*, *High School Social Studies Perspectives* (Boston: Houghton Mifflin, Company, 1962).

Johnson, Henry, *Teaching of History in Elementary and Secondary Schools,* revised edition (New York: The Macmillian Company, 1940).

Long, Clifford L. (ed), *Localized History Series* (New York: The Bureau of Publications of Teachers College, Columbia University, various dates).

Michaelis, John U. and A. Montgomery Johnston (eds), *The Social Sciences: Foundations of the Social Studies* (Boston: Allyn and Bacon, Inc., 1965).

Morrissett, Irving (ed), *Concepts and Structure in the New Social Science Curricula* (West Lafayette, Indiana: Social Science Education Consortium, Inc., 1966).

National Council for the Social Studies, *Interpreting and Teaching American History,* Thirty-first Yearbook (Washington, D.C.: N.C.S.S., 1961).

National Council for the Social Studies, *New Perspectives in World History,* Thirty-fourth Yearbook (Washington, D.C.: N.C.S.S., 1964).

National Council for the Social Studies, *New Viewpoints in the Social Sciences,* Twenty-eighth Yearbook (Washington, D.C., N.C.S.S., 1958).

Nugent, Walter T. K., *Creative History: An Introduction to Historical Study* (Philadelphia: J. B. Lippincott Company, 1967).

Parker, Donald D., *Local History: How to Gather It, Write It, and Publish It,* revised and edited by Bertha E. Josephson for the Committee on Guide for Study of Local History of the Social Science Research Council.

CHAPTER EIGHT

The Method of Discovery: Geographic Studies

Geographic study is at once very old and relatively new. As a field of inquiry, it dates from before the birth of Christ. Only history is more venerated as a social science discipline of greater age and longevity.[1] And although the first textbooks in geography were published in the United States shortly after the American Revolution, it was not until early in the present century that it was to become recognized in the United States as a discipline in the same sense as the other social sciences.

School Geography and Geography as a Social Science

A number of factors have operated to consign geographic inquiry to a special kind of limbo; it has still not been completely successful in effecting its escape. During the nineteenth century, there was no doubt of the importance of geography as a school subject. In fact, during this period it was viewed as an important instrument of the commercial community. Every elementary school child was taught the knowledge which was "thought useful for a merchant to know."[2] It was expected that the schools would prepare people by providing the kind of knowledge necessary for them to get along in a world in which the expanding American economy found its business. Therefore, children were taught to "bound the important countries of the world," to recite their major products, and to locate the cities from which the trade emanated.

[1] Chapter Two, the reader will recall, contains a brief review of the rise of the social science disciplines.
[2] C. R. Dryer, "A Century of Geographic Education in the United States," *Annals of the Association of American Geographers,* XIV (September, 1925), pp. 134-135.

The geographic textbook played an important part in defining the American Dream during these years. This was the period that has been termed the "good God in nature" era, and it was duly reported in the classroom text. During the formative years following the Revolution, the frontier and the unknown lands beyond began exerting an almost mystical influence which has only recently subsided. Unbelievable stories about the great west contributed to the concept of the special American Destiny. Who had not heard the stories of the geysers in Yellowstone, or the accounts of the unparalleled splendor of the Rocky Mountains, or the tales of trees so large a man was dwarfed by them? Through the study of geography, these stories, conceived and reported in the tradition of the American Dream, became symbols to generation after generation. And so these "eighth wonders of the world," all American, accompanied by accounts of the already discovered seven, became standard fare for the young in school.[3]

Although geography occupied an esteemed position in the curriculum of the elementary school, there were few scholars in America engaged in the task of advancing geographic knowledge; this was to have a lasting effect upon the school. It is true that there were Europeans of towering scholarship occupied in developing the discipline; but, as late as 1904, when William Morris Davis called a meeting of scholars to found the Association of American Geographers, there were not more than one hundred persons in the United States who could have been described as professional geographers. It was particularly in Germany that the major advances in geographic scholarship were taking place, under the leadership of such men as Humboldt, Ritter, Ratzel, and Hetner. By World War II, when the need for geographers in the U.S. became acute, the number had not reached one thousand.[4] James estimated there were about two thousand by 1954[5]. The number certainly does not exceed three thousand today. The American Historical Asso-

[3] For the Centennial Exposition held in Philadelphia in 1876, enterprising lumbermen sent a section cut from near the base of one of the giant sequoia trees in California for exhibition purposes. Although not the largest that could have been selected, the exhibit met with such disbelief on the part of the fair goers that the lumbermen found that their exhibit backfired. Apparently merely reading about these things did not accomplish what had been expected.

[4] A survey conducted in 1943 showed that fewer than one thousand competent geographers were at work in the United States. One third of these were working for the federal government. Of the total, only 291 held doctorate degrees in geography. P. W. Picklesimer, "The Craft of the Geographer," *School and Society*, LXXVI (November 15, 1952), pp. 305-308.

[5] Preston E. James and Clarence F. Jones (eds.), *American Geography: Inventory and Prospect* (Syracuse, N.Y.: Syracuse University Press, 1954), p. 3.

ciation, the comparable professional affiliation for the historian, meantime, has a membership in excess of twelve thousand.

Thus, when the call for curriculum reform went out, late in the 1800's, there were many historians to speak concerning the desirable curriculum for their subject but few geographers to assert the values of their field.[6] The whole pattern of recommendations for reform thus reflects a gradual lessening of emphasis upon geographic inquiry through the first half of the century, although the intervening years have been marked by increasing interest in providing geographic study in the school. In part this has come about because of bitter lessons learned during World War II (and because of the nature of international affairs), but it is also because there are beginning to be enough professional geographers to provide the leadership schools require if viable programs in geographic education are to be developed.

The Nature of Geography Today

The teacher's concern must be to understand the nature of modern geography if ways are to be found to teach valid geographic understandings within the curriculum of social studies. There is no question that geography is sorely misunderstood, not only within the teaching profession, but among the general public as well. Old notions persist and, because for so many years little geography has been taught, particularly beyond the elementary grades, few teachers have adequate preparation in the field. Consequently, the problem of improving the offerings of the geographic branch of the social studies is a difficult one to solve.

The word *geography* is derived from *geo* (earth) and *graphy* (writing). Thus, geography simply means "earth writing." Therefore, the study of geography is concerned with the patterns of things as they occur over the face of the earth, the relationships of these things one to another, and the importance of these things to man. It is concerned with the meanings of natural and man-made features as they occur from place to place around the globe, and with what these kinds of "writings" mean to man. For it is in the uneven distribution of things over the face of the earth that the geographer seeks to create meaning and significance. Why things are where they are and their relationships to other

---

[6] The American Political Science Association was also a relatively large and influential organization in the earlier stages of the school curriculum reform in social science to which reference was made in Chapter Two.

natural and man-made phenomena are therefore the "stuff" of geography and geographic inquiry.

Human beings have always been curious about the earth on which they live; they have always sought to learn more about it. From earliest times—those times extending far back into pre-history—people have sought to learn what was beyond their immediate horizon. But as civilization progressed, and as means for recording events and conditions were developed and refined, more accurate ways of studying and thinking about the earth came into existence. Tools were developed and concepts evolved to bring greater accuracy to the process of improving the precision of these descriptions. The Greeks were by far the most productive people in this regard. As early as 200 B.C., Eratosthenes, using a well to study the changing of the sun's shadow, concluded that the earth was round, and he calculated its circumference with considerable accuracy. Concepts of the grid (later known as latitude and longitude) were developed; these helped to locate places that were far apart with greater accuracy. Homer, Herodotus, and others wrote detailed descriptions of places they had been; and they recorded as accurately as they could the words of travelers. By these means, they sought to bring together ideas to help expand knowledge about the earth as the home of man. Much of what was "discovered" and written about was inaccurate; some of it was completely false. Yet it has been out of this constant search for understanding of the human habitat that the modern discipline of geography has sprung. Through the centuries, other disciplines have arisen as a consequence of a sort of splitting-off process. Climatology, physics, geology, all of the classic "natural sciences," arose from geographic study, thus giving rise to the assertion that geography is the mother of sciences.

Contributions to understanding about the earth have come, and continue to come, from many fields. Geography without history is incomplete. And modern geography also must utilize knowledge from other fields of the natural sciences and the social sciences. It has been correctly termed the bridge between the natural and the social sciences. Like history, therefore, it is a *synthesis* field: its subject matter is drawn from the widest experience and knowledge of man. Also like history, it is distinguished not so much by its nature of subject matter as by the ways in which that knowledge is utilized. But whereas history organizes ideas temporally, or in relationships in time, geography organizes its subject matter spatially. Modern geographic thinking stems basically from that point in time when systematic and objective means became employed to analyze spatial arrangements of things as they were found to be distributed over the face of the earth and to assign significance to those areal differences, patterns, or "writings," as they could be observed and studied.

THREE CONCERNS OF GEOGRAPHIC STUDY

Thus geographic study involves three major factors. First, it is concerned with *description*. That is, the things which occur in the environment may be described with accuracy, whether they are within the immediate view or whether they are far over the horizon. To aid in this process, concepts have been invented and terms developed. For example, at one level of generality, words like "delta," "mountain," "plateau," and "valley" assist in the process of description. Much more specific terms may be applied; for example, concepts of relative height are given more precise meaning through the use of terms such as "relief," "slope," and "elevation." These, in turn, may be subjected to even greater specificity of meaning by the application of still more technical terms, such as grade, feet, or inches above or below sea level.

Second, geographic study is concerned with the *location* of things, with the *direction* of these things, and with the positions and relations of these, each to the others. Again, concepts and terms have been developed to help locate natural and man-made things on the face of the earth and to show relationships between them. Concepts of direction and ideas about the relative location of things have been brought to very high levels of sophistication. Beginning with the simplest ones of "up and down," "left and right," these move on through conceptions of degrees of latitude and longitude to the means of calculating direction. Thus one may sense the extent to which man's thinking has developed over the centuries. In addition, he has worked out concepts of the relationships of things in space which transcend the *geomatical* (or the mathematics of location) in the sense of thinking about the *relative location* of things: relative in terms of time involved in travel, in terms of the importance of one area to another, in terms of the significance of certain relationships between one thing and another.

Third, geographic study is concerned with attaching significance or meaning to the things which may be described, located, and related to each other. The geographer always asks the question, "Why is this relationship important and in what ways is it of significance to man?"

Geographic inquiry is involved in making *judgments* and in seeking to form generalizations about man's occupancy of the earth. In the past, there was often an inclination to view the natural environment as a prime determiner of man's actions, the controller of his occupancy of the land. This view has been called "environmental determinism"; it is now largely disregarded. It is presently thought that human use of the environment is primarily determined by cultural and historical factors.

Further, it should be kept in mind that modern geographers are not merely concerned with the study of the interrelationships of people to place. They are also involved in the study of people in relation to other people. Similarly, the scope of geographic inquiry cannot be restricted to a consideration of physical phenomena.

THE METHOD OF GEOGRAPHIC RESEARCH

Like history, geographic inquiry involves certain concepts and methods of research unique to the discipline. To the geographer, these are best described as the *regional concept* and the *regional method*.

The Regional Concept. The usual dictionary definition of a region denotes it as a large and indefinite part of the earth's surface having about it some homogeneous quality. In thinking geographically, however, a more specific meaning is attached to the term. The geographer's concept of a region reflects his interest in studying the differences which occur from place to place. To study particular kinds of differences, the geographer first must select an area in which phenomena occur that engage his interest. In making this selection, he must be careful that the region he defines is large enough to provide the widest possible range of occurrence of the matters of interest to him but which is not so large that it becomes unmanageable. Thus, a region is (1) an area of any size which is (2) homogeneous in terms of specific criteria and which is (3) distinguished from bordering areas by a particular kind of association of areally related features; therefore, it possesses some kind of internal cohesion. The geographer's problem begins even before he commences his study. He must define a specific area, homogeneous in terms of the things he wishes to scrutinize, but not so large that other geographic phenomena occur too frequently for him clearly to observe the object of his inquiry.

The concept of the region has had great power for the geographer as he has sought to learn the nature and significance of areal differentiation. It has served as a device for illuminating an intellectual concept. There

are no such things as "true regions," but if this concept serves to illuminate, rather than to obscure, then its use is justified. And, it should be
added, there are as many regional systems as there are geographic
problems to be studied.

The concept of the region has assisted the professional geographer
in bringing new unity to his field. A few years ago it was commonplace
to specify the field in which geographic studies were being conducted as
if they were separate and discrete disciplines. For example, one still
hears a great deal of talk about "human geography" and "physical
geography," in addition to topical, economic, political, social, and many
other "geographies." These conceptions are largely outmoded, and it is
the regional concept which has brought about this change. It is recognized today that there is only one true geography, unified by the regional
concept and by its method of study. Although recognition of this fact is
relatively recent and acceptance of it still limited mostly to those of the
geographic profession, the subject matter of geography is not viewed as
being a unifying characteristic. In this sense, then, it is very much like
history, which also is unified not by its subject matter but by its point of
view and its method. Thus, the field of geography, rather than being
involved with several separate disciplines, is seen as being comprised of
various specializations, each of which employs the regional concept and
the regional method.

The Regional Method. The geographer utilizes the concept of a
region through what is termed the regional method. This approach to
the study of geographic phenomena consists of several steps and is
governed by criteria which establish objectivity for the research.
Basically, these steps include the identification of the purpose of the
study, which in turn determines the dimensions of the region or regions
to be analyzed, analysis through various geographic tools, and the
development of concepts and generalizations.

Selecting the purpose of the study clarifies the boundaries of the
region or regions which will be used in analysis. In some instances,
boundary lines may be very precise. For example, they may be defined
by city limits or county lines. In some instances, they may be composed
of boundary lines derived from grouping several states or provinces, or
nations or groups of nations, together. Regions may also be defined with
considerable exactness by using natural features such as rivers, mountain ranges, shore lines, and the like. But in other instances, regions may
be less precisely defined. Climatic zones, population concentrations,

the lands devoted to particular kinds of crops, the occurrence of certain religious beliefs, or other social phenomenon are examples of regions that might be utilized in geographic study for which boundaries cannot be drawn exactly.

In settling on the region or regions to which he will give his attention, the geographer attempts to satisfy a particular purpose. Perhaps he is primarily curious about a given region and wishes to study it in order to add to the store of knowledge about the place in question. An example of this type of study might be the study of the agriculture of a particular area. It may perhaps involve land-utilization patterns in a major city. Another purpose might be to secure information which differentiates two or more unlike regions. An example of this type of study might be the analysis of areas in which different types of crops are grown: what factors operate to bring about this condition? Other examples could be the study of differences in soil, vegetation, or climatic regions; or perhaps the analysis of factors involved in distinguishing urban and rural occupance of the land. A third purpose the geographer might attempt to satisfy through the regional method of study is to seek information which compares similar regions. Examples of this kind of study include analyses of regions with similar climatic conditions, physical situations, and land-use patterns. A further purpose in conducting geographic inquiry may be to satisfy some interest which calls for clarifying the way a region or its components function in a more inclusive area. Most geographers accomplish this goal by becoming specialists in one major region of the world, such as Latin America or the U.S.S.R.; they may then conduct studies of these very large regions, often working with colleagues who have interests in the same area. Finally, a geographer may be seeking answers to a question of cause and effect. An example of this type of study would be the analysis of the effect of water pollution on plant and animal life in a particular area. Another might be a study of the transportation network in a particular area, undertaken for the purposes of seeking better solutions to the problem of moving people from place to place in an urban complex.

Research Tools in Geographic Inquiry. The regional method employs a wide variety of sources of information and analytical techniques, some of which are common to other fields, others of which are more or less unique to geographic inquiry. The sources of information that the geographer consults include such widely diverse published and unpublished documents as descriptions of places and events, reports, statistics, photographs, and maps. Frequently, he will also turn to records and materials, concepts and generalizations from other fields in the social sciences. For example, he may use such information as the cultural stages suggested in anthropological research, population data compiled by demographers, and records showing climatic changes over the years.

Geographical inquiry relies heavily upon the first-hand study of phenomena. It is a characteristic peculiar to the geographer, therefore, to spend a good portion of his time out-of-doors, recording data on maps which are later combined with other information for further analysis. Air photographs, field mapping in which information of areal associations may be recorded on maps of relatively large scale,[7] collecting samples, taking photographs, and taking notes occupy much of his time. In addition, the geographer seeks out people in the region who may have information of significance to him. Interviews, both first-hand and by means of questionnaires, comprise an important part of the data-gathering process in the regional method. The geographer must be a person who likes the out-of-doors and one who can conduct himself easily in a wide variety of circumstances.

Geographers are required to develop some highly specialized techniques for analyzing data. Among these techniques are those of cartography (or map making), the use of statistical procedures (including the ability to utilize complex computers), and interpretation of photographs (especially in the case of aerial photography). Like the tasks of scholars in other disciplines, the processes of gathering and analyzing geographic data are rapidly becoming more complicated. Professional geographers being trained today, like their counterparts in other social science disciplines, therefore are required to become expert in several relatively new dimensions, in contrast to their colleagues trained only a few years earlier.

The Goal of Geographic Inquiry: The Development of Concepts and Generalizations. Clearly, no two points on the face of the earth are exactly alike. But if he is to develop our understandings concerning man's occupancy of the earth in this place and in that one, the geographer cannot merely examine each spot independently of all the others. He must seek to draw inferences within manageable limits and to formu-

---

[7] The large scale map, that is, a map showing in great detail a relatively small area, is one of the most important tools of geographic study. Strangely enough, the maps of large areas, such as continental or world maps, which are the main staple of geographic instructional materials in the classroom, are rarely of use to the practicing geographer. Because they represent such vast areas, it is not possible to show the detail necessary to geographic analysis.

late meaningful relationships. Thus, the geographer always attempts to generalize. As has been seen, the geographer is concerned primarily with formulating concepts and generalizations about the relationships of regions. He may also concern himself with establishing cause and effect relationships within a particular area. But since time brings changes in man's thought and technology, and since new data are constantly being discovered and modified in this process, it is not possible to say that the geographer is dealing with absolutes. The concepts and generalizations formulated at any one time therefore are subject to modification. They are always subject to study and criticism. One generation of geographers may establish regional divisions by careful means and for specific purposes; another generation may find it necessary, because of newer criteria, to revise these concepts. Each set of generalizations about geographic studies must be scrutinized just as carefully by each succeeding generation of geographers. Thus, geographic inquiry is a developing field; it is constantly being modified by time and by the discovery of new information. This new information, in turn, is adjusting itself to the changing times and conditions. It is not a static discipline consisting of a known body of information merely waiting to be enumerated in increasing detail.

The Importance of Thinking Geographically. It has been noted that geography, like history, cannot be identified by its subject matter. The entire range of human experience, past and present, may be the concern of either the historian or the geographer. What *is* unique about these disciplines is the manner in which they approach their studies. It is the concept of the region and the regional method (the historical method is the counterpart), not the subject matter, that sets geographic inquiry apart. And it is the process of employing the regional method which is the essence of thinking geographically.

Abilities to think geographically are not the exclusive property of the geographer, nor are geographic concepts and generalizations developed solely by geographers. Just as history has been and continues to be written by persons who are not strictly historians, so persons who are not professional geographers continue to contribute to geographical understandings. The criterion which determines one's capabilities either as a historian or geographer is the capacity *to think historically or geographically.* A person does not possess abilities to think in either of these modes without experience. To learn to think geographically, one must concern himself with geographic problems; then he must seek to solve

those problems using the concepts and methods of research characterizing geographic inquiry.

Everyone can learn to think geographically. Because most personal
and social problems contain elements that are geographic in nature, the
school should consider this to be a prime objective of the social studies
curriculum. Of course, there is important subject matter, as well; but
that subject matter cannot be taught successfully when divorced from a
meaningful context. Of equal importance are the consideration of geographic problems and the mode of inquiry employed in reaching solutions to them. Since children can begin to learn to think geographically
at a very early age, experience with geographic problems should be provided in the kindergarten and continue throughout the years the child is
in school. Clearly, one does not expect original contributions to geographic understandings from such a course, but one *can* expect to
develop the habit of thinking geographically about out-of-school problems. If the geographic strand of the social studies curriculum has been
underemphasized in the past, the need today is to reassert its importance
in a manner based on modern conceptions of the nature of geographic
inquiry.

The importance of the teacher's knowledge of his subject has been
mentioned several times. Special note of the problem must be made here
because of the fact that few teachers have had any formal preparation in
this field. For most teachers, geographic study has not extended beyond
the junior high school years. Although this situation is changing, many
teachers still find themselves without the basic concepts and understandings essential for them to "feel at home" working with children in
geographic studies. Consequently, several books and other sources are
listed at the end of this chapter; these contain the kinds of information
helpful in dealing with this problem. In addition, the reader may turn
to geographic works dealing with the particular topic or problem he is
teaching. Librarians in public and college libraries can assist in the selection of suitable books.

Mapping is the key technique in geographic inquiry and the essential tool in geographic thinking. In order to record accurately the information he secures from his field and other studies, the geographer therefore must possess *cartographic,* or map making, skills. It is by means of
the map that the basic analysis of geographic phenomena occurs. Maps
show the areal relationships of things which have been observed and
located as no other instrument can do, and they provide information

about the distribution of those things as well as the frequency with which they occur. It is from this kind of information that the geographer develops generalizations concerning the significance of the things he has studied. He will also use maps prepared by others, of course, particularly to compare his own findings with those of others. But the primary use of the map is for recording that information which is germane to his particular study.

The map is basically a condensed representation of a much larger area and as such can take innumerable forms. Techniques of map making have become exceedingly sophisticated over the years. As a consequence, there are now many different types of special purpose maps. For instance, land-use maps show variations in the purposes to which man puts land. A large land-use map might show distributions of forest land, desert areas, agricultural land, urban complexes, and so forth. A land-use map showing a relatively small area might show land devoted to dwelling space, streets, parks, civic purposes, and schools and colleges. Relief maps indicate degree of slope and elevation for a given area. Other maps show the distribution of such diverse things as population, climate, rainfall, soils, crops, and minerals. Sometimes maps show combinations of things, a common one being political boundaries and physical relief. In addition to the wide variety of types of maps, new techniques are being developed which aid in the discovery of areal relationships or that assist in showing the distribution of particular kinds of things. An example of the first type is the transparent overlay which makes possible the visual perception of distributions of different things by superimposing several maps on top of each other. By looking through these, patterns of associations may be observed which otherwise might become extremely difficult to plot. An example of the second type of development is in the area of printing advances. Color rendition has improved to such an extent that relief-like maps, rather than showing elevation changes with separate colors, actually make it possible to visualize the relief of an area. Other printing advances make it possible to produce maps and globes which actually represent relief as it occurs in nature (at a much reduced scale and with distortion controlled equally).

Not every geographer will become a professional cartographer, but every geographer must possess knowledge of cartography and know how to develop an accurate map. Without these abilities, and without the map, his data become a hopeless jumble of facts and other odd scraps of information. Children, too, require experience at map making, starting with the very fundamental concept that the map is a representation of a larger piece of the real world and extending through understandings which deal with the concept of the grid as a technique of achieving accuracy in the location of things in the real world on a globe or flat piece of paper.

Building Geographic Understandings in the Classroom

The preceding discussion has emphasized four major characteristics of geography which are important in thinking about ways of planning a classroom program for boys and girls. First, it was noted that geography is concerned with the *description of things,* with the location and direction or *position of those things* from place to place, and with establishing the *significance of the areal relationships of things.* Second, it was noted that geography as a field of study is unified not by its subject matter but by its point of view and by its method. In this connection, emphasis was placed upon the concept of the region and the regional method in geographic inquiry, and the uniqueness of these to geographic thinking was pointed out. It was also reiterated that geography, like history, derives its subject matter from the entire range of human experience, both past and present, and that one without the other was virtually meaningless. Third, the importance of the map and mapping to every aspect of geographic thought was noted. And fourth, the development of concepts and generalizations about areal relationships was seen as the major goal of all geographic study.

Each of these four aspects of geographic inquiry may be seen to have applications for thinking about ways of working with children in the geographic strand of the social studies curriculum. In the discussion which follows, an attempt will be made to relate each of the four aspects of geographic inquiry to classroom experiences suitable for boys and girls.

DEVELOPING CHILDREN'S DESCRIPTIVE ABILITIES

The ability of people to describe accurately things which occur from place to place around them is fundamental to all geographic understandings. Children must start, of course, with what can be seen and experienced in the immediate environment. But the goal is to move beyond the visual horizon and to develop meaningful understandings of what things are like beyond this view. It is very easy to assume that children are aware of the things that surround them in their everyday life when, in fact, such awareness does not exist. And terms are often used in class work to describe these things for which inadequate or insufficient understanding exists. One common example applicable at almost all instructional levels is the idea of a "river mouth." Most children have a very difficult time with this idea, but there are other concepts, seemingly very simple, which are also misunderstood. One teacher in the dry southwest area of our country, for example, was surprised to find out that his seventh grade pupils had no idea what a river with water in it looked like. They had all had experience with dry rivers, a common feature where these children lived. But when the teacher described the force enabling large rivers to carry logs down to the coast to be processed in a lumber mill, his pupils thought he was deliberately trying to joke with them. Instances paralleling this kind of misunderstanding may be discovered every day. Urban children, for example, often do not really know what common farm animals are like. Frequently, they are completely unaware of the existence of even the best-known landmarks in their city and, often, even in their own neighboorhood. They may be led to discover what these and countless other things are like. Ideas must be developed for such things as rivers, plains, mountains, hills, valleys, cities, towns, and numerous other things. Even the simplest ideas are likely to be missed unless the teacher maintains an awareness that the children may not understand all of the ideas behind the words being so freely used in the classroom—by children and teachers alike.

Geographers have developed a special terminology to help make description of things in the environment even more accurate and meaningful. Geographic education involves the gradual introduction of these specialized terms as teachers increasingly demand more precision in the child's thought. The teacher's role, then, is to heighten the child's sensitivity to the everyday things around him, to help him become increasingly more precise in the way he describes them, and to assist him in growing (considering his level of maturity and his capacity to conceptualize) in his ability to describe accurately and meaningfully those things which occur from place to place beyond his immediate horizon.

To accomplish this objective, experiences designed to sensitize the child to the things which he observes and experiences within his immediate environment are begun in the kindergarten and continued through the primary grades. In sharpening perceptual abilities and developing greater accuracy in observation, description of everyday events becomes important in geographic thinking. Perhaps the child is asked to tell what he sees when he comes to school; the teacher asks him to think about the houses he passes on his way (their color, size, and shape, plantings around them, people near them); the child is asked which route he takes and what things were passed or what he came across (the names of streets, how wide they are, what kinds of traffic are on them, was there a policeman, was there a milk truck?). The teacher engages the children in recall of immediate past experience; he asks them to notice more the next time the experience is repeated. He suggests that they ask questions of their parents and others. Or, perhaps the children describe the weather on a particular day, tell what they observed on a trip around the school grounds, around the block, or on a trip to a place of interest near the school. What kinds of trees did they see (trees with leaves or without them, big ones, squat ones, etc.)? Did they see any animals (bugs, dogs, horses)? What kinds of plants were there (colors, sizes, and shapes; differences between grasses, trees, flowers, bushes)? How sensitive can children become to the nature of those things and can they be helped to find the words they need to describe what has been observed?

Later, the teacher may move to descriptions of things experienced vicariously. The children may watch a motion picture, or they may be asked to watch a particular television program. The teacher may bring into the classroom some flat pictures, or he may secure a filmstrip containing objects that encourage the children to think and talk. In this setting, the children have an opportunity to express their conceptions of things in ways other than discussion: they draw pictures of mountains and valleys; they write or dictate descriptions of a study trip they have taken; or they collect and label objects found on their school grounds or during a neighborhood walk.

Obviously, this is the sort of thing which can go on incidentally much of the time, but the teacher can also plan so that descriptive sensitivities are increased by design. Gradually, words and phrases are introduced that represent concepts which help make descriptions more precise. Special terms help clarify descriptions involving both man-made and natural elements in the environment of children. The nature and extent of the things the teacher will talk about with children depends upon their maturity levels, previous experience, and their apparent abilities to visualize and describe the things about them. It is probably true, however, that children's capabilities in description are overestimated.

Not only do they lack adequate concepts, an inability which leads to the misuse of terms (such as the previous example offered of the "river mouth"), but they are amazingly unaware of the obvious.

The abilities involved in accurate and meaningful description are developmental. Gradually, as the child moves through the intermediate and upper grades, he is expected to acquire concepts that will make it possible for him to describe things more precisely. For example, a plain is not just a plain; it has certain topographical characteristics which distinguish this plain from others, or which affect the way a particular plain is used. Mountains may be characterized explicitly. The vegetation growing in a particular area has certain unique qualities which may be stated with considerable precision. Everything in the environment may therefore be described so that the picture of it conjured up in the mind becomes more and more vivid. For example:

Plains may be	*Mountains may*	*Vegetation may be*
gently sloping	be in a chain or system	natural
very flat	have steep valleys	tropical
stream eroded	have high sharp peaks	forests
desiccated	be volcanic	grassy
old or young	be old or young	evergreen
alluvial	be forested	deciduous
terraced	be glaciated	swampy
glaciated	etc.	sparce
etc.		etc.

Soils may be	*Minerals may be*
fertile	used for fuel
acid	accessible or inaccessible
alkaline	strip mined
rocky	gas or liquid
alluvial	pure or in an ore
in humid lands	etc.
deposited and eroded	
etc.	

As the child grows in his abilities to describe the things that occur in one place and in another, he should also be better able to visualize things beyond his immediate view. The effect of a mountain barrier may be appreciated whether the evidences of that barrier are found near the eastern seaboard, in the Andes of South America, or in the Pyrenees of western Europe. The hazards of and opportunities for human occupancy in the southeast Asian plains, or in those of central Africa, can be visualized and meaningfully described. But meaningful description, it should be pointed out, does not only mean writing or telling about something. Pictures may be collected, put in order, and briefly captioned; drawings and charts may be made; and, of course, maps can be constructed to show what another part of the world is like.

TEACHING ABOUT LOCATION AND DIRECTION OR POSITION

To find the position of anything and to see it in relationship to other things involves concepts of direction and distance. Of these two major ideas, the most complex and difficult is that of direction. To compound the teacher's problem, the developmental characteristics of young children are such that many of them may experience mild to severe perceptual confusions, which, in turn, interfere with the ability to deal with directional concepts meaningfully. Although these confusions in most cases automatically clear up by the time the child is between eight and ten years of age, teachers who work with youngsters in the kindergarten and primary grades must realize that many boys and girls do not find it natural or easy to use such terms as "up" and "down," "left" or "right," "north," "east," and the other compass referents. Signs of disorientation in space, such as confusion when asked to show which is the right hand, may cause difficulties in learning in several curriculum areas in addition to social studies, most notably the reading and writing areas. It is important to be patient with children, recognizing that they may wish to learn but are experiencing true perceptual difficulties which make it impossible for them to see the logic in some basic ideas associated with direction.

The position of things in space can be represented with greatest accuracy through mapping. Therefore teachers begin mapping activities early and systematically continue them through every grade. At the earlier ages, care must be taken to observe the restrictions necessarily imposed by the nature of children's thinking. Aside from the fact that many children in the kindergarten and primary grades experience some disorientation in space which neither explanation nor memorization nor drill will clarify, these little boys and girls must begin mapping those things that are within their immediate environment—those things which they can experience directly and continuously while they are engaged in locating and recording information on the maps they are making. At first, this means activities by means of which the child can

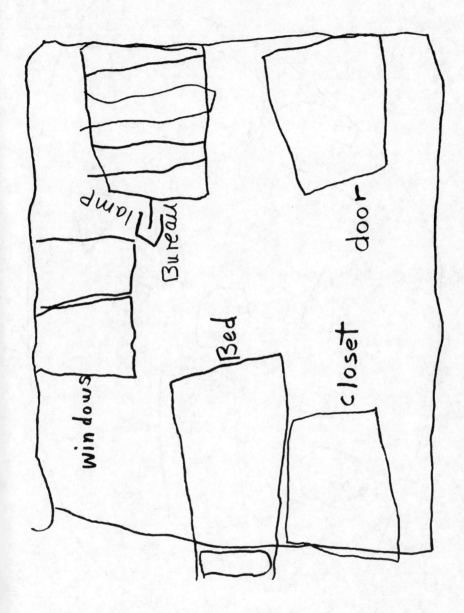

Figure 8—1: An example of a drawing of a child's bedroom at the kindergarten level. Note the interjection of three-dimensional qualities. This is
normal for this level of maturity. Labels of items have been added for clarity.

Figure 8–2: An example of a drawing of a child's bedroom at the kindergarten level. This illustration represents a less mature attempt at mapping than does Figure 8–1.

see everything he needs for his map. Three-dimensional figures are also helpful at these beginning stages. Usually, the teacher will begin with the classroom itself. Perhaps children will develop maps of their room at home. But one cannot expect children at this age in school to map their bedroom at home. They must be able to see and record what they see in one operation.

The first objective is to teach the concept of what the map is. In their own ways, children discover that a map is nothing more than a representation of a given space or area drawn to a reduced scale on which things are located and shown in proportion to each other and in proper relation to one another. Small children will struggle mightily with the problem of getting things in proportion, and they will be satisfied that everything *is* shown correctly long before the adult would be willing to give in. And, of course, the problem of proportion and proper positioning of things on the map is always going to be present. In the beginning, the teacher helps reduce the frustrations which come about by trying to get everything into proper relationship with other things by using standard objects. Model furniture, blocks, standardized sizes of paper to represent different classes of things all contribute to this end.

When children understand what purposes are accomplished by mapping, they can begin to develop maps for areas beyond their direct line of vision. However, they must be able to refer to those areas easily in order to see that items on the maps are properly positioned. For example, the teacher may first have children map their own school, or a portion of it, by using standard sized pieces of paper to represent the various rooms and places located nearby. First taping a piece of paper to the floor to represent their own room, the teacher asks the children what is next door, what is beyond this point or that, until many pieces of paper have been arranged to depict the area being mapped. In most instances, the children at this level will need to send out groups to *see* what actually *is* next door. Although they have been there many times, the problem of getting the proper location and direction of things in the school has not previously been considered. It is therefore a new problem and one for which evidence must be gathered. Gradually, this kind of activity can be extended to include the area immediately adjacent to the school, then to the neighborhood, and finally beyond. The criterion of being able to ascertain personally the proper location and direction of things is the important one.

When the area to be mapped has extended beyond the immediate horizons of the child and when information about the locations of things can no longer be verified by immediate first-hand observation, work must begin on the concept of the grid more directly. The squares made by city blocks, where streets form the grid or frame of reference within which things may be located, provide a convenient pattern with which to begin. Many areas in which recent building has occurred have used patterns other than the conventional rectangular one, and, in these instances, it may be difficult to make use of such areas in the classroom. Even so, many such new patterns are developed within a larger scheme which follow the rectangular one, and thus they are not as confusing as first observation might suggest.

By the time the child has entered the intermediate grades, he should be ready to deal with problems in location and distance that are not dependent upon his ability to check for accuracy the information recorded through direct experiencing. It is at this juncture that concepts of distortion are introduced. Since the only true representation of the earth must account for the fact that the earth is shaped more or less like a ball, any effort to render a portion of the earth to a flat surface results in some distortion. Obviously, the larger the area to be shown on a flat map, the greater the problems of distortion. Distortion also occurs in the sense that, when larger areas are shown on the map, the symbols which are used must often be larger than the space they occupy in real life or they must be generalizations of the area in question. Elevation, boundary lines, rivers, signs for railroads and highways are examples of the first problem. Relief, symbols which represent complex networks (e.g., the detail in a delta or a transportation system), signs which indicate the density of activity and its distribution (such as a population map), and those which show the distribution of some specific phenomenon (e.g., dominant crops grown in an area or land-use patterns) represent the latter type of problem.

Incorrect concepts and generalizations are easily encouraged by the use of the flat map. This is particularly true where considerable distance exists between things. Consider, for example, the commonly held notion that the coastline of the Pacific in the United States roughly parallels that of Asia. The flat map, and particularly the Mercator projection, encourages this kind of thinking. On the globe, it is readily apparent that these coastlines form one continuous line. Other examples of distortion might be cited (the size of Greenland, or of the U.S.S.R.; the position of South America in relation to North America; the most direct route to

Tokyo from the United States.[8] In teaching about spatial relationships which involve large portions of the earth's surface, the use of the globe is preferable to that of the flat map. Without doubt, the money spent on flat maps of the world for use in the elementary schools would be far better spent on large globes.

Another problem occurs with respect to the direction of "north" and other compass points. Since virtually every flat map shows north to be at the top of the page, children identify "up" with north and "down" with south.[9] Greater use of the globe and the selection of flat maps in which *north* is located at other positions can help to overcome this difficulty.

Location and direction, or position, can be mathematically described and can be indicated in relative terms. Children will gain an understanding of mathematical location by experiencing directly the problems of locating things in space by means of the concepts of latitude and longitude. Teaching these concepts didactically in the intermediate and upper grades is difficult, if not impossible. But if children have had previous experiences in preparing their own maps they will have the necessary background. Then increasingly they will be able to use mathematical modes for expressing position. One way to involve children in activities requiring the use of latitude and longitude is through the building of a model globe. This procedure is described in Chapter Ten. By the conclusion of the elementary school years, at the ages of thirteen or fourteen, every child should have had experiences in dealing with the mathematical concepts of position.

Relative location has to do with the idea that distance and direction vary according to the uses of things, or according to the purposes for which they might be used. In discussing the relative location of Los Angeles to New York, for instance, one might think of them as four hours apart by jet, three days apart by train, a few minutes apart in

[8] An attempt to combine the many practical uses of a flat map such as that of the Mercator projection with the advantages of the globe in seeing relationships was that of the Telecurve map. This consists of a Mercator map on which the curving lines of direction and distance are shown. Unfortunately, the idea did not prove popular with school people so these maps have never been as widely used as they deserve. Ideas shown through these maps would have considerable application particularly at the upper grades. For an explanation of these maps and their applications, see Felix Locher, "Reading Maps of the World," Fifteenth Yearbook, *Claremont College Reading Conference* (Claremont, California: 1950), pp. 87-118. Devices of this type assist in reading more accurately the orbits of space vehicles when those orbits circumscribe the earth.

[9] In medieval times, maps were drawn with east at the top. Hence maps are now "oriented." But the orientation is no longer to the east; instead, it is the north.

© United Feature Syndicate, Inc. 1966. Reprinted by permission.

terms of instantaneous communication. The distances and directions involved vary according to the modes of transportation (ship, plane, automobile, train). Many other spatial relationships exist between the two
cities: the markets which they supply in common, the political relationships between the two, the cultural ties. Concepts of relative location
along with those of geomatical (or mathematical) location are used to
describe geographic *position*. Many opportunities present themselves at
every grade level to work on concepts of relative location as well as the
more exact descriptions which are necessary in mapping and in reading
maps.

TEACHING CHILDREN TO ATTRIBUTE SIGNIFICANCE
TO AREAL RELATIONSHIPS

It is not enough to heighten sensitivity to things in the environment
and to build understandings of the relationships of things in space; one
must also raise the question of the *meaning* of the relationships perceived. Geographic studies with children are therefore concerned with
questions designed to help boys and girls think through the importance
of the things they observe. Why does the postman deliver the mail every
day? Why is it important to have trucks bring packages of mail to the
storage boxes we saw on our walks around town? Why are there so
many storage boxes? Why are they located where they are? From such
questions for beginners, the processes of maturation lead to increasingly
more complex ideas. Questions of this type are designed to help children
think about the importance of the areal relationships of things.

It has already been emphasized that it is easy to overestimate the
extent of children's understanding. Questions which draw out the
child's estimate of the significance of his observations provide an important guide to appreciating the degree of his understanding of the

relationships of things he has discovered. "Why?" and "What if?" questions help in this process. They are also valuable in heightening sensitivity to relationships for which awareness is low or nonexistent and in encouraging the child to evaluate geographic ideas systematically.

THE MEANING OF THE REGIONAL CONCEPT AND THE REGIONAL METHOD FOR TEACHING GEOGRAPHIC STUDIES

The concepts of the *region* and the *regional method* provide important frameworks for thinking about geographic ideas in the classroom. For example, the regional method provides a frame of reference for thinking about the size and composition of the area selected for study with children; also, it helps identify the problem or question, thus providing a focus for the study. The regional method, on the other hand, suggests ways the study of the region may progress, the kinds of tools needed to conduct the study, and ways geographic thinking may be encouraged.

The Concept of the Region in the Classroom. As noted earlier, the concept of the region proposes that the earth's surface can be divided into areas which are homogeneous with respect to certain characteristics. Any area so identified will not be entirely uniform or homogeneous— it might be subdivided continually until hardly any space or area were left (even the smallest patch of dirt is composed of different ingredients). James has suggested that the criteria for selecting a region must be based on whether the particular region illuminates a geographic problem. He points out that "regions are defined for specific purposes, and for each purpose a different regional system is needed. Regions are judged good or bad by the degree they illuminate a problem: regions that have the effect of obscuring area relationships are bad regions."[10]

If the comments of the geographer about the regions selected for developing geographic studies with children are considered seriously, the teacher will select regions that illuminate the problem or question uppermost in his mind. In choosing a particular study, then, the teacher should first ask himself: what problem are we seeking to understand and what region illustrates that problem? There are many kinds of regions; some will be good for our purposes and others will be unsuitable.

Geographic scholarship can make teachers more aware of the dangers and opportunities inherent in defining the regions used in studies carried

[10] Preston E. James, "Geography," in *The Social Studies and the Social Sciences* (New York: Harcourt, Brace, and World, Inc., 1962), p. 51.

out by boys and girls. For example, geographers warn that the traditional concept of the continents as viable regions needs to be examined. The splitting of Europe and Asia, and the impact of this on dividing the study of the U.S.S.R., is the most awkward example of this kind of regional differentiation. But strange things happen to other areas. Central America, Egypt, and Antarctica are examples where problems arise in such regional differentiation. Another traditional pattern of organization which is based on outmoded geographic thinking is that of climatic regions. Torrid, temperate, and frigid zones do not adequately describe the distribution of climates; in fact, gross misconceptions accrue from such divisions. The growing emphasis upon man's role in determining how the environment shall be used, rather than upon the old concept that the environment is the major determiner of his occupance of the land, has led to the development of the concept of culture regions. Instead of arbitrarily drawn lines, these provide a framework for thinking about areal differences based on the most important determiner of how space or area will be used—*man*. Geographers today generally agree that there are eleven culture regions; these, however, are being modified as times and events change man's relationships to his fellow man around the globe.

The Eleven Culture Regions of the World

European
  Western, southern, and northern Europe
Soviet
  The Soviet Union and eastern Europe
Anglo-American
  Canada and the United States
Latin American
  Mexico, Central America, South America, the Antilles, and the Bahamas
North African-Southwest Asian
  The Moslem countries from Morocco to Afghanistan and Israel
South Asian
  India, Pakistan, Ceylon, and border countries
Southeast Asian
  The "shatter belt" between India and China
East Asian
  China, Japan, and bordering countries

African
  The countries south of the Sahara
Australian-New Zealand
  The countries of British origin in Australasia
Pacific
  The islands of Melanesia, Micronesia, and Polynesia[11]

When planning a geographic study for even the very youngest child, one should identify the region; this helps the study find a focus useful in encouraging the development of geographic thinking. Beginning studies of the school, the immediate neighborhood, or the community provide opportunities to define the area of concern and to think about the common characteristics of that particular space or area, as well as to discover the nature of the differences that occur from place to place within it. Studies of the metropolitan area in which the children are living (about two-thirds of the people in the United States live within 216 regions called Standard Metropolitan Statistical Areas), of their state, or the region of states take place within regions as the geographer defines them. In each of these studies, the regional concept can be applied as a helpful means for setting limits on the dimensions of the study and for providing a frame of reference for identifying the geographic ideas which are the goals of teaching.

The Regional Method in the Classroom. As noted previously, the *regional method* is the term used to describe the way the geographer goes about discovering and evaluating geographic information. In this process, three considerations concern him: (1) he identifies the specific problem he wishes to investigate; (2) he utilizes various sources of information and tools of research, some of which are peculiarly "geographic"; (3) he attempts to develop concepts and generalizations about the areal relationships he has studied.

In surveying the areal association of things, geographic studies do not consist of simply developing inventories of all those things that can be described and located within a region. Rather, they focus upon those physical, biotic, and cultural features for which causal relationships can be established and which give the area under scrutiny its distinctive character. Thus it is important that the problems under investigation be stated clearly enough so that children can distinguish between significant and relatively unimportant information. Identifying the differences between the relevant and the irrelevant obviously takes

[11] *Ibid.,* p. 81.

time and practice, but well asked questions will help a great deal. Just as the geographer must devote considerable effort to defining the problem he proposes to investigate, so children with their teacher need to take time to clarify the questions and problems about which they want information.

Below are listed some kinds of problems which might be posed to children concerning important aspects of geographic study. The reader is asked to rephrase the questions so that they will apply to a geographic study focusing on an area which children at a particular grade level might study. Finally, it is characteristic of geographic inquiry to ask "Where?" and to endeavor to understand the "Why?" How might the reader state these questions so that they will ask "Why?" as well as "Where?"

1. Questions which illustrate problems of *population distribution*. (In a given area) Where do people live? Who are they? What do they do? How many are there? Ancillary questions include: Can the land support a greater population? What effects do such things as relief, slope, and elevation have on distribution? Are there relationships between weather, climate, soils, and water and population?

2. Questions which illustrate problems of *natural resources*. (In a given area) What are the natural resources? How are they used? Have they always been considered of value to man? Ancillary questions include: How can natural resources change in value to man? Can resources be destroyed? How can they be conserved?

3. Questions which illustrate problems of *land use*. (In a given area) What kinds of purposes does man find for the land? Where is his use of the land intensive and where slight? What natural and what human conditions influence land-use patterns? Ancillary questions include: What is the effect of the earth's size, shape, and motions upon land use? How do soils and natural vegetation differ? What makes land valuable?

4. Questions which illustrate problems about *surface features, climates, and vegetation*. (In a given area) What are the characteristics of the surface features? The climate? The vegetation? What interrelationships exist between these three factors? Ancillary questions include: What is the relationship between land and water features? What

is the relationship between climatic factors and weather conditions—rainfall and temperature. How are man's activities related to each of the three natural features of the area?

Since geographic study includes both human and natural elements, problems can be formulated which deal exclusively with either those human or natural elements in areal association with each other, or they may consider the interrelationships persisting between them. The range of geographic topics for which significant problems might be formulated could be very extensive. In human affairs, for example, the concern might be the economic, political, social, recreational, aesthetic, and other types of associations observable among men. The basic human activities provide a framework for appreciating how extensive those relationships might be. In the natural environment, one might also identify an extended list of elements, resources, or raw materials which describe the physical earth as the home of man. One such list developed by Kendall and his associates is useful as a basis for thinking about the elements in the natural environment which man utilizes in his occupancy of the earth:

Elements of the Human Habitat

Physical	Cultural
A. Atmosphere (Air)	A. Man
1. Weather	1. Population
2. Climate	a. Numbers
B. Lithosphere (Earth)	b. Distribution over the earth
1. Earth materials	c. Density
a. Bedrock	2. Cultural groups
b. Regolith,	a. Major groups
especially soils	b. Other groups
c. Minerals	3. Cultural institutions
2. Surface configuration	a. Languages
a. Continents	b. Religions
and islands	c. Political units
b. Major	B. Works of Man
landforms	1. Settlements
c. Minor landforms	a. Rural
C. Hydrosphere (Water)	b. Urban
1. Oceans and seas	2. Forms resulting from economies or ways of life

   2. Waters of the land   a. Hunting, fishing, and
      a. Surface water   gathering
      b. Ground water   b. Pastoralism
   3. Glaciers and icecaps   c. Agriculture
D. Biosphere (Life)   d. Exploitation of earth
   1. Native plants   resources, *i.e.*, lumbering,
   2. Native animals   e. Manufacture
                                         3. Routes of transportation and
                                            communication[12]

In the process of studying areal associations of various kinds, geographic study relies upon certain kinds of sources of information more than upon others. The map is *the* unique tool of geographic study, of course, not only because it provides a valuable source of information but because of its central importance in recording and analyzing data. Geographic study is also singularly concerned with direct observation in the field and with those substitutes for direct observation which come as close as possible to the thing itself, e.g., photographs, motion pictures, models, artifacts, and samples taken directly from the field. The following listing of resources for discovering information of a geographic nature suggests the wide range of places children may turn to in their search to discover answers to the geographic problems in which the teacher has interested them.

Sources for Locating and Gathering Geographic Information

Reading materials
    Books: textbooks, readers, trade books (fiction and non-fiction), encyclopedias, atlases, dictionaries, almanacs
    Periodicals: magazines, newspapers, reports, bulletins, government publications
Community resources
    Businesses
    Communication media
    Cultural opportunities
    Government: local, regional, state, national
    Historical places of interest
    Industrial enterprises

[12] H. M. Kendall, R. Glendinning, and C. H. McFadden, *Introduction to Geography*, second edition (New York: Harcourt, Brace and Company, 1958), p. 5.

Transportation services
Recreation and play
Interviews and guest speakers
Field trips
Community surveys
Motion pictures, filmstrips, and slides
Charts, graphs, posters
Recordings, radio, and television[13]

An examination of the above list suggests that geographic inquiry utilizes many modes of communication other than the written form. This is because it is extremely difficult to express spatial relationships in an expository manner. Too often, what is written turns into a series of statements listing facts and other data. It may laboriously describe relationships of things which could more easily and directly be told by using another manner of reporting. The preparation of maps, charts, and graphs; the collection of pictures and samples; and the construction of models consequently become prime means for expressing ideas about areal associations. Geographic studies should not be devoid of written expression, but they do offer opportunities to extend children's reporting experiences in dimensions other than the one which receives such heavy emphasis in other curriculum areas.

Developing Concepts and Generalizations in the Classroom. Geographic inquiry takes the child into a wide range of ideas, both from the physical and from the natural sciences. The concepts and generalizations to be developed are therefore not drawn exclusively from any one field of study. Their major common characteristic is that they are *thought about* primarily in terms of their power to describe the areal or spatial associations of things in the environment of man. It is therefore impossible to develop a comprehensive list of concepts which should be developed in elementary schools, although attempts have been made along these lines. It is possible, however, to identify certain concepts with technical meanings that are particularly relevant to problems which arise in describing the areal associations of things. The following list of terms represents one attempt along these lines.[14]

---

[13] Adapted from Ella C. Leppert, "Location and Gathering Information," *Skill Development in the Social Studies,* Helen McCracken Carpenter, editor, Thirty-third Yearbook, National Council for the Social Studies (1963), pp. 53-73.

[14] The reader should keep in mind that words and phrases stand for, but are not themselves, concepts. A concept is an intellectual construct representing all the ideas that a person may have about a particular thing.

continents
the poles
earth size and shape
earth motions
land and water
earth-sun relations
earth-solar system
    relations
earth-galactic
    relations
cardinal directions
compass
magnetic north
hemispheres
latitude
longitude
islands
isthmus
mountain
hill
summit
plains
equator
relief
elevation
slope
oceans
lakes
rivers
river mouth
river source
tides
underground waters
surface waters
streams
sun energy
seasons
precipitation
dry lands
ravines
irrigation
forest types
soil types
weather
climate (types)
vegetative cover
    (types)
company

pastoral
manufacturing
landscape
domesticated animals
farm animals
great circle route
agriculture
nation
meridian
    (prime and others)
homelands
province
state
nation
map symbols
    (various)
seasons
solstices
pastures
sea level
glaciated
desiccated
eroded
peninsula
canyon
delta
gulf
channel
strait
tropics
temperate zone
wells and springs
sources of fresh water
flood waters
frost
city
town
hamlet
capital city
truck farms
transportation
conservation
fertilizer
Arctic Circle
Antarctic Circle
Tropic of Cancer
Tropic of Capricorn
river system

volcano
rock (types)
floodplain
mountain peaks
cape
bay
valley
crops
natural plant life
natural animal life
timber and
    timber line
rain forests
population
Orient
boundary lines
routes
goods
town
navigable
mining
lumbering
seaport and port
foreign trade
renewable resource
time zone
armaments
suburbs
raw materials
natural resources
ore
coal
iron
miner
pasture
plantation
commercial crop
dairy
belt
petroleum
natural gas
trade
manufacturing
industrial country
factories (types)
power
barter
relative location

imports and exports	temperature	mathematical
immigration	altitude	location
transportation	hurricane	humid
(types)	equinoxes	middle latitudes
primitive man and	tundras	market
primitive ways	snowline	light industry
harbor	inhabitants	heavy industry
canal	settlements	hydroelectric power
coastline	customs	domestic trade
vegetation	raw materials	degrees of longitude
ocean floor	resources	and latitude
reefs	machinery	

Children should have experience with ideas relating to most of these terms by the time they complete their eighth or ninth year in school. Obviously, they will not develop concepts of this sort exclusively within the framework of the geographic studies planned for them. Studies which are essentially historical, economic, political, or perhaps those in the area of science, will provide many opportunities for contact with these geographic ideas lying behind these words and phrases.

Teaching Children to Generalize about Areal Relationships. The importance of generalizing, and some of the ways in which this process is accomplished, was discussed in an earlier chapter. Here, as in every other social study, teachers should plan studies so that children are encouraged to generalize about their experiences. Several excellent lists of generalizations dealing with geographic ideas are available and the reader is encouraged to consult them. Here the primary emphasis should be on the process of generalizing about areal associations discovered by the child.

Children learn to generalize when they are encouraged to try out their own ideas concerning what they believe they have observed. The teacher's questions can help a child develop skill in generalizing, but the teacher cannot supply the generalization for the child; the child must understand the concepts and facts behind it. Nor can children in the earliest grades of school be expected to go much beyond their own first-hand experience. As one youngster put it, "The Indians *we* studied about lived in places where they could get out of the cold in the winter time." She did not think it relevant to talk about what Indians living in other cold climates might have done to solve the heating problem. And at even a younger age, children will generalize, as one did quite adequately about why stop signs and warning signs had been placed on the streets around his school. But it is only later that children of this age will conclude that unknown streets and highways beyond their view (those they have not seen or experienced directly) also are marked with signs for similar purposes.

In the intermediate and upper grades, children experience a rapidly growing capacity to see areal associations and to generalize about them. For example, the pattern of agricultural uses of land is related meaningfully to population distribution and to the motions of the earth. Or, land productivity can be related to combinations of farming techniques, climate, soil fertility, and availability of a market. Children at this age are much more able to think logically and to relate direct experience to vicarious experiencing secured through reading books, seeing pictures, and combining information discovered in these and other sources on a map. Consequently, generalizing appears to be more fruitful at this age; but the processes of thinking about geographic ideas have their roots in the work of the primary grades. If children are encouraged then to express their ideas and to make mistakes as well as to give the "right" answers, they will use good thinking later on. If they learn that the teacher does not really want to spend time waiting for them to think, then they will short-circuit reasoning procedures in an attempt to supply the teacher with the answer they think he expects.

How does one learn *how* to help children generalize? Generally, not by reading a book but, rather, by being sensitive to the nature of the child's thinking by learning *how to ask good questions.* The best way for anyone to achieve this goal is to work directly with children.

The gaining of geographic concepts, the forming of generalizations in the area of geographic studies, can be filled with much excitement for a child. Using globes, beginning at an early age, in preference to flat maps may give him the feeling, described by Joyce Cary in *A House of Children,* that he is riding on a round world, that he can feel the roundness of the earth beneath his feet. Geographic studies can carry him far from his own doorstep, can feed his growing curiosity with all sorts of ideas from the natural and physical sciences. It can open windows for him upon the world.

FOR FURTHER READING

American Council of Learned Societies and the National Council for the Social Studies, *The Social Studies and the Social Sciences* (New York: Harcourt, Brace & World, 1962).

Broek, Jan O. M., *Geography: Its Scope and Spirit* (Columbus, Ohio: Charles E. Merrill Books, Inc., 1965).

Gopsill, G. H., *The Teaching of Geography* (London: Macmillan & Company, 1956).

Hanna, Paul R., *et. al., Geography in the Teaching of Social Studies: Concepts and Skills* (Boston: Houghton Mifflin Company, 1966).

Hartshorne, Richard, *Perspective on the Nature of Geography* (Chicago: Rand McNally & Company, 1959).

James, Preston E. and Clarence F. Jones (eds.), *American Geography: Inventory and Prospect* (Syracuse, New York: Syracuse University Press, 1954).

Hunt, Earling M., *et. al., High School Social Studies Perspectives* (Boston: Houghton Mifflin Company, 1962).

Michaelis, John U. and A. Montgomery Johnston (eds.), *The Social Sciences: Foundations of the Social Studies* (Boston: Allyn and Bacon, Inc., 1965).

Mitchell, Lucy Sprague, *Young Geographers* (New York: John Day Company, 1934).

Morrissett, Irving (ed.), *Concepts and Structure in the New Social Science Curricula* (West Lafayette, Indiana: Social Science Education Consortium, Inc., 1966).

National Council for Geographic Education, *Curriculum Guide to Geographic Education* (Publications Center, Illinois State Normal University, 1963).

National Council for the Social Studies, *New Viewpoints in Geography* Twenty-ninth Yearbook (Washington, D.C.: N.C.S.S., 1959).

National Council for the Social Studies, *New Viewpoints in the Social Sciences*, Twenty-eighth Yearbook (Washington, D.C.: N.C.S.S., 1958).

Peattie, Roderick, *The Teaching of Geography* (New York: Appleton-Century-Crofts, Inc., 1950).

Piaget, Jean, *The Child's Conception of Space* (New York: Humanities Press, 1956).

Thralls, Zoe A., *The Teaching of Geography* (New York: Appleton-Century-Crofts, Inc., 1958).

CHAPTER NINE

The Method of Discovery:
The Other Social Sciences

Historical and geographic emphases in social studies must be balanced against the contributions of other fields of the social sciences if a sound curriculum of social studies is to evolve. The overall curriculum pattern that results may be a combination of separate and unified disciplines approaches. Scholars active in proposing ways of improving social science education are not in agreement about the advantages of one approach over the other. Major projects representing both points of view are under way as part of the curriculum reform movement in social studies, leading one to the conclusion that the dichotomy is not likely to be resolved in the near future. Very likely it is not desirable to achieve agreement on this point since the rapidity with which knowledge is being discovered is altering the face of the traditional social science disciplines and causing new fields of inquiry to be created. To elect one view over the other may constitute an error since, it is clear, both approaches offer values for learning. Thus we may decide to study a problem in economic education, a separate disciplines approach, much like that being advocated by Senesh.[1]

Geography and history, then, are *synthesis disciplines;* that is, they may be identified not on the basis of their unique concern but through the manner in which data are organized and through the methods employed in creating significance for those data. Certainly, the history or geography of any topic may be studied; i.e., any matter of concern may be thought about either historically or geographically.

Such is not so clearly the case with the "other social sciences"; each

[1] See *Our Working World* by Lawrence Senesh (Chicago: Science Research Associates, 1964-65).

may be seen to have a special focus, a particular concern. Economics, for example, inquires into the nature of man's economic relationships. In the study of those relationships, it may draw upon geography, history, political science, and other disciplines; still, the focus is clear. Sociology, briefly defined, concerns itself with the study of man in groups. It, too, may utilize information from a wide variety of sources; yet, the limitations of what is appropriate to sociological inquiry are preserved with reasonable sharpness. Each of the "other" disciplines of the social sciences has its unique concern, some rather narrowly focused; others, such as sociology and anthropology, have a very broad view.

The "other social sciences" do not, however, possess uniquely different research methods. Although particular research techniques may avail the political scientist to a greater degree than to a researcher in another discipline, by and large the modes of inquiry of value to one may have equal value to another. As we shall see, economists, sociologists, political scientists, and anthropologists are all concerned that students learn to "think" in ways appropriate to the problems their field of inquiry is most concerned about. However, this objective does not carry with it the specificity that learning to utilize the historic method does to the historian or the regional method to the geographer.

Separate Disciplines or Unified Social Science Approach?

In planning the classroom program of social studies, the teacher may elect to draw upon concepts and generalizations selected primarily from one of the social science disciplines such as economics or government. Or, he may choose to focus on a problem or issue which utilizes ideas from several of them. Such a study could be followed by a study rooted in a multidisciplinary approach. An example of the latter is the long-term projects sponsored by the American Council of Learned Societies and Educational Services Incorporated.[2] It would appear that the greater value is to be gained for boys and girls not by adhering rigidly to one or the other of the approaches but by designing a social studies curriculum that engages children in classroom encounters with ideas that are vivid and stimulating.

[2] See *Occasional Papers*, The Social Studies Curriculum Program (Cambridge, Mass. 02138: Educational Services Incorporated, 1965). Descriptions of the programs as they are developing may be secured upon request.

Contributions of Economics to Social Studies

THE NATURE OF ECONOMICS AND ECONOMIC INQUIRY

Economics has been described as "the study of how men and society *choose,* with or without the use of money, to employ *scarce* productive resources to produce various commodities over time and distribute them for consumption."[3] Put another way, economics may be considered to be the study of (1) the ways societies allocate their resources, which are always in short supply, to produce goods and services and (2) how those goods and services are distributed to meet never-ending human needs and wants.

Recognition that the public in general and teachers in particular have had poor and frequently inaccurate notions of the nature of economics and the ways in which the economist goes about his work has led to the publication of a number of valuable materials in the recent past. Some of these materials will be mentioned here. The reader is encouraged to consult the bibliography listed at the conclusion of this chapter for more detailed information.

What Economics Is and What It Is Not. Although everyone is engaged in the practice of economics in his daily life, those experiences do not necessarily lead one to an understanding of economics. For example, compare your version of the nature of economics with the following statement of the Joint Council on Economic Education:

1. Economics is *not* the same as personal finance. While the consumer plays a vitally important role in the economy, an exclusive devotion to "wise buying," how to open a savings account, etc. is not by itself "economics." A study of the behavior of the consumer is *part* of economics but only part.

Economics *is* concerned with society as a whole and with the activities of the various groups who constitute society, including consumers, businessmen, farmers, workers, savers, investors, and federal, state, and local government. It is *a social science.*

2. Economics is concerned not only with the individual parts of our economy, such as the consumer, the business, the union, and the market for a particular product such as automobiles (which we call *micro-economics*) but also with the functioning of the economy as a whole—with how fast it is growing, for example, and how vulnerable it is to inflation or depression (which we call *macro-economics*).

3. While many economic concepts can be understood by reference to

[3] Paul A. Samuelson, *Economics: An Introductory Analysis,* sixth edition (New York: McGraw-Hill, 1964), p. 5.

personal experiences or through "role-playing" (e.g., being a consumer), real economic understanding requires an ability to reason abstractly and to consider society as a whole rather than just one's own position in it.

4. Economics is *not* just a study of current events and the weighing of the pros and cons of an issue in the morning newspaper. It is a *social science*, which seeks to develop the ability to define and analyze a problem in a rational way, using scientific methods; and to identify goals, the alternative ways of reaching them, and the consequences of following each possible line of action.

To have economic understanding does *not* mean that one has memorized "facts." It means that one has acquired certain "ways of thinking" about economic problems—a scientific method comparable to that involved in physics or chemistry, which permits one to make rational choices among alternatives. The real test of economic understanding is whether or not one has the ability to deal with future economic problems, as they arise, in an organized scientific way.

Thus, the heart of economics is the awareness of and ability to use a set of analytical tools which we call *economic theory*. In this respect, economics is no different from other disciplines. It is, as noted, a *social science*.

5. Economics is not concerned merely with static situations—with how institutions function at this moment alone—but also with the dynamics of change and adjustment to change. For example, in economics one studies the way in which prices are determined by supply and demand but one also studies the process of growth and the problems which arise as a result of the changes involved in growth over a period of time.

6. Economists *are* concerned with value judgments but *not* with making them. Both personal goals and broader social objectives are, of course, important. Rational choices among alternative lines of action can be made only in the light of clearly stated goals. Thus, economic goals (such as growth, stability, efficiency, justice, security, and freedom) need to be identified clearly. They represent the value judgments of our society and of the people in it. But, while economists operate within a framework of value judgments with respect to goals, they keep their prescriptions of them to a minimum.

7. Finally, to have economic understanding means that one possesses certain skills, including the ability to interpret statistics, the ability to use certain tools of analysis (economic theory), and a sense of the historical evolution of human events.[4]

The Nature of Economic Inquiry. The preceding statement emphasizes that the study of economic problems involves use of the "scientific method," and it asserts that economic inquiry incorporates unique "ways

---

[4] Adapted from James D. Calderwood, "Economic Ideas and Concepts," *Teachers Guide to Developmental Economic Education Program, Part One.* (New York: Joint Council on Economic Education, 2 West Sixth St., New York, N.Y., 1964), pp. 2-3.

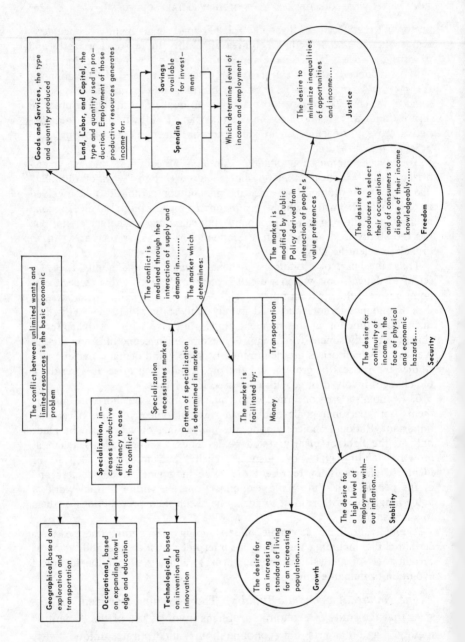

Figure 9–1: The Fundamental Idea Relationships of Economic Knowledge. (From *Our Working World: Neighbors at Work* by Lawrence Senesh. Copyright © 1965, Science Research Associates, Inc. Reprinted by permission of the publisher.)

of thinking." What, then, can be the distinguishing characteristics of the mode of inquiry one uses in thinking about economic problems? First, consider the type of problem in which the economist is interested. The field of economics is concerned with studying the economic relationships between human beings and their material world. An impression of the many parts of man's economic world, and the complexity of the inter-relationships between those parts, may be gained by studying the chart appearing on page 264.[5]

Second, economic questions are studied through application of the *scientific method*. In advancing their knowledge of economic behavior:

They gather the facts and figures which they judge to be economic in nature, often relying on the assistance of the accountant, historian, and statistician. They group those facts and figures which appear to be of the same kind or to belong together, thus bringing some order to the raw data and reducing the number of individual items that must be studied. Econo-mists study the groups of facts and figures to see if they can detect any relationship between them. Upon noting a possible relationship, they form a tentative hypothesis or explanation which they then proceed to verify or test by applying the hypothesis to additional facts of the same kind which had suggested the hypothesis. If testing indicates the correctness of the hypothesis, economists believe that an addition has been made to the stock of reliable economic knowledge.[6]

Economic inquiry therefore seeks objectivity. In achieving this objec-tivity it is aided by the fact that much information of an economic nature can be quantified. Thus the economist must also be skilled in mathematics and in employing statistics in seeking to establish relation-ships among his data. But economics remains a social rather than a physical science. Questions of value permeate his concerns. Why people behave the way they do—why they find economic value in some things more than in others—and the consequences of the value they place upon things make economic questions difficult to answer with the precision (and its accompanying predictive power) which people in the natural sciences may expect. This is why economists, in suggesting future courses of action and in conjecturing on the differing consequences of alternate economic policies, so often find themselves in disagreement.

[5] Lawrence Senesh, "The Fundamental Idea Relationships of Economic Knowl-edge," *Our Working World,* Teachers Edition (Chicago: Science Research Associ-ates, Inc., 1965).

[6] Ronald H. Wolf, "Economics," in *The Social Sciences: Foundations of the Social Studies,* John U. Michaelis and A. Montgomery Johnston, editors, (Boston: Allyn and Bacon, Inc., 1965), pp. 153-154.

Human motives and human behavior are so variable, so uncontrollable, that economic inquiry can never predict the future. But, by furthering understanding of man's economic relationships, one can further his understanding of the alternatives in the very complex economic system in which people live and illumine the manner in which that system functions to meet his material wants and needs. The result of this search for knowledge opens more opportunities to satisfy those wants and needs and provides a major means for improving the economic conditions affecting human endeavors.

ECONOMIC INQUIRY IN THE CLASSROOM

Arguments for including studies containing an economic emphasis propose that topics and problems be included at all levels of schooling. Although there has been disagreement whether the "dismal science" could be taught effectively, even at the secondary level, recent thinking emphasizes that it is not the nature of the subject matter but the ideas and the methods used in presenting them to children which are crucial.

As one examines the curriculum of the elementary school, the most noticeable quality to be observed is that social studies traditionally have been organized according to the *expanding communities concept,* with the scope of the program frequently determined by the *basic human activities.* Although these ideas may be interpreted in slightly different ways, the result is a program which emphasizes utilizing concepts from the social science disciplines primarily on a "unified social science approach."[7] The teacher whose social studies program is based on such an overall curriculum pattern will want to select economic ideas which will fit well into the types of studies within this framework for determining what the curriculum shall be. A recent development, as noted elsewhere, evolving as part of the curriculum reform movement, has been the creation of studies focusing almost exclusively on ideas derived from economics itself. The pioneer project designed to develop curriculum for teachers with this base has been directed by Senesh.[8] Several others are being sponsored through Project Social Studies. Therefore, other curriculum materials, in addition to those which might be developed by the teacher in the classroom, will become available in the years ahead. Like the materials which the teacher will

[7] The reader may wish to refer to the section which explains the rationale for the expanding communities—basic human activities curriculum of social studies. See Chapter Three, p. 70 ff.
[8] Senesh, *op. cit.*

wish to develop for classroom use, these represent attempts to identify major understandings, with appropriate concomitant concepts and generalizations.[9] In some instances the ideas so identified are being labeled the "structure" of the subject. This terminology is also being applied to similar attempts to identify major ideas for teaching in the other social sciences. Materials that may be used either in a separate-disciplines or a unified approach are in the meantime being published by the Joint Council on Economic Education.[10] In addition to a *Teachers Guide to Economic Education,* which identifies important economic concepts and generalizations and contains suggestions for classroom practice, the Council publishes other materials useful to the teacher in broadening his own understanding of economic questions.

Teachers can begin helping children deal meaningfully with ideas of an economic nature during the earliest years, expanding gradually on the base built at this time as they move through the school heirarchy. In the examples which follow, a major economic understanding is presented, and ways in which those ideas might be furthered in the classroom are suggested. Since good ideas are always fruitful sources for formulating worthwhile learning situations, the reader should not find it difficult to extend his own list of teaching ideas, using this list as a foundation.

1. The basic idea behind all efforts in the area of economic education is to introduce children to the fundamental conflict which exists in all economic relationships: that human wants, desires, or demands for goods and services outstrip the resources necessary to meeting those desires. Consequently, one must choose among the alternatives. The extent of the conflict between unlimited wants and limited resources varies from place to place, from one time to another, and from family to family. Each of us must learn how to make wise choices. Everyone as a consequence needs to apply the limited resources available to him in such a manner as to yield the greatest satisfaction as he selects among those things he wants to have. Since the necessity of making choices is omnipresent, no study can be undertaken which fails to present situa-

[9] In an Appendix may be found one such attempt to identify generalizations in economics appropriate for the elementary school curriculum. See pp. 525-529.

[10] See especially Joint Council on Economic Education, *Teachers Guide to Economic Education, Part I,* "Economic Ideas and Concepts"; *Part II,* "Suggestions for Grade Placement and Development of Economic Ideas and Concepts." (New York: Joint Council on Economic Education, 1964). A small charge is made for these materials.

tions in which the nature of the choices available and the conditions affecting those choices are not open for consideration. For example,

In the primary years:
a. Children can talk about why people buy, sell, or produce different items and services. When they go to the store, certain choices are made. Conversations with parents may be re-created, parent roles played out, and dramatic play centers used to capture the child's interest in purchasing processes.
b. They can study the work people do, ask them how they get the money and other things they need, compare their work with that of other people they know about.
c. They can read stories in which imagined people are required to make choices. Such choices can be evaluated (good, bad, "I wouldn't have done that, because . . ."), alternate possibilities considered, changed outcomes contemplated.
d. Imagined circumstances can be devised and courses of action plotted. "If you were going to buy food for your family for two days, how much money would you need to make a good selection? What kinds of things would you buy?"
e. Different types of needs may be discussed and equated. Is having a bicycle as important as having an automobile? A bed as important as a table? A refrigerator as important as a stove? What conditions alter the nature of choices?
f. Time alters the kinds of things available to us and the possible choices. In historical studies, children can note such differences and discover factors which have changed the nature of choices one might make.

In the intermediate years:
a. Role playing continues to provide an especially effective avenue for thinking through problems which involve elements of choice. Spending an allowance, imagining what one might do with a certain sum of money ("You have just won $500. in a contest, what will you do with it and why?"), "becoming" an adult who faces the problem of deciding whether he can afford to purchase a new automobile, create circumstances which can be acted out. Different individuals and groups will, of course, arrive at other conclusions; each should have an opportunity to play out similar questions. Why different decisions are reached may be discussed and reviewed.

b. Comparisons can be made between choices involving the ever-present conflict between limited resources and unlimited wants available to people living in past periods (in colonial times, during the Revolutionary War, in frontier days, during the early twentieth century) with the present. Dramatic play provides opportunities for children to "step in" to another period, become the colonial housewife or frontiersman, and act out the circumstances in which choices were made. Discussion can bring out the wisdom (or lack of it) of choices made by other people. For example, the decision to hold a "Thanksgiving" involved an unusual raid upon available food resources. Frontier men undoubtedly found it necessary to discuss their wives' needs and wants for materials from which they made their clothes.

c. Study of people living in other places today provides a rich source for making choice comparisons. Flat pictures, television programs, motion pictures, and filmstrips are among the good sources of information that help children see in a more realistic way that different elements of choice are entering into the lives of people living today in different places and under different economic circumstances.

d. Imaginative stories provide a vehicle for thinking through the elements of choice in an economic situation. Open-ended stories, in which the first part is given in sufficient detail to stimulate children to imagine a conclusion (a story may be read by the teacher, or he may recount orally a situation), ending soon enough to give them sufficient degrees of freedom to enter into the process of deciding how the matter might be resolved, encourage them to think through and write down their notions of the matters which must be weighed.

e. Current affairs—a local bond issue, national policy matters—provide many questions of choice which are economic in nature. The consequences of various choices facing local, state, national, and international organizations needs explication and evaluation in terms of the anticipated outcomes of various courses of action that are infused with economic considerations.

The question is not whether the teacher can find issues of importance which are of an economic nature. Everyone is surrounded by situations and circumstances in which choices must be made and in which the factors involved may be thought about in a wide variety of learning situations: through discussion, dramatic play and role playing, in writing and reading, and in art forms of different kinds. It is possible, however, to select economic questions for which there is too low a level of understanding. The problem is roughly equivalent to the matter of finding an adult who might be able to visualize a billion dollars and then tell how it should be spent to secure a given end (raising levels of living in an urban ghetto, providing an economic "floor" to keep the wheat farmer from bankruptcy, etc.). One should avoid the billion dollar question with young children, it is obvious, and search for those circumstances which they can comprehend meaningfully—not always an easy task, naturally, but one which might be aided by remembering that the tendency is always to select situations too difficult for the child's comprehension.

2. A second fundamental economic understanding relates to the specialization of labor. Wherever groups of people are found, specialization of labor occurs. In complex societies, where levels of living are high, specialization is advanced; it is the central factor in determining the degree to which the unlimited wants of a people can be satisfied since, as specialization increases, productivity rises. As more goods and services are produced, the resource base is expanded and the conflict between wants and the ability to satisfy those wants grows. In one way, the basic wants are, of course, met to a much greater degree and the conflict between the two is reduced. But, in another sense, the conflict is increased since productivity also brings with it a wider range of products from which to choose. Specialization of labor is, of course, directly observable. It may also be seen in a meaningful way in many other circumstances which are met as studies on different topics evolve. For example:

In the primary years:
   a. Children can talk to parents, friends, and professionals about their particular work. Comparisons can be made. Thought can be stimulated about why people do different kinds of things. How each one who specializes depends upon others to produce other needed or wanted goods and services may be discovered. Children can consider the reasons why people do certain kinds of work and not other kinds. They can distinguish between specialization which results as a vocation is pursued and that which results from interests in different avocations. In all lines of work the need for specialization can be observed and thought about.

b. They can draw murals, write individual and cooperative stories, and act out roles which elaborate on their understandings of the nature of different kinds of work.

c. In beginning cross-cultural studies and in considering historical ideas, comparisons can be made between the immediate experiences and knowledge of children and the area or period they are thinking about. What did a teacher do then and what does he do now? How were logs cut, building blocks cut or created, books and newspapers printed? How have the jobs changed and what kind of preparation does a person need to do one of these jobs well? Do people living in another part of the world do the same kinds of work we do? What differences can be discovered? What accounts for some of those differences?

d. Examples of the displacement of human labor by machinery may be uncovered. Some jobs are changing rapidly, others disappearing, new ones arising. On study trips, through interviews, and by reading and talking, children can gain ideas about the nature of these changes and begin to think of their origins and their consequences. Comparisons might be made between the "chores" of children a few years ago and those today.

e. Children can recall from their own experiences people they have known in different places and the kind of work they did. Some of those jobs are more or less the same everywhere; others seem to be found only in certain places. Vacation resorts call for certain specialized talents; bus drivers are needed only where there are many people who want to travel along the same route; in places where there are not many people there seem to be persons who are able to do a number of different jobs reasonably well. Boys and girls can begin to sense differences such as these and to recognize the reasons for them.

In the intermediate and upper years:

a. The significance of specialization can be examined in fuller scope. It can be seen that certain industries, such as aviation and electronics, rely upon a veritable army of skilled technicians as well as professionals. The measure of the importance of such specialization might be discovered as studies are made of specific or related industries. Regional studies also illuminate circumstances in which highly specialized manufacturing concerns have located.

b. Effects of automation may be observed directly in the community or vicariously, such as through studies of the problems of unemployment (either in a region or over a broader area) and the search for a fully employed society.

c. Specific professions or technical jobs might be analyzed to discover what general and special types of preparation are required. Parents, community leaders, or business people might be consulted as the class makes such a study.

d. A trip to a nearby junior college or four year institution, discussion with students, faculty, or perhaps administrators who know about the kinds of jobs their students are preparing for, leads to ideas about the ways in which young people select and prepare for different types of work.

e. Pupils might be faced on occasion with generalizations relating to problems of specialization, seeking discussion and raising questions about the causal relationships implied. For instance, pupils might be asked: "What do you think is the relationship between the level of living of a people, such as people in the United States, and education? Why do you believe the way you do?" Or, "Where would you be mostly likely to find a jack-of-all-trades? On a plains area? In mountains? On an island? What factors are important in deciding what your answer would be?"

3. The consequence of growing specialization of labor is, of course, increasing interdependence. By specializing in one aspect of the economic order, individuals become more dependent upon the capability of others to produce those things which are needed to sustain and enrich life. As people become more specialized, they make their own unique contribution to the economic community, become more productive, and raise their levels of living, thus enabling them to enjoy the greater benefits that increased productivity provides. Elements of this interdependence may be seen in all of the previous examples. In addition, the impact of this important idea might be brought to the attention of children through such activities as the following:

In the primary years:

a. Awareness of the origins of products commonly used and the variety of people necessary to produce them might evolve from any study. Or, one might make a special effort to increase awareness of the variety of sources from which one obtains things in everyday use. A meal might be one such activity subject for analysis. What children are wearing; things they can find in their living room; or a trip to a nearby food market would provide information of this type, to be followed by discussion in class, map reading and map making, writing imaginary stories, or, perhaps, dramatic play.

b. Talking with parents and others who work about what they do brings forth information not only about specialization but about the dependence of workers upon each other.

c. Safety conditions provide a number of opportunities to think about problems of interdependence. Traffic problems, safety rules at school or at home, or the way a particular business attempts to secure a safe working environment for its employees illustrate that safety precautions are as much for the other person as they are for oneself.

d. Working together in groups within the classroom itself is a daily lesson which one would hope might lead to a growing awareness of the facts, conditions, and rewards of interdependence.

In the intermediate and upper years:

a. Current events frequently are apt conditions for considering problems of interdependence in a very real framework. A transportation workers' strike may affect vacation plans, alter a parent's work, or prevent a planned visit by a valued friend or relative. International "incidents" frequently are of deep personal concern to pupils and point up the consequences of the need for many people, as well as their governments, to act rationally, particularly when under great stress.

b. Studies of certain manufacturing processes (for example, smelting iron ore, refining oil, the assembly line) illustrate concepts undergirding ideas of interdependence, frequently on an international scale since materials basic to the process itself and/or to its subsequent distribution to users involve sources or markets all over the world. Of course, local studies also point up conditions affecting one's dependence upon others: the "company town," the family dependent upon an absentee landlord, the resort community dependent upon good weather, the mining community facing a cave-in all represent dramatic examples. Other more common yet interesting examples may be taken from any community study.

c. Emphasis can be placed on positive aspects of interdependence (not merely that nothing will be accomplished if one or more key elements in an interdependent system fails to function properly) by following the ways people behave when a keystone of a system fails or is destroyed. Examples of such incidences are the "natural" calamities of flood, earthquake, or tidal wave, or the "human error" circumstances of ship collision, fire, massive power failure, and the like.

d. Historical studies always contain within them elements of the information necessary to draw important "then and now" comparisons to show what happens as economic systems become more complex. By taking time out from the historical study *per se,* but using history properly of course, the children can become more aware of the flow of history, seeing one of its consequences to be a rapidly increasing interdependent society.

4. As people become increasingly specialized and interdependent, the need to trade increases. A fourth major economic understanding, therefore, has to do with how and why various devices (money, credit) have been devised, businesses created, and rules enacted (laws passed, enforcement officers hired, courts created) to facilitate and regulate trade. The following situations suggest ways in which economic ideas of this type might come to the attention of boys and girls in social studies.

In the primary years:

a. The need for a monetary system to facilitate trade may be viewed from a number of vantage points. In studies of primitive cultures, the type of system which has evolved, the uses of it, and an evaluation of this system for assisting the processes of trading may be noted. The children can compare the monetary system of the primitive culture with that of their own. Then, studies of the local community (perhaps of the dairy or some other aspect of the business community—the supermarket, the bakery, etc.) may be utilized to bring out the role of our monetary system in facilitating trade. Dramatic play and role playing are particularly fruitful avenues for developing understandings.

b. Study trips to the following places in the immediate vicinity of the school can help bring out understandings of the ways different units participate in the economic interchange which characterizes the local area: the bank or building and loan association, real estate offices, transportation companies (bus lines, air line companies, motor freight services, railroads, steamship lines, etc.), or telephone and other companies engaged in facilitating communications (television broadcasting companies, firms manufacturing and selling communication equipment, the radio station).

c. Persons who are engaged in various aspects of regulatory functions governing the manner in which trade in the local community is carried out may be interviewed or invited to the classroom for discussion. Among the many such individuals readily available are the following: the county agricultural agent, policemen, firemen, and inspectors employed by local, county, state, and federal agencies. In thinking about regulatory aspects and the existence of laws affecting the trading community, emphasis should be placed particularly upon positive aspects of these situations. Violators are the exception rather than the rule. The function of law is not merely that of seeking out and prosecuting the violator, of course; law provides a framework or code which defines accepted behavior. It gives the citizen guides for determining what he should do as he participates in the economic life of the community.

In the intermediate and upper years:

a. Pupils may be introduced to more complex concepts relating to the function of the monetary system, including the role of credit in facilitating trade. Analysis of simple systems of utilizing credit, including processes of calculating interest, should be introduced. Examples may be taken from the local scene: from advertisements for automobiles, perhaps, or from the marketplace of the major appliances, home purchase plans, and the like. There is no shortage of such examples of the uses of credit. Speculation about the possibilities for increasing trade, as a consequence of credit, may be coupled with interviews with business people and others to determine their attitudes and feelings about the importance of this aspect of the economic system in facilitating trade.

b. The role of communication systems in trading can also be considered in some detail. Advertising (including codes of ethics bearing upon the advertisers and the media carrying the advertisements), the need for various communications media and the roles each plays, and the varying importance of different modes of communication to different parts of the trading community may be discovered through interview, through motion pictures and television, and through study trips taken independently or by small groups to convenient locations in the immediate community.

c. Pupils can become increasingly aware of trade in the broader sense, in which states, regions of states, national, and international aspects are of vital importance to the overall function of an economic system. The nature of the trade which occurs between one region and another may be read about in textbooks, of course, but there are other valuable sources: atlases, almanacs, newspapers, and periodicals are important sources of information. The financial section of the local newspaper provides a daily account of the economic situation, a ready source for following matters which are of vital interest to the trading community.

d. By utilizing current publications, older pupils particularly may follow circumstances and situations which over a period of time affect specific aspects of trade between states, regions, and nations as well as factors primarily of local interest. Pieces of legislation, a local bond issue which, if passed, will stimulate business elements in the local community, or an executive order designed to intensify an existing measure that regulates trade may be followed. Such an analysis may be carried on primarily through classroom discussion, through individual study resulting in preparation of a notebook or report, or through activities planned by the teacher to engage the attention of pupils more systematically and formally.

The above major economic understandings, with a few classroom projects designed to increase these understandings, provide only a beginning in considering ways in which concepts and generalizations drawn primarily from the discipline of economics might be brought into the elementary school classroom. There is general agreement among economists that these four understandings are among the most important ideas to be considered and that they provide a core of ideas from which others evolve.

However, one must go beyond these; other major ideas also bear attention. Boys and girls should gain some ideas about how the market price of goods and services affects the economic system. They need to develop concepts about the manner in which societies develop what the economist calls "allocating mechanisms." That is, pupils can learn how various factors in a society influence how much of what kinds of things will be produced and what the methods of production will be. It is this process which is described generally as the allocating mechanism of the economic system. A beginning awareness of some of these factors, economists believe, should commence in the earliest grades in school. They also think it is possible to lead children to understand that *society* decides that certain provisions may be desirable which the normal mechanisms of the economy will not supply. Examples are: an educational system, health care for certain constituents in a society, unemployment assistance, aid to handicapped or impoverished citizens, and other subsidies to particular groups within the society. That a society makes decisions of this kind implies that it holds to certain values with respect to its particular economic system. Senesh suggests that value preferences in this regard can be grouped into five major categories:

1. Economic growth: a rising standard of living for an increasing population.
2. Economic stability: full employment without inflation.
3. Economic security: protection of income against the hazards of old age, death of the breadwinner, accident, disability, and unemployment.
4. Economic freedom: freedom of choice of each individual producer and consumer as long as it does not unduly abridge the freedom of others.
5. Economic justice: economic opportunities for all.[11]

Implicit in such a statement as this is the view that learning situations in schools should facilitate the development of these values. It has already been pointed out that the learning of values has two aspects: one may learn about these values through rather direct encounters with ideas; one also learns to hold these values to himself, to assume them as guiding principles or beliefs. The latter behavior eventuates over the years and is cumulative in the sense that many experiences in a wide variety of settings determine what a person ultimately holds as right or good. To assume these economic values, therefore, is not the exclusive responsibility of one teacher or even of the elementary school. There are, of course, other statements of this kind, all varying to a certain degree. The reader may wish to analyze several to determine how

[11] Lawrence Senesh, "The Fundamental Idea Relationship of Economic Knowledge," *Our Working World*, Teachers Edition. (Chicago: Science Research Associates, Inc., 1964), p. 4. The major economic understandings suggested as a basis for beginning work in economic education in this section are based largely on Senesh's work and the suggestions of the Joint Council on Economic Education.

closely he agrees with the statement offered by Senesh and to what degree he would wish to elaborate or modify it.

There are other important ideas which it is believed may be introduced in an elementary way at the start of a child's school experience that may then be thought about in more complex forms at later stages in the educational program. A variety of sources is available to which one may turn for guidance in identifying the broad scope of these fundamental understandings. Reference has previously been made to the Joint Council on Economic Education. In addition, note has been made of the value of the Senesh materials. Others are becoming available as the curriculum reform movement in social studies gathers momentum. Included in an Appendix the reader will find another listing of understandings which economists have suggested as guidelines in selecting from the discipline of economics content that is appropriate to the curriculum of social studies.[12]

Statements such as these need to be reinterpreted by the classroom teacher in the sense that the ideas presented must be put in a form which is understandable to the elementary school child. These will vary according to the age and maturity of the particular pupils with whom the teacher is working. Not least of all, the methods must be relevant to the teaching situation and the goals (or understandings) that are being sought. In addition, there is once again the question of the teacher's knowledge of the subject matter involved. It is only realistic to be aware of the fact that most elementary school teachers are not skilled in all aspects of economic inquiry. It is suggested therefore, that a teacher begin by selecting only those aspects with which he feels a reasonable familiarity. Awareness of some of the major ideas to be taught should, over a period of time, result in a growing strength on the teacher's part to work effectively with children in those areas now relatively unfamiliar.

Contributions of Political Science to Social Studies

THE NATURE OF POLITICAL SCIENCE AND POLITICAL INQUIRY

The field of political science has its roots in ancient Greece. Yet, like each of the other social sciences, it is in reality a relatively new discipline. For although modern political scientists continue to look to Plato's

---

[12] See the section on Economics from the California State Framework for the Social Studies, "Basic Ideas or Concepts from the Social Sciences," Appendix 2.

Republic and Aristotle's *Politics* as two of the most important writings in their field, the discipline known as political science has come of age only in this century.[13] Today it is a rapidly evolving field of study. Like the other social sciences, it is profoundly affected by the knowledge explosion. The rapidly accelerated pace at which knowledge relating to questions of interest to political scientists has grown, of course, meant that the facts available for him to study provide a very broad base of information. But in addition, technological advances are having their effect. With the advent of the computer, for example, the political scientist is finding ways of gathering, analyzing, and storing tremendous quantities of information, which, if it had been available before, would have been totally unmanageable. These developments, then, are opening up study areas previously dimly seen, if at all perceived. Whereas in the past, political science might well have been labeled one of the *least* scientific of the social sciences, these advances have brought about a new emphasis upon science and the scientific method. As a consequence, there is within the field of political science a continuing debate over the nature of this discipline and the research modes which are most appropriate in dealing with the questions that arise out of the study of politics.

What is Political Science? No simple definition can be given. Practical politics, or the *practice* of politics, is usually considered to be primarily an art, not a science. Depending upon one's viewpoint, such practice can be a racket, a game, or the most noble of professions. But the *study* of politics, which is the concern of the political scientist, is something apart from politics as one sees it functioning in daily life. To appreciate what political science includes and what it excludes one must, therefore, have an understanding of the meaning of *politics* and what is meant by *political*. Harold Lasswell, one of the most eminent political scientists, perhaps described politics as succinctly as anyone could when he elected to title a book *Politics: Who gets What, When and How*.[14] This view highlights politics as the process by which people

---

[13] For instance, the first college professor of political science in the United States was appointed to his position in 1858. The American Political Science Association was not formed until 1903, and it was not until the 1940's and 1950's that colleges and universities commonly had separate departments of political science. Until then, prevailing practice included political science with another field, usually history. There are today about ten to twelve thousand political scientists in the United States. About half work for the government, and the other half hold appointments in colleges and universities. Relatively few are employed by private agencies.

[14] Harold D. Lasswell, *Politics: Who Gets What, When and How* (New York: McGraw-Hill, 1936).

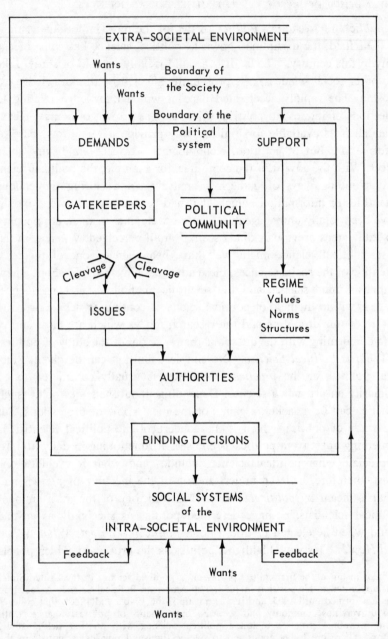

Figure 9–2: A Systems Analysis of Political Life. (Reprinted by permission of the author and publisher from Lawrence Senesh, "Organizing a Curriculum Around Social Science Concepts," in Irving Morrissett, editor, *Concepts and Structure in the New Social Science Curricula*, West Lafayette, Indiana: Social Science Education Consortium, Inc., 1966.)

organize themselves, both formally and informally, to resolve the inevitable value conflicts which arise whenever groups of human beings find themselves pursuing similar goals but where differing values are assigned to those goals and to the means which should be applied to achieve them. These formal and informal associations take a variety of shapes, from governmental units to churches, to local clubs, political parties, unions, and so forth. Taken together, they comprise what the political scientist terms the *political system* of a society. Political systems are obviously extremely complex as an examination of the accompanying chart suggests. And the relative importance of the various elements varies from one society to another. So the concerns of the political scientist, as he studies the various parts of a political system, can be seen to range over a good deal of territory.

The political system serves a most important function in society. That function is to make possible, through a series of processes and institutions, an effective means of arbitrating among the conflicting values in the society. Without such a resolution of conflicts which inevitably exist, there would be anarchy. Societies develop these processes and institutions to a greater or lesser degree. With them, as Easton states, it is possible to create "the authoritative allocations of values in society."[15] That is, through agreed upon processes and institutions, what the political scientist terms *public policy* emerges concerning those issues and questions which are deemed important to that society. In a highly complex one, these questions cover a multitude of topics, from local zoning ordinances to capital punishment, from medicare to international agreements, including treaties and other arrangements which affect both the private sector and the public one. The list is endless, and in our own country, we have developed an extensive set of institutions and processes through which public policy is designed to emerge. In the undeveloped portions of the world, political systems are more simple. And it is well to remember, too, that these undeveloped countries, along with much of the non-Western world, tend to rely less than developed countries upon formally established institutions. In such places, tradition, religion, family patterns, and familial ties are powerful factors in the development of public policy.

Political science, therefore, is concerned with the study of political systems. There are many specializations within the broad framework of

[15] David Easton, *The Political System* (New York: Alfred A. Knopf., Inc., 1953). See especially Chapter Five.

political science, and they include both the formal structures of government and the less formal means by which public policy emerges. According to Sorauf, political science examines political systems from four perspectives:

1. It studies the processes, behavior, and institutions of political systems in order to make systematic generalizations and explanations about the political.
2. It seeks generalizations about relations among political systems, especially the politics of nations in the international system.
3. It studies the end products, the public policies, of the political processes.
4. It studies, finally, ideas and doctrines about government and the political system, ideas such as the concepts of and justifications for democracy, justice, and equality.[16]

Differing Points of View. Political scientists can be divided generally into two groups representing basically different points of view: the traditionalists and the behaviorists. It may be helpful to contrast these two positions, since the former represents the "traditional" political science and the latter constitutes newer thinking within the discipline. Sorauf has commented on both viewpoints, indicating that the traditionalists have been mainly concerned,

with political and governmental institutions—with legislatures, executives, and courts; with political parties and elections; with international organizations and tribunals, with constitutions, public law, and international law. Conversely, they devoted little attention to behavioral decisions and processes within the institutions—to the political behavior of individuals or to the role behavior of officeholders, for example. Secondly, they shared a common disposition to historicism and chronology as a way of organizing their materials. Most of the textbooks in American government even today begin with the founding fathers and the writing of the American constitution. Lacking a systematic body of data, political scientists drew on historical examples; and lacking a body of theory and concepts, they sought the sequential, developmental analysis of history. Finally, these traditionists shared a distrust of generalizations and the probing for systematic explanation. Political scientists considered themselves practical men of action with a mission in the real world. They shared a confidence, which in hindsight seems more than a little naive, that readily observed facts would speak for

[16] Frank J. Sorauf, *Political Science: An Informal Overview* (Columbus, Ohio: Charles E. Merrill Books, Inc., 1965), p. 7. Reprinted by permission.

themselves. The layman's view of the world, they thought, needed no special form of political analysis.[17]

The behaviorist position took shape in the 1920's and 30's under the guidance of Charles Merriam at the University of Chicago and has been carried on by Harold Lasswell. It emerged after World War II as a powerful force in molding the field so that it has become, first, more rigorous and objective—more "scientific"—in outlook and, second, more focused on the behavior of those who engage in political activity. This is not to say that political institutions are ignored, but the emphasis upon behavior—the emphasis which causes political scientists of this bent to be called "behaviorists"—has been most important in the development of the modern discipline of political science. Sorauf contrasts the behaviorists' view with that of the traditionalists, above, by asserting that the behaviorists agree they want their discipline to adopt, albeit in varying degrees, the following posture:

1. *New data.* They would bring to the study of politics a new concern for the individual and group behavior that goes on within political institutions. They would, for instance, study the role of political leadership and elites and the influence of a congressman's role-perception on the way he carries out his responsibilities. In other words, they have sought to draw political science away from its almost exclusive concern with formal institutions and toward the political actors and processes.

2. *New methods.* The behaviorists have propounded a more rigorous and systematic empiricism, one that observes more closely, records more precisely, and uses more sophisticated concepts and tools of analysis than political science has in the past. Tables, graphs, scales, charts and mathematical models have become their trademarks; field work has virtually become their way of life.

3. *New concepts.* The new political science has drawn freely on the analytical vocabulary of the other behavioral sciences for new categories and concepts. Some, of course, they have developed for themselves. In either event, however, the goal is a technical vocabulary which will identify the more abstract, analytical relationships necessary for the development of theoretical generalizations. As a result, political scientists show a new ease with terms such

---

[17] *Ibid.,* p. 13. Reprinted by permission.

as *power, elite,* and *role,* not to mention *functional prerequisites* and *political socialization.*

4. *New theoretical goals.* Above all, the new mood in political science seeks to impel the discipline toward generalizations which will explain relationships within the political system. It is the old goal, more cautiously presented, of a science of politics. The behaviorists have brought the hypothesis and theoretical proposition back into even narrowly circumscribed research. At the same time they continue the search for the towering, over-all theoretical edifice which will integrate and unify the more specific findings and propositions of the discipline.[18]

Methods of Research in Political Science. The behaviorist position has had far-reaching effects upon the manner in which the political scientist studies his subject. Whereas the traditionalist emphasis upon philosophical discourse and historical analysis remains important, several trends, which are direct outgrowths of behaviorism, can be identified in political science research. Among them, those which have the most direct application in the elementary school classroom follow.

First, there is an increasing emphasis upon the utilization of a scientific methodology. This means that increasing attention is being given to identifying problems in political science worthy of research and to developing appropriate strategies for researching them. This means, also, that studies in this field are tending to have more clearly defined boundary lines. From the vast panorama of concerns in political science, one selects a problem small enough to be amenable to study using the scientific mode of research. For example, whereas one might have analyzed voter trends by state or regions of states, interpreting data on a rather broad scale, the newer approach suggests analysis of voting patterns and establishing reasons for voting on the basis of individual interviews within a much more restricted area such as that of the precinct or other limited electoral area.

Second, objective means are being employed to gather and analyze data. The political scientist's interests in employing primary sources in his research are reflected in the following list of materials he will use in addition to the traditional library resources:

Verbatim reports on legislative debates, on records of committee action, roll-call votes, and laws passed.

[18] *Ibid.,* pp. 15-16. Reprinted by permission.

Papers, messages, and statements of government leaders at all levels (including formal as well as off-the-cuff remarks).

Reports, records, and documents of government (including local, state, national, and international agencies as well as those of other nation states).

Informal sources, including memoirs, diaries, letters, personal papers, memoranda, and newspaper accounts.[19]

Also, quantification of data is being used increasingly. Statistical analysis and computer technology are of growing importance in this as in other social sciences. Use of objective means in analyzing data is not restricted to the more elegant machinery and techniques. Hence there is considerable use of techniques long familiar in education: the case study, the questionnaire, and the longitudinal study. However, mathematical treatment of data, whether no more complicated than computing means, medians, and standard deviations, is increasingly characteristic of research in political science.

Third, emphasis is upon the personal. The behaviorist has been particularly concerned with finding out why individuals behave the way they do in political situations, and this emphasis is being felt throughout the field of political science. That is, he seeks to discover how persons respond to the various political forces surrounding them, how they use power as they participate in roles which are of a political nature, and, of course, why they behave the way they do. To the behaviorist, particularly, the facts elicited through the study of individuals and small groups of individuals provide the framework for developing the basic concepts, generalizations, and theories of political science. That such an emphasis upon individual political behavior is the only way political science can develop a body of knowledge is the major argument for the approach of the behaviorist to his discipline. Although the argument is far from universally accepted, its impact upon political science as a whole cannot be denied.

Fourth, the political scientist is becoming more involved in field research. Information about some kinds of things simply cannot be discovered without employing interviewing, observing behavior, administering questionnaires, and seeking out public and private documents not available in libraries. But because some kinds of behaviors cannot be adequately analyzed through library study does not mean that the library is less important. Indeed, in many ways library research becomes more

[19] Adapted from Sorauf, *op. cit.*, p. 25.

important since it is there that one discovers the background information—the theoretical and integrative writings—necessary to the formulation of reasearchable questions in politics.

THE USES OF POLITICAL SCIENCE IN THE CLASSROOM

The teaching of "civics" has traditionally, of course, been a responsibility of both elementary and secondary schools. By "civics" one means a knowledge of the most important American institutions of government at the local, state, and national levels. It has meant that pupils have been expected to become familiar with the functions of governmental units in a democratic society; it has been hoped that they would also develop attitudes and understandings about the nature of "the good citizen." That is, it has been presumed that knowledge of the functions of government should also include a commitment to carry out the responsibilities of a citizen in a democratic society. In recent years, as the world has grown rapidly smaller and the United States has come to play an increasingly important role in international affairs, concepts of what a "good citizen" needs to know have been expanding. Of central concern has been the need to understand the nature of Communism.[20] Still, the basic consideration remains: to learn about the instruments of government and to gain the knowledge, understandings, skills, and attitudes which will lead to effective participation as a citizen.

The modern discipline of political science suggests ways this basic commitment may be better met in at least two ways. *First,* the expanded and changing nature of subject matter content helps one to see ways in which the findings of political science may be woven into the existing curriculum of studies. It also helps in clarifying goals in those studies which focus primarily upon topics or problems that are essentially rooted in concepts and understandings drawn from political science itself. A study of how a city governs itself, of the function of our national government, or of the United Nations are examples.

---

[20] The general success of efforts to teach "civics" has been discussed previously. See pp. 102-103. It should be remembered that there has been little agreement as to whether a dispassionate analysis of matters commonly included in "civics" is sufficient to long-term goals of developing an effective citizenry or whether some degree of indoctrination should not be attempted. Given an opportunity to reflect upon this question, most thoughtful persons disclaim indoctrination as inimical to the basic principles of a democratic society. The reader can decide for himself what types of classroom activities constitute indoctrination. However, it can be safely asserted that the familiar "civics" curriculum contains a large measure of indoctrination, particularly with respect to the handling of issues relating to Communism.

Second, the methods of research and the focus of concern of the political scientist suggest approaches to teaching children which may relieve, if not dismiss entirely, the concerns over factual presentation of topics versus indoctrination. For example, the growing emphasis upon the scientific method suggests increasing attention to identifying problems which are researchable as far as pupils are concerned. Problem setting, planning strategies for obtaining information, and learning to draw inferences from data collected that lead to new hypotheses—the essential elements in a scientific methodology—suggest that the questions children seek to answer should be specific. They should involve such issues as: how does the government act to prevent outbreaks of disease where we live?; how does our city government set safety, beautification, or other standards?; what steps did our congressman (or mayor, or other public figure) take in his bid for election?

The second trend in political science research is toward increased use of objective means in gathering and analyzing data. Like the historian, political scientists use primary sources wherever possible. The sources available to him are also available to the boys and girls in the classrooms: newspapers, letters, and other informal sources of information can be used along with the more formal reports and records of government agencies. Television and radio as well as interviews conducted in the classroom or elsewhere become important sources of information. Although not all data can or should be quantified, a great deal can and should be, even by younger children. In studying traffic regulations, for instance, boys and girls can count the number of vehicles, the different kinds they see, how the count varies from one day to the next, how many people cross streets during a given period, etc., as they discover the reasons police and other agencies attempt to develop safe conditions for living in an area. They can classify the number of different items which appear on a city council agenda or on that of some other agency of government. They can find out how many pieces of mail different postman carry on different routes, determine what the relationship is between first class and other types of mail, or explore the factors which determine the length and location of routes used in delivering mail. Older boys and girls can study the content of legislative records in very similar ways, and they can develop and analyze questionnaires and the results of interviews they conduct provided the problems they seek to solve and the questions they ask give them specific enough information. It is from such facts and details that concepts of government are expanded and generalizations about political behavior are developed.

The third trend emphasizes the development of understandings about individual behavior. The power of identification which is aroused through personal contacts with admired adults has long been recognized as a potent force in learning. The same strong elements can frequently be created through the use of biography and fictionalized accounts of persons whose own lives are worthy of emulation. Such personal and vicarious experiences help children understand how and why individuals with whom they identify reached the decisions they did and behaved the way they have. The mayor, policeman, or some other person in the community consequently becomes more real when he is interviewed than when someone describes him. The secretary-general of the United Nations or another world figure assumes human proportions when he is seen on television, when his words are heard as he actually speaks them, or as they are later read and analyzed.

From the local scene to the international, it is increasingly possible to study the day to day activities of political figures and to learn very directly what they are saying and doing, to think about the forces that are working upon them, and how they may be using the power of their office to gain certain objectives. This aspect for political science research has special power for the classroom teacher since it suggests that more may be learned about general trends and conditions through the careful analysis of selected groups and individuals with whom children can identify readily. The approach is not limited to the present, of course, but can be done in a historical context through the study of the personal writings and the first-hand knowledge of others living and writing in a period as well as through the use of historical novels.

Fourth, like the geographer, sociologist, and others interested in furthering understandings about the human estate, the political scientist increasingly is becoming involved in field research. By using field research techniques, such as the interview, questionnaires, direct observation of behavior, and by going to original documents, children, too, can obtain information that leaves not only vivid memories but which is more easily related and compared with other data than that dependent essentially upon vicarious experiencing. Searching the classroom, school, or community library for information is still essential, and absolutely necessary as a percursor of any extended activity falling within the general category of field research. It is the preparation ahead of time that yields the questions to be asked and the mode of inquiry to be used when seeking information outside of the classroom. For when children go outside of the classroom for information, they must be better prepared in the general background of their topic if they are to learn how to ask relevant questions and get answers to those questions. If children can learn to formulate questions in the areas listed below, for instance, they must "do their homework" in the classroom and school library ahead of time.

Types of Question Areas Which Encourage Field Research on the Part of Children

1. How government agencies function (city council, planning commission, police department, post office, legislature, etc.).
2. How the community has changed over a period of time (changes in land use, communication networks, attitudes of residents, etc).
3. How the community should be improved (what things need to be preserved, what things modified, what important community needs should be met, how attitudes differ with respect to these, etc.).
4. How groups express their concern to get change (how different groups organize, how they work together for common ends, what problems they encounter, etc.).
5. How laws come into existence, how they are enforced (processes at different levels, what kinds of roles are necessary to make laws operative, etc.).
6. How people are chosen for public office (how they decide to run for office, what they do, how they are chosen, how they are kept or not kept in office, etc.).

Applications of Political Science in the Primary Years. Developing understandings of the processes and institutions of government comes about gradually, and it would be a mistake to expect the younger children in our schools to demonstrate any great depth of knowledge in this regard. However, they should begin to develop a framework for knowing in this dimension, a framework which can become much more extensively developed in the later years. It may be helpful, in this respect, to think about the kinds of understandings that may be developed in three basic dimensions. First, children can become *practiced* in the ways of a democratic society. Second, they can experience the *rituals* and other modes of behavior we associate with living in a democracy. Third, they can begin to develop *concepts* about the processes and institutions of government which they will be expected to expand upon in later years.

By becoming *practiced* in the ways of a democratic society, one means having experiences in several distinct ways. First, but not most important for the very young child, is that of experiencing the processes of majority rule. This is mentioned first because it is most likely to be that aspect most abused in the classroom. It is true, of course, that the most crucial decisions in a democratic society such as ours are usually reached after people have an opportunity to weigh the pertinent arguments, arrive at a rational conclusion, and express themselves through the voting process. This is a very mature process, requiring understanding of the issues involved and the capacity to reason among them to the point of reaching a rational decision. There are a few classroom situations in which the processes of majority rule may be practiced, but it is dangerous to assume that practically anything can be decided this way and have the process remain a meaningful one in the child's eye. Therefore caution should be exercised in employing this procedure. Second, children can come into contact with people whose jobs include the formulating or carrying out of the will of the people as it is expressed through laws and regulations. Among the people who can make a contribution to children's understanding in this dimension, consider the following for classroom visits or interviews at their place of business:

city councilmen	lawyers
city engineers or other appointed officials	judges
public health nurses	school administrators
policemen	teachers
postal workers	social workers

Third, primary children should become familiar with the institutions of government as they are represented in buildings and other public places. Learning the location and function of city parks, transportation systems, public libraries, fire stations, post offices and other federal buildings, the city hall and associated buildings (if any) are examples of this type. Such learning can be undertaken for its own sake. And fourth, the child can become practiced in situations that require him to respond to leadership-followership roles. In certain circumstances and under specific conditions he may be asked to carry out the role of a leader. In others, he responds to those who exercise the leadership role.

Situations in which these roles are learned include the following:

1. He is chairman of a work committee (or member of a committee working with a chairman).
2. He helps formulate rules to be applied in the classroom, on the playground, or in some other specific situation.
3. He directs or stage-manages an impromptu play.
4. He takes part in a panel discussion.
5. He takes part in planning the arrangement of the classroom.
6. He acts as assistant to a teacher.
7. He helps a class of older children; of younger children.

From the moment they enter school, young children become acquainted with the *rituals* and other modes of behavior which are associated with living in a democracy through such activities as learning and singing songs associated with the American ideal, through saying the Pledge of Allegiance, by observing flag etiquette, and by learning how to show respect to those who have assumed leadership roles—both peer and adult. The young child is not expected to have a particularly well developed understanding of the meanings behind these rituals and routines. Some experiences will make one wonder whether the child has any understanding at all. Lack of mature understanding is not the criterion by which one judges whether such rituals should be observed. The point is that the child begins experiencing those events which form a common bond between all Americans as they demonstrate their love and respect for their country.[21]

Finally, of course, one expects the child to begin to develop understandings about the processes and institutions of government with which he will be brought into contact. Becoming familiar with the roles of persons in our society and the institutions that have been created to carry out the will of the people by bringing each child in touch with the people, places, and situations suggested above provides one of the

---

[21] A sobering yet amusing experience providing insights into the nature and extent of children's understanding in this dimension may be had by asking individual youngsters to either write or say the Pledge of Allegiance. Typical of third grade written responses are these examples: "I Plag Alegc to the flag of the Unit Stats of Amrac and to the repbc for wick it stans one Nash under god indavisabl with Libert and Jastis for all." An eight-year-old wrote: "I Placha a leejs to the flag of the Unitd saks of Amrek, and to the Replik from wichstans one Nachn under God indvisadle with ledrte and jaste of all." Another typical effort, this time from a ten-year-old, is also unchanged from the original: "I plage i leagun to the flag of the United Statey of i anmkar and to the re publick of with is stan one nasson undder god in the vibel and jus stis for all."

most important avenues in the development of these ideas. The observance of holidays and other special days constitutes another framework for giving attention to them. However, as Martin Dimond, a prominent political scientist, points out, one of the most important national holidays occurs during the summer vacation (July 4) and so our nation's birthday is not celebrated, as he thinks it should be, in our schools. Also, very young children frequently have hazy or inaccurate ideas about the meanings lying behind the observance of such common holidays as the following:

Approximate Date	Observance	Approximate Date	Observance
Sept. 11-15	Constitution Week	Dec. 15	Bill of Rights Day
Oct. 12	Columbus Day	Feb. 11	Race Relations Day
Oct. 20	United States Day	Feb. 12	Lincoln's Birthday
Oct. 24	United Nations Day	Feb. 22	Washington's Birthday
Second Tuesday in Nov.	General Election Day	Feb. 18-25	Brotherhood Week
Nov. 5-11	American Education Week	March 7	Arbor Day
Nov. 11	Veteran's Day	May 30	Memorial Day
Nov. 23	Thanksgiving Day	June 14	Flag Day

During the primary years most curriculums of social studies provide for specific emphasis upon local government and studies of such "community helpers" as the policeman, postman, and other civil servants. Such studies provide opportunities to become acquainted with people who are playing different roles in the governance of their community. Also during the child's primary school experience, the adult community will conduct an election. This event provides first-hand opportunities for the child to learn how people in a democratic society resolve important questions and select leaders for different roles in their government.

Applications of Political Science in the Intermediate and Upper Grade Years. Pupils at these levels can increasingly be provided experiences in each of the three major aspects of learning mentioned above: *becoming practiced* in the ways of a democratic society, *experiencing the rituals and other modes of behavior* which are associated with living in a democracy, and *developing concepts* about the processes and institutions of government.

With respect to the goal of becoming increasingly practiced in the ways of a democratic society, one might recall again Dewey's admonition that "democracy must be born anew with each generation." Such a statement means simply that classroom procedures must observe the principles of democratic behavior. Unless children grow up in a world in which there is faith in the use of intelligence in solving problems and clarifying issues, where there is a belief in the use of reason and persuasion rather than the force of authority in solving problems and settling controversy, one can hardly expect that as adults they will actively foster democratic principles and the democratic way of life on which our society is founded. It can be argued persuasively, in other words, that authoritarian procedures, in the classroom as elsewhere, abrogate democratic principles and consequently make the practice of democratic behaviors impossible. One does not learn the ways of democracy simply by studying or talking about them; they are learned as a consequence of years of actual practice.

Similarly, the observance of the rituals and other modes of behavior that one associates with living in a democracy requires systematic attention throughout the school. Sometimes it seems that the business of the classroom—particularly where that business is defined as "covering the subject matter"—does not leave enough time for such things. So there is often a tendency to brush over them lightly rather than linger and relish the moments which such observance takes. But beyond the daily pledge, song, or other observance, older children need to become aware of the significance of various routines, rituals, and other formalistic procedures that societies adopt, which reflect their point of view about government and which are so important in keeping the government functioning. This means becoming acquainted with:

1. The many applications of parliamentary procedure at local, state, and national levels.
2. The ways public officials are addressed.
3. The ways public and private bodies constitute themselves to carry out functions prescribed by the state (private corporations of different types, courts, city councils, legislatures, etc.).
4. How national bodies organize procedures to facilitate their work (Congress, Supreme Court, Executive Offices, etc.).
5. How protocol at the national and international levels functions.
6. How the United Nations and different foreign governments differ and are like our own country in this respect.

The meaning and importance of this aspect of life in a democratic society can frequently be developed through direct observation in the community. Television and the highly developed picture magazines such as *Life* and *Look* are also invaluable sources. An even more recent development, with wide use in the social study emphasizing understandings drawn from political science, is the "instant paperback." These are softbound books, including pictures as well as a narrative or text, published soon after a major event. Frequently, such books appear at the bookstand within a week or two of the event itself.

The intermediate and upper years provide the widest range of possibilities for extending understandings about the processes and institutions of government, both in the United States and elsewhere. Commonly observed content emphases in these years include studies of state and national government, of the governments of other lands, and attention to the United Nations and other international organizations such as the North Atlantic Treaty Organization, the Organization of American States, and the Southeast Asia Treaty Organization. Sometimes topics are woven into studies based on a unified approach to the social sciences; at other times they are primarily concerned with ideas drawn from political science. A major problem is encountered in such studies; it is difficult to avoid emphasizing the structure of governmental institutions and generalizing about the processes or ways different institutions function. For instance, it is easy for a study of the organization of Congress or the manner in which a bill becomes law to become quite dreary and, also, difficult to understand. Keeping in mind how the political scientist—particularly the behaviorist—approaches his studies may provide a suggestion or two for enlivening this process. For example, what would happen to studies of the functions and institutions of government (1) if pupils examined the ways in which one piece of legislation, one issue for a decision in government, or one example of a case which actually did reach court? (2) if pupils sought to understand the motives and found out about the actions of actual individuals involved in writing into law a piece of legislation, in an actual court case, in a foreign policy decision of the Executive Office, etc.? (3) if pupils used wherever possible such primary sources as pictures, written and spoken words of the principals in a particularly important circumstance, accounts of eye-witnesses or participants in an event, etc.? Recall that the four major trends in political science thinking and research included:

1. More emphasis upon the scientific method, defining problems which are specific, and developing strategies which will give detailed answers to the questions being raised.

2. Objective means increasingly being employed in gathering and analyzing data.
3. Inquiry more directed toward determining why individuals behave as they do when responding to issues or problems which are political in nature.
4. Field research assuming an increasingly important role along with traditional library study.

What other topics drawn from political science and what procedures which might be employed in studying them are suggested by these approaches to the study of problems in political science?

Contributions from the Fields of Sociology and Anthropology to the Curriculum of Social Studies

In the final section of this chapter the contributions of two other fields of the social sciences to the curriculum of social studies will be discussed. They are *sociology,* "the scientific study of society," and *anthropology,* "the science of man and his works." These broad and overly bold definitions nonetheless serve to emphasize the common focus which these fields of inquiry share. They are, truly, general sciences of man. That is, they are concerned with generating concepts and generalizations about human behavior as it is observed in a wide variety of contexts and situations. Each field has its special focus; still, it is worthwhile to contrast the intellectual concerns of sociology and anthropology with the other two fields of the social sciences which were considered in the earlier part of this chapter. For in economic and political inquiry, one looks at man's behavior in rather special circumstances. In these fields, one seeks to understand more fully the nature and quality of man's behavior in either economic or political situations. Sociology and anthropology encompass the totality of man's behavior within a different kind of framework. In sociology, for example, one thinks primarily about the consequences of group living. The sociologist wants to know how groups of different kinds function and how individuals are influenced by and, in turn, influence different groups in society. Anthropology, in contrast, is interested in all aspects of human life. It is not restricted in terms of time or place. Both physical and cultural elements leading to further understandings of human behavior interest the anthropologist.

Although the traditional concern of the sociologist has been contemporary, Western culture, and normally the society in which the sociologist has himself been living, sociology is beginning to concern itself with other cultures. Particularly is there a growing emphasis upon non-Western cultures. Meanwhile, the anthropologist has concentrated upon primitive, non-literate societies. His interests, too, are changing. A growing number of anthropologists are concerning themselves with aspects of contemporary, complex cultures. A growing area of interest among anthropologists in this country, for instance, involves studies of schools and the processes of schooling.[22] Thus, in some ways sociologists and anthropologists are investigating problems that are very closely related. Still, certain distinctions remain. Sociology maintains its interests in analyzing group behavior. Anthropology looks to a broader understanding of a total culture.

It is neither desirable, nor possible in the space available, to recount in any detail the specific concerns of either of these disciplines. Included at the close of this chapter, as well as in an Appendix, are references to books written by sociologists and anthropologists which comment upon the nature of their disciplines and upon some of the major concepts and generalizations that have grown out of recent research in each of these disciplines. The purpose here must be merely to introduce them and to point to ways significant ideas from sociology and anthropology may be drawn into the social studies curriculum.

Before proceeding to a more specific discussion, it is relevant to note that each of these disciplines is relatively young when compared with the other social sciences. One of the early great American sociologists, for example, was Charles Horton Cooley, who lived well into the present century (1864-1929). His discoveries concerning the significance of primary groups in shaping personality continue to have an important effect upon current sociological inquiry. Anthropological inquiry cast in the context of a discipline is even younger. It is not surprising, therefore, to realize that both sociology and anthropology continue to evolve as disciplines. Although they have reached a certain "maturity," it should be kept in mind that a continuing dialogue is sparking these intellectual communities over the basic issues evoked in discussions about the nature of any discipline: (1) what are the proper concerns of our area of inquiry and (2) what methods of research are valid?

[22] An outstanding collection of writings by anthropologists on the problems of schooling is contained in *Education and Culture,* George D. Spindler, editor (New York: Holt, Rinehart and Winston, 1963).

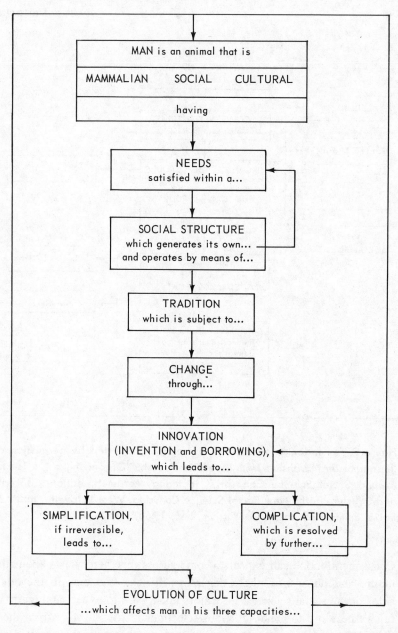

Figure 9–3: Fundamental Ideas of Anthropology. (Reprinted by permission of the author and publisher from Lawrence Senesh, "Organizing a Curriculum Around Social Science Concepts," in Irving Morrissett, editor, *Concepts and Structure in the New Social Science Curricula*, West Lafayette, Indiana: Social Science Education Consortium, Inc., 1966.)

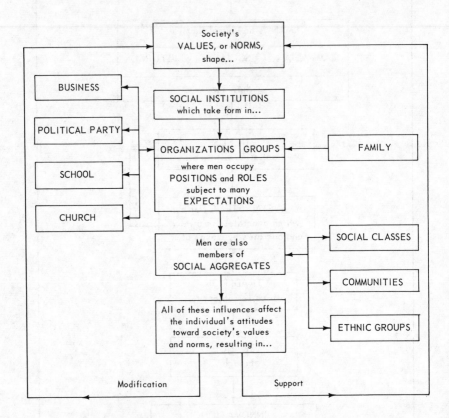

Figure 9–4: Fundamental Ideas of Sociology. (Reprinted by permission of the author and publisher from Lawrence Senesh, "Organizing a Curriculum Around Social Science Concepts," in Irving Morrissett, editor, *Concepts and Structure in the New Social Science Curricula*, West Lafayette, Indiana: Social Science Education Consortium, Inc., 1966.)

Consequently, one can expect to come across divergent views about the nature and purpose of these disciplines, just as one may in the other fields of the social sciences. Educators must learn to expect ambiguity in this respect and to make judicious selections of ideas drawn from these fields based on an understanding of the fact that eminent scholars are not in complete agreement about the nature of importance of different findings within their fields.

One of the major characteristics of the dialogue which is taking place throughout the social sciences, applicable as well to both sociology and anthropology, is the growing agreement upon the importance of basing inquiry upon scientific methodology. Here, as elsewhere, there is increasing emphasis upon the development of objective means for recording and analyzing data. There is also growing attention to the problem of identifying researchable questions and of developing hypotheses that are amenable to depth study, where raw data are drawn from first-hand or primary sources. Both the sociologist and the anthropologist, therefore, are heavily "field oriented." The use of mathematics and statistical procedures in studying human behavior, along with the development of other objective modes of analysis, is also becoming increasingly important. Although some people argue that there is real danger of "reducing everyone to a number" as man searches for means of studying such an infinitely variable subject as human behavior, there is little doubt that the emphasis upon objectivity has increased greatly the power of these fields in generating valid and usable ideas. The successes recorded to date are of such significance that there is no doubt objective research methods will play an increasingly vital role in the scholar's approach to his studies. It is the only means by which the social sciences can become truly scientific.

THE NATURE OF SOCIOLOGY

Sociological inquiry focuses upon the study of groups. Sociologists believe that by applying scientific methods of analysis to various aspects of group behavior they may identify common elements which will lead to a better understanding of why people behave and think as they do. In his analysis of behavior, the sociologist approaches his work primarily by comparing and contrasting the behavior he observes in one group with that of others. Although it is particularly true of complex, advanced societies, people everywhere belong to or become part of a large number of groups. Therefore, the scope of sociological inquiry can be seen to be very large. The breadth of interest becomes obvious as one reads Rose's description of the topics which interest sociologists.

. . . among other things, sociologists want to know why groups like the family, the tribe, or the nation persist over time even during war or revolution. Why does a soldier fight and face death when he might hide and run away? Why does a man marry and take on responsibilities for a family when he might just as easily satisfy his sexual impulses outside of marriage? What effects does group living have on the behavior of group members? Do people who live in isolated, preliterate tribes behave differently from those who live in New York or a Parisian suburb? Are the attitudes of a slum dweller different from those of an upper-class businessman and, if so, why?

Sociologists are equally interested in why groups change or fall apart. For example, they want to know why some marriages end in divorce. They are interested in why there is more divorce in some countries than there is in others and why the rates of divorce increase or decrease over time. They want to know if people behave differently after they move from the country to the city or from the city to the suburbs.

Finally, sociologists study the relationships among group members and among groups. What are the relationships between husband and wife and between parents and children in the United States today? Are these relationships like those in the early American family or like those in families in other countries? What causes conflict between Negroes and whites in the South? Do labor, industry, and government in the United States relate to each other in the same way as do similar groups in Australia or the Soviet Union? Why do some groups in the society have more material goods and more prestige than do others?[23]

The vast panorama of human behavior therefore sets the scope of sociological inquiry, but with a particular focus. That focus is upon the development of a science of social dynamics. It can be seen from Rose's description of the types of things which interest the sociologist that this discipline is basically a search for knowledge in three major areas. First, the sociologist studies the processes of social interaction. Second, he analyzes the structure of the social systems which have emerged over the years to facilitate and/or control social interaction. Finally, he seeks to learn how the social structure or system changes.

Differing Points of View. Like political science, modern sociology finds itself in a debate over the manner in which the study of human behavior as it is observed in groups should be carried out. The division occurs between those who advocate the broader use of scientific methods in conducting studies and those who argue for inquiry based on a definite value structure in which the development of a coherent theory precedes empirical research. Although the issues being raised are not of a totally either-or variety, the debate is based on clearly different viewpoints. Those advocating the view that basic sociological questions are disserted for action, that "objective" research is being undertaken without enough speculative consideration of the fundamental issues being studied beforehand, are in the best tradition of the type of sociological inquiry dominant during the first decades of the present century. It remains the position of a majority of sociologists in countries other than the United States. Proponents of this view claim

[23] Caroline B. Rose, *Sociology: The Study of Man in Society* (Columbus, Ohio: Charles E. Merrill Books, Inc., 1965), pp. 1-2.

with some justification that the romance with scientific methodology, which characterizes the newer sociology, results in investigations that are not only of too limited scope, they attack questions not related to the realities of the day. The shift to empirical research is viewed, Thomlinson suggests, "as being one which has gone from a preponderance of architects and thinkers to a domination by bricklayers and laundry-ticket counters."[24]

"Those pleased with this change contrast the 'soft' facts of armchair theorizers with the 'hard' facts of scientific data-gatherers." The noted sociologist Robert K. Merton has also typified the division by remarking that the person holding to an emphasis upon theorizing might say, "We do not know whether what we say is true, but it is at least significant." Meantime, the empiricist might reply, "We do not know whether what we say is significant, but it is at least true."[25]

Nevertheless, the dominant theme among American sociologists today emphasizes the *scientific* study of man in society. Sociology, like the other social sciences, follows the star of dispassionate, empirical research.

Concepts Basic to Sociological Inquiry. The evolution of any discipline brings with it a language reflecting the fundamental concepts with which scholars work. This is no less true of sociological inquiry than of other fields. In the previous half century or more, scholars have generated a series of basic concepts one finds wherever sociological inquiry takes place. These concepts, then, provide the framework for study. Since the terms which follow are generally used in conversation by lay persons, some mention of their technical meaning may be warranted. It should also be remembered that each of these concepts is composed of many others and that the ideas they represent are interrelated in a variety of ways.

Society and Culture. Sociologists distinguish between society—a large, organized, continuing group of people—and culture—the ways of life of a society. Culture refers to the way people think and behave; society to the associations and organizations which characterize the relationships of a large group of people. Culture emerges over a long period

---

[24] Ralph Thomlinson, *Sociological Concepts and Research* (New York: Random House, 1965), p. 20. The traditionalist view is argued in *Sociology on Trial.* Maurice Stein and Arthur Vidich, editors (Englewood Cliffs, New Jersey: Prentice-Hall Inc., 1963).

[25] Robert K. Merton, *Social Theory and Social Structure* (Glencoe, Illinois: Free Press, 1949), p. 83.

of time as human beings work out their relationships with each other and with the natural environment. Thomlinson suggests that,

culture has three aspects: technological, sociological, and ideological. (1) In man's struggle to wrest from his habitat the various necessary means of subsistence, he makes artifacts or physical objects. The material side of culture includes his tools, clothing, shelter, weapons, and so on. It also includes the techniques for the use of these artifacts. (2) The category of socio-facts or social organization includes the various groupings into families, clubs, religious sects, fraternities, and many others. This aspect also covers the economic and political structure. Culture is manifested through the social organization and the people in it. (3) The value system refers to the way of looking at life—philosophical tenets, religious beliefs, and rules of behavior. Values and beliefs upon which people build their lives. Major American values are success, efficiency, progress, material comfort, equality, freedom, nationalism, conformity, and democracy.[26]

Within every culture there are a variety of sub-cultures, each with its own set of values, codes of conduct, and ways of thinking and behaving. Sub-cultures range from those with religious, political, ethnic, and language patterns to those characterized by criminal behavior or other "social" issues, such as the conflict which is said to exemplify the teenager's relationships with adult authority in some societies.

Primary and Secondary Groups. Distinctions are also made between primary groups—those social groupings in which relationships are characterized by intimate face-to-face associations—and secondary groups, including all other groups to which people belong. Sociologists have been particularly interested in the effect of membership in primary groups upon the development of the individual. The pioneer sociologist, Charles Horton Cooley, identified the importance of group life upon the development of personality, especially in the setting of the primary group. The family, peer group, and other circumstances in which a person thinks in terms of "we" membership distinguish primary from secondary groups. The latter comprise an extremely broad spectrum, from political parties, to local social clubs, to vocational or professional organizations. Primary associations occur in those groupings with which a person identifies. Groups to which a person aspires, what the sociologist calls the *reference group,* provide situations in which face-to-face relationships evolve, in addition to those familial and other immediate associations, and which are powerful factors in controlling behavior and in developing values.

[26] Thomlinson, *op. cit.,* pp. 5-6.

Norms and Sanctions. Rules of behavior grow up over time. Some are formally compounded; others are included in the "unwritten law." Sociologists identify three major types of *norms,* or rules of behavior: folkways, mores, and laws. *Folkways* include the "correct" way of doing things. *Mores* are similar to folkways with the exception that moral values become involved to a greater degree. The "topless" waitress illustrates a violation of several mores held in the American culture. Being "topless" is construed as a sexual symbol which, combined with the puritan ethic of evil, means that being "topless" is therefore evil; the evil inherent in being "topless" therefore encourges promiscuity in a culture based on monogamous marriage, etc. The fact that there have been no *laws* directly bearing upon the state of being "topless" when serving as a waitress has caused no end of confusion. *Laws,* then, are the means by which a society controls those matters considered crucial to the existence of the culture. Complex societies necessarily evolve highly codified systems of laws whereas simpler ones get by with few, if any. Folkways and mores, in the end, are much more important and will vary markedly from one culture to another. Our "topless" example would not be an issue in a number of other cultures; it is an American phenomenon. *Sanctions* refer to the types of punishment meted out when norms are violated. These range from informal means of disapproval to the supreme penalty, also varying from one group to another depending upon the culture.

Stratification. Every society groups itself in such a way that levels or ranks appear. *Social class* is a term used to connote the system of social levels that evolve in a society which differentiates one group from another. Differences can be "told" in terms of such widely varying criteria as national origins of one's forebearers, church membership, occupation and income, level of education, type and place of residence in a community, clubs in which membership is held, the way one speaks, how he dresses, how he conducts himself, to mention a few of the major categories of difference. *Caste* is a term reflecting circumstances in which mobility, or the possibility for movement from one social class to another, is highly restricted. The nature of stratification within a society is a matter of much interest to sociologists since it yields an explanation of differences in values and ways of behaving.

Status and Role. Related particularly to concepts of social norms, commented upon above, are the ideas of status and role. *Status* refers to the position a person occupies in the group. One's status is usually defined in terms of how he is treated by the other members of the group. And, status changes from one group to another. Status may be ascribed, i.e., one's position is determined by the group to which one belongs because of age, sex, family, or perhaps caste; it may also be achieved in the sense that levels of education, particular talents, and choices made by the individual himself lead to participation in some groups and not in others. *Role* refers to the part one plays in the group. Status determines the role one plays. As father, teacher, faculty member, president of his club, a person behaves differently—he plays a different role. Status and role, therefore, help a person function satisfactorily in different groups by identifying appropriate forms of behavior; they smooth the way in social relationships by providing guides to behavior. Since most of us seek to behave in accordance with the expectations of others, the circumstances of status and role can be seen as facilitating group interaction. Therefore, sociological inquiry is concerned with these aspects of group dynamics.

Socialization or Enculturation. The processes by which a person becomes a member of society, termed socialization or enculturation, are also of concern to the sociologist. A person learns his value system, attitudes, habits, and the other things which characterize his behavior as a consequence of group living. The most potent influences are contributed by the primary face-to-face groups of which he is a member. The nature of those groups and the way they influence behavior results in personalities in tune or at odds with society.

Working from ideas such as these, sociological inquiry is based upon a variety of supporting concepts developed to facilitate the study of group behavior. There is a growing body of literature describing the work of the sociologist, the types of questions he raises, and the methods employed in seeking answers to those questions. Several references of this type are included at the close of this chapter. A reasonably full understanding of the dimensions of this complex discipline cannot be achieved without referring to these or similar books.

THE NATURE OF SOCIOLOGICAL INQUIRY

The methods the sociologist uses, although not completely unique to his field, are combined in such a way that he is able to facilitate his thinking about sociological questions. To the sociologist, like the geographer, economist, or other social scientist, it is important to "learn to think sociologically." That is, sociologists identify a mode of attack and methods for securing data which they consider more or less unique to their discipline.

Thomlinson identifies eight steps in the process of conducting inquiry into sociological questions:

1. *Selection of an interesting topic*—and perhaps, though not necessarily, a significant or useful one. The topic may be suggested by a theory, an apparent conflict between two theories, a gap in knowledge, or some other combination of inquisitiveness, creative hunches, and proficiency in the subject.
2. *Formulation of working hypotheses.* The translation of an interesting but quasi-specific question into an objectively testable hypothesis demands far more skill than might be supposed by the novice. This conversion of an interesting problem into researchable form is prerequisite to the determination of exactly what information will be relevant.
3. *Deciding on the manner of securing data.* This decision is generally restricted by decisions made in steps 1 and 2—and in practice the experienced researcher makes allowance for step 3 when formulating his hypotheses.
4. *Collection of relevant data.* This operation constitutes the actual performance of the study (the interviewing, for example), as opposed to the anticipatory nature of the first three steps. Sometimes suitable data are already available (the wise researcher always considers this possibility in contemplating steps 2 and 3), in which event, collection consists of copying.
5. *Analysis of the data by statistical and other techniques.* By computing percentages, averages, and more sophisticated measures, the investigator facilitates comprehension of what otherwise might be simply a chaotic mass of information too vast and complicated to be grasped by inspection.
6. *Interpretation of results.* Comparing the theory of step 1 and the hypotheses of step 2 with the findings of steps 4 and 5 has the objective of accepting or rejecting hypotheses and perhaps the theories or laws from which they were deduced. New generalizations may be advanced for later testing.
7. *Presentation of findings and conclusions.* Though the research paper is completed with step 6, publication or other announcement of results is desirable and customary. Otherwise the work is likely to be wasted.

8. *Application of results.* For maximum value of the research project, many sponsors prefer to see the results incorporated into an action program. It is this practical application that justifies the research to the public by making possible a faster rocket or a better mousetrap. The pure researcher, of course, is expected to disdain crass practicality in the tradition of certain ancient Athenians.[27]

Researchable questions in sociology run the gamut, from depth studies on highly specific questions involving relatively small groups to inquiries engaging large numbers of people covering a broad range of information. An example of the first type would be a study undertaken to discover how decisions are being reached in a local union, lodge, or other organization with a restricted membership. Such a study might employ as its major avenue for analysis a case-study approach where certain actions of the group are documented after gathering data through direct observation, interview, or the use of questionnaires. An example of the broad scale study is the classic one by Hollingshead where an entire community was subjected to analysis. The search in this case sought to lead the investigators to an understanding of the nature of the social structure of a typical American community and some of its educational implications.[28] The nature of this study was such that a large number of variables had to be considered. An inquiry frequently identified as primarily sociolgical involving a large population also, but in this case one spread over a large geographic area, is that of Alfred Kinsey and his associates who investigated sexual behavior.[29] A study falling in between these examples was conducted by Caplow and Mc-Gee,[30] who explored reasons college professors move from one institution to another. They analyzed the nature and reasons for vacancies occurring on the faculties of several major institutions in the United States, seeking to understand the factors causing professors to decide to move from one institution to another. Included in their study was

[27] Ralph Thomlinson, *op. cit.,* pp. 40-42. See especially Chapter Three, "Collecting Information," pp. 40-60. Reprinted by permission.

[28] August B. Hollingshead, *Elmtown's Youth* (New York: John Wiley and Sons, Inc., 1949) Other studies of this type include Lloyd W. Warner, *et. al., Democracy in Jonesville* (New York: Harper & Brothers, 1949); James West, *Plainville, USA* (New York: Columbia University Press, 1945) and the *Yankee City Series* by W. Lloyd Warner, *et al.* (New Haven: Yale University Press, 1963).

[29] Alfred C. Kinsey, W. B. Pomeroy, and C. E. Martin, *Sexual Behavior in the Human Male* (Philadelphia: W. B. Saunders Company, 1948); and *Sexual Behavior in the Human Female* (Philadelphia: W. B. Saunders Company, 1953).

[30] Theodore Caplow and Reece J. McGee, *The Academic Market Place* (New York: Basic Books, Inc., 1958)

an analysis of how the vacancies occurring over a given period of time were filled.

Some types of sociological research are indeed more speculative. They do not rely upon the gathering of empirical data to the extent studies such as those described above do. Examples of more speculative research include Waller's book on the family, in which he traces the influence of family life on personality from earliest childhood through the various crises of life,[31] and Sumner's classic, *Folkways*, in which he identifies the role of folkways, mores, and institutions in society and seeks to make applications of these concepts both to primitive as well as to more advanced societies.[32] Works of these kinds also make fundamental contributions to sociological knowledge.

THE NATURE OF ANTHROPOLOGY

To do more than sketch out in broadest terms the kinds of things that interest anthropologists and the ways they attempt to discover answers to their questions poses an extremely difficult task. This is simply because anthropology seeks to comprehend the most variable, difficult to understand subject on earth—man. The anthropologist, in all his boldness, sets out to learn such things as how human culture evolves, the roles of individuals and groups in shaping culture, the manner in which societies resemble each other, and the ways that they differ— all of the factors, elements, conditions, and so on that make human beings human, that cause variations from one culture to another, that show ways man has ordered his life so as to survive under a wide variety of conditions. Anthropological inquiry, then, is in a very real sense a synthesis discipline, much like history and geography but with possibly an even broader view. For as history seeks understandings through establishing temporal relationships between events, people, conditions, and the like, and as geography relates ideas within the scheme of spatial organization, anthropology takes as its focus *man*, wherever and under whatever conditions he may be found, either in time or place.

A single anthropologist cannot expect to achieve such a totality of view, of course, and so he specializes in his studies. In so doing he may draw upon ideas and research methods from virtually every field of knowledge. He may be more nearly a natural scientist, a social scien-

---

[31] Willard Waller, *The Family: A Dynamic Interpretation*, revised by Reuben Hill (New York: The Dryden Press, 1951).

[32] William Graham Sumner, *Folkways* (Boson: Ginn and Company, 1906).

tist, or a humanist at one time or another, depending upon the kinds of questions he seeks to answer. His work, in turn, contributes directly to a number of different fields of study. One major area of inquiry, for instance, is commonly called *physical anthropology*. Within this dimension of study, there are a number of subfields; among them one might seek to understand more fully the evolution of man, the nature of biological adaptation, genetics, or perhaps the relationships of nutrition and other factors to human growth and development. Information gained in such a search obviously may contribute important new knowledge to such standard fields as medicine, physiology, biology, chemistry, psychology, and many others.

Another major strand in anthropological inquiry probes more directly into the area of human behavior. *Cultural* or *social anthropologists* study in a more direct way human cultures. The major emphasis here is upon understanding how the characteristic elements of a culture have evolved as human beings live together. One important division of cultural anthropology is called *archeology*. The archeologist studies past human cultures through the human and other remains and evidences he discovers as he digs up old artifacts, human remains, and other traces of human activity. Other anthropological interests focus upon *linguistics,* or the study of language. Because of the importance of symbolic processes in the evolution of cultures, the nature of language provides a major means for understanding culture.

Because the concerns of anthropology are so broad, utilizing as it does information from many fields and, in turn, making direct contributions to many disciplines, it is sometimes difficult to assess what is distinctively anthropological and what might properly be thought to belong to another discipline. It was noted earlier that the lines demarking sociology and anthropology were probably the most blurred of all and suggested that distinctions between these two fields particularly were becoming increasingly difficult to note clearly. But anthropology also appears to have very similar interests to such fields as psychology (as reflected in its concern for understanding individual behavior), English (especially with regard for the singular importance of communication and the contribution of linguistics to the study of language), geography (in terms of its concern for analyzing human and natural phenomena in relation to their occurrences in space), or history (a major branch of anthropological inquiry is that of cultural history). Other fields might also be mentioned in this regard. The distinguishing characteristic of anthropology, of course, is its unrelenting interest in discovering knowledge about those things that link and unite and therefore explain *human behavior*. To do this, it must ignore the artificial boundaries that have been erected between disciplines and that have so frequently served to restrict intellectual inquiry over the years.

METHODS OF RESEARCH IN ANTHROPOLOGY

The breadth of interest represented by this field obviously means that many different research techniques are employed by those who seek to further anthropological knowledge. Depending upon the special interests of the anthropologist, it may be appropriate to utilize methods of inquiry from the natural sciences, the humanities, or the social sciences. Research advances of the recent past in all of these fields are serving the anthropologists well, just as they are those in the other disciplines. The electronic computer, the employment of radio-isotopes in establishing the age of artifacts, and various electronic marvels, such as the tape recorder, are widely employed.

Like the other disciplines in the social sciences, the trend in anthropological inquiry has been toward the establishment of more rigorous research techniques. Adherence to the principles of the scientific method has been particularly successful in the areas of physical anthropology and in archeology. Linguistic studies have also benefited, especially with the widespread availability of the tape recorder and computers.

As might be expected, cultural anthropology has been the last to yield to the insistent demands of science, and the relevance of empirical research methods to the classic field study of another culture is raising a spirited debate among modern anthropologists. Earlier it was noted that anthropological studies have tended to focus upon the analysis of non-Western peoples. In such studies, research techniques have relied mainly upon well established field work procedures—interviewing, observing, photographing, mapping, etc. Cultural anthropologists have sought to understand one culture in particular, primarily by living as a participant-observer with the people themselves. To this end, an anthropologist usually learned the native language in order that he might better establish rapport and so that he would have the best opportunity to grow in his understanding of what he was able to observe. In these earlier studies, unfortunately, the anthropologist frequently failed to give any specific data before generalizing about the culture he had studied, or else his writings might be held suspect because his examples followed few if any accepted standards for selection. The reader was generally expected to accept the anthropologist's findings—his generalizations—at face value. Although much worthwhile information came out of these earlier studies, criticism of them and the rising tide of science has led to increasing use of empirical or objective techniques. Standard tests, improved methods of employing the questionnaire and field interview, the utilization of census data and other public records, and the development of more systematic reporting procedures are among the means being used to show more clearly what data have led to the development of generalizations.

The invention of means and techniques for handling large quantities of information has brought about another important development. Whereas earlier research focused upon the study of one culture, it is now possible to compare and contrast data from many cultures. Thus, cross-cultural studies are assuming a more significant place in anthropological research. One of the most important sources of information for anthropologists interested in cross-cultural studies is known as the *Human Relations Area Files*. Here data about societies all over the world are placed. By utilizing modern information retrieval techniques, researchers now have information available that previously would have taken months or years of research to secure. The information now immediately available, based upon many lifetimes of work, are thus being built into a data bank of inestimable value to the anthropologist.

As is the case in all of the social sciences, as well as among other disciplines, anthropologists assert that there is a "way of looking at things" that is distinctive to their field. This "anthropological view" of things is probably best summed up in the anthropologist's concept of human culture. Culture, Robert Redfield, the distinguished anthropologist wrote, is a system of common understandings manifest in act and artifact. The emphasis upon "understandings" is most important. In this view, the anthropologist not only must comprehend man's organizational structuring and learn about those things, or artifacts, that are distinctively of his own making. He must, above all else, seek to understand the things held in the minds of men. Culture consists, therefore, of things understood (in their infinite variety) as well as of overt behaviors and material objects.

Resistance to the use of objective or empirical research methods in anthropology is based on the argument that the "anthropological view" may be seriously undermined if techniques are employed that may ignore the search for understanding those things held in the minds of men. There is the fear that anthropological inquiry will become involved exclusively in a search for those kinds of facts that can be coded and fed into a computer. If such data do exclude the important element in culture discussed by Redfield, then there is danger that the "new" anthropology may indeed mislead. The danger expressed by some sociologists and political scientists, particularly—that everyone may be reduced to a number, with the consequence that data collected, compared, and contrasted may not relate to anything important—is here echoed among the anthropologists.

APPLICATIONS OF SOCIOLOGY AND ANTHROPOLOGY IN THE CLASSROOM

The particular focus common to both sociology and anthropology is, of course, the attempt to understand and explain human behavior—to come to know man in the fullest possible way—in terms of comprehending the nature of the human condition as it is today as well as how it came to be. This emphasis means that inquiry in these diciplines and the knowledge deriving from them is characterized more by a point of view, as suggested, than it is by a concern for a particular aspect of human activity (as is more nearly the case in economics and political science), for the study of man's history, or for the manner he has evolved in the process of occupying the earth's surface. However, were one to view history in its very broadest sense as including an attempt to understand man and his development in every dimension of his being, then one might assert that anthropology, at least, bears a very close relationship to history. Indeed, they may be virtually one and the same thing.

Ideas drawn from sociology and anthropology, because of their sweeping concern, may be infused in every social study. The common emphases found in schools today, recounted in Chapter Two, clearly encourage the application of anthropological and sociological understandings. The common studies of preliterate societies, such as those of the American Indian or of ancient times, must draw heavily upon notions of the nature of culture, language, tools used, and social organizations formed to carry on those societies. Studies of the local community, of various world regions, and the like imply the need to draw upon understandings from these realms. Indeed, the "expanding communities concept" as a criterion for defining the scope of the social science curriculum is heavily weighted toward the sociological-anthropological view. These "activities in which all men engage," be they primitive or civilized men, regardless of the time or place, is in one sense a definition of the combined concerns of sociology and anthropology.

Increasingly, however, more direct applications of concepts and generalizations drawn from these fields are being evolved. The emphasis here is upon the development of studies based rather directly upon the work of scholars in anthropology and sociology. A prime example of the former is Jerome Bruner's "Man: A Course of Study," developed and field tested through the auspices of Educational Services Incorporated. Methods and materials have been developed to emphasize aspects of three fundamental anthropological questions: "What is human about human beings? How did they get that way? How can they be made more so?"[33] The purpose of the study, according to Bruner, is to,

. . . seek exercises and materials through which our pupils can learn wherein man is distinctive in his adaptation to the world, and wherein there is discernible continuity between him and his animal forebears. For man represents that crucial point in evolution where adaptation is achieved by the vehicle of culture, and only in a minor way by further changes in his morphology. Yet there are chemical tides that run in his blood that are as ancient as the reptiles. We make every effort at the outset to *tell* children where we hope to travel with them. Yet little of such recounting gets through. Much more useful, we have found, is to pose the three questions directly to the children so that their own views can be brought into the open and so that they can establish some points of view of their own.[34]

In this approach, children are asked to consider five subjects associated with the evolution of man as a species that define his distinctiveness as man and his promise for further evolution. These humanizing forces are "tool making, language, social organization, the management of man's prolonged childhood, and man's urge to explain his world."[35]

The approach of the social studies curriculum program, outlined briefly here, is designed to be used with children during their intermedi-

---

[33] Jerome S. Bruner, "Man: A Course of Study," Chapter Four in *Toward a Theory of Instruction* (Cambridge, Mass.: Harvard University Press, 1966), pp. 73-101. Also printed as Occasional Paper No. 4, by the Social Studies Curriculum Program, Educational Services Incorporated, 44-A Brattle Street, Cambridge, Massachusetts 02138. Available on request.

[34] *Ibid.*, p. 74.

[35] *Ibid.*, p. 75. The reader may wish to recall the description of a classroom that undertook a study of man's early tools, also heavily weighted in the anthropological dimension, contained in Chapter Six, "Teaching the Social Study."

ate grade years. Obviously, the dependence upon anthropological findings is direct. Similar types of studies are being based upon sociological inquiry, however. Lippitt and his associates, for example, are developing materials focusing on the study of human behavior in groups.[36] Materials and methods are being devised to help children become aware of the nature of human interaction through participation in planned experiences in the classroom group. Sensitivities are raised for the feelings of others under differing circumstances; ideas are introduced concerning the possibility of making informed guesses about expected behavior, if not actually predicting it. As in "Man: A Course of Study," Lippitt and his colleagues are emphasizing direct experiencing. Situations are developed and questions raised that draw directly upon the children's views; the approach is therefore primarily inductive and intuitive rather than deductive and analytic.

As is the case in drawing upon any of the social science disciplines for sustenance in planning a curriculum of social studies, the teacher's background and understanding of the concepts and generalizations in these fields is important. A teacher cannot be expected to tell well understandings that are foreign to his knowledge. And as mentioned before, the demands on the elementary school teacher are such that it is not possible to know, in advance, all that is needed to teach the broad scope of a particular curriculum of social studies. To assist in gradually overcoming problems in this area, a bibliography of books concerning the nature of sociology and anthropology are included at the conclusion of this chapter. References are also included with respect to teaching problems in these fields. In an Appendix will be found a bibliography of basic books selected to provide a broad background of understanding in the various dimensions of these and other fields of the social sciences. That it is important to consult references of this type is obvious. It is not feasible to include within the covers of one book the array of concepts and understandings necessary to teaching. That it is possible to teach (and to learn) incorrect ideas should be equally obvious. The realities of the culture of the American Indian, past and present, are not taught in our schools, by and large, because teachers are not aware of those realities. Ethnocentrism, the belief in the inherent superiority of one's own group and culture, accompanied by some degree of contempt for other cultures and other peoples, may be taught in our schools if we as teachers are not sufficiently well grounded in the important concepts

---

[36] To be published by Science Research Associates, Chicago, Illinois.

and generalizations—the major understandings that emerge from these important social science disciplines. In planning our work with children, as a consequence, we have a responsibility to select from these disciplines ideas and modes of inquiry that will extend in appropriate dimensions understandings about the nature of man, his works, his life as a member of a variety of social groups, his values, his aspirations. Seven persistent themes that may be woven into a curriculum of social studies and that may assist in achieving these objectives have been selected here to illustrate the manner in which concepts and understandings from the fields of anthropology and sociology might be considered in the classroom. Because these disciplines are general sciences of man, such broad vistas for study cannot be properly represented in such a listing as that following. However, these are the kinds of ideas that pre-adolescent children can cope with, growing in their awareness of the world about them, becoming alert to its many human problems, and developing an empathy for humankind through the power that this kind of knowledge about the human estate can give.

1. *The nature, variety, and purposes of social institutions.* Every society establishes a variety of social institutions in order to preserve and perpetuate its values. These institutions exist in endless profusion, differ markedly from place to place, and serve a wide variety of purposes. Some are central to the very existence of the society; others are more peripheral in nature. Their nature and extent also vary from one culture to another. A teacher will want to raise children's awareness of these institutions through direct study as well as by utilizing opportunities that present themselves either incidentally in the on-going work of the classroom or more deliberately as other studies proceed. Gradually children can become aware of the types of institutions their own and other societies have evolved over time, learn something of the changes time has wrought in them, and become familiar with some of the differences existing between institutions serving the same general purpose from one culture to another.

2. *The similarities and differences among world cultures.* Since most people tend to mistrust the strange and what at first blush appears to be unusual, empathy for other peoples is dependent upon knowing in sufficient detail about the ways others actually live. Human beings share the same common needs, responding in dif-

ferent ways according to the particular time, place, and conditions impinging upon them. All children may profitably consider the lifeways of other people, growing in their understanding, in the process, that every person places the highest value on what he considers to be *his* culture. The aim of such studies, of course, is to stem the tide of ethnocentrism, to cause the child to expand his capacities to empathize and understand others by expanding his awareness of the commonality binding people over the earth together.

3. *Elements and forces affecting group interaction.* In every society, man lives as a member of a variety of groups. Each of these groups has its particular structure within which individuals play different roles. Human behavior is characterized by this kind of patterning—groups assume certain structures, roles within them are learned—thus behavior is controlled or regulated to a greater or lesser degree depending upon the importance of the group to the well-being of the society. Pupils can be assisted to develop an awareness of the purposes of different groups, of their composition and importance in a society, and of ways behavior is regulated as a consequence of membership in particular groups. Gradually, they may understand that the scientific study of human behavior in groups assists in formulating principles and other guides for predicting behavior and that they, too, may, through the application of these understandings, grow in their power to understand the behavior of others.

4. *How communication and language facilitate understanding.* Human beings communicate in a number of different languages, some verbal, some non-verbal in character. Awareness of different modes of communicating may be heightened through attention to commonly used verbal and non-verbal signals, through contrasting languages, through "playing with" their own language to see how changes in syntax and grammar aid or otherwise affect powers of communication. The language of a culture, its values, attitudes, and objectives, are also communicated through the creative arts. Teachers would be remiss not to bring to the classroom a broad range of experiences that reflect a world view of the creative arts, including the performing arts as well as those of painting, sculpture, ceramics, etc. Sensitivities to the central role of language in cultural and social development, to the growth of intelligence,

may be raised through such activities as thinking about the ways
animals and other infra-human groups appear to communicate, relating this to human efforts, studying any one of the innumerable
aspects of a communications system, producing a classroom newspaper or textbook, etc., considering the many ways verbal and
non-verbal language is used throughout our own culture.

5. *The nature of leadership in a variety of settings.* Every group
    situation involves leadership and followership roles, some of a
    formal nature, others highly informal. The characteristics of
    leadership roles vary under different circumstances. Building
    awareness of roles comes about as a consequence of actually play-
    ing them out. Children should be given many different experiences
    involving widely varying roles. They may study, think about, con-
    sider in a variety of ways roles played by both people known to
    them personally as well as others whom they can observe.

6. *The development of attitudes, including prejudice.* Attitudes of all
    kinds begin their development in the child as soon as he becomes
    aware of other people. By the time he reaches school age, many
    of the attitudes and some of the prejudices that will color his
    thinking for the rest of his life are well along in their formation.
    One's own attitudes toward familiar things as well as attitudes
    as they are observed in others provide an important arena for
    study and discussion. Current events reported in the newspaper
    or picture magazine, accounts of situations observed in the
    classroom and the school, and circumstances in which changes
    in attitudes may be observed lend themselves to analysis and
    cogitation. Whereas we might think of an *attitude* as a readiness
    or predisposition to think or act in a certain manner, *prejudice*
    is an *unreasoned* and preconceived opinion or feeling about
    something. While both attitudes and prejudice can be either
    favorable or unfavorable in a given circumstance, prejudice is
    more often considered in its negative aspects. Studying and think-
    ing about prejudice as it can be observed, read about, discussed,
    and otherwise analyzed has a place in social studies, both in its
    contemporary forms and as it has emerged in different times and
    places. Although one would naturally adjust the classroom work
    in this regard according to the maturity levels of children, it re-
    mains true that one man's fact is another man's prejudice, and
    so there will always be a variety of opinion concerning the appro-

priateness of discussions with young children in this realm. Arguments for postponing or watering down if not glossing over entirely topics dealing with attitude formation and prejudice are for the most part based on what a public *might* accept rather than the degree to which children can understand. If it is true, as the song from *South Pacific* reminds us, "You've got to be carefully taught" and knowing that attitudes and prejudice begin forming at a very early age, the school certainly has a major responsibility to begin with the youngest children in explorations of the meanings and implications behind the development of attitudes of all kinds. We are not suggesting that children be taught what to think or believe, of course. Rather, we are concerned here primarily with two things: (1) that the child consider under objective guidance those elements and conditions surrounding him, which he is capable of dealing with meaningfully, that may stimulate his awareness of the existence of attitudes, including prejudice, and help him grow in his understanding of the nature, sources, and role of attitudes in thinking processes and in human relationships and (2) that he live in a warmly accepting classroom atmosphere where the adult personalities with whom he comes in contact are themselves relatively prejudice-free.

7. *The attributes that make man human.* During the course of a child's schooling he can come into contact with the basic informaation needed to understand how man in different environments and cultures differs and how he is alike. Not only are we concerned about similarities and differences; of course, there are those distinguishing characteristics which make man human, separating him from other animals. There is scientific information, discoverable much in the same vein as those approaches characterizing the work of the physical anthropologist, that are particularly suited to the intermediate and upper grade child. Children can explore profitably such questions as these: How does man differ in his physical measurements from place to place? What is the origin of the concept of the races of man? What are the measurable similarities and differences among races? How has man adapted to and utilized the earth's environment from place to place? What are some of the notions about the physical development of man over the ages? What evidences do we have about man's movements over the earth's surface in the distant as well

as in the recent past? How is the history of the earth's development related to the development of the human species?

In each of the foregoing, we are concerned also with emphasizing the
kinds of relationships existing among group members. How does primitive man, today and in past times, manage to survive in a world
whose natural environment is certainly more hostile than friendly? How
have people learned to bend the environment to do their will? What
kinds of groups and ways of living have they formed to achieve their
ends? How do these groups vary from place to place? How do the
roles various people play in them differ and change? What values, attitudes, and feelings do other people hold; how and why do they differ
from our own?

The questions raised by the work of sociologists and anthropologists
are therefore very broad. The focus is on the behavior of human beings
—what they are like, how they came to be the way they are. The contributions of these disciplines to our thinking as we plan a curriculum
for boys and girls should encourage us to develop many ideas that will
help raise sensitivities to our own behavior and to that of others.

For Further Reading

GENERAL

Berelson, Bernard and Gary A. Steiner, *Human Behavior: An Inventory
of Scientific Findings* (New York: Harcourt, Brace and World,
Inc., 1964).

Bierstadt, Robert, *et.al., Modern Social Science* (New York: McGraw
Hill, 1964).

Count, Earl W. (ed.), *Fact and Theory in Social Science* (Syracuse,
New York: Syracuse University Press, 1964).

The Encyclopedia of the Social Sciences, rev. ed. (New York: Macmillan, in press).

Handy, Rollo, *Methodology of the Behavior Sciences: Problems and
Controversies* (Springfield, Illinois: Charles C. Thomas, Publisher, 1964).

Hoselitz, Bert F., *A Reader's Guide to the Social Sciences* (Glencoe,
Ill.: The Free Press, 1959).

Kaplan, Abraham, *The Conduct of Inquiry: Methodology for Behavioral Science* (San Francisco: Chandler, 1964).

Morrissett, Irving (ed.), *Concepts and Structure in the New Social Science Curricula* (West Lafayette, Indiana: Social Science Education Consortium, Inc., 1966). See also various publications describing particular fields of the social sciences and their contributions to schooling.

National Council for the Social Studies, *New Viewpoints in the Social Sciences, Twenty-eighth Yearbook* (Washington, D.C.: N.C.S.S.: 1958).

Ray, Ronald P., *Trends in Social Science Research* (New York: Philosophical Library, 1961).

ECONOMICS

Economic Education in the Schools, a Report of the National Task Force on Economic Education (New York: The Committee for Economic Development, 1961).

Frankel, M. L., *Economic Education* (New York: The Center for Applied Research, 1965).

Harris, Seymore E., "Economics," Chapter 3 in *High School Social Studies Perspectives* (Boston: Houghton Mifflin Company, 1962), pp. 53-79.

Joint Council on Economic Education, *Teachers Guide to Economic Education Program,* Part I: *Economic Ideas and Concepts;* Part II: *Suggestions for Grade Placement and Development of Economic Ideas and Concepts* (New York: Joint Council on Economic Education, 1964).

Lewis, Ben W., "Economics," in *The Social Studies and the Social Sciences* (New York: Harcourt, Brace & World Inc., 1962), pp. 106-134.

Martin, Richard S. and Reuben G. Miller, *Economics and Its Significance* (Columbus, Ohio: Charles E. Merrill Books, Inc., 1965).

Social Education, Vol. XXX, No. 4 (April, 1966), a special issue on economic education.

Wolf, Ronald H., "Economics," Chapter 5 in *The Social Sciences: Foundations of the Social Studies* (Boston: Allyn and Bacon, Inc., 1965), pp. 137-69.

POLITICAL SCIENCE

Iredell, Vernon R., "Political Science," Chapter Four in *The Social Sciences: Foundations of the Social Studies* (Boston: Allyn and

Bacon, Inc., 1965), pp. 104-136.

Kirkpatrick, Evron M. and Jeane J. Kirkpatrick, "Political Science," Chapter 5 in *High School Social Studies Perspectives* (Boston: Houghton Mifflin Company, 1962), pp. 99-125.

Long, Norton E., "Political Science," in *The Social Studies and the Social Sciences* (New York: Harcourt, Brace & World Inc., 1962), pp. 88-105.

National Council for the Social Studies, *Political Science in the Social Studies*, Donald H. Riddle and Robert S. Cleary (eds.), Thirty-sixth Yearbook (Washington, D.C.: NCSS, 1966).

Sorauf, Frank J., *Political Science, an Informal Overview* (Columbus, Ohio: Charles E. Merrill Books, Inc., 1965).

Woll, Peter, "Recent Developments in Political Science," *Social Education*, Vol. XXX, No. 3 (March, 1966), pp. 168-172.

SOCIOLOGY

Alpert, Harry, "Sociology: Its Present Interests," Chapter Five in *The Behavioral Sciences Today* (New York: Basic Books, Inc., 1963), pp. 52-64.

Berger, Peter L., *Invitation to Sociology: A Humanistic Perspective* (Garden City, New York: Doubleday Anchor Books, 1963).

Cole, William E., "Sociology," Chapter Seven in *The Social Sciences: Foundations of the Social Studies* (Boston: Allyn and Bacon, Inc., 1965), pp. 191-219.

Inkles, Alex, *What is Sociology?* (Englewood Cliffs, N.J.: Prentice-Hall, Inc., 1964).

Page, Charles H. (ed.), *Sociology and Contemporary Education* (New York: Random House, 1964).

Rose, Caroline B., *Sociology: the Study of Man in Society* (Columbus, Ohio: Charles E. Merrill Books, Inc., 1965).

Sykes, Gresham M., "Sociology," in *The Social Studies and the Social Sciences* (New York: Harcourt, Brace & World, 1962).

ANTHROPOLOGY

De Bois, Cora, "Anthropology: Its Present Interests: Chapter Three in *The Behavioral Sciences Today* (New York: Basic Books, Inc., 1963), pp. 26-37.

Guthe, Alfred K., "Anthropology," Chapter Six in *The Social Sciences: Foundations of the Social Studies* (Boston: Allyn and Bacon, Inc., 1965).

Nimkoff, Meyer F., "Anthropology, Sociology, and Social Psychology," Chapter Two in *High School Social Studies Perspectives* (Boston: Houghton Mifflin Company, 1962), pp. 29-51.

Oliver, Douglas L., "Cultural Anthropology," in *The Social Studies and the Social Sciences* (New York: Harcourt, Brace & World, Inc., 1962), pp. 135-155.

Oliver, Douglas, L., *Invitation to Anthropology* (Garden City, New York: The Natural History Press, 1964).

Pelto, Pertti J., *The Study of Anthropology* (Columbus, Ohio: Charles E. Merrill Books, Inc., 1965).

Spindler, George D. (ed.), *Education and Culture* (New York: Holt, Rinehart and Winston, 1963).

Wolf, Eric R., *Anthropology* (Englewood Cliffs, N.J.: Prentice-Hall, Inc., 1964).

CHAPTER TEN

Using Globes and Flat Maps

Although maps are the major tool of the geographer and have special relevance to studies emphasizing geographic elements, they are also useful in every other aspect of social studies. It is hard to imagine a study which would not be more clearly presented by using maps and globes. Every study entails place and space. That is, every problem or topic children approach involves thinking about things occupying a position or place on the earth's surface; each is related to other things in space; all are separated by distance and direction. No other device shows these spatial relationships as well as the geographer's master tool: the map drawn on either a sphere or a flat surface.

In addition to the social studies uses to which maps logically may be put, there are long-term reasons for the development of map reading abilities. One cannot understand local, state, national, or international events and conditions without reference to maps. Newspapers, magazines, television programs, and books concerned with vital human issues rely heavily upon maps for the communication of ideas. Then, of course, an increasingly mobile population travels widely over the earth. The accurate and intelligent use of maps in getting from one place to jobs require map reading or other abilities closely related to it. The reading of blueprints and other drawings and plans, for example, in-another is self-evident. Not least in importance is the fact that many volves many of the concepts which are inherent in effective map reading. In short, a literate society not only reads words as they are printed on the page; it also reads the different types of symbols and other marks which the cartographer draws on maps.

Despite these needs, teachers have little reason to boast with respect to the effectiveness of efforts to develop good map readers. Almost all evidence which reveals anything about the abilities of either children or adults to read maps indicates that we remain, by and large, an illiterate nation. In addition, the effects of schooling are very difficult to find. One study, for example, showed that children in the first and second grades scored as well as children in the fifth and sixth grades.[1] This investigation sought information in only one of several areas of competence demanded in effective map reading. And it suggests, as does virtually every other investigation reported (of which there are unfortunately very few), that the methods being used to teach boys and girls to read maps are not as effective as they should be. However, this lack of a systematic program in developing competent map readers in the schools is attracting more and more attention; though individual schools may yet have a long way to go, valuable suggestions are becoming available for teachers who want to do something about the situation.[2]

Learning to read maps poses many of the same kinds of problems as learning to read books. For example, the wide variety of symbols that appear on maps cannot be read unless the child can visualize the things for which those symbols stand. The development of concepts about the natural and man-made things in the environment which are shown on maps is therefore a prerequisite to all effective map reading and is the point at which most boys and girls have difficulty. Similarly, children must be introduced to the special language of mapping. The cartographer, or map maker, has combined on his map a very complex pattern of colors, printed-word symbols, and other markings which show not only the location of things but their arrangement over the face of the earth. Thus, location or position is not haphazard but is determined by a complex set of rules. These rules appear in concepts of distance and direction and must be understood if map reading is to be effective.

As in printed-word reading, the ultimate goal in map reading is the

[1] Malcolm P. Douglass, "Some Relationships Between Laterality and Knowledge of Directions," *Elementary School Journal,* Vol. 66, No. 2, pp. 68-74.

[2] For example, see Bernice W. Casper, "Scope and Sequence of Geographic Education in the Modern School Curriculum Grades Four Through Twelve," published in two parts in *Transition,* Vol. 2, No. 3 and Vol. 3, No. 1 (Chicago: A. J. Nystrom and Company, n.d.).

Another helpful source is Ruby M. Harris, *The Rand McNally Handbook of Map and Globe Usage* (Chicago: Rand McNally and Company, 1959).

At the end of the Appendix section is a "Sequence Chart of Map and Globe Skills and Understandings: Kindergarten Through Grade Six" published by the Los Angeles Unified School District, Division of Instruction.

development of abilities to infer relationships. The map reader seeks to understand, as he looks at the patterns of things on the map, what kinds of relationships exist among the things shown. Is there a reason, for example, that cities are found in certain locations and not in others? Is there a connection between the routes of railroads and other transportation routes and the location of cities? What is the relationship between the location of mineral resources used in certain manufacturing processes, transportation routes, the location of manufacturing centers and the proximity of the market for the finished product? Various kinds of maps have been developed to aid in understanding the nature of these kinds of relationships. The ultimate goal with boys and girls in elementary schools is to help them grow in their ability to sense them through the critical study of maps of various kinds.

However, the beginnings must be modest. They must be developmental. That is, teachers cannot begin with the intermediate concepts of map reading, assuming that the children have progressed beyond the earliest stages of concept development and understanding the language of maps. And, finally, they should be sequential in that some kinds of understandings and abilities must precede others. Map reading should be introduced in the kindergarten. As in other aspects of the reading process, a good beginning can be had if major emphasis is placed upon making (or writing) their own maps. The emphasis upon making maps should not diminish throughout the elementary school years. It is the key to reading the maps made by other people.

Basic Concepts About the Model Globe

Since the earth is round, it is not surprising that the most accurate maps which can be used in the classroom must also be drawn on something round. To see things in their true relationship in every respect, one must therefore use the model globe. This is why the globe is the most accurate model of the earth.

Unfortunately, the model globe is often an inconvenient tool to use. It shows such a large area (the entire world) that it cannot be used to show any particular place in very much detail. Just the words "New York" cover over two hundred miles on a globe which is twelve inches in diameter. It cannot be rolled up and put away when not needed; nor is it very convenient to carry about. You can look at only one half of it at any one time, and, in addition, a good model globe is very expensive.

For these and other practical reasons, the model globe is not always the best map to use in the classroom.

However, it is essential that children in elementary school gradually learn the basic ideas that lie behind the model globe. This is because it is for some things the best tool to use in understanding worldwide relationships. For example, it is the only map which shows the *true* shapes, distances, directions, and equal areas or places around the world. It is the best device, for example, for understanding time changes and for plotting the shortest distance between any two points on the earth's surface. Of even greater importance, the model globe provides the basis for every other kind of map. Only by understanding the system of coordinates used to locate places accurately on the model globe can one understand and appreciate the uses and the possibilities for misunderstanding flat maps.

Another value of the globe in the classroom is in teaching how the earth's size, shape, and set of motions are related to the solar system. From such studies, children may gain a knowledge of the relationships of day to night, of the seasons, of wind and ocean currents, and other important information about the physical nature of their world.[3]

FLAT MAPS FROM THE MODEL GLOBE

When one attempts to render a curved surface, such as that of the model globe, to a flat one, something will be distorted, and every flat map is guilty of *some* distortion—it is out of shape in one way or another. Obviously, the larger the area shown on the flat map, the greater the distortion is likely to be. Flat maps of relatively smaller areas are likely to be more nearly accurate. In working with children, therefore, flat maps which show the entire world are least likely to be preferred. That is, use the globe wherever possible for mapping problems involving global concepts.

Everyone is familiar with the problem of peeling an orange or cutting up a soft rubber ball in such way as to make it as flat as possible. It will never become completely flat, of course, and the problem of slicing up a ball illustrates the problem with which the cartographer contends when he draws the parallels and meridians on a flat piece of paper. The rendering that results is called a "map projection" which means, as Greenhood states:

[3] Several references containing basic information about maps and globes are listed at the close of this chapter.

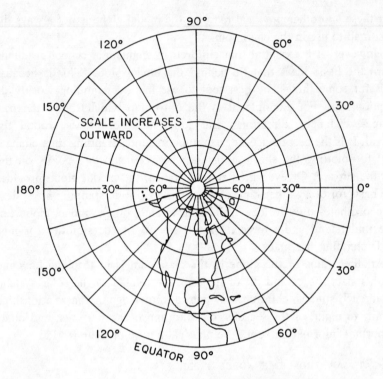

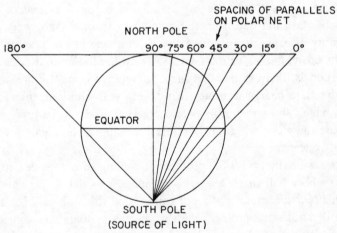

Figure 10–1: The Principle of Projections to a Plane. The projection shown, with the light at the opposite pole, is known as a stereographic projection. (Reprinted by permission from James M. Smythe and Charles G. Brown, *Elements of Geography*, New York: St. Martin's Press, 1959, p. 17)

Using a slang expression most literally, we might say a projection is a "take-off" on the globe. A plane trying to imitate a sphere.

The main job in transforming globes into flat maps is to have the precious coordinates. We may distort shape or sacrifice area; we may fudge on distances and connive about directions, take in a little here and let out a bit there, making one quality pay for building up another. But one function of a map is indispensable: showing *true location*. No map-user is going to stand for meddling with locations. They have to be right, no matter what kind of map we get: globular or flat, round, oval, triangular, square or polyhedral.

When we take that network of orderly lines off the globe and cast it upon a flat surface we must in all conscience be sure that the lands and seas which come off with it remain in the same corresponding positions as they had on the globe. Same for every city, bay, cape, island, lake, mountain peak, and what have we. If a certain place is located at the intersection of the 37th parallel and the 119th meridian on the globe, that's where it must be on the new map. No matter how much we bend, or curl, or flatten those netlines, or change the bearings, we must keep each location at its exact crossing of coordinates.

The verb "to project" means literally "to throw forward." A map projection is this network of coordinates picked off the globe and thrown forward upon a plane surface.[4]

The Mercator Projection. The most widely known "projection" is that invented by Gerard Mercator in 1567. It is today one of the most familiar of flat maps and probably the most misunderstood. Mercator's projection was originally devised to assist in navigation, and its prime purpose remains there. In Mercator's day, sailors could not use the globe to navigate from one place to another because it is impossible to plot accurately a ship's course on the model globe. Since all lines curve and distances between meridians vary, there were no tools which could be used easily and accurately. Mercator succeeded in developing the first successful map to employ the system of coordinates discussed above which could be useful to sailors. Although there were flat navigational charts in existence prior to this time, the most widely used ones (called Portolan Charts), although accurate for their day, were not calculated according to degrees of latitude and longitude. Despite Mercator's revolutionary map, however, it was a long time before it became widely used. Sailors could not see why they should use a map which had so many obvious errors. Their maps were bad enough, they said, and Mercator's just made a bad situation worse.

[4] David Greenhood, *Mapping* (Chicago: The University of Chicago Press, 1964), pp. 122-123.

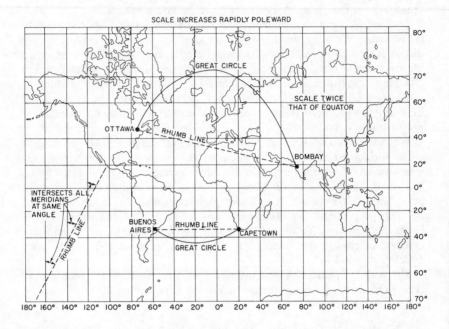

Figure 10–2: Mercator's Projection. Note: a rhumb line is the term given to a line of constant compass direction (the easiest route to travel). On Mercator's Projection rhumb lines are always straight lines. (Reprinted by permission from James M. Smythe and Charles G. Brown, *Elements of Geography*, New York: St. Martin's Press, 1959, p. 10)

What the sailors were objecting to was exactly the same thing which bothers us about it today—distortion. Mercator straightened out the converging meridians so that they no longer intersected; each meridian became a straight line, pointing north and south on the flat map but never meeting as they do on the model globe. Distances between meridians actually decrease as one nears the poles. To compensate for this, Mercator stretched everything in the latitudes as they approach the poles. Basically, he followed the principle illustrated below. By calling on mathematics for some additional help, he took the "projection" resulting when parallels and meridians are projected on a cylinder surrounding the model globe and equalized latitude and longitude in the extreme north and south latitudes.

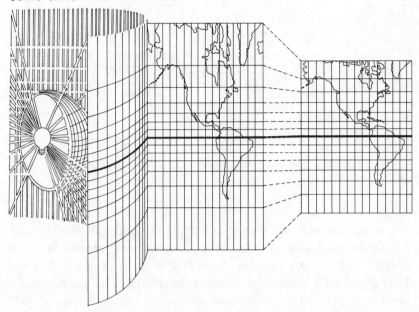

Figure 10–3: Central projection of globe upon a cylinder, and a sub-sequently modified map-structure, the Mercator, made to same scale along Equator.

Obviously, the Mercator projection is accurate where the cylinder touches the model globe—at the equator. Distances north and south of the equator grow increasingly inaccurate. They are so distorted that Greenland appears to be five times as big as India when it is actually less than half as large. It is therefore possible to gain some very strange notions about what the world is like by looking at Mercator's very valuable contribution to navigation. Without the model globe and other maps with which to compare it, Mercator's map is a poor one for school purposes. Aside from distortion in terms of the size of land and water masses, distance is badly stretched. The scale of distances on the Mercator, rather than being equal in every direction as they are on the globe, are different for different latitudes. So a scale for a Mercator map is printed like this, and the map reader must keep in mind to what extent the differences vary if he is not to be misled by what he thinks he sees.

Direction is also badly distorted on the Mercator map. The map showing the great circle route plotted along the route which appears to be shortest, appearing on page 328, illustrates this point. Other directional

STATUTE MILES

Figure 10–4: The Mercator Projection requires a "several-decker" scale of miles.

inconsistencies will appear upon examining the model globe along with a Mercator projection. For instance, the land mass nearest to North America *appears* to be Europe. Actually it is the land occupied by the U.S.S.R. directly across the North Pole. Plotting the course that a satellite launched from Cape Kennedy would take around the earth produces a waving line which extends first above the equator and then below on the Mercator map, seemingly an illogical path for a space vehicle to follow but one that seems completely reasonable when reference is made to the model globe.

Although the Mercator projection is not found in schools as often as it once was, a large number of these maps continue to be used. Children frequently see them on television where they are used on news programs and to illustrate such special events as the flight of a space vehicle. Whenever there is a need for a flat world map to show the distribution of phenomena over the earth, the Mercator is frequently the projection used to illustrate it. There are other world map projections that do not have as many combinations of undesirable features, but they, too, introduce peculiar qualities which must be understood to be appreciated. The best way out of this dilemma is to use many different kinds of maps and to refer always to the model globe rather than to the flat world map when it is possible to use the globe to illustrate the point.

Other Projections. Since Mercator's day, cartographers have developed scores of other map projections. Each has its special usefulness and value. The principles behind some of these maps are illustrated below. All maps are constructed with the aid of mathematical formulas, just as Mercator's was; some, such as the homolographic, or equal-area, are derived exclusively from mathematical formulas. Homolo-

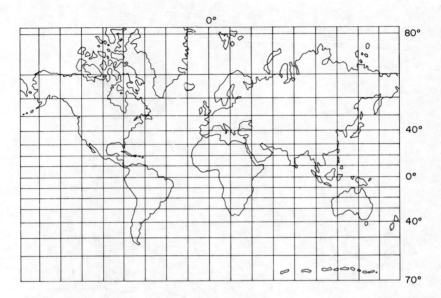

Figure 10–5: The Cylindrical Conformal, or Mercator, Projection.

graphic maps are best suited to showing worldwide distribution of things (see the discussion of distribution maps below) and may be considered superior to the Mercator map for this purpose.

In studying maps and map projections in the elementary school classroom, an interesting and worthwhile project for intermediate and upper grade children is the collection of as many different projections as can be found, posting them on a bulletin board with notes showing how alike and different they are from one another.[5]

In beginning a collection of this sort, select a world map or one which

[5] Some school districts have purchased a device which may be used to demonstrate the basic principles of projections for the Mercator (cylindrical), conic, and azimuthal projections. It consists of a transparent globe fixed with a small light in the center. By placing the plastic units supplied over the globe in a semi-dark room, the grid formed by the parallels and meridians, along with the major land masses, is projected onto the cylinder, cone, or flat surface when it is placed over or next to the globe. Paper can be attached to the plastic, the landforms traced, and then removed to show what happens when the map is viewed on a flat surface. This is undoubtedly the most vivid means of demonstrating problems of distortions of space, area, direction, and distance available. The device is manufactured by Farquhar Transparent Globes, 5007 Warrington Avenue, Philadelphia, Pennsylvania. Many naval reserve units have been supplied with these devices and frequently they can be borrowed from this source if unavailable in the school district.

"Gentlemen, before we release these satellite pictures to the public...."

Reprinted by permission from *Saturday Review* and Al Ross.

shows a sizable portion of the earth's surface (a hemisphere, perhaps, a continent, or a major culture area). As additional maps are collected, comparisons can be made of the ways the maps differ with respect to the four main properties all maps possess: those of shape, area, distance, and direction. To evaluate the maps with regard for these properties, questions such as these may be asked:

1. How do the maps vary in showing the proper shape of the land and water areas?
2. Do they preserve the relative size or area of one place in relation to the others shown?
3. How do the maps differ in showing distances from one place to another?
4. How accurately does each map show direction when relationships between one place and another are compared with those shown on the model globe?

A. Mollweide's Projection

B. Sinusoidal Projection

C. Aitoff's Projection

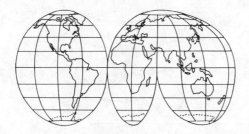

D. Goode's Interrupted Projection

Figure 10–6: Four types of homolographic, or equal-area, maps commonly used in school. Each is purely a mathematical projection. (Reprinted by permission from James M. Smythe and Charles G. Brown, *Elements of Geography*, New York: St. Martin's Press, 1959, p. 21)

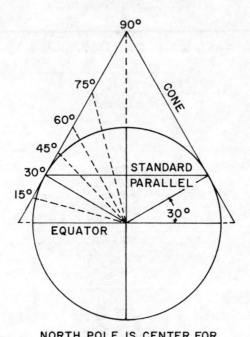

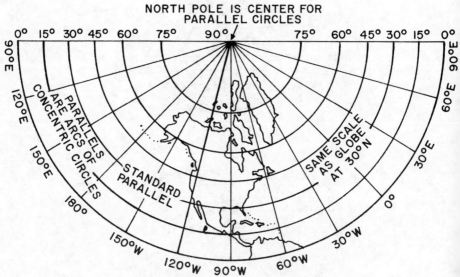

Figure 10–7: The Principle of Conical Projections. The standard parallel In this case 30° N. (Reprinted by permission from James M. Smythe and Charles G. Brown, *Elements of Geography*, New York: St. Martin's Press, 1959, p. 19)

Basic Concepts in Map Reading

Map reading is a much more complex process than one might at first suspect. No matter whether the map appears on a model globe or a flat surface, it can be read only when the reader can create meaning and significance for the wide variety of symbols the cartographer has employed in making it. The ways he has used color, for example, may depict the relief and elevation of different places. Or, color may communicate something about the uses to which the land is being put. It may also indicate how things are distributed over the earth's surface. In other words, color is used to tell different things on different maps, and the reader must be alert to the particular way it is used on the map he wishes to interpret or he will be confused.

The cartographer has also used a variety of symbols to show the location and distribution of things. Some of these symbols look very much like the thing itself or are suggestive of it, so the reader may be able to guess what the cartographer is trying to tell him if he does not already know the meaning of the symbol. Other symbols, such as those used to indicate location, size, and sometimes function of a city, for example, are much more abstract and require special knowledge before they can be interpreted accurately. Knowing how to use map legends is essential in understanding many of these kinds of symbols which are included on the map. In addition, the cartographer has used printed words to designate the location of one-of-a-kind features. Their interpretation requires printed-word reading abilities, often of a high order because place names frequently are quite unusual. Often cartographers are the worst offenders for not observing phonetic and other rules of pronunciation and spelling.

Finally, the cartographer has arranged all of these colors and symbols according to a complex grid or network of parallels and meridians. In reading the model globe, one expects the child gradually to acquire knowledge about the meaning of this grid system. In reading flat maps, one expects him ultimately to appreciate the fact that distortion is present, to know something about what special problems in distortion may be represented on the map he is attempting to read, and to interpret what he sees with this fact in mind.

Because of these very complex relationships, it is necessary to think about the kinds of ideas that are basic to map reading and to plan experiences with children which will make it possible for them to create meaningful images when they attempt to read maps—either those they have made themselves or those which the cartographer has prepared. Map reading activities are developmental and will be successful only when the maturity levels of children are respected. Since there is a general tendency to expect more of children than they are capable of, it is best to try not to assume too much. By involving children in map making at every level—beginning with the kindergarten—insights into the levels of understanding will be available against which the teacher can compare the difficulty of the tasks involved in reading maps prepared by others. During the years the child is in school, teachers should encourage development of five abilities basic to all map reading activities:

1. He should develop concepts about direction.
2. He should develop concepts of distance and scale.
3. He should be able to employ locational abilities.
4. He should be able to interpret map symbols of various kinds.
5. He should be able to draw inferences and develop generalizations from the study of a variety of different kinds of maps.

DEVELOPING CONCEPTS ABOUT DIRECTION

How many times every one of us has wondered at the amazing abilities of animals to travel, apparently unerringly, from one part of their world to another. The Pacific Coast salmon travels literally thousands of miles at sea and yet returns to spawn on the river where he himself was given life. Even the lowly ant traverses what for him are vast areas with an uncanny instinct for arriving at his destination. Were it thus for human beings! Not only are we not born with instinctive capacities for finding our way around, we often find it difficult to develop an adequate sense for direction even though others have labored long hours in attempts to teach us to think and act automatically whenever problems of telling "east" from "west" or even "right" from "left" arise. For without a good sense for direction, it becomes difficult for us to use these and the other intellectual tools which have been devised over the years to give expression to ideas about directions of things and the relationships of those things in space.

To appreciate the problem of the young child as he attempts to deal with directional relationships in and out of school, consider for a moment the manner in which the sense for direction appears to develop during the first few years of life. Prior to the time the child enters school, it is a rare youngster who has mastered the differences of "right" and "left," of telling where the sun rises or sets, and, of even greater difficulty, of using such concepts as "north" or perhaps even some of the other cardinal directions. The pre-school child is vaguely aware, at best, that there are places in the world other than the one he is occupying at the moment, that those places exist in a certain direction from the spot where he is, and that there is a vocabulary for telling one thing from another in spatial terms.

After the child enters school, when he is five or six years of age, his awareness of other places and of the ways one must go to get to them slowly increases. Although this awareness is partly the result of experience, it appears to be in large measure the consequence of development. Most seven-year-olds have learned to distinguish their right hand or foot from their left with a minimum of confusion, and most can point in the direction of north, whereas their five-year-old counterparts cannot. Many seven-year-olds can also address the major compass points, and some, those who seem to grasp directionality readily, can with very little direct teaching show where the intermediate compass points are. To the majority of seven- and eight-year-olds, these ideas appear to be completely logical, and they can begin applying these concepts in working with maps which they have constructed themselves. They are less able to apply them to maps made by others.

Clearly, not all primary children develop this sense for direction. Many remain confused over which is "right" and which is "left," where "north" or "east" may be, and so on. To them, there is no logic in these differentiations. After direct teaching (being shown or told by the teacher or other children) they seem not to be able to remember which is which even for a few minutes. Why this is, is still not known with any certainty.[6] However, about 25 per cent of all children will experience marked confusion in the primary years. Many of these children will not clarify their thinking with respect to direction until they reach the intermediate grades. Operationally, therefore, developing a sense for direction is not a function of intelligence but, rather, an extension of what is apparently an innate early perceptual lack of awareness. In addition, many of these children experience initial difficulty in printed-word read-

[6] See Bryant J. Cratty, *Movement Behavior and Motor Learning* (Philadelphia: Lea and Febiger, 1964), 332 pp.; D. H. Radler with Newell C. Kephart, *Success Through Play* (New York: Harper and Row, 1960), 140 pp.; Newell C. Kephart, *The Slow Learner in the Classroom* (Columbus, Ohio: Charles E. Merrill Books, Inc., 1960), 292 pp.

ing. Most of the problems will clear up more or less spontaneously some-time between the ages of eight and ten *if* the child has understanding teachers who recognize that the problem is not the result of orneriness or stupidity. Teachers of these children—and they are found in nearly every classroom—must be aware that what appears to every adult and most of the children of this age as simple, common-sense ideas are viewed by these boys and girls as *nonsensical,* without pattern and wholly arbitrary. Patience must be exercised with these youngsters; with-out it, they will get the idea that they *are* stupid or that school is a place where people do irrational and useless things, *or both.*

Direction during the Primary Years. The earliest years of school, like those which follow, call for an acceptance of a wide range of differences in abilities to sense and know about directional concepts. Much of the teaching in the earliest years, however, is informal and incidental. It takes place throughout the school day, in physical education classes as well as in the social study itself, for example. Activities which aid in the development of directional concepts include the following:

1. *Label directions on classroom walls.*
2. *Talk about the ways (directions)* children are moving on walks about the school.
3. *Play games* which involve using the right or left side of the body (example: Simon Says).
4. *Provide balance board and other kinds of equipment* where chil-dren play and also follow such directions as "Walk along the board with your right foot on the board, your left foot on the ground," etc.
5. *Label all maps* made in the classroom for direction and orient them accurately on the floor or table. The logic of orienting maps comes later. Toward the end of the primary years, move the map on the floor or table to the appropriate wall where directions are preserved.
6. *Look at and discuss maps* which show the school and immedi-ately surrounding area. Make maps of familiar things (the child's bedroom, his house, route taken to school, playground, com-munity or area in which the child lives and which he knows best).
7. *Study the apparent movement of the sun* and the movement of the earth by making a human sundial (have children stand on asphalt or cement surface at three or four intervals during the

day—one should be at noon. Outline the shadow with chalk, label the time, and paint in each figure with a different color of water base paint). Then, make your own sundials and study the ways they are constructed, how they are installed, and ways of reading them.

8. *Think about the earth's movements,* about the poles, and why they are named. Introduce the concept that north or south is the direction toward the pole. Be alert to the misconception that "north is up." Name and discuss the meaning of concepts of equator, grids on maps and their uses through construction projects.

9. *Develop the concept that the map shows the earth's surface* in a smaller space through having children make their own maps and other models of things, talking about the purposes of maps of different kinds.

10. *Experiment with devices which tell direction*—compass, gyroscope, weather vanes, marks on maps.

11. *Discover how directions may be told at night* by locating the North Star.

Direction in the Intermediate and Upper Years. Confusions with respect to "left" and "right," the compass points, and where the sun rises will have largely (although not completely) disappeared by the time children reach the intermediate years. Not infrequently, misconceptions about direction have been learned, however, and the teacher increasingly needs to be alert to the possibility that incorrect ideas are in danger of becoming firmly entrenched. The most common of these is the notion that "north is up" rather than that direction toward the North Pole and that "south is down" rather than the direction toward the South Pole. Greenhood's remarks are pertinent in this regard when he says:

A serious map-user should rid himself of the naive "up" and "down" geographical conceptions. They are picturesque but not true. "Down under" for Australia. *Lower* California. Lake *Superior*. We can't change these, but let's not refer to Indiana, for instance, as being just "above" Kentucky; or Borneo "below" the Philippines.[7]

These kinds of errors in thinking occur, in spite of good intentions, because so many maps appearing in school books as well as those displayed on classroom walls show these directions to be at the top of the page and at the bottom, respectively. Some activities appropriate for

[7] David Greenhood, *op. cit.,* pp. 69-70.

most intermediate and upper grade classrooms designed to foster accurate directional concepts include the following:

1. *Continue making a point of orienting all maps correctly.* Not infrequently, it is inconvenient or perhaps not possible to orient maps used in the classroom. Many modern classrooms are constructed so that wall maps cannot be oriented correctly, for example. In such cases, and when the type of map projection also precludes proper orientation, note should be made of the reasons in the class.

2. *Continue the study of the earth's rotation in relation to the sun and the moon as well as the uses of knowledge about the stars in telling direction.* Although younger children cannot understand many of the technical terms involved in describing the earth's size, shape, and movements, they can understand the principles involved. Gradually, specific terms can become associated with these principles. For example, they will come to understand the purposes of the *analemma,* commonly shown as a figure eight on most model globes, which indicates the latitude at which the sun's rays are vertical at noon on each day of the year. They will also become aware of the reasons for naming the *Arctic* and *Antarctic Circles* and the *Tropics of Cancer* and *Capricorn.* In the first instance, one is referring to the latitudes near the North and South Poles which mark the farthest position of the circle of illumination. The Tropics of Cancer and Capricorn mark the latitudes farthest North and South, respectively, that receive the vertical rays of the sun. The days on which these events occur are called the *solstices* and take place about June 21 at the Tropic of Cancer (in the northern hemisphere) and about December 22 at the Tropic of Capricorn, thus defining the "longest day" and the "shortest day" for people living north of the equator; for those living south of the equator, of course, the reverse is true. Pupils should also discover, that there are two times during the year at which the vertical rays of the sun cross the equator (about March 21 and September 23). On these days the circle of illumination extends from pole to pole and days and nights are of equal length. These are the *equinoxes*—equal days and nights. Although an illustration may explain, or re-explain, such concepts to the adult, elementary school boys and girls should work with model globes, controlled light (such as a flashlight provides) and should be able

to demonstrate the earth's movements since these are all ideas that can be discovered through experimentation. In addition to working with models, there are many books and articles which are of great interest to boys and girls bearing on these kinds of topics. Space science provides an exceptionally fascinating source of information, of course, but there are also accounts of earlier efforts to "know the earth" which hold great interest.[8]

3. *Study the compass or wind-rose—the chart showing the directions and their intermediate points.* Practice naming them and apply these directional terms to activities in and outside of the classroom. Differentiating between directions is as important in map reading as knowing the difference between addition and subtraction in arithmetic. Children should learn to use compass directions as a natural and normal part of their vocabulary. They can quickly gain a sense of the importance of accuracy in using directional terms through such activities as a class treasure hunt based on following a compass course laid out by the teacher or other members of the class.

4. *Learn about the value of parallels and meridians in telling direction.* Children should be introduced to the concepts of parallels and meridians during the earliest part of the intermediate years and should develop their abilities to apply the concept of a grid in map making throughout the intermediate and upper grade years. The grid used on maps, derived from the concepts of latitude and longitude on the model globe, is a fundamental tool which tells location as well as direction. Fourth and fifth grade children are capable of constructing their own model globe, starting with a blank sphere (either commercially prepared or made by the children themselves), meeting the problems of dividing the earth's surface through drawing parallels of latitude and meridians of longitude, and proceeding from there to locate the major land

[8] For example, the story of Stonehenge reads like a mystery story. This prehistoric stone structure in England apparently was constructed to chart the changing seasons. It is in fact an observatory; from it, it has been learned that even in prehistoric times there were people who had much knowledge about the earth and its relationships to the universe. See "The Eighth Wonder," *Time Magazine,* 1965, 86 (20), (Nov. 12), p. 98. Primary source: Gerald Hawkins, *Stonehenge Decoded* (New York: Doubleday, 1965). The many accounts and stories of the Age of Exploration — that period extending from about the time of Columbus' first voyage to the mid-1600's — also are of interest. Actual chronicles as well as fictionalized accounts of the adventures of the explorers who set sail during this period can become part of the literature program or can be made available for children to read on their own.

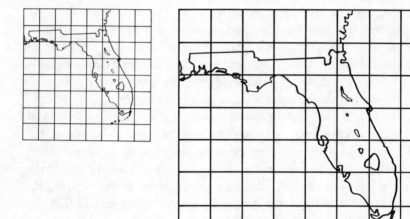

Figure 10–8: Here is a method of enlarging or reducing by squares. The simple geometrical principle of "similar figures" has been applied. Two squares, although they are not the same size, are similar figures because they are the same shape. As long as two or more figures are the same shape, the size can be varied as desired. They will vary only with respect to size. The angles will remain the same, and the corresponding lines will be proportional.

and water masses. A project of this sort is infinitely more valuable than a written description or a verbal explanation of the uses and value of the system used to tell the location, direction, and distance of things over the earth.[9] From such an experience, it is a natural move to use the grid in constructing flat maps which

[9] A description of the processes involved in constructing such a model globe is contained in the filmstrip, "Building the World in Your Classroom," produced by Loretta Belgrum, copyrighted 1961 by Herbert Elkins Company, distributed by the Curriculum Materials Center, 10031 Commerce Avenue, Tujunga, California.

show portions of the earth's surface. It must be remembered, of course, that children produce inaccuracies in the maps they make not only because they are struggling with ideas which are not always easily comprehended but because inaccuracies result from the inability to draw lines exactly where and how the young child would like them to be.

5. *Become acquainted with different types of instruments which help tell the direction of things.* Learning how a simple magnetic compass works, finding out something about how the radio is used in direction finding, examining and experimenting with a sextant, or constructing and trying out a simple astrolabe provide opportunities to understand and appreciate problems in telling direction accurately. The tools of the surveyors are also an interesting and valuable means for discovering more about problems in direction. Not infrequently, the social studies teacher feels that he does not have enough information himself about these things to launch studies of them in his classroom. But there are many resources which can be called upon. Particularly at first the teacher will want to ask the school district science consultant to assist him, perhaps with a demonstration lesson in the classroom. But there are other resources: parents, professional and business people in the community, and a wide range of inexpensive books and materials (available through discount houses as well as through scientific equipment firms) which will bridge the gap between the teacher's feelings of incompetence and sufficient knowledge to bring these kinds of experiences to children.

6. *Become familiar with different map projections and how direction varies on flat maps.* All flat maps distort direction (as well as distance) to a greater or lesser degree. Generally speaking, the larger the area shown on the map, the greater this distortion. It will be useful, especially when studies involve rather large areas of the earth's surface, to use a variety of map projections, in addition to the model globe. In this way, children can visualize how the area shown and the directions represented on it differ from one map to the next. They can also see that the directions shown on maps often vary markedly from the true directions as they can be seen on the model globe. Furthermore, they can learn that directions derived from the magnetic compass may be different still.

DEVELOPING CONCEPTS ABOUT DISTANCE AND SCALE

In addition to a knowledge of direction, effective map interpretation depends upon the ability to interpret map scales and to visualize the distances they represent on different maps. The options exercised by the cartographer in choosing a scale for his map are infinite, since primarily he is guided by the size of the paper he wishes to use and the amount of the earth's surface he wishes to show. Maps that stand for relatively small portions of the earth's surface can therefore normally be drawn to a scale which represents a low ratio between distance on the map in relation to distance on the ground. Maps showing much larger areas obviously must be drawn so that the distance appearing on the map represents a much larger distance on the ground. Particularly when larger areas are involved, maps drawn to different scales can lead to considerable confusion; it may not readily be apparent that the area on one map is considerably larger or smaller than that shown on another. For example, children's encyclopedias are frequently a source of such confusion because the maps used, particularly those of states, nations, continents, and even of the world, are all drawn to fit a standard page size. It is little wonder that children often think that the area shown on one map, perhaps that showing their own state, is little different from that of any other place appearing in the encyclopedia. This is likely to continue to be a source of confusion until they become aware of the signs included on every map that tell about the scale which has been used. Although considerable variation may occur, scale is usually shown graphically or as a representative fraction. Examples are shown below:

1. As a statement. For example: "One inch equals one mile."
2. As a graphic representation.
3. As a representative fraction. Examples include:

Scale 1:63,360   (in which 1 stands for any measurement on the map multiplied by 63,360, yielding the distance in the same units on the ground. If the unit of measure selected were inches, then 1 inch on the map would be equal to 63,360 inches, or one mile, on the ground.)

Scale $\dfrac{1}{100}$ (in which 1 also stands for any distance on the map and 100 the equivalent distance, in the same unit of measurement, on the ground.)

Thus the long-term goal in teaching is to help boys and girls relate concepts of distance in the real world to maps drawn in different scales. They should become alert to the fact that maps are drawn in different scales and be able to adjust their thinking in accordance with the scale which has been used, but, as in understanding about direction, the concepts underlying *distance* and *scale* as they are applied in map reading are quite complex. For example, one can see that mathematical concepts are important to understanding distance and scale. Just how much is an inch, a mile, a meter, or any one of a large number of other units employed to describe distance? Can the map reader convert one unit of measurement to another, and does he really understand that the map employs fractional concepts in its making? The mature map reader will also have a good sense of time and be able to relate this to concepts of distance. How long will it take to travel from one place to another if one uses different modes of transportation? A good sense of time is important in comprehending just how distant a place may be. And, perhaps of greatest importance, scale is important, along with the other symbols the cartographer places on the map, in helping one visualize the area shown on the map.

Distance and Scale in the Primary Years. Clearly, distance and scale involve a number of concepts which will not be understood well, if at all, until the child is enrolled in the intermediate or even the upper grades. For example, concepts of fractional representation, awareness of different units of measurement and their interchangeability, and abilities to visualize vividly areas beyond the immediate horizon and to compare them with other places represent the kinds of ideas which one would expect to be developed only in older children. In part, therefore, it is recognized that many aspects of understanding and interpreting maps made by others are geared to natural processes of growing and maturing. These can be encouraged by good teaching that has taken place when the children were younger. Emphasis at this stage should be upon map making, upon the development of critical abilities so that distance and scale are viewed as important concomitants in the construction and interpretation of every map, and upon concepts which are basic to the development of more complex aspects of distance and scale. The following examples of activities suggest the kind of basic concept building preparatory to the development of later, more advanced understandings:

1. *Take frequent walks about the school and neighborhood,* noting how long it takes to travel from one place to another using differ-

ent modes of movement—walking, bicycling, riding in an automobile. Use as many different kinds of measures as possible of the distances involved: how many blocks, steps, minutes does it take to get from one place to another?

2. *How people measure distances* is always an interesting topic for discussion. Collect examples of ways distance is measured and the tools and machines needed to measure distance: bring an odometer or a pedometer into the classroom and experiment with it; find out how people in different countries measure distances; how do you know where your house property begins and where it ends; how was distance measured in ancient times?

3. *Discuss events of common interest* and find out where they happened and how far away the location is from the children, eliciting thoughts about how far away *they believe* the event took place (how long it takes to travel there, how long it took the news to get to us, what different ways might one take to get there and actually see the place) and what it may be like there. Oral discussion, dictation, and other commentary (acting out through dramatic play, music, art) about places beyond the view of children is also of value. Although it should be recognized that most primary boys and girls conceive of places beyond their immediate view (those very close as well as those far away) as existing in a kind of disembodied world not really connected to the reality which the child is presently experiencing, young boys and girls are acutely aware of the existence of other places and frequently know a great deal about them. Opportunities to "say what these other places are like and where they are" provide practice and experience in visualizing places beyond their immediate view and relating them to the immediate world of the child.

4. *Begin early to make simple maps* of the classroom, a room at home, the playground, the area immediately adjacent to the school and other places about which the child feels he knows a great deal. Draw attention to questions of accuracy with respect to distances shown. Maintain third-dimensional qualities in these maps until the children begin to want to make their maps without this element. It pays not to rush toward two-dimensional maps.

5. *Building models of different kinds* helps the child gain insights into concepts of correct scale and the problems of accuracy in this respect.

6. *Make use of a variety of opportunities to measure distances.* How big is the classroom and the things in it? How far is it to each child's home? How far did they travel over the week end or during their vacation? How big is this piece of paper? How big will a piece be which is just half as large? How thick are the walls, the floor, the ceiling?

7. *Talk continuously with children about why we have maps,* what their uses are, and when they are helpful. Find as many ways as possible to use maps in the same way printed materials are used in order to gain information.

Distance and Scale in Intermediate and Upper Grade Years. The following suggestions presuppose a background in number and time concepts, experience in map making and model building, and that children have been encouraged to develop a geographical view of the area in which they live and go to school. By "geographical view" is meant first-hand experience coupled with classroom activities which have helped children to know the location of the things about them, noting distance and direction from each other, the purposes of those "things," and their importance in the community. Frequently, it will be found that older children have missed these experiences and understandings. It is necessary in such circumstances to review the concepts and generalizations which one would hope had been developed before moving into any consideration of more advanced ideas.

For Intermediate Children:

1. *Gain experience redrawing maps to another scale.* For example, construct a large map of the United States or one of their own state on the playground using an expanded grid and painting the outlines and other important information on it with tempera. Choose a time of the year when the weather is fairly predictable, or the map will soon be washed away. However, do not use permanent paint; the challenge of figuring out how to do it is the most important part of the experience. Subsequent classes should not find maps made by prior classes on the playground. Also, make maps in the classroom, using a large piece of plywood and working from a smaller map made by someone else.

2. *Make comparisons of different maps, noting how scale varies.* Compare the different flat maps with the model globe to account for variations in distortion.

3. *Become even more familiar with the size and shape of the earth,* how it rotates, and how distances are measured on it. Children should become thoroughly familiar with the concepts of rhumb lines, the "Great Circle Route," and be able to plot great circles on various flat map projections.

4. *Using different modes of transportation, travel measured distances,* noting the time it takes to get from one place to another. Discuss with the children their concepts of a hundred yards, a mile, ten miles, fifty miles, and greater distances. Study travel guides and timetables from different places around the world. Estimate time of travel, distances, directions, and earth features which must be overcome.

5. *Strive for greater precision in map making* and become habituated to considering scale and showing what scale has been used in preparing each map.

6. *Make a study of how maps are made.* Find out what a cartographer is and what he does, how maps are printed, and how model globes are constructed. Study the work of a surveyor. Visit the city engineer's office or invite someone from local government to describe ways areas are mapped and records kept of the property where children live and the uses to which other land is put.

7. *Use different kinds of map projections* and notice the different ways distance and scale are represented.

8. *Read books on the history of map making* (note references at the conclusion of this chapter which are appropriate for children as well as adults).

9. *Continue constructing maps of areas which children can traverse,* where they gather their own data and enter it on their map. Count paces for distance measurements and rely on rough estimates of direction as children travel over an area.

For Upper Grade Children:

1. *Make a serious study of map projections.* Emphasize problems of distance and scale. Also, study maps developed from mathematical formulas. Children should become familiar through such a study with the most common types of projections and the advantages of each over the others.

2. *Map familiar areas* using, in addition to the "footmade map," (1) the "compass traverse method"—distances computed by strides

and direction following azimuths (directions) derived from a simple compass; (2) the "plane table method"—employing basic concepts of triangulation but without complex equipment.[10]

3. *Become familiar with concepts of areas as well as direct-line distances* in thinking about maps and what they show. Familiarity with certain standard-sized areas (for example, a football field, the size of one's home state, a square mile) helps in making comparisons with other areas not well known.

4. *Practice converting scale* expressed in one mode to that of another (from fractional representation to graphic modes, for example), read graduated scales (such as that needed to read distance on the Mercator projection and those for polar projections), gain practice in selecting an appropriate scale for the size of paper on which maps are to be drawn and the size of the area to be represented.

DEVELOPING CONCEPTS ABOUT LOCATION

Probably the most frequent use of maps is simply to tell the location of things: where a particular city is situated, perhaps another country, a river, or any number of other natural or man-made features in the landscape. Sometimes the place is readily discovered. Using clues of various kinds (how far one thinks it is from known places, its direction from them, whether there are other features nearby which are already familiar), the eye travels meaningfully toward the object of search. And when it is discovered, the eye moves back and forth from the newly found location to the more familiar ones, gauging distance, direction, scale, and other cues. But sometimes one uses a "hunt and peck" method in locating things on the map. Perhaps one is not familiar with the area shown. Or, the clues the cartographer has left may not be easy to interpret for one reason or another. In such a setting, one is inclined to let his eyes meander over the map in the hope that they will come upon the object of his search more or less by accident.

However, merely being able to find things on maps through using rudimentary skills or happenstance is hardly the beginning in the development of the kind of locational abilities which one would hope serious map readers might possess. Location is expressed, and can be interpreted, in more significant ways. For example, location is sometimes an

[10] An excellent description of these "do-it-yourself" map projects, as well as one of the "footmade maps" noted above, is included in David Greenhood, *op. cit.,* Chapter Eight, "Basing Maps upon the Ground: Survey," pp. 203-239.

expression which contains the exactness of mathematics. Knowledge of the grid system—of the meaning of the parallels, or degrees of latitude, and of the meridians, or degrees of longitude—is a means of expressing location with great precision. And it is expected that children will gain experiences in school which will lead them to an understanding of the meaning of latitude and longitude as well as to the ability to use this mode in expressing the location of things that are found over the surface of the earth. All things have a location which can be expressed in terms of elevation above or below the level of the sea. This, too, can be expressed mathematically, and children can gain concepts of elevation through school experiences.

But the location of things is also a relative matter. Not only can the position of a place be described in terms of the coordinates of latitude and longitude and with respect to distance and direction from other places over the earth's surface, the relative location of each place is an important geographic consideration which may also be interpreted through map reading. Relative location refers to the circumstances surrounding a particular place which make it more or less accessible to man than are other places. In other words, relative location refers to the *judgment* one makes about the seeming distance and this, in turn, comes about as a consequence of how one values a place and of the use one would make of it. For example, mountains are frequently cited as barriers to human activity, causing the distances between plains areas on one side and those on the other to be relatively farther apart than the mathematical distance which intervenes. Of course, a strategically located pass and advanced technology which allows the construction of highways and railroads or perhaps the movement of jet airplanes reduces sharply or virtually eliminates the problem of the mountain barrier. Thus, in some places, mountains act more as barriers to human activity than in others. In judging the role of the mountain barrier one needs to know quite a bit about human aspirations and the level of economic activity before one can say a great deal about the relative location of the areas which seemingly are divided or separated by the mountain barrier.

Other factors which affect relative location are more of man's devising and less of nature's. For instance, barriers are erected by legal means in some instances (tariffs and immigration laws are examples) and in others private and government projects are undertaken to reduce distances (rural electrification and public inland waterways are examples). The political differences and basic antipathy between the United States and the Communist nations have also caused walls to be built—real ones as well as legal and emotional ones—which have almost literally created two worlds where physically there is only one. And so it goes. Economic, political, social, psychological, and other factors enter into spatial relationships demanding that one think of location not only in its exact sense but in its relative sense as well. Thus one would expect boys and girls gradually to acquire a background for understanding exact location, as well as the ideas which allow them to discover that the significance of different places varies according to the importance attached to them. Such ideas are in their fullest meaning complex, and all progress toward such understanding is itself a relative matter. Teachers need to work with children in this dimension, as in others, with a keen ear for sensing what they can contribute from their own experience to the meaningful interpretation of maps. But eventually children should be brought to an awareness of location in both its meanings: in its exact and mathematical sense and in its relative sense.

Developing Concepts of Location in the Primary Years. The first major idea which children need to acquire in developing locational abilities is to understand that maps can show them where they are in relation to other things, how to get from one place to another, and where other places and people are to be found. Ideas about exact and relative location develop slowly. Maps which the children make themselves contain the elements for deciding whether the things shown are located with reasonable accuracy. Maps made by others, such as community maps and road maps of areas the children have visited on trips, are also of value since direct experiencing can be recalled in thinking about the map and what it shows. Examples of experiences which help develop locational abilities include:

1. *Practice locating things appearing on maps* depicting familiar areas; tell as much about them as possible. Snapshots taken on a study trip and attached at appropriate places on maps prepared by the children or the teacher help children visualize the places they have been.
2. *Take walks about the school and neighborhood,* making a point of locating various things seen. Talk about them, how far and in what direction they are from other known places, and what their function is.
3. *Notice traffic levels on different streets and roads* and the kinds of vehicles which use them. Ask such questions as: What kinds of

things do you think are in the buses and trucks? Where did they come from? Where are they going? Why do they come down this street?

4. *Locate nearby railroad tracks, bus and truck routes, air terminals, and air lanes.* Try to discover what kinds of things are carried in these vehicles, where they come from, and where they are delivered. Observe the kinds of businesses which have grown up beside transportation terminals and think about their relationships to the commercial carrier.

5. *Always use every opportunity to refer to the model globe,* and, as indicated earlier, make a point when discussing areas and events distant from the child's experience to think about distances and directions involved. How far away is it? How long would it take to get there? How would you travel? Which way would you go?

6. *Look at pictures of different features in the landscape* (mountains, lakes, oceans and shorelines, plains, rivers, etc.) and consider how easy or difficult it would be to cross over them. Motion pictures and television programs frequently provide valuable topics for discussion, art expression, writing, and creative dramatics about other locations throughout the world. Creative expression stimulated by such programs extends children's insights into other places and their significance to them.

7. *Take a trip to a museum, aquarium, art gallery, or library; look at books, displays, and pictures* showing different animals; talk about where they are found and the type of vegetation existing there; relate this information to the kinds of animal life found in the area in which the children live. Games such as "Animal, Vegetable, or Mineral" sharpen perceptions in this and other areas of map reading.

8. *Listen carefully when children describe the location of things* they are talking about. Conceptual errors will be quite apparent if the child is given an opportunity to "talk himself out."

Developing Concepts of Location in the Intermediate and Upper Grade Years. Sometime between the ages of about nine and twelve, the child's awareness of the world appears to undergo a transformation. No longer is he almost totally consumed with the immediate, seeable world —the world he can touch, taste, feel, and enjoy moment by moment. Sensitivity to other places and the problems of people living in different parts of the world seem suddenly more real, important, and even interesting. The fact that this awareness appears to emerge at different times means that the intermediate classroom, particularly, is full of different kinds of children—of young people who are thinking about things beyond their immediate surroundings and of others who are still largely preoccupied with themselves and what is happening to them from moment to moment. Activities appropriate for such situations include the following:

1. *Build a model globe in the classroom.* (This project provides multiple learnings and is suggested elsewhere in this chapter in connection with the development of other concepts important in map reading.) Fourth and fifth grade children are capable of engaging profitably in this activity. Most children at this age cannot develop meaningful concepts of latitude and longitude without this or other first-hand experience in map making.

2. *Practice locating places according to their latitude and longitude.* One might select familiar landmarks as well as locations important in the social study for this purpose.

3. *Make a study of the ways airplanes, ships, and other vehicles plot their courses during a trip.* Invite a commercial or private pilot into the classroom to discuss how he solves problems of location when he is in the air.

4. *Through games of various kinds, make certain that children are familiar with the locations of key places in the social study.* For example, children in the fifth grade studying the "Northeastern States" should be able to locate and identify them on the map. Children studying other world regions should be capable of similar locational abilities. This suggestion should not be construed to mean that memorizing with little meaning large numbers of names and places is something which should be done in social studies. However, there are many interesting ways to keep the names of important places and their locations before children without involving them in endless mumbojumbo. To study a place without being thoroughly familiar with its location would seem to be pointless.

5. *Encourage the use of technical terminology* in both making and reading maps. Meanings for the following locational terms should be developed during these years and should gradually become part of the child's vocabulary:

Altitude   Mean Solar Day
Analemma   Meridians
Antarctic Circle   Nautical Mile and Statute Mile
Arctic Circle   Noon
Circle of Illumination   Orbit of the Earth
Elevation   Parallels
Equator   Revolution of the Earth
Equinox   Rotation of the Earth
Horizon   Sea Level
Inclination of the Earth's   Solar Day
    Axis   Solstice
International Date Line   Standard Time
Isobar and Isotherm   Sunrise and Sunset
Latitude   Tropic of Cancer
Local Time (Differences   Tropic of Capricorn
    from place to place)   Year
Longitude   Zenith
Map Projection

6. *Continue to emphasize location in classroom discussions* whenever appropriate. It is particularly important to consider the
   exact and relative location of places where current events attract
   attention. The model globe remains the most valuable tool for
   situations involving great distances.

7. *Plan a trip,* considering such factors as mode of travel, costs,
   changes in time as well as amount of time involved in making
   the trip, points of interest. Consult travel folders, chamber of
   commerce publications, and any other source containing pertinent information which might be available. Trips which involve
   travel across the Equator, the International Date Line, international boundary lines, or near the North Pole raise interesting
   questions which older children enjoy answering.

8. *Remember to consider questions of relative location when thinking about man's activities from place to place* and why he and
   his works (his cities, dams, highways) are located where they
   are. Some factors which are always important in questions of
   relative location are the following: source of water supply, terrain features, nature and extent of natural resources, climate,
   area nearby which is served by man's activities in a place (sometimes called service areas).

9. *Make a study of the problems in orbiting a satellite and bringing it back to earth.* How do we know where the satellite is at any given moment? How is it brought down on target?

10. *Study the ways elevation is determined, how it is represented on maps* (with color, shading, and contour lines), *and how it may affect man's activities from place to place.* Elevation is measured both above and below sea level, and concern can be developed for questions of land which is also either above or below sea level. It is described both in terms of exact distances and, in relation to other elevations, with respect to its *relief*. Relief refers to the amount of slope in a given place. Where slope is great, there is a great deal of relief, or "relief is marked." Where slope is slight, there is "little relief." Children should learn to consider during the intermediate and upper grade years simple problems brought about by relief and elevation. For example, they should become aware of the manner in which elevation affects climate and, as a consequence, the uses to which land with varying relief may be put at different elevations. Elevations with similar relief in different latitudes respond differently to man's attempts to use it. Other factors are also important, including the social and cultural heritage, educational levels, population density, and even religious beliefs of an area or place.

11. *Practice reading distribution maps* showing, especially, location of resources pertinent to particular industries; climate; population; soils; vegetation; land use; transportation routes for different modes of travel (air, sea, railroad, automobile and truck routes).

DEVELOPING MEANINGS FOR MAP SYMBOLS

Early in this chapter it was noted that learning to read the symbols appearing on maps calls for many of the abilities needed in reading the print in books. In some ways, however, it is an even more complex process since the variety of markings which are combined in making a map consist of so many different kinds of symbols. For, in addition to the conventional printed words, all maps also use a wide variety of special symbols invented by the cartographer and placed on the map following rigorous rules so that the locations of things will be as true as possible with respect to distances and directions between them. On many maps, as well, a system of color and shading is used to convey additional in-

formation about the land. Moreover, the symbols as well as the system
of colors and shading may differ markedly from one map to another.
The "language of maps" is not standardized, as is the printed language,
and this means that the map reader must be alert to the specific meaning
of the markings which he wishes to interpret.

As in reading printed words, the first rule in learning to interpret map
symbols calls for the development of a background of ideas for the
things for which the symbols stand. Probably the most common difficulty
in all map reading surrounds this point. Young children, or children of
any age for that matter, cannot be expected to read printed words for
which they do not possess adequate meanings. Similarly, one cannot expect a child to read map symbols without the ideas necessary to understanding what the symbols stand for. Put perhaps more simply, maps
show the locations of such things as rivers and lakes, cities, mountains,
forests, mineral resources, and many other things. If a teacher is to
help children become good map readers, he must make certain that they
understand what a river is, what a lake may be like, the various types of
cities, and so forth.

Naming things ranks among the simplest acts in the lowest levels of
intellectual activity. Although very young people, in reading their own
maps or those made by others, will be more likely to say, "That is my
street," "This is a mountain," or "That is a river," the overall objective
is to help the child understand that rivers, mountains, and everything
else in the landscape are eminently varied. Therefore, he is encouraged
to extend his descriptive powers to account for the peculiar nature of
places, to observe the subtleties in maps, and to grow in the ability to
sense whether mountains are "eroded," "forested," "steep," "high," or
whatever else might be appropriate. Growth in the ability to sense differences and to describe accurately and fully is a gradual process and
depends upon the extent and quality of the concepts which the child
possesses.

As often noted before, children do not automatically acquire concepts about anything. It has also been emphasized that learning is multi-
sensory. Children become aware of their environment through tasting
and touching, feeling and smelling, as well as through seeing and hearing. Most desirably, children would smell hay after it has been cut,
feel the chill of mountain air, touch the bark of huge trees in a virgin
forest, or strain to climb a steep hillside. Not all of these kinds of first-
hand experiences can be provided by every school, but many others
can. To build meanings which allow the child to make sense out of

map symbols, school cannot be confined to the four walls of the usual classroom. Children should be taken outside to observe, through all of their senses, the world about them. In this setting, the teacher can direct children toward the things which are worthy of their notice. Out-of-school experience can also be education in its best sense. And so, summer and week-end experiences, not to omit after school and before school events in children's lives—frequently encouraged by the teacher —when discussed in the classroom, are valuable. Unfortunately, some children come to school "sensorily deprived." They have not had anyone around them capable of helping them develop an awareness even for the simplest, most obvious things in their everyday world. For children with such meager and truly impoverished home backgrounds ways must be found to heighten sensitivities to the simplest things around them before one can move to map interpretation as one normally thinks of that process.[11]

Cartographers use four different major types of map symbols: (1) those out-of-proportion markings which show the specific locations of one-of-a-kind things such as rivers, houses, highways, and boundary lines; (2) those marks which represent quantities of things concentrated in an area, such as dots used to represent the population in different locations, regions colored to show levels of activity such as crop production, mining areas, or the major agricultural, desert, and mountain regions; (3) color and/or shading which shows topographic features or land use; and (4) those marks which show the relative flow of goods or people from one place to another, such as air traffic, the migrations of people, the movement of various raw materials from the source to the point of manufacture or distribution.

The first category of symbols, those showing the specific location of things, must, in order to be read, be drawn out of proportion to the space they actually occupy in the landscape. Some look more or less like the thing itself; others are pure abstractions. Clearly, those symbols that are close representations of the things man has placed in the landscape or that are found in nature pose less of a problem

---

[11] Within the very recent past, pre-school and kindergarten programs that are focusing on multi-sensory experiencing and developing an awareness for the immediate world of the child have been gaining much attention. For example, see Patricia Blake (text, including an interview with Martin Deutsch) and Burk Uzzle (photography), "A Big Break for Poverty's Children," *Life Magazine,* 56 (14) (April 3, 1964), pp. 78B-80. See also Fred M. Hechinger, ed., *Pre-School Education Today* (Garden City: Doubleday and Company, Inc., 1966). Teachers should consider the applications of these techniques and the goals which are being served for all children of elementary school age.

TOPOGRAPHIC MAP SYMBOLS

VARIATIONS WILL BE FOUND ON OLDER MAPS

Hard surface, heavy duty road, four or more lanes ..... (r)

Hard surface, heavy duty road, two or three lanes ..... (r)

Hard surface, medium duty road, four or more lanes ..... (r)

Hard surface, medium duty road, two or three lanes ..... (r)

Improved light duty road

Unimproved dirt road—Trail

Dual highway, dividing strip 25 feet or less

Dual highway, dividing strip exceeding 25 feet

Road under construction

Railroad: single track—multiple track

Railroads in juxtaposition

Narrow gage: single track—multiple track

Railroad in street—Carline

Bridge: road—railroad ..... (bl)

Drawbridge: road—railroad ..... (bl)

Footbridge ..... (bl)

Tunnel: road—railroad

Overpass—Underpass

Important small masonry or earth dam ..... (bl)

Boundary: national

state

county, parish, municipio

civil township, precinct, town, barrio

incorporated city, village, town, hamlet

reservation, national or state

small park, cemetery, airport, etc.

land grant ..... (r)

Township or range line, U.S. land survey ..... (r)

Township or range line, approximate location ..... (r)

Section line, U.S. land survey ..... (r)

Section line, approximate location ..... (r)

Township line, not U.S. land survey ..... (r)

Section line, not U.S. land survey ..... (r)

Section corner: found—indicated ..... (r)+

Boundary monument: land grant—other ..... (r)□

U.S. mineral or location monument

Index contour ..... (br)   Intermediate contour (br)

Supplementary contour (br)   Depression contours (br)

Cut ..... (br)

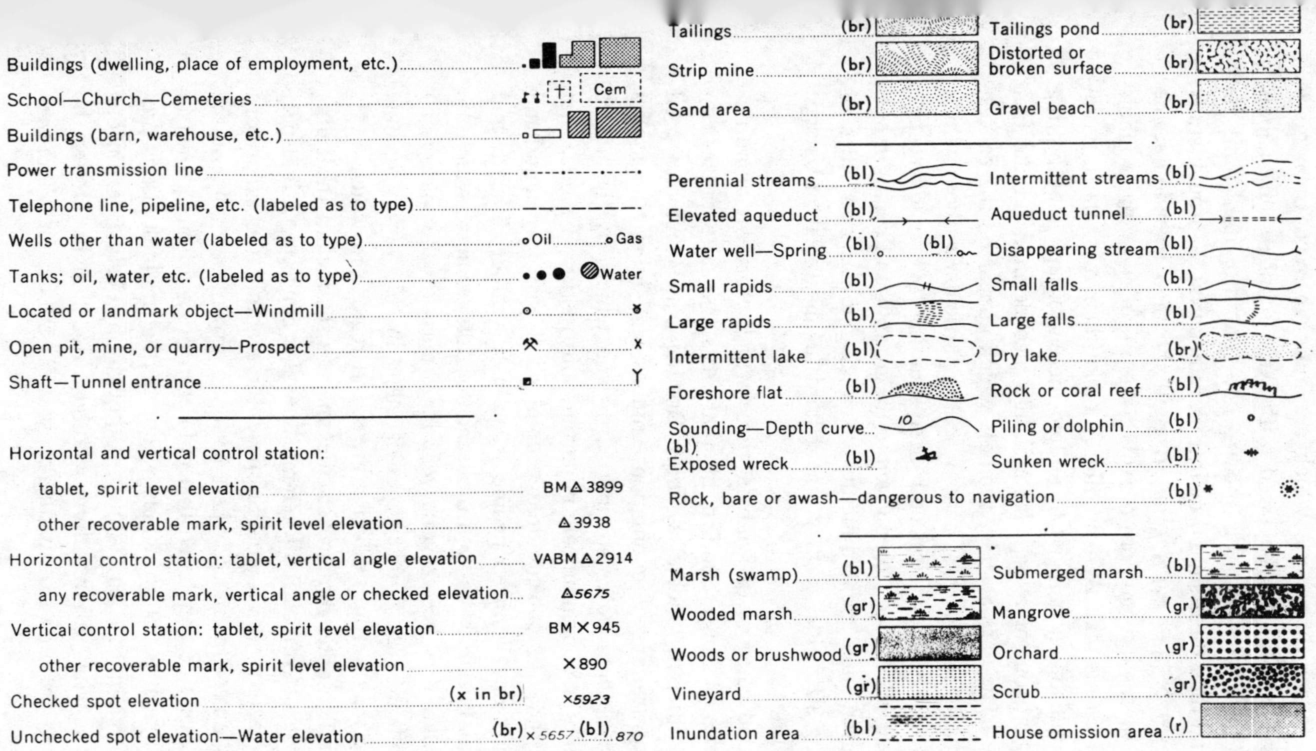

Figure 10–9: Major Map Symbols. Colors designate map features: black, man-made or cultural features; blue (bl), water or hydrographic features; brown (br), relief or hypsographic features; green (gr), woodland cover, with specific patterns to indicate type; red (r), important roads, built-up urban areas and public-land subdivisions.

for the map reader than those which are more abstract. Elementary school children should not be faced with large numbers of symbols which do not have the quality of "looking like" the thing itself until the later years, and then these should be introduced sparingly through study of the purposes of the *map legend*. It is in the map legend that the cartographer places information to explain the meaning of the symbols which appear on his map. When children make their own maps, therefore, they should be encouraged to imitate the cartographer by putting their own legend on their map. Note should also be made of the fact that there are some very abstract symbols which appear on the earliest maps used during the earliest school years, particularly those which designate cities of different sizes and those standing for boundary lines. Special consideration needs to be given to the meanings of such symbols because children have great difficulty visualizing towns and cities of vastly differing sizes, just as they find it hard to imagine the existence of boundary lines.

In the second category of symbols, those which represent quantities and/or qualities of things found in different areas, the cartographer employs several different kinds of symbols. Dot maps are commonly used to show concentrations of population, animals, and other things of a kind that can be counted reasonably easily and which, by the nature of their distribution, communicate important information. The idea that a dot might stand for one hundred people is not easy to comprehend since imagining one hundred people is, in itself, rather difficult, and comprehending hundreds or even thousands of dots, some of which are so close together they become one very large mass on the map, is an even more difficult task. Other types of maps in this variety include maps showing major crop producing areas and regions in which ore is mined or in which other human activities may be significant. In dealing with these kinds of symbols, children must develop concepts with respect to the level of activity in an area. Suppose, for example, the major corn producing regions or the places where cotton is grown are shown on the map. It may easily be concluded that only corn or cotton are grown in these places, that it is not grown elsewhere, or that nothing else is produced in the area marked on the map. Although obviously an erroneous conception, it is what children think who have not thought through the question of why the lines surrounding these areas are drawn where they are.

The third major type of map symbol, where color and/or shading may be used to show topography or perhaps land use, is also something with which the youngest children come in contact that frequently results in considerable confusion. In 1913 a worldwide agreement was reached among geographers as to what colors would be used to show different elevations on maps. The International Color Scheme resulted. For a variety of reasons, not least of which was the problem in printing many colors on one sheet (shading one color into another was expensive and required great artistic skill), maps for many years showed single colors for different elevations.[12] Thus, all elevations between sea level and 2,500 feet were printed with a green background, all those between 2,500 and 5,000 feet in a lighter shade of green, and higher elevations were shown in various shades of brown. Few of these maps are being printed today, but thousands remain in classrooms; and they are a source of great confusion. Not only do colors themselves convey ideas which lead to misconceptions of various kinds, the delineation of elevations in a system of layered colors does not suggest the relief which may be found in an area; it shows only the range of elevations. To the young child, such a scheme is likely to be meaningless and may even generate ideas which he might be better off without. During the past several years, however, maps showing the physical features in the landscape have been printed with what is sometimes termed a "relief-like" quality. That is, the earth's topographic features are drawn on the map much as they would appear if one were viewing them from a jet airplane.[13] Colors on the relief-like map generally remain those of the International Color Scheme, but they convey more realism than any system devised before. One problem which continues to arise, however, is that the coloration moves from greens for low elevations to the reds and browns for higher elevations. Death Valley, which is 282 feet below sea level, is colored green. Of course, every child knows that green on a map shows where things are green—where grass grows, cows chew their cuds, and

[12] However, map makers have been experimenting for years with more vivid ways of portraying topography on maps. European cartographers, particularly, have experimented with a wide variety of ways of showing differences in elevation. An interesting series of pictures both for the child and the adult depicting the development of techniques in representing relief and elevation on maps is contained in *The Global World Atlas,* by Frank Debenham (New York: Simon and Schuster, 1960), pp. 20-21.

[13] With the exception that the colors are more vivid on the map than those seen at high elevations over the earth's surface and the shadows shown depict light being cast from the northwest — highly unlikely, in the northern hemisphere, at least.

farmers arise at dawn—or does he? Middle and high elevations present similar kinds of problems.

Land-use maps present another set of problems. If one does not consult the map legend, he may believe he is reading a map showing physical features when, in fact, it shows the dominant uses to which the land is being put. Again, examination of the colors used for different areas forcefully brings to one's attention the fact that color can be confusing as well as enlightening. Most land-use maps show desert areas in a sandy beige color; certainly no better color could be found to convey the well-known desolation of the desert. But it should be remembered that some desert areas are among the richest producers of fruits and vegetables. Will the maps used with children reinforce incorrect concepts, such as this one, or will children have had sufficient acquaintance with the meaning of deserts and the human activities found there that the colors on the land-use or topographic maps will not cause them to gain totally erroneous ideas about the world around them? Maps in and of themselves cannot prevent people from developing strange or incorrect ideas. As in all reading, the meaning which may be derived from maps is dependent upon an adequate storehouse of ideas to begin with.

One further observation may be useful with respect to maps which show topographic features. For many years, *relief maps* have been available in schools. Only with the past few years have relief maps made out of plastic been available—thus replacing the heavy and easily damaged plaster maps. Children thus have available a map through which they may learn by their sense of touch as well as through seeing.[14] If children have not had experiences throughout their school years with building their own relief maps, they are going to have even more difficulty understanding that the relationships of height to distance on relief maps are highly exaggerated. And, of course, the larger the area shown on the map, the greater the exaggeration. A relief map of a state cannot be compared with one of the United States in terms of feeling or seeing relief. Intermediate and upper grade children may gain insights into the problem of exaggeration[15] not only by making their own maps and deciding

[14] Consult the list of sources in an Appendix for such maps. Some model globes are available which actually show relief; others are available which have relief-like qualities.

[15] A model globe which showed relief in true relation to distances on the map would have so little actual differences in elevation that it would, for all intents and purposes, be like any other model globe. Exaggeration on model globes is therefore 100:1, whereas on one widely used commercial relief map of the United States it is 20:1.

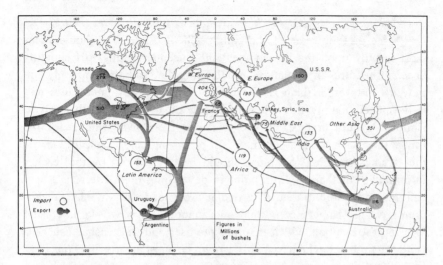

Figure 10–10: Flow maps show the movement of goods or people. This map shows international trade in wheat. (U.S.D.A. data)

how much vertical exaggeration they will wish to show but by learning to observe the map legend and practice converting elevations for given locations into actual feet.

Reading maps that show the flow of goods or people from one place to another (the fourth major type of map symbol which elementary school children should learn to interpret) requires the ability to sense differences in quantities of things by examining the relative thickness of lines drawn from one place to another on the map. The illustration above is typical of the flow maps which appear in texts and reference books children will consult. It asks the child to interpret width of lines, to sense significance in the relationships between locations connected by the flow lines, and, frequently, to infer differences and similarities through the colors used on the map. Such maps often report historical information as well as that which is more recent. Often such maps are used in historical studies. Children can gain experience in reading flow maps by constructing their own from data they collect. Traffic flow maps can be easily developed through direct observation. By counting traffic moving on streets adjacent to the school, for instance, they will have the raw data needed for such a map. There are, of course, other sources in the immediate community which can be used: municipal records, business data appearing in the newspaper, and handy references such as the *World Almanac*.

Developing Meanings for Map Symbols in the Primary Years. The first three or four years of the child's school experience should focus most heavily upon the development of concepts relating to frequently observed features in the landscape. Reading the symbols commonly employed to represent them is of growing but secondary importance and is developed mainly through maps made by the children themselves. Children should first be allowed to devise their own symbols for the things they wish to show on maps. In observing maps made by others, the symbols standing for things should be pointed out by the teacher informally, but there is little point in developing formal lessons to get children to be able to read a particular group of map symbols. As children grow in competence in their own mapping, they will be interested in using the symbols which map makers use; and the teacher can help children find out which symbols would be most nearly like the ones found on the maps in their classroom. Classroom experiences which will help children grow in their power to interpret map symbols meaningfully include the following:

1. *Look at flat pictures showing familiar landscape scenes.* Talk about the things which can be seen. Relate them to the out-of-school experiences of the children. Note differences, e.g., Which mountain is higher? Which is steeper? Which has more trees? Could you climb it? Which would be easiest to climb? Why? Which way would you go? Why? There is available in picture magazines and from commercial sources the widest variety of appropriate picture material which can be used to stimulate discussion about things found in nature.
2. *Recall walks and study trips taken some distance from the school and neighborhood.* Ask children to retell what they saw. Focus discussion on the variety of things seen, where they were in relation to one another (which things seen first, how far it was from one place to another, how long it took to get from one place to another, etc.), and how they differed (in kind and in quality).
3. *Talk about the kinds of markings they should put on their map* of the classroom, school, neighborhood to depict the things that they stand for in real life. Younger children will be happiest with three-dimensional "models" of things. Gradually realism will give way to abstract markings, but this process should not be hurried or stressed.

4. *Use a sand table to introduce the concepts of relief and elevation* (later primary years). Children living in suburban and rural areas, where the landscape has not been as drastically altered as in the cities, will be able to use the sand tray earlier. On the sand tray, represent any familiar area where slope can be noticed through direct observation.

5. After a vacation period or a time when children may have taken a trip, *look at road maps and talk about the markings on them.* Our highly mobile population creates an early awareness for the road map and its uses in finding one's way about. Primary children are interested in what the map shows and eager to tell what is on road maps. Fantasy frequently takes over in such discussions, but many ideas will be accurate and, always, reveal levels of understanding.

Developing Meanings for Map Symbols in the Intermediate and Upper Grades. Abilities to interpret abstract symbols expand rapidly during these years. By the ages of twelve to fourteen, children should be familiar with the meanings of the most commonly used map symbols and habituated to utilizing the map legend in gaining clues needed to read particular kinds of maps. Classroom experiences which can be planned by the teacher include the following:

1. *Develop a pictorial bulletin board* by collecting pictures of man-made and natural features in the landscape with the symbols commonly used to represent them.

2. *Make a collection of map legends* and discuss likenesses and differences among them. These, too, make a good bulletin board display.

3. *Study different ways relief and elevation can be shown on maps.* The historical development of the ways cartographers have shown relief on maps might be a project in itself.

4. *Build a model in the classroom which demonstrates the principles of the contour map.* By using modeling clay or some other plastic material (consult your hobby shop), build a mountain in layers which can be taken apart. Different colored material, or painting after construction, provides a more vivid model. Flat maps can be constructed from such models by tracing the outline of each piece on a piece of paper.

5. *Continue to practice visualizing places shown on maps.* Begin with familiar places, using the map as a stimulator of discussion

(ask pupils to tell about this place on the map, then another place, and so on, referring back to first-hand experience to confirm the observation). Later, collect pictures of an area and stimulate visualization of those places as they are shown on the map. Use the pictures as the reference in determining the accuracy of the observation.

6. *Find out how difference in quantity among similar things is shown on maps.* For example, how does one show that a river is large rather than small? Whether it flows all year or is intermittent? How can one tell that a city is larger than another? How can one make similar large–small judgments about other features in the landscape?

7. *Locate physical and cultural features of different kinds on outline maps.* Projects of this type have long been used in schools and too frequently they have consisted of merely copying a map appearing in another book. This procedure is of doubtful value. It is much better to select projects of this nature which require the pupil to gather data from several sources. He should either synthesize or reorganize his data so that he cannot possibly copy another map in its entirety. For example, use a broader classification system than that appearing on maps which will be consulted for information or have the pupil compile data from printed sources such as the *World Almanac* and present it in map form.

8. *Make a study of the different uses of isolines* (lines connecting points of equal value) in showing the location and distribution of things. For example, contours show points of equal elevation whereas isobars show points of equal barometric pressure on weather maps. Both are examples of the uses to which isolines (iso=equality, identity, similarity) may be put on maps. Isolines are used to show the distribution of such things as different kinds of agricultural production, levels of economic activity, soil types, the occurrence of natural vegetation, the presence of mineral resources.

9. *Continue map making activities* in connection with the social study, emphasizing the use of abstract symbols and the more precise use of color to show areal differentiation.

10. *Arrange for older children to gain experience in teaching young children* in this and other aspects of map reading. Teachers of

younger children will welcome the assistance, and the learning experience for both older and younger pupils will be invaluable.

DRAWING INFERENCES AND DEVELOPING
GENERALIZATIONS IN MAP READING

Abilities to read maps cannot be compartmentalized as simply as the foregoing has perhaps suggested. The ability to discriminate meaningfully between the different kind of symbols appearing on the map and to understand the concepts of location, distance, and direction are indeed important, each in its own right. But one cannot be satisfied with this. The symbols the cartographer has arranged on his map form patterns which yield important geographic information to the person who appreciates the kinds of interplay which can exist between these different kinds of map reading abilities. In fact, it is the ability to draw inferences and develop generalizations (as a consequence of interpreting the patterning of the various signs and symbols on the map) that distinguishes the true map reader from one who has barely made a start in understanding what maps are capable of communicating.

It is possible to go through life without learning that map reading ultimately involves processes of developing meaning and attributing significance to the patterns which can be observed through map study. But if a child's attention is consistently directed toward the possible meanings behind the patterns which emerge through map study, he will make steady growth in his capacity to use maps effectively. It is a slow process, of course, one that might be compared with learning to read print in books wherein the long-term goal is simply to help the child grow in his abilities to read between and beyond the lines of print. For in map reading, the primary concern is to help the child sense meanings and develop generalizations that may be illuminated only by a study of the relationships between and among things shown on the map.

Since the map is the major tool by which the geographer communicates his knowledge of areal relationships, as well as the most important device for discovering the nature of those relationships, the range and extent of the ideas that might be stimulated through map reading is as broad as the field of geographic inquiry. To read maps in this sense, therefore, is to engage children in the very heart of the process called geographic thinking. Consequently, every map in the classroom comprises a most important medium for encouraging children to think geographically, and so it is to be hoped that children will be encouraged to linger over their maps and that they will be stimulated to conjecture about the ideas which such contemplation brings forth.

Drawing Inferences and Developing Generalizations in Map Reading during the Primary Years. It was pointed out in previous chapters that young children do not draw inferences or develop generalizations on their own to any great extent; it is not that they cannot reason this way but that they particularly need challenging questions and situations if they are to be encouraged to think beyond the one-of-a-kind experiences of their immediate world which otherwise consumes virtually all of their energy and attention. To see the patterning which characterizes all maps, and to encourage the child to think about the quality of the areal relationships which can be discovered within these patterns, one needs to start with very simple ideas that are directly verifiable through recall of first-hand experience, or, better yet, which can be verified through direct observation under the guidance of the teacher. For example, young children can develop understandings about the pattern formed by a transportation network by beginning with a map of the area immediately surrounding the school. Beginning with a question such as, "Why are some of the roads shown on the map with darker, wider lines than others?" primary children can evolve ideas and experiment with the validity of generalizations in a broad area. For instance, these are the kinds of tentative statements elicited from discussions and activity, following such an opening remark as:

There are not as many "important" roads as other kinds of roads.
The "important" roads are usually wider, straighter, and smoother.
Houses are more likely to be found on the less important roads.
Businesses are usually found on or near the "important" roads.
Some businesses, like gas stations, are almost always found on the "important" roads, especially where they meet each other.
Important roads form a frame (or grid) which surrounds the less important ones.
The "important" roads "go somewhere."
Buses and trucks use the "important" roads more than the others.
People live near roads. The more roads, the more people there are.

What other kinds of statements might one expect boys and girls to evolve through the study of a community map? For example, consider the kinds of ideas which might be elicited after discussing (1) the effect of land forms on the location of roads; (2) how roads influence the location of telephone lines, power lines, sewage facilities; (3) how other natural and cultural features (rivers, parks, public buildings) relate to the network of roads in an area; (4) the location of safety devices in a community and its road system (traffic lights, fire stations and hydrants, crosswalks and other pedestrian safety devices, speed limits).

Drawing Inferences and Developing Generalizations in Map Reading during the Intermediate and Upper Grade Years. These are the ages during which the child's horizon of awareness expands rapidly. Growth toward abilities to reason inferentially and the capacity to generalize are also characteristic of this period. But since growth and development follows its own unique course within each individual, these are also years during which the teacher finds growing diversity in the classroom. Teachers of these ages consequently face much wider ranges of differences, with some children grasping abstract concepts readily and developing meaningful relationships among them with ease whereas others are still dependent upon their ability to recall specific experiences in order to attribute meaning and significance to ideas sensed as a result of map study.

The type of map used in the classroom influences the kinds of ideas which children may be able to generate through map study. Maps which show the distribution of soils, climate, or some other natural or cultural phenomenon obviously would serve to suggest quite different kinds of ideas than maps which show the location and distribution of physical or political features. Road maps show the areal patterning of certain kinds of phenomena. Maps showing the locations of raw materials needed in different kinds of manufacturing processes show other kinds of areal associations. The kinds of ideas which children will discover are closely related to the kinds of maps used in the classroom. Some thought should be given to the ideas considered central in each study and their relationship to the types of maps needed or the encouragement of geographic thinking through map reading will be difficult to achieve. Since there are many sources of maps beyond those supplied through school district purchases, the objective of securing a wide variety of maps showing the distribution of different kinds of phenomena for use in the social studies classroom is not a hollow objective. It may take some additional research to secure the maps, the listing to be found in an Appendix provides one source to which the reader may turn.

In summary, it may be observed that map reading is a complex process. One does not learn to read maps automatically, without systematic instruction based primarily on first-hand experience. The school has the important responsibility of providing a program of instruction which will lead to competence in map reading; this program obviously should begin in the primary years. If a teacher of older boys and girls should discover that important concepts about maps and mapping are lacking or inadequate, there is only one course open. That is to begin at the beginning. Some of the major elements of the beginning stages for developing competence in map reading and some of the more advanced stages in the development of mature makers and users of maps have been described here. When the first important experiences seem to be lacking, the teacher must move to the prior stages of development, adjusting judiciously the learning situations to fit the interests of children who are slightly older, if he is to help boys and girls grow both in the ability to prepare their own maps, using data they have discovered themselves, and to read maps prepared by others.

For Further Reading

Bagrow, Leo, *History of Cartography,* rev. and enl. by R. A. Skelton (Cambridge, Mass.: Harvard University Press, 1964).

Brown, Lloyd A., *Map Making: The Art that Became a Science* (Boston: Little, Brown and Company, 1960).

Brown, Lloyd A., *The Story of Maps* (Boston: Little, Brown and Company, 1949).

Cottler, J. and H. Jaffe, *Map Makers* (Boston: Little, Brown and Company, 1938).

Crone, G. R., *Maps and their Makers* (London: Hutchinson's University Library, 1953).

Deetz, C. H. and O. S. Adams, *Elements of Map Projection,* Special Publication #68, U.S. Coast and Geodetic Survey, 1945.

Greenhood, David, *Mapping* (Chicago: University of Chicago Press, 1964).

Mitchell, Lucy Sprague, *Young Geographers* (New York: John Day Company, 1934).

National Council for the Social Studies, *New Viewpoints in Geography,* Twenty-ninth Yearbook (Washington, D.C.; N.C.S.S., 1959).

Raisz, Erwin J., *Mapping the World* (London: Abelard-Schuman, 1956).

Raisz, Erwin J., *Principles of Cartography* (New York: McGraw-Hill Book Co., Inc., 1962).

Skelton, R. A., *Explorer's Maps* (New York: Frederick A. Praeger, 1958).

Smythe, James M. and Charles G. Brown, *Elements of Geography* (Toronto: The Macmillan Company of Canada, Ltd., 1959).

Steers, J. A., *An Introduction to the Study of Map Projections* (London: University Press, 1962).

Thralls, Zoe A., *The Teaching of Geography* (New York: Appleton-Century-Crofts, Inc., 1958).

CHAPTER ELEVEN

Using the Language Arts: Reading

Language takes many forms. Although one normally thinks of it as having some verbal attribute, such as spoken words or printed symbols of some sort, a moment's reflection reveals that human beings "talk" or communicate with one another through a wide variety of non-verbal symbols. Body gestures, facial expressions, and evidences of human activity left after an event all provide avenues for knowing which are not dependent upon the traditional modes of reading, writing, speaking, and listening. Then, too, the artist communicates, through his music, painting, sculpture, and dance, ideas and feelings which cannot be communicated with mere words.

Hence the languages one may learn to read or interpret, and through which one may find outlets for his own needs for expression, are of many kinds. Truly, the capacity one develops for both the verbal and non-verbal modes of communication determines the extent to which anyone may come to know and understand the world in which he lives. Learning in the curriculum of social studies cannot be limited to the verbal language abilities, as important and basic as they may be. In the discussion which follows, in this and the subsequent chapter, it should not be forgotten that the intellectual content of any social study depends upon the development of an appropriate balance between the verbal and non-verbal modes of communication. Unfortunately, most schools rely too heavily upon the traditional verbal modes to carry the intellectual content of the curriculum. How much more effective would teaching and learning be were the language of gesture, of the dance, of art, and of the myriad other non-verbal forms of language given "equal time" with the verbal curriculum.

The Varieties of Verbal Language

The verbal language abilities are usually classified as either receptive (listening and reading) or expressive (speaking and writing), and every elementary school provides a separate curriculum in language arts which has as its primary goal the further development of these language abilities in children. But since none of the modes of verbal language possess any inherent subject matter, the content areas of the curriculum play an exceedingly important role in helping the child grow in the use of his own language. Certain skills may be taught separately, perhaps; but children must have something to write about, to speak about, to hear about, and to read about. So it is to the social studies that teachers look for ideas to strengthen the language arts program, and to the language arts curriculum for learning situations which will extend understandings in the social study.

Some Facts About Language Development in Children in Relation to Social Studies

In thinking about ways in which language development may be fostered through social studies and what restrictions as well as opportunities the child's language ability places upon the work that he can do and the learning of which he is capable, knowledge about the nature of the child's evolving capacities to use his language becomes important. How the child has acquired and is acquiring his language leads to an understanding of why he expresses himself the way he does and provides insights into the quality of his social studies concepts, just as it tells something about the degree to which he may be expected to expand these understandings.

Although the quality of the child's receptive *and* expressive language modes will be discussed, this analysis will focus primarily upon his ability to listen in a variety of situations and his capacity to express himself orally, for these are the basic language abilities upon which the others are built. As teachers attempt to assess the conditions impinging upon the child's chances for learning well in social studies, they are concerned with (1) the richness of expression and the degree to which he is attracted to aural experiences which are themselves rich and full-bodied; (2) the extent and quality of both his oral and his aural vocabulary; and (3) the degree of flexibility with which he uses that vocabulary and the manner in which he responds in a variety of situations that demand listening abilities. Then, of course, in planning learning situations in social studies, one is interested in selecting from the vast array of possibilities those which have the greatest potential for extending the child's language abilities, both orally and aurally.

Although the intention here is not to provide an extended discussion of the field of language development, enough needs to be said about the subject to convey an idea of how important it is to be aware of *each* child's language and to understand that the language he uses as he works in social studies is a most significant manifestation of his thinking.[1] It is on the basis of this kind of information that realistic plans are laid. For although in one sense the elementary school child's language is rather fully developed by the time he enters first grade, it remains true that teachers tend to overestimate the child's comprehension of what he reads and are, as well, inclined *to read into* his oral language far greater understanding than actually exists.[2] It is also important to reflect upon the degree to which language abilities vary from one child to the next and the meaning this may have for working with youngsters in a social studies curriculum. For example, approximately two-thirds of the children in a given class will manifest abilities equivalent to the number of years they have been in school. The remaining third will go beyond these extremes: one-sixth of the class may be expected to fall below the second grade achievement level, and the remaining one-sixth will be achieving at the eighth grade level. Thus, a fifth grade class can normally be expected to range over six academic years in achievement —from "second grade ability" to "eighth grade ability" on whatever language criterion is selected (reading, writing, speaking, listening). Differences are indeed great in normal development. In utilizing the reading abilities of boys and girls in social studies, the teacher consequently needs to develop a particular sensitivity and awareness for each child's receptive and expressive language if he is to provide learning situations of value. By so doing, he may come closer to practicing the "art of the possible" in teaching.

---

[1] A bibliography of books in the area of language development useful to the social studies teacher is included at the end of this chapter.

[2] The average child's understanding vocabulary at six years of age is believed to consist of about 25,000 words; there are about 3,000 words in his oral vocabulary; his pronunciation system is virtually complete; and he uses the grammatical forms and syntax which will characterize his oral language throughout the remaining years of his life.

THE IMPORTANCE OF THE PRE-SCHOOL YEARS

The crucial years in language development are those between birth and about six years of age. Recognition of this fact is apparent in the development of Head Start and other pre-school language stimulation programs supported both by agencies of government and by private groups. For, as noted, it is during this time the child learns the pronunciation system of his native language and completes much of the learning of its grammatical structure. That is, the grammar the child will use throughout the remaining years of his life is, for the most part, learned by the time he is about eight years of age. Especially for those coming from economically impoverished areas and those growing up in homes where the native language is not English, much of the language which the child acquires may be non-standard; it differs markedly from that used by the majority of people and yet may, in fact, be used by most of the children in a particular class or school. Nonetheless, whatever language is learned, in meagerness or in richness, it obviously is learned early and learned with a high degree of permanence. To change one's language patterns is indeed difficult once it is learned. In the case of those boys and girls presently condemned to an impoverished language, either the young person will need to become highly motivated to change or be provided with especially effective instructional situations, or both. Such programs as Upward Bound and the Job Corps have been started in recent years, in addition to Head Start, to help young people in this respect. By improving the young person's facility with the various language modes, he can communicate better with others. Since language is the major means used in thinking, it is in this manner that he can be helped to improve his intelligence. If thinking can be improved markedly, then these youths will be able to take advantage of programs designed to help them acquire skills needed to survive in a world rapidly becoming more dependent upon highly trained workers. Public recognition is therefore being given to the problem of providing more effective language instruction programs than are presently being offered. The school has an obligation to discover and use learning situations for these kinds of youngsters that are more effective than presently exist This concern, therefore, must be taken into account in planning the curriculum of social studies just as much as in all other aspects of the work of the school.

Still, it is important to realize that although the language of children from economically impoverished areas tends to be "non-standard" (a sometimes euphemistically employed term used to connote those language forms, vocabulary, and the like, not acceptable in the generally middle-class culture of the schools), it is the purpose of the school to teach so that these boys and girls learn. The relative permanence of this language means that the teaching must occur in a climate of acceptance, where the non-standard provides the basis for initial instruction. Then, the setting for learning must be so varied, extensive, and rich that children experience the kinds of opportunities they need to serve as a firm base for developing a more effective language. The teacher's task, then, is not so much to attempt to mold the child's language to adult or other "acceptable" standards as it is to help the child grow in the capacity to manipulate his own language with increasing flexibility in gaining and expressing ideas.[3] This means putting him in touch with a wide variety of social studies materials, presented both in their written (printed) and oral modes (through tape recordings, listening to the teacher and classmates' oral presentations, motion pictures, television), and providing many opportunities for him to express himself through speaking and writing experiences.

ORAL SPEECH AS AN INDICATOR OF LANGUAGE DEVELOPMENT

The most important indicator to the social studies teacher of the child's total language development, and the clue which he will use in planning learning situations, is his oral speech. But since one cannot say accurately what he cannot hear, it is obvious that the basic language ability is listening. The fundamental importance of listening is well illustrated in the response of Helen Keller when asked if she were to have a choice between her afflictions of blindness and deafness which she would have chosen. She replied without hestitation that she would rather have been blind, for her inability to hear made it impossible to develop normal speech; hence, she found herself immeasurably more limited in her ability to communicate with others. The fact that profoundly deaf children never succeed in intellectual affairs to the degree that normal children or blind children do further points to the crucial

---

[3] The following recent news item emphasized this point: Salem, Ore., Aug 3— (AP). Children should be encouraged to use familiar slang or dialect in the classroom, the president of the National Council of Teachers of English says. Muriel Crosby of Wilmington, Del., told an Oregon State Education Department workshop that standard English usage can be taught more easily to a child who is fluent in his own dialect. "It is a question of whether you want pupils to write nothing perfectly or something imperfectly," she said.

role of hearing and listening abilities in language and intellectual development.

By listening to what the child says, the teacher can tell to what degree there is a congruence or correspondence between the child's oral language and the standard speech sounds. If there is a lack of congruence, that is, if the child is not able to reproduce with a reasonable degree of accuracy the sound units which make up words (called phonemes by the linguist), he will very likely have difficulties in reading and writing and in communicating his ideas in general. Although some deficiencies in this respect may result from an actual hearing loss, many are developmental; that is, they will be reduced as the organism matures. Thus, the seven-year-old who substituted the sound "menoh" for the letters m, n, and o, when "saying" the alphabet, was having considerable difficulty with reading and writing. When his ability to discriminate among the sounds which make up words improved, perhaps partly as a consequence of instruction but certainly in the process of maturing, he moved ahead rapidly. And so, for older children, it is not surprising that "when" is often spelled "whin" or "win" or that "library" is written and pronounced "liberry." That is the way some children hear the sounds, and that is the way they say them in their speech. How much should one criticize a child's written work in social studies when attention to his oral speech indicates that he is only being logical in translating the sounds he hears in his inner speech into written words? Perhaps a more effective approach would be to try to help him with the errors he is encountering in listening. The consequences of identifying more accurately the sound-symbol correspondence will be more accuracy in writing as well as in oral expression.

For children whose language backgrounds are different from the majority of the school population (or which are impoverished in other ways, developing for any reason more slowly, or whenever some anomaly is present), the social studies program must be adjusted, often radically. There is no future, nor even a happy present either, for the teacher or the children, where the oral language and listening abilities of any child must be used in an environment which is hostile to those abilities.

THE INTERRELATEDNESS OF THE VARIOUS LANGUAGE FUNCTIONS

The oral language facility depends, therefore, upon the quality of the child's listening abilities. To "say" a sound, he must be able to hear it.

It is not illogical, therefore, that the child whose oral speech is advanced can be expected to be high as well in listening abilities, but the analogy also extends to include both writing and reading abilities.

The child who is high in:	Will also likely be high in:
listening	reading, writing, and speaking
oral speech	listening, writing, and reading
writing	speaking, listening, and reading
reading	writing, speaking, and listening

Conversely, valid experience in one language mode tends to strengthen the others. Good writing experiences strengthen listening, speaking, and reading. Good speaking experiences tend to strengthen the child's ability to listen, to write, to speak, etc.

So although one may view a particular learning experience as focusing on reading, or perhaps primarily on writing, one cannot divide language experiences in the social study into discrete units. And if one thinks about the interrelatedness of these four functions, one may be helped to develop some ideas to use with children which otherwise might be overlooked, or at least one may get maximum use of an idea. For example, the classroom textbook—a book which the children and teacher write together about their experiences in a particular study— becomes not just a writing experience but a reading experience as well. Going just a bit further, one can see how it may also be an oral language experience as well as one in which listening abilities are practiced. One can also perhaps understand a little better why the child who is experiencing difficulty in reading can be expected also to have problems in writing; or why the child whose oral speech is poor will not perform well in other language activities in which he is asked to engage. Patience and a willingness to try to understand the language the child is capable of producing, even though it seems to be full of errors, will produce better results in social studies with children than will excessive criticism and demands for the production of "near perfect" language.

With this broad, general background concerning the development of language abilities in children, the specific language activities in each of the major modes to be utilized in any curriculum of social studies will be considered. In the remainder of this chapter, the role of printed-word reading is considered. In the chapter following, listening, writing, oral language, and some aspects of non-verbal communication are discussed. In dividing the discussion, it should be re-emphasized that all the modes of communication are interrelated. To separate them in this manner is an artificial device with which the reader must conjure as he thinks about their applications in the classroom. For as children

> read books
>> listen to the teacher, expert visitor, someone else
>>> observe and listen to motion pictures
>>>> hear music
>>>>> see and hear other people dance or use their bodies to "speak"
>>>>>> examine visually and with their other senses pictures, models, artifacts
>>>>>>> study filmstrips
>>>>>>>> and contemplate the meaning of things and ideas—

they have opportunities to

> write and speak
>> create their own pictures, music, models
>>> act out ideas formally and informally, singly and in groups
>>>> re-order and arrange the classroom to reflect their learning
>>>>> engage their own senses of touch, taste, smell, movement
>>>>> express their own and others' ideas through singing,
>>>>>> choral verse, plays (formal and unstructured), pantomime
>>>>>>> and in as many other ways *express* actively the concepts and understanding with which the teacher wishes them to become familiar.

Twelve Rules for Reading

1. Read
2. Read
3. Read some more
4. Read anything
5. Read about everything
6. Read enjoyable things
7. Read things you yourself enjoy
8. Read, and talk about it
9. Read very carefully some things
10. Read on the run, most things
11. Don't think about reading, but
12. Just read

Reading Experiences

Reading is a complex intellectual activity about which relatively little
is known. Such ignorance comes not from a lack of interest in trying to
find out what happens when a person "reads," for thousands of studies
have probed different aspects of the reading process. Rather, it comes
from the fact that every attempt to identify the elements involved in the
reading act shows us that the process called "reading" is much more
complex than was previously thought. Relatively simple definitions, such
as "reading is getting meaning from the printed page," have consequently given way to much more complicated ideas. One widely
respected authority in the field, for example, has said that "reading is
thinking."[4] DeBoer and Dallmann amplify this theme, saying.

We know that effective reading involves all of the higher mental processes. It involves recall, reasoning, evaluation, imagining, organizing, applying, and problem solving. Good reading requires good thinking. When
we teach reading, especially in the beginning stages, we must teach good
thinking.[5]

Increasingly, the emphasis is upon what goes on inside the reader—
how he recalls, recognizes, associates, creates meaning, and gives significance to what he reads. But throughout these definitions, the assumption
is made that only certain kinds of things can be read. Thus, DeBoer and
Dallmann say that reading is an "activity which involves the comprehension and interpretation of ideas symbolized by written or printed
language."[6] However, many believe that limiting the concept of the
nature of the reading process to printed stimulation limits one's ability
to think about what really happens when one "reads." This broader
view has considerable merit since it directs attention toward inner
processes rather than toward the correction through drill or practice of
errors in dealing with printed symbols. Its focus is therefore upon meaning, upon the abilities to associate past experience, and upon the ways
the youngster puts ideas together. Jennings has written a book which
casts reading in its narrow sense of creating meaning and significance for
graphic symbols in the broader perspective. Jennings comments:

[4] Emmett A. Betts, "Reading is Thinking," *The Reading Teacher,* Vol. 12
(February, 1959), pp. 146-151.
[5] John J. DeBoer and Martha Dallmann, *The Teaching of Reading* (New York:
Henry Holt and Company, 1960), p. 19.
[6] *Ibid.*

But reading, remember, is not restricted to the printed page. Actually, it never was. In one sense reading *is* the art of transmitting the ideas, facts, and feelings from the mind and soul of an author to the mind and soul of a reader, with accuracy and understanding, and much more. But throughout his history man has "read" many things: the flight of birds, the guts of sheep, sun spots, liver spots and the life lines on a hand. He has read the lore of the jungle, the spoor of the beast and the portents in a dish of tea. But whatever he has read and however he has read, it has always been for "reason." It was only when man invented symbols for the words in his mouth and the ideas in his teeming brain that other kinds of reading became more useful, possible or even desirable. . . .

Reading begins at the womb when the body first senses the universe, and the message center of the brain scans the scrambled reports of the senses. Reading gains precision as the sign of an ache or an emptiness is correctly translated into appropriate and soothing action. Reading gains in scope when faces and features become organized into personalities. Reading begins to encompass that universe when the mother standing with the child at the window "reads" the beauty of the day.[7]

In this section, problems and opportunities in utilizing reading abilities and in developing reading competence in its narrow sense of creating meaning and significance for printed-word stimulation will be discussed. The concern is with this kind of reading wherever it may occur: in books of various kinds, in magazines, in signs and charts, on television and motion picture screens, in things written by children and teachers, on bulletin boards, everywhere such symbols may be found and read. However, what appears here is written with the point of view of the broader conception of the reading process, that the major distinction between this kind of reading and other kinds is not one of differences in process but, rather, in the type of stimulus which is to be read. One might talk about listening as reading, but, in this discussion, the topic is limited to the type of stimulation (sounds versus printed words, for example). One could say that the process of creating meaning and significance for color and form (as in an artist's rendition) or for ideas symbolized by sounds arranged in patterns of melody, harmony, rhythm, and tonal color (as in music) or for ideas symbolized by facial expression, voice quality, gesture, and posturalization (as in observing and understanding the behavior of others) represent types of reading which also are a concern in social studies. That the problem for the reader is the same as he seeks to create meaning and attribute significance to each

[7] Frank G. Jennings, *This is Reading* (New York: Bureau of Publications, Teachers College, Columbia University, 1965), p. 11.

of these "reading problems" should be fairly obvious. The variable in each of these reading situations occurs outside of the reader and is related to differences in the type of symbolization to which the reader attempts to lend significance.[8]

READING A SILENT ACT

In any discussion of the role of reading in learning, it should be remembered that the behavior is always a silent one. The only way one can judge whether or what a person is reading is by inference. Also, judgment cannot occur until *after* the reading has actually taken place. It is, consequently, very difficult to know a great deal about another person's reading. One can ask him to talk about what he has read, to write about it, perhaps to paint a picture or act out something that will indicate the import which his reading has for him. Still, as one attempts to know about the meaning he has derived from reading, one can see that there are bound to be major communication problems.

THE NEED FOR MANY TYPES OF READING MATERIALS

Recent developments in social studies indicate clearly that curriculum researchers and developers of instructional materials are keenly aware of the need to have multiple materials in classes if optimum learning situations are to be encouraged. As indicated elsewhere, the concept behind using many different kinds of materials extends beyond that which is conventionally thought of with respect to reading materials. That is, motion pictures and video tapes, recordings and transcriptions, overhead projection materials, filmstrips, and other audio-visual devices are increasingly bringing to children in classrooms extended opportunities to read a wide variety of materials. Tape recordings are being produced, along with the traditional recording or transcription, which have been coordinated with printed materials in books and in filmstrip form. Frequently, the tape itself is enclosed in a self-contained package inserted into the machine, playing automatically, and then rewinding, ready for the next use. Similar materials are available in filmstrip form. Single concept filmstrips, actually a misnomer, which present to the reader a series of closely related ideas or concepts on a topic provide

[8] This view of the reading process is at variance with the popular view, which perceives reading as a specific set of responses conjured up by experiences with a limited set of stimuli (namely print). That reading of print is part of a broad behavioral developmental process involving all aspects of the human organism frequently evokes philosophical agreement but arguments at the level of practice.

opportunities for thinking in greater detail about a subject. Some of these filmstrips are also presented in self-contained packages, ready to be used many times by young children with a minimum chance of damage. Not infrequently, filmstrips and slide collections are coordinated with the tape recording or transcription which allows the learner to both see and hear independently or as a member of a group. All of these situations provide opportunities for developing reading abilities and for using reading capacities in gaining information.

In addition to the technological advances in this respect, of course, many improvements are being made in those materials with which teachers have long been familiar: in supplementary texts, trade editions, encyclopedias and other reference books, in maps, globes, and so forth. In the latter part of this chapter these diversified materials, sources from which they may be procured, and ways each is particularly suited to social studies are discussed.

First, however, the basic idea underlying the use of a wide range of materials and how classrooms might be organized to make efficient and effective use of them deserves some attention. It has been stated that it is preferable to engage children in studies in depth on selected problems rather than to attempt to cover a wide range of topics or ideas in a relatively superficial manner. This idea is based upon the widely accepted principle that to know something well is to make it one's own. That is, the child who has an opportunity to delve into a topic, to become as familiar with it as he possibly can, will have a better chance to know what he knows, to remember, and to apply his knowledge in other situations. But depth study also means employing a wide range of techniques or ways of gaining information. It requires a method of attack, the development of problem solving abilities, but this can never be accomplished with a limited set of materials. Problem solving, then, and utilizing a method of discovery require a variety of materials, not least of which are those which fall within the general category of "reading materials."

SOME SPECIAL PROBLEMS IN USING SOCIAL
STUDIES READING MATERIALS

In social studies, as in literature, science, mathematics, and all the other curriculum areas, the major problem in developing printed-word reading capacities is the proper utilization of the experience of the learner. Reading matter commonly available in the form of textbooks and related supplementary materials, it is readily agreed by all authorities in the field, presents too much content, in excessively condensed packages, which is almost universally replete with words and phrases likely to be unfamiliar to the pupil.[9]

Children are likely to find it difficult to cope with so much coming at them so fast and under conditions which seem to put the material and the ideas beyond anything they have known before. The first matter to be attended to in dealing with reading materials in the social study, therefore, is consideration for the closeness or distance which may exist between the child's own experience and understanding and that of the things he tries to read. The problem of concept development was discussed in some detail elsewhere, and here the reader will be referred to only a reconsideration of those ideas, for they are most pertinent.[10] The teacher, however, can assist pupils in comprehending the reading matter that comes before them if he will assume that even the phrases which appear to be most common are probably not understood by some of the pupils in his class and that there are many others which have, at best, only the vaguest definition. To prevent serious misunderstandings from developing, it is important to keep in verbal contact with the children by asking them to talk about what they are reading and to extend their understandings of words by relating those poorly understood words to more familiar ideas.

In addition to the problems of meaning, children meet difficulties in pronunciation which are peculiar to the social studies. Foreign words and phrases, often familiar to the child in his spoken speech, do not yield to ordinary word attack skills and may remain beyond his understanding even when "read" in context. Anticipating that children will confront words such as Zuider Zee, Viet Cong, and Taj Mahal provides the teacher with an opportunity to familiarize children with these words before they meet them in their reading. Since reading itself is an independent, individual activity, the teacher has no control over what the child will do when he meets these kinds of words in his reading. The only way he can be prevented from skipping, misinterpreting, and,

[9] For example, see discussions on this topic included in Helen Huus' chapter "Reading," in *Skill Development in Social Studies,* Thirty-third Yearbook, National Council for the Social Studies, 1963, pp. 95-101; and Leo Fay *et al.,* "Improving Reading in the Elementary Social Studies," Bulletin 33, National Council for the Social Studies, 1961, pp. 15-17.

[10] See Chapter Four.

in all likelihood, failing to comprehend entirely is to meet questions such as these ahead of time and to follow up with discussions and questions.

But of the two problems, pronunciation and meaning, the latter is of prime importance and poses major obstacles to the uses of reading in the social study. Problems of meaning range all the way from difficulties with proper names, to special terms, to words with more than one meaning, to words with shifting meanings or referents, to phrases and abstract terms that require special interpretation. Some examples of words and phrases in each of these categories follow:

Proper Names: Particularly in the primary grades, Plymouth Rock, Puritan, New York, Memorial Day, Massachusetts Bay, Sioux, Mississippi, etc.

Particularly in the intermediate and upper grades, Amazon, North America, Pharoah, Babylon, Federal Communications Commission, Congress, Morse Code, etc.

Terms: Community, conservation, interdependence, democracy, manufacturing, cartographer, industrialization, trade route, imperialism, colonial policy, etc.

Words with more than one meaning: Mouth, cape, plain, belt, quarter, cancer, range, bank, checks and balances, movement, pike, fork, etc.

Circumstances in which words shift their meanings or referents: For example: *It* was this loose, or *placer,* gold *that* Californians first discovered. Thousands of years in the making, nearly all such deposits had been found and worked out between 1848 and 1850. Then men began to search for the place from which the loose gold had come. They found *it* in the large quartz deposits of the Sierra Nevada. *These* mountains became California 'Mother Lode.' *Here,* deep mines were cut into the hillsides. Miners carried out the gold-bearing rock and separated the metal from *it*. But finding and mining underground gold took money, machines, and skill. *It* was no business for beginners."[11]

[11] This example is taken from John and Nancy Rambeau, *California Crossroads* (San Francisco:.Harr Wagner Publishing Company, 1963), p. 132. Italics added.

Phrases and   For example, these words appear in a single four-
abstract terms that teen-page chapter of a high-interest–low-vocabulary
require special   supplementary book[12] designed for intermediate and
interpretation: upper-grade use. Marblehead, maritime world, Salem,
                      East Indiaman, Sumatran, Calcutta, Canton, full-
                      rigged, East Indies, packet, China trade, Java Head,
                      around Good Hope, dory, in every line of her, to
                      hurl hostages to Fortune, immortalized in art, alba-
                      trosses, desolate headland, scudding clouds, con-
                      temporary sketch, log, squalls, beetling rock, wintry,
                      put in commission, epitaph.

Problems of this nature extend through the entire range of supplementary materials. Even children's encyclopedias are overly full of
difficult words and phrases. Among the least guilty are the magazines
and "newspapers" published especially for children; the mode of expression appearing in these publications reflects writing which is sensitive
to the nature of children's ability to understand and contrasts rather
sharply with what one sees in most other materials.

USING THE TEXTBOOK

Reliance on the textbook to the exclusion of virtually all other learning sources is obviously an unsatisfactory solution in teaching the social
study. But, in concert with a wide range of other materials, the text has
several major values. First, it may provide an overview of the topics or
problems to be studied. Second, it can make available to the children
in the class a common background of information, a starting point which
provides basic information for all. Third, textbooks provide opportunities to practice skills. Through tables, charts, maps, illustrations, etc.,
included in the text, which the class can study in group settings, the
teacher is able to provide practice in improving the abilities necessary to
comprehend and use this type of material. Fourth, textbooks frequently
serve as an excellent reference tool. Modern texts contain a wealth of
maps, charts, pictures, and other sources of reference-type information.
Glossaries, biographical sketches, recommendations for further reading,
and appendices containing a wide variety of information are found in
virtually all modern textbooks. Advances in technology make possible

[12] Mary Ellen Chase, *Donald McKay and the Clipper Ships* (Boston: Houghton
Mifflin Company, 1959), pp. 103-117. Although some of these terms are known
words, the meaning of which can be inferred from context, there are others that
require the use of a dictionary or some other source to secure their meaning for
the reader. Still others would not yield to such an analysis.

the inclusion of more accurate color renditions which bring increased realism to the pictures and which even make possible the inclusion of such a sophisticated cartographic technique as the overlay map.

SELECTING TEXTBOOKS

Not many years ago, the quality of textbooks in social studies was quite variable. Efforts on the part of teachers and administrators to select the best of these for school use combined with those of authors and publishers who sought to provide the best type of material possible have resulted in much improvement. Today, the textbooks published by the major publishing houses are of consistently high technical quality. Although one rarely finds errors of fact in the modern textbook, a criticism of their scholarly content is in order, however. Because they are produced for a mass market in an age in which drives for conformity are very strong, the content of textbooks tends to be accurate but bland. No offense is intended in producing them, and, as a consequence, many people and groups are inclined to take umbrage at the treatment, or lack of it, of topics they think are important. Although some critics are loudly calling for changes for selfish or perverse reasons, it is doubtless true that the search for a middle ground between critics, to the left as well as to the right, has resulted in the production of books which omit references to important topics and problems. This is particularly true with respect to the role of minority groups in the American culture and to issues which are controversial in nature. One would hope that social studies textbook writers and publishers in the future would concern themselves with presenting more balanced materials by refusing to be so intimidated by economic demands for "safe" material. It is likely, however, that the teacher who wishes to seek such balance and to include in his studies with children more relevant material will find it easiest to secure appropriate supplementary texts and trade books. In these publications one will find extended treatments of topics and problems usually either left out of the textbook or handled in a superficial way.

Thus the problem of selecting a "good" textbook is now primarily concerned with questions relating to how it is organized and whether its subject matter is appropriate to the studies which have been selected for emphasis in a particular school or district. In most schools, teachers have only an indirect responsibility for selecting textbooks. In some states, for example, state-wide committees recommend to the state board of education, which in turn requests money to purchase them from the state legislature, those books which it thinks are appropriate for the social studies curriculum. If other materials are in short supply, this scheme obviously puts severe limitations on the local district's choice of a social studies curriculum. In other instances, county-wide, or district-wide committees may recommend to their administration and, thence, to the local school board, the textbooks they would like to use. But the teacher does exercise a choice in the matter, for the manner in which he elects to use the textbook will determine for the most part whether he will be its master or its slave.

It should be pointed out that "textbook-like" materials are beginning to become available for younger children. These are programs incorporating a wide range of coordinated materials, including pupil books, suggested classroom activities, and other directions for the teacher and, not infrequently, filmstrips, recordings, and other devices which are to be used in the classroom during the course of the study. Among the first of these were the materials produced in economic education by Senesh and his associates.[13] These materials are based on a method of discovery with an emphasis on the "ways an economist studies." Taba and Robinson have been the major influences in the development of what is sometimes called the Contra Costa County Social Studies Curriculum Guides.[14] The concept behind their organizational pattern is that of a unified approach to the disciplines. Although none has been widely adopted as yet, it may be expected that instructional materials of this type will become increasingly available both for primary classrooms and for intermediate grades.

SOME GUIDES FOR TEXTBOOK USE[15]

The comments which appear here with respect to using textbooks in the school refer primarily to the intermediate and upper grades because

[13] Lawrence Senesh, *Our Working World: Families at Work* (Chicago: Science Research Associates, 1964).

[14] Contra Costa County Schools, Pleasant Hill, California, *Social Studies, Grade 1* (units on "Our School" and "Family Living"); *Social Studies Grade 2* (units on "Services to the Supermarkets," "Services in Our Community," and "The Farm"); *Social Studies, Grade 3* (units on "Primitives of Africa," "People of the Hot Dry Lands," "The Boat People of Hong Kong," and "People of Switzerland"); *California Yesterday and Today, Grade 4* (includes six major themes); *Anglo-America, Grade 5,* (includes eight major themes); and *Latin America, Grade 6* (includes six major themes).

[15] A number of writers have dwelt upon the place of the textbook in the social studies curriculum at some length. Two references the reader may wish to consult are Ernest W. Tiegs and Fay Adams, *Teaching the Social Studies* (Boston: Ginn and Company, 1959). See especially Chapter Thirteen. This material is most appropriate for intermediate teachers. See also: Morris R. Lewenstein, *Teaching Social Studies in Junior and Senior High Schools* (Chicago: Rand McNally, 1963), pp. 320-347. Especially suitable for upper grade teachers.

most social studies programs at the earlier grade levels are still formulated with the assumption that most children do not achieve the independence in reading required to use the conventional textbook meaningfully. Partly, too, it is because the social studies curriculum has focused upon the here and now world of the child. It is difficult to develop a textbook for a mass market that still meets individual needs. This does not mean that a large number of children are not reading independently before this time nor that learning in the social study may not depend upon reading activities. The numerous trade books, magazines, "newspapers," and the like designed for children of this age attest to this growing market of readers. It is just that traditional conceptions of the textbook have not been successfully adapted to the younger age levels in social studies—which may be a blessing. Nonetheless, in considering ways of using the text with older children, these points may be kept in mind:

1. No textbook can meet the reading needs of all the children in the class. Some will find the material too difficult; others will find that it lacks intellectual challenge. For children who have difficulty in printed-word reading, it should be remembered that the social studies textbook is *not* a "reader." A way needs to be found to present the information in the textbook to these children in some other form. Usually, the poorer reader will be able to comprehend most of the material if it is received aurally—if someone reads it to him. One way to accomplish this is to tape record the chapter and ask these children to listen while they follow the written material in the book. The teacher can interrupt his oral reading of the material with pertinent questions or other comments, if he wishes. For the rapid reader, arrangements should be made to get him into more difficult and challenging material as soon as possible. He should not be held back to the average child's progress in reading. Rapid readers may cover the entire textbook in a matter of a few days and should be allowed to acquaint themselves with their textbook very quickly, if they wish. They may also be called back to re-read the material so that the end result is thorough familiarity with it.

2. The textbook does not have to be used progressively, each chapter following the preceding one in order. Sometimes curriculum committees elect to "cover the material in the book in sequence" but that often is a consequence of the inability to think more creatively about the topics of the various studies. The "logical" order of the

textbook is often not the best "psychological order," either for the teacher or for his pupils. When the most desirable pattern of topics has been selected, then the textbook should be used in the sequence dictated by the choice of topics.

3. Major difficulties will be encountered, as already noted, by almost all children with the specialized vocabulary associated with each topic or problem. Rapid readers tend to slide over difficult words or phrases, getting the gist of the meaning but missing the precision in thinking of which these children are capable. Less advanced readers will often not understand these terms and will turn off their thinking, going through the reading process mechanically and with little meaning. Opportunities to discuss and think about these ideas ahead of actual reading helps to overcome these difficulties.

4. The various illustrations contained in the textbook (maps, charts, graphs, pictures, tables, glossaries, etc.) are among its most important sources for learning. There are advantages in each child having his own copy of these items since it provides for total-class instructional settings without a materials problem and makes it possible for the teacher to determine the ability of the class as a group, as well as of the individual, with respect to progress in reading these kinds of sources of information. Considerable time may be spent constructively in classroom lessons which linger over the different types of illustrations provided in the modern textbook.

USING SUPPLEMENTARY TEXTBOOKS

Frequently the local school district, or even the state, may supply certain kinds of books in limited quantities for classroom use. These books are most often ones which go into a topic in considerably more detail than the textbook. Rather than being supplied to each child, they are made available on some sort of ratio—for example, one book for every three or four children in the class. This makes possible smaller-group activities, and, eventually, every child in the class may have an opportunity to read and consider these materials. Usually, these books are written for a more local market than is possible in the textbook field. State histories, aspects of local or state government, special books dealing with map reading, and biographies of persons whose lives have had regional, rather than nation-wide, importance represent the kinds of materials most frequently available. Supplementary textbooks have advantages similar to those of the standard textbook although they cannot be realized in the classroom as readily: they are available to the total class, provide a basis for common experience and discussion, and are carefully organized and present information basic to the study.

USING TRADE BOOKS

In the recent past, with the advent of high speed presses, vastly improved color rendition, and a burgeoning market for sales, a vast array of materials have been published in what is termed "trade editions." These are books and related materials designed primarily for over-the-counter sales. In some instances multiple purchases are made by libraries. In contrast, textbooks are sold in large quantities primarily to schools. Their preparation is not affected by considerations of what the public market might be for them since sales to the public are insignificant. Unfortunately, many of the trade books published in any year are of poor quality, without any redeeming merit as far as school use is concerned and, perhaps, as far as the general public is concerned, as well. There is a profusion of valueless reading materials; yet they are readily available on any supermarket shelf and are purchased in profitable numbers by well-meaning parents, grandparents, and perhaps others. But a sizeable number of the "trade books" published every year are of the highest quality, and they play a valuable, even essential, role in the social studies. The problem for the teacher is to find out which books are of value and to make them available to the children, preferably in the classroom. Several sources may be consulted to this end:

1. Professional librarians provide the most valuable and immediately available source of information about books that are suitable for children to read. Although schools are seriously understaffed with professional librarians, many do employ them. No district with more than five schools should be without the services of such a person. In fact, no school should be without its own library and professional librarian although few schools are equipped either with adequate libraries or professional staff. Yet this source, when available, is invaluable to the development of a sound program of social studies. City and county libraries and their librarians can also be of invaluable assistance to the teacher, both with respect to professional advice and in helping supply classrooms with the needed books. But they cannot supplant the need for an adequate school library.

2. Nearby colleges and universities engaged in teacher education programs very often offer courses in children's literature and have
specialists on their faculties who are valuable sources of information and ideas for teaching.

3. There are a number of regular publications which assist in making
selections of books and in getting ideas for using them in social
studies as well as in other curriculum areas. The following list
represents the type of material which is available in most college
libraries and which should be available to some degree in every
school:

> A Basic Book Collection for Elementary Grades, American
> Library Association, Chicago, Illinois.
> A Basic Book Collection for Junior High Schools, American
> Library Association, Chicago, Illinois.
> A Reading List for Elementary School, Champaign, Illinois
> National Council of Teachers of English.
> *Reading Ladders for Human Relations,* fourth edition (edited
> by Muriel Crosby). Washington, D.C.: American Council on
> Education, 1963.
> American Library Association. *The Booklist and Subscription
> Books Bulletin.* Published semimonthly; annually reviews about
> 500 titles recommended for young adults. 50 E. Huron St.,
> Chicago 11, Ill.
> ————. *Top of the News.* Quarterly publication of the Chil-
> dren's and Young Adult Services Divisions. 50 E. Huron St.,
> Chicago 11, Ill.
> R. R. Bowker Co., *School Library Journal.* Monthly, September-
> May. 1180 Ave. of the Americas, New York, N.Y.
> Horn Book, Inc. *The Horn Book Magazine.* Published bi-
> monthly; reviews and news of children's books, authors, and
> illustrators. 585 Boylston St., Boston 16, Mass.
> *According To Us* (Priscilla Holton Neff, ed.), published annu-
> ally by the Claremont Reading Conference, Claremont Graduate
> School and University Center, Claremont, California. (There is
> a small charge for this material.)
> National Council of Teachers of English. *Elementary English.*
> Monthly, October-May, for elementary teachers. 508 S. Sixth
> St., Champaign, Ill.

————. *English Journal.* Monthly, September-May, for junior and senior high school teachers. 508 S. Sixth St., Champaign, Ill.

New York Herald Tribune. *The Lively Arts.* Published Sundays; book review and entertainment section. 230 W. 41st St. New York 36, N.Y.

New York Public Library. *Branch Book News.* Monthly. Fifth Avenue and 42nd St. New York 28, N.Y.

New York Times. *Times Book Review.* Published Sundays; semi-annual roundup of childrens' books. 229 W. 43rd St. New York 36, N.Y.

Saturday Review Corporation. *Saturday Review.* Weekly. Occasional reviews. 300 Madison Ave., New York, N.Y.

University of Chicago. *Bulletin of the Center for Children's Books.* Published monthly by the Graduate Library School. 5835 Kimbark Avenue, Roo. 206, Chicago 37, Ill.

Professional Books of special value for teaching social studies:

Huus, Helen, *Children's Books to Enrich the Social Studies: For the Elementary Grades.* Bulletin 32 revised edition, National Council for the Social Studies. Washington, D.C.: The Council, 1961.

Hanna, Geneva and Marianna K. McAllister. *Books, Young People, and Reading Guidance.* New York: Harper & Row, 1960.

Taba, Hilda and others. *Literature for Human Understanding.* Washington, D.C.: American Council on Education, 1948

Tooze, Ruth and Beatrice P. Krone, *Literature and Music as Resources for Social Studies.* Englewood Cliffs, N.J.: Prentice-Hall, 1955.

With the advent of federal funding of local school units, particularly with respect to instructional materials, trade books are becoming increasingly available to the classroom teacher. The above list of sources for selecting books provides an important key to obtaining books which relate to the many areas of interest in the social studies curriculum. Although there is no doubt that most schools will suffer from a shortage of these books for a long time to come, federal financing plus a growing level of support for public libraries will be beneficial to the teacher who who would like to employ these materials to a greater extent in the classroom. Most public libraries will allow teachers to withdraw a sizeable number of books on temporary loan. By going to the local public library, and by securing books from other libraries not in such close proximity, it is possible even under rather difficult conditions to obtain an adequate classroom library. The latter opportunity is more available to those who live in an urban complex, of course.

Other sources of reading materials are those paperbacks available at minimal cost to children through the "book clubs." Actually, these reading materials are being made available through the publishers of the classroom newspaper. Generally, they are of fair to good quality, are attractively bound, and are reasonably rugged. Although much of the material is fictional in nature, occasionally titles appear which are relevant to social studies.[16]

After solving the problems of quality selection and availability of books for classroom use, it must be recognized that the mere presence of trade editions does not guarantee that children will be attracted to reading them. Some further planning must be done, and although one would want to consider as many alternatives to the more or less formal assignment of a book to be read as possible, even the direct approach is not ineffective if used sparingly. However, in the long run the advice of librarians and others skilled in attracting children to books should be heeded. They consistently point out two important factors in getting others to read. First, the manner in which books are displayed is very important. Books on shelves simply are not read as frequently as books arranged in attractive displays. Second, it is important to consider who influences whom to read. Adults are more frequently attracted to read a particular book by hearing about it from a friend (the most effective motivator) or by reading about a book in a source they respect. And so it is with children. When a child expresses his enthusiasm for a book, his classmates will probably want to read it. It is this kind of enthusiasm for and about books which must flower in the classroom if boys and girls are to discover that there are books available that can be read for both fun and profit. To aid the development of an intrinsically motivated classroom setting for extending social studies learnings through the use of trade editions the following ideas are suggested:

1. *Make arrangements for a classroom library.* Fortunate is the elementary school with a library of its own and, even more fortunate,

---

[16] Among the better known sources of these inexpensive paperbacks are The Arrow Book Club, The National Scholastic Paperbacks, and the Macmillan Reading Spectrum.

a qualified librarian. Still, the school library does not completely fill the role of the classroom library, nor can it take the place of it. In developing a library in the classroom, children at any age will enjoy an opportunity to develop a classification system of their own which is related to the things they are studying. Very young children may decide they want to put all their "Stories About Pets," or "Books About Trains," together whereas older boys and girls will utilize a more adult-like scheme, as in "Historical Novels," "Atlases," or "Reference Books." Children of all ages prefer to have a place set apart for their library which has some special arrangements. An area rug by the bookcase may designate such a place, or movable book shelves or partitions may be used.

2. *Develop attractive displays of books which relate to topics being studied.* It is better to arrange six or eight books on a table where each can be easily seen than it is to attempt to put out all of the books which are available on a particular topic. The problem of changing the display is solved quite naturally. As children select books to read, new ones may be added.

3. *Designate a regular space on the bulletin board to display ideas emerging from the study.* Book jackets, pictures drawn by children illustrating episodes, moods, and the like from books they have read, and book "reviews" done by children are illustrative of the kinds of things which may be put together in various combinations to attract others to books and to communicate important ideas discovered through reading. Arrangements which feature children's work are better than those made exclusively by the teacher. In putting a child's work up for everyone else to see, it is suggested that he be allowed to display his work without the teacher's comments appearing on it. Sometimes this means the child will need to prepare a copy of his original material.

The basic objective in utilizing trade editions in social studies is to bring to the child a greater wealth of detail, presented in an inherently more interesting fashion than is possible through a textbook, information, and ideas which are relevant to his studies. This may be accomplished in a variety of ways:

1. *Oral Reading.* It is a commendable practice to spend some time each day reading aloud to children. It is therefore a simple task to select from time to time a book which relates to the social studies

curriculum. Ten to twenty minutes daily brings before the class, over a period of time, a great deal of information, some of which may be talked about, illustrated, or incorporated in other ways into the social study. Relevant selections used in this kind of setting may lead to worthwhile discussions, particularly with respect to values and attitudes represented in the book. Oral reading need not be restricted to the teacher, of course. As children read their own library books, they may be asked to present interesting or unusually valuable sections orally. Whenever anyone is asked to read to a group, sufficient time should be allowed for preparation. However, children, especially, should not be asked to read aloud material which they have not read before. Effective oral reading requires adequate preparation.

2. *Independent Study.* The presence of a number of trade books relevant to a particular study may be capitalized upon either as an adjunct to the reading program itself or they may, in a self-selection reading program, be completely integrated into the reading-language arts curriculum.[17] Teachers who plan a basal reading program with their pupils invariably include a library period, at least once a week, where children may become interested in books which present topics related to their study. However, it cannot be expected that every child will, or should, become so involved. A self-selection reading program provides greater opportunities to read widely from trade editions and, especially at the upper grade levels, may become the major avenue not only for improving reading abilities but also for supplying the basis for much of the information which children need in their social studies work.

3. *Group Study.* There are times when common problems may be identified by groups of children for study. In a study of the American Revolution, for example, pupils may become engaged in reading biographies of heroes of the period. Historical novels, such as Leonard Wibberly's Treegate Series, may be secured in multiple copies (three or four per classroom) or other books about the same people may be obtained. When the books children read are as vivid and arresting as Wibberly's, children quickly

[17] *See* Jeanette Veatch, *Individualizing Your Reading Program* (New York: G. P. Putnam's Sons 1959); Peggy Brogan and Lorene K. Fox, *Helping Children Read* (New York: Holt, Rinehart, and Winston, Inc., 1961); Dorris M. Lee and R. Van Allen, *Learning to Read Through Experience,* second edition (New York: Appleton-Century-Crofts, 1963).

develop a strong identification, not only with the heroic figures about whom the stories are written, but also for the distant times and places depicted.

USING FREE AND INEXPENSIVE "FUGITIVE" MATERIALS

Virtually every public and private agency of any size is engaged in the publishing business. That is, they print, and make available to anyone interested, information about the topics of concern to them and which they want the public to know about. These one-of-a-kind publications, printed from time to time as needs require, are usually called "fugitive" materials and are available at little or no cost. Although these materials are often of great value in teaching, there are also certain dangers associated with their use. Considering their source, for a moment, it is not surprising that fugitive materials usually present imbalanced points of view. Obviously, providing information is only one objective in making them available to the public. The major purpose, except for certain kinds of government publications, is to influence the reader in some way; improving the public image of the agency sponsoring the materials or encouraging people to purchase a particular product are but two reasons for going to the expense of preparing, publishing, and distributing these items. Some fugitive materials are blatant in this regard; others are more truly "public service" publications, but it is often difficult to tell which is which until the teacher and his pupils have an opportunity to examine them first-hand in the classroom.

With these biases in mind, such publications are still invaluable sources of reading materials for the social study. In planning a study, it is most worthwhile to write such diverse sources as foreign embassies, chambers of commerce, major private businesses in an area, and public utilities for information about the kinds of publications which are available on particular topics. From the large quantities of materials which such letters will elicit (best written on school stationery), selections of the most worthwhile can be made.

The uses of fugitive materials in the social study are extensive, and only a general notion of ways in which they might be employed in the classroom can be conveyed here. However, among the many ideas one might utilize, the following may prove helpful:

1. Because most fugitive materials are profusely illustrated, they make excellent sources for developing scrap books or bulletin

board displays, or they may be used to illustrate a classroom text-book or perhaps stories written by individual children.

2. Published material of this type also normally is a good source for current statistics for an area. These may be collected from a variety of sources, compiled, and compared with each other. Standard references and textbooks usually are not as current in their reporting of interesting data about a place. Fugitive materials may therefore be used as a source for updating other information, and they may also be used to determine whether there are discrepancies in the reports. Children may find it of value to speculate on why there are discrepancies.

3. Older children can read between the lines of different types of materials, asking what the purpose seems to have been in publishing this particular information, whether the presentation seems to be impartial or biased.

4. Train, bus, and airplane schedules may be used to plan imaginary trips and to provide interesting questions in arithmetic, such as judging the type of terrain existing between an area by noting the differences in time required to move from one area to another using different modes of travel.

5. Publications from embassies of different countries frequently reflect social and political attitudes and policies different from those of our own country. An analysis of materials of this type may stimulate interesting discussions and, perhaps, further research into the reasons such differences exist.

6. Special events, such as centennial celebrations or other anniversary or "special days," are frequently celebrated in part through the publication of local or regional histories or other special purpose collections of information which are truly of great value. The study of one's community or some other type of inquiry which is local or regional in nature may be enhanced immeasurably when such publications are available. Often, special collections of these materials will be worthwhile. In that way, normally expendable material of this type may be made available to pupils in subsequent years.

7. Although the telephone directory may not strictly be classified under this category, it serves as one of the most valuable resources available to the social studies teacher. Particular reference is intended here to the classified section, although public agencies,

foundations and other private organizations, foreign embassies, and the like are listed only in the main portion of the directory and are, of course, important resources. But within the classified section one will find reference to the widest assortment of businesses, services, and other economic and social activities of a region, complete with their address and telephone numbers. A study of the directory therefore yields a variety of near-at-hand resources for securing information, samples, sources for study trips, publications, and the names of persons who might come to the classroom to talk with children.

Systematic efforts to locate and record the source of free and inexpensive, or "fugitive," materials are reported in a variety of publications. Among the most comprehensive are those published by the Educators Progress Service, Randolph, Wisconsin. This company publishes four different books, revised annually, giving information about free curriculum materials, films, slidefilms, tapes, scripts, and transcriptions. These publications are frequently available in the school district curriculum laboratory or library. Other sources of information are available from the following:

The Joint Council on Economic Education, 2 West 46th Street, New York, New York (in the area of economic education only).

Division of Surveys and Field Services, George Peabody College for Teachers, Nashville, Tennessee (a general publication titled *Free and Inexpensive Learning Materials*).

Field Enterprises, Incorporated, Education Division, Merchandise Mart Plaza, Chicago, Illinois (publishes *Sources of Free and Inexpensive Educational Material*).

Bruce Miller, Box 369, Riverside, California (publishes *Sources of Free and Inexpensive Teaching Aids.*)

Furthermore, various professional magazines include lists of materials which business and industry, particularly, are making available to the schools. These frequently contain considerable advertising or are obviously promoting their product or service. Most publications of state teacher's associations contain such a listing as do professional periodicals such as *The Grade Teacher* and *The Instructor*. One of the most valuable sources of materials, however, is the Superintendent of Documents. The federal government, as well as the various state governments, publishes many materials which will be helpful in the classroom. Write to the Superintendent of Documents, Washington, D.C. for information and bibliographic material available on the topics which are relevant to the studies planned.

USING STANDARD REFERENCE SOURCES

Social studies classrooms should be equipped with a range of reference materials, appropriate to the maturity level of the children, which provide a ready source of factual information bearing on the problems or topics under study. In any classroom where the natural curiosity of children finds expression, there will be scores of questions, most of which are deserving of answers. The art of teaching includes some capacity on the part of the teacher to refrain from answering questions and to encourage the students to hunt for information which makes learning an exciting business. But how frustrating it is not to have the necessary reference materials.

Four major types of materials are available which provide ready sources of information on a broad range of subjects. These include almanacs, atlases, encyclopedias, and special purpose reference books. Some of these publications are expensive and are found in limited numbers in schools. Others are of the paperback variety and are consequently inexpensive. This type of material is becoming increasingly available and is proving to be a most valuable resource. One can now secure dictionaries, compendiums of useful information in growing number (*Information Please Almanac,* The New York Times, *U.S. Book of Facts, Statistics and Information, Encyclopedia of the World's Great Events,* etc.) and, books of quotations (*Bartlett's Familiar Quotations, Popular Quotations for All Occasions, Pocket Book of Quotations,* etc.) . Each of these is available for about one dollar per copy.

In considering the kinds of sources which are available, both in paperback and hardbound, it is important to remember that there are differences. As far as encyclopedias are concerned, for example, some contain relatively few comprehensive articles on topics. The remainder of the material includes basic information on a very broad range of subjects, and the treatment is relatively short. However, references may be included which are designed to help the reader discover other material in the encyclopedia which covers relevant topics. A few other publications offer extended discussions of fewer topics. If one were to use an encyclopedia rather heavily as a source for researching a fairly broad problem, the latter type of material would probably prove to be more useful. However, it is obviously desirable not to try to rely on one kind of publication; one would want to encourage children to go to a variety of such resources.

Older children will also find useful information in biographical publications such as *Who's Who in America* or *American Men of Science.* There are regional reference books of this type, such as *Who's Who in the East,* and there are a number of such publications for different fields of inquiry (including education, music, drama and art). Other types of special reference materials include the following:

Thorndike-Barnhart Junior Dictionary (Chicago: Scott-Foresman and Company, 1962).

Espenshade, Edward B. Jr. (ed), *Goode's World Atlas,* 12th edition (Chicago: Rand McNally and Company, 1964).

Book of the United States (Chicago: Rand McNally and Company, 1962).

Kunitz, Stanley J. and Howard Haycraft, *The Junior Book of Authors* (New York: H. W. Wilson, 1951).

Although there is available a wide range of school atlases, maps, and globes, most of which are of high quality, there are other sources for materials of this type which are not as widely known. Publications of the *National Geographic Magazine,* however, are popular and find wide usage. These cover a broad range of topics; the magazine treatments are highly readable and the illustrations outstanding. In addition, of course, carefully detailed maps and atlases are available through the parent organization. It is wise not to overlook local and county governments, and state governmental units as well, as resources for these kinds of materials. Still, one of the most valuable of resources is the U.S. Coast and Geodetic Survey, which publishes a wide range of maps (a source list is included in an Appendix) as well as a do-it-yourself globe that can be constructed in about an hour's time.

All of these types of references will be consulted in a variety of ways. They will be used to settle questions of facts of various kinds. They will be utilized in gathering data and in developing generalizations about the meaning of those data. They will cause children to consider where to find information, how to seek it out, and how to organize it so that it makes sense. For the teacher, there is the question of securing enough quality resources for learning for his classroom. There are variations among encyclopedias, in maps and globes, and in all the other types of reference materials he might want to use. It is frequently difficult to make a judgment about the major reference materials because they are rarely evaluated objectively; it is not easy to arrange for similar kinds of materials to be put side by side and comparisons made in that way. It is useful, however, whenever possible to make such comparisons and to attempt to judge the relative worth of these materials. A few objective evaluations done by others are also available. For example, encyclopedias are regularly evaluated by The American Library Association. Published evaluations appear in their bi-monthly review, *The Book List and Subscription Books Bulletin.*

With these thoughts in mind, some guides for using these materials in profitable ways with children are offered.

1. Develop the habit of "looking it up" when a question arises in discussion for which no one knows the answer and when a short diversionary trip to the encyclopedia or other reference source might seem profitable. The development of an inquiring mind seems to occur best where the business of conducting inquiry is part of the regular routine of the classroom.

2. In planning problems or topics worthy of research, try to avoid the type of subject which is treated in its entirety in the reference books available to the children. Such problems, and portions of them, which appear in reference books are likely to be copied and presented without much thought. An attempt should be made to pose simple questions that cause children to do considerable digging within an article. Others cause the pupil to look into more than one article—an effective deterrent to copying. In thinking through the kinds of questions that might be raised with children, a look at the reference books available in the classroom and the manner in which they cover topics within the area of inquiry planned by the teacher will provide guides to the kinds of questions that might best be posed.

3. Make a practice of comparing similar types of reference materials. Maps showing similar regions utilize different projections (causing land shapes as well as distances and directions to vary), give different kinds of data (perhaps one is a land-use map whereas another is a political one), employ symbols which are dissimilar, or vary on one or another count. Encyclopedias, dictionaries, and other reference materials contain differing descriptions for similar

topics. It is important for children to learn that the people who compile, edit, and write the reference books (as well as other written material, of course) do not have to agree on how information will be presented. There are differences of opinion concerning such matters as what is most important, what words may be used to prepare descriptions which will communicate most effectively; indeed with respect to every aspect of preparing printed material of all kinds for use by others.

4. Encourage the use of various types of reference materials at home. Homework assignments that call for securing specific information or which might precipitate family discussions (but not arguments) are helpful. For instance, questions such as the following might be researched at home: What does one feed a turtle? Or a hamster? What are the main differences between the English Parliament and the Congress of the United States? Between a Canadian province and one of our states? What different kinds of houses or shelters did the Indians of North America build? Why were there differences in the ways they built them? Questions of the "compare and contrast" variety are likely to stimulate discussion as children search for details which demonstrate similarities and differences. They are also applicable in reading pictures as well as printed words. It is frequently advisable, especially for younger children, for the teacher to prepare questions in multiple copies so each child may take home a written item rather than relying on children's often inaccurate memories of assignments given verbally.

5. In the classroom library, provide a special place for reference materials. Designate it as the "reference section," similar to any library. This will help children to begin to realize that there are certain types of books that serve specific functions—among them reference books—to which one might turn when various types of questions arise. They will also become familiar with the idea that other categories of questions cannot be resolved in a satisfactory manner merely by consulting standard reference materials; more extensive research is necessary in resources which provide much more detailed information.

6. Maps especially, and on occasion other types of reference sources, may be bound together to make a permanent collection. A class studying its state might collect road maps which show parts of the

state in greater detail than would be available in an atlas. A similar collection could be made for a larger region. Materials of this type may be bound into books by the children. By preparing book covers, stitching or stapling the pages, and gluing cover and pages together, they may produce their own books on special topics. Such items are usually highly valued and, consequently, used.

USING MAGAZINES AND NEWSPAPERS

Both magazines and newspapers have extensive uses in social studies. Increasingly, periodicals of value are being published which relate directly to the kinds of studies which are commonly taking place in schools. Like newspapers, they are also of value in discussions of current events. There are generally two types of magazines and newspapers available to the teacher: those prepared primarily for children and those gauged to a broader public but which children can use profitably also. In the former category are such publications as *My Weekly Reader* and *Boys' Life.* In the latter, one finds *American Heritage Magazine, Caravan,* and the better quality daily newspapers.

Materials prepared especially for children are highly readable, and the format is attractive to young people. Publication and distribution problems make it difficult for such publications to include true "current events." There is a considerable time-lapse between putting the paper or magazine together and the publication and distribution of it. Good foresight often leads to the inclusion of articles about topics that have considerable current interest, however. It is the daily newspaper which can meet the problem of presenting current issues, and, where high quality newspapers are available, many intermediate and upper grade teachers find it valuable to have a subscription delivered to the school. Magazines and newspapers are of special value in the following situations.

1. Both serve as the major source of information to which children turn in discussing current events. Subscriptions to a major news magazine and to one of the better newspapers for each class beginning with the fourth or fifth grade is strongly advised to provide ready sources of current information. Without these subscriptions, teachers must rely upon faulty memory systems to relay factual information secured at home, or upon the pupils for bringing clippings to school. In the latter instance, items selected often

concentrate on the sensational rather than the significant events of the day.

2. The major picture and news magazines also are useful sources of information to be included in scrapbooks. Pupils might become involved in following a political campaign, a program to further conservation of natural resources, or some other related series of news events which would be reported upon regularly in these sources.

3. Newspapers prepared especially for children may be made available, either in limited numbers or in quantity. Reading and discussing, role playing and dramatic play, stimulating further research on a topic may emerge as these materials are used from time to time. Teachers' guides are provided to suggest appropriate classroom procedures. Among the more widely available "newspapers" of this variety are the following:

   My Weekly Reader (graded editions, 1-6) and *Current Events* (upper grades) published by The American Education Press, 400 South Front Street, Columbus, Ohio, 43216.

   The Junior Review (upper grades) published by The Civic Education Service, 1733 K. Street, N.W., Washington, D.C., 20006.

   NewsTime (intermediate grades) and *Junior Scholastic* (upper grades) published by Scholastic Magazines. 50 West 44th St. New York, N.Y.

   World News of the Week (intermediate and upper grade editions) published by News Map of the Week, Inc., 7300 N. Linden Avenue, Skokie, Illinois, 60676.

4. Material appearing in magazines prepared mainly for an adult market often may be read orally to younger children with success, older pupils will find value in reading selected articles independently. It is sometimes necessary for the teacher to edit judiciously in reading aloud: some of the material will be beyond the comprehension levels of the class; or simpler words may be substituted for more difficult ones as the teacher reads to the children. Magazines which frequently contain information of value to social studies include:

   Holiday, published by Curtis Publishing Company, 641 Lexington Avenue, New York, N.Y.

   Arizona Highways, 2039 W. Lewis Avenue, Phoenix, Arizona.

National Geographic Magazine, published by National Geographic Society, 17th and M. Streets, N.W., Washington, D.C.

Natural History, published by American Museum of Natural History, Central Park West at 79 St., New York, N.Y.

Life, published by Time, Inc., Time and Life Bldg., Rockefeller Center, New York, N.Y.

Look, published by Cowles Communications, Inc., 488 Madison Ave., New York, N.Y.

Sports Illustrated, Time and Life Bldg., Rockefeller Center, New York, N.Y.

Caravan, New History Foundation, New York 1, N.Y.

American Heritage Magazine, published by American Heritage Publishing Company, Inc., 551 Fifth Avenue, New York, N.Y.

Sources of this type are usually exceptionally well illustrated. Pictures may be mounted separately, projected, or merely shown to children at appropriate moments.

5. Magazines particularly, but feature articles appearing in newspapers as well, provide a useful source of information on a wide variety of subjects which relate to social studies. Over a short period of time, magazines may be searched for relevant articles which are then cut out and put in attractive folders. These then become a regular part of the classroom library and a valuable source of detailed information on topics only given passing treatment in other books.

6. A number of magazines and other publications prepared primarily for boys and girls are valuable sources of information and ideas. The following publications are noteworthy:

School Bulletins of the National Geographic Society, 17th and M Streets, N.W., Washington, D.C., 20036.

Focus, published by the American Geographical Society, Broadway at 156th Street, New York, New York, (10 issues yearly for $1.00)

Nature and Science, published for the American Museum of Natural History by the Natural History Press, Garden City, New York, 1·1531 (biweekly October through November and January through May; monthly in September, December, June and July for $1.40).

Class activities may be planned around specific articles, or back issues may be saved to serve as background and resource material at a later date.

USING CLASS-MADE READING MATERIALS

Many of the products of children's thinking may find their way into usable reading materials for the social study. There is tremendous power in such class-made materials. Everyone should be aware of the attraction which his own words have for himself. A person frequently will prefer to re-read his own writing instead of that of someone else. Still, to read the writing of one's friends may be more interesting than reading something written by someone totally unknown to the reader. The analogy of reflecting on one's own behavior in looking at a group photograph in which he is included is an apt one. One first looks at his own picture and then at the others, but he will usually spend much more time observing his own image than any other. There is indeed, something very fascinating about our own selves and the things which we do or make, including the words that we write.[18]

This involvement and identification with one's own writing can be capitalized upon in scores of ways in social studies. For example:

1. Stories dictated to the teacher about a study trip, or some other vivid experience, may be illustrated and combined with others to make a record of a particular social studies experience.
2. Stories either dictated or written by individuals may be duplicated, illustrated, and "bound" into book form for individual use as well as being placed in the classroom library for future reading.
3. In a similar fashion, a classroom "textbook" may evolve. A series of writing experiences, duplicated, and distributed to members of the class may be put in a looseleaf binder. Contributions may come exclusively from the children in the class or from both the teacher and his pupils. The work of younger children will usually be placed on a chart rack, a moveable roll of paper, an easel, or some other place where large items may be displayed.
4. The teacher may prepare a class book which tells about a specific experience the class has had. A classroom play, for example, might be the basis for preparing "illustrations" (pictures taken by the teacher), the script for the play, "reviews" offered by other

[18] An old Chinese proverb asserts: "Every man admires most his own writing and his neighbor's concubines."

classes who observed the play (actually thank-you notes written
by those classes invited to see the play), and other mementos of
the experience that seem appropriate.

5. A picture file that relates to the social study may serve as a
stimulus for writing. Such contributions may be collected according to topic or on some other basis and stapled together with a
cover to make another book for class use.

These are the kinds of language experiences which provide lasting and
vivid impressions upon boys and girls. Through writing their own stories
in a variety of settings, collecting them, and including them in the classroom library, children derive a great deal of pleasure. Furthermore, children are being provided opportunities to go back and think again about
things which have been done, ideas which have been discovered, and
generalizations which have been developed in the course of the study.

USING MAPS

The important place of maps in social studies has been emphasized
several times. The teaching of the abilities to use these tools is the direct
responsibility of the social studies curriculum. Because of this and because the processes involved in reading these kinds of materials are
particularly complex, an entire chapter is devoted to the problem of
teaching these specialized reading abilities and to ways of using them
in social studies.

USING OTHER SOURCES FOR READING EXPERIENCES

Other sources for reading are either present naturally in the environment of the reader or may be employed deliberately in teaching. The
concern here is with building sensitivities for reading opportunities
which may occur on the television or motion picture screen, or on filmstrips, as well as in things for which the child may develop an awareness
through first-hand experiencing in his environment. Words and phrases
appear on signs that communicate a wide variety of ideas: places are
named, directions given, or products advertised, for example. Captions
on filmstrips or motion pictures explain what the pictures are about or
perhaps tell about the kinds of ideas the readers should look for in
the pictures. Boys and girls need specific guidance if their sensitivities
for these kinds of reading opportunities are to be brought to a satisfactory level. Street signs need to be noticed, discussed, and their meaning or significance recognized, or streets the primary child uses every

day will remain more or less nameless entities. Other things—the things which adults often take for granted and assume children, too, are familiar with—will also remain nameless, and purposeless, unless children can learn to develop an awareness for them.

The significance of these kinds of reading opportunities needs to be stressed for it is in this kind of reading situation that much of the persuasive communication so prevalent in our society takes place. In social studies one is concerned that children learn to read the advertisements which seek to persuade us to purchase a certain kind of automobile, a particular brand of soap, or one cigarette over another. One should be equally concerned that children become aware of the need and the difficulty in reading labels on packages of various kinds, to follow printed directions, etc. This kind of awareness begins when children are taught how to read the many things which need to be read outside of books and outside of conventional classroom reading situations. It begins with the "obvious," with road signs, with the names of things printed on trucks and store signs, with slogans and other kinds of simple persuasive materials (the Red Cross, "We Give"; the March of Dimes slogan of the year; the trade mark or phrase associated with a product or an idea). It expands as rapidly as meaningful discussion can be obtained; and it proceeds on the assumption that learning to read a textbook or some other book is not a sufficient guarantee that the persuasive "literature" which demands our attention on television, in the motion picture, or in advertisements in newspapers and other sources will be read as critically.

Examples of the variety of activities which may be planned in this area suggest many more approaches to raising sensitivities in this dimension of the reading process.

1. By providing a set of relevant filmstrips and a small projector, an individual study booth can be set up which will allow youngsters to view pictures and captions independently. Study centers of this type are similar to the idea of a listening center described in the next chapter.

2. Younger children can collect containers of different sizes and shapes formerly containing products purchased at the store. Various approaches can be used to see whether they hold more, less, or the same quantities as other containers. Older youngsters can read the indications of quantity on the container and draw inferences about the reasons for using different shapes. Differences in cost may also be noted.

3. Cartoons pose a variety of reading problems since they are abstractions of real life situations, each meant to convey a certain type of information. By projecting or duplicating material of this nature, presenting it in a form so that each child has ample opportunity to study the material, discussions may be stimulated that will extend understandings of the issues at point in the material. Cartoons, both current and those which might be used in a historical context, are often quite subtle. Care should be exercised to give children an opportunity to express themselves fully. Cartoons are useful in helping the teacher understand the extent to which ideas are comprehended.

4. Advertising as it appears in newspapers, magazines, and posters can serve as a point of departure for considering the nature of the messages intended, the techniques used, the manner in which questions of quality or quantity are implied, etc.

5. Graphs also pose specialized reading problems. The length of the two axes in relation to each other, the type of symbol used, and the sources of data provide opportunities for observing the different ways one may tell the truth with statistics as well as lie with them.

6. Similar situations may be encountered as one studies tables that purport to communicate certain information. Questions such as the following encourage discriminative thinking: What source or sources of data have been used in compiling the table? Have important categories been left out or is the table reasonably comprehensive? Are the data recent and could changes have been expected since the publication of the information recorded here which would make the situation appear differently today?

7. Children can be encouraged to read the signs that abound—on street corners, in shopping centers, within the stores themselves, on vehicles, in parks—wherever they go. The messages such signs convey are partly accomplished with words and partly through characteristic shapes, colors, and locations in which they occur. These matters can be brought out through discussion, by collecting and displaying things observed, through writing, and through dramatic play.

For Further Reading

Barzun, Jacques and Henry F. Graff, *The Modern Researcher* (New York: Harcourt, Brace & World, Inc., 1957).

Bernstein, Basil, "Aspects of Language and Learning in the Genesis of the Social Process," *Journal of Child Psychology and Psychiatry,* Vol. 1, 1961, pp. 313-324.

Harvard Educational Review, *Language and Learning,* Vol. 34, No. 2 (Spring, 1964).

Jennings, Frank G., *This Is Reading* (New York: Teachers College, Columbia University, 1965).

Lee, Dorris M. and R. Van Allen, *Learning to Read Through Experience,* second edition (New York: Appleton-Century-Crofts, 1963).

Loban, Walter D., *The Language of Elementary School Children,* Research Report No. 1, The National Council of Teachers of English, 1963.

National Council for the Social Studies, *Improving Reading in the Elementary Social Studies,* Bulletin 33 (Washington, D.C.: N.C.S.S., 1961).

National Council for the Social Studies, *Skill Development in Social Studies,* Thirty-third Yearbook (Washington, D.C.: N.C.S.S., 1963).

Taba, Hilda, *Literature for Human Understanding* (Washington, D.C.: American Council on Education, 1948).

Veatch, Jeanette, *Individualizing Your Reading Program* (New York: G. P. Putnam's Sons, 1959).

CHAPTER TWELVE

Using the Language Arts in Social Studies

Children are placed in the role of listener in a wide variety of situations in social studies. The teacher's directions must be followed, and reports are presented by other pupils. Discussion activities require listening before speaking. Recordings are played; a variety of other sounds (many of which may take some form other than words or music) may be "read" by the listener if he is so inclined and has the experience necessary to make sense out of what he hears.

Although everyone spends much of his life listening to a wide variety of things, the listening process itself is not well understood. But, one can differentiate listening from hearing much in the same way that one can distinguish reading from seeing. In many respects, listening may be compared with reading. It contrasts, perhaps, only in the sense that listening involves careful discrimination of sound differences, interpretation of those differences, and some response or reaction to what has been sensed aurally. Listening differs from reading, however, in that one cannot easily bring the sound back in order to review and analyze what has been heard. One must remember the sounds he hears and, in some respects, pay far more attention to the differences in pitch, intonation, stress, and the other characteristics of the thing being heard. But listening will be enhanced if the listener can also use other senses to help him confirm what he has been hearing. Seeing the speaker as one listens to him is an important aid to accurate listening. In fact, the combination of seeing and hearing is so beneficial to the listener that he will invariably intently watch a tape recorder or record player if he is straining to give his undivided attention to material that has been previously recorded.

Listening also may be described as involving levels of attention. If teachers would not talk so much, their pupils might listen more carefully. But, in any case, it is clear that the degree to which one attends to what is being heard is a matter of motivation. The child's level of attention—the degree to which he listens—varies according to his interests. Developing listening abilities is, therefore, as much a matter of motivation and interest as anything else.

Listening Experiences in the Classroom

There are two basic types of things to which the child turns his attention in listening. First are the listening situations in which the content of what is being presented might be described as discursive. These are situations in which ideas are being presented in some form or logical order. It is content which informs, explains, gives details, resolves issues, apprises or makes aware, or asks questions. Much of the content of social studies falls into one or more of these categories. The second type of listening situation may be described as consisting of non-discursive content. When the child listens to the teacher read fiction or poetry, when music is played, or when other sounds are made (the wind in the trees, a tire screeching on the pavement), other kinds of sensitivities come into play in reading the sounds, in listening accurately and meaningfully. Content of this type involves emotional responses and aesthetic judgments, whereas discursive content encourages analytical and logical thinking.

In developing social studies activities which help children improve listening abilities, Jacobs suggests that the teacher focus on considerations such as these:

In the kindergarten and early elementary grades, ideas needing emphasis include:

1. Listening differs from just hearing.
2. Listening to directions, announcements, important information is different from listening to music, poems, stories.
3. Listeners must be ready to use their ears and minds—must start with and adapt to the speaker.
4. Listeners think and feel while they hear.
5. Listeners remember the important things that have been said.
6. Physical comfort is important in listening.
7. Listening requires putting what has been heard in some order or sequence.

8. Listeners realize that different persons speak in different ways.
9. Listening implies recognizing the difference between fact and fancy.
10. Listeners interpret what they hear in terms of their own past experiences.

In the late-elementary grades, such considerations as the following may help students to be better listeners:

1. Listening requires recognizing the different viewpoints of speakers.
2. Listening calls for sorting out what is important to remember or retain.
3. Listening demands self-discipline with regard to distractions.
4. Listening may call for quick, brief note-taking as one continues to hear the speaker.
5. Listening means giving attention to the vocabulary and the expression of the speaker.
6. Listeners recognize when ideas are not well supported with evidence.
7. Listeners know that their own beliefs and feelings affect what they hear or are willing to hear.
8. Listening implies noting ambiguity or vagueness on the part of the speaker.
9. Listening calls for thinking ahead, anticipating what will come next.
10. Listeners are aware of the effects of the speaker's voice and the beauty of rhythm and expression in his speaking.

In the junior high school, further extension of the skills of listening may need to be taught. Some suggestions for this extension follow:

1. Listening means noting what has not been said as well as what has been said.
2. Listening calls for critical appraisal of facts, information, opinion, viewpoints as used in a given context by a speaker.
3. Listeners recognize central ideas and total meanings, and are able to summarize.
4. Listeners must be able to spot emotion-laden words, emotion-arousing ideas.
5. Listeners are able to take well-organized notes of main ideas and major supporting ideas.

6. Listening implies deciding how a speaker achieves various effects.
7. Listeners note the speaker's use of "either-or" or "always-never" thinking.
8. Listening implies observing how words are being defined, how evidence is being used, how examples are being presented.
9. Listening includes spotting new ideas, inspecting new data, observing unusual uses of known facts and information.
10. Listening takes into account propaganda techniques, the speaker's prejudices, and the methods he uses to affect his audience.[1]

Many social studies situations are particularly dependent upon the development of adequate listening abilities. Among them, the following are especially important.

LISTENING TO DIRECTIONS

Listening to and acting upon directions assumes a special importance in social studies where the class becomes involved in different activities at the same time, where opportunities for movement away from an assigned seat may be allowed or encouraged, and where classes often leave the school grounds to observe and gather data about their study. If all children are to be engaged in the same activity and if that activity is to take place at individual desks, the children will lose much of their interest in the study; but the teacher will have little difficulty in communicating what it is he wishes his class to do. However, in directing children so that they may have the maximum opportunity to think and act responsibly and on their own initiative within the limits set by their age and maturity level, it is well for the teacher to give considerable thought to the kinds of directions the children can comprehend and how experiences in learning to follow directions might be extended for them. In helping children grow in their ability to listen to directions, the following guidelines for the teacher's consideration may prove helpful:

1. If the teacher knows what the class can reasonably be expected to accomplish, the kinds of directions needed will be clear. Some directions deal with day to day classroom activities, others extend

[1] Leland B. Jacobs, "Speaking and Listening," Chapter Eight in *Skill Development in Social Studies,* Helen McCracken Carpenter, editor, Thirty-Third Yearbook, National Council for the Social Studies (1963), pp. 144-146. Reprinted by permission.

over a day, a week, or more. Where more time is involved than the daily lesson, a record should be kept of the directions given.

2. All directions should be stated in the simplest possible way. If directions involve several steps, take one step at a time, ascertaining that the children understand each step as it is introduced to them.

3. Create a climate for listening. If the child's attention is elsewhere, the teacher is wasting his time. Only the most mature children can be expected to accept the consequences of not listening, and in such situations the teacher must make certain that every opportunity is provided to make directions clear.

4. Ask questions of children to learn whether they are prepared to act upon the directions given them.

5. Give children experiences in giving directions and in setting the stage for listening to them.

6. Recognize that listening is dependent upon feeling involved in the study. If children feel it is being planned and executed by the teacher and that they have little part in it, the necessity for listening to directions will be viewed as a dull routine calling for calloused responses.

LISTENING TO REPORTS

Since "there is no impression without expression," children need to talk about the things they have been studying. Such reporting takes many forms in addition to the more or less formal report. Class plays, debates, panel discussions, dramatic play, talking about pictures, maps, and charts which have been developed during the course of the study all represent forms of reporting.

For every reporting situation there must be good listeners; children should be expected to give the speaker all the courtesies granted the adult. Normally, children are more interested when their peers speak, and accept more readily minor errors and problems in making a sensible presentation, than they are when adults are speaking. But the teacher can aid greatly by helping the children plan what they expect to do before their own or other classes. The teacher will know approximately how long reporting activities will take and can make certain that each child is reasonably familiar with his material before allowing him to step before the class. Other conditions that will facilitate reporting so that those who listen will also be engaged in an educational experience include the following:

1. Be certain everyone has a comfortable place to sit during the time planned for reports.
2. Encourage speakers to enunciate clearly so that all may hear. Some thought to room arrangement ahead of time will help. The smallest children will often find it difficult to speak so that everyone may hear. In classrooms where there are older children, the teacher may elect to sit farthest away from those reporting to judge how clearly everyone hears.
3. Limit reporting time to the maturity levels of the children—usually not more than ten or fifteen minutes for the youngest groups, although dramatic presentations will hold attention longer.
4. Find ways to tell how much the listeners gained from the reports; questions following a report or at the end of the class time is one way. Finding natural opportunities to refer to the reports on subsequent days is probably better. Older children may take brief notes occasionally.
5. Stimulate good listening by making certain children know what is going to happen—who is reporting, what the topic is, what is expected of the listeners in the way of gaining ideas.
6. Dignify the child's role as reporter and the listener's role in every possible way.

LISTENING TO OUTSIDE SPEAKERS

Readily available in most communities are a wealth of human resources which may be called upon in the social study. Parents, business people, civil servants, and others with special knowledge on the widest variety of subjects respond enthusiastically to invitations to talk to elementary school children. In order to get the most out of these exceedingly valuable resources, and so their experiences will be such that they will want to help the children and their teacher again, these suggestions are made:

1. Make certain that the topic which the outside speaker will discuss fits the current work of the class.
2. Help the speaker understand what the class has been studying and give any other assistance which will help him adjust his material to the vocabulary and experience of the children.
3. Give the guest speaker clear directions on how to get to the classroom, when he should arrive and how long he is expected to talk with the children.

4. Make all necessary arrangements for audio-visual aids and other special needs far enough in advance so that no embarrassment is possible.

5. Familiarize the children with the speaker and his topic in advance; children should know something about the speaker as a person, why he is coming, when to expect him, and what he will talk about.

6. Plan with children the kinds of questions they might ask and the ways they can go about getting satisfactory answers. Common rules of courtesy should be observed, but not so rigidly that children are stilted and afraid to be "natural."

7. Plan follow-up activities which allow children to recall and reorganize the information gained from the speaker.

LISTENING ON STUDY TRIPS

Listening in its broadest sense involves much more than comprehending and making sense out of verbal sounds. It also occurs when one hears and interprets other kinds of sounds—the sounds in a manufacturing plant, the blast of a train whistle, and the "noises" of animals in a zoo. Creating meaning for non-verbal sounds is an important aspect of listening, and the study trip offers particularly fine opportunities for developing these abilities as well as the more conventional ones. In addition, the study trip is especially well suited to multi-sensory experiencing, the most vivid circumstance for learning. Things can be felt; their shape, weight, and texture can be assessed through direct tactile experiencing. Things can be tasted, they can be smelled, and their heat or coldness can be felt. And all of these things can happen at one time as seeing and hearing processes combine with them. Listening sensitivities under these circumstances can become heightened in a manner unlikely to take place in any other situation.

Listening in its broadest sense, as well as in its narrower one, will be enhanced if these suggestions are observed in thinking about the most appropriate kinds of study trips for children:

1. The teacher should be completely familiar with the place(s) he expects to take the children. If at all possible, this means visiting the place before the class trip. If this is not possible, he should read whatever materials are available and discuss the trip with those who have actually taken it.

2. Select only those study trips which relate *directly* to the social study.

3. The purposes for the study trip should be clear and very simple. Avoid study trips to places where the complexity of the function being observed outstretches the maturity level of the children. In a trip to a museum, for example, do not try to see too many things. Even so, some study trips need to be repeated.

4. Children should know the purpose of the trip, what to look for, and how to record information gained on the trip.

5. Classroom experiences which capitalize upon information gained on the study trip are planned as an inherent part of the entire activity.

LISTENING IN LARGE- AND SMALL-GROUP SETTINGS

In recent years much interest has focused upon organizational schemes which result in the formation of various-sized class groupings. Different terms have become associated with specific schemes for reorganizing the traditional self-contained classroom, but most of them tend to be classifiable under the general one of *team teaching*. Although no pattern has yet emerged which is being followed in any great number of schools, experimentation is widespread. Central to virtually all of these plans is the idea that optimum learning situations cannot be planned for children unless it is possible to regroup them according to the purposes teachers hope to accomplish with those children. The assumption is that some kinds of learning situations should involve a fairly large number of children—perhaps two classes or more, making groupings which contain sixty or more youngsters—whereas others should be much smaller than has normally been the case in the past. Some particular points which may be emphasized in listening activities under such circumstances should be noted.

When any large number of children are brought together, the opportunity for direct participation in class activities declines rapidly. For the timid, reticent child and for the youngster who tends not to experience great amounts of success in the classroom, these opportunities are likely to disappear completely. The quick, verbal, self-assured child still can hold his own in the large group. The problem for most children in such a situation is to learn primarily through listening and observing. Authorities on team teaching agree that teachers must be provided ample planning time in preparing for large-group presentations. Concepts need to be particularly well organized and teaching aids employed skillfully if learning is to be at all effective in the large group. Without careful planning, the teachers' presentation to the large group is likely to degenerate into a drab lecture, or worse. If value is to be derived from large-group instruction, the teacher must exercise considerable self-discipline and creativity. It must be recognized, in deciding whether to plan work with children under such circumstances, that many teachers are not equipped to be effective in large-group settings.

The advantage of the large group is that it provides teachers opportunities to develop their own knowledge and skills in more limited areas of social studies. The consequence of this is presumed to carry over into more effective instruction in the classroom. Evidence supporting this assumption has not been forthcoming, however, and the planning of large-group activities is defended logically rather than empirically. However, there is one clear advantage to large-group instruction: it makes possible the formation of smaller than normal groupings. It is within these settings that individualized help can be given. Perhaps the passivity demanded by the large group is offset by the small-group opportunities. As yet, the evidence is inadequate.

The large-group setting in elementary schools is probably most effective if used with great restraint and usually when resources need to be shared with other classes. An author of books about the American Revolution may be available to give one talk to boys and girls, or a historian can be called upon to speak about his specialty, or a geographer may give an interesting talk on map projections; these are among the most productive large-group settings. But where teachers are called upon under some systematic rotation of classes, extra care must be exercised to keep the quality of such presentations at a high level. Otherwise, the organizational scheme can readily be seen as the matter which is controlling the nature of learning opportunities rather than the particular needs of the pupils.

Oral Language Experiences

If one is to learn, one must have opportunities to talk about the things that interest him. For speech has a confirming attribute about it; through talking one organizes his thoughts, clarifies ideas, and moves his thinking forward. If one is restricted in opportunities to express himself orally, his ideas seem to be set adrift and become strangely uncapturable when one has a need to recall them.

Talking presupposes an audience of some kind, someone to talk *to;* there must be a sounding board or, better yet, a reactor to what one says. And in a classroom with thirty or more children, all eager to express their ideas, there frequently is a good deal of impatience. After all, most people are more interested in hearing what *they* have to say than what their neighbors have to talk about. Little wonder, then, that many teachers approach oral language activities with some hesitancy. The factors involved in too much uncontrolled speaking are more than most people want to risk without considerable thought. However, with just a little care, children can be encouraged to engage in extended oral language activities without bringing about major classroom discipline problems. When oral language experiences are conducted according to simple yet clear-cut rules, and when a wide variety of types of experiences are provided, the values in oral language experience can be achieved within a manageable framework.

USING DISCUSSION EXPERIENCES

One of the most important oral language experiences which can be provided in social studies is that of discussion. It can take a number of different forms: a panel discussion before the total class, several small groups working on ideas at a given time, or, perhaps, a discussion, under the direction of the teacher or one of the pupils, which engages the entire class. Whatever the conditions, discussion differs from what one might term "conversation," nor is it the same as the common classroom situation in which the teacher asks questions and pupils are expected to respond. True discussion takes place when pupils and teacher become engaged in a talking-listening situation in which the focus is upon a theme or problem and in which the ideas of the participants are molded or shaped as a consequence of the discussion experience.

There are three elements basic to any discussion. First, there is a specific purpose to be achieved—some question or problem which calls for an exchange of ideas. Discussion starts with identifying that problem or question and clarifying the dimensions of it so that all participants are aware of the focus for the discussion. Second, ideas relating to the problem are interchanged. This aspect of discussion involves the greatest amount of time and calls for some preparation on the part of the participants. In some circumstances, the children may have spent a considerable amount of time in advance reading, thinking, and gathering data. The teacher may have given specific assignments designed to build background. Or, in preparation the children may have organized ideas out of their own experience for a few moments before moving into this stage of the discussion. In the latter situation, children may draw upon experiences encountered in the classroom (a study trip recently completed, a motion picture viewed) or upon events or conditions existing outside the class (something that has happened in the community about which most children are aware, circumstances on the playground which call for improvement). Finally, discussion always calls for some degree of resolution concerning the question or problem before the class. The discussion leader is responsible for encouraging participants to generalize about the problem, to draw some conclusions about it.

Participation in discussion calls forth a number of skills, attributes, and abilities which do not come easily to children. The capacity to participate effectively emerges gradually and is a consequence of experience. Boys and girls should be encouraged to develop standards to serve as guides in evaluating the quality of their discussion experiences. These standards should be viewed as developmental, and they should come about as a consequence of direct experience with discussion situations. With extended experience in discussion, most groups will decide that a good participant should:

> Talk only when he has something to say or a question to ask which will clarify the discussion or carry it forward.
> Speak so he can be easily understood.
> Use increasingly effective language.
> Back points of discussion with evidence when necessary.
> Listen with an open mind to what others have to say.
> Weigh opinions of others.
> Be willing to change his mind when he thinks another idea is better.
> Be courteous, even when he disagrees.
> Be thoughtful of the need for many people to participate in the discussion.[2]

Discussion in Committee Work. Frequently, at various stages of a study it is desirable to identify subgroups or committees to explore particular aspects of the larger problems being considered by the class. In these circumstances, pupils will be called upon to engage in discussion sessions. Purposes most frequently met through such meetings include planning to conduct research, sharing information discovered, organizing to develop reports, and planning ways of reporting to the total class.

[2] Dorris M. Lee and R. Van Allen, *Learning to Read Through Experience,* second edition (New York: Appleton-Century-Crofts, 1963), p. 39.

Committees in social studies may vary in size from two to five or six children; older boys and girls can work effectively in larger groups. Since they will normally meet when other committees are also conducting discussions, care must be taken to help each group work effectively. The following suggestions will help the teacher in organizing small groups for discussion purposes in the classroom:

1. Identify a chairman for each committee. Meet with these boys and girls in advance to help them clarify the purposes of their discussion. Remember that committees cannot be expected to function very effectively without prior experience in discussions involving the total class.
2. Limit the amount of time for discussion and make those time limits known at the beginning of the period. To begin, ten to fifteen minutes is sufficient for intermediate grades, fifteen to twenty minutes for upper grades.
3. When the children are gathered in committees, reaffirm that each group understands the goals of their discussion. In checking with groups as they conduct the discussion, the teacher should refrain from active participation with any group.
4. Have committee chairmen report to the entire group about the progress made during their discussion.

Panel Discussions. In this type of discussion, a group of from four to six or seven children explores a topic, usually under the guidance of a student chairman. Discussants do not make formal presentations; rather, they present their ideas in a free-flowing exchange which the chairman stimulates as needed by interjecting questions designed to encourage as wide a range of views as possible. Normally, the panel is given an opportunity to engage in its own dialogue before persons who are listening are invited to ask questions or to comment.

Three major roles need to be played where the panel technique is used: those of audience, participant, and chairman. Children learn to play each of these roles by observation and through direct involvement in each. Obviously, the chairman's role is the most difficult to learn, and few children will come by the chairman's skills naturally. Clearly, the teacher should select for this role, especially in the beginning, those boys and girls whom he feels will be most capable in this role. As children gain experience in panel discussion, and as standards for the different roles are developed, it will be observed that a majority in most classes will at one time or another be able to fill satisfactorily the chairman's role. Nearly all children will be able to experience success as members of the panel. Success in each of the roles, but particularly that of chairman, comes about as a consequence of observing and talking about what makes a good audience member, a good participant, and a good chairman. Although standards for each of these roles will emerge gradually as teacher and children experiment with these techniques, the teacher assists by setting the stage for children's beginning experiences.

1. The chairman should: be informed about the problem to be discussed; have any help he needs in thinking about ways of introducing it to the group; be prepared with some key questions which can be anticipated in advance; be prepared to redirect discussion when it veers away from the topic; be able to intercede politely when the discussion becomes too heated; be helped as needed in developing skills in summarizing; have a notion of how much time is to be devoted to the panel's comments and how much to questions from the audience.

2. The panel members should: have some knowledge and ideas about the topic to be discussed; speak clearly so everyone can hear; be alert to the problem of dominating the discussion; be directed in speech patterns which will set a tone of civility (especially always refer to the person who expressed a different view as "I disagree with Donna's statement because . . . ," avoid derogatory adjectives, as "I think that's a crazy idea."); if the topic warrants it, have sources of information available; listen carefully to, and be sensitive to, the comments of the other panel members.

3. The audience should: recognize the important role of the chairman; listen carefully, make notes if appropriate; try to ask clear questions when the time comes to speak; comment but not deliver a long talk on the subject; utilize courteous speech patterns.

Successful panel discussions can be developed around the widest range of possible questions. The teacher will want to select chairmen and panel members according to their knowledge and preparation, of course, but also with the recognition that children will be more successful with certain topics than others. With appropriate guidance and by exercising care in the selection of topics to be discussed, the panel technique can be employed very successfully beginning toward the end of the second grade. It cannot be emphasized enough, however, that the topics must be simple, and they must relate to the lives of the children. Emphasis must be placed on growth in skill with this approach rather than on the expectation of a mature performance.

It is frequently valuable in utilizing the panel technique to repeat topics with different chairmen and panel members. Such repetition helps children learn how to play the different roles involved and provides opportunities for bringing in a broader range of ideas on some kinds of topics. In certain instances, for example, a panel of boys will respond differently to a topic than will a mixed panel or a panel of girls. Other combinations will be suggested by the topics selected, but often repetition solely for the purpose of letting other pupils express their ideas on the topic is reason enough.

Debate. Another valuable means of encouraging oral language is through some form of the debate. Although it may be claimed that debate is more like arguing than discussing, this is not true if children are taught to observe the general form of debate. There must also be adequate time for preparation before the debate. In general, debate is a device most appropriate for the upper grade pupil; still, it can be modified and used effectively on occasion with many intermediate grade children. Again, the degree of success depends upon the appropriateness of the topic. Current events are often viewed as being particularly valuable sources for debate topics. In utilizing current events in this manner, it should be realized that some current topics cannot be adequately researched. When information is lacking, appeals to emotionality and bias are all too evident. A second point to keep in mind is that many questions have political and philosophical aspects. Children should experience the problems of participation in a debate that utilizes points of view with which they are not in agreement and which may grow out of debate based on "current" topics. But aside from the current scene, historic events, now seen in some kind of perspective, provide opportunities for children to relive arguments which engaged the thought of men in other times and places. The debate over slavery, arguments in which Americans engaged during the Revolutionary War, and questions raised over the expansion of the United States provide rich sources for utilizing the debate technique. Many others should come quickly to mind: Should the United States enter the League of Nations? Should we get out of Vietnam? How about capital punishment? Our treatment of the Indians? Orientals in California? Japanese during World War II?

Successful debate, therefore, requires the selection of a topic for which the children can clearly establish sides "for" and "against." Next, it requires the selection of pupils who have the intellectual skills and resources to prepare adequately. Third, it involves setting up rules for conducting the debate. These can vary from class to class but, once adopted, they should be adhered to. Fourth, the teacher should not relinquish his role as moderator until he is certain the class has had sufficient experience to conduct the debate fairly, according to the rules. Finally, there should be no emphasis upon who "won." Rather, the concerns in debate are effective preparation and forceful and cogent presentation of argument, regardless of the position taken.

USING REPORTING EXPERIENCES

Another important oral language experience in social studies is that of reporting, or talking about, information which has been discovered on a particular subject or topic. Reporting experiences can be rather formal in nature, or they can occur in a casual setting. They may provide opportunities for individual youngsters to organize and present information on topics which they have researched more or less independently, or each child's contribution may be closely related to and derive its meaning from reports given by other boys and girls in the class. The sources of information which are utilized may be part of the classroom library, or they may be sources consulted outside of the school. Generally speaking, growth in reporting abilities moves from the informal to the formal, from closely interrelated topics to independently researched ones, and from the utilization of resources primarily obtainable within the classroom and school to widely scattered sources.

Basically, reporting requires the pupil to select, organize, and present in an interesting and informative manner information collected from a range of sources which he has consulted on a particular topic. This may be a formidable task when viewed in its more mature form, but it is relatively simple if the topics and sources are appropriate to the interests and maturity level of the child. The foundations for more formal types of reporting are laid in the earliest grades and begin with merely telling about things that have been experienced.

The youngest boys and girls tell about the pictures they have painted after a study trip to the nearby fire station or other local site of interest. Each child's "report" need not exceed two or three sentences, and the teacher interjects questions or comments as needed to stimulate the speaker. Or perhaps they tell what they discovered while doing homework assigned by the teacher. Or the teacher may ask them to tell about the most important thing they learned from a motion picture. In each instance, the teacher helps them to select the more important from the less important, to organize their presentation, and to speak clearly and confidently. This kind of reporting is brief, almost always informal, and takes place in a positive, accepting atmosphere. Every child has something worthwhile to say; if others listen carefully, they will find something worthy of approbation. *Negative comments, expressed or implied, will never help anyone gain the confidence or develop the necessary abilities for communicating things he believes have value and significance to others.*

By the time the child reaches eight or nine, he should be able to utilize two or three sources of information, selecting from them the ideas he wishes to use in illuminating his topic, and presenting them clearly, confidently, and interestingly to the class. Prior to this time, his attention in speaking has been primarily to the teacher and incidentally to his classmates. At this age he is asked to begin switching his focus so that in two or three years, his standards for reporting will be considerably closer to those of the formal reporting processes.

Several warnings are in order with respect to using reporting experiences in social studies. Most important of all, the topic of the report must be meaningful to the child. Otherwise, there will be a tendency for him to memorize or read words copied down from a textbook or encyclo-

pedia. The teacher needs to help the child find topics which are worthwhile, interesting, and which require some degree of original thinking.
Unless he is guided in this manner, the child will be the prey of someone else's ideas. For example, rather than ask a child to write something
about the French painter Degas (about whom information is available
in the classroom encyclopedia), why not ask him to describe Degas'
painting technique or, perhaps, to compare one of his paintings with that
of another French painter of the same period? Or, rather than telling
about Meriwether Lewis (basic biographical data is also readily available to be copied), ask him to compare Lewis' personality with Clark's.

A second problem in reporting is that of timing. Reports should be
reasonably brief and to the point. Wandering discourse defeats the purpose of reporting and should be controlled rigorously. And listening to
reports given long after the topic has lost its pertinence to the current
work of the class is also an enervating experience for everyone. A third
situation to be avoided is the presentation of reports without the active
participation of the entire class. Listeners cannot remain passive ab-
sorbers of information; they must become involved in the reporting
process through questioning and commenting upon the information presented to them. Passive response is an indication that listeners are not
paying attention. Finally, reporting experiences without some kind of
evaluation on the part of pupils and teacher will result, the next time
reports are scheduled, in little improvement. Children at every age need
opportunities to set standards or guides for preparing and presenting
reports. As in discussion experiences, however, such standards emerge as
a consequence of experiencing opportunities to present and listen to
reports in the social studies classroom.

USING DRAMATIC EXPERIENCES

To the young child, reality and the world of imagination are very
close; for many children, they are virtually interchangeable. Of course,
any adult can tell the difference between reality and fantasy. Too often
the achievement of adulthood is synonymous with the final loss of the
ability to enter wholeheartedly into a world created by the imagination.
That children are able to project themselves into another time or place—
to truly "become someone or something else"—seems incomprehensible
to some adults. It is hoped, however, that the child's teacher will believe
the imagined world to be just as real, and often more vivid, as that
rather limited vista forced upon him by adulthood.

Several types of dramatic representation that draw upon this marvelous gift for making imagined things vivid and real can be used effectively in social studies. Each stimulates and encourages imagination in its own way, but all provide a means for the child to enter his other world, the world glimpsed by only a few privileged adults. Through dramatic experiences children can become explorers, famous inventors, mothers and fathers, and movers of nations; through the imaginative experiences of dramatic representation they can project themselves into the past, into the future, and to distant places. When the child's creative imagination is brought into play, new dimensions are added to understanding the world in which the child is living. All of these experiences provide invaluable opportunities for oral language experiences, some informal and spontaneous, others more structured.

Dramatic Play. In this form of dramatic representation, the natural and spontaneous language of children is stimulated by providing a few props, a "center of interest" which provides the basic situation to be acted out, and time for playing whatever role the center of interest suggests to the child. Perhaps the teacher has provided, with the help and assistance of the children, a post office, a supermarket, a fire station, or some representation of a home (the baby's room, the kitchen, the study): This is sufficient to involve children in a wide variety of activities. In dramatic play, there is no audience, no script, and no adult direction or other participation. Through careful observation, the teacher will learn a good deal about the concepts and understandings growing out of the social study, and he will develop an appreciation for the quality and extent of the language expressed by the children in his class. From this information, he will have cues for other kinds of experiences to be provided in the study and will also develop an understanding of the language usage he can expect from youngsters in other, perhaps more formal, situations.

Dramatic play has found its greatest uses in the kindergarten and first grade. There are valuable uses in the remaining primary years as well as in the intermediate years. A corner of a fifth grade classroom in which children are studying Colonial life might be devoted to an interest center depicting a home of that period, for example. Children find value in dramatic play situations throughout the primary and intermediate years, at least; and the topics normally studied during the later years also can provide the basis for this kind of experience. These youngsters, too, need to get the "feel" of the times, the people, and the place just as they did when they were younger.

Creative Dramatics. A somewhat more structured form of dramatic play is sometimes called creative dramatics; in it, some preparation is usually necessary, there is frequently an audience, the conditions or circumstances surrounding the actual "acting out" process are more clearly defined, and there normally is an evaluation by the audience and participants. This approach to dramatic representation uses fewer props than does dramatic play; but, like it, there is no script, no rehearsing of parts, no memorization of lines. It is most useful at the intermediate and upper grade levels.

In creative dramatics, children are encouraged to act out their versions of an event or circumstance. They are asked to project themselves into other personalities and to reflect on how those people thought and reacted. At the upper grade level, for example, children might re-enact their version of one of the Lincoln-Douglas debates, or they might form a panel to dramatize a meeting of leaders in Western Europe as they discuss the problems of the Common Market. At the intermediate grade level, re-enactment of the Boston Tea Party, the first Thanksgiving, or the discussions among the Sons of Liberty during the Revolutionary War period might provide a focus for creative dramatics. Every social study provides opportunities for this kind of dramatic representation. Although some preparation is necessary, many such experiences can grow naturally and easily out of the work of the class. The teacher's participation in creative dramatics is usually limited to suggesting the topic, giving whatever assistance may be necessary in preparation, and helping children evaluate. Once the children begin enacting the dramatic event itself, the teacher's role is one of observation. As in the panel discussion, where repetition of certain topics has value, some creative dramatic situations also may be repeated with value. Time limits must be enforced carefully in any event. Otherwise, children are inclined to "carry on" too long, finding it difficult to terminate their play.

Role Playing. This approach, also called *sociodrama*, provides situations in which children act out problems arising from interpersonal relations that are of concern to them. Perhaps they plan to conduct field interviews in connection with their study and want to know how they should ask adults questions under these circumstances. By acting out interviews in the classroom, they gain the skills and insights they will need in getting information from the adults with whom they plan to talk. There are a variety of other situations in which role playing has value. For instance, interpersonal problems in classroom behavior or on the school grounds may be viewed with more insight if the children have an opportunity to act these out in the classroom. Leadership roles required by chairmen of panel discussions, committees working on special subtopics, and the like can be analyzed through role playing. Any situation which will help the child view behavior without reference to his own personality or that of others in the class is a proper subject for a role playing experience, since the primary value in this kind of dramatic representation is that the children assume roles and act them out according to their own perceptions without having to admit to or be identified as playing a particular role. As the child steps outside of himself, others can also gain a view of behavior which is divorced from particular personalities, leading to a broader understanding of their own behavior as well as that of others.

Role playing should be planned around specific problems in the classroom setting. The teacher or pupils may identify the situation which is to be acted out, or he may select a *reaction story*. In the reaction story, the teacher reads a selection depicting a problem with which the children are familiar but which is "open ended," i.e., there is no conclusion. Groups of children in the class are then asked to act out the ending which they think is most appropriate. Since all role playing is situational and its course depends upon the people involved in it, the different kinds of solutions available are infinite. Replaying situations is therefore usually valuable.[3]

Choral Speaking. The field of literature offers opportunities for choral speaking experiences in social studies. In this form of dramatic representation, children read and speak in unison a selection of verse or prose which lends itself to dramatic oral presentation. There is a limited body of literature which is designed specifically for choral speaking, but many selections can be adapted to choral speaking. Boys and girls are not required to memorize the material selected for this kind of presentation; but they will, of course, practice to achieve appropriate inflection, emphasis, and pronunciation. As a result of practice, they may memorize the selection. If this happens, it is an extra dividend.

Choral speaking encourages the reticent child to speak out, it emphasizes the importance of communicating meaning through tonal pattern and inflection, and it provides a situation in which some pieces of valuable literature are learned thoroughly. It is an enjoyable experience for children of all ages and is much like a musical experience. Most anthol-

[3] Fannie R. Shaftel, *Role-playing for Social Values* (Englewood Cliffs, N.J.: Prentice-Hall, Inc., 1967).

ogies and many social studies textbooks include selections which can be used in choral speaking experiences with children in social studies. If sufficient copies of the piece selected are not available they are, of course, easily duplicated.

Formal Dramatization. It is valuable for children to become involved in more formal presentations from time to time. These efforts may still be quite casual, but they are different from all the prior forms of dramatic representation in that they involve a script, memorization of lines to speak, practice before presentation, and performance before an audience (usually consisting of children from other classrooms and, perhaps, parents). Costumes, a stage, or a polished performance are not particularly important, except that the greater the effort devoted to these, the less likely is the dramatization to make a direct contribution to the major goals of the social study. Considerable criticism has been directed toward formal dramatizations because of the problems involved in preparing an extensive stage production for the final performance. Much of this criticism is just, and the emphasis here is not on that type of formal work with young children. The formal play is best left to the high school and college years.

Most frequently, formal dramatization is the consequence of the pupil's desire to write and act in an original presentation. This may or may not take the conventional form of a play. It might, for instance, be an illustrated tour of some place the children are studying; it might be a tape recording done in the fashion of a radio program; it might be an "audio-visual" presentation with the television motif in mind; and it might be a play done in the no-prop "Our Town" technique in the classroom. Whatever the form, it should require very simple staging and costumes. Rarely, however, will a play written by someone else serve a useful purpose in any social study. And only on the rarest occasion is it appropriate to plan any formal dramatization which requires anything but the barest amount of staging and the easiest kind of costuming.

INTERVIEWING

Books are obviously only one source of information in social studies. Among the many other kinds of sources, community leaders provide one of the least used yet most valuable of resources. When children can learn to tap this source of information, many valuable ideas will be added to the study. Young people should be taught how to behave when interviewing and how to ask the kinds of questions which will elicit useful responses. Citizens who come to the classroom or who are interviewed outside of the school usually do not know specifically what information is most likely to be needed and useful to the class. Consequently, they will rely heavily upon the questions asked to guide them in selecting their responses. Children need considerable assistance in thinking through the kinds of questions which they might ask; in the intermediate and upper grades, methods of note-taking and ways of clarifying points which are not clear to the interviewer also need to be considered. Children can be helped by discussing both of these points ahead of the actual interview. As they gain experience in the process, the need for pre-planning in such detail will diminish, but it will never disappear entirely.

GUIDES FOR CONTINUITY IN ORAL LANGUAGE EXPERIENCES

It was pointed out earlier that the child's oral language reflects his background of experience as well as his intellectual capacity. It was emphasized that language facility is a gradually developing phenomenon, unique to each youngster; that one must learn to work with the language each child brings to school if one expects the child to realize effective growth in the development of that language. The child cannot be expected to use language patterns not within his experience; he cannot be expected to use standard English usage if his language is nonstandard. But one can help the child use the language he brings to school if he is encouraged to use his own language with gradually increasing degrees of sensitivity and discrimination. Language development is therefore characterized by its continuity—by its dependence upon what has come before and by its tendency to evolve slowly, based on the totality of prior experience—rather than discontinuity, or the relative lack of evolutionary elements in its development.[4]

Jacobs has suggested some guides for achieving continuity in oral language experiences which are useful in proposing expectancies for elementary school children in social studies. He warns that these must not be considered as absolutes, of course, but as cues to practice. In that respect they are relevant to this discussion.

---

[4] For further reading see Basil Bernstein, "Aspects of Language and Learning in the Genesis of the Social Process," *Journal of Child Psychology and Psychiatry* (1961), I, pp. 313-324.

Five- to Seven-Year-Olds

Discussion: Topics of immediate moment. Not much individual preparation. Teacher responsible as group leader in application of discussion skills.

Reporting: Begins with sharing of stories, personal experiences, objects brought from home, and the like. Ordering of content done quite spontaneously, without extensive individual preparation. Teacher immediately available to assist, in ways sought by the reporter, in the giving of the talk.

Interviewing: Largely cooperative group interviewing of persons invited to the classroom. Questions to be asked planned by children and teacher in advance. Teacher's role that of seeing that various children get to participate, cuing the visitor of meanings of oblique questions, and introducing and closing the interview.

Dramatics: Almost entirely dramatic play and creative dramatics. Acting done spontaneously, with free interpretations.

Eight- to Twelve-Year-Olds

Discussion: Topics of increasingly more precise dimensions. Direct attention to the nature of discussion. More student responsibility in the use of discussion skills. Individual preparation for many of the discussion sessions. Teacher's role that of participant and of observer of needs for further teaching. Some beginnings of panel discussion, under teacher guidance, may be introduced.

Reporting: Topics individually explored and ordered. Introduction of simple note-taking in preparation for reporting. Preparation of report and accompanying notes done individually, with such teacher assistance as reporter and teacher cooperatively agree on. During reporting and follow-up question or discussion period, reporter takes major responsibility for control of the situation. Teacher's role during the reporting largely that of astute listener and assessor of what needs further to be taught about reporting skills.

Interviewing: Introduction of individual interviewing, with continuation of group interviews. Understandings of nature and evaluation of the interview introduced. Use of results of individual interviews in reporting sessions. Consideration of interview skills as used in the mass media.

Dramatics: Largely creative dramatics; occasional experiences with scenes or sections from well-written plays. Some original playwriting. Attention by the teacher to the student's creation of character, his contributions to the action and dialogue, and his ability to contribute to the mood of the dramatization.

Twelve- to Fourteen-Year-Olds

Discussion: Broad exploration of topic under consideration. More precise self-evaluation by the student of his contributions to discussion and his behavior as discussant. Increased uses of panel discussion, with greater discernment concerning the nature and procedures of panel discussion and concerning the roles of discussant, moderator, and audience member.

Reporting: Skillful in selection and ordering of topic or problem. Considerable independence in note-taking and in preparing for the style of the report or talk to be given. Quite independent control in the reporting situation itself with regard to language, speech, and social skills.

Interviewing: More individual interviews and reporting, with precision, the results of the interviewing done. Increasing skill in assessing interviews presented on radio or television.

Dramatics: Continued use of creative dramatics, individual or group playwriting, and interpretation of scenes, episodes, and one-act plays. Depth of characterization, in acting and in comprehending interactions among characters in portraying plot and action. Authenticity of the spirit of the play sensitively comprehended.[5]

---

[5] Leland B. Jacobs, *op. cit.*, pp. 139-140. Reprinted by permission.

Writing Experiences

Social studies provide as richly varied topics for stimulating writing experiences as any area in the curriculum. Since anything children talk about can also be written about, the entire range of concepts and understandings, attitudes and feelings growing out of the social study may provide topics for children to write about. There are events to be recounted, classroom experiences to be told about, plays to be written, notes to be taken, talks to be prepared, signs and markers to be developed, poems to be recorded; all of which are engaging activities. Determining the kind of writing opportunities, how many of them are to be provided, and when, are probably more dependent upon the number of ideas the teacher can develop than upon any other single factor. All children are interested in writing and are capable of producing written material of surprisingly high quality if given the chance.

Opportunities to express in writing ideas growing out of social studies start in the kindergarten. The very youngest children should have regular experiences in recording their ideas in written form, just as they are expected to speak and listen. It begins with dictating experiences in which the teacher transcribes the verbatim accounts of individual children as well as the cooperatively produced stories in which the material to be written by the teacher is agreed upon through group discussion. This is a true writing experience, and, like all things written, the products of these dictation sessions deserve to be read and re-read. The earliest materials therefore provide important sources of reading activity. At first, these will be read to the class by the teacher and then by other children as they learn the stories and as they associate words in those stories with the symbols the teacher has recorded on paper.

As children move through the first and second grades, they will be able to read their own stories, and they will want to write them as well. Gradually dictation will diminish, but probably the need for it will never completely disappear. There will always be a few children in the class whose ability to express themselves will be hampered by their lack of writing skills. In those circumstances, the taking of dictation remains valuable.

"Writing," someone once remarked, "is just talk wrote down," and this is true as far as it goes. But writing demands degrees of precision in expression not required in speaking. Oral language designed to communicate without reference to print often appears to be not only disjointed but, frequently, absolutely meaningless. In its verbal mode, such language communicates. But in its written mode, it is, at best, unclear. These examples, from a study by Loban, illustrate typical oral language productions for elementary school children showing these character-istics:

I'm goin' . . . I'm goin' to build a flying saucer but I can't think how yet.

When I was fixin' ready to go home, my mother called me up in the house an' an' an' have to I have to get my hair combed.

I saw a hunter program last Sunday an' he, an' snow time he had to have lot uh, kah-h when he, uh, not too many dogs, he . . . and that's all I think of that picture.[6]

Adults are not much better. This example was produced at a conference of psychologists and linguists:

As far as I know, no one yet has done the in a way obvious now and in-teresting problem of doing a in a sense a structural frequency study of the alternative syntactical in a given language, say, like English, the alter-native possible structures, and how what their heirarchical probability of occurrence structure is.[7]

Obviously writing, whether produced as a consequence of dictation or physically transcribed by the child himself, requires that a conscious effort be made to express ideas more precisely than in oral language. Even then, when the words are finally recorded, they remain there to remind us of our failure to "say" exactly what we had in mind. Conse-quently, growth toward fluency in writing may be viewed as a continu-ing struggle toward an always illusive exactness.

In considering the efforts of boys and girls to write, one should remember that they, too, are struggling to record on paper exactly what they would like to say. And what they are able to say, is limited by all the factors which were described in the opening portion of the previous chapter. The "talk" which he elects to write down is limited by the richness of his oral language. Moreover, his oral language is a function of his intellectual capacity and his experience background. Social studies

[6] Walter D. Loban, "The Language of Elementary School Children," *Research Report No. 1,* National Council of Teachers of English, Champaign, Illinois (1963), p. 9.

[7] Roger Brown and Ursula Bellugi, "Three Processes in the Child's Acquisition of Syntax," *Harvard Educational Review,* Vol. 34, No. 2 (Spring 1964), p. 136, quoting H. MacClay and C. E. Osgood, "Hesitation Phenomena in Spontaneous English Speech," *Word,* XV (1959) pp. 19-44.

provide opportunities to affect his experience background, and it is out of his experiences as he continues his study that he will find things to write about.

One should remember also that demands for excellence in the skills of writing (spelling, punctuation, grammatical construction, and legibility in writing) can diminish clarity, fluency, and creativity in expression. One does not exist without the other, of course, but meaning and ideas must take precedence over skills. If too much attention is paid to the mechanics of writing, productivity will wither away and a frequently observed situation will result—a child who writes as little as he can and still "get by."

The rule in social studies, therefore, is to encourage children to write as much and as often as possible directly out of their experience. Just as it is true that the more one reads, the better he is likely to read, the more one writes, the better his writing will be. Too many corrections of grammatical construction, punctuation errors, and spelling errors and too little notice of the ideas which the child has attempted to capture and put down on paper will produce children who will not write any more than they have to. This is true for the very youngest child as well as for older children. Joos has some sound advice for the teacher who would help children grow in their power to express themselves in writing and who would find an important place for their writing in the social study:

Your aim should be to make the child's own resource available to him. He comes to you able, apparently, only to write simple sentences eight to twelve words long. Why? He is afraid to write the long compound sentences which he can and does use lavishly in conversation, because he has been regularly condemned for "comma-faults"; he is afraid of complex sentences because his teachers have foolishly insisted that he was making the wrong clause subordinate; he has not been encouraged to experiment with devices like saying "without noticing" and "heedlessly" instead of adding two more clauses to the sentence, but has instead been slapped down for beginning a sentence with "The trouble being . . ." He confines himself to the eight-to-twelve word simple sentence for one reason only: self-defense. In other words, *he is inhibited.*

Your ostensible goal for him should be nothing but completeness: finding room in his composition for everything that needs saying, including the linkages between the items. You find awkwardnesses in his drafts; each one is to be treated as an obstacle to completeness: it has interfered with something that he surely wants to put in.

Can you tell him how to clear away the obstacles? No, you can't; he has to invent his own devices. All you can do is to encourage, experimenting with grammatical and derivational transformations—the only proper employment of grammar-theory in composition—by demonstrating them and *never condemning any that he performs.* Condemnation is nothing but inhibition again; just encourage him to make still more transformations until he accidentally hits upon one that satisfies him. *If his ear is still too young, it isn't you that can age it.*[8]

USING A VARIETY OF WRITING EXPERIENCES

If children are to develop permanent interests in writing, they need a variety of opportunities to express their ideas in written form. Nothing is likely to dull the habit of writing quite so rapidly as selecting a limited number of ideas and repeating them over and over again. The following list of ideas is suggested as a starting point for thinking about different activities and situations in social studies which can stimulate children to write. Not all of these experiences require the child physically to write in a standard, acceptable form; in line with the emphasis upon the importance of ideas and the problem of expressing them in writing, the role of mechanics should not be over-emphasized. In some of these cases, the teacher will take dictation from individuals or from a group. In other instances, the first or second effort of the child will be taken by the teacher to be typed into usable form (modest corrections or changes aded as the teacher sees fit). In other instances, the child's effort will be accepted and valued without any attempt to "correct" it. No specific rule can be applied in deciding when a child and his teacher should feel satisfied that a particular written piece is finished. The time allowed for preparation, the reasons for writing it, the language facility of the child attempting to get his ideas down on paper, and his ability in handwriting or typing are some of the most important variables which the teacher will want to consider.[9]

Note-taking:	Some of the common situations arising in social studies for which the taking of notes suggests itself include the following: study trips, interviews, presentations in the classroom by talented citizens, motion pictures, television programs, lectures. Younger children, especially but

[8] Martin Joos, "Language and the School Child," *Harvard Educational Review,* XXXIV, No. 2 (Spring 1964), p. 210. Italics added.

[9] The search for perfection in *form* is just as illusive as it is for *content* in writing. It is rare indeed that even the simplest printed document does not contain some "error" in it (perhaps of punctuation, grammatical expression, or clarity in expression). Even authorities disagree on the finer points in describing what actually is "standard English."

not exclusively, need assistance in organizing their note-taking in advance of the actual event. By discussing the kinds of things to look for and preparing questions or categories of things of which they should be aware, they will be helped to get down the kind of information which will be most useful to them.

Writing letters: Frequently there is a need to write letters in order to gain information, to invite parents to attend a special event in the classroom or to inform them of activities in the class, to thank someone who has spoken to the class or performed some other favor, or just to communicate with a pen pal or some other person with whom the class has made a contact.

Classroom textbook: Information discovered in the course of a study may be preserved and collected to form a class textbook. Stories may be dictated or actually written by individuals or groups. The teacher can duplicate written materials selected for inclusion in the book so that everyone may have his own copy. Younger children particularly like to illustrate their books.

Displays and bulletin boards: Materials prepared for classroom displays of various kinds often require short written explanations and captions. Experiments or their results may be described. Processes may be followed, and findings recorded.

Charts: Descriptions of processes (How Bread is Made, How Water is Purified, etc.), records of events (Our Study Trip to the City Hall), or lists of important words and their definitions may be displayed in chart form before the class. Illustrations may accompany written descriptions, and material of this kind may eventually find its way into "book" form.

Dramatic representations: The writing of plays, television shows, or radio programs frequently involves the preparation of a script.

Outlining: For older children it is often valuable to outline material read or heard orally in class. The skills required in outlining are generally too advanced for most younger children; they will tend to return to the full source of information rather than attempt to listen, organize what they hear, and write, all more or less simultaneously. Older children need help and practice in developing outlining skills.

Reports and papers: Many intermediate and most upper grade children are capable of securing information on a topic, selecting important ideas out of that information, and putting it down in written form. As in the assignment of oral reports, however, the kind of topic which the child attempts to write on is extremely important. Problems or questions which have not really captured the child's imagination or which can be answered by copying from a convenient source should be avoided. It might be postulated that the tendency to copy is inversely related to the degree to which the child becomes interested and involved in the problem to be researched.

Essays and term papers: Older children are capable of planning term papers and preparing for situations in which they are asked to write short essays in response to questions asked by the teacher. Essays and term papers require planning in advance, and they require the ability to gather information in time to meet classroom deadlines; these require considerable maturity on the part of the pupil. For younger children, the time elapsed between assignment and completion should not be more than a few days.

USING IMAGINATIVE OR CREATIVE WRITING

The richness of children's imaginations and their wonderful ability to move back and forth between fantasy and reality can mean that creative or imaginative writing will provide a particularly apt avenue for developing and using writing abilities in social studies. Many of the techniques noted above for encouraging children to write lend themselves to writing in an imaginative vein. Perhaps the key in determining to what extent the child's creativity can be released is the teacher's own imagination. For example, these illustrations are drawn from the writer's own experience in observing creative teachers working with elementary school children:

> After talking about ways in which the mountains near their home might be described, children drew pictures and dictated stories telling about the mountains they had drawn. (kindergarten)

> In a study of Mexico, children secured bus schedules, chamber of commerce materials, and other descriptive brochures. They then developed an imaginative diary of a trip taken from their home to Mexico City. (sixth grade)

> A picture file serves as a source to which children may go to stimulate ideas for writing imaginative stories. (several grades)

> Children in several classes campaigned for and conducted an election to a model legislature. Issues, campaign talks, and the legislative session grew out of the imaginations of the boys and girls themselves. (eighth grade)

> The teacher's interest in poetry resulted in encouraging children to express ideas about topics in the study using different poetic forms. (fourth grade)

> In a historical study, children drew and captioned cartoons depicting issues of the particular era and the people associated with different sides of those issues. (fifth grade)

> In a study of the ancient world, children produced newspapers, complete with editorials, describing life and events as they imagined them to have existed. (seventh grade)

> A play written by the class, the problems in producing it, the actual production, and the compliments received for it were captured in photographs, drawings, and written records (the script, the reviews, the response of other classes) and put into book form as a permanent classroom reminder. (fourth grade)

> After studying kites, the children in a third grade wrote poems expressing how they would feel and what they would see were *they* the kites.

ENCOURAGING HIGH STANDARDS IN WRITING

As children grow older, individual differences in abilities to write increase rapidly. So wide is the variation in the average class that it is not possible to set a "grade standard" to serve as a guide for "acceptable work." Rather, ways need to be found which will encourage each child constantly to seek improvement in his own writing. Probably the least effective device toward this end is the teacher's sharp-pointed, critical pen. Other means, such as those listed below, are more likely to encourage the child to write while providing non-threatening avenues through which he may gradually increase his facility in written expression.

1. Every written effort deserves a complimentary remark from the teacher.
2. A little criticism goes a long way. The most able writers are more likely to be able to tolerate critical comments than average or below average writers.
3. Much of the written work which children do should not go beyond the first draft. If succeeding drafts are produced, there should be a clear reason for seeking to "perfect" the original. Children need to see the reason for, and value themselves the need for, eliminating any obvious errors that occur in their written work.
4. Getting assistance in writing should be made as easy as possible. Words which may be used and for which spelling may pose a problem should be made easily available (posted on charts or bulletin boards, in "word boxes," written on the chalkboard ahead of time by the teacher, etc.). Punctuation helps and other appropriate "guides for writing" should be on display.
5. Each child's writing should be judged individually: "Is this the kind of written work which this child is capable of producing? What suggestions should I make and which ones should I forget?"
6. Much of the "first draft" material may be retyped by the teacher, duplicated (with obvious errors corrected), and distributed to be taken home or put into books in the classroom.
7. Children can serve as members of editorial committees which ferret out errors in papers and help prepare them for inclusion in classroom books, bulletin board displays, or for some other use.

Aside from these suggestions, the most important thing the teacher can train himself to do is to accept and find value in each child's written work. No teacher is expected to like or admire everything the child writes or approve of the way he writes it. But just as one would not step up to a child's painting, mark it up, or demand that he make changes in it, the youngster's written material and particularly the imaginative or creative paper deserves the same kind of respect from the teacher. If the child senses this respect, his next work will in all likelihood be entered into with enthusiasm, and the result will be a step forward in his ability to express his ideas in writing.

Varieties of Non-Verbal Language

Non-verbal forms of communication in social studies, as well as the four verbal modes of reading, writing, speaking, and listening, should be considered. The child learns to read non-verbal language at a very early age and continues this activity during his years in school. Every teacher's facial expressions, gestures, tone of voice, and dress, for example, are constantly being read by the pupils in his class. Sometimes teachers are not aware that they communicate with pupils through these non-verbal avenues, nor do they realize that they are using their own senses to read other people and other things through largely non-verbal attributes which can be assigned to the things they observe.

The school program should not allow the non-verbal language with which human beings communicate to evolve and be developed accidentally. Sensitivities to non-verbal means of communication can be developed systematically, and non-verbal language may be used as a means to communicate ideas and as an important source in learning. Ruesch and Kees have developed a useful framework for thinking about non-verbal language. They define three major varieties of non-verbal language—sign language, action language, and object language—as follows, providing examples which have ready application in classroom situations.[10]

Sign Language

Sign language includes all those forms of codification in which words, numbers, and punctuation signs have been supplanted by gestures; these vary from the "monosyllabic" gesture of the hitchhiker to such complete systems as the language of the deaf.

[10] Jurgen Ruesch and Weldon Kees, *Nonverbal Communication, Notes on the Visual Perception of Human Relations* (Berkeley: University of California Press, 1956), p. 189.

Examples: *pictographs and ideographs from primitive to modern times*—pictures used to express ideas in sequence
comic strips
works of art—including traditional and impressionistic, abstract and non-objective art
the dance—all forms, including "image or mimetic" dance, "gesture dance," etc.
pantomime, or *"dumb-show," growing out of the dance*—by comedians, clowns, silent movie actors, etc.

Action Language

Action language embraces all movements that are not used exclusively as signals. Such acts as walking and drinking, for example, have a dual function: on one hand they serve personal needs, and on the other they constitute statements to those who perceive them.

Examples: *systematized action languages*—the automobile driver's signals, referees' and umpires' signals, signs used by surveyors and others where noise or distance prevent verbal communication.
reflex motions—feelings thought to be linked to certain expressions, such as rage with teeth gritting, fright with recoil, horror with facial contortions.
expressive movements—voluntary and involuntary internal and external smooth muscle movement such as "a look of curiosity," an upset stomach brought on by some fear or disturbing anticipation of an event or condition.
adaptive behavior as a form of language—biologists interpret the action signals of animals (fright, love, dam building, etc.), sociologists study slums and slurbs through "behavior" of residents.
gestures—deliberate motions designed to illustrate, emphasize, point, explain, or interpret, some of which are highly cultural in their origin.
traces that action leaves—the wake of a ship, automobile tires on sand, worn spots on floors and doors, shoes, chairs, doorknobs, etc.
occupational stigmata—grease on the mechanic's hands, missing fingers on the carpenter, calluses and variously

developed muscles on the musicians, the circus performer, the guitar player, etc.

posture—indicating experience as a professional bicycle racer or parade-ground soldier, attitude or feeling toward an event, level of energy available at a particular moment.

materials used in the art of writing—various kinds of material on which writing has taken place and the instruments themselves.

handwriting—as an expression of personality, profession, guilt in crime, authenticity for great acclaim, etc.

facial expression—as a reflection of interest, boredom, pain, remorse, both voluntary and involuntary in nature.

general appearance related to constitutional psychology and anthropology—studies of physiognomy and human nature reveal parallels between general appearance and behavior. Body parts have also been subject to study as sources of revelation about human attitudes and behavior, for example, the study of the hand.

appearance—attractiveness based on cultural expectations of beauty or ugliness, reflections on the meaning of obesity, attraction or rejection in sex.

clothing—reflecting that designed to protect, beautify, hide, expose, etc.

hairdress—exposing the wearer's social grouping, fastidiousness, barber, length of time since last shorn, cultivation of other hirsute adornment.

masks—from theatrical to Halloween, other objects used thereon, such as glasses and their frames, contact lenses, monocles, etc.

Object Language

Object language comprises all intentional and non-intentional display of material things, such as machines, art objects, architectural structures, and the human body and whatever clothes or covers it. The embodiment of letters as they occur in books and on signs has a material substance, and this aspect of words also has to be considered as object language.

Examples: *variations in material, shape, and surface*—any material evokes tactile and thermal images of smoothness, roughness, hardness, softness, coldness, warmth; and these images are strengthened or reduced in light of the manner in which they are arranged, singly and in combination. The whole effect may differ from that of any part.

words and numbers in relation to objects—form of type and lettering suggest utility, subject matter, are dependent upon seeing the object itself to make sense to the reader, etc. Style of print, type of paper, width of margins, and the nature of the material on which it is used (paper? metal? cardboard?) convey a message beyond those of the words themselves. There are languages of abbreviations (arrows, abbreviated words, other "symbols" which stand for the statement itself) which are "read" just as words are read. In combination with words, they take on added meaning, poignancy, potency, clarity.

atmosphere—the arena in which things are found provide a language (the downtown business area, the residential block with "old world charm," the industrial park or the industrial slum) rich and full of meaning.

appeals to perception—"atmosphere" is deliberately constructed to attract and to convey what it is all about (the "Tahitian" restaurant, the elegant and respectable silver dealer). Some appeals are not consciously constructed (the advertisements in grocery store windows occupy all available space), but a perception of the whole tells what may be found beyond without recourse to the information conveyed by the words themselves.

summons to action—road signs use form and word to convey messages (octagon form for stop signs, variously designed shields for route markers), barbed-wire fences, mailboxes, overflowing trash cans, each has its special message.

design for meeting—furniture arrangements, types of furniture, various other objects suggest "dentist waiting room," tete' a tete', public meeting, put mail here, etc.

design as a reflection of the designer—homes, classrooms, offices, stores all reflect the character of the work, behavior, or living of the designer. Pictures, dustcovers and doilies, knick-knacks, room arrangements in general tell about the arranger(s).

USING NON-VERBAL LANGUAGE MODES IN THE CLASSROOM

How does one help children develop a sensitivity to the non-verbal world, and how might one use these ideas in developing an awareness for the world around us? The ways are legion, but here are a few: Collect a wide variety of objects which relate to the social study and which appeal to the different senses (soil samples, many pictures both photographic and artistic, other "realia" which are drawn from the period, the place, or the process under study). Discuss what is being seen, touched, tasted, and what the seer, toucher, and taster is experiencing. Provide opportunities to re-create the people, the time, the place, or the process through creative dancing, artistic effort of all kinds, dramatic play, any expressive mode of a formal or informal nature on a verbal level as well as with a minimum involvement of the verbal attributes. Linger over simple objects, for example, by providing a picture of a subject under study and inviting children to react to it in writing or in some form of discussion (general class discussion, symposium, debate, individual or small group "reports"). Or, provide the same circumstances with music, or music and dance through motion pictures, or with the re-creation by a pupil in the class of a person or people being studied. For example, one teacher illustrated the manner in which Egyptian pictographs might have been drawn by asking a few children to assume the postures represented in pictures observed in the textbook and by asking the remainder of the class to render the real form observed in the class on their papers. Conduct class activities through pantomime, through structured or previously agreed upon signals, or through other modes which avoid verbal clues. Have children develop their own sign language, write their own pictographs or comics, develop artistic modes without words to represent material being studied. Find similarities and differences in pictures, art forms, etc., in clothing, hair style, general appearance of contrasting people in various times and places. Develop sensitivity for "atmosphere" by providing opportunities for such analysis through pictures, dance, observations in the classroom, and in other directly observable situations. Have individuals and small groups re-create people under study at crucial periods or times and seek to have other children in the class "read" the circumstance being depicted.

The teacher should seek out those experiences which will help children interpret situations which present the three modes of non-verbal language: sign language, action language, and object language. In thinking about the variety of non-verbal forms of communication which might be utilized in any particular study, one can see readily the opportunities for teaching and learning which suggest themselves. Non-verbal language can and should occupy a major place in social studies. It is easy to develop many different ideas from the listing above which will find ready application in the current study. Non-verbal modes of communication comprise an important avenue in learning, and the school has a responsibility for teaching children so that they improve their abilities to express themselves through these modes of communication. Moreover, many "non-verbal" children in the schools find avenues for successful expression here when the verbal modes pose difficulties for them. For such youngsters, non-verbal communication is a major avenue for learning; when absent from the classroom, these boys and girls are unduly handicapped in acquiring the concepts and understandings which one hopes they will develop.

In this and the previous chapter, the place of the various forms of verbal and non-verbal language in social studies has been considered. In making various suggestions for classroom practice, several overarching principles have served as guides in thinking about learning situations which are appropriate for children:

1. Language behavior is exceedingly complex. Growth in ability to use language in facilitating communication and thought does not occur merely as a consequence of adding skill upon skill. A large factor in language growth is intuitive in nature. Our understandings of the optimal conditions under which language in each and all of its modes may be developed to its fullest extent are still evolving.

2. It is expected, in normal development, that there will be a wide range of language abilities within and among children in the classroom. Teaching boys and girls in social studies recognizes and accepts this condition of variability.

3. The child's language is a window to his innermost being. By observing, listening, and in every way seeking to understand each child as he uses his language, one may come to know him better —to know what he understands, how he feels, and to what he aspires.

4. No sword is sharper than words written or spoken to another which, by implication or intent, communicate the idea that he is

an inadequate person. Criticism of the child's language is the same as criticizing the child himself; one should be extremely careful in his use of criticism.

5. A child cannot grow in language power unless he has many opportunities to use the language he presently possesses.

With these principles in mind, it is suggested that learning situations in social studies, to be productive of language growth and to facilitate the child's power to think about socially significant ideas, must be carried out in an environment where the child's language finds acceptance. By this it is meant that:

1. Whatever the language mode used, it is viewed primarily as an attempt to communicate.

2. Language production is essential to improvement. Teaching tactics and techniques which reduce productivity (such as excessive "correcting" of written work or requiring pupils to read materials which are too difficult) are not appropriate in the social studies classroom.

3. There should be a constant attempt to achieve balance in utilizing the various language modes, including non-verbal as well as verbal modes of communication.

4. Every child has something worth saying or writing; every one wants to achieve success in reading and to use reading to extend his understanding. The teacher's responsibility is to emphasize the positive aspects of the child's attempts to communicate. By accepting his present capacities to utilize language, by minimizing the negative or "incorrect" aspects, teachers will be most effective in helping children grow in their language facility and in their power to think.

For Further Reading

Applegate, Mauree, *Helping Children Write* (New York: Row Peterson and Co., 1954).

Association for Supervision and Curriculum Development, *Nurturing Individual Potential* (Washington, D.C.: A.S.C.D., 1964).

Brogan, Peggy, *Helping Children Read* (New York: Holt, Rinehart and Winston, 1961).

Chesler, Mark and Robert Fox, *Role-Playing Methods in the Classroom* (Chicago: Science Research Associates, 1966).

Claremont Reading Conference, *Claremont Reading Conference Yearbooks,* 1935 to date.

Harvard Educational Review, *Language and Learning,* Vol. 34, No. 2 (Spring, 1964).

Lee, Dorris M. and R. Van Allen, *Learning to Read Through Experience,* 2nd edition (New York: Appleton-Century-Crofts, 1963).

Loban, Walter, *The Language of Elementary School Children,* Research Report No. 1, National Council of Teachers of English, 1963.

MacCampbell, James C., *Readings in the Language Arts in the Elementary School* (Boston: D.C. Heath, 1964).

National Council for the Social Studies, *Social Studies for the Middle Grades* (Washington, D.C.: N.C.S.S., 1960).

National Council for the Social Studies, *Skill Development in Social Studies,* Thirty-third Yearbook (Washington, D.C.: N.C.S.S., 1963).

Nichels, Hildred and Lois Williams, *Learning About Role-Playing* (Washington, D.C.: Association for Childhood Education International, 1960).

Pease, Don, *Creative Writing in the Elementary School,* (New York: Exposition Press, 1964).

Sears, Pauline S. and Vivian S. Sherman, *In Pursuit of Self-Esteem* (Belmont, California: Wadsworth Publishing Company, 1964).

Shaftel, Fannie R., *Role-playing for Social Values* (Englewood Cliffs, N.J.: Prentice-Hall, Inc., 1967).

Shaftel, George and Fannie R. Shaftel, *Role-Playing: The Problem Story* (New York: National Conference of Christians and Jews, 1952).

Stuart, Marion F., *Neurophysiological Insights into Teaching* (Palo Alto, California: Pacific Books, 1963).

Tooze, Ruth and Beatrice P. Krone, *Literature and Music as Resources for the Social Studies* (Englewood Cliffs, New Jersey: Prentice-Hall, Inc., 1955).

University of Chicago, *Conference on Reading,* 1939-1966.

Zirbes, Laura, *Spurs to Creative Teaching* (New York: Putnam's and Sons, 1959).

CHAPTER THIRTEEN

Evaluating Learning in Social Studies

It is important for at least four major reasons to make systematic efforts to determine the quality of learning which is taking place in social studies. First, evaluation is the only way to determine if the objectives sought in teaching are being obtained to any significant degree. Second, it provides the kind of information necessary if teaching procedures are to be improved. Third, from evaluating, the consequences of teaching, data are obtained which make it possible to assess the progress of individual learners and to compare that progress with that of other pupils in the class. And fourth, the data obtained in evaluation programs involving many children from a large number of classes provide the most important objective source of information for determining how well the overall objectives of the social studies are being achieved in American schools.

Making judgments about progress in learning is a complex task, particularly complicated in the social studies because of the broad nature of the objectives valued in this particular curriculum area. The reader will recall that in the opening chapter of this book, four major objectives were listed for all social studies teaching:

1. The teaching of subject matter content.
2. Teaching thinking and problem solving.
3. Teaching skills.
4. Teaching values and attitudes.

The importance of developing specific objectives for each of the studies children engage in during their school experiences was emphasized. Since teaching purposes cover such a wide area, one needs to be prepared to assess the effects across a wide range in terms of both the quality and the extent of pupil learning.

Criteria for a Balanced Evaluation Program

A program of evaluation seeks to strike a happy balance among these four major social studies goals. In developing sound ways of assessing progress in classroom learning, one should keep in mind that some of the desired goals are more easily evaluated than others. For example, it is much simpler to devise techniques of evaluating the learning of content than to tell of growth in thinking and problem solving abilities. And it is much easier to assess skill learnings than to judge changes in values and attitudes.

A balanced evaluation program at every level of the child's school experience means that:

1. *There is a systematic program for assessing progress in learning.* There is an orderly, planned set of procedures which includes both informal and more formal evaluation tools and techniques.
2. *The program of evaluation is not excessively time-consuming.* Too much testing can take away opportunities to learn.
3. *Evaluation occurs in a wholesome atmosphere.* Experiences which are "evaluative" for the teacher can be, and often are, anxiety producing for pupils. Although the dangers in this respect fall mainly in the upper grades, younger children can also feel the lash of the test.
4. *Evaluation takes place throughout the course of each study.* Achievement of the broad purposes of social studies cannot be determined merely by attempting to evaluate learnings at the conclusion of the study. Progress in learning is assessed continuously as the study develops.
5. *Evaluation includes a wide variety of tools and techniques.* No single method of assessing growth in learning, nor any particular group of tools and techniques, is clearly superior to any other. Two factors will determine the means which the teacher employs in building a balanced program of evaluation for social studies: (1) the maturity and intellectual levels and the cultural backgrounds of the children themselves and (2) the preferences of the teacher and his skill in using different devices effectively.
6. *Evaluation involves keeping records.* Without a system of record keeping, evaluation procedures will depend upon opinions and impressions rather than upon concrete evidences of a child's work.
7. *Responsibility for evaluating progress is shared.* Self-appraisal by

children of their progress in learning is as basic an element of a balanced evaluation program as is assessment by the teacher. Parent participation is an equally important element and one for which systematic plans should be developed.

8. *Information resulting from evaluation is used in a variety of situations.* Data secured in the evaluation program are not put away and used only to report progress to parents or others interested in comparing individual or group performance with that of others. Information is also used to guide daily planning of the social study. It provides a basis for selecting more appropriate methods and materials in teaching, and it serves to inform the pupil about his own progress in learning.

Planning a Workable Evaluation Program for the Classroom

The question before every teacher concerned with developing a useful and practical evaluation program is this: "What devices and procedures should I select? Will they give me the kind of information I need to work most effectively with boys and girls?" Easy answers are not readily apparent, despite the many tools and techniques of evaluation from which to select. The personal choice of the teacher remains exceedingly important in building the classroom evaluation program because (1) the specific goals for teaching are developed by the individual teacher, and the tools of evaluation must be highly individualized if meaningful information about progress toward those goals is to be obtained; and (2) some devices are "right" for some teachers and not for others. Each teacher will want to employ those tools for evaluating learning which provide directly useful information, avoiding those which they find unwieldy and difficult to use. As a consequence, experience and experimentation with different assessment procedures is essential before a suitable evaluation program can be developed.

COMMON ERRORS IN ESTABLISHING AN
EVALUATION PROGRAM IN SOCIAL STUDIES

As one views assessment practices in schools, three common errors become apparent. First (perhaps because of the wide range of evaluation devices from which the teacher may select and because the goals of social studies are so broad), there is the frequent tendency to develop a program of evaluation containing too many elements. One simply cannot teach when he is testing all the time. It is easy to make the error of using too many evaluative devices. When this happens, so much energy is channeled toward finding out what has been learned that there is little left for forwarding the learning itself.

A second error poses the opposite problem. In some instances, teachers seem to believe that social studies evaluation can be accomplished in a wholly informal and unstructured atmosphere; they rely upon intuitive appraisals of daily progress in the classroom. Although no one can deny that valuable information about learning progress may be derived in this manner, dependence upon such modes for collecting and evaluating evidences of learning provides an inadequate base for a sound evaluation program.

A third error occurs when measures of learning progress are utilized in too limited numbers. This happens when the goals for teaching and learning are excessively narrow. For example, when high value is placed on the learning of subject matter content (to the exclusion of almost everything else), frequently there is overdependence upon one or two devices which tell something of progress in this particular dimension of learning but provide little information about anything else. Teacher-made objective tests and written assignments frequently dominate such evaluation programs. In other instances, high value may be placed upon social development. In such classrooms, evidence of progress in the ability to participate effectively in various class groupings is used as the primary basis of evaluation.

Although these are called "common errors" here, the examples are polarized for the sake of clarity. These are the issues at stake when one is planning a program of evaluation capable of yielding useful information while still remaining manageable in the classroom setting. Such a program basically:

1. Employs a balance between informal and formal procedures.
2. Emerges as a consequence of experience and as a result of experimenting with a variety of tools and techniques.
3. Is designed to yield information across the broad range of goals in social studies.

Tools and Techniques in Evaluation

OBSERVATION IN THE CLASSROOM

One of the richest sources of information about pupil progress is the observation of boys and girls as they are engaged in study. Inevitably every teacher judges the quality of what he sees going on before him;

gradually the daily impressions received in this manner take on added meaning. As he comes to know each child better, the behavior observed takes on meaningful patterns. In such informal settings, the professional person seeks to be objective in his interpretations of classroom behaviors; yet, as in all human relationships, frequently the daily experiences which characterize teaching and learning make it difficult to judge accurately and to evaluate objectively.

So, although it is true that informal observation can lead to useful and valid judgments about pupil progress, more formal techniques for assessing growth in learning are also appropriate. The teacher sets aside times when he may direct his attention from the daily routines of teaching in order to concentrate on the meanings of the behaviors elicited by involvement in the social study. He observes several groups as they work on side-studies or special projects; he notes behaviors of children engaged in dramatic play, in writing, in reporting to the class. All of the activities which involvement in the study have brought about may be subjected to this type of observation.

The demands placed on the teacher by the immediate needs of children may seem to forfeit any opportunities to achieve an objective view of the classroom, but planning ahead of time will yield the kinds of opportunities required. Teachers of young children, especially but not exclusively, will find it valuable to secure the assistance of outside persons from time to time as the elements of a workable observation program take shape. One important source of assistance consists of parents and other adults in the community who are interested in helping out at school. Older boys and girls in the school itself, or in a neighboring high school, comprise another source. The growing use of teacher aides may be another place to which the teacher may turn. Colleges and universities, when situated close enough to the school, provide an excellent source of assistance, since many young men and women enrolled in institutions of higher learning are eager to help young children in school.

Observation provides opportunities to evaluate learnings which are difficult to assess in other ways. As one observes children working together in small groups, for example, he gains information about growth in social skills and research abilities. Listening to reports and discussions tells something about the development of concepts, facts, and generalizations. Watching children attempt to research problems or organize facts in preparing reports yields information about skill development. Ideas expressed on controversial or value-laden topics may provide information about the development of attitudes and values. But the specific growth, development, and change can best be determined when the particular objectives of the study are known. Without a clear view of these objectives, classroom observation, like any other tool of evaluation, loses much of its power as a tool for appraising progress in learning.

Checklists. A device which has considerable merit in helping to organize the observation itself and in establishing criteria for determining what dimensions of learning are to be evaluated is the *checklist*. The simplest form which can be devised merely lists objectives with space for notes and comments.

Evaluation of Work Habits in Small Groups

Teacher:	Works consistently; stays with topic	Participates effectively with other members	Contributes relevant ideas	Is accepting of ideas of others	Uses materials wisely	Completes responsibilities to the group	Uses imagination in researching problems
Date of Observation:							
Group I							
Joe							
Donald							
Randy							
Marsha							
Susan							
Group II:							
John							
Arthur							
Eloise							
Sharon							
Martha							
Group III							
Group IV							

Any group of objectives may be listed across the top of the checklist with names arranged on the other coordinate. When objectives are clear and can be stated, this device may be easily developed and used at regular intervals as a guide to observation.

Anecdotal Records. Anecdotal records are descriptive accounts of episodes or events in a child's life. If collected over an extended period of time, they increase insight into the causes of an individual's behavior. Although anecdotal records are used most extensively in conducting intensive studies of a limited number of children, some applications of the techniques used in developing these records are of special use in social studies.[1] For example, many social studies teachers find it worthwhile to maintain a notebook in which entries are made approximately once a week for a portion of their class. During a period of ten to fifteen minutes set aside about once a week, the teacher writes a brief comment summarizing the behavior of from ten to twelve children during the prior week. As weeks pass, the comments the teacher accumulates begin to form a meaningful picture for each child in the class. In social studies, such records are particularly useful in helping to evaluate growth in social relationships. However, it is possible to select a particular focus and to limit entries made by the teacher within that framework. For instance, the teacher's comments may deal with growth in study habits, in research abilities, or on attitude changes. Any specific objective of the study might appropriately be evaluated in this manner.

At times, it may seem advisable to maintain a more intensive record of the behavior of one or two children in the class, and, in such cases, the techniques for keeping anecdotal records will probably encompass behavior in other curriculum areas as well as in social studies. The reader should be warned, however, that keeping anecdotal records is a time-consuming process and one which demands that the teacher train himself to describe behavior without allowing his remarks to be influenced by value judgments about the meaning of that behavior. Anecdotal material is valuable only when the behavior described is an honest account of what happened, not what seemed to happen, or why. Words suggesting that the record is injecting subjective interpretations of behavior should not be part of the record itself. Writing and analyzing anecdotal remarks, perhaps with the advice of someone

---

[1] For a comprehensive discussion of anecdotal records and their uses in the overall curriculum of the school, see Millie Almy, *Ways of Studying Children, A Manual for Teachers* (New York: Bureau of Publications, Teachers College, Columbia University, 1959), especially Chapter Two, "Observation: The Basic Way to Study Children."

experienced in describing behavior objectively, reveals rapidly what types of tendencies an individual teacher may have as he attempts to describe the behavior of others objectively. Of the examples following, for instance, only the fourth is truly anecdotal because it is the only one which specifically describes behavior. The others are either evaluative, interpretive, or generalized remarks, or a combination of these.

An *evaluative* statement:

Julius talked loud and much during poetry; wanted to do and say just what he wanted and *didn't consider the right working out of things.* Had to ask him to sit by me. Showed a *bad attitude* about it.

An *interpretive* statement:

For the last week Sammy has been a perfect Wiggle Tail. He is *growing so fast he cannot be settled. . . .* Of course the *inward change* that is taking place *causes the restlessness.*

A *generalized* description:

Sammy is *awfully restless* these days. He is *whispering most of the time* he is not kept busy. In the circle, *during various discussions,* even though he is interested, his *arms are moving or he is punching the one sitting next to him.* He *smiles when I speak to him.*

A *specific* description:

The weather was so *bitterly cold* that we *did not go* on the playground *today.* The children played games in the room during the regular recess period. *Andrew and Larry chose sides* for a game which is *known as stealing the bacon. I was talking* to a group of children *in the front* of the room *while the choosing was in process* and *in a moment* I heard a loud altercation. Larry said that *all the children wanted to be on Andrew's side* rather than on his. Andrew . . . remarked, *"I can't help it if they all want to be on my side."*

Mixed *description, evaluation,* and *interpretation:*

Lately Larry has shown marked interest in a little girl in the grade [*generalized description*] . . . . I am a little concerned over this particular friendship [*evaluation*]. The girl comes from a much better home than most [*evaluation*] but has a stepmother toward whom she is antagonistic [*interpretation*]. She has spent her life from earliest childhood pretty much as she pleased [*interpretation*]. . . . Briefly she is a child who has obtained sex knowledge in the wrong way [*evaluation*] and she is anxious at all times to impart her learning to others [*interpretation*]. She is a very attractive looking child but most tempestuous [*generalized description*] Every boy in the room seems to be attracted to her [*generalized description*] and she is well aware of the fact [*interpretation*]. Perhaps Larry is only one of the herd, but I can already tell that Alice's influence is making itself felt [*interpretation*].[2]

Observing Work in Progress. Since social studies are characterized by a wide variety of activities, the objects which classroom activities yield provide an important basis for evaluating learning progress. As murals and paintings are planned and executed, stories and "books" written, articles for display gathered and arranged, information collected and notes taken, dramatizations prepared and practiced for presentation, and all the other activities which have been planned proceed—each at its own pace—there will be a need to record individual and group progress in completing them. As the teacher moves from child to child, and group to group, he will find it useful to keep a record of progress since individualized activities of this nature require coordinating and planning as some projects approach completion and others require more time or demand special assistance. Entries made on a card which the teacher carries with him provide a simple means of record keeping and, with the passage of time, an important record of progress.

Dramatic Play and Role Playing. Situations in which children project themselves into other roles are particularly valuable for noting the quality and extent of generalizations which are developing and of attitudes being fostered through the social study. The spontaneous quality of dramatization stimulates the imagination and capitalizes upon intuitive thinking processes in a unique way. The teacher whose pupils feel free to engage in both dramatic play and role playing is privileged to observe aspects of the child's world frequently hidden from adults.

DISCUSSION

Note has been taken of the vital importance to teachers of learning to listen to children. It is truly an imperative of teaching that the art of listening be well developed in assessing learning progress in social studies because the child's oral language provides one of the most important windows for viewing the quality and extent of his understandings. In discovering what children know, discussion techniques may involve the total class, smaller groups of children, or oral interchange between the teacher and individual boys and girls. Discussing means drawing from the child responses which reflect his thoughts.

[2] *Helping Teachers Understand Children,* American Council on Education, Commission on Teacher Education (Washington: American Council on Education, 1945) pp. 33-34.

These are not times for the teacher to teach in the sense of attempting to direct or redirect the intellectual traffic in the classroom. These are times to stimulate the child to speak his own thoughts freely and as extensively as possible. This can be achieved by emphasizing:

1. Open-ended questions (Who? How? What do you think?), avoiding those for which only one answer is correct. Questions beginning with *when* and *which* and sometimes *what* frequently have only one correct response and can often be answered with one word.
2. Questions which stimulate thinking about goals (How much more work do you need to do? What do you need to find out next?).
3. A maximum of child commentary, a minimum of comments by the teacher. (Questions which stimulate interchange among children are more fruitful than those which encourage the child to talk to or tell the teacher without regard for the other children in the class.)
4. Drawing out children who tend to remain silent. Encourage all children to find successful oral experiences in discussion. A classroom discussion can seem lively and worthwhile yet actively involve only a small portion of the class.

A useful technique which will assist teachers and pupils in analyzing interaction during classroom discussions is the following: Have a child or observer in the classroom record the initials of each child who participates in discussion in the order in which each speaks. At the end of the discussion, chart the results so that it appears something like one of the examples shown on page 462.[3]

Large-Group Discussion. The teacher will wish to use large-group discussion situations to appraise individual and small-group progress in learning; this device is also useful in getting an overall picture of the manner in which the whole class is moving toward its goals. The large-group setting is particularly powerful: it provides a common frame of reference by informing individuals and small groups engaged in related projects about the total progress of the class. It also provides a basis upon which individuals may judge their own progress in relation to that of the other members of the class.

Small-Group Discussion. When boys and girls become involved in sub-studies of various kinds, it will be useful to provide opportunities to discuss aspects of their work with these small groups. Out of such

[3] Millie Almy, *op. cit.*, p. 30.

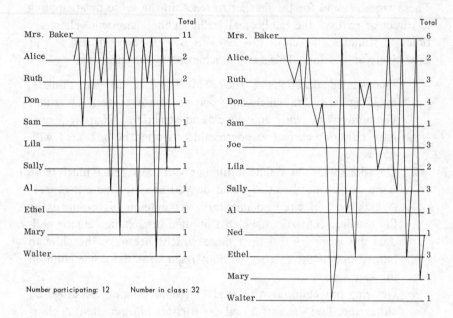

Figure 13—1: Participation Charts. In the example at the left, each pupil had spoken. In the example at the right, the discussion involved more inter-change among the children who contributed, yet fewer out of the total class entered into the deliberations. If both examples were representative of discussions occurring in a classroom in which thirty or more were enrolled, it would be obvious that a majority did not become involved in it. Such a situation might suggest the need for encouraging the silent ones to enter into the give and take orally at the next opportunity. (Reprinted with the permission of the publisher from, Millie Almy, *Ways of Studying Children*, New York: Teachers College Press, 1959. © 1959 by Teachers College, Columbia University)

situations, the teacher discovers a great deal about individual and group learning problems, and he is able to help children who are having difficulty to move ahead with a minimum of wasted time. Such problems as discovering the right kinds of references in researching a topic, locating construction materials, assisting with particular skills, and helping to solve interpersonal conflicts illustrate situations with which the teacher can deal effectively as he moves from one group to another. As the teacher thinks about pacing the study to suit the abilities and interests of his pupils and as he plans the next steps with the total class, discussion in small groups will provide him with essential information.

Individual Conferences. Although the classroom setting provides many opportunities for exchange between a child and his teacher, often these are neither long enough nor completely satisfying. Occasionally each child has a right to the teacher's individual attention for a reasonable length of time. In some circumstances conferences might be held after school; in others, at some time during the school day. *When* such conferences occur is not important. It *is* important that the child understand that the experience is designed to help him, not punish him. Frequently, of course, a personal conference with the teacher spells trouble to the child involved as well as to his classmates. Te serve its purpose, individual conferences should be arranged so that they are in no way threatening; they should be a part of every child's experience. Certainly, they should not be associated with attempts to correct individual learning or behavior problems. As is the case with other evaluation techniques, it is well to maintain some written record of the conference, including the date on which it was held and a pertinent remark or two about the topics discussed with the child.

WORK SAMPLES

A basic problem in all evaluation is one of telling the forest from the trees. That is, in judging the progress children are making toward the goals of social studies, day to day changes are difficult to see. How can one tell, for example, that a particular behavior demonstrates growth in learning to read maps? How can the teacher tell that a child's comments *today* represent an increasing ability to generalize or that his remarks made in a discussion indicate a deepening grasp of important concepts? Or, how can growth in the use of skills be measured? In fact, how can progress in learning of any kind be measured without the element of time?

Clearly, measurements which show "before" and "after" are as essential in evaluating progress in social studies as they are in evaluating progress toward any goal. For this reason, record keeping has been emphasized even in the more informal evaluative situations which classroom observations and discussions provide. Only the *pattern* which emerges from such records over a period of time is meaningful in evaluating the child's progress in learning.

One of the most useful techniques for assessing progress in learning involves collecting samples of children's work over an extended period of time. In this manner the teacher is provided the most extensive and complete evidence of classroom learning. Careful examination, in which comparisons are made with prior work as well as with similar efforts by other class members, reveals much valuable information.

Samples of Individual Work. The materials which the teacher collects and puts in a large file can obviously be of several varieties. Written work (including stories, written tests, logs, diaries, etc.) is perhaps the most obvious but certainly not the only type. Pictures, maps and graphs, scrapbooks, and bulletin board materials may also be included. The collection resulting should ultimately consist of work which the teacher views as typical of the child's efforts. It should not be limited to items which have passed through several stages of revision and correction nor to things judged as outstanding examples of the child's work. In addition, the work collected should be selected with some system in mind. Periodic collection is better than remembering from time to time to collect samples. Usually the work of all children will be filed at one time, and all materials will be dated so that time lapses between one sample and another will be readily apparent.

Samples of Group Work. Children working as members of committees often produce items which can serve useful functions in assessing progress. These may include large maps, models, class-made "textbooks," tape recordings, bulletin board displays, dramatizations, and collections of objects that have eventuated from group endeavors (rocks, minerals, soil samples, utensils used in past times). The item may be retained in the classroom, with indications of individual contributions to the project. At other times the evidence will need to be distributed among the children to take home; occasionally perhaps it will be discarded altogether. Such events as dramatizations, participation in symposiums and debates, and role playing are transitory, seemingly impossible to capture. The teacher's camera and the tape recorder are handy tools in recording these categories of activities; evidence collected in this manner can then be evaluated at a later date. All of these things can be combined with other work samples to provide evidences of growth in learning as well as to help children summarize and evaluate their own experiences. The class textbook is but one outstanding example of this type; a recording of a play is another. One teacher used photographs she had taken of the play, the script, program, letters of invitation to other classes to see the play, responses and "critical reviews," and even pieces of material used in costumes and scenery to help children develop a book about their own experience. Things of this type which result from the varied activities in social studies serve several purposes: as a means of evaluation, as useful reading material, as a class record of a venture in learning worth preserving for its own sake.

OBJECTIVE TESTS

Objective tests, in their many forms, comprise another category of testing devices available to the teacher of social studies. Published standardized tests frequently are considered to be among the most "objective" of objective tests, of course, and they are used widely (perhaps too widely) in schools. In the curriculum of social studies, relatively few standardized tests are being published. Of those available, most are inadequate for the purposes they are intended to achieve. Objective testing is not limited to published materials, of course. The teacher may develop evaluative devices which observe the principles of objective test construction and which are more suitable for use in his own classroom than are standardized tests.

Standardized Tests. Standardized tests are of two general types: (1) those which have been developed and published for use throughout the country and (2) those developed within states and in the larger school districts and which are designed for use within those school units. Of the tests published for the widest possible audience, there are a limited number which deal with what might be termed purely social studies information. However, many of the standardized test batteries—tests which probe knowledge in a number of different curriculum areas—contain sections which deal with content normally considered to be within the realm of the social studies curriculum. Nevertheless, the total number of standardized tests in social studies is low in relation to those in other curriculum areas, e.g., reading and arithmetic.

Several problems present themselves to the classroom teacher when he considers using standardized tests in his evaluation program. First, there is the question of the adequacy of the tests in evaluating progress toward the broad range of goals which characterizes objectives in teaching social studies. Standardized tests are most efficient in measuring knowledge of specific content and of certain abilities associated with reading maps, graphs, and charts. They do not lend themselves to assessing the development of concepts and generalizations, growth in attitudes and values, or in abilities to think and solve problems. True, *some* standardized tests attempt to probe learning growth in these dimensions, but they are relatively few. Of those which do, even fewer are successful.

A second problem has to do with the relationship of the test items to the specific objectives of a given social study. Because standardized tests are designed for universal use and because classroom programs are usually highly individualized, it is not surprising that published tests often bear little relationship to the underlying purposes of the daily work in the social studies classroom.

A third problem deals with the range and number of tests available. In a recent evaluation it was discovered that only forty-seven separately published tests are available for use in elementary and secondary school social studies programs.[4] An analysis of these forty-seven tests reveals that thirty of these are designed for high school and college use. Of the remaining seventeen, two include sections possible for use in the primary years (third grade only); nine contain items announced as appropriate for the intermediate years (one is limited to sixth grade); and fifteen items deemed useful only at the upper grade levels. These figures illuminate a fact which applies to all standardized tests in social studies: relatively few have been specifically designed for younger children.

A fourth problem has to do with the adequacy of standardization procedures. Of the forty-seven tests evaluated, no less than thirty-six were classified as unfavorable when they were reviewed for adequacy of technical data—an almost universal sign that data supporting norms for the test are inadequate. In a number of cases, there were no norms given. Since test batteries are used more widely in schools than separate tests, in every curriculum area, norms for scores obtained from standardized tests are more likely to be adequate. However, test batteries provide sub-scores on relatively fewer test items than do separately prepared tests. Therefore, social studies sub-scores generally represent a

[4] Barbara A. Peace, "Bibliography of Social Studies Tests," in an Appendix of *Evaluation in Social Studies*, Thirty-fifth Yearbook, National Council for the Social Studies (Washington, D.C.: National Education Association, 1965), pp. 230-247.

sampling problem; there are only a few questions being asked within the dimensions of the curriculum of social studies.[5]

Because of the general inadequacy of standardized tests in social studies, there is little value at present in using them to evaluate progress in learning in the classroom. Scores secured as a consequence of administering a test in many classrooms may be meaningful to administrators and the public generally if the limited scope of the questions is clearly understood. However, before schools and school districts can rely on standardized tests in social studies to any great extent, better tests must be devised and the norms used in interpreting the meaning of the scores obtained must be more adequately derived. In the absence of useful national norms, and because local conditions vary markedly, school districts should attempt to establish local norms for any test in social studies which they elect to use over any extended period. Such data, if collected over a period of time and with proper statistical controls applied, will be useful in long-range curriculum planning and development.

Teacher-made Tests. At least three major advantages over standardized tests are realized when the teacher, employing principles of objective test construction, develops his own tests. First, the test can be closely related to the objectives of the social study. Second, the teacher can select as many different test items as necessary to give a valid picture of the child's understanding on selected topics. Third, test items can be constructed which reveal growth in learning across the broad range of objectives held for social studies; i.e., questions and situations can be devised which appraise knowledge not only of factual information but of higher levels of knowledge as well as growth in quality of attitudes and values relating to the particular study.

The difficulty in devising useful classroom tests is simply that good objective tests are difficult to construct. Generally speaking, the easier one finds it to prepare a test based on "objective" principles, the more likely it is that the matters being assessed are trivial. Since time is always limited in teaching, good tests for evaluating social studies learnings will, of necessity, be infrequent.

[5] Critical reviews of virtually all currently published tests in the United States appear in O. K. Buros, *Sixth Mental Measurements Yearbook* (Highland Park, N.J.: The Gryphon Press, 1965). Previous yearbooks were published in 1939, 1940, 1949, 1953, and 1959. The reader who wishes information about tests no longer available in print may consult previous yearbooks.

When composing items to be included in tests based on principles of objective test construction, general knowledge of the techniques most commonly used in preparing objective type tests is needed. The reader should be aware that the techniques used most frequently in social studies are indeed those which apply to the broad field of objective testing. The details of constructing objective test items will not be discussed. Reference to one or two of the books listed at the end of this chapter will introduce the reader to the major problems and issues in the field of testing, so there is no justification in repeating that material here. One should be reminded, however, that there are four basic types of questions which may be constructed: the dichotomous statement (or some variation on the true-false theme), the matching or organizing type of question, the extended response or essay question, and the multiple-choice or best answer item. Typical of these four kinds of questions are the following:

The dichotomous statement (requiring the student to decide whether a statement is true or false, right or wrong, incorrect or correct, etc. This type of question can be combined with "short-answer completion" in instances where the statement is false or wrong when the pupil is asked to correct the incorrect information.)

Examples:

T	F	The natural environment has little influence on man's religious beliefs.
T	F	Though many substitutes for wood products have been discovered, man's dependence upon forests is increasing.
R (ight)	W (rong)	The City Manager is elected just like the City Councilmen.
R (ight)	W (rong)	Longitude is the measurement of distance east and west of the International Date Line. (If this were a test in which the pupil was to correct the incorrect statement, the correct answer would require him to indicate that distance is measured east and west of the Prime Meridian.)
T	F	GNP stands for Gross Normal Profit. (Again, if the pupil were being asked to give the correction needed to make the statement read properly, he would need to know that

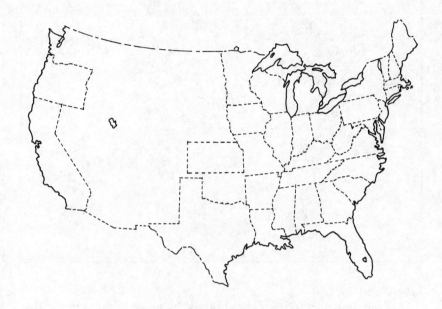

GNP stands for Gross National Product. He might add a definition: the value of all goods and services produced in a country during a fiscal year.)

Short-answer completion (requiring simple recall of information or a brief explanatory statement).

Examples:

Explain the postal service's motto, "The Mail Must Go Through." (Sufficient space is presumably provided for the pupil to record his answer.)

What were the three main points expressed in the Monroe Doctrine?

   1 _____

   2 _____

   3 _____

What famous man was the publisher of the Pennsylvania Gazette?

Matching or organizing (requiring recognition of information supplied and reorganization of it so that relevant items are properly connected).

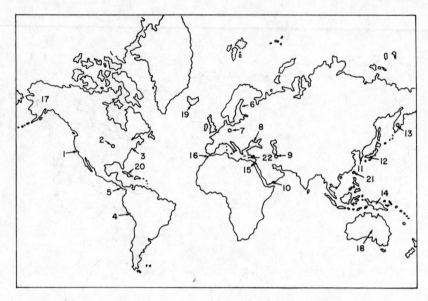

Examples:

On the desk map[6] of the United States, name and color (1) the free
states in 1863, (2) the loyal slave states, and (3) slave states which
seceded.

Write in the space shown the number indicating the location on the
map of each place listed below.[7]

1. ( ) Korea
2. ( ) Finland
3. ( ) San Francisco
4. ( ) Lebanon
5. ( ) Formosa
6. ( ) Aden
7. ( ) Member of SEATO

8. ( ) Permanent home of the
United Nations
9. ( ) City on which first
atomic bomb was
dropped
10. ( ) Site of first use of
United Nations police
force

In the blank after each date, put the number of the event which
took place in that year:

1. Zebulon Pike's Expedition
2. Expedition of Lewis and Clark
3. George Washington elected President

1. 1789 _____
2. 1803 _____
3. 1823 _____

---

[6] E. J. Thompson, *A Pupil's Guide to Accompany The American Story* (Boston:
D. C. Heath and Company, 1959), p. 98.
[7] Adapted from Thompson, *ibid.*, p. 106.

 4. Napoleon invaded Russia   4. 1796 _____
 5. Monroe Doctrine declared   5. 1801 _____
 6. Louisiana purchased from France   6. 1804 _____
 7. United States declared war against Tripoli   7. 1812 _____
 8. Congress passed the Missouri Compromise   8. 1820 _____
 9. Whiskey Rebellion took place
10. Washington's Farewell Address

Extended response (requiring verbal or written communication in some length in response to questions raising complex issues or principles. This is the most difficult type of question to evaluate since a wide variation always exists among responses obtained from any one question).

Examples:

Imagine you are Thomas Jefferson writing a letter to Lewis and Clark telling them what you hope they will accomplish on their expedition. What would you write to them?

Do you think man is naturally war-like? Tell why you believe as you do.

Why was it important for our expanding nation (1800 to 1860) to develop a better system of transportation?

Multiple-choice (requiring recognition and association of information supplied where choices provided include only one clearly relevant or "best" response).

Examples:

The most important reason people left England to come to North America during the colonial period was:

 1. to gain religious and political freedom
 2. for adventure
 3. the search for a better living
 4. to establish a colony for England
 5. the desire to convert the Indians

World War II spread to the Pacific Ocean area when the Japanese attacked:

 1. Dutch Harbor
 2. Guam
 3. Singapore
 4. Pearl Harbor
 5. The Philippine Islands

People are most likely to be dependent upon one another if they live on:
1. plains
2. mountains
3. lowlands
4. deserts

The Mississippi River might be of more value to the United States if it flowed into the Atlantic Ocean because it would:
1. flow in the direction of principal trade routes
2. reduce the eroding effect of the river
3. place the rich agricultural region nearer the industrial east
4. place the rich delta region in a more favorable climate

An additional word of warning concerning the value of objective-type tests: their usefulness will be heavily dependent upon the child's ability to read and write. Although other means may be used, for example, pictures may be substituted for words and the child's verbal language or his ability to draw or act out his responses utilized in place of writing, still it remains true that the most widely used procedures require considerable facility in both reading and writing. It follows that there are limited uses for assessment procedures of this type in the earlier school years. And for those older children who are experiencing difficulties in mastering these language modes, or for whom the language modes are simply not appropriate as is the case with many so-called culturally disadvantaged children, paper and pencil tests can be grossly unfair. Whatever of value the child has learned will be difficult to assess when the device selected presents such a communication barrier between pupil and teacher.

For the teacher, experience is one of the most important factors in learning how to construct tests useful for the classroom. Practice in writing test items and experience in administering and scoring tests are almost the only ways to learn how to prepare clear and unambiguous test questions which will elicit responses indicating growth toward major social studies goals. In the early stages of test writing, therefore, it may prove helpful to ask another teacher to read and criticize any new test devised. Frequently, another reader can identify problems or errors in test construction more readily than can the author. And it is obviously unfair to administer a test to pupils which might cause confusion or lead to misunderstanding.

Another useful reference in test construction is the *Taxonomy of*

Educational Objectives, developed by Bloom and his associates.[8] The levels of intellectual activity described in the *Taxonomy* provide useful guideposts in determining the quality of questions which one has developed in his social studies test.

Values of Discussion and Review. If tests constructed by the teacher are to have maximum value in the classroom, there should always be opportunity for discussion and review. This should occur a short time after the formal testing. It should take place while the purposes which the test was designed to serve are still fresh in everyone's mind. The objective-type test provides opportunities for diagnosing individual and group problems in learning. It may also stimulate discussion which focuses upon those things that the test has revealed as needing additional attention, helping to clarify learnings that may be confused or ambiguous. In checking over papers—"correcting them" is one term used to describe this behavior—it is usually valuable to record the number of correct or incorrect responses to each item and to note individual problems encountered in taking the test. For example, one may notice that two or three items were answered incorrectly by a large number of pupils, indicating a need for continued attention to the matters which that question sought to probe. Or, one may learn that a group of pupils had difficulty with certain of the items. Such a discovery may, as a consequence, lead to a meeting with those boys and girls to help them clarify their thinking with respect to the ideas which those questions sought information about. On the other hand, test items which were answered correctly by most pupils may serve as an indication that the question was either too simple, or that more time than necessary was devoted to that topic, thus providing him some additional guidelines for teaching in the future.

Cooperatively Designed Tests. Because constructing useful tests is a difficult and time-consuming job, teachers sometimes are attracted to the idea of developing tests which may be used with several classes. *If* teachers agree on goals and are successful in developing test items truly related to the evaluation of learning progress toward those goals, such an approach to evaluation may prove useful. There are some dangers in joint efforts of this kind, however, the primary one being that individual teachers may be inclined to "teach for the test." They will

---

[8] Benjamin Bloom (ed.), *A Taxonomy of Educational Objectives: Cognitive Domain* (Chicago: University of Chicago Press, 1956).

not wish their pupils to appear in an unfavorable light in relation to other classes. This problem becomes even more pronounced if the test resulting from such cooperative effert is concerned mainly with assessing knowledge of specific information.

SOCIOMETRIC TECHNIQUES IN SOCIAL STUDIES

The nature of social relationships may be studied through sociometric techniques, and the information gained can be used both in evaluating and in planning in social studies. The major tool of sociometric study is the sociogram, a diagram depicting aspects of the social relationships which exist in the classroom. The sociogram is derived from an analysis of responses to questions asked of the pupils. Quite understandably, therefore, the nature of the questions one asks determines the pattern which emerges as the sociogram is developed. For example, if each child were asked to list the two children with whom he would like to work on a social studies committee, the answers would provide a different pattern than if the pupils were asked to list the two people they would most like to have as members of their baseball team. Additional factors influence the type of pattern which emerges as the sociogram is constructed. The passage of time alone brings certain changes.

Figure 13–2: (on facing page) This simplified worksheet may be used to develop a sociogram quickly and, with a little practice, quite easily. In the example shown here, intermediate children were asked to respond to these statements: "We are going to need committees to work on special topics in our study. Put your name at the top of the 3 x 5 card I have given you. Then write the names of two people with whom you would like to work. I will keep your choices in mind and arrange the committees so that everyone will be with one or more of the people he has named." In this example, the teacher did not ask the children to think specifically about the possibility of naming either boys or girls. If he had, there might have been more crossing over. The fact that the sexes segregated themselves is typical of the age levels participating. Younger and older boys and girls will make more cross-sex choices as a rule. In the case of the younger children, the teacher might have asked each child to come to the desk to whisper the names of those with whom he would like to work. Limiting choices to two names greatly reduces the complications of manipulating these data, making the sociogram much easier to construct.

	BOYS (Chosen) 1	2	3	4	5	6	7	8	9	10	11	12	13	14	15	GIRLS (Chosen) 1	2	3	4	5	6	7	8	9	10	11	12	13	14	15
BOYS (Choosers) 1						+			+																					
2									+				+																	
3													+		+															
4								+							+															
5																					+		+							
6									+					+																
7						+								+																
8					+								+																	
9						+				+																				
10									+			+																		
11					+										+															
12										+			+																	
13			+			+																								
14											+				+															
15								+			+																			
GIRLS (Choosers) 1																	+						+							
2																			+		+									
3																	+			+										
4																						+					+			
5																		+					+							
6																		+					+							
7																+					+									
8																					+			+						
9																					+		+							
10																	+				+									
11																									+		+			
12																				+						+				
13																										+				+
14																									+		+			
15																										+		+		
Total	0	0	1	2	4	0	2	4	2	2	1	4	2	4	0	1	3	2	1	2	6	1	5	1	2	3	3	1	0	1

Class Roster

Boys:
1 John
2 Paul
3 Mark
4 Robin
5 Chris.
6 Jack
7 Bobby
8 Ricky
9 Jim
10 Randy
11 Ronnie
12 Peter
13 Don
14 Gordon
15 Brian

Girls:
1 Betty
2 Norma
3 Clara
4 Judy
5 Michele
6 Margaret
7 Jane
8 Susan
9 Martha
10 Jean
11 Mona
12 Shelly
13 Marian
14 Jenifer
15 Enid

As children live together in the classroom, they become aware of and learn to appreciate the talents of others around them. Friendships change. Even ten-year-old boys eventually discover that girls are acceptable and perhaps even useful in certain circumstances in the classroom. The number of choices which the teacher asks for will also alter the choices themselves and the pattern of relationships which the sociogram may show. And the classroom climate itself changes from day to day, influenced by events in school and out. A stormy day, the teacher's disposition on the day the pupils are questioned, or the absence of one or two children may influence markedly the responses which children give on a particular day.

Even so, information derived from analysis of the sociogram may be useful. In social studies, the data are particularly valuable in forming effective sub-groups and in increasing the teacher's understanding of the role individual children are playing in their peer relationships. Because so many factors cause differing patterns of relationships to emerge over a period of time, one needs to be especially careful in determining the meaning of differences which appear from one sociometric study to another. The teacher may observe changes which are most meaningful in indicating how leadership and followership roles are changing, whether children who were chosen less frequently than others are gaining greater acceptance in the group, and how preferences of the pupils in general may be shifting when similar types of questions are asked. However, it is always dangerous to generalize about data obtained from sociograms, and it is wise to remember that they are at best imprecise tools of evaluation.

Figure 13–3: (on facing page) Working with the raw data compiled on the worksheet, the teacher then develops a sociogram which illustrates graphically the nature of the choices made. Numbers are used only to simplify the sociogram itself. By referring to the totals of choices for each child, those mentioned most frequently are identified and a circle and appropriate number for each is arranged on a sheet of paper. Plotting these "leaders" first facilitates the placement of the remaining data. Lines are drawn from one to the other which indicate the direction of choice. Some practice is necessary before a completed sociogram can be drawn after only one or two drafts since one must learn how to arrange the given data so that the crossing of lines is reduced to a minimum.

COMPLETED SOCIOGRAM

BOYS   GIRLS

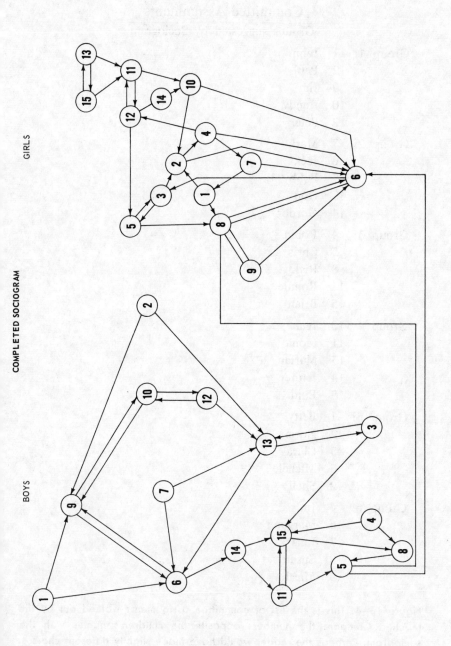

Committee Assignments

Groups suggested by Sociogram

Group 1: 1 John
          2 Paul
          9 Jim
         10 Randy
         12 Peter

Group 2: 3 Mark
          6 Jack
          7 Bobby
         13 Don
         14 Gordon

Group 3: 4 Robin
          5 Chris
          8 Ricky
         11 Ronnie
         15 Brian

Group 4: 10 Jean
         11 Mona
         13 Marian
         14 Jenifer
         15 Enid

Group 5: 1 Betty
          2 Norma
          3 Clara
          5 Michele
         12 Shelly

Group 6: 4 Judy
          6 Margaret
          7 Jane
          8 Susan
          9 Martha

Figure 13–4: This is the list of committee assignments worked out by the teacher. Compare the numbers opposite the children's names with the sociogram. Perhaps the reader would have made slightly different choices. Or, if fewer committees were being planned, the complexion of the groups might have been altered markedly.

Two rules must be observed in using sociometric techniques. First, when children are asked to state preferences, the information they provide *should be treated confidentially.* Older children need to be assured of this. Second, the questions asked *should lead to action.* For example, if the teacher asks children to list choices for working on committees, then committees should be formed based on the data collected. By following through on his initial question he will help pupils feel there is real utility in supplying the requested information.

ENCOURAGING SELF-APPRAISAL

Inevitably, a balanced program of evaluation in social studies includes attention to procedures that encourage boys and girls to appraise their own learning progress. When pupils have opportunities to evaluate their own accomplishments and those of the groups in which they are participating, they learn how to make realistic judgments about the quality and extent of the work they have done; they gain experience in clarifying goals and in planning more effective means for reaching them.

One needs to gain experience in self-evaluation, however. The ability to look realistically at one's accomplishments does not come about easily or as a matter of course. Frequently, it is difficult, if not impossible, to see oneself in an objective light. But a number of opportunities present themselves to the teacher every day which may foster growth toward the kind of objective thinking-about-oneself in relation to his own expectations and in terms of group progress in learning which is so essential to the establishment of good mental health. Situations in which self-appraisal may be encouraged include the following.

In Total-Class Discussion. Whenever the entire class joins together with the teacher in discussing some aspect of their study, there is always the opportunity to elicit views from children concerning their appraisal of the work they have done. Comparing accomplishments with previously agreed upon objectives provides criteria for evaluating progress objectively. The teacher may raise questions which help children evaluate the discussion session itself (Did we stay on our topic? Were we calling upon evidence gathered in our study or on opinions and personal experiences? Were we attentive when others were talking? Did everyone get a chance to participate? Did we have enough time to explore the discussion topic in sufficient detail? etc.). Or, discussion may center around an evaluation of progress in the social study itself (How is each group progressing toward its goal? Are special materials needed? Is every member of the group having an opportunity to make a contribution? What other problems is each group having which need to be discussed?). In addition, the total class should have an opportunity to evaluate particular activities and experiences. A debate held before the class, a symposium, perhaps a role-playing situation or other form of dramatization, provide settings for discussing the quality of the particular experience. Finally, such common experiences as study trips, visits to the class by talented citizens, or viewing a motion picture, play, or television program provide opportunities to consider the values of such experiences.

In Small-Group Discussions. When smaller groups work together toward some objective, the teacher can encourage the development of self-appraisal. Committees may be asked to spend part of their work time evaluating among themselves. The chairman may then report conclusions to the total class. Or, the other members of the class may observe a group evaluate its performance. For example, in a debate or symposium or perhaps merely an informal discussion which takes place before the entire group, an evaluation period may follow in which the observers do not participate directly.

In Discussion with Individuals. As children work independently or in small groups, it is always appropriate for the teacher to confer with individuals about their progress. Talking with a child about what he is trying to accomplish not only helps the teacher clarify purposes and set attainable goals; it also is invaluable to the teacher in determining how clearly the overall objectives of the study are being perceived. Individual conferencing may be formalized, particularly with older children. However, informal conferences, carried out as the regular work of the class goes on, without the atmosphere of testing or checking on people, are always appropriate.

Using Charts. Charts which state objectives are valuable aids in helping children establish standards against which they may judge their progress in learning. Charts can be developed that deal with social behavior or the development of skills, or they may relate more directly to content objectives. In general, charts which are developed cooperatively with the pupils are most advantageous. Such charts tend to mean more to boys and girls since the ideas expressed on the chart reflect their own ideas. However, it is not inappropriate for the teacher to prepare a chart to be used with children. These charts can be discussed and explained in a useful way, and they are undoubtedly superior to those ostensibly cooperative devices which, in actuality, are teacher-made. It is not difficult to direct a discussion with children so that the ideas expressed on the chart are those of the teacher rather than of the pupils. Younger children will not recognize what is happening when a chart is developed in this manner; however, such charts will be relatively meaningless to them. Older children will know that their ideas are not on the chart, and they will actively reject the thoughts or guidelines recorded on them.

Reporting to Parents

There are no completely satisfactory methods for reporting to parents the progress their child is making in social studies learnings. Some parents and teachers appear to believe that only the traditional letter grades can convey sufficiently specific information. They think that letter grades—in their infinite variety, ranging from A's and B's, through E's (Excellent) and N's (Needs to Improve), to 1's and 2's (another form of A and B)—are capable of communicating how much a child has learned, not only as an individual but in relation to his classmates and to the larger world of fourth graders, eighth graders, kindergartners, or whatever grouping may identify him. There is an opposing view, of course, one that maintains that meaningful communication about progress in learning can occur only through extended interpersonal contact between the teacher and each child's parents. Letter grades, and even extended written comments cannot, they feel, supply the vital information needed to give a proper evaluation of a child's progress in learning. Of course, between these two positions lies a range of compromises. Because most evaluation programs consist of compromises among widely differing opinions about what constitutes an appropriate program for reporting progress in learning to parents, school district procedures are constantly under revision. Within one of these widely varying patterns, the classroom teacher must attempt to find some way of working which reflects his own philosophy about reporting to parents while remaining loyal to the method adopted by his school system.

The problem of finding a satisfactory way of communicating pupil progress in learning applies to all areas of the curriculum, of course. But if it is difficult to represent accurately a child's progress in such areas as reading and arithmetic, just think how much more difficult it is in social studies. In the first place, parental misunderstanding of the nature and extent of the curriculum of social studies provides a formidable barrier to communication. Beyond this, and with special reference to specific studies, parents find it hard to understand that there is a broad range of legitimate goals in teaching. The learning of skills and of highly specific content may be all that a parent thinks can be worthy of study. He may easily consider emphasis upon ability to generalize, to think, to solve problems, or upon the whole question of attitude development, to be frills. He may even believe the school should not be concerned about such areas.

Satisfactory communication between parent and teacher therefore can be achieved only when both have reasonably clear conceptions of teaching goals. It is only against this measure that progress in learning can be discussed intelligently. The teacher's responsibility is not merely to report to parents. He must also *educate* parents so that they will understand the goals of teaching social studies.

THE TROUBLE WITH REPORT CARDS

Regardless of what one might privately determine to be an ideal program for reporting progress to parents, the practicalities of existing reporting programs must be considered. No teacher is completely satisfied with the tools provided. The vast majority of schools rely upon the report card as the basic instrument for communicating progress to parents. The letter grade, in one form or another, forms the system of ranking and rating. Some schools supplement the report card by encouraging the teacher to write extended accompanying remarks. Many have adopted programs of parent conferencing in which parents are invited once or twice a year to the school for discussions with the teacher. In addition, almost all schools plan one or two "Open House" meetings during the year at which time general questions about the school program may be answered; however, individual discussions about particular children may be discouraged or even avoided entirely.

Reporting programs can include additional aspects; these involve little work by the teacher in relation to the amount of value derived from them. These programs are discussed in later paragraphs. First, however, a closer look at the problem of the report card itself is relevant to this discussion. It has long been recognized that systems employing some version of the letter grade, in addition to serving as poor communicators to parents, can be detrimental to children's learning. Particularly is this true when the child becomes overly aware of the importance parents or teachers attach to such symbols of learning success. The tyranny of grading can be very real! Where letter grades (or some similar system) obtain, children should not be impressed with notions about their importance or value in social studies (or in any other curriculum area). For primary and most intermediate children, this means refraining from assigning letter grades to projects or papers completed in the classroom and not calling attention to grades recorded on report cards. To avoid the detrimental consequences of grades on children, ideally report cards would be mailed to parents, with the request that the children not be involved in discussions or questions about the grades assigned. Even older children, who are more aware of grades as such, undoubtedly would be spared much worry and concern if adult conceptions of the meanings of grades were not emphasized so much. Probably such dreams are utopian, yet a number of fallacies are widely accepted as facts, not only among parents but teachers as well, where grades and the common grading system are involved, namely:

1. Anyone can tell from the mark assigned what the student's level of achievement is or what progress he has made.
2. A student can achieve any mark he wishes—if he is willing to make the effort.
3. A student's success in his after-school life compares favorably with his success in school.
4. The student's mark is comparable to the worker's paycheck.
5. The competitive marking system provides a worthwhile and justifiable introduction to competitive adult life.
6. School marks can be used as a means to an end without their becoming thought of by students as ends in themselves.[9]

Research suggests two other concerns: (1) women teachers are likely to give higher marks than men teachers; and (2) both men and women teachers tend to give better grades to girls than to boys and to children who come from the higher socio-economic levels than those who come from lower ones.

Attaching special rewards or awards to successful accomplishments in social studies, either by the teacher or the parent, is also of little positive value in learning and has dubious distinction in developing a

---

[9] William L. Wrinkle, *Improving Marking and Reporting Practices in Elementary and Secondary Schools* (New York: Rinehart and Company, 1947), pp. 36-49.

valid program of reporting to parents. This is simply because such extra signs of achievement are almost consistently given to relatively few students—those who are consistent high achievers. Over a period of time, the pattern which emerges serves only to highlight the non-achiever and to reinforce his feelings of inadequacy; meanwhile, the recipients of such recognition hardly need more attention to their successes.

Although written comments may be added to the report card, several problems are involved when one attempts this in order to extend understanding of the school's grading system. First, rarely is there sufficient time for the teacher to write comprehensively about each child. To overcome this difficulty, it is suggested that, as the end of the formal report period approaches, the teacher select eight or ten children to write about each week rather than attempting to do all at once. Second, space is rarely sufficient. Writing on a sheet of paper and attaching it to the report card reduces some problems in this respect. Third, it is difficult to be original and to find positive things to say. Most of us need not only practice in writing comments about the behavior of others but also experience that will help us to recognize the unique qualities of individuals. To write with insight, and at the same time to record those things which will be of value in the growth of the child, the processes of preparing written comments need time to mature. Beginning teachers, especially, will benefit from the guidance which an older, more mature teacher may be able to provide through reading and criticizing the teacher's comments. Perhaps if this had happened, the teacher who wrote on the first report card that "Johnny is trying," and, on the second one, "Johnny is very trying," would have found another way to communicate with parents if such a procedure had been followed.

Parent Conferencing. Some schools provide for regular conference periods within their formal framework of reporting to parents. It is expected during this time that the teacher will find opportunities to discuss the child's progress in all areas of the curriculum, not just the social studies. This is a formidable and rarely achieved objective. The conferences themselves take a great deal of the teacher's time, in addition to the amount of preparation which must precede each one. At the conference, probably held twice a year, each child's parents are allowed a period of twenty to thirty minutes to talk to the teacher. This situation is likely to be frustrating or even embarrassing for some parents and even for some teachers who find the time inadequate for establishing both rapport and an effective avenue for communicating information about the child. Keeping a file of the child's work in social studies, as well as in other areas, provides something objective to talk about and keeps the conference on the topic of mutual concern to the participants —the child.

Two other problems deserve mention. First, many parents find it difficult to come to school during the hours scheduled for conferences. Therefore, many will not have such a conference unless the teacher meets the parents' time schedule, usually in their homes. Home visitation has always been a valuable means of communicating with parents, particularly before trouble or difficulty in learning is identified by the teacher. Conferences in the home are therefore appropriate, but, of course, the climate of the home, where other family members are likely to be present, alters the manner and the topics which might be discussed. A second problem is that most conferences exclude the child who is, after all, the prime subject of the meeting and the reason the meeting is being held. Why should children, particularly intermediate and upper grade children, be excluded? No good reason has yet been offered. The child looks upon his teacher and his parents as a team, with him, in the whole process of schooling. When all the members discuss problems together, the resulting plans and suggestions for action make more sense to the child and are much more powerful factors in motivating him to learn than when he is excluded from the conference, only to hear from either his parents or his teacher what has been decided about him.

SOME FURTHER SUGGESTIONS

A number of less formal, but no less effective, means for communicating with parents may be utilized. The advantage of such approaches is not restricted to their ability to inform parents of their child's progress and to help parents compare that progress with that of other children; they are particularly important in communicating the goals of the social studies curriculum in its broader sense. The suggestions which follow summarize these approaches. Creative teachers will be able to find many variations on them.

1. Invite parents to observe classroom activities. There are stages in studies when children summarize their experiences. These frequently lend themselves to parent observation. Any situation *for which there has been enough preparation so that no child will be embarrassed* may be appropriate. This does not mean that only formally prepared programs should be open to parents. However,

children should know enough about what will transpire while adults are present so that everyone will be at ease.

2. Share as many classroom products of learning as possible. Many activities in social studies result in artifacts of one kind or another, some of which are more easily shared than others. With a little imagination some things which seem to be classroom-bound may be shared with others. For example, the class textbook can be duplicated in sufficient numbers that each child has a copy to take home; or group projects may be dismantled and individual efforts distributed appropriately.

3. Prepare information sheets for parents which reflect aspects of the study. For example, collect responses of children to a common question (What do they do in city hall? What I want to find out in my study of our community? How we are learning to read maps?), mimeograph them, and send them home. This is a particularly good technique for the primary grades; first names only identify the author. The teacher may also prepare a short statement from time to time which will tell parents something about what the children are studying, what kinds of questions they may expect from them, and what kinds of materials or other resources they may find useful. Or, a suggested list of study trips relating to the year's curriculum of social studies, book lists, television shows or radio programs, and the like, may be prepared and distributed.

4. Use parents as classroom resources. A questionnaire asking parents about special talents they might contribute to the social studies is one way in which one may identify talented persons who can enrich the curriculum itself while opening avenues of communication. Wide ranges of talents can be discovered among the parents of children in every classroom who will make genuine contributions to social studies learnings. In addition, some parents will also be able to fill the role of teacher-aide or assistant teacher from time to time.

5. Make home visitations. Informal conferences *arranged in advance*, preferably not in connection with any particular behavior or learning problem, provide a valuable means of communicating to parents the objectives the teacher hopes to achieve with his class. Through knowing parents, the teacher not only becomes more familiar with the child and is led to understand him better as an

individual, he also learns to know the community in which he is teaching. Through such understanding, he may learn whether his objectives are realistic as he discovers nearby resources which may be valuable in his teaching.

Evaluating Social Studies in the Total School Setting

In the opening chapter of this book, it was noted that the social studies curriculum is in a state of ferment and change. The curriculum reform movement was referred to, and it was pointed out that it promised far-reaching changes which are now being felt in a significant way. Vast quantities of federal money and, increasingly, state moneys are being expended on research and development in the social studies curriculum in behalf of this movement. As Michaelis points out, the expansion appears to be taking place at an accelerating rate; the number of social studies projects increased fivefold in the first three years and doubled in the last two of those three years. We seem only to be at the threshold of research and development in conducting cooperative investigations designed to improve teaching and learning in social studies, yet no one can say for sure where these developments will take us.[10] These and other projects are not merely causing materials to be created which will fit existing patterns of curriculum in social studies, of course. Although some of the research and development projects are designed to strengthen the traditional historic and geographic strands of the social studies, a large proportion of them emphasize the teaching of concepts and of thinking processes derived from fields in the social sciences which have not yet found a very large or permanent niche in most school programs. The outstanding examples of this type are those in economics, anthropology, and sociology. A recent trend in such projects, too, is the multi-disciplined approach in which understandings from several aspects of the social sciences and humanities are being blended together.

Although sound educational practice calls for establishing a comprehensive evaluation program regardless of any other conditions, the curriculum reform movement adds a particular sense of urgency in the social studies. In the future, new procedures, materials, and approaches will be offered as substitutes for present practice. There is no doubt that

[10] John U. Michaelis, "Social Studies," Chapter Eight in *New Curriculum Developments* (Washington, D.C.: Association for Supervision and Curriculum Development, 1965), pp. 68-77.

these teaching and study materials will vary widely in their usefulness in schools. It is likewise true that the social studies curriculum demands improvement. However, how can teachers and principals, supervisors, and others whose job it is to help the teacher teach, resist the pressure to adopt the "new" merely because it is new and, by definition in our culture, "better"? The only alternative would appear to be knowledge of the strengths and weaknesses of the existing program of studies coupled with a critical awareness of the "new" programs which are being made available to the schools.

Evaluation in the broader sense is the concern of the school, of the school district, and of county and state educational units. Since there is a tendency in our culture to rely upon the results of standardized testing, procedures in which assessment of the social studies curriculum will place heavy reliance upon such instruments used with many children will undoubtedly arise. However, the existing standardized tests are generally inadequate to this task. Besides, a comprehensive evaluation program will necessarily rely upon a much broader base than that provided by one type of evaluation instrument. Thus, programs designed to assess the effectiveness of social studies in schools will depend upon a variety of approaches, some more objective in their nature than others. In addition, new instruments will have to be developed to replace the inadequate ones presently available.

There is a reasonable fear among teachers and other professional persons that evaluation programs involving large numbers of children will become unmanageable. There *is* real danger if evaluation programs are limited to the so-called objective-type assessment instrument, administered to all at specific points in the school experience of the children. Historically, the consequences of incessant testing of this type have been to put unnecessary constraints upon the creative teacher and to force conformity in teaching and learning in general. If the curriculum of social studies is an area which by its nature should be diverse and in which different approaches to topics are encouraged, an assessment program with such a heavy emphasis upon conventional evaluation procedures may be even more out of place.

LOOKING AT THE SOCIAL STUDIES CURRICULUM IN THE SCHOOL

Every faculty which systematically reflects upon the nature and effectiveness of the social studies curriculum being provided in the school is participating in an activity that has significant value in the overall evaluation program. Such discussions provide opportunities to share experiences, re-define objectives, and identify problems in teaching—each of which is a basic activity in evaluating the worth of any program. Regular faculty meetings provide one opportunity for focusing on such concerns, but there are other times and places which should not be overlooked. The organizational framework provided by a team teaching arrangement is especially valuable since it brings together those teachers within the larger faculty whose needs and interests are most closely related. In team teaching, three or more teachers jointly plan the overall curriculum for all of the children under their direction. When planning social studies for several classes, decisions must be based on the extent of progress in learning in all of the groups for which the teachers are responsible. Cooperative teaching, or arrangements in which two teachers share planning and teaching responsibilities with a group of children, provides another framework encouraging a broader consideration of teaching problems than is available to the teacher whose principal assignment is with one group of pupils. But even in the classroom where more conventional organizational arrangements are in effect, small groups can be encouraged to consider the effects the curriculum of social studies in its broader aspects is having upon boys and girls.

Several other advantages accrue to faculties which from time to time discuss the consequences of their teaching of social studies. Every faculty will boast one or two teachers who by interest and training have special facility in teaching social studies. Other faculty members can draw upon these teacher-specialists for information and guidance, especially with respect to new developments in their fields of interest, from new interpretations and theories in their subject areas to assessments of new teaching and study materials which may be available. It is through thinking jointly about problems of teaching that other elements important in improving quality in teaching are considered: those of in-service needs, extending knowledge of teaching resources useful in individual classrooms, and in planning more effective programs for communicating progress to parents.

LOOKING AT THE SOCIAL STUDIES CURRICULUM
FROM THE VANTAGE POINT OF THE SCHOOL DISTRICT

The central office or district staff has two important functions in appraising social studies: (1) the development of objectives and purposes for the curriculum which are appropriate for the schools and classrooms of the school district; (2) arranging the means and securing the materials teachers need to become more effective in their work. Usually, school districts adopt a course of study in an attempt to fulfill the first function, that of establishing goals and purposes appropriate to the children and the schools under its jurisdiction. The course of study varies from place to place and is developed in different ways. Some are relatively brief statements whereas others are comprehensive guides not only to objectives for teaching but to methods and materials which the teacher may use in the classroom. In some instances, these guides to teaching are developed by groups of teachers and administrators who work together over an extended period of time. In other cases, the course of study is developed primarily by the administrative and supervisory staff. Especially in smaller school districts, it may have been developed by the county or even by a larger school district elsewhere (although usually within the state) and adopted in whole or in part by the local unit. There are differences of opinion of the value which one type of guide has over another and the worth a course of study has for teachers when it is developed cooperatively by teachers and administrators or by those in the administrative hierarchy alone. However, regardless of its origin, such statements are merely a beginning in helping clarify goals for teaching social studies. Much more work must be done. Without further clarification and thought, the criteria which such statements provide are far too broad to be used as a basis for a detailed analysis of the success a curriculum may have in helping children achieve goals in teaching social studies. Like school district faculties, therefore, it is important for personnel thinking through curriculum problems at the district level to work intensively on defining specific goals of instruction, if adequate criteria are to be developed against which judgments of progress in learning are to be made.

Comparisons of the objectives for social studies agreed upon in the school district with whatever relevant data the central office staff may be able to collect provide the basis upon which action is taken to help teachers in their work with children. There is a body of data dealing with the conditions under which curriculum change may be encouraged, and the reader is referred to references at the end of this chapter for detailed information on this most important topic. However, the course of action open to schools is limited by the type of people upon whom teachers can call for guidance. It is becoming increasingly clear that the kind of specializations, or lack of them, in the social science disciplines represented among school district personnel will govern the manner in which one proceeds. Most supervisors of instruction and administrators can be classified as "generalists." That is, although they have broad understandings of curriculum, are acquainted with sources of specialist help, and are skilled in organizing resources and using them to solve curriculum development problems, they do not have the depth of understanding in a specific content area necessary to provide the teacher with the help he needs. The growing trend in curriculum supervisory work is toward securing people who are educated in depth in the content area for which they will serve as supervisor or consultant and who are specialists in how that area may best be taught. However, few districts as yet employ resource people whose background in subject matter content is specialized enough for the task at hand. Since the social sciences themselves cover a broad range of content, represented singly and in various mutations and combinations in the curriculum teachers are expected to teach, securing specialists within the several areas which are emphasized in the social studies curriculum poses even greater difficulties than in such areas as science or mathematics. For these reasons, it is usually necessary for the school district to locate specialists who can be brought into the school from time to time to serve as consultants to the generalist supervisory staff as well as to the teachers. Clearly the role of the consultant who knows both content and methods of instruction is therefore of growing importance in the schools.

A careful evaluation program yields other evidences which the district staff may act upon to help teachers improve their teaching. In addition to the specialized help of the subject-matter specialist-consultant, for example, nearby universities and their extension divisions may be requested to offer courses that will be of value to the teachers in the district. Research projects may be developed to probe specific questions arising as a consequence of findings from the assessment program, and experimental curricula may be tried. Local instructional materials, found wanting in certain aspects of the social studies, may be prepared; or efforts may be directed toward securing those materials available elsewhere which are in limited supply within the school district. In short, a systematic program of evaluation yields the evidence necessary to reach decisions about the needs of teachers. As teacher's needs are met, teaching procedures become more directly related to fulfilling the goals of the curriculum of social studies.

VIEWING EVALUATION IN SOCIAL STUDIES
FROM A BROADER VANTAGE POINT

It is extremely difficult to devise and carry out a sound evaluation program at educational levels beyond that of the local school district. This is true of all aspects of the curriculum, as illustrated by this newspaper article (only the names have been changed) which appeared in one of our populous states where a systematic and comprehensive testing program has been in effect for a few years.

Increasing Criticism of State Testing

Norlandia's statewide testing program is coming under increasing criticism.

Members of the State Board of Education and the State Department of Education's top research executive voiced critical comments when the results of last year's testing program were announced at the Board's October meeting.

Robert Sorris, board member from Intermedia, said, "We're spending so much money on statewide testing, but all we get are some vague data showing how we're doing now compared to three years ago. I really don't see what value there is in this. It doesn't really show us what we are accomplishing."

Tom Gibson, board member from Yellow Springs, said current testing fails to measure abilities of culturally disadvantaged children. "What we need are new tests."

Frank Bottoms, board member from Mountain City, questioned whether the tests really indicated a pupil's ability to think.

Jack W. Johnson, chief of the Bureau of Educational Research for the State Department of Education, answered Bottoms' request for new tests with the comment that a special test for disadvantaged children would cost at least $500,000 to develop.

Board members questioned the need for annual testing, which they said costs more than $1 million each time the tests are given. Johnson agreed, suggesting testing on an every-three-year or five-year basis. "But," he added, "the Legislature has ordered us to do it annually."

Results of last year's testing program of 5th, 8th and 11th grades revealed that:

Norlandia's pupils scored virtually the same as they did in the previous two years of testing in their mastery of reading, mathematics and English.

Norlandia pupils continue to equal or exceed the national average. Pupils get lower IQ scores as they advance in school. Norlandia fifth graders had an average IQ of 106, it is 102 at the

8th grade and 100—exactly the same as the national norm—at the 11th grade.

Girls continue to perform better than boys.

Manfred Lohmon, board member from Triton, noting that achievement scores have not improved during the past three years, wondered if that meant new school programs were not paying off.

John X. Walden, Board Chairman from Silver Beach, said he thought the influx of 200,000 out-of-state children into Norlandia each year would prevent improvements from showing up on the test scores.

Johnson thought it was still too early for recent improvements in the schools to be reflected in test scores. He predicted, however, that new reading programs should improve test scores next year.

Dr. Mario Salvatori, state superintendent of public instruction, said the state's new compensatory education program and class size cuts should cause a definite improvement in the next few years.

Beginning next year the state will launch a three-year statewide testing program in reading. This will be followed by testing of the "new math."

Salvatori said 2.3 million children have been tested in the program since it was started three years ago.

Virtually all of the major issues in developing a broad-scale assessment program are illustrated in this short article.

1. The cost of testing large numbers of children is very high.

2. When a large population is tested, scores obtained are more nearly likely to mirror national norms since the population itself is virtually a mirror of the population used to establish the norms in the first instance. As a consequence, growth or improvement is likely to be difficult, if not impossible, to discern; and comparisons of scores grow increasingly meaningless as the size of the test sample is increased.

3. Tests which can be administered successfully to large populations of children do not measure the wide range of objectives of the school. Hence, subject-matter and skill ability scores are obtained and the "pupil's ability to think" and other equally worthy objectives left out.

4. When governmental units legislate in the area of curriculum, the consequences are frequently interference with the educative process, let alone causing the costs of education to rise.

5. Tests are not "culture fair" to individuals who do not grow up

in homes that reflect the dominant culture upon which the norms for the test have been developed. Their scores therefore do not properly reflect their capacity to learn or what they know.

6. People use a wide variety of irrelevant arguments to explain away the meanings of test scores obtained from large samples.

7. All tests are truly "tests of reading," perhaps more than of anything else.

8. Wishful thinking will not improve test scores.

9. A great deal of pupil time and effort is being enlisted to test the presumed past effects of the educational program.

When evaluators become engaged in assessing learning involving large numbers of pupils spread over a wide geographic area, the so-called objective test must necessarily be the prime source of data, particularly as long as the testing of large samples is valued. As a consequence, the inherent dangers of social studies objective tests, discussed previously, virtually preclude any valid wide-scale sampling of pupils in this curriculum area. Doubtless, devices for measuring the effectiveness of the social studies curriculum will increasingly be applied over broad portions of the school population, in spite of these dangers. This result can be anticipated because of the growing general concern about the quality of education being provided children in the American culture and the desire being expressed for improvement. The willingness of the American people to spend money to obtain improvement is evidenced in the support being given to state and federal projects designed to achieve this end.

If there is to be a valid assessment of the curriculum of social studies on a broad scale and if, consequently, accurate directions are to be charted with respect to the kinds of improvement which are desirable in this curriculum area, it is obvious that major changes need to be effected in the approach to assessment which is used. Instead of submitting all children at certain points in their educational experience to standardized tests—the present trend in testing generally—social studies will best be evaluated through depth studies conducted among restricted populations selected because they typify important segments of the general school population. Such studies will emphasize a wide variety of techniques of evaluation, utilizing many of the approaches described on the previous pages. Such a change in emphasis in evaluation is desirable not only because of the serious limitations in the standardized test materials currently available in social studies, of course. The very nature of this curriculum area is such that the standard test, even in well developed form, is not capable of assessing adequately the several realms or purposes which social studies are designed to serve. This is a project which must be accomplished if new directions being plotted are to be successfully followed by teachers and pupils. Without doubt, the task is a formidable one.

FOR FURTHER READING

American Council on Education, Commission on Teacher Education, *Helping Teachers Understand Children* (Washington, D.C.: ACE, 1945).

Bloom, Benjamin (ed.), *Taxonomy of Educational Objectives,* Handbook I: *Cognitive Domain* (New York: Longmans, Green & Co., 1956).

Educational Testing Service, *Making the Classroom Test—a guide for teachers* (Princeton, N.J.: Educational Testing Service, 1959).

Evans, K. M., *Sociometry and Education* (London: Routledge and Kegan Paul, 1962).

Fox, Robert, *et al., Diagnosing Classroom Learning Environments* (Chicago: Science Research Associates, Inc., 1966).

Green, John A., *Teacher-made Tests* (New York: Harper & Row, 1963).

Hoffman, Banesh, *The Tyranny of Testing* (New York: Crowell-Collier Publishing Co., 1962).

Jennings, Helen H., *Sociometry in Group Relations, A Work Guide for Teachers* (Washington, D.C.: American Council on Education, 1949).

Kearney, Nolan C., *Elementary School Objectives* (New York: Russell Sage Foundation, 1953).

Krathwohl, David R., Benjamin S. Bloom, and Bertram B. Masia, *Taxonomy of Educational Objectives,* Handbook II: *Affective Domain* (New York: David McKay Co., 1964).

Medley, D. M. and H. E. Mitzel, "Measuring Classroom Behavior by Systematic Observation," in N. L. Gage, *Handbook of Research on Teaching* (Chicago: Rand-McNally Co., 1963).

Melton, Arthur, *Categories of Human Learning* (New York: Academic Press, 1964).

National Council for the Social Studies, *Evaluation in Social Studies,* Thirty-fifth Yearbook (Washington, D.C.: N.C.S.S., 1965).

Thomas, R. Murray, *Judging Student Progress,* 2nd edition (New York: Longmans, Green & Co., 1960).

Wood, D. A., *Test Construction: Development and Interpretation of Achievement Tests* (Columbus, Ohio: Charles E. Merrill Books, 1960).

Wrinkle, William L., *Improving Marking and Reporting Practices in Elementary and Secondary Schools* (New York: Rinehart and Company, 1947).

Appendices

APPENDIX 1
THE CENTRAL PRINCIPLES AND VALUES
OF A FREE SOCIETY*

The search to establish criteria for selecting the most important ideas to be taught through the curriculum of social studies is a never-ending one. The fifteen themes, with an explication of the meaning of each appearing here, is one major effort in this regard. Developed by a committee of the National Council for the Social Studies, these themes are an attempt to provide guidelines for selecting the content which should be taught through the social studies. The final statement of this sort will never be written, of course. These "central principles and values," stated here as societal goals of American democracy, have themselves been under constant revision. However, such a statement is useful in that it provides one source of assistance to the person planning a curriculum of social studies by describing in the broadest strokes long-range purposes authorities believe should be achieved through social science education. One should not assume that there is universal agreement that the school should undertake the achievement of each of these lofty goals. Further, there are controversies as to whether some of the matters included actually can be taught success-fully in the school; there are other institutions and situations in our society that serve as effective means for educating children and youth. The degree to which they should share responsibilities with the school in the attainment of these high aims raises issues that should not be overlooked.

* Dorothy McClure Fraser and Samuel P. McCutchen (eds.), *Social Studies in Transition: Guidelines for Change,* Curriculum Series Number Twelve, National Council for the Social Studies, 1201 Sixteenth Street, N.W., Washington, D.C. 20036, 1965. pp. 11-50. Illustrative concepts and generalizations to be used in the development of each of these themes are suggested in this document. Reprinted by permission.

Theme 1: Recognition of the Dignity and Worth of the Individual

The uniquely distinguishing quality of Western democracy is its insistence that the individual is the all-important unit of society. Following the philosophy of John Locke, it is the individual man who possesses inalienable rights, derived from God and Nature. This in turn springs from the Judaic-Christian and Stoic value of the preciousness of the individual human life. In this system of values, government is an implementing agency, a means to the end of protecting and guaranteeing these rights. The state is therefore not an end in itself, as totalitarianism would maintain. The rights which are inalienable and which democratic governments should sustain, include life with at least a minimum standard of living, liberty compatible with the rights of others, freedom of thought and speech with their concomitant responsibilities, freedom of religion and from an established church. In his relations with other men, the democratic individual should treat them as individuals, avoiding stereotyped thinking, and looking for the essential worth and dignity of each. This is not an uncritical sentimentality, for some men may have little worth and no dignity. When we try to see why persons act as they do, however, we understand them better. We need to know better the interpersonal competences, the skills of getting along with people in individual contacts and in groups. The social ideal is that each man, by his own work and his own effort, may make what he wishes of himself.

Any comprehensive analysis of American history and its society, however, does discover instances of intolerance and prejudice; they illustrate our imperfections and sins. Stereotyped preconceptions are widespread; we generalize in terms of race or religion. Society's evaluation of the individual is based in too large part on what work he does. The nature of the work is the major element in establishing social class, which while more fluid than in some other societies, is distinguishable here.

Theme 2: The Use of Intelligence to Improve Human Living

As one of its essentials, democracy assumes intelligence, actual or potential, in every man. Because of this assumption, democracy promises the freedom of the mind. It offers the free competition of the market place for ideas and values. Freedom of the mind involves the right to knowledge, the freedom to learn, and the freedom to teach. As democracy requires intelligence, so its perfecting depends upon open-mindedness and critical thinking. The processes of inquiry and investigation are involved in the right of the individual to participate in decisions on matters which affect him. If there is to be open competition of ideas and values, there must be a wide dissemination of knowledge and opportunity for independent value-judgments; communication and education become social tools. This means that the schools and the mass media of communication have a direct social responsibility both to the dissemination of knowledge and its use, and to the maintenance of the free market place for ideas and values. As our pattern of living grows more complex, experts are trained in various fields. The intelligent citizen knows how to discern and select the expert—and to avoid the demagogue—but he also comes to know how far to use the expert and at what point he must take the responsibility of making decisions which affect him and/or his democratic society.

Individuals, like institutions, have responsibilities commensurate with their freedoms. With the freedom to learn and teach goes the discipline of scholarship. Academic freedom denies itself subservience to an external and *ex officio* authority. The individual's right to decide carries a responsibility not to permit authoritarian usurpation of decision-making by default. Superstition stands as the enemy of knowledge and has not yet been routed. The mass media do not use their opportunity to teach, and instead cater to a growing appetite for thrills. Emotional bias contests, still successfully, with open-mindedness and known facts; preconceptions remain rooted, though shaken by education. Where ignorance is widespread, greedy and selfish groups can organize irrational, cruel, and selfish programs. The cure may require a study of man himself—the relation of his biological make-up to his drives, desires and ambitions. If groups come naturally to be formed of like-minded folks, the study of greater intelligence in the roles of leadership and followership would be profitable.

Theme 3: Recognition and Understanding of World Interdependence

The most important influence of modern technology has been exerted through modern communication and transportation. Communities which were once isolated and self-contained have been made neighbors to distant continents. Distinctive institutions which have developed because of basic differences in cultures have been brought into contact with each other and into competition. A Moslem world of nomads must deal with complex Western economic organization. Economic activities have changed from self-sufficiency to specialization, as modern industry has come to depend on imports of scarce materials from far places, and as the reciprocal export trade has grown to be essential, markets have become global. Freedom of movement to all parts of the world has become a feasible luxury, verging upon tomorrow's necessity, and if we are not citizens of the world, we are world members. The stage upon which our nation's role is cast has already become the planet so that we be affected by Asians, Africans, Australians, Argentinians, and Austrians.

The world has shrunk but it is more complex and harder to understand. In it can be found, existing now, nearly every stage of social evolution from the savage, through barbarism and feudalism, up to the experimental patterns for day after tomorrow. The intricate machinery of modern industry clanks and roars by the side of ancient handicrafts and both must make adjustments. "Democracy" has taken on a dozen conflicting meanings. No part of the world is more than 24 hours away, no Iron Curtain can completely shut out free ideas; but neither can we quarantine successfully against communicable disease, ignorance, or intolerance. News of happenings on the other side of the globe may reach us almost instantly but our mass media do not necessarily provide us with a representative or objective view. Our best hope for physical health and a free society is to extend technology and education so that poverty and ignorance may be overcome. We greatly need an appreciation of the value of difference. We need to know and accept responsibility for the effects of our actions on other peoples and cultures.

Theme 4: The Understanding of the Major World Cultures and Culture Areas

Western culture developed historically in relative isolation from that of other parts of the world. In an area centering around the Mediterranean Sea, men developed institutions, morals, and values which became the elements of a civilization which is homogeneous in spite of rival nationalities, differing languages, and competing economies. This Western culture migrated to the American continents with the white man and found in the breadth of the Atlantic Ocean a new basis for isolation. The 20th century, however, has seen this isolation destroyed. The technology of transportation and communication has brought non-Western cultures into immediate juxtaposition with Western civilization and the two worlds face the urgent needs to understand each other.

In the 20 years following the end of World War II, the number of free and independent nations has more than doubled. These new nations, in the main in Asia and Africa, were once colonial possessions of European empires and their nationalism is sharp and obvious. Proud of their independence, they tend to emphasize their distinctiveness, their equality, and their differences.

If this shrinking world is to grow in peacefulness, we must make formidable efforts to know these peoples and their cultures.

Theme 5: The Intelligent Uses of the Natural Environment

The world of nature in which man finds himself and of which he is a part has conditioned where and how men live. In the earliest phases of primitive life, the physical environment was the dominant force in determining economic activities, religious practices and beliefs, social and political institutions. Indeed, the considerable differences in these institutions which may be found throughout the world, historically and today, may be accounted for in part by differences in natural environments. Each great stride in technology of land usage and adaptation to physical environment has caused or permitted changes in basic institutions. That adaptation has ranged from complete conformity to natural mandate to developments such as irrigation, improvements in building, and modification of plants and domesticated animals so that the original mandates have been negated. While man satisfies his basic physical needs in a habitat, the improvement in transportation may alter basically the use of that habitat by encouraging specialization for which the region is especially suited rather than by requiring self-sufficiency within regions. In many other ways, men are constantly studying the natural world and are finding ways to use its forces and resources intelligently.

The physical environment still stands unconquered in many important aspects. Floods, droughts, and major storms are threats to physical and economic security; the scanty depth of soil fertility and the falling water table stand as threats to growing populations. Human ingenuity, however, has so far kept ahead in the race with the exhaustion of basic earth resources by ferreting out new deposits and by inventing substitutes. In today's world, men are looking to the stars not only for poetic inspiration, but as new horizons of the natural world which beckon to today's explorers and pioneers.

Theme 6: Vitalization of Our Democracy Through an Intelligent Use of Our Public Educational Facilities

If we would preserve and use our major freedoms, each person must recognize the cause-and-effect connection between his freedoms and the social responsibilities which they entail. In an earlier American society, both responsibilities and freedoms were easier discerned, and participation in social affairs came more naturally for the young. In our present, more complex society where social, political, and economic relationships are more impersonal, society's dependence upon formal education has become greater, and its assignment to the public schools has also become more complex.

The role of education in training for vocations, or of providing the knowledges and skills which vocations require, is generally accepted and and relatively easy to implement. The task of education to make persons more intelligent and skillful in taking their places in society, and in improving that society, is less generally accepted or understood. Democracy demands a higher level of self-discipline and social morality than does an authoritarian government; a responsible social role is harder to perceive and fulfill in a complex urban society than in the simpler groups of the past century. Modern production, distribution, research, and utilization of services are largely group rather than individual functions; today's politics are impersonal, social groups are large, and it is difficult for the individual to find his place in them. The American public school system is unique in providing our society with a major instrument for bringing together all of its people in an attempt to teach individual members how to carry out satisfactorily their responsibilities.

With a rising birth rate and a rapidly increasing population, with an expanding curriculum in the schools as our society wants more subject fields taught, and as modern education learns to use more specialized facilities in the better accomplishment of its assignments, public education grows more expensive. One of our serious lags has been a failure to find appropriate ways of financing these added costs. School taxes still fall predominantly on real property, and wide variations in educational services exist between rich and poor communities and between sections of the nation. Discrimination still curtails the quantity and quality of education of segments of the population. We need to recognize that ignorance and other effects of inadequate education in any part of the country can threaten the whole nation as surely as an infectious disease.

Theme 7: The Intelligent Acceptance, by Individuals and Groups, of Responsibility for Achieving Democratic Social Action

If, as Theme 1 asserts, the individual is the central value of Western democracy, and his rights and their defense are the basic justification of government, certain central responsibilities devolve upon him. The individualism of the 18th and 19th centuries insisted that the welfare of the individual was his own direct responsibility, hence failure was due to lack of ability or effort. The 20th century has become aware of a social responsibility to provide equality of opportunity—hence universal education—and to accept some of the blame for failure—as governmental relief agencies attest. But the 20th century, at its "mid-stride," has not absolved the individual from his concern for his own destiny. He is still the master of his own fate. Indeed, his responsibility has broadened, for we have begun to make explicit his concern for the general welfare. More, perhaps, than ever before, man is becoming his brother's keeper; the competent citizen has an active and positive desire to contribute to the common good. A greater national and global population has complicated this assignment, and there are several levels of government in which intelligent participation is required of the citizen, but greater skills are required for him to relate to the several groups of which he is a part and the effectiveness of his social participation is increasing. Not only is this true for persons, but groups are becoming more alert to their social responsibilities. Political parties, corporations, trade union, trade associations—all furnish examples of such group acceptances.

As with other goals, our grasp has not always attained our reach. Individualism is too often merely acquisitive and selfish. Conserving and planning for the future are set aside for self-gratification and aggrandizement in the present. People who fail rationalize their lack of success and blame everything but themselves. Institutions provide an anonymity for their members so that both the individuals and the group can evade the demands of social conscience. The general welfare becomes formalized and the provision of it institutionalized, and as society undertakes to see that no one starves, the defeated pauperize themselves and accept a parasitic existence. While men's sense of realism leads them to expect and tolerate some inevitable failure, faith leads them to expect a measure of success for themselves and for the majority of their fellow men.

Theme 8: Increasing the Effectiveness of the Family as a Basic Social Institution

Institutions are social inventions designed to implement ideals or to bridge the gap between a less than satisfactory situation and the desired result. In this sense the family achieves the perpetuation of the species, the building of basic values, the maintenance of the culture, and the induction of the young into it. Western culture has deemed the monogamous family its most effective unit. Originally patriarchal in structure, the Western family has been exposed to many dynamic factors. The growing importance of women in industry has given them the basis of economic independence. The disappearance of the artisan crafts has sharply decreased the number of sons who learned their trade from their fathers, and technology's impact on urban living has tended to make chores obsolete. As children have lost the economic value they once represented as wage earners in the early industrial revolution, the size of the family has diminished, and the social value of children, of childhood and youth has changed. Such changes have not all been for the best, and today young people tend to behave like overvalued but displaced persons, since they may no longer learn the skills of participation in primary groups. Medical advances have extended the span of life so that the care of the aged now looms as an ever-larger family responsibility. The family is more than a means of biological reproduction, and more than an economic unit of producing or spending; it is the basic means of giving the security of belonging to persons.

The problems of today's families may not be new but they may require new solutions. Housing is one of these persistent problem areas, as the growth of slums keeps up with new building. Broken homes caused in part by a high divorce rate create new problems in child training and juvenile delinquency, and those problems are accentuated by faulty popular understanding of the newer principles of child psychology.

Theme 9: The Effective Development of Moral and Spiritual Values

Democracy, in the long run, will rise or fall according to the extent that individual citizens live by accepted ethical, moral, and spiritual values. In our interdependent society the individual rights guaranteed in our Constitution become meaningless unless they are exercised in a manner harmonious with the moral and ethical principles that are the foundation of Western democracy. The greater the freedom enjoyed by the individual, the more urgent it is from society's point of view that he hold to these principles. The reverse is equally true: the more fully that all individuals accept and implement these principles, the greater the freedom they may enjoy in society. These principles—such as moral responsibility, devotion to truth, and the brotherhood of man—grow out of the one that is basic to them all: recognition of the dignity and worth of the individual. (Theme 1) Inextricably bound up with these ethical concepts are spiritual values which mankind has ever sought to realize, both as a means of self-development and as an anchor in an uncertain world. Responsibility for helping young people develop moral and spiritual values is shared by the three great institutions of home, church, and school. Working within the context of freedom of religion and separation of church and state, our public schools cannot become involved in theological teachings. However, the school can and must carry its share of responsibilitiy for developing moral and spiritual values. It can focus directly on problems of social ethics. And by teaching about the institution of religion, the school can help young people appreciate the great part that organized religion has played and does play in the growth of an individual's moral and spiritual values.

The need for more effective development of moral and spiritual values is dramatically demonstrated in many of our current problems. These include delinquent acts by juveniles and such things as adult crime, unethical behavior, immorality, and bigoted behavior by adults. The need is tragically demonstrated by the rising tide of mental illness, attributable at least in part to the tensions of our times. By helping young people develop moral and spiritual values, we can help them find security in an insecure, changing world. We cannot give them solutions to problems not yet formulated, but we can help them arrive at moral and spiritual standards against which to evaluate both the problems of the future and the solutions that will be proposed for them.

Theme 10: The Intelligent and Responsible Sharing of Power in Order To Attain Justice

Governments are instituted among men in order to guarantee inalienable natural rights but men have to surrender some alienable freedom in order to have a society. Social order requires law, and laws must be

made, interpreted, and enforced, so the legislative, judicial, and executive functions are defined. The concept of justice implies a government of law, not of man, and its ideal is an equal justice for all. Pure democracy, as practiced in the Greek city-states and in New England town meetings, permitted the citizen to take part directly in government, but the increasing size of political units and their populations has developed the machinery of representation and of federalism. In the latter, the balancing of local and central control has been a varying equation depending upon the efficiency of communication and transportation available at any given time. The ability of the central government to extend its powers to the borders of its realm has varied over the centuries and has seen many machineries of empire, none so effective as that established by the Northwest Ordinance of 1787.

The government of any society at any period has represented some balance of freedom and security for its people, ranging from the Jeffersonian ideal of little government and much freedom, to the dictatorships with some security sometimes; privilege, not equal justice for all, has at times been rampant. Economic specialization and competition have produced elements of hidden government through lobbies and other pressure-tactics on legislation. In the making of laws today, 51 grist mills, dominated by lawyers, grind out laws which often conflict and overlap bewilderingly, to the confusion of the citizen. Every generation relearns anew the hard tasks of democracy.

Theme 11: The Intelligent Utilization of Scarce Resources to Attain the Widest General Well-Being

From earliest times men have confronted a scarcity of material resources, and systems have been established to economize these resources. In the system of private enterprise, economic value is determined by scarcity, utility, and desirability; prices of goods and services vary with these factors. The price mechanism, operating in the marketplace, has served as the regulator of both supply and demand. By another basis of analysis, the consumer by means of dollars as ballots, has become the regulator of the market, determining what shall be produced, the quantity, and how it shall be distributed. Other societies have delegated work to one social class, leaving an upper class whose only social services were governing and fighting, to live upon the efforts of the workers. Industrial technology has both proliferated the specializations of labor and has made work a necessity for all except those few who live upon inherited wealth. As a regulator of the market, the consumer is also the allocator of manpower.

In any system permitting private property, the concentration of wealth and power will be a recurrent problem. In our system today the mammoth corporation and mammoth union, and their normative tendency toward monopoly, become the most serious manifestation of the problem. Growing from the central stem is the phenomenon of the business cycle with its phases of boom and bust. Wealth or power concentrated in private hands can lead to the rapid exploitation of irreplaceable natural resources which from a social point of view should be conserved. The government representing the people, has a role to play in regulating monopoly, in controlling the extreme results of the business cycle, and in the preservation of natural resources.

Theme 12: Achievement of Adequate Horizons of Loyalty

In simple agrarian societies, in the depths of the Dark Ages, the allegiance of men reached no farther than the valley in which they lived. A widening sense of belonging extended the concept of allegiance to the country, then to the duchy, and at last to the kingdom. In the American picture within the past century, men forced to choose between the Nation and State decided: "I am first a Virginian." The concept of loyalty to the national sovereign state is one of the important understandings in today's world. Sovereignty may be simply defined as the power to make the final decision, and its resides where there is no higher authority which can coerce. The past century has seen the extension and intensification of nationalism all over the world. It has witnessed the unification of important nation-states in Europe, the intensification of nationalistic awareness in Europe, Asia, and Africa, and rivalry among nations everywhere.

Nationalism has given its meaning to citizenship, and the functional analysis of that term would define the areas of civic activities and responsibilities at local, state, and national levels. Some pioneering

efforts have been made to catalogue the skills of effective social participation in the various groups of which we are members; more work in
that direction would be profitable. Nationalism has expressed itself at
times in a glorifying, uncritical patriotism which has resulted too often
in isolationism and has been used too much as a cloak to cover reac-
tionary movements and to gild private greed. The social objective
becomes a sane and reasoned patriotism, and an understanding, appreciation, and identification with the various groups of people with whom
we interact, beginning with the family and extending through the local
community, state and nation to all mankind. However, loyalty to wider
groups requires a kind of knowledge and of intellectual grasp which is
not needed for loyalty to the small face-to-face group. It becomes important for the educator to think through the problem of teaching for an
intelligent loyalty to groups which cut across national boundaries, and
a part of this teaching should consist of a thorough exploration of the
question of conflicting loyalties as between nations and interest-groups
which cut across national boundaries.

Theme 13: Cooperation in the Interest of Peace and Welfare

The achievement of nuclear fission may have removed the cork and
released the genie of total destruction. At best it has clarified the alternatives in international relations so that nations must endeavor earnestly
to resolve differences or run the risk of human annihilation. Cooperation
is the corollary of such interdependence. At an earlier and perhaps
simpler time, aggressors could expect that initiative and their superior
strength would bring them gains greater than their losses. Balance of
power diplomacy developed to oppose these aggressors. Its techniques
were the discovery of common dangers, of common interests, and the
need for common action. The cooperation they achieved was partial and
short-lived but the precedent is important. In other instances of danger
and crisis, whether of war or disasters of nature, people have shown
that they can subordinate selfish interests and act for the common good.

Machinery of cooperation has developed in labor-management relations and instead of strike and lock-out, riot and police rule, there has
been an increase in conference and conciliation, mediation and arbitra-
tion, seeking a consensus. Unfortunately we stand today far from the
goal. The bargaining table, whether diplomatic or industrial, finds the
pride and prestige of the individuals who are bargaining too often the
operating values, instead of the greatest good for the greatest number.

The earlier polite language of conciliation, insincere though it may have been, has been discarded for the language of conflict. The race for superiority in atomic weapons continues, and when the gun of final destruction is loaded, some fool may pull the trigger.

Theme 14: Achieving a Balance Between Social Stability and Social Change

The bicameral legislature has often been justified because it balanced the rashness and urge to change of the popular house with conservatism and power to delay of the Senate or Lords. Those two basic factors, progress and stability, exist and operate in many social institutions. The dynamics of modern society proposes and urges change; social conservatism resists and controls the degree of modification. When both forces operate together within an institution, orderly progress can result; when conservative forces are dominant, the institution or the society may become static or stagnant. At times the critics of the existing order and the innovators take control and fundamental and revolutionary changes come about.

The rate of modification among institutions in a society may vary markedly. Technological developments have made basic and rapid changes in our economic institutions, but conservative forces have slowed the rate of change of the political and social institutions. The resultant "cultural lag" has caused strains and maladjustments. For example, governmental machinery to control the new situations created by changes in transportation has not kept pace with crime or big business or congestion. However, in spite of sensational and visible changes in some phases of living, basic institutions stay on; tradition holds things in place. Our society reaches its decisions, either frontally or obliquely, about values which at one time were sharply controversial, and the problems then change to those of implementation. Perhaps the most important function of history is to record the conserving and maintaining, not merely the changing.

Theme 15: Widening and Deepening the Ability To Live More Richly

While man is a social being with obligations to and rewards from the groups of which he is a part, he is also an individual. A goal of living and of education, then, should be the multiplication of his sources of enrichment and the enhancement of his powers of enjoyment. Generally the arts, both fine and practical, are the avenues by which perceptions and sensitivities are increased, and the improvement of both appreciation and creative powers should be sought. But in the humanistic scheme of values, any learning, any discipline, can contribute to personal enrichment. The humanist climbs a mountain because it is there; he learns for the joy of learning and for the sense of victory over ignorance; he is not restricted to the horizons of the useful and the applicable. Most persons, of course, combine the humanist and the utilitarian and are potentially both the scientist and the engineer. Esthetics and emotions, therefore, can be used to make both the humanist and the humanitarian. In our dominant values, work becomes both a means and the end of personal enrichment.

Much still needs to be done to improve the constructive use of leisure and to improve mass tastes. In an earlier day, leisure and good taste belonged exclusively to the aristocratic leisure classes. In an age of mass media, the patron of the arts is the common man. The quality of culture in a democratic society depends upon how the great mass of the people use their leisure time. Mass media without education may lead to vulgarity and cultural mediocrity; with education the common man may build a culture equal in taste to the historical aristocracies and more varied in its patterns, because of the new contributions of many people from many lands.

A challenge for any democratic society is to find some means for preserving individual choice in an age of mass media which could lead to cultural conformity. One aspect of this problem is to help each person develop individual tastes and preferences, and to encourage like-minded groups of individuals to insist upon their share of the time and services of the mass-oriented cultural institutions.

APPENDIX 2
BASIC IDEAS OR CONCEPTS
FROM THE SOCIAL SCIENCES*

The recent past has been characterized by attempts to identify the major concepts and generalizations in the social sciences. It is being suggested that such lists of ideas provide a base point for selecting subject matter content in the classroom. An important state-wide effort in this regard is represented by the material following. Social scientists were asked to suggest to the state curriculum commission the central concepts and generalizations of their disciplines. The listing here is the result of their deliberations.

To invest generalizations with meaning, one must necessarily possess understandings of the concepts and facts undergirding them. Such a list is therefore useful not only in helping the teacher identify the broad dimensions of those disciplines with which he is familiar, it also is useful in pointing out to him those aspects of the social sciences where his understandings are weak and in need of strengthening.

Each of the eight social sciences contributes certain basic ideas or concepts to the social studies program. These are broad, central generalizations that should become progressively more meaningful, even though they are not specifically introduced, through organized learning experiences at the various grade levels.

To prepare the generalizations which are presented on the following pages, groups of social scientists throughout the state were asked to review the content of their particular discipline and to assess its contributions to competent citizenship in our modern, complex society. The findings of these groups were then studied and analyzed by educators and other interested citizens on a statewide basis. As the generalizations were developed, "goals of understanding" were formulated. These were appropriate for application to adults rather than to a particular grade. Therefore, the curriculum planner must decide what subgeneralizations, concepts, and factual information are appropriate for youth in each of the grades that comprise the elementary and secondary school programs.

---

* California State Department of Education, *Social Studies Framework for the Public Schools of California,* Part III, Prepared by the State Curriculum Commission. Sacramento, California: California State Department of Education, June, 1962, pp. 89-109. Reprinted by permission.

These subdivisions then become reference points for planning and organizing instruction and for preparing courses of study and other classroom materials. The reference points need to be cumulative so that understanding in the social studies is moved in the direction indicated by the generalizations.

Although these goals for understanding will be invaluable in guiding school district personnel in the selection of specific units of instruction, in determining learnings to be stressed, and in appraising pupil progress, they must necessarily be supplemented by understanding applicable only to the local community.

It is also recognized that the content of the social studies does not come exclusively from eight social studies. When children and youth study topics related to this aspect of the curriculum, they utilize information from additional fields. Such is particularly the case in the elementary school, where pupils sometimes need information about the natural and physical sciences, art, music, literature, health, and safety to comprehend the significance of what they are studying. Although a setting for the practical application of information from these fields is thus established in a way that enhances learning in the social studies, the fields also receive attention in other parts of the instructional program.

The social studies simply provide an opportunity to bring the contributions of related social disciplines into a meaningful context for children and youth. In so doing, they serve as an essential and central aspect of general education and as a background for successful living in our American society. Contributions of the eight social sciences, however, do more than indicate the basic sociocivic learnings that relate to general education. In addition, they reflect persistent contemporary problems. Influences of general trends in our society—such as population growth, increased mobility of the population, and changes in the pattern of family living—can be noted in a number of the ideas or concepts.

These social science generalizations should not be taught but should emerge as conceptualizations from what has been studied. Acquiring of new information is essentially training, but the discussion and relation of new facts to other knowledge from which generalizations may be drawn constitute education.

Curriculum specialists know that pupils can generalize only to the extent that the breadth and depth of their knowledge will permit and that limitations in this process cannot be overcome by pupils through learning to verbalize a mass of words that have little or no meaning to them. Children and youth acquire meaning only from a broad base of experience and learn to generalize at ever higher levels only through skillful guidance from informed teachers.

Generalizations from Geography

OVERVIEW

Geography deals with areal arrangement. Its principal orientation is toward the earth's surface and the varying distributional patterns created by nature and man. It seeks to define the earth's physical and cultural features, to show their distribution, to make them understandable by explaining the basic forces or factors that affect them, and to present the more fundamental of their interrelationships. Because of its dual nature, geography is both a natural and a social science and, as such, helps to integrate both. As part of its educational responsibility, geography seeks to help pupils become earth-minded (even universe-minded) and spatially oriented, to build a useful mental image of the world and its parts, and to develop the pupils' sense of space in a manner similar to the way in which history seeks to develop their sense of time.

PHYSICAL GEOGRAPHY

It is the task of physical geography to describe and explain the distribution of surface features and to define natural regions that are caused by and continuously affected by forces and processes in nature.

1. Life on the earth is influenced by the earth's (global) shape, its size, and its set of motions.
2. The shape of the earth causes the unequal distribution of sunlight, or energy, from the sun, which in turn influences the circulation of the atmosphere and causes differences in climate and natural vegetation.
3. Earth movements of rotation and revolution are basic to understanding climate and time: rotation of the earth on its axis is a measure of time and causes night and day; seasons are caused by a combination of revolution, inclination, and parallelism of the earth's axis.
4. Earth movements and earth-sun-moon relationships also offer bases for the understanding of the geography of outer space.

5. Weather, climate, and earth crustal movements affect the surface of the earth and cause regional differences in landforms, minerals, drainage, soils, and natural vegetation.

6. Climate is determined by sunlight, temperature, humidity, precipitation, atmospheric pressure, winds, unequal rates of heating and cooling of land and water surfaces, irregular shape and distribution of land and sea, ocean currents, and mountain systems.

7. Because of various combinations of heat and moisture and the distributions of these two factors, the earth is divided into climatic regions, consisting of tropical, middle latitude, polar, and dry lands; each of these types has several subtypes. These classifications are a means of organizing information about the earth.

8. The crust of the earth consists of various types of rocks that influence topography. It contains useful mineral deposits and is the parent material of soils.

9. Soil, water, solar energy, and air are the natural resources most indispensible to man. The great source of all activity and life on earth is heat from the sun.

10. Soil and vegetation may be thought of as the cover over the non-living surface configuration. This cover provides the landscape with character and color.

11. Major climatic regions coincide approximately with major vegetation zones because vegetation is related to climatic conditions. Natural vegetation is a great resource utilized by man.

12. Soils are altered by nature and man. Nature combines the action of climate, vegetation, and animals on parent materials to produce regional variations in soils.

13. The physical elements of the earth are a unit, and no part can be understood fully except in terms of its relationship to the whole.

CULTURAL GEOGRAPHY

Cultural geography is concerned with the distribution of man and his activities on the earth's surface. Since man's occupation of an area is affected by the physical environment, cultural geography is also concerned with the adjustments that he must make to this environment. The nature of these adjustments depends upon man's stage of technology and on the controls of social behavior and nature.

Cultural geography involves not only population distribution but also settlement patterns; land-use activities; ethnic, linguistic, and religious characteristics; and features of political organization. Since cultural geographers are interested in the activities of people in relation to their spatial organization, they seek to interpret the various world, regional, and local patterns of economic, social, and political behavior.

1. Man constantly seeks to satisfy his need for food, clothing, and shelter and his other wants; in so doing, he attempts to adapt, shape, utilize, and exploit the earth. Some aspects of the natural environment, however, are not significantly altered or utilized by man.

2. The significance of the physical features of the earth is determined by man living in his environment. The natural environment may set the broad limits of economic life within a region, but it is man who determines its specific character within the limits of his culture.

3. To exist, man must utilize natural resources. Groups develop ways of adjusting to and controlling the environment in which they exist. Human change, and even the whole structure of civilization, may depend upon the nature and extent of man's supply of energy and his ability to utilize and control it.

4. The extent of man's utilization of natural resources is related to his desires and to his level of technology.

5. The processes of production, exchange, distribution, and consumption of goods have a geographic orientation and vary in part with geographic influences. The nature of the organization of economic processes within an area (spatial organization) results from the kinds of resources, the stage of technology, and the sociopolitical attitudes of the population.

6. The location of production is controlled by the factors of land (natural resources of the physical environment), labor, and capital. In most cases, the attainment of maximum efficiency, as motivated by competition for the factors of production, determines location of production. In some cases, the location is determined by political or other social controls rather than by economic efficiency.

7. Land is less mobile than the other basic factors of labor and capital and has a dominant role in determining the location of

production. Since people, in general, prefer to live near their work, this location becomes significant in the distribution of the population.

8. The kinds of climate, soil, native vegetation and animals, and minerals influence the nature and extent of man's achievements within each region. The amount and the kind of food needed for health vary with climatic conditions and man's technology.

9. Factors of production, including technology, are subject to change. Therefore, geography is concerned with changing patterns of land use.

10. Understanding the location of political or other social institutions is contingent upon a knowledge of the economy of an area. Since understanding of this economy depends in part upon a knowledge of the natural environment, it follows that political and social institutions are related to this environment.

11. The sequence of human activities and culture patterns is related to geographic location and accessibility and to the particular time in which human beings live. People in different stages of civilization react differently to similar environments.

12. Man and animals may, by their activities, upset the balance of nature. Man is different, however, in that he may do something— such as undertake conservation—to regain the balance.

13. Competition for the acquisition of the earth's natural resources sometimes results in political strife, and even in war.

14. Political cooperation and strife between nations are related to their geographic locations.

SUMMARY

Geography encompasses more than a description of the earth's surface. Its prime concern in the social studies is the way in which man utilizes the raw materials and resources of his natural environment. The study of geography, therefore, has a major role in the development of civic competence. The problems of mankind cannot be fully understood or successfully solved without a knowledge of the geographic factors involved. Man's geographic distribution and his utilization of the resources of nature are basic to understanding many contemporary problems that have local, regional, and international implications. Geography is also closely related to all the social, biological, and physical sciences.

Generalizations from History

OVERVIEW

History is the record of what has happened to man. It is the effort to grasp the whole of human experience within a chronological framework. History is interpretive, imaginative, and normative. It is the script of human drama and also the drama.

Because of the interpretive role of history, the principal ideas—or major generalizations relative to it—necessarily involve other social sciences. The social sciences deal with man and his experience, but history alone presents a chronology of human experience.

The past furnishes a base from which to understand the present and from which to project into the future. The maturity of men and women is built upon reflections from the past. We are thus continuously indebted to the past and to the historical record of human activities.

CHRONOLOGY, SEQUENCE, AND CHANGE IN HISTORY

1. Space and time form a framework within which all events can be placed. All of man's experience has occurred within a space and time framework; however, the same relationship does not necessarily apply to events as they have occurred in various parts of the world.

2. Man's struggle for freedom and human dignity has occupied a relatively brief period of time, as compared with the total span of man's existence.

3. The past influences the present, and the present cannot be adequately understood without knowledge of the past. Life goes on against the intricate tapestry of the past. History does not repeat itself, but events tend to occur in some sort of sequence. Events in nature usually occur uniformly. Human events are predictable, but to a lesser extent.

4. History contributes much to man's preparation for his social and political life. It is possible to derive basic principles and implications for thought and action in contemporary affairs from the historical backgrounds of our society.

5. Change has been a universal condition of human society. Change and progress are, however, not necessarily synonymous. Many civilizations have risen and fallen, but only some have contributed

greatly to our present civilizations. The tempo of change has increased markedly in the recent past.

MAIN TENDENCIES IN THE GROWTH OF CIVILIZATIONS

1. History reveals a degree of homogeneity in mankind during all periods of recorded time. Environments in many places and regions have been altered physically, but human motives or drives within them have remained nearly the same.

2. Brotherhood, in the sense of peaceful cooperation, is one of man's worthiest and earliest historical concepts. Conflict and hostility are also within man's experience. Men of all races have many basic physical similarities. Geographical variations and time variations in man's environments help explain his past actions and continue to influence his behavior in the present.

3. In the contemporary world, historical events may have a significance that reaches far beyond the limits of a state or province or the place of their origin. The worldwide implications of such events must be understood.

4. Although certain historical customs and institutions have characterized individual civilizations or nations in the past, men in every age and place have made use of basic social functions in adjusting themselves to their world.

5. Past and present civilizations represent our cultural heritage. The races, cultures, and civilizations in most areas of the world and of most historical periods, beginning with the dawn of recorded history, have made some contributions to the growth of our present civilizations.

6. Interdependence has been a constant and important factor in human relationships everywhere.

HISTORICAL INTERPRETATION

1. Such factors as the passing of time and advances in the techniques of scholarship have brought new perspectives and understandings of history. New interests and controversies of our own day and past centuries have also marked effects on the interpretation of events and ideas. Use of the historical method in fact finding and problem solving has made possible the discovery and use of new data and perspectives.

2. Human motives, drives, and ideas of many kinds, whether correct

or incorrect in terms of historical progress and human improvements, have markedly influenced local, national, and international actions. The interpretation of these motives is one of the most critical tasks of historical analysis.

3. There are various traditional and contemporary interpretations of historical processes and movements of a national and international scope that may illuminate the study of history. Such historical processes are sometimes referred to by such terms as action and reaction, rise and fall, and growth and decline as they are applied to civilizations, nations, and empires.

4. The efforts of people, great material achievements, and important ideas are delineated, assessed, interpreted, and placed in perspective by historians.

5. History demonstrates that mankind has been motivated by morals and ideals and by material wants and needs. The demand for moral standards has persisted throughout man's experience. The ideals of men in all parts of the world and in all ages have been rooted in the value systems of large and small groups.

SUMMARY

History is especially responsible for pointing up and interpreting the similarities and differences within man's experience. It serves as a yardstick of evaluation for the actions, institutions, and events of men. History, together with other of the social sciences, should show the great basic and universal values that comprise man's efforts to reach the worthiest of human goals. The study of history thus provides contemporary man with a basis for intelligent action now and in the future.

Generalizations from Political Science

OVERVIEW

Political science is the study of government—of the theory and practice of man in organizing and controlling the power needed to formulate public policy and administer the public services. It is divided into several branches.

Political theory is that branch which seeks to formulate principles, conclusions, and valid generalizations concerning the state and man's many relationships to it. The political theorist attempts to synthesize and integrate existing knowledge about the state, utilizing data and analyses of specialists both within and outside the social sciences.

Political scientists have been concerned with such basic questions as the origin of the state; the purpose or justification of the state; the nature of law, justice, and liberty; where the authority of the state should be reposed (i.e., in a monarch, an aristocracy, the whole people, a dictator, an elite, the proletariat); and, especially in the twentieth century, how far the authority of the state should extend into the realms of business, social life, and individual conduct.

Other branches of political science are *public law,* which embraces constitutional law, international law, administrative law, and criminal law; *politics,* which encompass the institutions, processes, and methods of governing; *public administration,* which deals with the theory and practice of the executive branch of government; *national, state, and local government,* which includes study of the Constitution and the functions and services of government; *comparative government,* which includes comparisons of institutional phenomena and of political behavior and political values of foreign political systems; and *international relations,* which encompasses diplomacy, international law, economic policies, ideological competition and propaganda, military power, and international organization.

THE STATE OR GOVERNMENT

1. Throughout history, the peoples of the world have experimented with a wide variety of governmental forms. While Americans are engaged with their own governmental problems, the peoples of all other countries are endeavoring to resolve their problems of government.

2. Government is but one of the institutions serving society. The state or government is essential to civilization, and yet many human needs can best be met by the home, the school, the church, the press, and private business.

3. Two essential functions of government are to serve and to regulate in the public interest. The ultimate responsibilities of government are divided into five major categories: (a) external security; (b) internal order; (c) justice; (d) services essential to the general welfare; and, under democracy, (e) freedom. Perhaps the clearest indication of the importance of the state in the twentieth century lies in the fact that, although it has exclusive responsibility in none of these fields, it has residual responsibility in all.

4. In a democracy, government is the servant of the people; people are not the servants of government. Government is by right an institution made by man for man. The source of authority resides in the people.

5. It is the business of government to do for the people what they cannot do or what they cannot do as well for themselves. Philosophies of government range from laissez-faire, in which a minimum of services is provided, to totalitarian collectivism, in which every phase of the individual's life is dictated for him. Government is indispensable to assure internal order and external security. Since order is indispensable if freedom is to have any genuine meaning —indeed, if life itself is to be tolerable—its establishment and maintenance are prime tasks of government.

6. No one yardstick is adequate for comparing different political systems. It is particularly important for citizens in a free society to understand the ideas and techniques characteristic of authoritarian political systems and to develop attitudes that will permit them to cope objectively with problems arising from the real or potential hostility of those systems.

7. When government is organized, it is essential that leaders be authorized power with which to act and that they be held responsible for its wise use.

8. Government cannot be effective unless it has the flexibility to cope with new conditions. Adaptation, social invention, and gradual change provide the best safeguards against political revolution. To fulfill its role in a democracy, government must be adaptable. The Constitution of the United States provides for flexibility to meet changing conditions.

9. Political parties and special interest groups perform certain necessary services in the governing process. The political parties of this country and of every free nation were formed so that citizens having common beliefs and interests may seek to mold basic policies and choose government leaders. Parties and interest groups both have a check-and-balance and force-and-counterforce role, which leads to evolutionary changes and growth. The politician generates interest and musters popular or legislative support necessary for formal approval or adoption of policy.

10. All nations in the modern world are part of a global, interdependent system of economic, social, cultural, and political life. The

evolution of the international law of war has been paralleled by the effort to develop an international law of peace and by the attempt to devise and build international political institutions and organizations capable of making such laws effective. Consideration for the security and welfare of the people of other nations remains the mark of the civilized man and has now become the price of national survival as well.

DEMOCRACY

1. Democracy implies a way of life as well as a form of government.
2. Democracy is based on certain fundamental assumptions. Among these are the integrity of man, the dignity of the individual, equality of opportunity, man's rationality, man's morality, man's practicality, and man's ability to govern himself and to solve his problems cooperatively.
3. Man develops his fullest potential in a climate of freedom. Much of the progress of civilization can be traced to man's search for a larger measure of freedom. For the truly civilized man, no amount of material wealth can ever compensate for lack of freedom. A society benefits when its individual members are relatively free to develop their creative talents.
4. Human beings are creatures of self-interest. For democracy to function, however, self-interest must be curbed to a degree in favor of public interest.
5. A chief goal of democracy is the preservation and extension of human freedoms. Freedom is unworkable, however, unless it is balanced by corresponding responsibility. Freedom appears to range from legal to political freedom, and from political to genuine economic and social freedom.
6. Civil liberty—freedom of thought, speech, press, worship, petition, and association—constitutes the core of freedom. With civil liberty, all other kinds of freedom become possible; without it, none of them can have any reality.
7. Basic to democracy is belief in progress. A free society is hospitable to new ideas and to change and encourages the unfettered search for truth. Peaceful action rather than violence is one of its hallmarks.
8. Certain factors are necessary for democracy to succeed and survive. These include (a) an educated citizenry; (b) a common

concern for human freedom; (c) communication and mobility; (d) a degree of economic security; (e) a spirit of compromise and mutual trust; (f) respect for the rights of minority groups and the loyal opposition; (g) moral and spiritual values; and (h) participation by the citizen in government at all levels.

9. Opportunity for the individual to choose his type of occupation voluntarily is a concept that has flourished under democratic philosophy and practice and the capitalistic system.

CITIZENSHIP

1. The well-being of the state is dependent upon the education of its citizens.
2. A citizen can do his part in making democracy work only if he is sufficiently informed to think intelligently on the issue of the day. Information can best be provided by free and responsible mass media of communication.
3. The citizen has civic responsibilities as well as rights.
4. A democratic society depends on citizens who are intellectually and morally fit to conduct their government. Civic responsibility and moral courage are balanced wheels in a democracy. To fulfill their obligations of citizenship, individuals must be aware of the quality of service that must be performed by the government; they must also be willing to participate actively in community affairs. The capable citizen should evaluate objectively information received through mass media of communication in making political choices.

SUMMARY

Political science helps individuals to become more keenly aware of their opportunities and obligations as citizens. It provides perspective for the study of such current problems as recruitment of personnel for civilian and military services, costs of defense and other public services, raising of revenues to underwrite these costs, and achievement of security. To be a capable and conscientious citizen, the individual needs (1) to understand the structure and function of government; and (2) to develop citizenship skills. These include knowing how to read newspapers, speak in public, and conduct meetings; and how to be an action-minded participant in the affairs of the school, community, state, nation, and world.

Generalizations from Economics

OVERVIEW

Economics is concerned with analyzing information, issues, and public policies connected with the production, distribution, and consumption of wealth and income. This discipline begins with the study of scarcity and unlimited wants and proceeds through specialized production, interdependence, exchange, markets, prices, costs, and public policy. Emphasized are economic stability and growth; the allocation of resources to their most important uses; and equitable distribution of income; and, in our economy, a wide range of economic freedom for workers to choose their jobs, consumers to choose goods, and investors and entrepreneurs to own property and choose their investments.

All problems that may properly be termed "economic" must be considered in these categories whether they originate in capitalist, socialist, fascist, or communist countries. Economic theory has been defined as "a method rather than a doctrine, an apparatus of the mind, a technique of thinking which helps its possessor to draw correct conclusions." The study of economics is thus important to the individual and society for both the knowledge which it provides and the thinking processes which it requires. Valid information about our economy and the ability to use it effectively are indispensable to effective citizenship in assessing many of the most pressing public issues of the day.

Consideration of specialized areas in economics must be based firmly on this approach. Included in economics are the study of money and banking, business cycles, public finance and taxation, industrial organization and public policies toward business, labor-management relations, accounting, finance, statistics, consumer economics, international trade and finance, economic growth and development, and comparative economic systems.

ECONOMIC ENDS AND MEANS

1. Economic welfare is a goal in most, if not all, modern societies. It is believed that it is beneficial for people to have more rather than fewer economic goods and that poverty *per se* is not desirable. Many economists believe that economic welfare is an important quality of society; that economic progress makes the other qualities of society more readily obtainable; and that the creative arts—such as painting, music, and literature—flourish more fully in a highly productive economy.

2. Productive resources are scarce, and human wants are unlimited. Since man cannot satisfy all of his desires for material goods, he must make choices. The essence of "economy" lies in making wise decisions with regard to such matters as saving, spending, purposes of expenditures, kinds of investments, and types of jobs to be undertaken. The "real cost" of any end product is thus the alternatives sacrificed in producing it. This is known as the "opportunity cost principle."

THE GROSS NATIONAL PRODUCT—A MEASURMENT OF ECONOMIC ACHIEVEMENT

1. The size of the Gross National Product (consisting of the total value of all economic goods—products and services—produced annually) depends upon many conditions. Among these are (a) the extent and richness of natural resources; (b) the number, quality, and motivation of the working population; (c) the amount and nature of capital goods (factories, houses, bridges, roads, machines and tools of all kinds) created through saving and investment; (d) the effectiveness of investors and entrepreneurs in organizing and developing productive activity; (e) the existence of a large free-trade area, in which the free flow of goods permits each locality to specialize in the production of those goods in which it has the greatest relative advantage and to obtain other goods by trade (the "principle of comparative advantage"); and (f) the presence of political institutions that are conductive to and encourage creative and productive effort on the part of all people. To maintain the conditions upon which high productivity (and consequently our high standard of living) depend, conservation must be practiced.

2. The size of both the GNP and population greatly influences economic welfare. This welfare depends upon the balance between population growth and depletion of resources and upon improvements in production techniques and expansion of capital goods. When population growth exceeds the capacity of the land and capital goods, output per worker declines unless there are compensating improvements in technology. This principle is known as the "law of diminishing returns."

3. The full use of productive facilities directly influences economic welfare. Fluctuations tend to be more severe in industrially

advanced nations than in those that are primitive. In the former, specialization and complexity are vastly greater, shifts in demand and changes in techniques are more frequent, a larger proportion of resources are devoted to the production of durable consumer and producer goods, and substantial changes in the volume of investment expenditures are dependent upon the people's desire to save a fairly stable part of their incomes.

4. Government can contribute to the maintenance of high-level production and employment, rapid economic growth and progress, and the stability of the dollar by proper use of its authority through sound fiscal and debt-management policies.

5. High per-capita income is the result of high productivity of labor. The total income of a society is its total output of goods. Therefore, if American labor is ten times as productive as foreign labor, American wages can be ten times as high without curtailing the ability of American industry to sell its products in world markets. High wages thus rest on high productivity, not on tariffs.

THE COMPOSITION OF INCOME—THE ALLOCATION OF RESOURCES

1. Basic to sound economic organization is securing effective cooperation among specialized producers. The type of economic system determines how much of each commodity and service is to be produced and how each resource unit is to be allocated to its most important use.

2. In a competitive, private-enterprise system, prices indicate the relative value of goods and services. On the one hand these prices reflect the willingness of buyers to buy and sellers to sell; and, on the other hand, they influence the decisions of both consumers and producers. A relatively high price tends to restrict present consumption and to stimulate production of a larger supply in the future. A relatively low price has the reverse effect. Raising or lowering a competitive price by artificial means, whether by private monopoly or governmental authority, is likely to aggravate the situation that the action is designed to alleviate, unless the change in price is accompanied by the power to affect directly future demand or supply in an appropriate manner.

3. A market price system works best when both buyers and sellers are highly competitive, well informed, and able and disposed to act in accordance with the information available (competition—

knowledge—mobility). Thus, a free-enterprise system is supported and strengthened by government action designed to keep markets free (antitrust policy), buyers and sellers informed (prohibition of false advertising and laws against misrepresentation), and the system mobile. At the minimum, government must maintain order and justice, protect property, enforce contracts, and provide a sound money system in some fields if free enterprise is to be effective.

4. Because of special conditions in such fields as public utilities, government has been authorized to regulate prices to assure that they are not discriminatory. The quality of service rendered by electric power, gas, and telephone companies has also been regulated. In some cases, the government has directly undertaken the provision of services such as those required in the operation of post offices and distribution of the water supply.

5. There are many ways to organize economic activity. Most national economies in the world today, though differing in fundamental respects, make considerable use of the price system to ration goods, providing incentives for productive services, and allocate resources to their best uses. A free society provides opportunity and incentives for the individual to invest what he owns in an effort to make a profit.

THE DISTRIBUTION OF INCOME

1. In a competitive system, the prices paid for productive services also serve to divide the total output of goods among those responsible for their production. Thus, the wages of workers, the dividends of investors, and the rents of landlords all provide the incomes that determine the size of each individual's claim to actual goods and services.

2. In a competitive market, each productive agent tends to receive as income a sum equal to the value of his productive contribution to society. The greater the demand of the public for the particular service or product and the smaller the supply, the larger is the income. Those possessing the greatest skills demanded by the public tend to receive the highest incomes. Inequality in the distribution of income thus is the result of unequal payments for services and of unequal ownership of property. At the same time, the opportunity to acquire a larger income furnishes an incentive

to develop individual abilities, to save and acquire property, and to use resources most efficiently and productively.

3. Imperfections in competition create important public problems. The power of monopoly, whether exercised by buyers or sellers, management or labor, or private groups sometimes supported by government, usually distorts the allocation of resources and distribution of income.

4. The way to improve the standard of living for all the people is to increase productivity. Such has been the tremendous economic achievement in the United States. Industrial output per man-hour has increased six times since about 1850. Half of this gain has been realized in shorter hours (and more leisure) and half in more goods. Thus, the average length of the work week has been reduced 50 percent and, at the same time, real income per capita has tripled. The grinding poverty in which a large part of the world's population lives today is caused by the sheer unproductivity of human labor, not by deficiency in purchasing power or imperfection in the distribution of income.

SUMMARY

Since the world's resources are insufficient to satisfy all wants, the study of economics, both theoretical and applied, is essential to the general education of all people. The individual makes economic decisions throughout his life. Through voting and other types of community participation, he helps to decide problems involving the economic welfare of all people.

Generalizations from Anthropology

OVERVIEW

Anthropology is the comparative study of man. It is concerned with his evolution and present characteristic as a biological form; with his various modes of organizing group life; and with his utilization of the natural environment. Thus, anthropology is a social science with a special relationship to the biological sciences.

Specialists in the field include physical anthropologists; anthropological linguists, who study the numerous unwritten languages of the world; archeologists who seek to understand the story of prehistoric man by unearthing and studying remains of his activities; and cultural anthropologists, who investigate the cultures and modes of organization of extant societies to reconstruct prehistoric life and formulate generalizations about the essential characteristics of human social life.

Although anthropology may be primarily identified with the study of preliterate societies, many modern anthropologists devote all or part of their research to the study of major civilizations.

Anthropology has perhaps made its greatest contribution to social science by developing the concept of culture as its central theme, which has illuminated all the disciplines concerned with the study of human group life. Research method in anthropology is notable for its emphasis on long-term intimate observation and participation in the day-to-day life of the society under study.

DEVELOPMENT THROUGH BIOLOGICAL EVOLUTION

1. Many persons believe that man has developed his present form through the same processes of biological evolution by which animals have developed, and that the process of man's evolution has involved approximately one and one-half billion years. During this period, it is believed that a multitude of plant and animal forms have also evolved.

2. Physical anthropologists generally believe that man's separate stem of evolution spans several million years; however, in the scale of biological time man is a relatively new phenomenon.

3. Fossil remains of early man illustrate the ultimate evolution of distinctively human characteristics. The most important include a large brain, upright posture, manipulative hands, keen vision. and mouth and throat structures that make speech possible.

4. Man attained essentially his present-day biological attributes many thousands of years ago; his development since that time has been overwhelmingly cultural. Man's survival no longer depends chiefly on further biological evolution but rather on cultural development.

DEVELOPMENT OF CULTURE

1. Although man is identified with other living creatures, he differs profoundly by virtue of his development of culture.

2. Culture is a product of man's exclusive capacity to comprehend and communicate by means of language. Culture is socially learned and consists of the knowledge, beliefs, and values which

humans have evolved to establish rules of group life and methods of adjusting to and exploiting the natural environment.

3. The variety of cultures developed by human societies affords man more diverse ways of living than animals. At a specific time and place, every society has a culture to some degree different from that of any other society, past or present.

4. Culture can be altered rapidly to cope with new conditions, and a society can borrow ideas readily from another culture. The superiority of man's cultural adaptations is thus emphasized in contrast with the slowly developing and constrictive biological adaptations of animals. Man's superiority illustrates the desirability of encouraging the continuance of many different cultural streams and of fostering sympathetic understanding of them. Such diversity enriches all of human life.

CULTURAL HERITAGE

1. No modern society has evolved more than a small fraction of its present cultural heritage. Each is deeply indebted to the contributions of other civilizations.

2. Man has left evidences of his presence in the Old World for at least the last 500,000 years. Paleolithic ("Old Stone Age") men invented and developed languages; made crude tools of chipped stone and probably less durable materials; eventually developed primitive clothing and learned to control fire; and still later domesticated the dog.

3. Some nine or ten thousand years ago, men living near the east end of the Mediterranean Sea first domesticated food plants and animals, thus beginning the Neolithic ("New Stone") Age. Such control of the food supply constituted one of the most far-reaching revolutions in human history. Populations increased rapidly where farming developed and permanent towns sprang up. The increased density of population and the additional security and leisure made possible by the relatively assured food supply gave man his first opportunity to develop those parts of culture which are the basis of civilization: writing, mathematics, and science; specialized technologies, such as weaving, pottery making, and metallurgy; organized philosophy and religion; and legal, political, and economic organizations. These advances and their improvement began soon after the agricultural base was established.

4. No real break exists between the cultures of the ancient Neolithic farmers and the great civilizations of today. But the rate of cultural progress and the dissemination of new knowledge have accelerated tremendously. This speed-up—particularly in science and technology—has created new opportunities and new and pressing problems for man. How the great cultural advances are put to use is the most urgent problem in the modern world.

CULTURE AS AN INFLUENCE ON SOCIETY

1. The culture under which a person matures exerts a powerful influence on him throughout his life.
2. Since the culture of a society has such an impact upon an individual's personality, he feels, thinks, and acts in accord with its imperatives, not only to be accepted by his fellows but also to maintain his self-respect and confidence. The world into which every individual must fit is defined by his culture.
3. Language is an essential, effective, and exclusively human tool for the invention and transmission of culture. Art, music, and other symbolic and aesthetic expressions are also effective means of transmitting culture.
4. Culture, the creation of human activities, may be altered by them. Norms of culture are derived historically but are dynamic and thus may be subjected to planned change.
5. All cultures provide for the essential needs of human group life but differ, sometimes markedly, in the means by which they fulfill these needs. Different cultures result in different modes of thought and action. People generally prefer the culture of their own society but should recognize that they would probably prefer another culture if they had been subject to its influences to the same degree.
6. Anthropologists have been unable to discover a scientific basis for evaluating cultures as absolutely inferior or superior.
7. A major problem in the modern world is to discover ways in which social groups and nations with divergent cultures can co-operate for the welfare of mankind and yet maintain as much respect for one another's cultural patterns as possible.

HUMAN BEINGS AS MEMBERS OF HOMO SAPIENS

1. Since long before the beginning of written history, all human beings have been members of a single biological species, the

Homo sapiens. For convenience of description and classification, anthropologists divide the species into "races," each of which has distinctive, observable *physical* traits. These traits, however, merge imperceptibly into one another so that most men posses characteristics of more than one race.

2. Populations have seldom remained isolated long enough, nor have they been subjected to sufficiently intensive natural selection, to become homogeneous races. Modern, worldwide interdependencies and rapid transportation and communication make it clear that such isolation cannot be expected in the future.

3. Anthropologists distinguish three main stocks or extreme limits of human biological variability: Mongoloids, Caucasoids, and Negroids. The great bulk of humanity is intermediate between the extremes.

4. Physically, all human beings are much more alike than different. Geneticists estimate that all human beings have more than 99 percent of their genes in common and that the most extreme variation results from genetic differences in less than 1 percent of the genes. Differences between members of the same main stock are frequently greater than differences between persons of different groups.

5. A common misconception is that groups can be identified as "races" on the basis of differences in language, religion, or nationality. These differences are cultural and nonbiological. So-called "ethnic groups" are generally regarded to have one or a combination of these characteristics. Even when biological traits are considered to identify a group, wide physical variations are likely to exist within it. Such an ethnic group is, in general, a minority, either in numbers or in power, whose culture differs to some degree from the majority group of the locality. If cultural differences are to be cherished for their enrichment of human life, ethnic groups should not suffer disadvantages or discrimination merely because they vary culturally from the norm of the majority.

CULTURAL PARTICIPATION AND CONTRIBUTIONS

1. Human beings, regardless of their racial or ethnic background, are nearly all capable of participating in and making contributions to any culture.

2. The environment in which a person lives and his opportunities for

personal growth have profound effects upon the development of every individual. When these opportunities are limited by cultural poverty or repressive action, society loses as much as the individual.

3. So-called "race problems" are cultural problems arising from conflicts between ethnic groups or an ethnic group and the majority population. If the positive social value of cultural diversity is recognized, ethnic differences can add to the general richness of life.

SUMMARY

The person who has gained some anthropolgical knowledge about the range of human variation, both physical and cutural, and who understands and accepts the anthropological viewpoint about the causes and positive values of such differences will understand more fully his own behavior and that of others. Study of a variety of cultures increases a person's understanding of his own culture and reactions to life situations. The study of anthropology can also increase a person's effectiveness in daily life by helping him to understand the viewpoints of others and to be more effective in adapting to, introducing, or controlling social and cultural changes. Through knowledge of anthropology, a person can learn to appreciate man's universal qualities.

Generalizations from Psychology

OVERVIEW

Psychology is the science of human behavior. Its aim is the understanding and prediction of behavior. Broadly speaking, psychology is concerned with the scientific study of all its forms, such as learning, growth and development, thinking, feeling, perceiving, social behavior, personality development, and atypical behavior; and with the physiological process underlying behavior. Psychology is closely related to both the social studies and the biological sciences.

Individual psychology is concerned with the description and understanding of the patterns of behavior exhibited by the person. Included are the nature of growth and development, appraisal of personality characteristics, measurement of individual differences in various aspects of behavior, and the discovery of the pattern of influences producing given forms of behavior, such as aggression, withdrawal, delinquency, and creativity.

Social psychology is a bridge between sociology, which focuses attention on understanding large social settings and group structures, and psychology, which focuses attention primarily on understanding individual behavior and personality. Social psychology deals with such problems as the effects of social pressure on the behavior and personality of individuals, differences in the behavior patterns of individuals living in the same culture groups, and the processes through which the behavior of individuals is influenced by their culture groups.

BEHAVIOR

1. Behavior is caused and is not its own cause. Each form of individual behavior has a pattern of causes that are multiple, complex, and interrelated. Behavior is not capricious or random. The discovery of causes leads to an understanding of behavior.
2. Human behavior is purposive and goal-directed. The individual may not always be aware of basic purposes and underlying needs that are influencing his behavior. The study of psychology attempts to bring about a great awareness of the underlying causes of behavior.
3. Behavior results from the interaction of genetic and environmental factors. Through genetic influences, all individuals have a potentiality for development and learning; yet these genetic factors produce differences among individuals. The character of the physical and social environment promotes or limits the degree of realization of the individual's potentialities.

INFLUENCE OF SOCIAL GROUPINGS

1. As a biologic organism, the individual possesses at birth certain physiological needs, but the methods of satisfying these needs and their subsequent development are to a great extent socially determined by his particular cultural unit.
2. Through the interaction of genetic and social and physical environmental factors, the individual develops a pattern of personality characteristics. This pattern includes motives for action, the organization and development of self, values and standards of conduct, and relationships with other individuals.
3. Individuals differ from one another in personal values, attitudes, personalities, and roles; yet, at the same time, the members of a group must possess certain common values and characteristics.

4. Social groupings develop as a means of group cooperation in meeting the needs of the individuals. The basic unit of the family makes it possible for two individuals to cooperate in producing and training children. Similarly, other social groupings—such as communities, social organizations, and nations—enable individuals to work together toward satisfaction of common needs. The nature and structure of groupings tends to change and become more complex with the circumstances under which man lives.

5. Every individual is a member of several social groups, each of which helps to satisfy his needs. The child starts life as a member of a family but soon establishes additional memberships in school, neighborhood, church, and other groups. As he matures, he extends his membership into a greater variety of groups.

SOCIETY AND THE INDIVIDUAL

1. Each of the social groups to which an individual belongs helps shape his behavior. Members of different societies learn different ways of acting, perceiving, thinking, and feeling. Groups exert pressures on their members so that they will accept and follow group ways and mores. The behavior of any individual reflects in many ways the influences of group pressures.

2. Differences are important in the personality structure and behavior of individuals and make possible the infinite variety of work and recreation that characterize modern culture. Differences also furnish a basis for flexibility and creativity, which are essential to social change and development. In any social group, the range of differences among individuals is likely to be greater than the differences between any two groups.

3. Socialization processes, such as methods of child training, differ markedly in different social classes, groups, and societies. Personality structure and behavior are largely influenced by these processes. Individuals develop standards of values that reflect these influences as they seek to relate themselves to the group and to satisfy personal needs.

4. The satisfaction of social needs is a strong motivating force in the determination of individual behavior. Values placed in learning, as well as levels of aspiration, are largely attributable to the mores of the individual's "reference groups." What sometimes appears to be nonconforming behavior may be in reality

conforming behavior in terms of a particular group in which an individual seeks status. The strong human tendency to conform to social pressures often prevents individuals from seeing reality. The stereotyping of individuals because of racial or cultural backgrounds is another example. In general, noncooperative, aggressive behavior indicates that the individual's need for social acceptance has been frustrated. The individual displaying such behavior usually has been forced, through repeated experiences of rejection, to develop an attitude of defeat and inferiority.

5. The behavior of individuals is related to the structure and organization of the group in which they are placed. A range of roles, such as leadership, followership, aggression, and submission, may be exhibited by the same individual in different groups. The "need-satisfying" quality of a group and the member-to-member relationship influence behavior.

6. For preservation of its identity, a social group resists change through the phenomena of cultural lag and conservatism. A social group also changes in various degrees to preserve its identity when new conditions arise.

SUMMARY

Psychology contributes to the social studies through its content and method. Both are important to those who guide learning experiences. Generalizations that deal with relationships between individual behavior and group structure illustrate important considerations in the development of content and method.

Generalizations from Sociology

Sociology is a scientific study of the social relations which men develop in their interaction with one another. Sociologists analyze the basic structures and functions of societies and of associations and groups within societies to discover how they became organized, to identify the conditions under which they become disorganized, and to to predict the conditions for reorganization.

GROUPS, SOCIETY, AND COMMUNICATION

1. The work of society is performed through organized groups. Group membership requires that individuals undertake varied roles involving differing responsibilities, rights, and opportun-

ities. Groups differ because of their purposes, their institutions, heritage, and location. Nevertheless, they are generally similar in organization, structure, and properties. Every person belongs to many groups, and, therefore, groups overlap in membership. In an open-class society, an individual may move up or down in the social system and thus experience significant changes in group membership. An individual's participation in several groups may produce conflicting demands and involve him in several roles that have varying responsibilities and opportunities. Moreover, any group may change its membership and its objectives. Therefore, the individual needs to analyze his relationship to various groups to discern the conflicting demands made upon him and to recognize that he must identify himself as a person as well as a group member. There are differences in the significance of importance of membership in various groups. Many stereotypes ignore their important characteristics.

2. Communication is basic to the existence of culture and groups. Individuals and groups communicate in many ways other than language. However, every type of communication involves symbolism of varying meanings. These differ from one group to another. Basically communication takes places between individuals. Therefore, the tools of communication are vital to every individual. Stereotyping and ethnocentrism are serious distorting elements in the communication process.

PERSONALITY AND THE SOCIALIZATION PROCESS

1. The expression of man's biological drives are influenced by his social environment.
2. The realization of self is modified by contacts with others.
3. Socialization results from the methods of child training and the experiences of childhood. Social controls and pressures tend to lead to the child's acceptance of the folkways and mores of his culture.
4. Role is determined by the expectations of others. Nonconformity, for example, is perceived in one culture as leadership behavior. In others, it may be regarded as damaging to society. Man occupies different social roles as he moves from group to group.
5. Status within a culture is achieved by means of the prestige attached to natural and artificial differences, such as caste, vocation, class, age, sex, and individual traits.

6. Individual or group organization or disorganization reflects the presence or absence of coordinated and integrated behavior.

SOCIAL RELATIONS AND CULTURE

1. An established society, association, or social group gradually develops patterns of learned behavior accepted by and common to its membership. These patterns, together with their accumulated institutions and artifacts, make up the cultural "way of life" of the society and its associations and groups.
2. Social relations and their complexes are generally shaped by culturally defined rights and duties shared by members of a group.
3. Cultures vary from society to society. Any given culture changes in the course of time. Some behavior and institutions within a culture are universal while others vary widely, even during the same period.
4. Changes and variations may result from factors generated by the culture itself, such as the invention and use of machines, or contact with other societies and cultures.
5. Children growing up within a society tend to learn that its particular behavior patterns, folkways, and institutions represent the "right" values and that those of other societies are "wrong" values.
6. Within any large and complex society, subsocieties with varying cultures exist. Often, these subsocieties consist of peoples who have migrated and are regarded as minority groups in the larger society.
7. People with a common culture sometimes become grouped as social classes and think of themselves as having (a) status or position; and (b) roles or functions quite distinct from those of other classes. A society which becomes so rigidly stratified that it allows little, if any, significant interaction between classes is described by sociologists as having a social caste system.
8. Culture tends to standarize human behavior and to stabilize societies by developing many interrelated and elaborate institutions.
9. Societies that fail to evaluate continuously these institutions and modify them intelligently are subject to cultural lag. This is a maladjustment between parts of a culture that leads to social disorganization. Cultures that fail to make adjustments rapidly

enough tend to be absorbed or exploited by more aggressive and rapidly developing cultures. Sometimes societies are eliminated in the process.

10. Internal cultural crises tend to provide social revolutions. These purport to bring about sweeping changes in the old social order.

DEMOGRAPHY AND HUMAN ECOLOGY

1. Many individual, social, and physical problems are influenced by changes in population. These problems may involve considerations of old age, youth, migration, war, housing, famine, employment, government, transportation, recreational activities, education, vocational opportunities, sanitation, social controls, living habits, and medical facilities.

2. National migration develops cultural diversity within a group and cultural diffusion among groups.

3. The environment influences man's way of living, Man in turn modifies the environment. As he becomes more technically efficient, man is less influenced by his environment and more able to modify his environment. The spatial and temporal distribution of populations and their institutions, as well as the processes that bring about their establishing of patterns, is called human ecology. This is the study of the reciprocal relationship between the community and its physical and social environment. It involves for example, climate, clothing and shelter, natural resources, water and food, social environments and institutions, and folkways and mores.

4. Individuals generally function as members of communities. A community has a fixed geographic location, but its essence lies in the interaction of the persons that comprise it. They are grouped in a locality to cooperate and compete with one another for sustenance, survival, and cultural values. Communities have been increased and developed by modern inventions.

SOCIAL PROCESSES

1. Societies develop in accordance with recurrent sequences of interaction called social processes. Social interaction and communication are the general processes through which more specialized processes evolve. These include association, dissociation, and stratification; cooperation and accomodation; competition and conflict; and assimilation.

2. In association, human beings in interaction continuosuly organize and join groups and "societies." Dissociation is illustrated by the fact that groups tend to dissolve in time, losing members to new groups. Stratification is the tendency of individuals, families, and groups to become ranked by society into a hierarchy of social classes based on heredity, wealth, education, occupation, group membership, and other status factors.

3. Cooperation is illustrated by the way in which members of families and other more intimately related social groups tend to work together in performing functions of community living and in attaining common goals. Those persons who cannot fully accept other members of their intimate groups, other groups, or the way of life of these groups, often make the necessary compromises or adjustments to remain in the groups or larger community and to enjoy their high priority values. This process is known as accommodation.

4. In competition, persons become rivals of other group members or groups. This may compete as well as cooperate. Conflict occurs when a rivalry precipitates a clash or struggle because either side feels it must defend its social institutions and values or impose them on the other side.

5. Assimilation is the process through which persons and groups migrating to a new environment lose previously acquired modes of behavior and gradually accept those of the new society.

SOCIAL CONTROL

1. Societies require a system of social control to survive. This control is based upon uncodified rules of behavior (mores and values). Infraction of the rules will bring ostracism or pressure to conform to the controls.

2. Some of the techniques of social control that are used by groups or individuals to secure conformity are shunning, ostracism, gossip, jeering, praise, approval, and acceptance. Informal social control is the strongest factor in securing conformity to group standards.

3. Social control, particularly in complex societies, is also partially secured by formal, codified rules of behavior (laws), infractions of which result in formal penalties. The formal, legal controls are imposed upon those areas of social life which are too important to be governed by informal controls. When a "power group"

seeks an objective which cannot be reached by other means, it may attempt to impose legal controls.

SUMMARY

The study of sociology reveals and clarifies the structure of groups, group phenomena, and the role of the individual in various kinds of groups. Sociologists endeavor to predict social behavior by use of the scientific method and social research. These means of investigation and the application of what is known about group processes help to solve social problems. Thus, sociology contributes directly to the social studies.

Contributions of Philosophy

OVERVIEW

Within the past two hundred years, fields which were once considered a part of philosophy have been developed as separate social sciences. Before their emergence, philosophy and history were the disciplines within which students of human behavior inquired into the conditions and consequences of institutionalized life. Philosophy continues to be concerned with questions, concepts, and valuations related to the study of man and appraisals of his conduct. Thus, it is similar in subject matter to other social sciences. Philosophy has an essentially critical role in the analysis and valuation of concepts and generalizations contributed by these fields. It is the responsibility of philosophers to explore methodology, foundations of theorizing, and judgment criteria concerned with man's activities and values.

Although philosophy is not studied separately in elementary and secondary schools, it contributes to all social studies undertaken in the spirit of *inquiry*. If the study is to enlist pupils as effective participants, they must acquire and employ intellectual skills requisite for following arguments, clarifying ideas, and submitting claims to tests. Social studies conducted to develop the spirit of inquiry must utilize these skills.

LOGIC, SCIENTIFIC METHOD, AND ETHICAL ANALYSIS

1. Philosophy contributes to social studies the tools of logic, scientific method, and ethical analysis. It contributes also to social philosophy, political philosophy, and the philosophy of history. These tools and areas of study equip individuals to cope critically

with questions, problems, concepts, theories, and value judgments that arise in discussion of race, private property, the
family, the state, human nature, obligation to others, socialism,
free enterprise, civic responsibility, civil disobedience, classes
and class conflict, self-government, the rights of man, and the
relation of religion to morality.

2. Because of the influence of interests and emotionally charged
   words in discussions of human affairs, the teacher needs to make
   clear the "how" and "why" of requirements laid down for testing assertions on the basis of evidence and right reasoning and to
   point out the pitfalls that trap discussions that do not fulfill these
   requirements. By utilizing the requirements and developing respect for them, pupils learn to make intelligent choices and
   decisions as citizens. They learn how to face up to controversial
   issues through objective examination of ideas and arguments.

ABILITY TO MAKE JUDGMENTS

1. The study of philosophy, either as a separate discipline or in conjunction with other social sciences, helps pupils to develop the
   ability to make well-considered judgments.
2. The processes by which sound conclusions are reached need to be
   emphasized to pupils continually and utilized in their oral and
   written discussion. Thereby pupils engage in the work of critical
   analysis essential to judgment. They will not be satisfied with
   ready-made answers or with the omission of issues that can stimulate the spirit and practice of inquiry.

SUMMARY

For its own well-being, a free society must keep open the path of free
inquiry and develop in its future citizens those habits of study which
result in responsible commitments in thought and action. Conducted as
an inquiry to which philosophy contributes tools and areas of investigation, the ability of pupils to make well-reasoned judgments. Concepts,
generalizations, and doctrines which pupils encounter will be subjected
to questioning. Reasons for their acceptance or rejection will be reviewed, their applications investigated, and their implications explored.
In this way, the examined life which Socrates declared to be the life
most worthy to be lived by man will be developed and encouraged in
the pursuit of social studies in all grades.

APPENDIX 3
A BASIC BIBLIOGRAPHY
OF BOOKS IN THE SOCIAL SCIENCES

The following bibliography is intended to provide the reader with a list of basic references in each of the six major social science disciplines considered in this book. Suggested by social scientists, the books were selected to provide both breadth and currency of scholarly views regarding the nature and concerns of each discipline.

HISTORY

*Allen, Frederick Lewis, *Only Yesterday: An Informal History of the Nineteen-Twenties* (New York: Harper & Brothers, 1931), a Perennial Library paperback.

Billington, Ray Allen (ed.), *The Reinterpretation of Early American History* (San Marino, California: The Huntington Library, 1966).

*Commager, Henry Steele, *America in Perspective,* abridged (New York: Mentor Books, 1953), a Mentor Books paperback.

Gabriel, Ralph Henry, *The Course of American Thought,* 2nd ed. (New York: Ronald Press, 1956).

*Handlin, Oscar, *The Uprooted: The Epic Story of the Great Migrations That Made the American People* (Boston: Little, Brown, 1951), a Universal Library paperback.

*Higham, John (ed.), *The Reconstruction of American History* (New York: Harper, 1962), a Harper Torchbooks paperback.

Nevins, Allan (comp. and ed.), *American Social History as Recorded by British Travellers* (New York: Oxford University Press, 1948).

*Potter, David Morris, *People of Plenty* (Chicago: University of Chicago Press, 1954), a Phoenix Books paperback.

*Probst, George E. (ed.), *The Happy Republic* (New York: Harper & Brothers, 1962), a Harper Torchbooks paperback.

* Available in paperback edition. Addresses of publishers are included at the end of this bibliography.

GEOGRAPHY

Broek, Jan O. M., *The Compass of Geography* (Columbus, Ohio: Charles E. Merrill Books, 1965).

Hartshorne, Richard, *Perspective on the Nature of Geography* (Chicago: Rand McNally & Company, 1959).

James, Preston E., *One World Divided: A Geographer Looks at the Modern World* (New York: Blaisdell, 1964).

James, Preston E. and Clarence F. Jones (eds.), *American Geography: Inventory and Prospect* (Syracuse, New York: University Press, 1954).

National Council for the Social Studies, *New Viewpoints in Geography,* Twenty-ninth Yearbook (Washington, D.C.: National Council for the Social Studies, 1959).

Raisz, Erwin J., *Mapping the World* (London: Abelard-Schuman, 1956).

Raisz, Erwin J., *Principles of Cartography* (New York: McGraw-Hill, 1962).

ECONOMICS

Alchian, Armen and William R. Allen, *University Economics* (Belmont, Calif.: Wadsworth Publishing Company, 1964).

*Heilbroner, Robert L., *The Worldly Philosophers* (New York: Simon and Schuster, 1961), a Simon and Schuster paperback.

*Henderson, Hubert D., *Supply and Demand,* Cambridge Economic Handbooks (Chicago: University of Chicago Press, 1958), a University of Chicago Press paperback.

Knopf, Kenyon A. and James H. Stauss (eds.), *The Teaching of Elementary Economics,* Conference of College and University Teachers at Merrill Center for Economics (New York: Holt, Rinehart and Winston, 1960).

*Robinson, Marshall A., Herbert C. Morton, and James D. Calderwood, *An Introduction to Economic Reasoning,* 3rd ed. (Washington, D.C.: The Brookings Institution, 1962), an Anchor Books paperback.

Samuelson, Paul A., *Economics: An Introductory Analysis,* 6th ed. (New York: McGraw-Hill, 1964).

GOVERNMENT
(POLITICAL SCIENCE)

Davies, James C., *Human Nature in Politics: The Dynamics of Political Behavior* (New York: Wiley, 1963).

Diamond, Martin, Winston Fisk, and Herbert Garfinkel, *The Democratic Republic* (Chicago: Rand McNally, 1966).

*Hoffer, Eric., *The True Believer: Thoughts on the Nature of Mass Movements* (New York: Harper, 1951), a Perennial Library paperback.

*Lipset, Seymour, *Political Man: The Social Bases of Politics* (Garden City, N.Y.: Doubleday, 1960), an Anchor Books paperback.

*MacIver, Robert M., *The Web of Government* (New York: The Macmillan Company, 1947), a Free Press paperback.

*Neustadt, Richard E., *Presidential Power: The Politics of Leadership* (New York: Wiley, 1960), a Signet Books paperback.

*Schubert, Glendon, *The Political Role of the Courts: Judicial Policy Making* (Chicago: Scott, Foresman & Co.), a Scott, Foresman paperback.

*de Tocqueville, Alexis, *Democracy in America* (New York: Knopf, 1945), Edited by Phillips Bradley. A Knopf paperback.

Truman, David, *The Governmental Process: Political Interests and Public Opinion* (New York: Knopf, 1951).

Wolin, Sheldon, *Politics and Vision: Continuity and Innovation in Western Political Thought* (Boston: Little, Brown, 1960).

SOCIOLOGY

*Coleman, James S., *The Adolescent Society* (New York: Free Press, 1961), a Free Press paperback.

*Greer, Scott, *The Emerging City: Myth and Reality* (New York: Free Press, 1962), a Free Press paperback.

*Goffman, Erving, *Asylums: Essays on the Social Situation of Mental Patients and Other Inmates* (New York: Doubleday-Anchor Books, paperback, 1961), an Anchor Books paperback.

*Janowitz, Morris, *The Professional Soldier: A Social and Political Portrait* (New York: Free Press, 1960), a Free Press paperback.

Mills, C. Wright, *White Collar: The American Middle-Class* (New York: Oxford University Press, 1951).

*Sykes, Gresham, *The Society of Captives: A Study of a Maximum Security Prison* (New York: Random House, 1956), an Athaneum paperback.

*Whyte, William F., *Street Corner Society* (Chicago: University of Chicago Press, 1943), a University of Chicago paperback.

ANTHROPOLOGY

*Benedict, Ruth, *Patterns of Culture* (Boston: Houghton Mifflin, 1934), a Sentry Editions paperback.

*Harris, Marvin, *The Nature of Cultural Things* (New York: Random House, Inc., 1964), a Random House paperback.

*Herskovits, Melville F. J., *Cultural Dynamics,* abridged from *Cultural Anthropology* (New York: Alfred A. Knopf, 1964), a Knopf paperback.

*Kluckhohn, Clyde, *Mirror for Man* (New York: McGraw-Hill, 1949), a Premier Books paperback.

*Kroeber, A. L., *Anthropology: Culture Patterns and Processes* (New York: Harcourt, Brace & World, 1923, 1948), a Harbinger Books paperback.

*Linton, Ralph, *The Cultural Background of Personality* (New York: Appleton-Century-Crofts, Inc., 1945), an Appleton-Century-Crofts paperback.

*Linton, Ralph, *The Tree of Culture,* abridged by Adeline Linton (New York: Random House, 1955), a Vintage Books paperback.

PAPERBACK PUBLISHERS

Anchor Books, Doubleday & Co., Inc., 277 Park Avenue, New York, N.Y. 10017.

Appleton-Century-Crofts, Inc., Division of Meredith Publishing Co., 440 Park Avenue S., New York, N.Y. 10016.

Athaneum Publishing Company, 162 E. 38th Street, New York, N.Y. 10016.

Free Press Paperbacks, a division of Macmillan Co., 866 Third Avenue, New York, N.Y. 10019.

Harbinger Books, Harcourt, Brace & World, 750 Third Ave., New York, N.Y. 10017.

Harper Torchbooks/The Academy Library, Harper & Row, Inc., 49 E. 33rd Street, New York, N.Y. 10016.

Knopf Paperbacks, Alfred A. Knopf, Inc., 501 Madison Ave., New York, N.Y. 10022.

Mentor Books, New American Library of World Literature, 1301 Avenue of the Americas, New York, N.Y. 10019.

Perennial Library, Harper & Row, Publishers, 49 E. 33rd Street, New York, N.Y. 10016.

Phoenix Books, University of Chicago Press, 5750 Ellis Ave., Chicago, Ill. 60637.

Premier Books, Fawcett World Library, 67 West 44th Street, New York, N.Y.

Random House, 457 Madison Ave., New York, N.Y. 10022.

Scott, Foresman & Co., 433 E. Eric Street, Chicago, Illinois 60611.

Sentry Editions, Houghton Mifflin Co., 2 Park Street, Boston, Mass.

Signet Books, New American Library of World Literature, Inc., 1301 Avenue of the Americas, New York, N.Y. 10019. Also: Science Editions Paperbacks, John Wiley Sons, Inc., 605 Third Avenue, New York, N.Y. 10016.

Simon & Schuster, Inc., 630 Fifth Avenue, New York, N.Y. 10020.

The Universal Library, Grossett & Dunlap, Inc., 51 Madison Avenue, New York, N.Y. 10010.

University of Chicago Press, 5750 Ellis Avenue, Chicago, Ill. 60637.

Vintage Books, Random House, 457 Madison Ave., New York, N.Y. 10022.

APPENDIX 4
FACT-FINDERS THREE-FOOT SHELF
FOR AMERICAN HISTORY*

Because of the present heavy emphasis not only upon American history but upon state and local history as well, it is imperative that social studies teachers be well-informed in this aspect of the work of the school. The listing that follows represents a comprehensive bibliography of the most valuable reference books available. Certainly, every junior and senior high school library should possess these books. And all elementary school teachers should have ready access to them in the school district professional library and curriculum laboratory.

A list of the Basic Guides and volumes most useful for helping one who wishes information about some aspects of the American past to find his way through the jungle of printed material (25,000 books are printed annually in English) that libraries contain:

1. *Harvard Guide to American History.* Handlin, Oscar, et. al. (eds.). (Cambridge: Harvard University Press, 1955).

    The core of this volume (Part III) is a bibliography with the most complete listing of significant books and periodical essays (chiefly before 1950) on every topic and major event in American history from the Norse discovery to the election of Eisenhower in 1952. Parts I and II contain 66 specialized chapters on such topics as "Principles of Historical Criticism," "Newspapers" as sources, and selected Historical Novels, "How to edit a document," etc., etc. The tricks of the trade of the serious searchers for historical information. The prime weakness of the bibliographies, however, is the titles are mostly unannotated and unevaluated. If a student can afford only one reference work, this is it.

2. *A Guide to the Study of the United States of America (Library of Congress Guide).* 1960.

    The outgrowth of questions addressed to the Library of Congress especially by Europeans regarding the "best works" on American Civilization, History, Art, and Literature. This Guide is superior to the Harvard Bibliography in being more selective and printing crit-

---

* Prepared by Professor Douglass G. Adair, Claremont Graduate School and University Center.

ical evaluations and summaries of the titles listed. Less weighted toward narrative and political history, it is especially strong on leading American authors and their writings. Next to the *Harvard Guide,* the most useful single volume for the student's library.

3. Morison, S. E., and H. S. Commager. *The Growth of the American Republic.* 2 vols., 5th ed. (New York: Oxford University Press, 1962).

This is the best narrative—analytic survey of American history—best in terms of literary skill, stylistic vitality, and scholarly soundness. It is the classic among American college text books, and is detailed enough to serve as the easiest source of ready reference for the whole course of our history. Well indexed, and good selective bibliographies attached to each chapter.

4. Spiller, R. S., Willard Thorp, T. H. Johnson, and H. S. Canby. (eds.). *Literary History of the United States.* 3 vols. (New York: Macmillan Co., 1948).

A comprehensive, standard history of American literature from the colonial period to 1948. The third volume is a collection of literary bibliographies, with sections on "Literature and Culture," "Movements and Influences," and "Individual Cultures." "Literature" is defined broadly enough to include sections on folk lore, traditional ballads, and other sub-literary genre. An abridged edition of 1953 adds a "Postscript on Mid-Century Authors," but cuts the bibliography to the bone in the interest of the lay reader rather than the researcher.

5. Larkin, Oliver W. *Art and Life in America,* rev. ed. (New York: Holt, Rinehart, and Winston, Inc., 1960).

A fine survey for the intelligent layman of American arts and the ways in which they have expressed our manner of living. For the general student of American civilization it is a serviceable introduction to American art history, with its bibliographies an extremely useful guide thereto.

6. *Dictionary of American Biography.* 21 vols. and index. (New York: Charles Scribner's Sons, 1943). Two supplements.

The great biographical dictionary of the more than 13,000 American men and women who have most distinguished themselves as makers of American history. No entry for a living person so the original entries are for persons dead before 1935. The supplements contain biographies of those dying after original publication and before 1940. The index catalogues subjects by state or country of birth, by school or college attended, by occupations, etc.

7. Kaplan, Louis. *A Bibliography of American Autobiographies.* (Madison: University of Wisconsin Press, 1961).

A listing of more than 6,000 American autobiographies published from colonial times to 1945. A descriptive statement for each title indicates something of the subejct's career and experience, the time and the place he lived. Good subject index.

8. Matthews, William, and Roy Pearce. *American Diaries: an annotated Bibliography of American diaries written prior to the year 1861.* (Boston: J. S. Canner & Co., Inc. 1945).

Coverage extends from 1629 to the outbreak of the Civil War. Each diary is listed under the year of its first entry. The authors' major interests are noted. Also an index of localities is given.

9. Nevins, Allan. (ed.). *America Through British Eyes.* (New York: Oxford University Press, 1948).

Substantial extracts from 30 British travelers dating from 1794 to 1946. For the student the annotated biblography of the chief British visitors gives this collection its special value. cf. Handlin's *This was America* (1949) with a variety of continental accounts; and H. S. Commager's *America in Perspective: The United States Through Foreign Eyes* (1947) which is made up of quite short generalized and interpretative passages.

10. Barbun, Jacques, and Henry Graff. *The Modern Researcher.* (New York: Harcourt, Brace & World, Inc., 1957).

A manuel and handbook, wittily and wisely written, so that it will be both instructive and entertaining to anyone who is concerned with gathering facts, checking them for accuracy, and reporting on them in an effective manner.

APPENDIX 5
SOURCES OF MAPS

There are many sources of excellent maps, not a few costing little or nothing if the correct source were only known. The following lists contain the major sources, both public and private, to which the teacher may turn. Also included is a reference chart to be consulted in ascertaining the major advantages and disadvantages of the different types of map projections commonly employed.

Government Maps

Selected types of maps and charts published by government agencies are listed below. Information concerning specific maps may be obtained from the publishing agency. Some of these maps are available from the publishing agency, but others (as indicated) are available only from the Superintendent of Documents.

Further information concerning Geological Survey maps and other maps may be obtained from the Map Information Office, Geological Survey, Washington, D.C. 20242.

Type	Publishing agency	Available from
Aeronautical charts	Coast and Geodetic Survey	Coast and Geodetic Survey
Boundary information:		
United States and Canada	International Boundary Commission	International Boundary Commission
United States and Mexico	International Boundary and Water Commission	International Boundary and Water Commission
Congressional districts	Bureau of the Census	Superintendent of Documents
Electric facilities	Federal Power Commission	Superintendent of Documents
Geologic quadrangle maps	Geological Survey	Geological Survey

Type	Publishing agency	Available from
Geological investigations maps	Geological Survey	Geological Survey
Geophysical investigations maps	Geological Survey	Geological Survey
Ground conductivity	Federal Communications Commission	Superintendent of Documents
Highways: United States	Bureau of Public Roads	Superintendent of Documents
State and county	State Highway Departments	State Highway Departments
Historical: Reproductions from historical and military map collections	Library of Congress National Archives	Library of Congress National Archives
Explorers' routes	Library of Congress	Superintendent of Documents
Treasure maps and charts (bibliography)	Library of Congress	Superintendent of Documents
Hydrographic information: Nautical charts of U.S. coastal waters	Coast and Geodetic Survey Corps of Engineers, U.S. Lake Survey	Coast and Geodetic Survey Corps of Engineers, U.S. Lake Survey
Charts of Inland Waters Great Lakes and connecting waters River charts: Middle and upper Mississippi River		

Type	Publishing agency	Available from
and Illinois Waterway to Lake Michigan	Corps of Engineers	Corps of Engineers, Chicago
Lower Mississippi River	Corps of Engineers	Corps of Engineers, Vicksburg
Missouri River	Corps of Engineers	Corps of Engineers, Omaha
Ohio River	Corps of Engineers	Corps of Engineers, Cincinnati
Foreign waters	U.S. Naval Oceanographic Office	U.S. Naval Oceanographic Office
Hydrologic investigations atlases	Geological Survey	Geological Survey
Indian reservations	Bureau of Indian Affairs	Bureau of Indian Affairs
Mineral resources maps and charts	Geological Survey	Geological Survey
Minor civil divisions	Bureau of the Census	Superintendent of Documents
National Atlas of the United States	Various government agencies	Superintendent of Documents
National forests:		
Forest regions	Forest Service	Forest Service
National forest index	Forest Service	Superintendent of Documents
National parks:		
Topographic maps	Geological Survey	Geological Survey
National park system	National Park Service	Superintendent of Documents
Natural gas pipelines	Federal Power Commission	Superintendent of Documents
Population distribution of the United States	Bureau of the Census	Superintendent of Documents
Railroad map of the United States	Corps of Engineers	Army Map Service

Type	Publishing agency	Available from
Soil survey maps	Soil Conservation Service	Superintendent of Documents
Time zones:		
United States, Canada and Mexico	Interstate Commerce Commission	Superintendent of Documents
World	U.S. Naval Oceanographic Office	U.S. Naval Oceanographic Office
Topographic map series of the United States	Geological Survey	Geological Survey
Indexes to published topographic maps for each State, Puerto Rico, and the Virgin Islands	Geological Survey	Geological Survey
Status indexes to aerial mosaics, aerial photography, and topographic mapping in the United States	Geological Survey	Geological Survey
Township plats (reproductions):		
Illinois, Indiana, Iowa, Kansas, Missouri, and Ohio	National Archives	National Archives
All other public land States	Bureau of Land Management	Bureau of Land Management
United States base maps	Coast and Geodetic Survey	Coast and Geodetic Survey
	Geological Survey	Geological Survey
	Other government agencies	Superintendent of Documents
Water resources development map	Geological Survey	Superintendent of Documents

Type	*Publishing agency*	*Available from*
Weather map	Weather Bureau	Superintendent of Documents
World maps	Army Map Service	Army Map Service
	Coast and Geodetic Survey	Coast and Geodetic Survey
	U.S. Naval Oceanographic Office	U.S. Naval Oceanographic Office

Publishing and Distributing Agencies

Army Map Service
San Antonio Field Office
Building 4011
Fort Sam Houston, Texas 78234

Bureau of the Census
Department of Commerce
Washington, D.C. 20233

Bureau of Indian Affairs
Department of the Interior
Washington, D.C. 20242

Bureau of Land Management
Department of the Interior
Washington, D.C. 20240

Bureau of Public Roads
Department of Commerce
Washington, D.C. 20235

Coast and Geodetic Survey
Department of Commerce
Washington, D.C. 20230

Corps of Engineers
536 S. Clark Street
Chicago, Illinois 60605

Corps of Engineers
U.S. Lake Survey
630 Federal Building
Detroit, Michigan 48226

Federal Communications
    Commission
Washington, D.C. 20426

Forest Service
Department of Agriculture
Washington, D.C. 20250

Geological Survey
Department of the Interior
Washington, D.C. 20242

International Boundary
    Commission
United States and Canada
441 G Street, N.W., Room 3810
Washington, D.C. 20548

International Boundary and
    Water Commission
United States and Mexico
United States Section
Mart Building, 4th Floor
El Paso, Texas

Corps of Engineers
P. O. Box 80
Vicksburg, Mississippi 39180
Corps of Engineers
205 N. 17th Street
Omaha, Nebraska 68102

Corps of Engineers
P. O. Box 1159
Cincinnati, Ohio 45201

National Park Service
Department of the Interior
Washington, D.C. 20252

Soil Conservation Service
Department of Agriculture
Washington, D.C. 20251

State Highway Departments
State Capitals

Superintendent of Documents
Government Printing Office
Washington, D.C. 20402

Interstate Commerce Commission
Washington, D.C. 20423
Library of Congress
Map Division
Washington, D.C. 20540

National Archives
General Services Administration
Washington, D.C. 20408

U.S. Naval Oceanographic Office
U.S. Naval Supply Depot
5801 Tabor Avenue
Philadelphia, Pennsylvania 19120
            or
U.S. Naval Oceanographic Office
Clearfield Annex
Clearfield, Ogden, Utah 84015

Weather Bureau
Department of Commerce
Washington, D.C. 20235

Private Firms

Aero Service Corporation, 210 E. Courtland St., Philadelphia 20, Pa.
    (photogrammetry, molded plastic relief)
American Map Company, 3 W. 61st St., New York 23, N.Y.
Chicago Aerial Survey, 10265 Franklin Ave., Franklin Park, Ill.
George F. Cram Company, P. O. Box 426, Indianapolis 6, Ind.
Dennoyer-Geppert Company, 5635 Ravenswood Ave., Chicago 40, Ill.
Fairchild Aerial Surveys, Inc., 224 E. 11th St., Los Angeles 15, Calif.
Farquhar Transparent Globes, 5007 Warrington Ave., Philadelphia, Pa.
    (terrestrial, celestial)
General Drafting Company, Inc., Canfield Rd., Convent Station, N.J.
    (road)
Geographia Map Company, 636 11th Ave., New York 36, N.Y.

The Geographical Press, a division of C. S. Hammond & Company
 (graphic depictions of surface features, geological)

H. M. Gousha Company, 2001 The Alameda, San Jose, Calif. (road)

Hagstrom Company, 311 Broadway, New York 7, N.Y.

C. S. Hammond & Company, 515 Valley St., Maplewood, N.J.

Hearne Brothers, First National Bank Building, Detroit 26, Mich. (wall;
 school, office)

Mark Hurd Aerial Survey, Inc., 345 Pennsylvania Ave., South, Minneapolis 26, Minn.

International Map Company, 140 Liberty St., New York 6, N.Y.

Jeppesen & Company, 8025 E. 40th Ave., Denver 8, Colo.

H. P. Kraus, 16 E. 46th St., New York 17, N.Y. (antiquarian)

Map Corporation of America, 316 Summer St., Boston 10, Mass. (city)

A. J. Nystrom & Company, 3333 Elston Ave., Chicago 18, Ill.

Panoramic Studios, 179-189 W. Berks St., Philadelphia 22, Pa. (relief
 globes and models)

Erwin Raisz, 107 Washington Ave., Cambridge 40, Mass. (graphic depictions of surface features)

Rand McNally & Company, P.O. Box 7600, Chicago 80, Ill.

Replogle Globe Company, 1901 N. Narragansett Ave., Chicago 39, Ill.

Thomas Brothers, 550 Jackson St., San Francisco 11, Calif.

Weber Costello Company, 1212 McKinley St., Chicago Heights, Ill.

Identification of Map Projections*

1. *Meridians*	2. *Parallels*	3. *Projection*	4. *Suitability*
1. *Straight lines,*	Straight lines,		
(a) Parallel	parallel		
	(a) Widest apart in Equatorial regions	Cylindrical Equal Area	World on one sheet Africa S. America Tropical regions
	(b) Equidistant	Central Cylindrical (Plate Carree)	Rarely employed Tropical regions least distorted
	(c) Widest apart in polar regions Difference:		
	(i) Slight	Gall's Stereo-	World on one sheet
	(ii) Marked	graphic	Rarely employed
	(iii) Very marked	Central Cylin- drical Mercator	Navigation maps and charts

* T. W. Birch, *Maps: Topographical and Statistical* (London: Oxford University Press, 1964) pp. 109-110. Reprinted by permission.

(b) Radial	*Circles, concentric*		
	(a) Equidistant	*Polar cases of:* Zenithal Equidistant (Clarke's practically equidistant)	Polar areas to intermediate latitudes
	(b) Widest apart in Polar regions Difference:		
	(i) Slight	Zenithal Equal Area	Polar areas to intermediate latitudes
	(ii) Marked	Orthographic	Polar areas Other projections usually preferable
	(c) Widest apart away from Pole Difference:		
	(i) Slight	Stereographic	Polar areas
	(ii) Marked	Gnomonic	Charts of Polar Seas Straight lines are parts of Great Circles
(c) Converging	*Arcs, concentric*	Simple Conic with One or Two Standard Parallels	Countries in temperate latitudes without great latitudinal extent
2. *Curved lines,* *(a)* Equally spaced along any given parallel	1. *Arcs,* *(a)* Concentric	Bonne's	Countries in temperate latitudes Europe Australia Topographic maps
	(b) Not concentric	Polyconic	Modified for Topographic maps
	2. *Straight lines,* parallel *(a)* Equally spaced	Sinusoidal	World on one sheet Africa S. America World on interrupted projection
	(b) Slightly wider apart in	Mollweide's	World on one sheet or in hemispheres

	Equatorial direction		Africa S. America World on interrupted projection
(b) Closer together along any given parallel as distance from central meridian increases	*Straight lines,* equally spaced	Orthographic (Equatorial case)	World in hemispheres (others preferable) Africa S. America (others preferable)

SEQUENCE CHART OF MAP AND GLOBE SKILLS AND UNDERSTANDINGS
KINDERGARTEN THROUGH GRADE SIX

THE EARTH — SIZE, SHAPE, AND MOTION

Kindergarten	Grade One	Grade Two	Grade Three	Grade Four	Grade Five	Grade Six
—Begins to understand that a globe is a small model of the earth, which is very large	—Understands that a globe is the most accurate map because it is a model of the earth	—Understands that the earth is a sphere and that it can be divided into hemispheres on globes and maps	—Learns that any part of the surface of the earth can be shown and located on a map	—Understands that portraying the earth's surface on a flat map involves distortion of land and water areas	—Learns about the vast size of the earth, its circumference, and diameter	—Learns about some ways that the earth's shape, size, and set of motions influence plant and animal life on earth
—Begins to understand that the globe is round because the earth is nearly round	—Understands that the earth is made up of land and water and is surrounded by air	—Begins to understand that the earth is a planet	—Learns that the earth is not a perfect sphere	—Begins to learn about the inclination of the earth's axis and its effect upon light, dark, and seasonal change	—Compares various map projections with globes and notes distortions between land areas on maps compared with land areas on globes	—Learns about some ways in which the shape of the earth affects the distribution of sunlight, vegetation, circulation of air, and climatic conditions
—Begins to understand that the earth turns	—Understands that globes and wall maps are symbols for all or parts of the earth	—Understands that the earth rotates from west to east, and demonstrates this with a globe	—Uses the globe frequently to develop correct map concepts of shape, area, distance, and location	—Begins to understand the concepts of the earth's rotation on its axis and the earth's revolution around the sun	—Compares photographs of the earth's surface, taken at great distances above the earth, with a globe; generalizes about the curvature of the earth from this evidence and first-hand observation (horizon, eclipse)	—Compares various problems of cartography in projecting the globe to a plane or flat map by such methods as cylindrical, conical, and equal-area projections
	—Begins to understand that on earth the sun appears to rise in the east and set in the west because of the rotation of the earth	—Understands the relationship between the earth's rotation and day and night	—Begins to understand that the position of the earth with relationship to the sun changes, causing the seasons to change		—Traces and understands the orbits of the earth around the sun and the orbits of the moon around the earth	—Compares and contrasts the size of the earth to other planets, the sun, and the moon
					—Traces and understands the orbits of man-made satellites around the earth	—Understands the relationship between the rotation of the earth and time
					—Is introduced to the analemma as an indicator of the latitude where the sun's rays strike the earth vertically at noon each day of the year	

DIRECTION — ORIENTATION

—Begins to orient self as to location in relation to things in the environment	—Understands that up is away from the center of the earth and that down is toward the center of the earth	—Finds north by facing his shadow during a sunny noon; understands that south is behind him, east is on his right, west is on his left	—Knows that cardinal directions are determined by the poles and understands that north is the direction of the North Pole	—Learns that imaginary east-west and north-south lines form a grid on globes and maps	—Uses the intermediate directions accurately in establishing or describing location	—Extends understanding of latitude and longitude
—Begins to place objects in relationship to one another	—Uses left and right correctly	—Understands that the equator divides the earth into two hemispheres, Northern Hemisphere and Southern Hemisphere	—Learns that the North Star or Pole Star can be used to determine the direction of north	—Begins to learn that the Northern and Southern Hemispheres are divided by the equator and that the Eastern and Western Hemispheres are divided by the prime meridian and the 180th meridian	—Orients maps of different projections	—Understands the relationship between meridians and time, and compares time in various parts of the world
—Uses the terms up and down with understanding	—Understands that there is a North Pole and a South Pole	—Begins to understand that north is toward the North Pole and south is toward the South Pole; finds north and south on a globe	—Begins to understand the difference between true north and magnetic north as shown by a magnetic compass	—Understands that the earth can be divided into various hemispheres	—Understands the meaning of northern latitudes and southern latitudes	—Understands the meaning of the low, middle, and high latitudes: low latitudes—the area between the Tropic of Cancer and the Tropic of Capricorn middle latitudes—the area between the Tropic of Cancer and the Arctic Circle; and also the area between the Tropic of Capricorn and the Antarctic Circle high altitudes—the area between the Arctic Circle and the North Pole and the area between the Antarctic Circle and the South Pole
—Becomes aware of left and right	—Understands that the North Pole is the point farthest north on the earth and on globes, and that the South Pole is the point farthest south on the earth and on globes	—Learns that cardinal directions are determined by the poles of the earth; uses directions with understanding	—Understands the functions of a magnetic compass and the purpose of a map compass or compass rose as direction finders	—Begins to understand the meaning of parallels and meridians on globes and maps	—Understands the meaning of and uses the terms low, middle, or high latitudes correctly (rather than torrid, temperate, and frigid zones)	—Understands that most places on the earth's surface can be reached within a few hours by using great circle routes

SEQUENCE CHART OF MAP AND GLOBE SKILLS AND UNDERSTANDINGS (continued)

Kindergarten	Grade One	Grade Two	Grade Three	Grade Four	Grade Five	Grade Six
DIRECTION — ORIENTATION (continued)						
—Becomes acquainted with areas of the school and makes simple floor maps of the school with blocks	—Begins to use the cardinal directions	—Uses the sun and a shadow stick to establish east-west directions	—Understands that north may be shown on a map at places other than the top of the map	—Begins to learn that north-south lines are called meridians of longitude	—Reviews parallels and meridians on globes and on flat maps	
—Becomes familiar with street addresses and the names of cardinal directions; north, south, east, and west	—Makes floor maps of the community (floor blocks and other materials) and orients them, with teacher help	—Learns to read directions on large maps correctly oriented by being placed on the classroom floor	—Uses the intermediate directions (northeast, northwest, southeast, southwest)	—Begins to understand that latitude means the distance north or south of the equator	—Develops the concept of the great circles as any circle that divides the earth into hemispheres; compares distances of great circle routes (air routes) with other routes	
—Begins to make simple maps of the immediate school community on the classroom floor and orients them as to direction (floor blocks)	—Understands that a map can be used to determine the direction and distance of one place from another	—Begins to understand the use of a magnetic compass	—Learns that the earth is commonly divided into four major hemispheres (Northern, Southern, Eastern, and Western)	—Begins to learn that east-west lines are called parallels of latitude		
		—Learns to follow a simple diagram of the route to be taken on a class trip		—Begins to understand that the zero or prime meridian is the meridian from which east-west distances are measured; understands that the prime meridian was arbitrarily chosen to pass through Greenwich, England		
LOCATION		—Locates a place on a simple map by following given directions				
—Begins to describe relative location of various objects in the environment (near, far, up, down, right, left, over, under, back, front, here, there)	—Understands that things are located in definite relation to, or direction from, one another	—Recognizes his city, state, and country on a map or globe and understands that they are in a large land mass or continent called North America	—Understands the concept of continents as large masses of land and oceans as large bodies of water; locates them on maps and globes	—Locates places in relation to the equator or Northern and Southern Hemispheres	—Locates areas in the news on a world map or globe	—Locates major cities in the Western Hemisphere and the world

LOCATION (continued)

—Locates specific areas within the school	—Observes landmarks in the community	—Locates major natural features of the community on maps and globes	—Locates places in relation to continents and bodies of water	—Finds and understands the meaning of North Pole, South Pole, equator, Arctic Circle, Antarctic Circle, Tropic of Cancer, and Tropic of Capricorn	—Relates the United States to other parts of the world	—Uses the grid system to find exact locations
—Begins to locate features of interest on pictures and simple picture maps of the community	—Observes locations, sizes, and shapes of land and water areas on a globe	—Generalizes about his environment, such as, "We live in a hilly place," or "We live in a valley"	—Recognizes specific land and water areas by their shapes and sizes (peninsula, isthmus, island, bay)	—Locates the three major oceans (Atlantic, Pacific, Indian) and notes the lands which they touch	—Locates the chief physical features of the United States and Canada	—Traces and compares trade and travel routes (air, land, and water)
—Uses a globe to understand that it shows the earth's land and surface water	—Understands that a globe contains all the countries in the world but may not show all of their boundaries	—Locates his country on a globe, and compares its size and shape with other areas	—Recognizes similarities between areas introduced on a globe and the same areas on a map	—Locates continents (commonly identified as North America, South America, Europe, Asia, Africa, Antarctica, and Australia) and notes their relationship to one another	—Locates places on a map or globe with reference to distance from the equator	—Understands the division of the globe into 360°
—Recognizes that friends and relatives live in various places in the community, state, nation, and other parts of the world	—Locates North America in relation to other continents on a globe, as they are brought up in discussion	—Locates his state in relation to the rest of the nation and the world	—Understands the need for reference points on a globe or map (North Pole, South Pole, equator) to describe locations exactly	—Distinguishes continents by their sizes, shapes, and positions	—Locates places of national historical significance	—Locates and uses the International Date Line to interpret time zones
—Learns the names of his city, state, and country and locates them on a globe	—Finds the equator on a globe; recognizes that it is a great circle halfway between the poles, dividing the earth into a Northern Hemisphere and a Southern Hemisphere	—Locates the community or city on a globe or on a map of an area much larger than the community			—Locates and compares areas of basic natural resources in the United States and Canada	—Finds and understands the meaning of standard time zones in the United States
—Uses the globe to discover that there is more water than land on earth	—Locates places of interest as situated north or south of the equator	—Reads maps to find the principal natural features of his community and state			—Locates and compares areas of great population density in the United States and Canada	—Compares time in the community with that of time in other localities
—Begins to use a simple globe to point out approximate locations of places discussed						
—Uses streets and avenues as a simple grid system; makes avenues go north and south, and streets go east and west on floor maps made in the classroom						
—Locates places he has visited in and out of the community on a map and describes them using geographical terms correctly						

SEQUENCE CHART OF MAP AND GLOBE SKILLS AND UNDERSTANDINGS (continued)

Kindergarten	Grade One	Grade Two	Grade Three	Grade Four	Grade Five	Grade Six
LOCATION (continued)						
—Locates places of vital current interest in the community, state, nation, and world on maps or globes	—Uses the globe and wall maps to locate areas in the news and to relate them to his community		—Learns about the use of a grid system to aid in locating places on a map	—Reads maps to find the principal man-made features of his community and state	—Traces routes of explorers and settlers of the Americas	—Locates air and ocean currents which affected historical exploration and understands their role in the development of countries
			—Learns to identify specific landmarks, such as an unusual coastline or other conspicuous natural feature, and uses the information to locate places on a map or globe	—Maintains understanding of the purpose and uses of a grid system in locating places on a map	—Locates and compares resources of various states	
			—Relates current happenings in the state, nation, and world to areas on maps and globes	—Locates ocean currents, such as the California current and other currents affecting the Pacific Basin	—Locates natural barriers which influenced exploration, the movement of people, and settlements	
					—Compares natural and man-made boundaries	
SCALE — DISTANCE						
—Begins to express distance and size in relative terms (nearer, farther, bigger, smaller)	—Expresses familiar distances (as number of blocks between home and school) with understanding	—Observes relative lengths of familiar units of measure (inch, foot, yard, block, mile)	—Understands that differences in distance on maps and globes are relative to differences in distance on the earth	—Compares the mileage scale on the legends of various maps	—Understands that latitude is the distance north or south of the equator and is measured in degrees	—Understands that distances on a map can be measured by using fractional parts of the scale unit of measurement
—Begins to understand that places on earth which are far apart appear to be close together on maps	—Distinguishes relative sizes and distances in describing or representing things in the environment	—Begins to estimate short distances in the environment (blocks from school)	—Makes large maps of familiar areas drawn to a predetermined scale	—Begins to learn that mileage scales are expressed in different ways on different maps	—Understands that distance from the equator may be measured in miles or degrees	—Measures and compares different travel routes (air, land, and water)
—Generalizes that some toys are small-scale models of real things	—Makes and uses picture maps showing relative sizes of things represented (school size to home size)	—Estimates and checks familiar distances in terms of number of blocks	—Compares amounts of time taken to travel over familiar distances by various means of travel	—Understands that large-scale maps show more detail than small-scale maps	—Extends understanding of linear and areal mileage scales	—Uses various mileage scales with understanding (scales expressed graphically, in words, or as a representative fraction)

—Understands that maps show relative size —big things on earth are made relatively big, and small things are made relatively small	—Understands the relationship between distance and time in travel	—Uses the mileage scale to find the distance from one place to another on a map	—Estimates distances on a map and checks them by using the mileage scale			—Estimates and computes linear distances which cannot be directly observed or measured
—Begins to understand the need for scale reduction on a map	—Compares aerial photographs of a small area with maps and pictures of the same area					—Uses with understanding maps of identical areas drawn to different scales
—Recognizes that small things on a map represent large things on earth	—Understands that mileage scales on maps are given to indicate the distance from one place to another					
—Understands that places distant from one another on the earth appear to be close together on a map or globe	—Learns to recognize the mileage scale in the map legend					

SYMBOLS

—Begins to understand that the globe is a symbol for the earth	—Interprets his environment in pictures painted	—Uses his own symbols correctly in mapping out communities studied	—Finds several illustrations of symbols used in the map legend	—Consults map legends before interpreting various maps	—Consults the map legend and finds several illustrations of the symbols given on the map	—Devises map symbols and legends for outline maps used for special purposes
—Begins to learn that pictorial symbols on a map stand for real things on earth	—Associates the correct pictorial symbols with pictures of various natural features	—Observes landscape features in his environment and learns about commonly-used symbols for them	—Uses special map symbols (directions, water areas, land areas, cities, highways, railroads) as needed	—Understands the use of color to show elevation or altitude	—Uses a variety of symbols with understanding	—Compares the various uses on different maps for the same kinds of symbols, such as lines and dots
—Begins to identify color or symbols for land and water on simple maps and globes	—Interprets simple map legends, such as color keys for land and water, and symbols for rivers, lakes, and mountains	—Uses a directional sign (map compass) correctly on his own maps	—Develops and uses appropriate map legends on outline maps	—Begins to understand the use of the International Color Scheme on relief maps	—Compares map legends on several different maps and generalizes about standardized symbols	—Understands that the surface of the earth is irregular (above and below sea level, and in the oceans)

SEQUENCE CHART OF MAP AND GLOBE SKILLS AND UNDERSTANDINGS *(continued)*

Kindergarten	Grade One	Grade Two	Grade Three	Grade Four	Grade Five	Grade Six
SYMBOLS *(continued)*						
—Paints pictures of things in the environment according to his maturity and interest	—Makes use of pictorial and semi-pictorial symbols on maps as symbols as needed, such as symbols for house, school, church, and road	—Extends familiarity with map symbols; understands how the map legend helps to interpret a map	—Learns to interpret symbols, such as lines, dots, and colors, as needed	—Learns about colors other than the International Color Scheme used to designate elevations	—Understands that there may not be symbols given for all the information on a map or globe	—Understands relief on a map or globe as it is shown by merged colors, shading, contours, and hachures
—Describes features of the environment verbally; understands that they can be described through pictures and other materials	—Begins to understand some non-pictorial symbols, such as dots used on maps as symbols for whole cities	—Understands that the keys in a map legend may vary from map to map	—Learns that color as a symbol on a map is used for special purposes, such as on relief maps or political maps	—Learns abbreviations commonly used on maps		—Compares aerial photographs with relief maps and contour maps of the same area
		—Generalizes from using various maps that map makers use some standardized symbols		—Uses color symbols which provide specialized information, such as those used for rainfall or vegetation		—Uses the map legend to interpret the special use of color to present various kinds of information, such as food production, languages, and population concentrations in different areas of the world
				—Recognizes boundary lines, such as county, state, national, and international		
USE — INTERPRETATION						
—Interprets pictures	—Makes and interprets diagrams of the classroom correctly	—Reads simple maps and globes with understanding; relates information to his geographic environment	—Uses various kinds of maps to find places of interest in the community, city, state, and nation	—Traces routes of explorers significant in California history	—Grows increasingly skillful in interpreting many kinds of maps	—Uses a variety of maps and globes (political, physical, economic, special features) for different purposes
—Reads simple picture maps	—Makes and uses large-scale picture maps of familiar areas of the school and community	—Understands that maps are made for different purposes, to give different kinds of information about the earth	—Uses the globe frequently as a source of information	—Identifies natural and man-made features of his state on a map	—Makes inferences from maps, noting relationships, such as those between livestock production, corn and grain production, and proximity to transportation systems	—Uses both physical and political maps of the same areas for clarifying concepts

USE — INTERPRETATION (continued)

—Uses simple globes showing land and water areas	—Makes maps showing the distribution of houses and people in a given block	—Makes pictorial maps showing kinds of businesses or occupations within a given area of the community	—Compares aerial photographs of specific localities with large-scale maps of the same area	—Identifies areas of low, middle, and high elevations on various kinds of maps	—Compares physical and political maps of the United States and Canada	—Consults more than one map for information about an area
—Begins to understand the purposes of maps and globes	—Makes maps showing the distribution of schools in a given part of the neighborhood	—Understands that the United States is of vast size, and compares its size on various maps and globes	—Uses inset maps	—Begins to understand the relationship between climate and other factors, such as elevation, ocean currents, or location, in reference to the equator	—Determines from a relief map, the direction in which rivers flow, and traces the course of a river from its source to its mouth	—Compares maps and text descriptions of an area to draw inferences from them
	—Begins to use maps as a source of information	—Uses wall maps with globes to compare the same areas (shape and size)	—Learns to compare maps and makes inferences from them	—Interprets resource maps in terms of possible occupation of a region in California	—Translates specific information from maps and globes into bar graphs, and reads information from bar graphs	—Uses maps to increase understanding of current and past history
	—Finds familiar points of interest on a large map of the community; compares them with the actual places	—Understands and uses simple map terms correctly, such as equator, North Pole, South Pole, continents, oceans, lakes	—Increases geography vocabulary to meet requirements of a widening study of the world	—Translates geographic data into simple box graphs	—Becomes aware of the effect of ocean currents on the history and geography of the United States and Canada	—Refers to dates of maps and globes before interpreting information from them
	—Compares photographs of community features with pictorial maps of the same area	—Becomes aware of some resources of his country through the use of maps and globes		—Reads and makes inferences from facts given in maps, graphs, and tables	—Uses outline maps to record specific information discovered by study	—Compares old and new maps to learn about changes man has effected on the earth
	—Becomes aware of the unity of the earth's surface features			—Uses various kinds of maps for different purposes (topography weather)		—Uses a variety of maps to discover the relationship between physical features, man's use of the land, and population distributions; generalizes from the information
				—Learns about the effect of the prevailing westerlies on vegetation, forests, and agriculture		—Habitually consults maps and globes as resources for a variety of information
				—Relates the effect of ocean currents to the history of California		—Translates information derived from maps and globes and into line and circle graphs

Index